Fashion Cultures

From the catwalk to the shopping mall, from the big screen to the art museum, fashion plays an increasingly central role in contemporary culture. *Fashion Cultures* investigates why we are so fascinated by fashion and the associated spheres of photography, magazines and television, and shopping.

Fashion Cultures:

- readdresses the fashionable image, considering the work of designers from Paul Smith to Alexander McQueen and Hussein Chalayan
- investigates the radicalism of fashion photography, from William Klein to Corinne Day
- considers fashion for the 'unfashionable body' (the old and the large), football and fashion, and geographies of style
- explores the relationship between fashion and the moving image in discussions of female cinema icons – from Grace Kelly to Gwyneth Paltrow – and iconic male images – from Cary Grant to Malcolm X and Mr Darcy – that have redefined notions of masculinity and cool
- makes a significant intervention into contemporary gender politics and theory, exploring themes such as spectacle, masquerade, and the struggle between fashion and feminism.

Stella Bruzzi is a Senior Lecturer in Media Arts at Royal Holloway, University of London. She is the author of *Undressing Cinema: Clothing and Identity in the Movies* (Routledge 1997) and *New Documentary: A Critical Introduction* (Routledge 2000). She is currently working on a book on fatherhood, masculinity and Hollywood.

Pamela Church Gibson is a Senior Lecturer at the London College of Fashion. She is co-editor of *Dirty Looks: Women, Power, Pornography* (BFI 1993) and the *Oxford Guide to Film Studies* (Oxford University Press 1998). She has published essays on film, fashion, fandom, history and heritage.

Fashion Cultures

Theories, explorations and analysis

Edited by

Stella Bruzzi and
Pamela Church Gibson

London and New York

First published 2000
by Routledge
11 New Fetter Lane, London EC4P 4EE

Simultaneously published in the USA and Canada
by Routledge
29 West 35th Street, New York, NY 10001

Routledge is an imprint of the Taylor & Francis Group

Typeset in Perpetua and Bell Gothic by
Florence Production Ltd, Stoodleigh, Devon
Printed and bound in Great Britain by
TJ International Ltd, Padstow, Cornwall

British Library Cataloguing in Publication Data
A catalogue record for this book is available from the British Library

Library of Congress Cataloguing in Publication Data
Fashion cultures : theories, explorations, and analysis / edited by
  Stella Bruzzi and Pamela Church Gibson.
    p. cm.
  1. Fashion—Social aspects.   2. Mass media—Social aspects.
  I. Bruzzi, Stella, 1962–   II. Gibson, Pamela Church.
  GT525 .F37 2000
  391—dc21   00–059191

ISBN 0–415–20685–5 (hbk)
ISBN 0–415–20686–3 (pbk)

To our mothers, Zara Bruzzi and Josephine Church

Contents

Illustrations

Notes on contributors

Fiona Anderson is a freelance Curator and Lecturer. She assisted on the Paul Smith True Brit exhibition (Design Museum 1995), the Cutting Edge exhibition (V&A 1997) and has also worked as Curator of the Conran Foundation Collection. In addition she has taught Fashion and Textile History and Design History at a range of institutions, including Brighton University and the Royal College of Art. She has previously published on the subjects of late nineteenth century Savile Row tailoring and twentieth century men's dress.

Sarah Berry is author of *Screen Style: Fashion and Femininity in 1930s Hollywood* (Minnesota University Press 2000) and writes on film, media and design. She has taught at City University of New York and Murdoch University and works as an interactive media designer.

Christopher Breward is a Reader in Historical and Cultural Studies at London College of Fashion, The London Institute. He is the author of *The Culture of Fashion* (1995) and *The Hidden Consumer* (1999, both Manchester University Press), and several articles relating to fashion and masculinity in the nineteenth and early twentieth centuries, fashion and its representation in print culture, and the historiography of fashion.

Réka C.V. Buckley is completing a PhD at Royal Holloway, University of London on female film stars and popular culture in post-war Italy.

Edward Buscombe was formerly Head of Publishing at the British Film Institute and is currently Visiting Professor in the Faculty of Media Arts, Southampton Institute. His next publication will be *The Searchers* in the BFI Film Classics series.

Sarah Cardwell is a Lecturer in Film and Television Studies at the University of Kent. Conference papers and forthcoming articles include work on literature-screen adaptations, nostalgic fictions, the medium-specificity of film and television, and television drama.

Catherine Constable is a Lecturer in Film Studies at Sheffield Hallam University. She has a PhD in Philosophy from the University of Warwick. Her thesis entitled 'Surfaces of Reflection: Re/constructing Woman as Image' analyses psychoanalytic and postmodern constructions of woman as a trope of the surface and discusses these constructions with reference to the films of the Dietrich-von Sternberg cycle. She is co-editor with C. Battersby, R. Jones and J. Purdom of, 'Going Australian: Reconfiguring Feminism and Philosophy', *Hypatia*, 15 (Spring 2000).

Louise Crewe is currently a Reader in Economic Geography at the University of Nottingham. Her main research interests are in retailing and consumption, the fashion sector, the cultural industries and local economic development. Recent work includes two ESRC projects on informal consumption spaces (car boot sales, charity shops and retro clothes shops) and a Leverhulme Trust project on the cultural industries. She is currently working on a book on consumption entitled *Second Hand Worlds*.

Rachel Dwyer is a Senior Lecturer in Indian Studies at SOAS, University of London. Her books include *Gujarati* (1995), *All You Want Is Money, All You Need Is Love: Sex and Romance in Modern India* (2000), *The Poetics of Devotion: The Gujarati Lyrics of Dayaram* (2000), and she has co-edited *Pleasure and the Nation: the Politics of the Consumption of Public Culture in India* (2000). She is currently finishing a book on Yash Chopra and is working on design in Bombay cinema.

Caroline Evans is a Senior Lecturer in the Cultural Studies Department at Central Saint Martin's College of Art and Design, London, where she is also Senior Research Fellow in Fashion. Additionally she is a Visiting Tutor at Goldsmiths College, London, and is on the editorial board of *Fashion Theory: The Journal of Dress, Body and Culture*. She has taught and written widely on the history and theory of fashion, ranging from exhibition catalogues to academic articles. With Minna Thornton, she is co-author of *Women and Fashion: A New Look*. She is currently working on a book on contemporary fashion and its historical origins in modernity.

Jane M. Gaines is a Professor at Duke University where she directs the Programme in Film and Video. She co-edited *Fabrications: Costume and the Female Body* (Routledge 1990) and has recently finished *Fire and Desire: Mixed Race Movies in the Silent Era* (Chicago 2000).

Lorraine Gamman is a Senior Lecturer in Cultural Studies at Central Saint Martin's College of Art and Design in London. She is co-editor of *The Female Gaze: Women As Viewers of Popular Culture* (The Women's Press 1988), co-author of *Female Fetishism: A New Look* (Lawrence & Wishart 1994) and author of *Gone Shopping, the Story of Shirley Pitts, Queen of Thieves* (London Signet Books 1996). She is currently researching the subject of visual seduction thanks to a funded research leave award from the AHRB and Central Saint Martin's College of Art and Design.

David Gilbert is a Senior Lecturer in Geography at Royal Holloway, University of London. His recent work has concerned the geographies of the modern city, particularly the influence of imperialism on the landscapes of London, and the development of tourist cartographies and understandings of London and New York. His publications include *Imperial Cities: Landscape, Display and Identity* (Manchester UP 1999) with Felix Driver, and *Class, Community and Collective Action* (Clarendon 1992).

Sarah Gilligan is a Lecturer in charge of Media at Hartlepool College of Further Education. She is currently working on a PhD at Royal Holloway, University of London, entitled 'Gender, Clothing and the Female Spectator in Contemporary Cinema'.

Alison Goodrum is a postgraduate reasearch student in the Geography and Environmental Management Research Unit (GEMRU) at Cheltenham and Gloucester College of Higher Education. She is currently completing her PhD which looks at British fashion and the effects of globalisation on the industry from a critical cultural geography perspective.

Stephen Gundle is a Senior Lecturer and Head of the Department of Italian at Royal Holloway, University of London. He is the author of *Between Hollywood and Moscow: The Italian Communists and the Challenge of Mass Culture, 1943–91* (Duke University Press 2000) and of many articles on Italian history, politics and popular culture. He is currently completing studies of glamour and of feminine beauty and national identity in Italy.

Nathalie Khan studied at Royal Holloway and then Birkbeck College, University of London. She is currently working for the Donna Karan Company. Her research interests are centred on the role of the designer in the Fashion Industry.

Clare Lomas is Research Assistant in Historical and Critical Studies at the London College of Fashion. She is currently using oral history in her PhD research on the relationship between fashion and gay male identities in England in the post-war period.

Moya Luckett is an Assistant Professor of Film Studies in the English Department of The University of Pittsburgh. She is co-editor with Hilary Radner *of Swinging Single: Representing Sexuality in the 1960s* (University of Minnesota Press 1999).

She has extensively published in *Screen and the Velvet Light Trap*, and her articles have been widely anthologised.

Noel McLaughlin is a Lecturer in Film and Cultural Studies in the School of Arts at the University of Northumbria at Newcastle. He has published work on popular music and Ireland.

Angela McRobbie is Professor of Communications at Goldsmiths College London, and author of *Postmodernism and Popular Culture* (Routledge 1994), *British Fashion Design* (Routledge 1998), *In the Culture Society* (Routledge 1999) and *Feminism and Youth Culture* (2nd Edition 2000). She is also co-editor of *Without Guarantees, In Honour of Stuart Hall* (2000); he is writing a book on music and cultural identity.

Hilary Radner is Associate Professor in the Department of Film, Television and Theater at the University of Notre Dame. She is the author of *Shopping Around: Feminine Culture and the Pursuit of Pleasure* (1995) and the co-editor of *Film Theory Goes to the Movies* (1993), *Constructing the New Consumer Society* (1997) and *Swinging Single: Representing Sexuality in the 1960s* (1999).

Jacqueline Reich is Assistant Professor of Italian and Comparative Literature at the State University of New York at Stony Brook. She has published articles on Italian cinema, Italian literature and Italian American cinema in numerous anthologies and journals. She is presently working on a book-length study of the films of Marcello Mastroianni.

Elliott Smedley is a freelance fashion stylist whose work has appeared in magazines such as *Arena, Dazed and Confused, Dutch, Italian Glamour* and *Vogue Homme International*. His advertising credits include styling campaigns for clients such as Armani, Banana Republic and Gucci.

Carol Tulloch is a Research Associate in Visual Culture at Middlesex University and a part-time Lecturer at the Royal College of Art. She has contributed to a number of exhibitions on fashion, design and photography, and to several publications on the culture of dress in the African Diaspora. Her recent publications include *That Little Magic Touch: The Headtie in Black British Culture and Society*, edited by Kwesi Owusu, and 'There is no place like home: home dressmaking and creativity in the Jamaican community of the 1940s to the 1960s' in *The Culture of Sewing: Gender, Consumption and Home Dressmaking*, edited by Barbara Burman.

Acknowledgements

We would like to thank our editor Rebecca Barden and our assistant editor Alistair Daniel, whose tireless practical help and patience have enabled us to complete this book. The Arts and Humanities Research Board have given research grants to Pamela Church Gibson and to Caroline Evans for her 'Fashion and Modernity' project. We need to thank all our contributors, many of whom have worked under great pressure – both personal and professional. In particular, Jane Gaines gave us vital support in the genesis of this project, Chris Breward provided invaluable advice throughout and Elliott Smedley assisted us greatly with, amongst other things, our picture research. Within the world of museums Deirdre Donohue of the Metropolitan Museum of Art, Pamela Golbin of the Louvre and Valerie Steele were very generous with their time and expertise. Richard Dyer, Pam Cook, Ginette Vincendeau and Phil Crang should be thanked for their interest in the project. For their support and friendship, especially during a difficult and momentous time, we want to thank: Celia Britton, Mick Conefrey, Mike and Bridget Craig, Patrick Fuery, Andrew Gibson, Roma Gibson, John Hill, Avril Horsford, Beth Millward, Mervyn Poley, Marlene Rolfe, Michael Talboys, Charles Wallace, Nick Weaver and Paul Willemen. We are also immensely grateful to our copy-editor Sandra Jones for all her work on the manuscript. Lastly, we should like to thank our families.

Stella Bruzzi and
Pamela Church Gibson

INTRODUCTION

A S THE AREA OF FASHION STUDIES gradually sheds its under-
valued status to become a valid concern of different academic disciplines –
indeed, the journal *Fashion Theory* would have had no forum ten years ago – there
is obviously a need for more investigation and informed discussion. 'Fashion' as
a term has several connotations, some specific, others far wider and this anthology
aims to span both types. In the early days of Hollywood, to entice women to the
cinema, short films were made about fashion shows and what we would now call
'lifestyle'. Interestingly, perhaps, these have turned out to be the dominant concerns
of this book. At the end of the twentieth century, on both sides of the Atlantic,
there has been a proliferation of television shows about home making and make-
overs, clothes, cooking and now gardening. The assumption is, many would think,
that such programmes as *Home Front*, *Changing Rooms*, Delia Smith's *How to
Cook*, *Better Homes*, *Real Gardens*, *Looking Good* and *She's Gotta Have It* are
aimed at a largely female audience. Although gardens and chefs' kitchens are traditionally male domains (whilst 'cooking' is a feminine activity, 'being a chef' tends
to be a masculine one), the lifestyle and clothes strands are presented by women.
Until the 1980s (with exceptions) fashion and clothing were likewise perceived as
areas of specifically feminine interest. Both of these may turn out to have been
misplaced assumptions. Given a wide brief, more of our contributors than we would
have predicted chose to write about issues around masculinity: male images and
icons, patterns of male consumption and shopping, footballers, fashionable men of
history. The whole notion of 'fashion' and what constitutes the fashionable has
shifted.

The threads running through *Fashion Cultures* seem to be: masculinity, spectacle,
Italy, urban spaces and lifestyles, performance – and where the essays focus specifically on fashion, there is a profound interest in the work of the more conceptual

designers. Whereas ten years ago it was possible to identify a dominant interest in womenswear and in women, Vivienne Westwood, Paris couture and the problems posed by commodity fetishism, these concerns have currently been replaced – if not entirely superseded – by those in the pages of this anthology.

The emergence of different debates in the decade around fashion imagery, theories of consumption and the body led to new and significant work. Nevertheless, it sometimes seems as if the debates in these areas proceed along parallel tracks, never to converge. We have tried in this book to achieve two things; we wanted to draw together the disparate areas of discussion in one volume and examine the varied methodologies deployed to investigate fashion, while suggesting alternative ways in which fashion might be theorised. Within the body of existing work there are still surprising omissions. In published work on gender studies, for instance, fashion is conspicuous by its marginalisation. Even books that try to incorporate fashion into a broader discussion of gender (including works of popular theory such as those by Natasha Walter and Rosalind Coward) are either obliged to view fashion as a negative force or vilified for seeing it as a positive one. Similarly, studies of consumption do not generally differentiate between the consumption of fashion and everyday items, whether frozen pizzas, washing powder or lavatory paper. Shopping for clothes is surely not on an emotional and psychological par with shopping for functional household gadgets or groceries. Work on popular culture has included the consideration of fashion but this needs to be extended and formalised, highlighting the influence of film and music; subcultures and radical streetstyle have perhaps been given too much emphasis. Work on the body has often minimised the role of fashion in the imaging of the desirable body; further-more, clothes have been seen as an extension of the wearer and as semiotically meaningless without this affiliation.

Our book is an attempt to bring together and examine in one volume the different areas of previous research around fashion and make links between different sectors of the relevant industries. We think it is important that academic writing here and elsewhere allows varied voices to be heard and deploys a diversity of registers; so, a discussion of Gazza's wedding or of contemporary 'gastroporn' is as valid within an academic context as the more familiar referencing of high theory – from Jean Baudrillard and Judith Butler to Joan Riviere and Susan Sontag. Part of the perceived problem of fashion has been that academics in particular have not always known with what tone to approach and write about it – it's too trivial to theorise, too serious to ignore. These difficulties are intensified by the unfortunate legacy of some earlier writings that have ranged from the purely descriptive to the hagiographic, with precious little in between. Fashion has developed its own grand narrative around the centralisation of the individual couturier; a canon of designers has emerged, treated with the same veneration as the old masters of conventional art history. Finally, fashion's fundamental dilemma is that it has inevitably been predicated upon change, obsolescence, adornment and, in the so-called First World, it has been inextricably bound up with the commercial; this has led to the assumption that it is therefore superficial, narcissistic and wasteful.

Clearly, the importance of fashion reaches far wider than the narrow para-meters of the couture world that these derogatory dismissals target. The way in which fashion is disseminated, for example, or the creation of spaces in which it is consumed and enjoyed have, in the first section on 'Shopping, Spaces and Selling', been articulated by two cultural geographers. The discipline of fashion is thereby shown to have become in itself much less rigid in its definition. Partly as an acknowledgement of fashion's breadth and eclecticism, certain supposedly key areas for debate — such as the relevance of fashion to eating disorders and excessive thinness — have not proved dominant concerns within the chapters of this book. When the issue of food is approached, it is its relationship to fetishism, seduction and modern concepts of the grotesque that is highlighted. Image and the body generally have been rather unexpectedly marginalised by many of our contribu-tors, not because they do not have a place within the discourse of fashion, but because they are no longer perceived as the definitive factors they were once thought to be; hence the emphasis, for example, on the spectacularity of the catwalk show over the frail beauty of the models who participate in them. Likewise, the cult of fitness and the healthy body is of only marginal concern to many of our contributors, even those who focus on masculinity. The emergence of a growing men's health and fitness magazine market in the 1990s is not, perhaps ironically, directly linked to the increased emphasis on men's fashion. A love of fashion does not automatically signal an obsession with the body, and the chapters here that discuss men take quite specific but divergent approaches: the significance of Malcolm X as a black icon to women as well as men, not just as the natural father of 'cool'; the dandy; the non-narcissistic appeal of stars such as Cary Grant even to straight men; the fashionable sportsman.

Somehow inscribed into the book, though not necessarily occupying space for elaborate exposition, is the notion of same-sex looking. A seeming consensus linking many of these pieces is the idea that the fashionable image is not created for the purposes of sexual titillation. Instead, it is seen as part of a complex process involving self-expression, same-sex rituals which vary from mothers and daughters going shopping together to adolescent groups of both sexes roaming the high street shops and the non-erotic, non-judgemental pleasures of dressing up and looking at the different dress codes of others. It is because fashion no longer is seen as irre-trievably linked to sexual display that we have omitted the discussion of the televisual personality, for instance, whose function as fashion icon is to present an image of exaggerated sexuality — Denise van Outen would seem a perfect example, with her range of Top Shop swimwear. Van Outen is a constructed icon in as much as she exists in and through the media. What is interesting about the icons discussed in this book and the process by which they are created is that, whilst some are likewise shaped by their media context, others only accidentally (such as Colin Firth's synonymity with the persona of Mr Darcy) have achieved iconic status.

Bridget Jones's fixation with the moment when Darcy emerges wet from the lake raises the current concern of what constitutes the spectacular. The understand-ing of spectacle that emerges from various chapters in this book is multi-faceted, encompassing contemporary music, artistic practice, subculture, football and cinema. The second section, 'Catwalk and After', develops these notions of spectacle, masquerade and performativity whilst also examining the continued role of photography in the generation of what constitutes the fashionable image at given historical moments. And finally, 'Modes and Methodologies' seeks to bring together concepts that have underpinned the rest of the book but which also move the discussion forward: the notion of glamour, the silent struggle between fashion and feminism, the place given to oral testimony and the changing function of the museum as it seeks to showcase fashion as part of a complex discourse rather than simply a collection of garments.

The scant mention in the following pages of the writings of the fashion historian James Laver is maybe just one indication of how theory, like fashion, is ephemeral and goes out of vogue. To reconfigure Laver's own familiar axiom, that which is ten years old is hideous, that which is twenty years old is quaint, whereas after thirty years or more, fashions become increasingly attractive. Laver himself, of course, could not have foreseen the current inability to move beyond retro chic, which means that fashions of the 1980s are now being recycled. In a mere five years' time, if theory follows fashion, *Fashion Cultures* may well be the academic counterpart of cargo pants.

PART ONE

Shopping, spaces and selling

Chapter 1

David Gilbert

URBAN OUTFITTING
The city and the spaces of fashion culture

'WELCOME TO THE DIESEL PLANET.' This is the greeting given to telephone callers to Diesel Industries HQ in Molvena, Italy. Diesel makes no secret of its globalising philosophy: its founder, Renzo Rosso, has stated that 'we at Diesel view the world as a single-borderless macro-culture', and the view of Earth from space has been a recurring icon in its advertising and catalogues (Polhemus 1998: 20). In 'The World according to Diesel' national boundaries lose meaning and cultures overlap. For Rosso, 'the obvious triumphs of this nationless, raceless company make a very attractive statement about the benefits of seeing the world without strict divisions – not as "us" and "them", but simply as one giant "we"' (quoted in Polhemus 1998: 10). The idea of globalised, borderless fashion has become something of a millennial fixation. The first edition of *Elle* for the year 2000 proclaimed that 'what used to be key looks by key designers for key cities has now reached out to a broader audience – the entire planet' (Kraal 2000: 100).

It's easy to read Planet Diesel as an avatar of the globalisation of fashion culture at the beginning of the twenty-first century. Diesel's company strategies, and particularly its knowing, ironic advertising, seem to be the highest stage of global branding. Unlike the sartorial imperialism of American brands such as Gap, Nike or Levi's, Diesel strives to appear not as an aggressive multinational corporation, but as the first transnational clothing supplier, producing global styles for a global market. But like most supposedly global phenomena, the geography of Diesel is particular, partial and complex. Most obviously, Diesel is firmly rooted in what has been referred to as the 'Third Italy' (see Belussi 1991), operating within a regional production complex of flexible specialisation. Diesel also operates within a regional design and marketing culture (with Fiorucci and Benetton as the most obvious precursors) which has appropriated the stylistic conventions of mid-century

American workwear, and transformed them into relatively cheap designer clothing associated with a strong and distinctive brand image (Braham 1997: 158).

However, there are other geographies to this self-proclaimed global company. Unlike Benetton, which has hundreds of franchised stores, Diesel has created a more concentrated network of flagship shops (or 'StyleLabs') in certain major cities: New York, London, Berlin, Paris, Barcelona, Rome, San Francisco. While Diesel clothing can be bought in outlets in other cities, or through catalogues or on the Internet, the flagship stores are a vital part of Diesel's branding strategy, literally finding the company a place in the market. The location of these flagships plugs Diesel into fashion's symbolic order of world cities. In turn the presence of the flagship becomes one small but significant element both in the wider profile of the city in which it is situated, and in its intricate internal geography of the spaces of fashion.

Even (or perhaps particularly) in an era of globalisation, the connections between the geographies of fashion culture and the modern city remain vital for both. This chapter explores those connections. It first suggests that claims for globalisation of fashion culture are overplayed. Just as the globalisation of the world financial system of the 1980s and 1990s increased the significance of strategic cities, so changes in the structure and technological contexts of fashion have had parallel effects on its world order. While developments such as the rise of out-of-town shopping and e-commerce seem to presage the homogenisation and de-urbanisation of consumption, there are aspects of fashion culture which actively encourage production of active and differentiated urban spaces. The second section of this chapter looks in more detail at those long-term processes that established certain cities as key sites in the cartographies of fashion, and discusses their continuing significance. The final section thinks about the cities themselves as fashion objects, subject to fashion cycles, and visual accessories in fashion's iconography.

Spaces of fashion: the global and the urban

High fashion (an increasingly slippery and problematic concept as one-time elite designer companies like Ralph Lauren, Gucci or Prada compete with mass-market brands like Gap or Benetton) has witnessed a substantial globalisation of brands in recent years. Just as globalisation produced massive mergers between banks and other financial institutions to create supranational companies, so recent changes in the fashion industry have seen the creation of global players, capable of surviving in a world of cross-national and cross-media marketing. The consolidation of fashion companies (such as Hermès' recent takeover of the Jean-Paul Gaultier label, or Prada's acquisition of Helmut Lang and Jil Sander)[1] combined with the spectacular expansion of e-commerce seems to suggest the approach of a homogenised world fashion culture, segmented by purchasing power alone (Kraal 2000: 104–6).

This overlooks a number of contradictory (or at least complicating) trends in the geography of fashion culture. Consolidation necessarily entails concentration of control – and concentration usually takes place in or around the established world centres. Previous technological changes which have supposedly annihilated distance or made possible simultaneous contact with remote others (railways, jet aircraft, telephones, radio, television) have signally failed to eliminate the distinctivenesses of particular places. Indeed, those changes that have been most bound up with what David Harvey terms the 'time-space compression' of capitalism have increased economic unevenness and political inequality, both globally and locally (Harvey 1989: 240). The comparison with the process of financial globalisation is instructive. For example, far from disrupting and decentring the established geography of financial institutions, globalisation enabled the City of London to reinforce its importance and distinctiveness and to 'rearticulate its social power' (Pryke 1991: 211). The networks of contacts, face-to-face meetings and established social institutions of the City took on a new global significance. A parallel process has accompanied the globalisation of fashion in the late 1990s and early 2000s. The established contact networks and institutions of particular fashion cities have been reformed within new global contexts. The annual round of big city fashion collections are often criticised in the press as self-indulgent side-shows of the impossibly rich watching the impossibly thin wearing the unwearable. This may be fair comment on the immediate surface performance of the collections, but it misses the established significance of the collections as social institutions for the controlling elites of global fashion culture. The unhappy history of London Fashion Week and the repeated and desperate attempts to fix a London event into the cycle of Paris, New York and Milan collections give some indication of the perceived costs of exclusion from this geography of connection and influence.

A second influence on the geography of fashion culture is that certain cities are among the strongest and longest-established of global brands. This is best understood as a symbolic ordering of cities, for the connection between, say 'Paris' as a word on a label and the actual city is often hard to specify. In a world of subcontracting and franchising, the article labelled 'Paris' is less and less likely to have been designed, made or even sold in the city. It may be that a certain image or name is used for the value of its associations without any 'real' connection. No one expects Elizabeth Arden's globally promoted perfume '5th Avenue' to be made from the crushed petals of Central Park blossom, or even (despite the slogan 'It Takes You There') to have the authentic aromas of traffic fumes and sweaty summer tourists. But these signs of the sanctified sites of fashion are not completely free-floating and detached from the places to which they refer. The mythologising of Fifth Avenue in the name and promotion of perfume makes a small contribution to popular understandings of the district and the status of New York as a fashion city. These understandings in turn influence the decisions of shoppers, tourists and urban planners, the state of the commercial rent market, and the price of goods within the shops themselves. Similarly, the continued cachet of the name 'Paris' depends not just on the sustained intensity of the virtual city of promotion campaigns and the fashion press, but also on the credibility of the city as a centre of fashion consumption and particularly as an embodied experience of fashion.

The continuing importance of this experiential dimension of fashion culture is a further influence on the spaces of fashion. One dominant reading of contemporary consumer culture (which we might call the 'mall and modem' model) emphasises the erosion of local distinctiveness, and a loss of an *urban* experience of consumption. The West Edmonton Mall, the Metro Centre, Bluewater and hundreds of other out-of-centre developments, all stuffed with chain retailers selling mass-market global brands, seem to anticipate a future in which the established city centre, with its mix of shops and public streets, will be superseded by privately owned and controlled spaces. To some extent, mall-like developments have also entered traditional city centres, creating consumption spaces dependent upon a high degree of planning and visual coherence, and on strict but unobtrusive security (at least for 'unproblematic' middle-class consumers) (Zukin 1998: 836). For some the process of 'de-urbanising' consumption culture extends to threaten the whole experience of the modern city itself. The 1990s have seen New Yorkers railing against the 'Disneyfication' of Times Square, as investment by the Disney Company transformed the Square into a safer, but far more controlled corporate public space. For Sharon Zukin, this specific threat to Times Square is emblematic of a greater danger in which 'a single corporate vision could dominate Manhattan', turning it (or at least its best-known spaces of consumption) into a gigantic theme park or open-air mall (Zukin 1998: 836).

In the late 1990s and early 2000s, the rapid development of e-commerce has also prompted some commentators to mourn the imminent death of a diversified, embodied and peculiarly urban experience of consumption. Like many digital developments, e-commerce seems to bring to fruition many of the apocalyptic visions of the consequences of earlier technologies. The idea of the 'dissolution' of the city – that developments in communications will turn large metropolitan cities into anachronisms – is at least as old as electronic communication itself (Graham 1998: 169). For Marshall McLuhan the emergence of the global village would mean that the city 'must inevitably dissolve like a fading shot in a movie' (McLuhan 1964: 366). More recent work has explicitly anticipated a technological demise for the urban experience of consumption. Writing in 1992 (before e-commerce), Harvie Ferguson suggested that television and advertising had already destroyed the processes and pleasures of embodied shopping: 'we no longer need to be educated in consumption. – The shop window now opens directly into the home: the *flâneur* has become the somnambulist' (Ferguson 1992: 32). The Internet seems to promise a step further, where the whole has moved into the home, and where the physical distance between promotion and purchase has been eliminated: perhaps even sleep-walking has become too much effort.

While the 'mall and modem' vision of the near-future highlights some important developments in the geographies of consumption generally, and of fashion culture in particular, there are good reasons for doubting that the modern city will disappear as the pivotal element in the landscapes of fashion. Within the fashion process itself are elements that are resistant to the standardisation and control of the spaces of consumption, or their substitution by the virtual spaces of the web. Perhaps the most significant of these features is the importance of fashion as an experience rather than a disembodied and unplaced act of consumer choice and purchase. In drawing attention to the symbolic significance of consumption and the relationship between its practices and identity formation, recent work has stressed the important role played by consumption sites and spaces in self-signification (Crewe and Beaverstock 1998: 299). The pleasures of shopping (and its tensions and anxieties) are of continuing significance in the fashion process. For the individual consumer, the significance and meaning of a particular item are bound up with the process of shopping. Clothes, perhaps more than most other goods, can bear the imprint of the effort and enjoyment spent in finding and choosing them. A shirt or skirt bought as a part of an expedition to the big city can have a quite different personal meaning from an identical item bought locally or over the Internet.

Modern urban tourism often demonstrates an extreme version of this phenomenon in which it is the experience of shopping in significant sites which is valued more than the commodities themselves. (Indeed, on such trips the bags bearing precise geographical indicators of the experience of purchase may be more meaningful and prized trophies than the clothes themselves.) As the *Rough Guide* to London comments for the Diesel StyleLab in Covent Garden, 'the building itself is half the attraction, with a vast shattered-mirror wall – The clothes, from cropped shimmery jackets to artfully-cut own-brand jeans aren't cheap, but you are paying for the carrier' (Humphreys 1997: 537). The notion of paying extra because of where a shop is, or for a particular name and address on a plastic bag, may seem to be the most extreme and delusional form of commodity fetishism. Yet such behaviour, generally undertaken knowingly and often pleasurably, has been endemic in capitalist consumer societies for at least the past 250 years, and has been by no means limited to elite consumers of high fashion. The growth of homogenised shopping spaces and instant home purchasing may increase rather than eliminate the premium paid for a particular experience of shopping.

Too often accounts of consumption end at the point of purchase, or at least at the end of the experience of shopping. Some of the most satisfactory work on the spatialities of fashion has emphasised the way that fashion is an intrinsic part of the performance of urban life. Elizabeth Wilson, in *Adorned in Dreams*, points to the significance of fashion in the nineteenth-century city: 'New and more complicated "codes of dress" developed, for in the metropolis everyone was in disguise, incognito, and yet at the same time an individual more and more *was* what he wore' (Wilson 1985: 137; original emphasis). She points to the interdependent ambiguities of modern fashion and the modern city – both can be vital, alluring and liberating, yet both are potentially oppressive, manipulative and exclusionary. In a subsequent commentary on fashion and postmodernism, Wilson again emphasised the way in which clothing has the potential to lend 'a theatrical and play-acting aspect to the hallucinatory experience of the contemporary world' (Wilson 1992: 8). To be sure, this performance of fashion is not limited to urban spaces. Indeed, as Jennifer Craik has suggested, fashion works as a 'technique of acculturation' within a wide range of local milieux, each with different codes of behaviour and rules of ceremony and social position (Craik 1994: 10). However, the modern fashion process at its most frenetic, creative and transitory seems still to be closely bound up with metropolitan spectacle and performance. In many ways the expansion of the modern fashion media through the twentieth century – from advertising, cinema and television to the Internet – succeeded in spreading and popularising the metropolitan experience. Those techniques of acculturation, which were once highly localised within the stores and streets of metropolitan centres, are approaching what Christopher Breward describes as 'a kind of contemporary Esperanto' (Breward 1995: 229).

The cultural critic Frank Mort emphasises the performance of fashion in his influential reading of the changing urban geography of London's Soho (Mort 1996).

What we find in Mort's work is an emphasis on consumption in general, and fashion in particular, as an actively transformative influence on urban landscapes. He introduces the term 'topographies of taste' to indicate not the static mapping of different fashion areas in the city found in shopping and tourist guides, but rather the role of 'consumption spaces as sites for human creativity and action' (Mort 1998: 900). Thus while the reinvention of Soho during the past twenty years cannot be understood without reference to wider economic and political processes, its success has also been dependent upon the performance of fashionability on its streets. Mort points to the role played by new forms of masculine literature – both for a gay audience and more 'mainstream' publications – in providing information about 'how to be oneself in the city' (Mort 1998: 897). The new Soho is therefore not just a collection of shops from a particular segment of the fashion market, or just a metropolitan gay village, or just a centre for media-related industries. Binding these together and fuelling ongoing urban change is a highly visible consumer culture, in which the interplay between dress codes and identity is central.

Mort places the urban performance of Soho within a distinctively 1990s context. While the promotion of Soho drew upon its particular history as a 'continental' or 'bohemian' space within London, similar places have become 'endemic to so many contemporary cityscapes', and 'part of a diaspora of style-led consumption' (Mort 1998: 898). Some of the specific markers of these new urban consumption sites are particular to our times (for example, the rise and partial 'democratisation' of elite designer labels, or the ubiquitous presence of the café-bar), and they are perhaps more internationally interconnected than ever before. Yet the role of fashionable performance in the making of urban districts is by no means new, nor limited to those quarters used by elite global consumers. For example, the transformation of Carnaby Street and the King's Road in Chelsea in the 1960s was also dependent on their role as performative spaces – these were not simply collections of boutiques but places where fashion was displayed, watched, imitated and transformed. More recently the performance of fashion has become part of the nighttime urban rituals that have reinvented the public spaces of northern English cities, such as Newcastle's Big Market or Manchester's Canal Street.

A distinctive feature of the fashion culture of these cities over the past twenty years has been the development of local 'taste constellations' based not only around fashion, but also music, dance and clubs (Crewe and Beaverstock 1998: 301). While some designers and companies from these cities have made an international mark (such as the very different examples of Nottingham's Paul Smith and Manchester's Joe Bloggs), the fashion cultures of these cities have often had an intensely local dimension. This is not to say that these cities have not experienced the extension of international designer brands found across Western consumer societies and beyond. But while many inhabitants of these cities may be fluent in the Esperanto of high fashion, this is mixed with a local dialect of (often more affordable) street labels and locally derived brands. Rarer local labels may lack the international recognition of designer brands but can indicate 'higher cultural competence on the part of consumers', at least in the eyes of others in the local 'taste community' (Crewe and Beaverstock 1998: 301; Mort 1996: 11). In these cities, and in parallel cases in Europe, North America and Australasia, relatively small, independent designers and retailers may sustain a viable independent fashion culture, often within distinctive districts of the city, such as Nottingham's Lace Market or Paddington in Sydney.

Such districts and taste communities also exist within, say, New York or London, but in world centres of fashion the relationship between small-scale entrepreneurial fashion operations and high fashion is more complex and fraught, particularly in an age of global branding and fashion multinationals. For example, London is now almost routinely celebrated as a dynamic source of ideas and trends for world fashion, coming out of its design and fashion schools, its club and street cultures, its blossoming multiculturalism, its open-air markets, and its independent designers and retailers. London is portrayed as a different kind of fashion capital – not the source of authoritative edicts on 'the look', or the headquarters of globalising corporations, but a place where high fashion reinvigorates and renews itself, as it bumps up against the rawness of the real city. In fashion's continuous search for marketable expressions of the 'spontaneous' or 'authentic', this trope of the city as a diverse and unpredictable 'hotbed of creativity' can be very powerful. In his recent eulogy to contemporary London, Andrew Tucker idealises the relationships between high fashion and different spaces of the city:

> What would Chloé's Stella McCartney do without the markets of Portobello Road, where she rummages for antique trims with which to embellish her simple slip dresses? – To whom would Alexander McQueen boast of his East End roots and (supposed) descent from a victim of Jack the Ripper? They, and many others, are products of their environment – and that environment is London.
>
> (Tucker 1998: 17)

For a generation of British designers who have gone 'international', these claims for rootedness in the spaces of London provide a kind of worldly certification of innovation and iconoclasm (which may, ironically, liberate them to 'experiment' with more conservative styles in their new contexts). Angela McRobbie suggests that the export of talents like McCartney, McQueen and John Galliano to French post-couture houses is symptomatic of a wider failure of the British fashion industry to exploit both British design talent and London's dynamic fashion culture (McRobbie 1998). Clearly the disparity between London's profile in the international landscape of fashion, and the relative commercial insignificance of the British fashion industry (particularly in terms of the marketing of global fashion brands) is a matter of concern for British governments. Yet it may be that the character and success of London's fashion culture, and by extension its distinctive position within a world order of fashion spaces, depend in part on the relative absence of global players from its immediate environment.

World cities of fashion

One enduring cliché of high fashion advertising is a list of great cities following a brand or designer name. Two or three city names are permutated from a limited range of possibilities: Paris, New York, Milan, London, and maybe a few others.

In extreme cases of this symbolic geography, the city name itself becomes an integral part of branding – DKNY is the most obvious current example. The formula is so familiar that it has become an almost completely transparent sign, absorbed and understood without reflection. But by playing with the elements, the force of this formula becomes clear. Put the name of a mundane high-street brand in front of 'Paris, London, New York' and the effect is immediately pretentious and comic. Play this game the other way round, substituting new place-names for one of high fashion's established centres, and the dissonant combinations say much about the inclusions and exclusions of fashion's world order: Paris, London, New York – and Tokyo, Barcelona, Sydney (probably); and Manchester, Seattle, or Hamburg (perhaps, but only for a certain kind of fashion); – and Detroit, Birmingham Alabama or Birmingham West Midlands (almost certainly not).

The construction of this world order of fashion cities has a complex history. There is some overlap with what Saskia Sassen has termed the global cities – those places that play a key role in the world economic system, and which are often marked by extreme concentrations of wealth (Sassen 1991). The emergence of New York as a world city of fashion in the early twentieth century, or the development of Tokyo as an international fashion centre from the early 1980s, was not unrelated to the position of those cities in rising economic super-powers. Yet the symbolic and economic geographies of the fashion industry are different from those of finance and business services. Even in cities that are global financial and fashion centres, like London and New York, there is often a distinct spatial and cultural separation between the spaces of finance and those of fashion. This is not to suggest that Wall Street or the City of London has been untouched by fashion. Breward has suggested that through much of its modern history the City has been a contradictory fashion space. The Square Mile has been characterised by both intense occupational and social differentiation through the detailing and quality of masculine clothing, but also by a culture which associated more overt demonstrations of fashion with effeminacy, creating 'particular problems for the communication of masculine values by sartorial means' (Breward 1999: 241). There were some shifts in the 1980s when the Hugo Boss suit became an aggressive symbol of the newly deregulated financial markets of London and New York. The same kind of ungainly compromises between decoration and domineering bulk that were to be found in the new landscapes of Battery Park City and Canary Wharf were matched in the personal architecture of double-breasted façades and reinforced shoulder-padding. As women became more significant in these corporate landscapes, there were uneasy negotiations between different fashion codes. Some senior women began wearing adaptations of masculine conventions ('power-dressing') to claim equal status, while others adopted elite designer fashions of the West End or Fifth Avenue to differentiate themselves from women in subordinate secretarial jobs (McDowell and Court 1994).

However, to understand the position of the handful of elite fashion's world centres we need to look beyond what Arjun Appadurai (1990) has described as the finance-scapes of global flows of money and capital. But we also need to look beyond the internal processes of the fashion industry itself, such as the couture and collection systems. If any sense of this geography were to be found in traditional fashion history, it usually entailed an uncritical reference to certain sites of elite fashion design and consumption. In effect Simmel's trickle-down theory was extended from the social to the spatial. Standard accounts of the fashion process contained an implicit geography of emulation in which elite fashion was simultaneously metropolitan fashion – it's not just that I want to look like someone 'better' than me, it's also that I want to look as if I come from a better place. The archetypal example was the couture system, which projected Paris as world fashion's central place – the source of actual designs for a small elite, and of pronouncements on the 'look' for the rest of the fashion world. Even at the height of its powers, the claims made for the stylistic influence of the couture system were exaggerated and the relationship between elite design and mass-market fashion was complex. Moreover, this kind of account had little to say about the processes by which Paris and other cities established and maintained their positions. The continuing status of London, New York, Milan, and particularly Paris has to be understood through the long-term intersection of a number of cultural and economic processes bound up with the development of the modern city. In thinking about the long-term development of the geography of fashion's world cities, it is useful to identify five main themes. These can be characterised as:

- the urban consumer revolution of the eighteenth century,
- the economic and symbolic systems of European imperialism,
- the development of rivalries between European fashion cities,
- the influence of an American engagement with European fashion, and
- the development of a symbolic ordering of cities within the fashion media.

Discussions of the emergence of modern consumption now conventionally stress the importance of an urban renaissance and 'consumer revolution' of the late seventeenth and early eighteenth centuries, rather than the later industrial revolution. Glennie and Thrift (1992) suggest that European and new North American urban contexts were central both to the learning of new consumption practices and to their pursuit. Yet clearly not all cities were equally suited to the development of the fashion process. If knowledge of consumption was essentially practical, acquired less through instruction or advertising than through 'quasi-personal contact and observation in the urban throng', then some cities (and particularly London) were more thronging than others (Glennie and Thrift 1992: 430). And if the rise of fashion was dependent on the prioritisation of novelty, then some cities (and again particularly London) were in positions in the networks of world trade which enhanced the supply of novel experiences, and encouraged the acceleration of the fashion cycle. Part of the shock-value of the extreme figure of the *Macaroni* on the London streets of the 1770s came not just from the speed at which his fashions changed, but also from the seemingly wasteful and indulgent geographical reach of his clothing. As Miles Ogborn has suggested, the *Macaroni* was 'understood within the international chains of commodities that made London itself a dangerous place through the ways in which its endless varieties of consumption brought together the produce of the world' (Ogborn 1998: 139). These early developments were of vital significance for London's long-term status as a fashion centre; while fashions themselves came and went rapidly, the overall spatial ordering of fashion proved remarkably stable.

The 'consumer revolution' also shaped London's internal geography, establishing a pattern that appeared in other important fashion centres. In a sense, London's geography remained pre-industrial, with an economic structure characterised not by factory production but by small-scale workshops, often involved in the finishing of fashions and luxury goods. Fashion was therefore significant not only in the elite 'front regions' of the city, where it was displayed, purchased and worn, but also in 'back regions' where it was made, finished and often copied. Despite the development of an international division of labour, where many mass-market fashions are produced for a pittance in the Third World, the existence of a finishing trade has remained an important feature of fashion's world cities. Indeed, the fashion industry's dependence on an accessible and flexible local manufacturing sector has often encouraged a miniature version of the international division of labour within the metropolis, in sweatshops exploiting immigrant labour. The proximity of these front and back regions remains one of the key characteristics of fashion's world cities, and can produce unexpected crossings and blurrings of the boundaries between different social worlds: modern Parisian shoppers who abandon the Rue du Jour to slum for bargains among the workshops of the Passage du Caire are following a journey made many times before, perhaps in late-nineteenth-century Whitechapel, or the Garment District in the 1930s. In a beautiful essay on her childhood as the daughter of a Jewish master tailor in the London rag trade, Ruth Gershon has described how her life was saturated with experiences of the latest styles and cuts: 'swaggering around Hendon Central in a copy of a 1961 Cardin suit in a brilliant blue-and-black tweed with a fur collar' (Gershon 1999: 82). Fashion's great centres have long contained overlapping fashion cultures and spaces, in which conventional models of the fashion process — trickle-down emulation or bubble-up street innovation – prove hopelessly inadequate as descriptions of the interlocking circuits of production and consumption, imitation and intimidation.

If in the late eighteenth century London's position as a commercial city created new forms of the fashion process, by the mid-nineteenth century London's imperial centrality was the most significant influence on its development as one of fashion's world capitals. During the nineteenth century, London came to be understood as a site of both innovation and of fashion authority, in the British Empire and beyond. For example, the development of London's department stores in the second half of the nineteenth century was accompanied by a rhetoric and performance of world significance and centrality. Thus Harrods of Knightsbridge was able to style itself 'the most elegant and commodious emporium in the world', while increasingly exotic displays of commodities took place in stores like Liberty and Selfridges (Nava 1996). These stores rapidly became part of an idea and image of London promoted to the provinces and the colonies, developing the established reputation of the West End as a site for the purchase and performance of elite fashion. Shopping, particularly for women's fashions, became one of the essential tourist acts in the city, and guidebooks for those arriving from the colonies stressed the significance of London as a capital of style and luxury (Gilbert 1999).

The modern character of fashion culture in cities like London and Paris cannot be understood without reference to their imperial past and post-imperial present. Most obviously, the economic ordering of the fashion industry has been shaped around the international divisions of labour established in the imperial age. Imperialism also shaped profoundly the ideological context of fashion, so that the stylistic incorporation of 'exotic' elements took place within an imaginative geography that set the imperial cities at the centre and the colonised at the margins. A dramatic feature of the fashion culture of these cities in a post-imperial age is the way in which this ordering has been disrupted by recent social and cultural change. While London and Paris have provided homes for non-Europeans for as long as they have been cities, post-war migration has created distinctively new sites of hybridity and cultural fusion. The elite fashion of these cities still regularly creates 'new looks' through crass pillaging of stylistic tropes from other cultures, but the 1990s also saw the local development of transcultural fashions, directly related to the emergence of new forms of social and cultural identity. The recent transformation of Brick Lane in London's East End is indicative of this development. One of fashion's archetypal back regions, a district characterised by a long history of immigration, a sweatshop economy, and a huge weekly flea-market, Brick Lane is gaining a reputation as one of the emerging fashion districts of twenty-first-century London.

Across nineteenth-century Europe high fashion became part of the promotion of a certain ideology of distinction and distinctiveness, in which constructions of historical depth and cultural superiority were reinforced by the demonstrable political and economic dominance of European 'civilisation'. The age of Empire was marked not only by highly unequal relations between Europe and the rest of the world, but also by intense economic, political and cultural competition between the European powers. Like the magnificence of the architecture of capital cities or the size of the great exhibitions, the influence of high fashion became another of the ways in which European national cultures could measure themselves against each other. As the London fashion industry was only too well aware, it was Paris which proved best able to position itself as the world capital of fashion.

The idea of Paris as the source for the diffusion of high fashion has a history that predates the couture system, stretching back at least as far as the courtly fashion systems and *marchandes de modes* of the seventeenth and eighteenth centuries (Jones 1996). Neil McKendrick has argued that the veneration of Paris was a significant dimension of the consumer revolution centred on eighteenth-century London. Fashion that was 'expensive, exclusive and Paris-based' was translated into something that was 'cheap, popular and London-based' (McKendrick 1983: 43). It was vital that the process of translation from exclusive Parisian fashion to popular London fashion was incomplete, and that a residue of Parisian origins remained on clothes that were intended for consumption outside the traditional elites. There has been a remarkably consistent tension between the fashion cultures of London and Paris; in London, Parisian fashions have long been derided as elitist and decadent, while being copied and incorporated into designs for popular commercial fashion. Similar processes to those identified by McKendrick for the eighteenth century can be found in the example of the appropriation of Dior's 'New Look' by British working-class women in the 1940s and 1950s (Partington 1992). While only a small international elite could afford the actual clothes, Parisian designs, and perhaps as importantly, the ideal of Parisian fashion, could be part of the repertoire and dreams of a vast number of distant consumers.

A long tradition in urban guides and topographies has used London and Paris as indicators of the doubled-sided nature of the modern city (see Hancock 1999). The feminine 'capital of pleasure' was routinely contrasted with a more masculine city of work and business. Despite London's incontrovertible economic and political supremacy, it is Paris which is remembered, in Walter Benjamin's phrase, as the 'capital of the nineteenth century', not least because its cityscape was remade as a global object of desire and consumption (Hancock 1999: 75). The 'Haussmannisation' of Paris changed more than its street pattern and its architecture; it also altered the imagined geography of the city, locking together a strong visual trope of the material city with ideas about its cultural life, in which the consumption and public display of high fashion were key elements. International tourism was one of the growth industries of Second Empire Paris, and by the end of the nineteenth century developments in transatlantic travel helped to turn the city into the hub of the European tour for thousands of upper- and middle-class Americans. Guidebooks for Americans increasingly stressed Paris's position at the centre of the fashion world. London was slow to respond to these developments, and by the beginning of the twentieth century English publicity for travelling American women featured rather desperate pleas to support the 'English-speaking races' by buying in 'tariff-free London' (D.H. Evans & Co. 1902: 25).

This, to put it mildly, was missing the point. Transatlantic tourists were not interested in acts of political or economic solidarity, but in experiencing the pleasures of elite consumption. Very often for middle-class Americans these experiences did not extend to actual purchases of clothing or perfume (which in any case were increasingly available in the major stores of New York or Chicago). The fashion object that was being consumed was the city itself, and the spectacle of high fashion *in situ*. Those Americans who travelled to experience Paris were just part of a wider process of the popular consumption of the idea of Paris as an elite space. As Craik (1994: 74) suggests, the development of fashion in the early twentieth century was schizophrenic, marked by an unprecedented democratisation as more and more people had access to fashion clothing and fashion imagery, but also by a concentration of the control of style and design. There was a strong interdependence between Parisian and American fashion. Craik emphasises what Hollywood did for Paris – 'Paris took off as the fashion heart because of Hollywood' (1994: 75) – but Paris, or more accurately the aura of Parisian fashion authority, was a critical feature in the systematisation of the American fashion cycle.

In the early twentieth century New York City itself came to enjoy the status of a new world city of fashion, and became established as another place which existed both as an actual site of elite fashion consumption and as an imagined space of fashion fantasy. Since the late eighteenth century New York had been the dominant economic city of the United States, and a public culture of socially choreographed displays of fashion, taste and difference on Broadway and Fifth Avenue was well developed by the 1860s (Domosh 1998). By the late nineteenth century the city was the match of London and Paris in both its scale and its 'intensely urban qualities', which stimulated the development of a vibrant commercial culture (Hammack 1991: 37). Like the great European capitals, it also possessed a highly flexible local manufacturing sector able to respond rapidly to changes of style, at least in part due to the heterogeneity of a population in which immigrants formed a majority.

A number of factors pushed New York into the front rank of fashion cities. To some extent, this was a direct reflection of the rise of American political and economic power. The development of New York's international fashion prestige depended on the development of a class of the super-rich resident in the apartments and hotels of the city. As the novels of Edith Wharton and Henry James indicate, this new elite often sought to validate and consolidate their status through connections with established European aristocratic families. High fashion formed part of the performance of this new status; but what was significant was that this performance was increasingly one with a global audience. The image of elite New York consumption was one element in an unprecedented promotion of a city as a spectacle of commercial culture. Alongside the emerging vertical city of skyscrapers, and Broadway's 'great white way', the high fashion shops of Fifth Avenue became a familiar part of a cityscape which was celebrated in film, song and literature. One 1924 tourist guidebook indicated that public displays of fashion were among the sights of the city, and that fashion culture touched parts of the city far beyond the 'gorgeous shops of Fifth Avenue':

> Another characteristic of New York, and one that applies to all grades of society, is the lavish and conspicuous mode of dress adopted by New York women on the public streets. The styles for street wear change more rapidly and more radically than any other costumes; and no sooner has a new mode found favour on Fifth Avenue than cheap imitations of it make their appearance on Fourteenth Street and the lower East Side.
>
> (Rider 1924: xlv)

Urban outfitting: the city as fashion object

The landscape of fashion in the twentieth century was mediated by film, photography and the fashion press. What the media did for New York City was indicative of the way in which certain sites of fashion were sanctified by the increasingly significant fashion press. Many major American magazines (which were to become the backbone of the international fashion press) were based in the city and increasingly promoted the city as the centre of a new and distinctively American metropolitan culture (Harris 1991: 73). Similarly, for consumers outside of a tiny elite, what actually went on in the couture houses was less significant than the virtual Paris celebrated and revered on the pages of *Vogue*, *Elle*, *Harper's Bazaar* and other magazines. While the direct influence of metropolitan designers on the fashion habits of ordinary women and men may have been limited, New York, Paris and a few other cities became major elements in the 'hallucinatory' projection of images of desire (Wilson 1985: 157).

It is therefore useful to think of cities as the objects of fashion, as well as the physical context for fashion. Since the 1950s, one manifestation of this has been a kind of fashion cycle of places as well as of styles. One of the established tropes of the international media is the identification and celebration of *the* dynamic, defining centre of contemporary fashion culture. Perhaps the classic example of the genre was *Time* magazine's description of 'Swinging London' in the spring of 1966:

Every decade has its city. During the shell-shocked 1940s thrusting
New York led the way, and in the uneasy 50s it was the easy Rome
of *La Dolce Vita*. Today it is London, a city steeped in tradition, seized
by change, liberated by affluence – In a decade dominated by youth,
London has burst into bloom. It swings, it is the scene.

(*Time*, 15 April 1966: 32)

In the thirty-five years since 'Swinging London', Barcelona, Seattle, 'Mad-chester',
Tokyo and others have all had their fifteen minutes of fame. The identification of
Zeitgeist cities is just an extreme manifestation of a wider change. Fashion has
taken its place alongside music, gastronomy, clubbing, museums, galleries and
urban tourism as a key 'cultural industry'. Across the world, governments are
paying increasing attention to middle-class consumer demand for distinctive, high-
quality cultural commodities in efforts to regenerate or promote particular cities.
Making a city fashionable (in both narrow and wider senses of the term) is now
a common and often explicit aim of urban policy. In this post-New Right 'cultural
turn' in urban politics, public initiatives return not to address social division and
exclusion, but to subsidise elite arts institutions, to stage spectacular events, or to
'aestheticise' public spaces in prominent districts of cultural and commercial
consumption. Attracting a branch of an elite fashion store – as for example the
opening of Harvey Nichols in Leeds in the mid-1990s – is now seen as a significant boost to the urban 'symbolic economy', particularly for cities below the top
ranks of the urban cultural hierarchy (Zukin 1998: 826).

However, if fashion culture enjoys inventing and reinventing its urban geography, it retains a certain conservatism about its world centres. For those cities,
the rhetoric is not so often of newness and dynamism, so much as an almost organic
sense of fashionability growing out of the rich culture of metropolitan life. In the
December 1999 edition of *Vogue Australia*, editor Kirstie Clements provides a classic
example of the genre:

But my enthusiasm wasn't entirely fired by the action on the catwalks,
although there was a lot to get excited about. What was more
compelling was watching the utterly chic men and women of Milan
going about their business. Seventeen-year-old models in transparent
shirting have nothing on some of the grand dames of Milan, with their
thick silvery hair and impeccable dress sense. It's these incredible
women – with their soft leather jackets, amazing jewellery and elegant
shoes and bags – who are the real head-turners. For while the frenetic
pace and hype of the shows is always intoxicating, it's what people are
buying, wearing and living in that provides the full fashion picture. –
In Italy, the transition from high fashion to real life is seamless.

(Clements 1999: 16)

These clichés may be inflected by the local characteristics of fashion culture, and
by established traditions in the representation of particular cities. London, for
example, has had less stable and more ambiguous readings of its fashion culture,
both because of the significance of street styles in its fashion culture, and long-

running English ambivalence about high fashion. The strength of competing representations of New York (particularly in cinema and literature) makes it harder to reduce its fashion culture to a landscape peopled just by the utterly chic. None the less, the fashion press in almost all consumer cultures has routinely presented selective readings of London and New York alongside more generalised interpretations of Paris, Milan and Rome as the distant objects of aspirations and dreams.

The imagined cities of fashion press rhetoric become visualised as the city is presented as a fashion object by photography. Fashion photography has had a close relationship with the representations of cities on postcards and in tourist guides. In both cases there is value in those symbols that are unambiguous identifiers of a particular city. The bottom of the Spanish Steps or the view towards the Eiffel Tower from the balcony of the Palais de Chaillot, are clichéd sites for fashion photography, because they are such readily identifiable markers of Rome and Paris. The close relationship between shopping and urban tourism means that fashion photography may even mimic the snapshot. Fashion photography is very good at accessorising the city by drawing upon everyday iconographic elements as markers of place: red buses, pillar boxes and black cabs, or water hydrants, steam vents and yellow taxis.

Fashion photography also draws upon a more generalised urban aesthetic. Elizabeth Wilson has suggested that the 'love affair of black and white photography with fashion *is* the modernist sensibility' (Wilson 1985: 157). It is no coincidence that black and white photography has also been crucial in the visualisation of the modern city. In the post-war period the two have often been firmly fused, particularly through the development of what art historian Martin Harrison has described as 'Outside Fashion' photography (Harrison 1994). Hilary Radner has argued that this move towards dynamic 'action' photography of female models, and away from more formal, framed and contained studio shots, signified the construction of a more active image of women (Radner 1999: 89). This shift towards *mise-en-scène* photography, often of a woman moving purposefully through city streets, formed a contradictory moment in fashion's gaze on the female body. While the studio shot controlled the image, rendering the model herself anonymous, even abstract, the street shot created an impression that she had an independent existence, beyond the gaze of the camera. This new photography, which was to become a staple of the new individualistic and aspirational women's press of the 1970s (particularly in *Cosmopolitan*), seemed to celebrate (some) women's social empowerment and growing confidence in the pleasures of independent conspicuous consumption and urban life. Yet the shift in photography also moved the viewer outside into the street; the gaze of the male *flâneur* is re-invented and re-inscribed on the bodies of the women in the pictures (Radner 1999: 95). During the 1960s photographers like Terence Donovan, David Bailey and John Cowan broke with the existing conventions of British fashion photography by using working-class districts, factories and urban wasteland as their settings. This movement was particularly significant in redefining the image of fashionable masculinity. Drawing upon the increasing visibility of street styles, and on new portrayals of masculinity in American cinema, this new urban photography produced a grainy, dirty glamour, which was more resistant to earlier criticisms of male fashion as elitist or effeminate.

This move prefigured a more general aestheticisation and romanticisation of the marginal and dangerous spaces of the late twentieth-century city. This shift, visible in both masculine and feminine fashions, with gay and straight variations, is most apparent on the uneasy meeting grounds of street, mass-market and high fashion. A significant section of the fashion industry now seeks to mark and market clothing as 'urban', rather than 'metropolitan'. In 1997 Malcolm Gladwell introduced the term 'coolhunt' to describe the current systematisation of a much longer relationship between the fashion industry and sub-cultural street styles. Global sportswear companies now routinely sample trends and prototype new lines among young blacks and latinos in those US cities most emblematic of the urban edge: New York, Los Angeles, Chicago, Detroit and Philadelphia. What the 'coolhunt' achieves is a commodification (and expropriation) of that urban edge, which can be sold-on (and of course sold-back) bearing the mark of street authencity. A trainer that has been through the process sheds its geography of company head-quarters and product design (perhaps in Oregon or Germany), while its 'flexible' geography of production (one month the Philippines, the next Vietnam) becomes ever more invisible. Dereliction and decay now compete with sophistication and affluence as markers of urban style; an imagined Watts and a virtual South Bronx have become objects of fashion.

Note

1   Jil Sander split, acrimoniously, from Prada, but her label (called 'Jil Sander') remained in the Prada portfolio – an extreme example of the transformation of designer names into corporate brands.

References

Appadurai, A. (1990) 'Disjuncture and difference in the global cultural economy', *Theory, Culture and Society* 7: 295–310.

Belussi, F. (1991) 'Benetton Italy: beyond Fordism and flexible specialization. The evolution of the network firm model' in S. Mitter (ed.) *Computer-Aided Manufacturing and Women's Employment: the Clothing Industry in Four European Countries*, London: Springer-Verlag.

Braham, P. (1997) 'Fashion: unpacking a cultural production' in P. du Gay (ed.) *Production of Culture/Cultures of Production*, London: Sage.

Breward, C. (1995) *The Culture of Fashion*, Manchester: Manchester University Press.

—— 1999) 'Sartorial spectacle: clothing and masculine identities in the imperial city, 1860–1914' in F. Driver and D. Gilbert (eds) *Imperial Cities*, Manchester: Manchester University Press.

Clements, K. (1999) 'Editor's letter', *Vogue Australia*, December: 16.

Craik, J. (1994) *The Face of Fashion*, London: Routledge.

Crewe, Louise and Beaverstock, Jonathan (1998) 'Fashioning the city: cultures of consumption in contemporary urban spaces', *Geoforum* 29: 287–308.

D.H. Evans & Co.'s Handy Guide to London for the Use of American Tourists (1902) London: D.H. Evans & Co.

Domosh, M. (1998) 'Those "Gorgeous Incongruities": Polite politics and public space on the streets of nineteenth-century New York City', *Annals of the Association of American Geographers*, 88: 209–26.

Ferguson, H. (1992) 'Atrium culture and the psychology of shopping' in Rob Shields (ed.) *Lifestyle Shopping: The Subject of Consumption*, London: Routledge.

Gershon, R. (1999) 'A life in clothes', *Granta* 65: 77–102.

Gilbert, D. (1999) '*London in all its Glory – or how to enjoy London*: guidebook representations of Imperial London', *Journal of Historical Geography* 25: 279–97.

Gladwell, M. (1997) 'The coolhunt', *The New Yorker*, March 17: 78–88.

Glennie, P. and Thrift, N. (1992) 'Modernity, urbanism, and modern consumption', *Environment and Planning D: Society and Space*, 10: 423–43.

Graham, S. (1998) 'The end of geography or the explosion of place? Conceptualising space, place and information technology', *Progress in Human Geography*, 22: 165–85.

Hammack, D. (1991) 'Developing for commercial culture' in W. Taylor (ed.) *Inventing Times Square: Commerce and Culture at the Crossroads of the World*, Baltimore: Johns Hopkins University Press.

Hancock, C. (1999) '*Capitale du plaisir*: the remaking of imperial Paris' in F. Driver and D. Gilbert (eds) *Imperial Cities*, Manchester: Manchester University Press.

Harris, N. (1991) 'Urban tourism and the commercial city' in W. Taylor (ed.) *Inventing Times Square: Commerce and Culture at the Crossroads of the World*, Baltimore: Johns Hopkins University Press.

Harrison, M. (1994) *Outside Fashion: Style and Subversion* (exhibition catalogue), New York: Howard Greenberg Gallery.

Harvey, D. (1989) *The Condition of Postmodernity*, Oxford: Blackwell.

Horowitz, R. (1975) 'From elite fashion to mass fashion', *Archives Européennes de Sociologie* 16: 283–95.

Humphreys, R. (1997) *London. The Rough Guide*, London: Rough Guides Paperback.

Jones, J. (1996) 'Coquettes and Grisettes. Women buying and selling in Ancien Régime Paris' in V. de Grazia with E. Furlough (eds) *The Sex of Things: Gender and Consumption in Historical Perspective*, Berkeley: University of California Press.

Kraal, N. (2000) 'World domination', *Elle Singapore*, Millennium edition (January): 100–6.

McDowell, L. and Court, G. (1994) 'Missing subjects: gender, power and sexuality in merchant banking', *Economic Geography*, 70: 229–51.

McKendrick, N. (1983) 'The consumer revolution of eighteenth-century England' in N. McKendrick, J. Brewer and J. Plumb (eds) *The Birth of a Consumer Society: The Commercialisation of Eighteenth-Century England*, London: Hutchinson.

McLuhan, M. (1964) *Understanding Media – the Extension of Man*, London: Sphere.

McRobbie, A. (1998) *British Fashion Design*, London: Routledge.

Mort, F. (1995) 'Archaeologies of city life: commercial culture, masculinity and spatial relations in 1980s London', *Environment and Planning D: Society and Space*, 13: 573–90.

—— (1996) *Cultures of Consumption: Masculinities and Social Space in Late Twentieth-century Britain*, London: Routledge.

—— (1998) 'Cityscapes: consumption, masculinities and the mapping of London since 1950', *Urban Studies*, 35: 889–907.

Nava, M. (1996) 'Modernity's disavowal: Women, the city and the department store' in M. Nava and A. O'Shea (eds) *Modern Times: Reflections on a Century of English Modernity*, London: Routledge.

Ogborn, M. (1998) *Spaces of Modernity: London's Geographies 1680–1780*, London: Guilford Press.

Partington, A. (1992) 'Popular fashion and working-class affluence' in J. Ash and E. Wilson (eds) *Chic Thrills: A Fashion Reader*, London: Pandora.

Polhemus, T. (1998) *Diesel: World Wide Ware*, London: Thames & Hudson.

Pryke, M. (1991) 'An international city going "global": spatial change and office provision in the City of London', *Environment and Planning D: Society and Space* 9: 197–222.

Radner, H. (1999) 'Roaming the city: proper women in improper places' in M. Featherstone and S. Lash (eds) *Spaces of Culture*, London: Sage.

Rider, F. (ed.) (1924) *Rider's New York City. A Guidebook for Travelers*, London: Geo. Allen & Unwin.

Sassen, S. (1991) *The Global City: New York, London, Tokyo*, Princeton: Princeton University Press.

Shields, R. (1992) 'Spaces for the subject of consumption' in R. Shields (ed.) *Lifestyle Shopping*, London: Routledge.

Tucker, A. (1998) *The London Fashion Book*, London: Thames & Hudson.

Wilson, E. (1985) *Adorned in Dreams: Fashion and Modernity*, London: Virago.

—— (1992) 'Fashion and the postmodern body' in J. Ash, and E. Wilson (eds) *Chic Thrills*, London: Pandora.

Zukin, S. (1998) 'Urban lifestyles: diversity and standardisation in spaces of consumption', *Urban Studies* 35: 825–39.

Chapter 2

Louise Crewe and Alison Goodrum

FASHIONING NEW FORMS OF CONSUMPTION
The case of Paul Smith

Introduction

THE BRITISH FASHION INDUSTRY is currently enjoying a level of international success not seen since the heady years of 1960s Swinging London. From being neglected by government and industrialists alike, and dismissed as frivolous, narcissistic and economically marginal for several decades, fashion designers are once again headline news. *Vanity Fair*'s European editor argued that 'London is once again a city on the international fashion agenda that sets the pace of what is style. London is now gale-force in its speed' (Talley 1997). And Chanel's Karl Lagerfeld recently proclaimed, in a similar vein, that 'London is *hot* . . . there is a resurgence of ideas, techniques and energy among designers, sculptors, film-makers, the music industry . . . in fact right across the board in London now there is daring and finesse' (*Vanity Fair*, March 1997). Designers are again being seen as creative entrepreneurs, the seed-bed of innovation and as emblematic of a certain version of Britishness, one that is progressive, transformative and visionary. As the think-tank Demos argued recently,

> Britain has a new spring in its step. National success in creative indus-
> tries like music, design and architecture has combined with steady
> economic growth to dispel much of the introversion and pessimism of
> recent decades. Cool Britannia sets the pace in everything from food
> to fashion.
>
> (Leonard 1997: 13)

At the same time questions of cultural production and consumption have come to occupy a central focus within social-scientific enquiry, and recent research is exploring how the creative industries such as fashion (Crewe and Beaverstock 1998), film (Clarke 1997) and music (Leyshon *et al.* 1998) are powerful markers of place and identity, and are sites and spaces through which processes of self-signification can be played out. A key strand within this work involves an exploration of the ways in which fashion has the ability to articulate national identities (Goodrum 1998).

Our aim in the following discussion is to explore the ways in which British fashion design is a site central to both the re-branding of Britain and to contestations about British identity. In particular we are interested to understand how the apparently straightforward and economically driven process of the internationalisation of fashion is, in fact, a far more culturally nuanced and locally embedded encounter. Using the case of Paul Smith, Britain's most successful and arguably most influential contemporary menswear designer, we shall explore how Smith's evolving corporate strategy and international expansion have led to the export of a particular form of Britishness abroad, one that is progressive and yet at the same time deeply nostalgic, even parochial. In doing this, we shall explore the ways in which Smith has mobilised, and indeed shaped, emergent narratives about new forms of gendered consumption. More broadly, we are concerned here to understand the means by which Paul Smith negotiates the contentious and problematic discourses surrounding British fashion, which is at once seen as a deeply under-resourced and neglected industry, yet at the same time is being hailed as the country's flagship industry, a vibrant and progressive cultural symbol capturing the creative spirit of Cool Britannia and helping to make London swing again. We begin, however, with an exploration of the current state and status of the British fashion industry.

British fashion design: the state we're in

Design and related activity in Britain is worth £12 billion per year and employs more than 300,000 people. The cultural industries are increasingly being seen as alternative sources of employment within deindustrialising cities and encouraging the creative city is beginning to bring together cultural and economic policy at an ever more strategic level (Landry 2000; Leadbetter 1999; McRobbie 1998, 1999a, 1999b; Scott 1999). Britain ranks among the world's top five nations for design skills (Design Council 1996) and nearly one-third of the 300,000 student designers who graduate each year from Europe's design colleges are trained in Britain (Central Office of Information 1996). British manufacturers now spend £10 billion on product development and design while British design consultancies earn nearly £400 million a year abroad (Cunningham 1997). The value of cultural exports stood at some £10 billion in 1998 and the cultural economy of fashion is an enormously important component within this creative industries sector. Yet against this backcloth, the fashion industry has endured several decades of poor trading performance, escalating costs and mounting pressures of recession and redundancy.

Paul Smith has been unusual in that he has nurtured his business through one of the longest and deepest world recessions, and continued to increase sales whilst many around him failed. Sales in Japan were up 2 per cent in 1992 compared with Armani's decline of 20 per cent. What is perhaps more remarkable is that Paul

Smith has succeeded against a background of government neglect in the UK and in a retail environment dominated by middle market retail chains. Britain is unique amongst developed market economies in having an under-valued, under-financed, under-developed fashion industry. In the world of international luxury goods, more money is made from designer clothing (23%) than luxury cars (21%), yet British fashion firms rarely figure on any international league table. It seems, argues Smith,

> that one can no longer mention the British fashion industry without enquiring as to the state of it. And what a state it's in . . . The lack of investment from government and industry these past few decades has had an appalling effect on the business, with designers going bust or moving abroad . . . We are still considered to be the poor relation of our continental cousins in Paris and Milan . . . We used to be a nation of shopkeepers, whereas now we are little more than a themepark without a theme.
>
> (Smith, cited in Jones 1995: 56–8)

The reasons for the failure of British designer firms are not difficult to identify, and relate to an undervaluing of the design profession by the government and by industrialists, to a concentrated retail environment dominated by middle-market chain stores, to a clothing production system afflicted in large part by mass-productionitis, to a consuming public wedded to notions of quantity rather than quality, and more specifically, to a cultural legacy which feminises and trivialises clothing consumption and until recently dismissed male consumption practices as insignificant and unimportant. As Paul Smith himself was quick to point out in an interview,

> We are dealing with a history of negativeness . . . It's all about attitude, investment, the attitude of government and of management to creative people. A designer in the UK is not a designer. They are sent out to copy. It's despicable. Whoever wanted yesterday's news? In Italy a designer creates, on a board, from a blank page. It's a massive difference. For example, if M&S ask for a new sock range, the UK manufacturer comes up with black and brown and hideous designs. Japan come up with hundreds of colour ranges. We lose designers all the time to Europe. This year I placed sixteen students in jobs. None are in the UK . . . We have a unique situation in the UK, dominance by the chain stores. The British man is brainwashed into cheap and cheerful. Lots of bad clothes.

For many years, then, it seemed as if British fashion was trapped in a vicious circle. Our domestic market is tiny, generating annual sales of designer clothes of £265 million, compared with £1.9 billion in Italy and £1.4 billion in France. Those designers who stay in the UK face an incredibly difficult struggle against the structural and cultural barriers to success within the fashion industry, yet those who venture abroad face intense competition from the generously resourced, high-calibre fashion houses of France and Italy. Yet our designers continue to provide the inspiration on which other countries feed. What is surprising, then, is that 'in a global fashion market dominated by the resources of France and Italy and the wealth of the US, it is to Britain that the world still looks for new ideas' (Brampton 1997). As the think-tank Demos recently argued,

> Britain is a peculiarly creative nation. We have a history of eccentricity and quirkiness, and an ethos that values individuality, non-conformity, new ideas and difference . . . cultivating that creativity requires us to (see) . . . creative fields not as marginal but as central to our economic future.
>
> (Leonard 1997: 52)

But for so many the equation between design and profit is rarely made, and the realms of art & design, and business & commerce remain separated, inhabiting different imaginary worlds. As Smith himself laments, 'the designers trained at the RCA are now designing for Sony, for Braun but not for the UK clothing industry' (author's interview). 'Why do Katharine Hamnett, Jasper Conran and all the rest have to make it in Italy? Because there is nobody over here who understands how to back them' (cited in du Cann 1990: 53).

And so in many ways British style is suffering from a crisis of representation. The backward-looking and hidebound projections of 'Britishness' propagated by the creative industries have become hackneyed and clichéd in the minds of both domestic and overseas consumers. Consequently, 'Britishness embarrasses British business' – a sentiment endorsed by British Telecom, Gas, Home Stores and the Airport Authority, through their recent jettison of all things 'British' from their corporate names and identities (Leonard 1997: 9). According to McDermott (1987), British design has quintessentially been identified with Burberry macs, Morris textiles and Chippendale furniture. Alternative British traditions to do with non-conformism, eccentricity and anti-establishment feeling have been subdued within the national picture and made marginal.

The supercilious nature of, and bad press attracted by, unorganised and unstrategic national design industries signify a potentially ruinous period for British fashion. Paul Smith bemoans the fact that 'the UK is a goldmine of talent . . . [but] we are truly useless at handling design talent' (interview). Following his snubbing of the Designer of the Year Award in 1992 (he deemed it too self-congratulatory), Paul Smith has headed up a campaign not only to salvage British fashion and design but also to bring it up to speed in terms of competition both in the global marketplace and in the new millennium. Paul Smith, then, is championing a personal and national crusade to fashion new forms of British identity. In 1997 he was invited to join the newly elected Labour government's Department of Culture, Media and Sport Creative Industries Task Force. The remit of this Task Force is to offer government assistance to the creative industries of the UK in order to help achieve their full economic potential. Through his membership of this committee, we see Paul Smith peculiarly positioned as both ambassador to, and critic of, the national fashion industry. As such, Paul Smith offers a unique commentary on both the state of British fashion, and more importantly, an insight into government initiatives and public policy towards fashion and cultural identity.

These government initiatives set to recover the flagging national fashion scene play host to previously undervalued modes of style through the creation of what we have termed 'discourses of renewal'. These discourses refer to the language used by government and national institutions in their description of future directions for national identity. The advent of the new millennium coinciding with devolution and increasing European integration necessitates a 're-newal', 'renaissance' and a 're-branding' of British identity (Leonard 1997). This is in line with more generic debates on cultural identity in which 'identity only becomes an issue when it is in crisis' (Mercer 1990: 43). Challenges to any community customarily produce a reactionary crystallisation of identity and a pressing need to define 'who and what we are, and comprise' (Cohen 1997; McCrone 1998). In the past, 'commentators have struggled to find ways of expressing the schizophrenic nature of Britishness'. From Michael Frayn's 'herbivores and carnivores' to Peter York's 'punk and pageantry' there has been conflict over the presentation of national identity (*Sunday Times*, September 1997). However, new forms of Britishness actualised through fashion and couched in terms of national regeneration and transformation have enabled alternative versions of national identity to enter the spotlight. Stalwarts of traditional British style such as Aquascutum, Margaret Howell, Clarks and Burberry have become innovators of fresh takes on an otherwise dated national 'look' stereotypically personified by the country squire. Burberry, for example, outfitter to the British 'county set', has recently been labelled as 'born-again' after 'cleaning up its collections' and making the move from being priggishly 'mumsy' to displaying 'sharp-as-a-knife' tailoring modelled by Stella Tennant and sported by Britpop's Gallagher brothers and Jarvis Cocker (*Independent on Sunday*, August 1998). Mulberry, another iconic British label synonymous with the selling of an elitist rural idyll, also made headline news when it went 'grungy' and sent female models down the catwalk with cropped, spiky hair, body piercing, daringly placed tattoos and low-cut tops (*Daily Mail*, April 1999). Here we see how British fashion design is central to a renewal of British identity but additionally we show how these emerging versions of Britishness are controversial and sit uneasily alongside more mainstream sartorial styles.

True Brit?

Just as there are fashions in clothing and style, so too are there fashions in academic thought and geographical discussion. The much vaunted 'cultural turn' of the early 1990s endorsed a trend towards 'spectacular geographies' of consumption and commodification and of an attendant vogue in elegant semiotic analyses of the built environment (Jackson 1995: 1875). This 'theme-parkisation' of both retail space and popular culture was deemed to be a consequence of the clodhopping forces of globalisation and was said to result in a (well-documented) erosion of local uniqueness and spatial homogeneity (see Harvey 1989; Hopkins 1990; Kowinski 1985; Ritzer 1993; Sack 1988; Sorkin 1992). Whilst the fashion industry with its global reach and influence bolsters these ideas of homogeneity it, simultaneously, is able to commentate on matters of a more proximate nature to do with notions of the self, personal identity and the immediate spaces of our life-worlds. There is a well-promoted backlash against the oppressive – and passé –

dictates of omnipresent, entrenched multinationals. The Spring/Summer 1999 Sisley collection for example sells its high-fashion, ready-to-wear clothes with the byline, 'A man flattened by an opponent can get up again. A man flattened by conformity stays down for good'. The emergent fashion sentiment, then, is towards an eclecticism of styles, away from the cloning of a global consumer. As such we find the fashion industry, in negotiation with local and global discourses, offering a potent lens through which to examine and challenge the simplicity of the globalisation thesis in more multiple and complex ways (Cox 1997; Crewe and Beaverstock 1998; Crewe and Lowe 1995, 1996).

Doubtless there remains a series of fashion brands (for example, Benetton, Gap and Levi's) that lay testimony to the homogenising influence of a rapidly globalising marketplace (Crewe and Lowe 1996). The ubiquity of these labels forms part of a 'logo culture' intent on appropriating contemporary consumption practices regardless of location or space (Klein 2000). However, just as Jackson and Thrift (1995) call for a departure from the tyranny of the single retail site towards a more heterogeneous conceptualisation of consumption spaces, so too is there a need for a more comprehensive profile of the fashion scene and the players within it. Quite simply, the exhibitionism and extravagance associated with the megamall or the conspicuous fashion brand offer us only a partial snapshot of the consumer scene. Eulogistic accounts of shopping malls as cathedrals of late-capitalist consumption – sanitised, supervised and surveyed (Goss 1993; Gottdiener 1986; Shields 1992) – overshadow less spectacular but just as vibrant modes of retailing (Crewe and Gregson 1998; Crewe *et al.* 2000; Gregson *et al.* 2000a, 2000b). Similarly, the global dominance of flagrant designer brands has eclipsed more complex explanations of locally sensitive and flexibly specialised modes of clothing provision and consumption.

Kevin Robins (1997) tells us that globalisation is about a growing mobility across frontiers. This mobility is characterised by a host of both economic and cultural complexities nowhere more evident than in the world of fashion. Whilst fashion and the consumer culture to which it is related have previously been trivialised as mere surface effects (Raban 1974; Wark 1991), it is possible to re-evaluate this view through the spatial politics and locally grounded practices of the Paul Smith organisation. The globalisation process brings together international cultural elements with national and regional influences, thereby combining different spatial scales as well as the related forces of change and continuity (Allen 1995; Massey 1991; Massey 1995; Meegan 1995; Robins 1991). This combination is inherent to the fashion industry. For example, haute couture designers are described as possessing a 'magpie mentality' intent on 'plundering the world of its ideas' (Craik 1994; Jones 1995: 22; McDermott 1987: 28) to reveal an array of different cultural, spatial and temporal influences across their seasonal collections. Furthermore these influences are continually being manipulated and reinterpreted, not only by the designers themselves, but also by the various cultural intermediaries found within the fashion system. Thus there exists a constant reinvention of identities within fashion that refutes the notion of homogeneity and the 'dulling down' attributed to globalising cultural industries.

As far as Paul Smith is concerned, the fusion between change and continuity is a crucial component of the brand identity. The phrase 'classic with a twist', which has now passed into common fashion parlance, was first coined by the organisation (*Scotland on Sunday*, October 1995; *The Guardian Weekend*, February 1998) to describe a look that is 'in many ways traditional, but at the same time, funky' (*Elle*, October 1995).[1] From this description it is possible to view the way in which Paul Smith juxtaposes varying temporal styles to mark out a unique brand identity which simultaneously borrows from the familiar, or traditional, as well as the avant-garde. To cite an example, recent Paul Smith menswear collections have exhibited classic suiting taken from long-standing British tailoring traditions and re-presented it in unorthodox velvets, overblown checks and pistachio-coloured Harris tweeds. Rather than a uniformity emerging out of this growing mobility then, through the case of Paul Smith, we see an integration of sartorial identities and styles which makes for eclecticism in terms of both cultural persistence and cultural innovation (Hannerz 1992; Nederveen Pieterse 1995).

The nature and effects of globalisation are also made manifest in the transformation over recent years of manufacturing and signifying practices. The growing emphasis on communication and information technologies symptomatic of time-space compression has resulted in a shift away from standardised techniques of mass production to more specialised systems of carefully targeted provision. This move from Fordism to Benettonisation, from a principally industrial economy to one that is information- and service-led, has been instrumental in the fashion industry (Belussi 1992; Phizacklea 1990; Purvis 1996). The lifestyling of consumer goods enabled by flexible and smaller-batch production initiatives has meant that clothing can be employed as a mechanism through which entire lifestyles are sold to specified niche consumer groupings (Leiss *et al.* 1986; Maffesoli 1988; Shields 1992; Tomlinson 1990).

This culturisation of clothing and accessories via flexible specialisation is heavily endorsed by Paul Smith. According to him, unlike other British labels which suffered from an ambition to monopolise the global fashion scene during the 1980s, Paul Smith chose instead to foster a brand identity based around values of exclusivity, individuality and uniqueness (interview, November 1991):

> I've always tried to design clothes which allow the person to be an individual, rather than making them look like part of a high fashion gang . . . I want my customers to put their own personality on what they buy, and the clothes allow people to express their character rather than have it overwhelmed.
>
> ('True Brit' exhibition catalogue, 1995: 2)

It is apparent, then, that through the lifestyling of his designs, Paul Smith markets ideas of individualism to potential buyers around the world rather than conformity and a globally homogeneous, singular style.

In a globalising world where there are concerns over the eradication of difference, heightened importance is continually being placed on this notion of distinction and on how we manifest our differences. The disorientation and the rootlessness that are said to characterise global times have given rise to a reactionary search for stability and the pursuit of a palpable 'sense of place' (Allen 1995; Jameson 1988; Lash and Urry 1994; Massey 1991; Massey 1994; Ohmae 1990). In consequence, the niche marketing of fashionable lifestyle brands is one mechanism that has tapped into this consumer longing for 'placed identities for place-less times' (Robins 1991: 38). Certain fashion labels have become invested with spatial meaning and place-specific iconography and mythology (for example, Laura Ashley with rural Wales; Mulberry with Somerset and the south-west of England). In turn, this means that by buying particular articles of clothing, we are also able to acquire a sense of place and a slice of locally grounded identity. This process is an antidote to the speed and chaos of high-flying global exchanges, since the return to roots marks out the search for coherent cultural asylum.

One of the ways through which Paul Smith grounds this sense of localeness is via an association of his products and organisation with senses of Britishness. Most notably this attachment with national identity has been created via the 'True Brit' phenomenon – a catchphrase with which Paul Smith has become synony-mous. The title 'True Brit'[2] was first coined in October 1995 when the Paul Smith exhibition celebrating his twenty-five years in business was launched at the Design Museum in London. The 'Paul Smith: True Brit' exhibition details the evolution and development not purely of the organisation, but of the man, his personality and idiosyncrasies. On show is a deeply anecdotal and personalised history, describing the cycle-mad teenager and allowing a glimpse of school reports and photographs. The exhibition is a snapshot of Paul Smith's life and work, candid and unpretentious and cultivating a sense of tradition and heritage as a counter-measure to the placelessness and blandness so often linked to globally expansive companies. The story makes much of Smith's family and upbringing in Nottingham, and underscores, above all else, his ordinariness. The description of Paul Smith as a *true* Brit reinforces the notion of authenticity and genuineness in a global-ised world that prizes the hyper and virtual reality of simulated and electronic exchanges where 'real-ness', it has been argued, is defined by residence in any one place and the internalisation of subjective dispositions (McCrone 1998; Smout 1994).

Narratives of ambiguity

Paralleling these complex negotiations between the local and the global, the story of the Paul Smith organisation is also one based on a curious set of juxtapositions and ruptures. The narratives surrounding Smith's emergence as a sartorial authority hinge around a series of ambiguities: Paul Smith is at once a symbol of pro-vincial parochiality and an icon of the new urban metropolitan chic; his style is at once deeply nostalgic yet also progressive and avant-garde; he is anarchic and dismissive of big business yet at the same time a spokesperson for British design and very much part of the fashion establishment; he is steeped in British sartorial tradition yet disrupts conventional design aesthetics and scrambles fashion's signs and symbols: the floral suit, the photo-printed budgie waistcoat, the strip-cartoon trousers. Such discourses of ambiguity (Pratt 1992) are significant in that they have shaped the evolution of the organisation and continue to form the basis for its marketing strategy. Quite how these narratives of juxtaposition unfold will be explored below. First, however, a note about the evolution of the organisation.

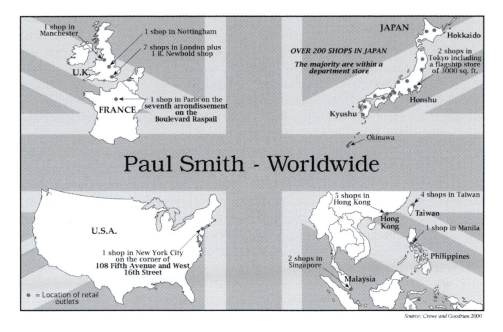

Source: Crewe and Goodrun 2000

Figure 2.1   Location of Paul Smith stores worldwide. © Louise Crewe.

Paul Smith began in 1970 in a small shop in Byard Lane on the edge of Nottingham's Lace Market that remains the site of his store today. The shop was pioneering in the sense that it was the only one outside of London to stock emergent designer names such as Kenzo and Margaret Howell. By 1976 Paul was acting as a consultant to the International Wool Secretariat and to an Italian shirt manufacturer, and it was at this point that he decided to go it alone and to show his first collection in Paris. The collection was founded on British tradition and a tailored look but with a keen eye on contemporary influences. He went on to open a clutch of shops in London, and others in New York, Paris, Hong Kong, Singapore and throughout Japan. There are currently ten Paul Smith shops in England, seven in London, one in Manchester, one in Nottingham and one R. Newbold shop in London. There are over 200 shops in Japan (see Figure 2.1) and Paul Smith sells more there than his Italian rivals Versace and Armani. He is considered to be the leading European designer in Japan, and argues

> I often talk at business conferences and one of the first things I'm always asked is 'How do you break into a lucrative market like Japan?' You can almost see them dribbling at the prospect. But it's not about breaking into a market. It's about building relationships . . . A lot of designers like Lauren, Armani, Gianfranco Ferre have got licence agreements but they've either never been there or have been there once, travelling from their hotel for a sort of waving ceremony. The difference is that we really work at it.

> (Interview)

The company remains entirely self-financed and has an annual turnover of £171 million. Worldwide sales have experienced a year on year growth of between 50 and 60 per cent since 1993. Two-thirds of all sales are made up from exports and four-fifths of turnover comes from Japan.

In many ways, then, the dominant story surrounding Paul Smith is that of humble, self-effacing, Nottingham-boy-turned-style-guru who has transported his successful retail formula around the world whilst remaining firmly tied to the Nottingham local economy where he was born and began his business. His official story is emphatically local in origin, even parochial, and much is made of his Nottingham roots and continued connections with, and allegiance to, this provincial British city. Yet the relationships between Paul Smith's Nottingham roots and his emergent place in the global fashion arena are ambiguous – and intentionally so, for they form part of the marketing strategy of the organisation. Biographical accounts of Smith's early years in Nottingham and his connections with local art colleges and clothing firms in the Lace Market, Nottingham's fashion quarter, form a dominant discourse throughout much of the company's marketing and promotional literature. This emphasis on local roots and heritage is mobilised through notions of tradition and provinciality. This discourse of localism, of family ties and of history is deliberately set against the dominant narratives of the global fashion media which hinge around ideas of centrality and of an aesthetic that is resolutely international and, most importantly, metropolitan and spans the fashion centres of London, Paris, Milan and New York. Here, then, we see an intriguing paradox between the nostalgia of 'home' and localeness and its articulation by a fashion organisation involved in the global business of outward show, depthlessness and facade.

Also ambiguous are the connections (and confusions) between Paul Smith the designer, Paul Smith the label and Paul Smith the organisation. This ambiguity is central to the retail strategy of the organisation since notions of idiosyncrasy, eccentricity, intimacy and the personal are the foundations upon which the corporate identity rests. The importance of Paul himself is continually underscored in the literature. He ensures that all of his offices are above the shops in which he sells his clothes and he is frequently found serving behind the counter of the Floral Street shop in London, or advising customers on tailoring and accessories. This, together with allowing the public a peek at the usually cloistered depths of a chairman's office, conveys a sense of the personal, of approachability and firmly grounded reliability. Smith celebrates a golden age of British retailing, before the arrival of the mass-market giants, when retailers were shopkeepers and when shops were located in, and grew out of, their home town, their local place. He very much models himself on the traditional shopkeeper, and runs his global business as if it were a local shop, with a hands-on management style and a commitment to creative independence. He argues, 'I prefer the individuality and oddness of corner shops or food shops, or shops where old and modern utilitarian items are sold together' (Blackwell and Burney 1990: 99).

The design aesthetic of Paul Smith's stores also hints at a sense of incongruous juxtaposition. Throughout the world his stores are replicas of the Paul Smith shops in England and are fitted out in the style of a traditional 1950s English gentleman's dressing-room or tailors, with mahogany fittings, wooden floors and glass cabinets. Entire wooden interiors have been shipped from England to Japan. The Kobe shop, for example, was originally a chemist's in Sheffield and the Tokyo shop a choco-latier's in Newcastle. Yet amidst such traditional English grandeur we see a range of incongruous fixtures, including not only classic British memorabilia such as turn-of-the-century decorative shell boxes, selections of 1920s and 1930s oil paintings and objets d'art by young British designers, but also personal gadgetry such as toy cars and water pistols which provide an atmosphere of 'homely retail anarchy' (Jones 1995: 16), a decidedly British trait and particularly in couture where the British look is characterised by individualism and off-beat eccentricity. The eccen-tric tastes and foibles of this 'down-to-earth Nottingham lad' (*Observer*, 1995) are accentuated by the organisation who is quick to describe his office as Santa's rather old grotto with tatty books, cameras strewn everywhere, antique jewellery and dismembered radios. Smith owns a collection of 350 robots and frequently produces absurd and incongruous props such as rubber chickens at board meetings.

What we are seeing then are clear references to traditional notions of elegance and Britishness which are underscored by reverential discourses about quality and cut and hark back to traditional notions of craftsmanship. Yet at the same time another set of cultural vocabularies is superimposed upon this aesthetic of tradi-tionalism, namely notions of irony, of kitsch and of the surreal. Through the display of commodities that evoke memories of 1950s Britain, and particularly of post-war childhood, we see a deep sense of knowing irony and nostalgia at work. As Sean Nixon acknowledges in his appraisal of menswear retailing in the 1980s, these narratives of traditionalism and the avant-garde came to dominate the design aesthetics of a great many British retailers:

> The significance of these design elements across the markets consolidated two dominant repertoires of cultural values: a sense of 'modernity' and a sense of 'tradition' in the presentation of menswear. From the stark austere minimalism of Comme des Garçons to the softer dark-wood interiors of Paul Smith, menswear outlets mixed – to varying degrees – the aesthetics of non-reference and placelessness of an aggressive moder-nity with the nostalgia of a particular re-imagined Edwardian past.
>
> (Nixon 1996: 58)

Yet while others were looking towards either the futuristic, end-of-millennium look or to the minimalism of earlier versions of modernity, Paul Smith was mobil-ising a very explicit sense of kitsch and irony within his store design process. Parallels can be seen here with other retail pioneers such as Café Pop in Manchester and Wayne Hemingway's Red or Dead chain, both of which, like Paul Smith, rely extensively on witty incursions and crass juxtapositions into an otherwise predictable and mind-numbingly dull retail environment. Both Hemingway and Smith, for example, draw on unlikely sources for design inspiration and mobilise the absurd for aesthetic effect.

> The flotsam and jetsam that people discard fascinates Hemingway and has proved a rich source over the years. The walls of his office are covered with car-boot sale finds, every available surface filled with glass animals, snow-scene paperweights, straw donkeys and kitsch holiday

souvenirs . . . Wedgwood china has to be one of the saddest things anybody could ever collect. Garden gnomes too . . . those pictures of doe-eyed boys and girls . . . the artificial wood-grain print taken from those 1960s Formica tables.

(Kingswell 1998: 22)

Irony chic, it seems, is suddenly terribly fashionable. But what is important about this is that the celebration of trash is not a political act of 'identification with the poor' but rather an exhibition of middle-class knowingness. Those invest-ing in alternative and ironic forms of cultural capital – such as Paul Smith's 'witty' shirts and satirical fabrics – are what Bourdieu terms the 'new style autodidacts' (cited in Sconce 1995: 376); people who can transgress conventional taste bound-aries and invest in unsanctioned culture because they have already acquired the requisite cultural – and economic – capital. The important point, of course, is that in reality some people have access to both high and low culture, but the majority only have access to low. In other words, those who have access to the codes and practices of consuming both 'high' and 'low' culture are in the privileged state of having what Gripsrud calls 'double access', and double access is essentially a class privilege (Sconce 1995: 383). In this way, a taste for kitsch, irony and bad taste may ultimately be an act of unintended, middle-class condescension. As Wayne Hemingway explains, 'Probably my favourite car-boot find of all time is the Tretchikoff Lady . . . She sums up the naff style of the 1960s and 70s – it's the archetype of what people with "taste" wanted on their walls' (Hemingway 1998: 24).

Such celebrations of trash, it seems, are ways of mapping out one's taste territories whilst remaining safely within one's own elite taste culture.

It requires a certain level of sophistication. It's nostalgia with an ironic distance. It's kin to another semi-highbrow activity, the deliberate culti-vation of bad taste. 'I like wearing the leisure suit because it looks weird and outdated. *I know that.*' It's this absolutely essential know-ingness, then, which creates that safe distance, that prevents you actually looking like the dweeb who would have worn that in the real 70s.

(Sconce 1995)

The 1990s, it seems, was the time to make the uncool cool. And while Paul Smith employs the naff image of Mills & Boon romance novels as a marketing tool, Wayne Hemingway opts for the immeasurably uncool Geography Teacher collec-tion in 1997:

We wanted to get across the way that often the coolest people in the world are those who are the most uncool, and geography teachers embody that for me. It was like a really witty collection . . . taking styles and fabrics that would be classed as unwearable – corduroy, plus-fours, geeky specs, dodgy tattershalls and shirts – all the clothes that my geography teacher wore.

(Hemingway 1998: 28)

Paul Smith's latest retail venture, the outlet in Westbourne House, Notting Hill, further reveals the sense of ambiguity that pervades the entire organisation. Westbourne House is a magnificent mews house that is reminiscent of nineteenth-century maison de couture retailing. Smith's mission has always been to provide an alternative to the dull uniformity and mind-numbing predictability of mass-market retailing, and the opening of Westbourne House can be seen in many ways as the realisation of this dream to have a shop-in-a-home. He commissioned Sophie Hicks to redesign the interior in a way that plays on the idea that this shop is a home. Throughout, Hicks has abstracted ideas from residential traditions, and has deliberately played with and scrambled the symbols and styles of residential design so that Westbourne House reads subliminally like 'home' yet is quite clearly a privately run, highly profitable retail venture. By scrambling the conventional boundaries between home and work, the public and the private, retailing and domesticity, Smith continues to furnish our consumptional imaginations with new vocabularies of style. Unlike other 'flagship' stores such as Ralph Lauren's Rhinelander Maison on Madison Avenue in New York, which replicates an English country house, Westbourne House takes an ironic, even surreal approach (Menkes 1998). The pictures on the wall are a rogues' gallery from Paul Smith's life – again an example of the indivisibility of the man and the organisation. The children's room includes a bubble gum machine and an igloo and at the top of the staircase is a 'deliriously bad painting' (Lancaster 1998) of a couple on their country estate which is altogether more ironic and knowing than the conventional design cues adopted by other flagship stores. Into this mélange go the clothes that include tailored jackets for £400 and custom-made suits with bright lining beginning at £1,000.

Designing desire, transforming consumption

New man, old man

The early 1990s have seen an unprecedented amount of media attention on the meanings of masculinity and the possibilities for 'new man': television programmes such as BBC2's 'From Wimps to Warriors' series argue that 'it's a myth about masculinity being fixed and natural' (*The Times*, 1991); *The Times* went on to argue that masculinity is becoming the issue of the 1990s, and the author of the radical men's magazine *Achilles Heel* argued that 'the feminist movement left a gap in which anti-sexist men are . . . struggling for an identity . . . they want something to call themselves' (*The Times*, 1991, quoted in Brooks 1999). Confronted by the loss of traditional gender roles and thrown into a sense of unstable disorientation, masculinity, it is argued, is in crisis. Yet the fashion sector welcomed such hand-wringing uncertainty as an entirely positive move, in that it created new possibilities for the (re)definition of multiple masculinities. New markets were opening up and the creative possibilities of menswear were acknowledged. 'There's suddenly more scope and a new market in between classic suits and sporty casual clothes' (*The Face*, November 1984: 87, quoted in Nixon 1996: 34). And while many British men clung on to the last vestiges of their conventional wardrobes, 'an unpleasant mac, a dowdy overcoat, a shaggy jumper and slacks for week-ends, an insistence on dour colours from the sludge spectrum unique to GBM, and a sullen resistance to sock-changing' (Spencer 1992), there were at least signs of a new breed emerging. 'Only the creeping arrival of Euroman, with his suspect peacockery and his handbags threatens the dull purity of the strain [of Great British Men]' (Spencer 1992). While the creation of new man may always have been as much the creation of the media as of men ('I know they wear Paul Smith, said one magazine editor, but I've never met one', wrote Spencer [1992] in his search for new men), Paul Smith was also undoubtedly a key player within this transformation of male consumption. Most known for his revolutionary work on the male wardrobe, he is argued to be 'the leading fashion designer who persuaded British men that well-cut cloth was not just for pretty boys' (*The Times*, October 1995). He brought to the business a keen awareness of global variation in consumption patterns and lamented what he calls the 'Englishman's disease', typified by a tendency to buy 'vast quantities of bad clothes. Here, no-one breaks the rules about appearance. There's a terrible sameness.' In contrast, Smith argues that 'if you live near Prato you have beauty all around you. Great food. Great dressing. It's absolutely okay' (interview). Yet Smith managed to introduce a European sense of style, quality and design into the male British consumption scene and has successfully instilled his products with a strong sense of identity, suggestive of understated style:

> With his stuff you get kudos and credibility – it shows you're an inter-esting person, maybe a cultured or artistic person. The barristers and solicitors and all those people who are considered very boring might wear Paul Smith in the evening and at the week-end to prove they're not.
>
> (Prosser 1990: 8)

In many ways, then, Paul Smith emerged as a cultural authority in determining the codes of a new form of masculinity. He did this by offering a repertoire of styles, from his iconic boxer shorts and filofaxes in the mid-1980s, through to his quirky and humorous printed shirts and his immaculately styled couture suits. For young men, taking an interest in one's appearance was no longer seen as trivial and superficial, it had become a legitimate means of self-signification, a 'tangible demonstration of self-worth' (Mort 1996: 123). As such, it has been argued that 'the masculinity which the British have held so strongly . . . may be changing messily, unevenly and with great resistance into a more feminine identity' (Dodd 1995: 24). However, and as we go on to show here, the emergence of this new masculinity in 1990s Britain is an uneasy and, for some, unsettling process. While new man was envisaged as a softer, more reflexive and altogether more stylish individual, the plurality of significations enmeshed within the construct has given rise to a certain level of anxiety and anxiousness. 'The original new man welded together the possibilities of the nurturer and the narcissist in a flawed whole; but in reality the new man was always an uneasy mixture' (Rutherford 1988: 230). It has been argued that new man is a contradiction in terms, 'one who is becoming more self-conscious of what it is to be a man, and one who sees through the farce of masculinity and all the entrappings that accompany it' (Gentle 1998: 98).

We illustrate such tensions and ambivalences through a reading of some of the key sartorial motifs within Paul Smith's ranges. First, there is an evident middle-class romanticising of a past, working-class masculinity that is seen as more authentic, more gritty, more honest than its middle-class counterpart. The R. Newbold range in particular provides an interesting discourse on the theme of utility design and its influence on British fashion. The collection was inspired by the factory of the same name which Paul Smith bought in 1991 and which supplied the army and the great British stores Harrods and Browns. The first collection included several styles and garments that the factory was famous for having produced in the past. The Spring/Summer 1998 'Network' collection echoes the Utility wear of garments worn by early servicemen and technicians during the construction of the telecommunications industry. What is important here is the way in which Paul Smith has foregrounded workwear and utility as dominant motifs within the collection. At one level the value accorded to workwear is indicative of a celebration of working-class masculinity, and suggests a reverence for a time when real men grafted and life was uncomplicated. What is interesting here is that it is the *work* wear of earlier eras that is being celebrated, not the leisurewear. This is, then, a celebration of the world of male, manual work, the very world that, if not quite lost, is rapidly disappearing. It is thus about labour and loss, about the loss of particular (supposedly uncomplicated) masculine workplace identities and – consequently – is suggestive of the uncertainties and provisionalities of masculine identities in contemporary Britain. New man looks back to old man for a sense of security and stability in a fast-moving and slippery style-world.

Second, there is a strong sense, as we have outlined above, in which Paul Smith man is a knowing, witty ironist. The range of commodities on display, from the infamous boxer shorts to the cheeky cufflinks and kitsch office accoutrements suggests another version of new man; new lad, with his ironic knowingness and laddish posturing. A reaction to the media-scorn which was increasingly being piled upon the 'supposed "new man" with his phoney nappy changing . . . ways' (*Observer* 13/11/94) perhaps, 'new lad' was born. Fuelled by men's magazines such as *loaded*, men could once again be themselves, could revert to laddish behaviour and boys' toys. Paul Smith very much captures this sense of fun and frivolity within men's consumption, this ironic stance towards the canons of good taste, and plays to an audience who appreciates the sartorial satire embedded within the Pythonesque stage which is the store.

Finally, there is a version of new man which is elitist and classist, which builds on a certain traditional English craftsmanship and quality and which reaches its apotheosis in the spectacular space of Westbourne House. With an emphasis on understated inconspicuous consumption, such sartorial elites employ an intelligent and knowing prose in their consumptional vocabularies, and draw on discourses of quality, design and exclusivity to legitimise their excessive expenditure. This version is resolutely middle class and employs the classically Bourdieuian tactics of the controlled cultivation of taste in order to carve out a sense of distinction. Dismissed by Rutherford as a 'chauvinistic, elitist, a narcissistic toad' (1988: 232), this version of new man buys into the stereotypical iconography of the 1980s yuppie and 1990s cultural intermediary: a creative and discerning professional who knows quality when he sees it and is prepared to pay for it.

This leaves us with Paul Smith's three versions of masculinity: the hedonistic, ironic new lad; the elitist and expensive new man; and the nostalgic 'new old man', who looks longingly to an earlier version of straightforward masculinity when real men worked and were proud of it. Together, it could be argued that such motifs of masculinity are reinforcing the 'existing power structure by producing a hybrid masculinity which is better able and more suited to retain control' (Rutherford 1988: 235). Moreover, the rise of new men who are gentle yet strong, sensitive yet sexy, stylish yet knowingly ironic, suggests the 'feminisation' of men's consumption (Dodd 1995). Such incursions into the traditionally feminine spheres of domesticity and consumerism are seen by some as a sign that 'having secured the heartland of the public, men are now moving into the private' (White 1990, quoted in Brooks 1999). The emergent multiplicity of masculinities may not be the transformative and liberating force it at first appears; nor may it challenge the enshrined gendered power bases in 1990s Britain.

> If what we define as female qualities will be highly valued in our brave new future, then to maintain hegemony it is in men's interests to co-opt femininity . . . the future may be female, but I fear it will still belong to men.
>
> (Chapman 1988: 248)

Exporting Britishness

What, then, does the foregoing discussion tell us about sartorial style, national identity and global fashion brands? The national look is a notoriously slippery concept to define. Consensus wavers between British style as starched, upright and earnest, and as Britain, the streetstyle capital of the world. David Shilling, revered British milliner, articulates this identity fracture:

> Britain has not just one national fashion identity, but two. I call this 'Monarchy and Anarchy'. Monarchy is the classic look, in which ladies in hats still figure as do men in formal tailoring: the traditional British look. Anarchy is the experimental free-spirited look in which Britain excels, whether seen through 'pop' or 'streetstyle', or commercially interpreted by a whole range of design talent from market stall to international market-place. The look is funky, eccentric, often humorous, and above all innovative.
>
> (Shilling in de la Haye 1996: 196–7)

Whilst Britain has made its name selling a look based on classic and class-oriented clothing, increasingly there are drives to promote Britain's funkier subcultural scene. Clothing and the fashioning of identity through strong sartorial styles is a crucial aspect of British subculture (Hebdige 1979) and therefore opens up an avenue for the selling of a renewed national identity both domestically and overseas, involving alternative British looks and ideologies. It may be argued that British fashion and its export is as much an element of the tourist industry as it is an industry based purely around design and retailing. In their latest edition of *UK: The Guide*, The British Tourist Authority (BTA) see the national fashion scene as a valuable marketing tool in 'altering perceptions of Britain' and the development of a 'reputation overseas as an exciting and contemporary destination' (BTA press release, February 1998). *UK: The Guide* offers

> essential reading for any hip young visitor who wants to be in the know about 'the scene' in Britain. It moves away from the more traditional icons that are often used to promote Britain and features the nation's hottest dancefloors, football, fashion, pub bands and cult British TV.
>
> (BTA press release, February 1998)

Here we see how British fashion is being used to entice tourists and tourism into the UK. Interestingly however, the national fashion scene is not only about this one-way cultural exchange. As well as inward flows and the strengthening of the internal tourism industry, the BTA also view the 'cool' fashion scene as a route to raising Britain's profile overseas and to the expansion of outward British investment in foreign markets. Following this, it is possible to see how the export of national fashion is being employed as part of a two-pronged policy to profitable cultural exchange couched in both inward and outward flows of touristic discourse.

Fashion, in terms of haute couture and streetstyle, is by no means composed of two entirely separate spheres. Couture often relies on subversive styles for its inspiration. 'British style, quirky, undulating is never simply one look, one packaged idea. "After all", says Jasper Conran, "this is the country that has produced John Galliano *and* Aquascutum"' (*Vogue*, August 1987). Vivienne Westwood, now the 'grande dame' of British fashion, first launched her career in the radical underworld of punk and revolutionary style. Alexander McQueen made his name with morbid runway shows inspired by gothic culture. Paul Smith follows in a similar, if slightly more subdued vein, selling an amalgam of influences drawn from all manner of cultural spheres.

> Most people think of English style as Savile Row and country house tweeds. What Paul does is say yes, we have a tremendous tradition of classic tailoring but we also have punks and mods and street style and weird eccentrics like Cecil Beaton . . . what you see on the Paul Smith catwalk is the length and breadth of English style in all its complexity.
>
> (Howarth 1993)

The notion of Britain as a nation of eccentrics is a common thread in nationalist discourse (Aslet 1997; Davies 1997; Paxman 1998; Samuels 1992). In part, this eccentricity is manufactured and reinforced by the occupants of the national fashion scene. Paul Smith is a self-appointed 'John Cleese of fashion' (*Elle Style* 1995: 74) and he transports his idiosyncrasies, through his designs, via exports around the globe under the banner of British individualism. 'I suppose', says Smith, 'my thing has always been about maximising Britishness' (*True Brit* catalogue, 1995: 2). In this case, Britishness is the Paul Smith cross between 'Savile Row and Carnaby Street, the Eton schoolboy and the East End bad boy' (*The Face* 1994: 76).

Because of the evasive nature of Britishness, national identity is often usurped by designers and fashion organisations alike for their own means. Burberry stores, with their proliferation of Union Jacks and imperial memorabilia, are described as 'a kind of British experience for tourists' (*Independent on Sunday* magazine, February 1996) and additionally, the territorial boundaries of England, Scotland and Britain are frequently muddied in marketing rhetoric to be used interchangeably at the industry's convenience. Historically, the shape and edges of British identity are changing, often vague and also malleable – an aspect which has been termed as the 'fuzzy frontier' of Britishness (Cohen 1994: 35). Thus we see that, 'whether inadvertently absorbed or fully exploited by fashion designers, national identity offers a route to product differentiation and makes good business sense' (de la Haye 1996: 11–12). With Paul Smith, however, there is an additional cultural imperative to the utilisation of notions of Britishness that goes beyond hard-nosed economics and a sense of doing good business. Paul Smith employs the eccentricity ascribed to British fashion to authenticate his own personal style message. His eighty or so shops 'have to have a heart' and around the world are, 'little oases of discreetly English eccentricity, invariably fitted out with antique mahogany counters, display cabinets, shelves and oak flooring stripped from redundant premises around Britain. He even imported a 100-year-old floor for one of his Tokyo stores' (Miller 1993).

On the surface, then, the emerging narrative that we see here is indeed one of colonisation and the appropriation of foreign markets by Paul Smith using the accoutrements of a bygone age. His highly visible presence in Japan in particular relies on the use of traditional design cues and typically British fixtures and fittings, many of which are historical imports, the 'stuff that lets you know you're in a Paul Smith shop, not just some tacky olde English emporium in Regent Street where they put tartan in the window and sell marmalade at the tills' (Garfield 1990: 4). Japan spends $12 billion on clothing imports, which amounts to 40 per cent of the $30 billion clothes market, but very little of this comes from the global fashion centres of Paris, New York or Milan. Rather, it is the hallmarks of British lifestyle such as Burberry, Aquascutum and Paul Smith that are increasingly evident in Japan (*Nikkei Weekly*, 22/12/97). Such brand names, in Japan, possess a mystique, a cachet that creates an impression of sophistication and taste (Clammer 1992: 210). They also play a significant role in appearance management and self-identity, where great emphasis is put upon having the 'correct' appearance, for which read immaculately laundered and ironed garments of impeccable quality which leave the store in elegant packaging, and retain their hallmarks of brand name and quality (Clammer 1992).[3]

But if we scratch beneath the surface of this dominant narrative, we see that Smith's extraordinary success relates to far more than the simple transplantation of his quirky Britishness abroad. Rather, his internationalisation strategy displays a remarkable awareness of global variation which he uses to great effect. Smith displays a strong ability to seek out the right local conditions in order to maximise competitiveness and uses local specialisms to his advantage, be it printed fabrics from Como, linens and wools from Florence, mohair from West Yorkshire or retro memorabilia from 1960s London. In many ways, then, he uses the global division of specialisation not for conventional cost-reduction reasons, but in order to tap into local pools of excellence on a global basis. Turning again to Smith's phenomenal success in Japan, where he is the number one selling men's brand name in the country which now accounts for four-fifths of his world turnover, it can be seen that this success relates not simply to clever packaging of a particular version of traditional Britishness, but to his detailed personal knowledge of the cultures, customs, consumers and systems of economic organisation at work there. He enjoys a close working relationship with the Japanese trading house Itochu, which still manufactures, wholesales and retails Paul Smith and R. Newbold across Japan, and visits personally at least twice a year. His ability to penetrate the markets of the Far East, then, is firmly rooted in his craft of fashion, his fabric selection, tailoring skills and attention to detail. He has recently launched a new jeans range, for example, called Red Ear. The inspiration for the collection stems from his pursuit of quality and longevity. The concept reflects the Japanese obsession with detail and quality. It relies on meticulous dyeing and weaving processes and precision cutting, making and finishing with rivets, studs and stitching. It is this unfailing attention to detail and to understated quality which in part explains his Japanese success. This awareness of global markets is also revealed through the 'True Brit' exhibition, which was expanded and added to for its tour of Japan in order to tap directly into the peculiarities of this local market. This shows that Paul Smith's global voice is also locally sensitive and attuned to the demands and preferences of local cultural groupings. As well as the addition of a 'Famous People' photo gallery featuring famous Japanese individuals wearing Paul Smith clothing, a noteworthy inclusion was a custom made 'artcar' – a Mini sprayed in stripey citrus colours mirroring the Paul Smith Summer 1997 collections and set to tempt the Japanese obsession with the miniature.

Paul Smith's approach to the export of his products and his philosophy mark him out as uniquely positioned amongst other global fashion competitors. Unlike blatant conspicuous consumption brands that have little regard for local distinctiveness, Paul Smith exhibits a comprehensive grasp of differing traits between markets. Furthermore, Paul Smith has bypassed the 'imperialist nostalgia' route (Rosaldo 1993) and the selling of his goods via strategies of 'imperial camp' (Driver 1993) a 'glamour of backwardness' (Nairn 1977) and the regurgitation of romanticised tropes to do with an older British Empire. In fusing the aspirational images of classic British labels with the gaining momentum of streetstyle, Smith has suggested one way in which the contentious task of representing 'Britishness' on the globalising high street and the fin-de-siècle catwalk might be managed. Whether the distinctly gendered forms that the fashion system mobilises and perpetuates will be quite so easily negotiated remains to be seen.

Notes

1   The 'classic with a twist' catchphrase is, of course, a traditional feature of British menswear fashion, which has been characterised by eccentric tendencies and offbeat styling for many years (Polhemus 1994), and particularly so in shops such as John Stephen's His Clothes on Carnaby Street of 1960s Swinging London, where narcissistic dressing-up was a male and a female option and drew on Mod style and 'city gent' influences.

2   The use of the slogan 'True Brit' is a telling take on the macho and reactionary *True Grit* film starring John Wayne, presumably intended as a witty comment on a particular version of masculinity.

3   And see too McVeigh (1997) on how the wearing of uniforms in Japan is a means of disciplining minds and bodies, of, quite literally, wearing ideology.

References

Allen, J. (1995) 'Global worlds' in J. Allen and D. Massey (eds) *Geographical Worlds*, Oxford: Oxford University Press/Open University Press, 105–42.

Ash, J. and Wilson, E. (1992) *Chic Thrills: A Fashion Reader*, London: Pandora Press.

Aslet, C. (1997) *Anyone for England? A Search for British Identity*, London: Little, Brown & Company.

Belussi, F. (1992) 'Benetton Italy: beyond Fordism and flexible specialisation' in S. Mitter (ed.) *Computer Aided Manufacturing and Women's Employment*, London: Springer-Verlag, 73–92.

Blackwell, L. and Burney, J. (1990) *Retail Future*, London: Thames & Hudson.

Blomley, N. (1996) 'I'd like to dress her all over: masculinity, power and retail space' in N. Wrigley and M. Lowe (eds) *Retailing, Consumption and Capital*, Harlow: Longman, 238–57.

Bourdieu, P. (1984) *Distinction*, London: Routledge.

Brampton, S. (1997) 'The empire strikes back', *Elle*, June.

Brooks, K. (1999) 'Media discourses and masculinity'. Unpublished paper (mimeo) available from author.

Central Office of Information (1996) *Britain 1996: An Official Handbook,* London: HMSO.

Chapman, R. and Rutherford, J. (1988) *Male Order: Unwrapping Masculinity*, London: Lawrence & Wishart.

Clammer, J. (1992) 'Aesthetics of the self: shopping and social being in contemporary urban Japan' in R. Shields (ed.) *Lifestyle Shopping: The Subject of Consumption*, London: Routledge, 195–215.

Clarke, D. (1997) *The Cinematic City*, London: Routledge.

Cohen, A.P. (1997) 'Nationalism and social identity: who owns the interests of Scotland?', *Scottish Affairs* 18.

Cohen, R. (1994) *Frontiers of Identity: The British and Others*, London: Longman.

Corner, J. and Harvey, S. (1991) *Enterprise and Heritage: Crosscurrents of National Culture*, London: Routledge.

Cox, K. (1997) *Spaces of Globalization*, London: Guilford.

Craik, J. (1994) *The Face of Fashion*, London: Routledge.

Crewe, L. and Beaverstock, J. (1998) 'Fashioning the city: cultures of consumption in contemporary urban spaces', *Geoforum* 29 (3): 287–308.

Crewe, L. and Gregson, N. (1998) 'Tales of the unexpected: exploring car boot sales as marginal spaces of contemporary consumption', *Transactions of the IBG* 23: 39–53.

Crewe, L. and Lowe, M. (1995) 'Gap on the map: towards a geography of consumption and identity', *Environment and Planning A*: 1877–1989.

Crewe, L. and Lowe, M. (1996) 'United colours? Globalisation and localisation tendencies in fashion retailing' in N. Wrigley and M. Lowe (eds) *Retailing Consumption and Capital*, Harlow: Longman, 271–83.

Crewe, L., Gregson, N. and Brooks, K. (2000) 'Retro-retailers and the production of consumption'. Article submitted to *Society and Space*.

Cunningham, S. (1997) 'British at forefront of designer-led revolution', *The Times*, 27 October.

Davies, F. (1997) *Fashion, Culture, Identity*, Chicago: Chicago University Press.

Davis, P. (1992) *This England*, London: Little, Brown & Company.

De la Haye, A. (1996) *The Cutting Edge: 50 Years of British Fashion*, London: V&A Publications.

Design Council (1996) *The Contribution of Design to the Economy*, London: The Design Council.

Dodd, P. (1995) *The Battle over Britain*, London: Demos.

Driver, F. (1993) 'Editorial: imperial camp', *Society and Space* 11: 615–17.

Du Cann, C. (1990) 'Material worlds', *Marxism Today*, Jan.: 50–3.

Featherstone, M. (1991) 'The body in consumer culture' in M. Featherstone, M. Hepworth and B. Turner (eds) *The Body: Social Process and Cultural Theory*, London: Sage.

Franklin, C. (1996) *Franklin on Fashion*, London: HarperCollins.

Garfield, S. (1990) 'Yen and the art of fashion design', *Esquire Special Supplement*.

Gelder, K. and Thornton, S. (1997) *The Subcultures Reader*, London: Routledge.

Gentle, K. (1988) 'The new male: myth or reality', in J. Ash and L. Wright (eds) *Components of Dress*, London: Routledge, 89–98.

Goodrum, A. (1998) 'Wearing Britishness: designing the fashionable body politic in British clothing exports and retailing'. Paper presented at BSA Annual Conference, 'Cultural Representation and the Body' session, University of Edinburgh, 6–9 April.

Goss, J. (1993) 'The magic of the mall: an analysis of form, function and meaning in the contemporary retail built environment', *Annals of the AAG* 83: 18–47.

Gottdiener, M. (1986) 'Recapturing the centre: a semiotic analysis of shopping malls' in M.Gottdiener and A. Lagopoulos (eds) *The City and the Sign*, New York: Columbia University Press, 288–302.

Gottdiener, M. and Lagopoulos, A. (eds) (1986) *The City and the Sign: An Introduction to Urban Semiotics*, New York: Columbia University Press.

Gregson, N., Brooks, K. and Crewe, L. (2000a) 'Bjorn again? Rethinking 70s revivalism through the reappropriation of 70s clothing', in V. Steele (ed.) *Fashion Theory: The Journal of Dress, Body and Culture*, New York: New York University Press.

Gregson, N., Brooks, K. and Crewe, L. (2000b) 'Narratives of consumption and the body in the space of the charity shop', in P. Jackson *et al.* (eds) *Commercial Cultures*, Oxford: Berg.

Hannerz, U. (1992) *Cultural Complexity*, New York: Columbia University Press.

Harvey, D. (1989) *The Condition of Postmodernity*, Oxford: Blackwell.

Hebdige, D. (1979) *Subculture: the Meaning of Style*, London: Methuen.

Hopkins, J. (1990) 'West Edmonton mall as a centre for interaction', *Canadian Geographer* 35: 268–79.

Howarth, P. (1990) *Esquire*, special supplement, Oct.

Jackson, P. (1995) 'Guest editorial: changing geographies of consumption', *Environment and Planning A*: 27, 1875–76.

Jackson, P. and Thrift, N. (1995) 'Geographies of consumption' in D. Miller and N. Thrift (eds) *Geographies of Consumption*, London: Routledge, 204–37.

Jameson, F. (1988) 'Cognitive mapping' in C. Nelson and L. Grossberg (eds) *Marxism and the Interpretation of Culture*, Basingstoke: Macmillan, 247–58.

Jones, D. (1995) *Paul Smith: True Brit*, London: Design Museum.

Kingswell, T. (1998) *Red or Dead: The Good, The Bad, The Ugly*, London: Thames & Hudson.

Klein, N. (2000) *No Logo*, London: HarperCollins.

Kowinski, W. (1985) *The Malling of America: An Inside Look at the Consumer Paradise*, New York: William Morrow.

Lancaster (1998) 'Fashioned but no longer made', *Telegraph*, 23 May 1998, 1093.

Landry, C. (2000) *The Creative City*, London: Earthscan.

Lash, S. and Urry, J. (1994) *Economies of Signs and Space*, London: Sage.

Leadbetter, C. (1999) *Living on Thin Air*, London: Penguin.

Leiss, W., Kline, S. and Jhally, S. (1986) *Social Communication in Advertising: Persons, Products and Images of Well-being*, London: Methuen.

Leonard, M. (1997) *Britain TM: Renewing our Identity*, London: Demos.

Leyshon, A., Matless, D. and Revill, G. (1998) *The Place of Music*, London: Guilford.

McCrone, D. (1998) *The Sociology of Nationalism: Tomorrow's Ancestors*, London: Routledge.

McDermott, C. (1987) *Street Style: British Design in the 1980s*, London: The Design Council.

McRobbie, A. (1998) *British Fashion Design: Rag Trade or Image Industry?* London: Routledge.

—— (1999a) 'The return to cultural production: case study, fashion journalism', Paper presented at OU seminar, mimeo.

—— (1999b) *In the Culture Society: Art, Fashion and Popular Music*, London: Routledge.

McVeigh, B. (1997) 'Wearing ideology: how uniforms discipline minds and bodies in Japan', *Fashion Theory* 1 (2): 189–214.

Maffesoli, M. (1988) *The Time of the Tribes: The Decline of Individualism in Mass Society*, London: Sage.

Massey, D. (1991) 'A global sense of place', *Marxism Today* 35 (6): 24–9.

—— (1994) *Space, Place and Gender*, Cambridge: Polity Press.

—— (1995) 'Imagining the world' in J. Allen and D. Massey (eds) *Geographical Worlds*, Oxford: Oxford University/Open University Press, 5–52.

Meegan, R. (1995) 'Local worlds' in J. Allen and D. Massey (eds) *Geographical Worlds*, Oxford: Oxford University/Open University Press, 53–104.

Menkes, S. (1998) 'Going home, with Paul Smith', *International Herald and Tribune*, 6 Feb.

Mercer, K. (1990) 'Welcome to the jungle: identity and diversity in post-modern politics', in J. Rutherford (ed.) *Identity: Community, Culture, Difference*, London: Lawrence & Wishart, 43–71.

Miller, A. (1993) 'Wheels of fortune', *Draper's Record* 26: 25.

Mort, F. (1996) *Cultures of Consumption*, London: Routledge.

Nairn, T. (1977) *The Break-Up of Britain*, London: New Left Books.

Nederveen Pierterse, J. (1995) 'Globalization as Hybridization' in M. Featherstone, S. Lash and R. Robertson (eds) *Global Modernities*, London: Sage.

Nixon, S. (1996) *Hard Looks: Masculinities, Spectatorship and Contemporary Consumption*, London: UCL Press.

O'Connor, J. and Wynne, D. (1996) *From the Margins to the Centre: Cultural Production and Consumption in the Postindustrial City*, Aldershot: Ashgate Publishing.

Ohmae, O. (1990) *The Borderless World: Power and Strategy in the Interlinked Economy*, London: Collins.

Paxman, J. (1998) *The English: A Portrait of a People*, London: Michael Joseph.

Phizaklea, A. (1990) *Unpacking the Fashion Industry*, London: Routledge.

Polhemus, T. (1994) *Streetstyle*, London: Thames & Hudson.

Polhemus, T. and Procter, L. (1978) *Fashion and Anti-Fashion: An Anthropology of Clothing and Adornment*, London: Thames & Hudson.

Pratt, A. (1992) 'Book review of Sebba, A. (1990) Laura Ashley: A life by design', *Journal of Rural Studies* 8 (1): 126–7.

Prosser, N. (1990) 'True Brit: Paul Smith – Leader of the pack', *Esquire*, Oct.

Purvis, S. (1996) 'The interchangeable roles of the producer, consumer and cultural intermediary. The new pop fashion designer', in J. O'Connor and D. Wynne (eds) *From the Margins to the Centre: Cultural Production and Consumption in the Postindustrial City*, Aldershot: Ashgate Publishing, 117–40.

Raban, J. (1974) *Soft City*, London: HarperCollins.

Ritzer, G. (1993) *The McDonaldization of Society: An Investigation into the Changing Character of Contemporary Social Life*, California: Pine Forge Press.

Robins, K. (1991) 'Tradition and translation: national culture in its global context' in J. Corner, and S. Harvey (eds) *Enterprise and Heritage: Crosscurrents of National Culture*, London: Routledge, 11–66.

—— (1997) 'What in the world's going on?' in P. Du Gay (ed.) *Production of Culture/Cultures of Production*, London: Sage.

Rosaldo, R. (1993) 'Imperialist nostalgia' in R. Rosaldo, *Culture and Truth*, Boston: Beacon Press.

Rubenstein, R. (1995) *Dress Codes: Meanings and Messages in American Culture*, Boulder, Col.: Westview Press.

Rutherford, J. (1988) 'Who's that man?' in R. Chapman and J. Rutherford (eds) *Male Order: Unwrapping Masculinity*, London: Lawrence & Wishart, 21–67.

Sack, R. (1988) 'The consumer's world: place as context', *Annals AAG* 78: 642–64.

Samuels, R. (1992) *Patriotism: the Making and Unmaking of British National Identity*, volume 3, London: Routledge.

Sconce, J. (1995) 'Trashing the academy: taste, excess and the emerging politics of cinematic style' *Screen* 36 (4): 371–93.

Scott, A. (1999) 'The cultural economy: geography and the creative field', *Media, Culture & Society* 21: 807–17.

Shields, R. (1992) *Lifestyle Shopping: The Subject of Consumption*, London: Routledge.

Smout, T. (1994) 'Perspectives on the Scottish identity', *Scottish Affairs* 6.

Sorkin, M. (1992) *Variations on a Theme Park: The New American City and the End of Public Space*, New York: Hill & Wang.

Spencer, N. (1992) 'Menswear in the 1980s' in J. Ash and E. Wilson (eds) *Chic Thrills: A Fashion Reader*, London: Pandora Press, 40–1.

Talley, A. (1997) 'London fashion-streets ahead', *Vanity Fair*, March.

Thornton, S. (1995) *Club Cultures: Music, Media and Subcultural Capital*, Cambridge: Polity.

Tomlinson, A. (1990) *Consumption, Identity and Style: Marketing, Meanings and the Packaging of Pleasure*, London: Comedia.

Wark, M. (1991) 'Fashioning the future: fashion, clothing and the manufacturing of a post-Fordist culture', *Cultural Studies* 5: 61–76.

Wilson, E. (1985) 'Fashion and the postmodern body' in J. Ash and E. Wilson (eds) *Chic Thrills: A Fashion Reader*, London: HarperCollins, 3–16.

Wrigley, N. and Lowe, M. (1996) *Retailing, Consumption and Capital*, Harlow: Longman.

Chapter 3

Sarah Berry

BE OUR BRAND
Fashion and personalization on the web

THE OTHER DAY MY COLLEAGUE Rob looked up from his web browser and said, 'Look, Sarah – it's me!' On the screen was a three-dimensional rendition of a slightly pear-shaped woman in chinos and an oxford shirt. Beneath her image was the caption,

> This is Robert. You can try clothes on her more easily than you can on yourself. If she looks more or less like you, then you're ready to start. Explore, try on the clothes and have fun. A good place to begin is style advice. If you don't think she's an accurate reflection of you, return to MY MODEL to make changes. Be sure to tell us what you think!
>
> (landsend.com, April 2000)

Rob explained that this was the Land's End web site's 'Personal Model™', generated by the user's selection of body measurements, hair colour, and skin tone – a feature available only for women. Robert's transgendered use of the model to try on a new pair of chinos made this example of e-commerce 'personalization' particularly comical, but in some ways typical. Increasingly sophisticated technology is being used to 'micromarket' clothing to consumers through techniques called 'mass customization', 'one-to-one marketing' and 'relationship marketing' (cf. Pine 1992; Peppers and Rogers 1997; Newell 2000; Gilmore 2000). The Internet has become a Mecca of micromarketing, from the reflect.com site, which offers customized cosmetics, to barbie.com, which lets you construct your own Barbie from a range of style features (though not from a range of body types).

Like landsend.com, these fashion sites make product recommendations based on shoppers' personal information or past purchases. They also do things like:

remind you to stock up on things you buy often, answer your fashion questions by e-mail, and offer online chat with personal shoppers who know your purchase history. Some clothing sites emphasize the social nature of fashion by providing online chat with other shoppers or matching your shopping habits with similar customer profiles to make recommendations in a process called 'collaborative filtering'. A teen site called bolt.com offers personal fashion advice via e-mail, lists the top-ten and most recent ten items sold on the site, and has a bulletin board where shoppers can post comments or critiques of the merchandise (bolt.com, April 2000). Marketers are banking on the fact that personalized online shopping will become faster and more convenient than a trip to the mall. The payoff to manufacturers, of course, is that all the personal data collected online can be used to pinpoint valuable consumers, make them more loyal, and develop new products based on their profiles. Considered revolutionary by marketing pundits, the concept of personalization has a long history in the fashion industry. This chapter will look briefly at that history in order to evaluate current predictions that in the near future, personalized shopping will make fashion design more diverse and consumer-driven (Goldbogen 1999).

McCustomization on the web

Mass Customization, the 1992 book by management consultant B. Joseph Pine II, heralded the arrival of a new economy that is said to benefit both consumers and producers. Mass customization combines micromarketing and post-Fordist production (also known as 'flexible specialization'), the use of a fluid workforce for small-batch production that can quickly adapt to market and consumption patterns. In order to succeed, Pine argues, companies will need to increase their product variety and shorten product life-cycles through 'just-in-time' production methods. According to Pine, this is necessary because 'customers can no longer be lumped together in a huge homogeneous market, but are individuals whose individual wants and needs can be ascertained and fulfilled' (Pine 1992: 6, 34). This, he says, is possible because of new technologies for micromarketing, like collecting databases of e-commerce activity, credit-card transactions, and purchase histories. Analysing this information ('data mining') allows marketers to define consumer behaviour in ever-narrower ways, hence the term 'one-to-one' marketing (Peppers and Rogers 1997).

The surveillance of web browsing and shopping represents a significant contribution to the market in consumer information, and one that is fraught with privacy problems (Macavinta 1999). Not only can online businesses track your every mouse click on their web sites (and see what site you came from and what kind of browser you use), they can combine that information with your offline purchase history *and* match it with similar data purchased from other companies. Web site surveillance is known as 'implicit' data gathering, and it uses both server-based software and 'cookies' set on your computer when you visit a site. It is said to help consumers by giving them streamlined access to the goods and services they want, but research shows that most people have a healthy distrust of such practices. While they are less opposed to 'explicit' questionnaires about their personal preferences, in general people want to know *and* control how such information will be used (KPMG/ Indiana University 1999: 21). Not surprisingly, given the anti-regulation ethos of American business, US web shoppers are simply told to trust corporate privacy policies – a dubious protection given the absence of oversight and sharing of corporate assets through mergers.

On the other hand, product customization can be seen as a benefit to consumers – the Dell computer site, which allows customers to select from a laundry-list of components and features, is held up as a good object of mass customization. Web portal sites have long been asking users to make custom home pages by prioritizing features and content. The new cosmetics site reflect.com uses this approach to personalize both its products and the look of the web site itself. As a new visitor to the site, I was greeted by the image and voice of Vicky, who claimed to be my 'personal shopping assistant'. I was then prompted to answer a series of questions about myself, including:

If I were a house, I would be:
1   A beautiful mansion filled with art from the hottest artists
2   A penthouse apartment in the heart of a big city
3   A maintenance-free townhouse with an exercise room
4   A cosy house with a meditation room and a garden
5   A historic home in an established upscale neighbourhood
6   A ranch in the country

and:

My personality is best represented by:
1   A peacock
2   A hawk
3   A swan
4   A dove

I was also shown four collage images and asked to choose the one I found most 'visually pleasing' (reflect.com, April 2000) (Fig. 3.1). 'None of the above' was not an option, leaving me to decipher the images and pick which category I would be grouped with. Using the science of semiotic cliché-spotting, I saw the following categories: a 'feminine' type (yellow flower in the foreground), a 'glamorous' type (a woman's face with lots of make-up), an 'ethnic' or 'athletic' type (a dark-skinned woman, stopwatch, and helmeted woman in the background), and a 'natural' type (large leaves, two young women with little make-up). At the end of this questionnaire I was told that I could now enter my 'personal reflect.com site' featuring images, colours and fonts corresponding to my taste. At that point a new series of prompts asked me to create custom make-up, under the banner, 'Cosmetics: I am the artist and I am the canvas. Create your basic cosmetics product line to reflect your needs and wants.' Like television ratings, the reflect.com strategy claims to help give consumers what they want when it is really asking them to choose from a few pre-packaged options. The basic categories have been predetermined by economic, demographic, and 'lifestyle' research, leading

Figure 3.1   Reflect.com web site.

consumer analyst Morris Holbrook to call such marketing 'McCustomization' (Holbrook 1999: 23).

Proprietary biometrics: 'It's a fun thing'

There are predictions that micromarketing and 'lean' production strategies will make clothing manufacture and retail so efficient that customers will soon be able to order custom-made clothes for the cost of ready-to-wear. Levi Strauss & Co., for example, estimates that by 2004 customized clothing will account for 25 per cent of its sales, even though the company gave up selling its clothing online due to 'channel conflict' with partner retailers. In 1995 Levi's introduced the Personal Pair programme, which allowed women to order customized pants based on their measurements. In 1998 this strategy was turned into Levi's Original Spin, which allows both men and women to design custom-fit jeans and choose from among thirty style options (Peppers and Rogers Group 1997a, 1997b, 1998). In 1999 Original Spin went high-tech at the company's flagship San Francisco store. Customers there are invited to enter a booth that electronically scans their bodies and displays detailed measurements. But the relatively modest price of tailored jeans is not all that Levi's customers are asked for: they are also encouraged to use in-store kiosks to create a personal profile that actually stores their finger-prints. Gary Magnus, Levi's retail director, told a reporter that 'We use biometrics so we can track people. If [customers] don't want to participate they don't have to. It's a fun thing' (Glave 1999). All the data collected in these personal profiles – from body shape and fingerprints to the music selected at store listening kiosks – is used by Levi Strauss & Co. for marketing.

Wired Digital News reports that the Levi's store represents 'the first large-scale voluntary collection of biometric marketing data in the country, if not the world', and adds that fingerprint information could be subpoenaed by a range of govern-ment agencies (Glave 1999). More frightening than government use, perhaps, is the fact that only the company's privacy policy governs the commercial circula-tion of this data. The electronic body measurement system used in the Levi's store was developed by the Tailored Clothing Technology Corporation, an industry R&D consortium known as [TC]2. According to the consortium's web site, three other [TC]2 systems have been purchased so far, one by the US Navy and two by fashion training colleges (tc2.com, April 2000). The consortium site states explicitly that the apparatus was designed to help develop mass customization in retail clothing, and two members of the consortium have written a book proclaiming the future of personalized clothing. As Holbrook points out, this paradigm 'retains the cost economies of Taylorism while capitalizing on the marketing advantages of tailoring' (Holbrook 1999: 23). Of course, the consumer may be paying more for this conve-nience than is immediately apparent – as Levi's 'customization director' admits, the personal data they collect from customers 'is a gold mine' (Glave 1999).

From a fashion history perspective, it's interesting that Levi Strauss & Co. has been in the vanguard of garment customization. Back when there was only one kind of Levi's, the mass-produced, unchanging style of these jeans was an anomaly in the world of fashion. The fashion system is based on change, and women's fashion, in particular, never fully adopted the methods of mass production. At the turn of the century, while the rest of the manufacturing world was turning towards large-batch production and mechanized labour, the introduction of the sewing machine and the paper pattern simply increased the complexity of women's ready-to-wear clothing and stimulated greater fashion change (working-men's clothing like Levi's, by contrast, became factory-produced and relatively fixed in style). The combined effects of new print media, department stores, and faster distribution meant that middle- and working-class women began to adopt new styles at the same pace as the traditional fashion elite (Fine and Leopold 1993: 95; Richards 1951: 21). Clothing wholesalers found that this rapid turnover in styles could be profitable as long as production was divided between many small contractors who used underpaid, 'sweated' labour. Middlemen hired new immigrants on a per-batch basis, exploiting an entirely flexible labour pool who even had to supply their own sewing machines. Retailers were able to place orders at the last minute in tiny production runs, making new fashions affordable for the masses (Fine and Leopold 1993: 101–2, 107). In other words, the new mass *consumption* of fashion was not the result of mass production, but of an early form of mass customization.

Calls for 'just-in-time' production methods thus elicit a sense of déjà vu when it comes to the garment industry: in 1909, the *Dry Goods Economist* suggested that 'The way out of overproduction must lie in finding out what the woman at the counter is going to want; *make it; then* promptly drop it and go on to something else to which fickle fashion is turning her attention' (cited in Leach 1993: 94). Similarly, the *KPMG Consumer Markets* newsletter recently asked,

> Who will be powerhouse of the fashion industry as we leap into the next millennium? Will retailers reign? Will manufacturers call the shots? If we look at history, either is possible – but in the coming reality neither is probable. Industry members expect to bow before a new deity: the consumer.
>
> (Goldbogen 1999)

While it's unclear in the *Dry Goods Economist* just who determines the 'fickle fashion' producers must follow, these days it is commonplace to say that consumer taste must be followed rather than dictated. Some argue this is because contemporary consumers no longer have time for browsing in shops and must simply be catered to (Loewe and Bonchek 1999: 2). In addition, the Internet has facilitated comparison shopping (pricewatch.com), bulk-buying (mercata.com), discount bidding (priceline.com), and auction shopping (ebay.com), empowering consumers in new ways. But the need for mass customization is attributed by Pine to the same kind of 'overproduction' that worried the *Dry Goods Economist* in 1909: a plethora of goods on the market means companies must work harder to carve out new markets. Pine comments, 'in the past twenty years, the number of different items on supermarket and pharmacy shelves has exploded, allowing manufacturers and retailers to reach ever-finer granularities of consumer desires'. But this 'reach' does not amount to a consumer-driven economy, since he argues that the pioneers of mass customization have found that 'reducing product life cycles and fragmenting demand can yield powerful advantages for those causing these changes' (Pine 1992: 6, 7). This simply amounts to planned obsolescence and niche marketing in overdrive, not a new responsiveness to individual consumer desires.

'Customer category management'

The idea of 'fragmenting demand' by associating goods with a variety of personalized qualities is also hardly new. In the early twentieth century, the success of the consumer fashion industry inspired manufacturers of all kinds to use product styling changes to create planned obsolescence in everything from cars to kitchenware. The concept of personalization was seized on as a way to create a flexible set of categories for this expanding range of styles. Take, for example, the Lady Pepperell linens campaign of 1929, which offered Hollywood stars as personality types:

> Doris Kenyon's bedroom is decorated to Miss Kenyon's colorful personality. Doris Kenyon knows how well color expresses personality . . . You can make your bedroom express your personality, easily and inexpensively, by using Lady Pepperell sheets of a becoming color that best expresses you – precisely as you express yourself in choosing becoming clothes.
>
> (Lady Pepperell 1929)

Women's clothes had previously been categorized according to when they would be worn; by the 1920s, however, clothing production had exceeded basic use categories, and marketers began to 'fragment' the market into smaller segments. The most successful new merchandising strategy was the concept of the fashion type, whereby clothing was categorized according to certain kinds of feminine personality. For consumers used to straightforward fashion dictates, the idea of defining their own personal fashion type was unfamiliar. Fashion guides offered advice on 'How to Discover Your Style', noting that 'Many girls have a style of their own, but are unconscious or indifferent to it. Are you one of these girls? If so learn about yourself' (McFarland 1936: 71). Another fashion guide noted that,

> In the following pages we shall attempt brief character sketches of six fundamental temperaments. And you must decide which one is yours. Then study the wardrobes suggested for that type and see how you can make them fit in with your requirements.
>
> (Byers and Kamholz 1938: 116)

Fashion types were marketing tools for classifying customers and organizing demand, couched in terms of finding the right style for one's own personality. In *The Economics of Fashion* (1928), an early marketing textbook by Paul H. Nystrom, fashion types are included in a chapter on 'Standardization of Sizes and Types', indicating that standardized classes of consumer were as important to early fashion marketing as consistent product sizing. The most basic classifications of women began with three 'fundamental' types (dramatic, ingénue, and athletic), but by the end of the 1930s the number of fashion personality types had proliferated dramatically (Nystrom 1928: 480). Though less refined than the use of collaborative filtering or a 'personal model' to recommend styles according to body type, the basic concept is the same. This is made clear in a business consulting newsletter that describes mass customization as a form of 'customer category management'. The article claims that 'moving a company to a customer-centric business model is a fundamental shift in operating philosophy . . . through which to understand buying behavior and merchandise movement from the customer's point of view'

(Brogan *et al.* 1999). But, as with the earlier fashion-personality type, the basic categories are predetermined. The subtitle of the article, 'Employing Your Customers to Manage the Business' reveals more about the strategy, since personalization simply asks consumers voluntarily to submit the information that market researchers used to compile.

Marketing difference

For Georg Simmel in 1904, fashion typified modern individualism in its tension between conformity and the desire to express individual subjectivity (Simmel 1971). Postmodernity, on the other hand, is in some ways typified by mass customization because it reveals the gap between the diverse ways people use and enjoy consumer goods and the market's attempts to exploit that diversity. Consumer capitalism is predicated on the process of 'fragmenting demand' through endless stylistic differentiation – the creation of new markets and the multiplication of existing ones. This 'symbolic economy' was said by Baudrillard to regulate social value rather than enable social communication. In fact, Baudrillard questioned the concept of commodity 'personalization' back in 1988. He cited Pierre Martineau's book *Motivation in Advertising*, which described personalization as, 'an interaction between the personality of the individual and the so called "personality" of the product itself'. Baudrillard acknowledged that 'people define themselves in relation to objects', but he saw this process as 'a gamut of distinguishing criteria more or less arbitrarily indexed on a gamut of stereotyped personalities' (Baudrillard 1988: 16). The multiplicity of objects one could identify with did not, he argued, produce an 'abundance of choice' and freedom:

> let us not be fooled: objects are categories of objects which quite tyrannically induce categories of persons. They undertake the policing of social meanings, and the significations they engender are controlled.
> (Baudrillard 1988: 16–17)

But others have argued that consumer goods are 're-socialized' and given meaning every day by those who use them, a process that is particularly evident when it comes to fashion (Appadurai 1986; Miller 1987, 1995). The irony of mass customization is that it claims to break out of the 'categories of persons' used by traditional marketing, when in fact it represents an intensification of the process Baudrillard described. Market fragmentation mimics the social plurality of fashion's use, but reduces it to the capture of individual idiosyncrasies in order to offer mix-and-match variations on a mass scale. The results can be both sinister (the collection of teenagers' fingerprints) and comical (Robert's female 'Personal Model').

Ethnic diversity is an aspect of social difference that Western fashion has explored throughout its history through the appropriation of 'exotic' cultural motifs (as in Orientalism and Africanism). Cosmetics, in particular, have been marketed in terms of exotic ethnicity, if only because there was a limited range of products that could be sold in association with a demure 'English complexion'. In 1928 fashion marketer Paul Nystrom noted that complexion types, like personality types, offered a way of identifying consumers with a wide range of products (Nystrom 1928: 480). For example, in 1928 Max Factor changed the name of his cosmetics line from 'Society Make-Up' to 'Color Harmony Make-Up' on the advice of his marketing agency, Sales Builders, Inc. Their research showed that if the need to buy personalized and 'harmonized' products was stressed, women would buy more items in the same brand. The result was the Max Factor 'Color Harmony Prescription Make-Up Chart', which indicated the complementary shades of powder, rouge, and lipstick to be used according to complexion, hair, and eye colour (Basten 1995: 80). This personal colour-matching system was widely copied, and is still used today by brands like Clinique and reflect.com. It avoided issues of race by describing differences in skin tone as 'complexion types', although cosmetics advertising of the 1930s increasingly used specific exotic stereotypes like 'Tropical', 'Chinese', and 'Gypsy' product lines. Other brands simply referred to women of colour with European euphemisms: a 1937 advertisement for Richard Hudnut 'eye-matched' make-up features the Mexican-born star Dolores Del Rio, and describes her as having a 'Parisian' complexion type. The advertisement claims that the 'eye-matched' line of cosmetics is 'scientifically keyed to *your* own personality color – the color of *your* eyes!' (Richard Hudnut 1937).

Ethnicity has recently been rediscovered as a growth area by some American marketing consultants, who encourage companies to 'capitalize on the nation's growing ethnic diversity'. Mainstream retailer Wal-Mart now runs print, television, and radio advertising in Spanish, and Sears has opened a line of urban outlets featuring 'ethnic' apparel lines like 'Selina', designed by Sandra Salcedo. J.C. Penny now sponsors a Hispanic Model Search and throws a yearly Hispanic Designer Gala. For the past six years J.C. Penny has targeted African-American women with its 'Fashion Influences' catalogue, and recently introduced Diahann Carroll as a spokeswoman for a line of clothing and accessories (Reese 1999). The attempt by large manufacturers to colonize minority markets brings to mind Stuart Hall's essay 'The local and the global: globalization and ethnicity,' which addresses the way that Western multinational capitalism increasingly requires partnership with local political elites and the negotiation of cultural differences. One result, Hall argues, is that the universalized Anglo-American male subject, which was always defined in opposition to 'ethnicity', is increasingly seen as a kind of ethnicity. He suggests that the homogenization associated with global mass culture is never complete because global capital 'cannot proceed without learning to live with and working through difference' (Hall 1997: 179, 181).

From this perspective, mass customization can be seen as roughly analogous with global capitalism. For example, Armand Mattelart has pointed out that the globalization of corporate reach does not necessarily require the standardization of marketing strategies. Although he sees an inexorable movement toward 'world brands' being marketed by more concentrated corporate capital, he cites the often-quoted lines of Saatchi & Saatchi's 1985 *Annual Report*, to the effect that global marketing can 'camouflage' itself as local culture:

> [S]ophisticated marketers are recognising that there are probably more social differences between midtown Manhattan and the Bronx, two sectors of the same city, than between Midtown Manhattan and the 7th

arrondissement of Paris. This means that when a manufacturer contemplates expansion of his business, consumer similarities in demography and habits rather than geographic proximity will increasingly affect his decisions. . . . All this underlines the economic logic of the global approach.

(Mattelart 1991: 52–3)

John Sinclair has referred to this as global capitalism's 'multidomestic' strategy, whereby different national and geographic markets are simply analysed as demographic distinctions (Sinclair 1987: 164).

Like 'glocalization' – the use of regional marketing strategies and product designs by multinational corporations – mass customization uses consumer profiles to create a 'multidomestic' marketing strategy while maintaining economies of scale in production and (theoretically) a coherent brand identity. In the case of fashion, this means that direct surveys of consumer tastes will supplement existing practices of fashion forecasting and ethnographic research. Such consumer feedback may formalize the 'trickle-up' movement of fashion innovation that has marked the industry since the rise of consumer fashion in the early twentieth century. For example, the reflect.com site has a 'trends' area that invites customers to send the company email about fashion fads they've noticed in their community, while bolt.com's 'shopping board' asks teenagers to comment on the site's merchandise, providing valuable information about teen fashion trends. In the past, such companies had to hire professional ethnographers to do trend-spotting, or pay teenagers to gather information about their friends' favorite colours, games, and clothing (Astroff 1997). Ever since the youth-subculture research of the Birmingham Centre for Cultural Studies (Hall and Jefferson 1976), cultural studies of fashion have focussed on such local uses of fashion rather than mainstream design. This orientation was influenced by Raymond Williams, who saw 'both the designing and wearing of fashions and clothing as versions of forms of creativity . . . As such, fashion and clothing are productive of the world in which we live' (Barnard 1996: 44). Fashion is no longer seen as simply imitative of the upper classes, a perspective underscored by the fact that mainstream design increasingly appropriates and repackages the stylistic innovations of 'peripheral' social groups. For the fashion industry, mass customization on the web represents an attempt to shorten its response time to new trends on the street by getting hot fashion tips directly from consumers.

Conclusion

The proliferation of style cultures stimulated by consumerism will most likely be accelerated by the consumer-feedback loops of mass customization. But there is an aspect of popular fashion that remains resistant to these strategies, and to the conformity associated with commercial fashion, no matter how narrowly marketed. For example, the bolt.com 'shopping board' recently contained the following exchange:

BlackOrchidz We need more Punkish or Gothic clothes out there in this place. It sucks having just preppy crap. Ya know? Am I the only one that feels this way? If not . . . add a message under this one. Thanx.

nirvanakat I absolutely agree. There is not enough good goth clothing available! But on the other hand, making your stuff is so original . . .

PunkgrrrrL agreed . . .:)

spiceychick007 totally agreed!

harleykOrn We definitely need some goth and punk shit! I'm sitting here in a black toga made from my curtains!

The bolt.com postings are a reminder that this virtual-mall context is a social space not entirely circumscribed by its commercial aims. The social underpinnings of fashion often include a desire to reject existing commercial categories and bond with others over that gesture. No matter how closely individual tastes can be predicted and pre-packaged, there will be those who reject even their own taste once it is presented to them as a tailor-made marketing category.

References

Appadurai, A. (ed.) (1986) *The Social Life of Things*, Cambridge: Cambridge University Press.

Astroff, R. (1997) 'Market research as capitalist ethnography' in M. Nava, B. Richards and Macrury, I. (eds), *Buy This Book: Studies in Advertising and Consumption*, London: Routledge.

Barnard, M. (1996) *Fashion as Communication*, London: Routledge.

Basten, F.E. with Salvatore, R. and Kaufman, P.A. (1995) *Max Factor's Hollywood: Glamour, Movies, Make-Up*, Santa Monica, CA: General Publishing Group.

Baudrillard, J. (1988) 'The system of objects' in M. Poster, (ed.), *Jean Baudrillard: Selected Writings*. Stanford, CA: Stanford University Press, 10–28.

Brogan, B., Hoeller, J. and Abramo, G. (1999) 'The accelerated business solution for retail: employing your customers to manage the business', *KPMG Consumer Markets* (http://usserve.us.kpmg.com/cm/article-archives/actual-articles/pcfinal2.html). August.

Byers, M. and Kamholz, C. (1938) *Designing Women: The Art, Technique, and Cost of Being Beautiful*, New York: Simon & Schuster.

Fine, B. and Leopold, E. (1993) *The World of Consumption*, London: Routledge.

Gilmore, J.H. (ed.) (2000). *Markets of One: Creating Customer-Unique Value through Mass Customization*, Cambridge, Mass.: Harvard Business School Press.

Glave, J. (1999) 'Levi's Brave New World', *Wired News* (http://www.wired.com/news/news/business/story/21268.html). August 16.

Goldbogen, J. (1999) 'Fashion's crystal ball: industry executives prepare for the future of apparel retailing', *KPMG Consumer Markets*, (http://usserve.us.kpmg.com/cm/article-archives/actual-articles/Fitsem22.html). August.

Hall, S. (1997) 'The local and the global: globalization and ethnicity', in A. McClintock, A. Mufti and A. Shohat (eds) *Dangerous Liaisons: Gender, Nation, and Postcolonial Perspectives*, Minneapolis: University of Minnesota Press.

Hall, S. and Jefferson, T. (eds) (1976) *Resistance through Rituals: Youth Subcultures in Post-war Britain*, London: Hutchinson.

Holbrook, M.B. (1999) 'Higher than the bottom line: reflections on some recent macromarketing literature', *Journal of Macromarketing*, 19 (1): 4–74.

KPMG/Indiana University (1999) 'Retail technology in the next century: what's 'in store' for consumers', *KPMG Consumer Markets*, (http://www.us.kpmg.com/cm/home.html). August.

Lady Pepperell advertisement (1929), *Photoplay* 35 (3): 80.

Leach, W. (1993) *Land of Desire: Merchants, Power, and the Rise of a New American Culture*, New York: Vintage Books.

Loewe, P.M. and Bonchek, M. (1999) 'The retail revolution', *Management Review* (http://www.strategosnet.com/articles/retail_rev.htm).

Macavinta, C. (1999) 'Privacy advocates rally against doubleclick–abacus merger', *CNET News.com* (http://news.cnet.com/news/0–1005–200–1461826.html). Nov. 22.

McFarland, F.W. (1936) *Good Taste in Dress*, Peoria, IL: The Manual Arts Press.

Mattelart, A. (1991) *Advertising International: The Privatisation of Public Space*, trans. M. Chanan, New York: Routledge.

Miller, D. (1987) *Material Culture and Mass Consumption*, Oxford: Basil Blackwell.

—— (1995) 'Consumption as the vanguard of history', in D. Miller (ed.) *Acknowledging Consumption: A Review of New Studies*, London and New York: Routledge.

Newell, F. (2000) *Loyalty.com: Customer Relationship Management in the New Era of Internet Marketing*, New York: McGraw-Hill Professional Publishing.

Nystrom, P. (1928) *The Economics of Fashion*, New York: Roland Press.

Peppers and Rogers Group (1997a) 'Elements of an effective channel strategy', *Marketing 1to1: INSIDE 1to1* (http://www.1to1.com/publications/inside1to1/i1–9–25–97.html). 25 Sept.

—— (1997b) *The One to One Future: Building Relationships One Customer at a Time*, New York: Bantam Doubleday Dell Publishers.

—— (1998) 'Levi's buttons up a new customer', *Marketing 1to1: INSIDE 1to1* (http://www.1to1.com/publications/inside1to1/i1–12–3–98.html). 3 Dec.

Pine II, B.J. (1992) *Mass Customization: The New Frontier in Business Competition*, Cambridge, Mass.: Harvard Business School Press.

Reese, S. (1999) 'No longer color blind, retailers eye ethnic markets', *KPMG Consumer Markets* (http://usserve.us.kpmg.com/cm/article-archives/actual-articles/sr-ethni.html). August.

Richards, F.S. (1951) *The Ready-To-Wear Industry 1900–1950*, New York: Fairchild Publications, Inc.

Simmel, G. [1904] (1971) 'Fashion' in D. Levine (ed.) *On Individuality and Social Forms*, Chicago and London: The University of Chicago Press.

Sinclair, J. (1987) *Images Incorporated: Advertising as Industry and Ideology*, London: Comedia.

Web sites

http://www.barbie.com (April 2000) ('My Design' pages).
http://www.bolt.com ('Shopping Board' page, April 2000).
http://www.landsend.com ('Personal Model'™ page).
http://www.levi.com/Original_Spin/.
http://www.reflect.com.
http://www.tc2.com, 'History' page.

Chapter 4

Lorraine Gamman

VISUAL SEDUCTION AND PERVERSE COMPLIANCE
Reviewing food fantasies, large appetites and 'grotesque' bodies

THIS CHAPTER IS WRITTEN around two body parts – the eye and the mouth – and it attempts light-heartedly to discuss familiar issues about food, fashion and representation, before moving on to look at eating disorders and so-called 'grotesque' bodies. The first section discusses visual seduction and food and argues that in a cultural context where designer food fashions are becoming significant, women's eyes should always be bigger than their bellies and bodies. The second section uses theory about performative gender identities to explain why this is so. It goes on to discuss women's relationship to food in regard to issues about body weight and perverse compliance through excessive dieting. It raises questions about ingestion and the self regulating gaze when discussing the British TV chat show host Vanessa Feltz in terms of Foucault's account of 'the power of normalization'.[1]

Eyes bigger than bellies – reviewing food fashions and the case against ingestion

Peering into other people's food trolleys is a voyeuristic game we can all play when queuing at the checkout (as French gastronome Brillat-Savarin put it, 'Tell me what you eat and I'll tell you who you are').[2] Aspirational food shoppers may be more entertaining than the compulsive-obsessive chocolate types. Chocoholics are often very serious, despite Dawn French's best endeavours in Terry's chocolate advertisements to parody the extremity of the nation's passion for chocolate.[3] Class fantasies articulated via gourmet foods and/or supermarket ranges are far more humorous in terms of aspirational styling – to me at least – than those articulated through property and fashion statements. I've never really believed that you are what you have or wear, so the notion that 'you are what you eat' seems really rather funny. Yet in the social arena humour may be an inappropriate response to the subject of image when so much emphasis is placed on appearances and the relationship of 'looking good' to success.[4] Indeed, survey evidence presented by Shelley Bovey, for example, reveals that in the West the culture of slenderness dominates social discourse and that fat has a negative connotation.[5] From Germaine Greer (1971) to Naomi Wolf (1990) many feminist critics have complained about the culture of slenderness.[6] Some have also identified how fat men and women do less well at job interviews than their slender counterparts, who may not be as gifted or qualified.[7] Social definitions about the meanings of body type are complex, as Peter Stearns points out in *Fat History: Bodies and Beauty in the Modern West*.[8] He discusses how the contemporary obsession with fat ran parallel with the growth of consumer culture, women's equality and changes in women's sexual and maternal roles. It is clear that Western cultural assumptions – from medicine right through to fashion – underlie many negative perceptions of the fat or fleshy body, as discussed by critics in books as diverse as Emily Martin's *Woman in the Body*[9] and Mary Russo's *The Female Grotesque*.[10] Yet few of the writings I have found on the fat body address the food we eat, unless through linking the buying and preparation of food to women's nurturing and maternal role. This is why I want to focus here upon that recent phenomenon – mass-produced designer food – to see what new cultural processes this recent cultural form may have produced and to consider how actually eating food (or not eating it) has a connection to sexual and gender identities.

Mass-produced designer food may be more surprising than mass-produced designer frocks and houses decorated by interior designers. This is because it's taken for granted that we actually know what people really *do* with their frozen gastroporn TV dinners and their gourmet chutneys. But once you accept that food is the subject of women's erotic fixations and sexual fetishism, what your friends eat may start to play on your mind as well as with their bodies.[11] Indeed, larder displays take on new visual meanings when connected to the notion that 'display might be the best method of concealment'.[12] This is perhaps a completely opposite way of understanding 'a love [for an object] that dare not speak its name', or erotic fetishism linked to a secret closet of shoes or stockings.[13] What I am suggesting then, is that food can be the subject of erotic projections because at this moment in history food is rarely eaten simply for nutrition. Indeed, food has become a commodity subject to trends and sexual display, just like everything else in what has been described as the post-modern 'Society of the Spectacle'.

In Guy Debord's book *Society of the Spectacle*, the argument that all social life is saturated by commodity culture is put forward, and developed to suggest that an excess of display has the effect of concealing the real conditions of existence of society.[14] The point being made is that social relations are objectified far beyond the promotions we associate with mere advertising or the public relations industry. It is claimed that everything is objectified via television and other communications media associated with consumer society, so that we can see everything even if we understand very little about what it all means. The society of spectacle has 'provided the viewer with an unending stream of images that might be best understood, not simply as detached from a real world of things, [as Debord implied] but as working to efface any trace of the symbolic'.[15] Cooke and Wollen, writing about visual display and culture beyond appearances, go on to suggest that this never-ending stream of images 'condemns the viewer to a world in which we can see everything but understand nothing – allowing us, as viewer victims, only a "random choice of ephemera"'.[16]

In the case of food, the choices at stake are far more complex than simply the choice between carrots or peas. Since the post-war consumer boom, food has become part of, and subject to, 'lifestyle fashions' as described by Stephen Bayley,[17] and 'new identifications' by consumers as described by Rob Shields.[18] Indeed, it is hard to tell whether or not food is really bought to be eaten or to be seen with; such is the intensity of the consumer sales pitch. Food and everything it takes to cook it have also been subjected to the designer gaze, so that it is not always what it seems. Claire Catterall has argued that 'today food is a mass produced consumer commodity and as such has as much right to claim to be a designer object as the Ford motor car'.[19] The food design to which Catterall refers is not the obvious mass-produced designs for processed food or that which is genetically modified. She suggests that *all* food is designed, not just the sort we associate with mass production or 'overkill'. For example, it can be observed that even organic foods haven't quite escaped the issue of design or the designer gaze. Assorted vegetables can be found at any supermarket contained in packaging that mobilizes the grunge aesthetic often expensively designed to connote 'no design' at all.

Fashionable food, by design, invites you to look but not to touch, or at least to consider photographing the plate before chewing. Its production is all about visual rather than other sensations, and certainly food consumption has a relationship to sexual and gender identities. I once read that Jerry Hall ate before she went out to dinner because she understood that ordering food in a restaurant had little to do with actually eating. And she certainly didn't want to be photographed with her cheeks bulging with food, as this would not be good for her image. Perhaps she felt it would link her to what Mary Russo has called the 'female grotesque', a discussion to which we shall return later.[20] She may even have been concerned about associations with the American underclass, as fat is increasingly perceived as linked to wider social problems about poverty and poor nutrition.

As we start the new millennium, the celebrity status of food has intensified. Supermarkets and fast-food outlets surround us, while celebrity cooks and restaurants speak to us about recipes and ingredients in almost supernatural terms.[21] The society of the spectacle has cast its gaze further upon our daily bread and lives. Food has become not only the subject of hyperbolic connotations associated with the advertising of mass-produced food products (everything from Hovis bread to Quorn) but also the subject of more specialist media advice about *How to Eat*[22] as well as the sort of foodie 'connoisseurship' critics like Mathew Fort in the *Guardian* expound. Food has also been colonized to sell back to us a sanitized version of different class positions, ethnicities as well as changing cultural practices. We can eat the world on our high street (will it be Indian or Thai tonight?), so long as we conform to bourgeois colonial understanding, namely that any meal cooked in the West, despite its origins, should be served with wine, three courses and coffee at the end of it.

Most supermarkets offer a celebrity range of items, for example from Paul Newman's salad dressing to Lloyd Grossman's pasta sauce, as well as a choice between personality cooks and celebrity and or ethnic restaurant cookbooks. Italian fantasies, for example, appear to be very popular at the moment, perhaps as compensation for the imagination (as well as the stomach) from what are imagined in contrast as otherwise dull British food and lives. *The River Café Cookbook* is clearly different from the sort of 'back to basics' offerings by Delia Smith and Nigel Slater, or the 'let's add more cream' approach associated with *The Two Fat Ladies*.[23] It provides class aspiration and gastroporn at the same time – or simply manual relief on a plate. All types of food fantasies seem to appeal to women and men who can't cook, anorexics that won't eat, and it has to be said anxious 'new' women types (like sad fictional anti-heroines Bridget Jones and Ally McBeal), who, in their diaries at least, express real post-modern feminist angst when confronted with lunch or the bathroom scales:

> Monday 24 February 15st (combined weight of self and unhappiness), alcohol units 1 – i.e. me, cigarettes 200,000, calories 8.477 (not counting chocolate), theories as to what's going on 447, no of times changed mind about what to do 448.[24]

The questions raised by the popularity of celebrity cookbooks are not those that concern true foodies (who simply love eating). These are instead linked to the fact that these cookbooks appear at a time when women's eating disorders are rampant – appearing, then, almost as forbidden food for the imagination. Indeed, even today women are expected to enjoy preparing food for others rather than to be seen to eat it themselves. As Susan Bordo argues, slenderness has become a cultural value for women that is pursued by many beyond other pleasures.[25] Slenderness may be an attempt to embody 'masculine language' or masculine values like self-control, strength and determination, within the female body.[26] Certainly, the changes that have followed women's entry into the full-time labour force have produced many worries about femininity. Judith Butler is fascinating in her account of femininity construing gender, not as an expression of what one *is*, but something that one *does*. She talks about gender 'performativity' and suggests gender is 'an identity tenuously constituted in time, instituted in an exterior space through a stylized repetition of acts.'[27] Her point is that the body is subjected to styling, so that femininity is fluid and not something that is essentially given. R.W. Connell also takes up this argument and raises issues about compliance and 'emphasized femininity' in her book *Gender and Power*. She suggests that 'some types of femininity are performed, and performed especially to men'.[28] Eating becomes the subject of anxiety to women when society at large does not construe it as appropriately 'feminine' behaviour. Consequently the performativity associated with women eating may involve taking meagre portions in public, serving others huge meals, or not eating at all, offering an ascetic response to bodily pleasures. In such a context it is clear, that femininity is not the product of choice, but as Judith Butler points out in *Gender Trouble* 'the forcible citation of a norm, one whose complex historicity is indissociable from relations of discipline, regulation, punishment'.[29]

Certainly some women, like the fictional anti-heroine Bridget Jones, appear to have taken on board the punitive aspects of some types of femininity in relation to weight control. Her entry for 'Monday 27 January' reads: '9st 3 (total fat groove), boyfriends 1 (hurrah), shags 3 (hurrah!), calories 2,100, calories used up by shags 600, so total calories 1,500 (exemplary)'.[30] Her narrative also appears to exhibit heterosexual panic – humorously exaggerated – when confronted with activities that compromise femininity, such as eating dinner! Reduced calorific intake of food is linked to finding the right male companion to sit next to in the designer restaurant itself (and of course to live and bear children with later). For Bridget Jones, and many real life women, there is some fear that heterosexual resolution might not happen if too much is eaten and fat is accumulated. Consequently food causes great fear, as S.L. Bartky confirms when she points out that 27.3 per cent of women compared to 5.8 per cent of men when surveyed (UCLA 1985) said they 'were terrified' of getting fat.[31]

This concern about being slim enough to attract a partner to be *seen with* may also have been exacerbated in Britain by the fact that designer types such as Ron Arad, Richard Rogers, Nigel Coates, as well as artists such as Damien Hirst, have recently done things to restaurant interiors aimed at inspiring envy, rather than gluttony. You may not be what you eat, but your ethnic, class and gender subjectivities may be articulated through where you are seen to eat, and these highly emphasized interiors implicitly demand a trophy companion to sit next to.

Appearances are important in a society of surfaces. While we can own food commodities, and all the expensive objects needed to cook and serve food, the tragedy for women is that they frequently feel unable to own their own bodies. This obviously affects what they put into their mouths. As Susie Orbach has argued,

> [Women's] bodies are quasi-commodities, elusive but essential parts of their personae rather than the place in which they dwell. The woman may create a split between what she describes as herself and what she describes as her body'.[32]

This split is not helped at all by a culture of slenderness that promotes a form of misogynistic revulsion against the fleshy female body. The irregular female form must be abhorred and contained, if not entirely repressed from representation. As Foucault comments, the power of normalization imposes homogeneity; but it individualizes by making it possible to measure gaps, to determine levels, to fix specialties and to render the differences useful by fitting them into one another'.[33] Consequently, there are few large women represented in the media. Model Sophie Dahl and TV personalities Lorraine Kelly and Lisa Tarbuck are exceptions. To some extent it could be argued that excluding larger women from representation, or focusing only on extreme representations of fat women with all the negative grotesque associations, functions to keep the rest of the female population on diets. Or certainly constrained by invisible corsets, worried about how they look when eating.

The social spectacle of being seen eating at the restaurant with a partner in the context of gender performativity, may then be very significant, in both gay and heterosexual contexts for achieving 'normalization'. The emphasis on being seen (rather than just being) is also more often about being desired than desiring, or simply being with the one we love. Indeed, the partner and the food served may be less significant than being able to be viewed, and to view others looking back; designer restaurants facilitate this sort of bourgeois display very well.

Indeed, designers have done extraordinary things to restaurant interiors these days to promote the art of looking, and assorted scopic regimes.[34] Some restaurants are almost as interesting as museums, featuring low-fat architectural experiences, from Japanese minimalism to what I call the 'open prison look'. Often moulded metals and Formica create a sort of post-industrial chic that wouldn't look out of place on the film set for *Blade Runner*. No one ever remembers eating food in these restaurants, as much as feasting their eyes on the décor and hoping to see not just celebrity design, but a celebrity too. Everything is so 'showy', it seems to hint 'star' quality could be present.

The fabulous delicacies that appear on plates at Quaglinos and Mezzo by Conran, or the more trendy designer eateries like Belgo, the Oxo Tower or Mash and Air in Manchester and Central London, connect designer chic to eating. This is precisely why it has become appropriate for eyes to become bigger than bellies or bodies in designer restaurants. It's not just that the ideal body has an extremely flat abdomen, but the pleasures of voyeurism and performativity on offer are there to be enjoyed by men and women, perhaps far more than the food.

Of course, for some men and women, unless they resort to bulimia, it is impossible to eat much of the food on offer and actually still fit into the slim designer chairs which are de rigueur in such restaurants. For women who suffer from the illness in epidemic proportions, bulimia is a 'coping strategy' that operates in the context of complex emotional and interpersonal problems. It's often an unconscious and irrational response to what is happening in their social lives and appears to be linked to anxious perceptions about body size. In the last ten years it is interesting that men have increasingly started to show up in the bulimia statistics (10 per cent of all sufferers are male) because this occurs at a time when men's bodies have become increasingly commodified too. Indeed, jeans and after-shave ads regularly feature 'men without heads', as a consequence of the over-accentuation of the super-fit male torso. With so much emphasis on the body and consuming to groom and please, no wonder men as well as women have resorted to bulimia as a practical aid to trying to have it all.

Yet when bulimia is referred to as a coping strategy by therapists and clinicians, the argument is about complex rather than literal responses. Melanie Katzman describes a bulimic student, Rebecca, as using the bulimic ritual as a way of trying to look good while still avoiding the autonomy her life demanded from her. The bingeing and vomiting took up so much time that Rebecca, like so many other bulimics, found it difficult to get on with other things. Indeed, Katzman's emphasis suggests that the weight problem became the focus of Rebecca's worries, in order to hide more complex problems about individuation and sexual identity.[35] Obviously, bingeing and vomiting are not always irrational or unconscious responses as the Romans demonstrated with their habit of puking after feasts in order to keep on eating. Yet bulimia, as well as being a painful and debilitating illness (one that may involve levels of addiction), is perhaps to the culture of consumption what potlatch was to earlier communities who periodically burned all their possessions.[36] Bulimia is not simply wasteful or even abnormal in response to many of the cultural contexts in which we live, but it may seem logical to some individuals, as potlatch did. Of course, bulimia is ultimately damaging to the health of body and mind. We know only too well the horror stories associated with the deaths of Lena Zavaroni and Karen Carpenter who suffered from bulimia before the onset of anorexia. More recently the BMA reported that the gap between the perceived ideal body shape and reality is widening.[37] Even though generally women are getting larger, 'every family doctor in the country is treating two patients suffering from anorexia and eighteen with bulimia.'[38] Bataille does not discuss bulimia (he was writing in the 1930s) but he provides us with an aptly catastrophic metaphor of the social effects of potlatch:

> The living organism, in a situation determined by the play of energy on the surface of the globe, ordinarily receives more energy than is necessary for maintaining life; the excess energy (wealth and [food]) can be used for the growth of a system (e.g. an organism); if the system can no longer grow, or if the excess cannot be completely absorbed in its growth, it must necessarily be lost without profit; it must be spent, willingly or not, gloriously or catastrophically.[39]

Those of us who have little time to cook, let alone think about food and catastrophe, or to go to designer restaurants, can be found at stores like Waitrose and Marks & Spencer buying mass-produced gourmet food instead. Frozen foods have become increasingly popular since the late 1960s: indeed Findus started selling frozen lasagne in 1972, forty-three years after Heinz first offered spaghetti in tins.[40] Recent surveys such as the Rennie *Eating into the Millennium Report* of 1997 as well as the Mintel *Guide to British Lifestyles*, confirm that huge numbers of us now buy our gastroporn from the chill counters, as well as low-fat, ready prepared slimmers' meals. Even the British are more adventurous about what they eat than ever before. According to recent surveys, they are perhaps more health conscious and less obese compared to neighbours in the USA and Germany, although certainly are getting fatter as each year passes.[41] Evidently, in Britain alone £1m is spent on chilled dinners per day. As Claire Catterall points out this represents a growth of 24 per cent from the 1970s to the 1990s.[42] The latest research also reveals that nearly half the population no longer sit at the table to eat their food but tuck into the edible mass-produced fantasies while watching the visual equivalent on the telly.[43]

It seems that 'couch potatoes' – children as well as adults – are now an international phenomenon, causing the rising obesity figures to become one of the World Health Organization's most serious concerns in the First World.[44] No wonder, when not thinking about gastroporn, that the rest of us appear to be starting a new slimming diet, or oscillating between feasting and fasting or even manic exercise routines. Our lives are full of such contradictions about self-regulation. Ros Coward called the visual consumption of high-fat luxury food recipes and images, while dieting on beans on toast or low-fat meals, a form of 'food pornography'.[45] We appear easily seduced by visual images into wanting what we know is probably not good for us or even 'real' in the first place. Anorexia may not have been simply caused by the ideological effect of the health and beauty industry, (or virtually all women in the West would suffer from it)[46] but according to Dally and Gomez it was probably not at all common until the latter half of the nineteenth century.[47] Indeed, it has been argued that the fashion of thinness is linked historically to the development of photographic media and moving images.[48] Stephen Mendell suggests that not only is anorexia a now 'very familiar illness in Europe and North America' but also that 'there appears to be a clear connection with the reliable and plentiful availability of food . . . anorexia nervosa is not reported from countries where there is still danger of widespread famine.[49] Today, wanting to look like Kate Moss, whilst also needing to consume huge quanties of chocolate, ice cream and women's magazines, is a practice that seems peculiarly Western and female. It is perhaps comparable to the male use of lager and pornography.

While half the world's population starve as a consequence of famine, the rest of us try to diet whilst being absolutely obsessed with consuming, often inspired by the visual seduction of so many gastroporn and ultra-thin sexual images. 'Eat twice as much for half the calories' we are told by advertisements when trying to fight the flab. 'Lose weight without feeling hungry', suggests the sales pitch for *Slimmer's World*. Dieting has become a cultural obsession with women in the West. Consequently, Jeremy MacClancy points out, in the First World we spend more on diet products than it would take to feed the entire world's hungry twice over.[50] Elizabeth Wilson reminds us that 'photography accentuates width' and that 'both film stars and fashion models have, especially since the photograph came to dominate fashion journalism, contributed to the fashion for extreme thinness and length of leg.'[51] Whilst we cannot simply blame photography for anorexia or other eating disorders, it is clear that the cultural reproduction of values about slenderness – generated by the visual media – may be harmful. Indeed, Harvard anthropologist Ann Becker noted in 1998 that 'a sudden increase in eating disorders among teenage girls in Fiji may be linked to the arrival of television in the 1990s and to "Western ideals of beauty"'. She found that 75 per cent of Fijian girls questioned felt they were 'too big and fat' and that 15 per cent said they had vomited to control their weight.[52] In the UK the 'Body Image Seminar' chaired by Tessa Jowell at Downing Street on 21 June 2000 appears to be thinking through how to make a cultural intervention on the subject. Fashion editors, designers and journalists were invited to attend and discuss why the self-esteem and confidence of 95 per cent of women who do not have the genetic disposition to be fashionably thin[53] must be compromised by fashion images of superthin models. The situation is perverse, however you look at it.

And look at food we do. Our bodies, our homes, kitchens, food, all our consuming habits in the Western world, now more than ever before seem also to function as aspirational signs of status lifestyles. Even our toilet seats have been subjected to the over-designed gaze. Our lavatories are no longer just to shit in but are to be *seen in* too. The intensification of the commodity form has reached more parts perhaps even than Guy Debord envisaged in his pessimistic account of the forward movement of the society of the spectacle.[54] The success of recent British TV programmes such as *Home Front* and *Changing Rooms* has meant that the 'before and after' identity makeover formula – so successful is the cultural discourse aimed at slimmers and others locked into the need for transformation – has now colonized the perspective of designers too. Our private spaces are no longer just that, or places in which we can remain invisible any more because the distinction between the public and private is collapsing. The need to perform all our identities everywhere, with anyone, at all times, becomes the subject of more and more cultural imperatives, so that we take pride even in our toilet seats. Often, what it looks like is presented as more important than what it feels like or tastes like. It's in this arena too that food has become 'fashionable', particularly to those in the West who aspire to middle-class values as signs of social status.

In contrast to images of lifestyle culture and designer food, Martin Parr's gritty photographs of lardy potato food (his sequence found in *A British Feast* for instance) have always cheered me up.[55] They are so antithetical to the lifestyle approach. They conjure up people who eat deep-fried anything – including Mars bars – and have a rather less designerly relationship to food and their bodies than anything you will ever seen in *Vogue*, *Elle* or *Wallpaper* magazines. Parr's images of iced buns and cakes from baker's shops in working-class districts contrast powerfully against the middle-class aspiration of the *River Café Cookbook*'s delicacies. In this nutritional scenario, Parr's photos of lardy potato food or cakes with garishly synthetic icing on them, are possibly the visual equivalent of *Readers' Wives* in porn mags. Parr's images of street food disrupt the foodie fantasy world of magazine spreads, where the wafer-thin girls are poised ready to eat (but never actually seen chewing). Yet these wafer-thin female models are part of a more common British feast too. Indeed, Mary G. Winkler has observed that the codes and conventions of female representation are such that in the UK, like everywhere else, the usual 'centerpiece of the feast is the model – the model of fashion and the model woman. This woman is the end to which all articles on grooming, diet, business savvy, gynaecological tips, and political issues are directed.'[56] In contrast, Parr's lardy

Figure 4.1   Lucie Russell, 'Cakes in Windows'. © Lucie Russell

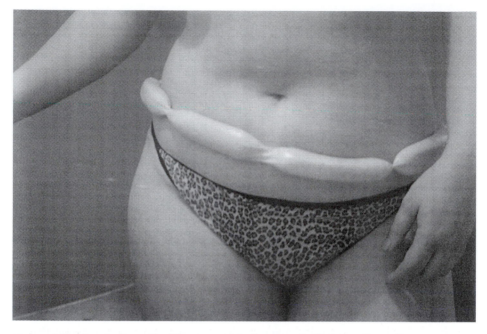

Figure 4.2   Lucie Russell, 'Tummy with Sausages'. © Lucie Russell

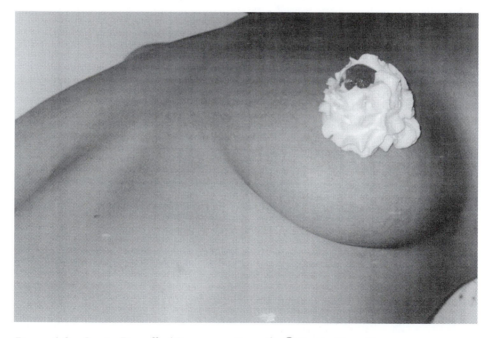

Figure 4.3   Lucie Russell, 'Cream on Breast'. © Lucie Russell

food images are powerful because they make us think about the presence of absence; of people who consume too much of the 'wrong' sort of foods – and of bodies that are not designer-shaped at all.

Before and after objection – Vanessa Feltz – or why I'm glad and sad she's still got a big mouth

It's not just anorexics that get fantasy and reality confused around body shape. It appears that many ordinary women are able stoically to maintain thin bodies even when starving, such is the persuasive power of wanting to conform to an image that involves body work. Jennifer Craik in *The Face of Fashion* identified respondents of a survey undertaken at UCLA in 1985 who appeared to identify with supermodels in terms of ideals about body shape.[57] Seventy one per cent of them also said they disliked their thighs, their bottom (58%) breasts (22%) hips (40%) legs (32%) and upper arms (17%). These facts and figures confirm what S.L. Bartky noted some years earlier: most women surveyed about their weight appear to want to weigh less, whereas men surveyed don't exhibit similar problems.[58]

Indeed, being able perversely to comply with the disciplinary norms and rules about body shape reified by the culture of slenderness takes a lot of energy. It's no accident that women focus more than men on reshaping thighs, bums and tums, because being the right shape, taking up so-called 'appropriate' amounts of space with the female body, is all part of the performance of femininity. Failure to master the language of femininity, as Angela McRobbie points out, means to be seen as lacking,[59] usually not just in terms of self-control but also in 'essential' female grace. However, the codes governing the articulation of femininity may not be completely rigid – differences in terms of age, race, class and sexual orientations are allowed, and to some extent there is some fluidity. Indeed, the masquerade of femininity is articulated differently by women from different cultures. Nevertheless, there is a tradition of imposed limitations that operates to keep binary oppositions in place between the 'female ideal' and the 'female grotesque'.

Some women never 'transgress' much or stop aspiring towards the female ideal. They appear to enjoy the power of controlling their gestures, postures and movements associated with normative femininity: or they simply like keeping trim and healthy, and get pleasure as well as endomorphins from exercise. Even though many women are not able to ignore the social consequences of being fat, they nevertheless enjoy being fit, and their relationship to exercise is linked to pleasure more than stoicism, and is certainly not perverse. Other women are not so lucky. Despite being a healthy body size and shape, they suffer from perceived inferiority. Consequently, for the last thirty years feminists have been writing about the harmful effects of objectification of women's bodies, promoted by the culture of slenderness. They complain not only that many women have to starve to meet the cultural ideal, but also that feeling out of control around food makes women feel both helpless and worthless. Yet there is another side to understanding what is at stake in dieting. Indeed, perverse compliance to accentuated signs of 'small' and 'superthin' femininity may be part of a powerful female masquerade adopted even by those who know that femininity is fabricated and fictional. Simply to dismiss women who diet as colluding in their own oppression, for example focusing on their bodies rather than on more material goals, rather misses the point about how women negotiate power. It also misses the point that there is a lot of pleasure involved not only in looking good but actually feeling good. For some women the discourse of 'fat liberation' offers a way towards better mental health. The problem occurs only when fat turns to serious obesity with health-related restrictions or when women do not feel at ease with their bodies, which brings me to Vanessa Feltz.

Vanessa Feltz is a very powerful British TV personality and perhaps an appropriate person to focus upon in order to raise questions about the body, as she has been talking about hers a lot lately. Her approach to the female masquerade raises questions about how the docile female body is constructed by culture and often disciplined and punished into shape, by behaviour that is powerfully and perversely compliant.

Until recently Vanessa was one of a rare species, a famous fat lady who had become successful in the British media, who wasn't a comedienne and who took being 'fat and happy' very seriously. As one newspaper put it, 'As the fat woman's champion, Vanessa always insisted it was possible to have a successful career, perfect marriage, beautiful home as well as two lovely daughters – and still eat Mars bars and profiteroles'.[60] Unlike Victoria Wood and Dawn French – who have already made a space for the fuller figure by mocking everything and everyone who suggested fat ladies should not make themselves either seen or heard, Vanessa Feltz did not go in for aggressive subversion of misogynist thinking. Nor did she try and play with ideas about the female grotesque in regard to playing with the image of the 'fat lady eating excessively', in the way that Jo Brand has done. When presenting breakfast TV and her chat shows, Vanessa certainly did not challenge the status quo through her political discourse, which was often conservative. Although her appearance and her body hinted at the contradictions of her story, her thinking appears to have found much in common with the 'you can have it all' business amazons, as she tried to do just that.[61] Husband, children, chat show, designer clothes and huge quantities of chocolate profiteroles – which she bored us about endlessly. In performing her success, Vanessa Feltz, like Roseanne Barr, seems to have ignored what has been described as a matronizing edict, namely 'Thou Shalt Not Make a Spectacle out of Oneself'. Mary Russo develops this argument and suggests that women learn how to behave from other women:

> 'Making a spectacle out of oneself' seemed a specifically feminine danger. The danger was of exposure. Men, I learned somewhat later in life 'exposed themselves' but that operation was quite deliberate and circumscribed. For a woman, making a spectacle out of herself had more to do with a kind of inadvertence and loss of boundaries: the possessors of large, aging and dimpled thighs displayed at the public beach, of overly rouged cheeks, of a voice shrill in laughter, or a sliding bra strap – a loose dingy bra strap especially – were at once caught out by fate and blameworthy. It was my impression that these women had something wrong, had stepped, as it were, into the limelight out of turn – too young, or too old, too early or too late – and yet anyone, any woman, could make a spectacle out of herself if she was not careful.[62]

Vanessa was a spectacle even though she kept her large body charmingly presented or at least well covered. (In one TV programme she took the camera into her bedroom and revealed to the audience racks and racks of brightly coloured suits which were the trademark of her TV chat show.) One of her more attractive qualities in wearing bright colours and being large is that she did not completely appear to understand the danger involved in a woman transgressing the invisible codes of femininity. And she transgressed all the time, which is perhaps why she got so much flak and criticism from the media.

But she has since worked it out – she says . . . Vanessa has entered the twenty-first century five and a half stones thinner and minus a husband (who gave her an ultimatum to lose weight but still left her anyway), a slim yet much sadder woman. One whose chat shows have been repeatedly axed. Indeed, Vanessa's saving grace is that even though she is seen everywhere showing off her new slim body, she is no longer performing 'happiness'. In fact she is now even starting to talk about what she interpreted as the hostility in the national press to her Jewishness, her fatness and her success. Yet her alleged compliance to her husband's demands for her to be thinner ('Believe me, everything came second to him. Any money I earned went into a joint bank account and if he said "Jump", I'd say, "How high?"')[63] have somehow made her a more grotesquely interesting figure than she was before. Even though she is now thin, she still hasn't completely grasped why her husband's complaints about her 'self-loathing' and 'inability to keep anything private'[64] seem to be very pertinent. In fact, in the way she discusses losing weight in the newspapers or on other people's chat shows, such as that hosted by Michael Parkinson, Vanessa appears to demonstrate that she has lost something far more significant than five stones: she appears to have lost her happier self. Watching the public spectacle of Vanessa trying to be hyper-normal and slim is a lot more scary than looking at her previously large body.

Whilst I don't deny the power of the sort of hysterical conformity that Vanessa Feltz's body, as well as her mouth, seems to articulate, I do think her behaviour raises some interesting questions about perverse compliance. Estelle Weldon has argued that 'if psychoanalysis began with the study of hysterical non-conformity, [perhaps future] development will be stimulated by the study of perverse compliant deception.'[65] In Vanessa's case what I am suggesting is that her self-deception – publicly she denies any culpability in the break-up of her marriage, except for admitting she was fat – leaves her with only the possibility of reinventing herself. And she does so, every time she is interviewed, telling the *Daily Record*, 'I hope I never do an Oprah Winfrey and pile it all back on',[66] and admitting to other newspapers why she now thinks it is 'impossible' to be desirable and fat. Consequently, the trauma Vanessa has lived through about her negative feelings towards her body, and now her husband, takes the form of her presenting herself as hyper-feminine. She has even appeared in a bathing costume in some newspapers. 'I'm thin the pink', joked the front page of the *Mirror* (13/3/00), connecting her new body to stereotypical notions of femininity. Perhaps Vanessa has to try to be hyper-slim, hyper-feminine and hyper-normal because she feels so Other. In contrast, whilst Oprah Winfrey made a big fuss about losing weight when she turned up on her TV show in 1988 with a trolley of lard, I don't remember her – in any of her body incarnations – exposing quite so much flesh as Vanessa, and consequently Vanessa's behaviour worries me. The process of self-reinvention may not be an easy or happy process to live through, but no doubt it will be one with many sequels. Inevitably, the popular media in teasing (and perhaps humiliating) Vanessa over her previous fatness, and now in helping her celebrate her slim success, have ultimately set her up for failure. To consume too many profiteroles again would make her more than a laughing stock, it would also make her a blatant failure (something that would be obviously difficult on top of having her TV shows cut). No doubt the papers will wreak their revenge, as the British media appear to enjoy setting up celebrities just to tear them down later. And after all, Vanessa has always transgressed, so doesn't she deserve it? She has been a woman who loved too much, who ate too much; and now I fear she may have dieted too much (or at least over-publicized her dieting) to be truly acceptable. By breaking the unwritten rules of femininity, she has inevitably linked herself to the comic grotesque, in the Bakhtinian sense,[67] a female figure to be laughed or sneered at rather than taken seriously. Indeed, the spectre of the fat woman and the anorexic are twin faces of the female grotesque today.

Vanessa has clearly ingested too many chocolate profiteroles to be shaped ideally feminine, and having controlled her 'grotesque' body, now the mouth she shoved them into erupts with accounts of her problems of self. She has swallowed the thin beauty ideal, and now spits out experiences of it. In so doing she draws attention to the mouth as an abstract – 'the orifice of profound physical impulses', as Bataille defines it[68] – and it is through the mouth that she is linked to the grotesque. For as Mary Russo points out, 'the grotesque body is open, protruding, irregular, secreting, multiple, and changing; it is identified with official "low" culture or the carnivalesque, and with social transformation.'[69]

My account of the representation of Vanessa may sound harsh, but it is not meant to be. I wish Vanessa well, and a place to experience her life outside of the society of the spectacle. However, I suspect her addiction to fame and to media performativity will be more damaging to her in the long run than her fat ever was. Indeed, media performativity appears to be linked to a more damaging form of self-harming than her weight 'problems' ever were.

Conclusion

This chapter has emphasized two body parts – the eye and the mouth – in order to argue that the emphasis on fashionable food and eating out in designer restaurants conceals real problems women have about eating. It has suggested that it may be relevant to understand the way women eat and relate to food in terms of ideas about gender performativity and transgression. The designer restaurant may offer a space where normative gender and sexual performativity can take place, but the point I have tried to make is that the irony about this context, and the emphasis on designer food, may *conceal* problems women actually have about eating. Femininity is obviously not fixed by the media. It is often experienced as both fluid and flexible. Nevertheless, it is ultimately a regulative and disciplinary practice. It generates both anxiety and insecurity, particularly around issues of self-regulation, not least because the image of the fat female grotesque is the repressed of normative femininity. Indeed, images of grotesque women operate to keep the ideal feminine norm in place, just as the positive emphasis placed on ultra-thin women serves to keep other women worrying about their diets.

Clearly, the culture of slenderness is a perverse development of the culture of plenty, and in this chapter I have tried to understand how fatness in women, in the West at least, is linked in representation (and in life) to a fear of female transgression that serves to keep women in their place, worrying about their bodies. This chapter has tried to use humour to make some new points about some old contradictions about women's food obsessions, even their eating disorders. Indeed, it has tried to look at the feelings of power enjoyed by women who manage to adhere to a perverse compliant rigid form of thin femininity, and not to under-estimate the pleasures on offer, while implicitly suggesting that there are worse things in life than being fat. Yet when discussing the case of Vanessa Feltz, the argument has been made that hyper-normality can be very scary, particularly if it appears to correlate with self-harming. Finally, the chapter has tried to understand how gourmet cookbooks and designer restaurants offer women access to what I have jokingly called 'gastroporn lifestyles': a perverse cultural form of the post-modern period that allows female desire to be confronted without being articulated, or acted upon. Here's looking at you, kid – *bon appetit*!

Acknowledgement

Lorraine Gamman would like to thank the AHRB for research leaving funding in 1999/2000 to complete this chapter.

Notes

1   Michel Foucault, *Discipline and Punish: the Birth of the Prison*, trans. Alan Sheridan, New York, Vintage Books, 1979, 184.

2   Cited in J. MacClancy, *Consuming Culture*, London, Chapman, 1992, 5.

3   Surprisingly, Europeans eat more chocolate than do Americans. Source: 'Sweet news: chocolate consumption rises'. Online at *http.//www.candursa.org.sweet-ness.html*, accessed 10/7/00.

4   Shelley Bovey, *The Forbidden Body: Why Being Fat Is Not a Sin*, New York, New York University Press, 1994.

5   Ibid.

6   Naomi Wolf, *The Beauty Myth*, London, Chatto & Windus, 1990; Germaine Greer, *The Female Eunuch*, London, Paladin, 1971.

7   Wolf, op. cit.

8   Peter Stearns, *Fat History: Bodies and Beauty in the Modern West*, New York, New York University Press, 1997.

9   Emily Martin, *Woman in the Body: a Cultural Analysis of Reproduction*, Milton Keynes, Open University Press, 1989.

10   Mary Russo, *The Female Grotesque: Risk, Excess and Modernity*, New York and London, Routledge, 1994.

11   Sexual fetishism of food is discussed by Lorraine Gamman and Merja Makinen, *Female Fetishism: a New Look*, London, Lawrence & Wishart, 1994.

12   L. Cooke and P. Woollen (eds), *Visual Display: Culture beyond Appearances*, Seattle, Bay Press, 1995, 9.

13   Gamman and Makinen (op. cit., 102), locate a woman stocking fetishist.

14   Guy Debord, *The Society of the Spectacle*, London, Zone Books, 1994.

15   Cooke and Wollen, op. cit., 9.

16   Ibid.

17   Stephen Bayley, 'Food as fashion' in C. Catterall (ed.) *Food Design and Culture*, Italy, Lawrence King Publishing in association with Glasgow, 1999, 34–53.

18   Rob Shields (ed.), *Lifestyle Shopping: the Subject of Consumption*, London and New York, Routledge, 2.

19   Catterall, op. cit., 3.

20   Russo, op. cit.

21   The claims made for ingredients in advertising sometimes seem so inflated that they acquire almost supernatural referents more commonly associated with religion. For example, in the way water and bread, employed in the rituals of baptism and the Eucharist, have connotations that symbolise the body of Christ and participation in the Christian faith.

22   Nigella Lawson, *How to Eat*, London, Chatto & Windus, 1998.

23   Rose Gray and Ruth Rogers, *The River Café Cookbook*, London, Ebury Press, 1996; Delia Smith, *How to Cook*, London, BBC Consumer Publishing, 1998; Nigel Slater, *Real Cooking*, London, Penguin Books, 1999; Jennifer Paterson and Clarissa Dickson Wright, *Two Fat Ladies' Obsessions*, London, Ebury Press, 1999.

24   H. Fielding, *Bridget Jones. The Edge of Reason*, London, Picador, 1999, 111.

25   S. Bordo, 'The body and the reproduction of femininity' in K. Conboy, N. Medina and S. Stanbury (eds), *Writing on the Body: Female Embodiment and Feminist Theory*, New York, Columbia University Press, 1997, 90–110.

26   Ibid., 96.

27   Judith Butler, *Gender Trouble: Feminism and the Subversion of Identity*, London, Routledge, 1990, 140.

28   R.W. Connell, *Gender and Power*, Oxford, Polity Press, 1987, 80.

29   Butler, op. cit., 232.

30   Fielding, op. cit., 3.

31   S.L. Bartky, 'Foucault, femininity and the modernization of patriarchal power' in I. Diamond and L. Quinby (eds), *Feminism and Foucault: Reflections on Resistance*, Boston, Northeastern University Press, 1988, 61–8.

32   S. Orbach, 'Psychological processes of consuming', *British Journal of Psychotherapy*, 10 (2): 196–9.

33   Foucault, op. cit., 184.

34   Pasi Falk, 'The scopic regimes of shopping' in Pasi Falk and Colin Campbell, *The Shopping Experience*, London, Sage, 1997, 181: 'the scopic regimes that facilitate this are more about the glance than the gaze, as both shops and restaurants appear to facilitate space for a seriality of quick looks . . . which gives priority to the *glance*.'

35   Melanie Katzman, 'Is it true eating makes you feel better?', *The Bulimic College Student*, New York, Haworth Press, 1989, 75–87. Consequently, issues raised by some clinicians and theoreticians about eating disorders link female problems with individuation and sexual identity and have led to bulimia being described as a coping strategy that involves a type of fetishism.

36   The annual potlatch ceremony practised by the Kwakiutl Indians offers a site
      where accumulated wealth and possessions were not just redistributed but wholly
      used up. The anthropologist Marcel Mauss raises a discussion of 'the gift' in
      relation to dispersal. Baudrillard has drawn upon this work to discuss a form of
      potlatch where a community's wealth is used up in order to prevent accumula-
      tion. Jean Baudrillard, *Selected Writings*, Stanford, Stanford University Press,
      1988, 93.
37   V. Nathanson, *Eating Disorders, Body Image and the Media*, London, BMA, 2000.
38   Cherry Norton, 'Rise in eating disorders', *Independent*, 31/5/00.
39   G. Bataille, *The Accursed Share, Vol. 1*, trans. R. Hurley, New York, Zone Books,
      1991, 21. Comparing potlatch to bulimia may be problematic. Bulimia does not
      eliminate value because the supply of food commodities, in the First World at
      least, appears never-ending and does not disperse desire nor enable gratification
      but instead defers it. Indeed, the bulimic is rarely satisfied by the food binged
      upon and then vomited up, but appears caught in the cycle of feasting and fasting.
      Mary Douglas, by contrast, describes the complexities of the social processes
      through the anthropological use of potlatch when discussing the Indians of Puget
      Sound in relation to their behaviour and food cycle. See Mary Douglas and Baron
      Isherwood, *The World of Goods: Towards an Anthropology of Consumption*, London
      and New York, Basic Books, 1979, 46–7.
40   Bayley, op. cit., 34.
41   J. Laurence, 'The world's fattest nations', *Independent* (5/9/98: 3), revealed that
      of the fattest nations in the world, Samoa is at the top of the list before the
      USA, Germany and Britain.
42   Catterall, op. cit., 26.
43   Ibid.
44   Laurence, op. cit.
45   R. Coward, *Female Desire: Women's Sexuality Today*, London, Paladin, 1984,
      99–106.
46   'It is a popular view, for example, that fashion design for the youthful, even
      prepubertal, body and the use of very young fashion models from the 1960s
      onwards, starting with Twiggy, has in some sense "caused" anorexia . . . Many
      women follow fashion, perhaps diet from time to time, but are not anorexic.
      Nor has anorexia decreased during the 1980s, a decade when fashions were not
      uniformly prepubertal, as they were in the mid 1960s'. E. Wilson, 'Fashion and
      the postmodern body' in J. Ash and E. Wilson (eds), *Chic Thrills: A Fashion
      Reader*, London, Pandora, 1992.
47   Dally and Gomez are quoted in S. Mendell, 'On the civilising of appetite', in
      M. Featherstone (ed.) *The Body, Social Process and Cultural Theory*, London, Sage,
      1991, 150.
48   E. Wilson, *Women and Fashion*, London, Virago, 1992.
49   Mendell, op. cit., 150, 151.
50   J. MacClancy, *Consuming Culture*, London, Chapman, 1992.
51   Wilson, *Adorned in Dreams, Fashion and Modernity*, London, Virago, 1985, 116.
52   This point was made and quoted in the 'Notes to Editors' given in the Cabinet
      Office press release, 'Better for Women, Better for All', CAB 229/00,
      20/06/00.
53   Ibid.
54   Debord, op. cit.

55 These are helpfully reproduced in Claire Catterall, op. cit., 64–77.

56 Margy G. Winkler, 'Model women' in M. Winkler and L.B. Cole (eds) *The Good Body: Asceticism in Contemporary Culture,* New Haven, Yale University Press, 1994, 221.

57 Jennifer Craik, *The Face of Fashion: Cultural Studies in Fashion*, London, Routledge, 1994.

58 Bartky, op. cit.

59 Angela McRobbie, '*More!* New sexualities in girls' and women's magazines' in J. Curran, D. Morley and V. Walkerdine (eds) *Cultural Studies and Communications*, London, Arnold, 1996, 176–94.

60 Sue Caroll, *Mirror*, 18/1/00.

61 Leah Hertz, *The Business Amazons*, London, Methuen, 1986.

62 Russo, op. cit., 53–4.

63 Sue Carroll, 'How Vanessa won a 12 week challenge', *Mirror*, 18/1/00, 12–13.

64 Winkler, op. cit., 221.

65 E. Weldon, review in *British Journal of Psychotherapy*, 1996, 12 (4).

66 Kathleen Morgan, 'Switched on', *Daily Record*, 2/2/00, 14–15.

67 Russo, op. cit., 53–4.

68 Georges Bataille, *Vision of Excess: Selected Writing 1927–39*, translated and edited with an introduction by Allan Stoekl, Minneapolis, University of Minnesota Press, 1985, 59–60.

69 Russo, op. cit., 8.

Chapter 5

Pamela Church Gibson

'NO-ONE EXPECTS ME ANYWHERE'
Invisible women, ageing and the fashion industry

> I am always greeted with the question, 'Is this for yourself?' as though I
> must be buying for someone else, as though I didn't buy clothes for myself
> – as though I must have some supply somewhere in an old trunk, left me
> by my mother, waiting for me to wear when I reached the right age.
> (Macdonald 1984: 74)

SO WROTE LESBIAN ACTIVIST Barbara Macdonald when in her sixties.
Her book, *Look Me in the Eye*, has nothing to do with fashion and everything
to do with the phenomenon of invisibility. It is in her extraordinarily powerful
indictment of the way that, even within the feminist movement itself, ageing
women are ignored or treated with embarrassment that the phrase, 'No-one expects
me anywhere', is to be found. I do not wish to demean Macdonald's work by
using it as an epigraph for an essay on retailing and the ageing population; rather,
I see within advertising, marketing and the fashion industry the best example of
the way in which Western society treats its ageing population.

In theory, we could be approaching a time when the demographics of American
and European society – the moment when the 'boomers' who so lionised youth
are themselves confronted with the realities of their own middle years and the
prospect of what lies ahead – might bring some changes for the better. It is
frequently suggested within the mass media that this generation, with its economic
and political power, with so many of its members safely in positions of power and
influence, and with its proven ability to activate social change, will finally change
not only the socio-economic realities of ageing but our perception of age; that
they may even possess the wherewithal to defy temporality. 'I won't grow old
like my parents did', is the unspoken message that so many middle-aged celebrities – rock stars, actors, ex-models, whatever – seek to stress within interview

or profile, in each posed photograph. The current vogue for female celebrities to remove their clothes and pose semi-naked, even if they have never before been seen in such a state of *déshabillé* (as is the case with demure cake-maker Jane Asher and Aga-saga writer Joanna Trollope), is part of the defiance of this generation. These images are their proof that the passage of time has not and will not affect them as it did their unfortunate mothers, aunts and grandmothers. These photographs appear everywhere – even in that bastion of Middle England, the *Radio Times*. This particular trend for older self-exposure in fact began in the pages of *Playboy*, when Ursula Andress celebrated her sixtieth birthday by recreating her famous emergence from the Caribbean, bikini-clad, in the very first James Bond film.

Within the confines of an essay, it is not possible to examine fully our perception of age and the ways in which this might – or should – be changed by more sober, socially beneficial actions. But I shall nevertheless try – through an outline of the current situation in the supposedly callous world of retail and fashion – to assess the climate and the likelihood of change. I have included a foray into oral history as testament to the experiences and emotions of several fashion-literate 'boomers' as they roam within current retailing spaces.

For those who are already in late middle age and older, changes if they come will be too late; many have already experienced a feeling of being unwelcome and have donned a sartorial cloak to suit their social invisibility. Ted Polhemus, working with Lynn Procter, wrote his first book on fashion in 1978. Writing from an anthropological perspective, he posited the notion of 'fashion' against that of 'anti-fashion'; inevitably, the latter is easier to define. It seems relevant to do so within this context:

> With the exception of the unfashionable (those who can't keep up with fashion change but would like to), 'anti-fashion' refers to all styles of adornment which fall outside the organised system or systems of fashion change. The Royal Family, at least in public, wears anti-fashion; my mother wears anti-fashion; Hell's Angels, hippies, punks and priests wear anti-fashion . . . in no case is their dress or adornment caught up in the mechanism of fashion change, neither do they want it to be . . . While anti-fashions most certainly do occur within the context of Western and Westernised societies, the most readily identifiable forms are the folk costumes of primitive and peasant peoples.
>
> (Polhemus and Procter 1978: 34–5)

Although the late Princess Diana did a great deal to change both the reality and the perception of royal style, the Queen herself still falls into Polhemus's wide-ranging categorisation – or massive generalisation – of 'anti-fashion'. Twenty years after these definitions, we can still identify his original examples, and other, newer groups who seem intentionally impervious to 'fashion' and who ignore current trends and eschew change. But what about the 'unfashionable'? And is there any overlap? Is there anyone who might actually feel excluded from fashion, for reasons other than financial? Is anyone actually prevented from being fashionable, even if they would like to participate in some way?

There is an obvious answer here. Look around any social gathering, watch carefully on the high street – the majority of women in their sixties and upwards seem to be following their own sartorial rules. During the day, there is in the summer, a profusion of floral or other prints, usually of man-made fabrics. Over the frocks – or skirts and blouses – there is a white cardigan or, if colder, a beige blouson jacket (also worn by men of a similar age). In winter there are pleated skirts, cardigans again, pull-on trousers or a very unfashionable, non-designer, non-sporty tracksuit, possibly made of velour and pastel-coloured. Shoes are usually beige and bear little relation to current styles. There's a preponderance of neutral colours, a seeming desire for camouflage and anonymity.

Do these women dress in this way from choice or necessity? Obviously there are both financial circumstances and the desire for comfort to be considered, particularly as women reach their seventies. The man-made fabrics are both relatively inexpensive and low-maintenance, but they are sometimes worn by those who could afford natural fabrics and the cost of their upkeep.

Women in this older age group from a different socio-economic category, who have more money and wish to proclaim their class allegiance or merely to display their 'taste' (in Bourdieu's sense of the word), spend their money differently. But they still seem to don a uniform – Liberty scarves, silk blouses, navy blue skirts and pearls, for example. A foray into the places frequented by those within this age category who wish to make known their cultural capital, the tea-rooms in London galleries, say, will provide plentiful examples of this particular form of protective colouring.

If you observe and take notes over a sustained period of time, as I did, one thing is interesting; you see these women and their friends wearing virtually identical outfits, give or take the details, just as teenage girls still finding their fashion feet tend to do. As with young girls, they will often have interchangeable hairstyles. Have they consciously adopted this regimented appearance or has it been forced upon them by an unsympathetic industry? Have they given up on fashion, perhaps through self-consciousness, and opted for the security of a peer group style – or anti-style? Men too are affected – particularly after retirement, when a suit is no longer an option.

Do these older people dress as they do because they only feel welcome in certain retail outlets? There are of course exceptions, but they are just that – exceptions to the norm. In Italian towns, however, stylish older women and elderly ladies who still have and display an interest in their appearance are far more plentiful. In the villages, of course, there are still older women in *lutto* – the all-black garb of deep mourning, adopted after the death of a partner and worn for life. Any historian of costume will tell you that in different societies and at different historical junctures, certain styles of dress and particular garments – a shawl, an embroidered cap – have signalled the onset of later life. Have these English women been forced by an unsympathetic industry, or have they actually chosen to create a modern-day equivalent? Are they, in fact, wearing a form of fashion *lutto* – adopted unwillingly?

In order to investigate this question – surely vital in the light of current demographic trends and their implications – I first looked at the available literature and noted the worrying gaps. Cultural theorists, for instance, are not usually interested in ageing; some writers have begun to address the issues, but overall there is a paucity of theoretical work; only gerontologists and other scientists have really examined the issues that confront an ageing population. I interviewed some of those involved in the fashion industry, who should by rights be aware of these trends and preparing for the consequences – journalists, buyers, and retailers. Lastly, I selected and interviewed in depth a focus group – choosing women born between 1947 and 1952.

Those theorists who do discuss the negative perceptions of ageing, particularly concerning the ageing woman, must refer to two seminal and highly negative accounts of female ageing, both written in the early 1970s. Susan Sontag's well-known and overly influential 'The double jeopardy of ageing' includes the categorical statement: 'That older women are repulsive is one of the most profound aesthetic and erotic feelings in our culture' (Sontag 1972: 37).

Indeed, those of us who have read Bakhtin's description of the three 'naked, pregnant old hags' quoted by Kristeva and used by Mary Russo in her work on the female grotesque (Russo 1996: 69) will know that for Bakhtin the combination of old age, nudity and fecundity was the apotheosis of the abject.

De Beauvoir, in her seminal work on the treatment of the elderly in Western culture *Old Age* (de Beauvoir 1972b) paints an equally grim picture, stressing senility, sterility and impotence, both sexual and personal. When interviewed by *Harper's Magazine* she advocated a similar argument to Sontag – she emphasised throughout that ageing was more 'traumatic' for women because they are always judged primarily on their sexual allure (de Beauvoir 1972).

Interestingly, de Beauvoir herself defied the conventions of ageing in her mode of self-presentation. Margaret Simon, in her tribute to de Beauvoir published immediately after her death, reveals as much about her own prejudices, and those of the society she inhabits, as she does about de Beauvoir when she describes their first meeting: 'I was shocked – although she was old and wrinkled, she had the audacity to wear red lipstick and bright red nail polish' (Simon 1986: 204).

Eileen Fairhurst, who recently worked with a cross-gender control group to assess their feelings concerning their own appearance and their preferred modes of self-presentation, found that Sontag's notion of the 'double standard of ageing' seemed to be refuted by her own findings: 'concern with physical appearance may cross-cut gender . . . there is other research which also leads to a re-examination of this thesis' (Fairhurst 1998: 263). Fairhurst's interviewees spoke eloquently of their reactions to physical change and to their perceived invisibility, but both men and women referred repeatedly to their belief that it was their duty to 'make the best of themselves'. She therefore concludes: 'I would suggest that this has implications for the ways in which gender is claimed to operate' (p. 272) having noted that 'in the growing corpus of knowledge on ageing amongst gay males, great concern was expressed' (p. 271).

So it is not only women who feel that they should try to present their changed physicality to best advantage. This is something, she notes, that was apparent in the first book on ageing written by the two academics who have done most to open up this area within the remit of cultural studies, namely Mike Featherstone and Mike Hepworth. *Surviving Middle Age*, which Fairhurst references to emphasize her conclusions on gender-specificity, appeared in 1982; since then, Featherstone and Hepworth have written widely on the topic of ageing and have co-edited various anthologies (Featherstone and Wernick 1995; Featherstone *et al.* 1991; Hepworth and Featherstone 1982, 1988). The impetus for the first book was, they explain in the Preface, the evening when they overheard the prolonged taunting of their local barman by his friends; he was teased about his plumpness, his beer belly, and his obvious need to get himself into better physical shape. The authors chronicle the new ideas of 'body maintenance' and care for appearance; they describe what was becoming apparent as 'the new image of middle age – one whereby the battle against ageing becomes a social duty' (Hepworth and Featherstone 1982: 95). That this 'duty' is one for both men and women is not necessarily reassuring – tyranny does indeed cross-cut gender.

These authors have throughout the last two decades drawn attention to the negative stereotyping of older people within advertising and within popular culture. However, despite their efforts, we are still presented with the two kinds of extreme image noted by Andrew Blaikie (1999: 95–105). Grandma Giles, *Driving Miss Daisy* and Thora Hird in *Talking Heads* are lined up against Joan Collins.

Kathleen Woodward, investigating the portrayal of ageing in literature, examines 'youthfulness as . . . masquerade' – the presentation of a youthful appearance through artificial aids (Woodward 1991: 147). She uses the work of Joan Riviere in a very sympathetic analysis of the various motives behind the adoption of such a mask, which may in fact be resistant and subversive as well as a denial of reality. Masquerade in age is merely a 'cover-up through which old age, none the less, speaks' (p. 148) and she is very clear that it is our duty to 'add age to the recent debates on difference . . . which have resulted in some of the most important criticism in the last few decades in the areas of social difference, colonialism, ethnicity, race and cultural difference (p. 157). She discusses fully the contemporary disciplining of the ageing body; she describes elderly Americans as 'in hiding amongst the population' (p. 161).

Nowhere is the predicament – and the paradox – of the ageing boomers and their attempts at concealment expressed more clearly: 'At precisely the historical moment that the elderly are appearing on the historical stage in record numbers, many are vanishing into the crowd, no longer marked as old' (p. 162). This is not the triumphalist stance of the older rockstar, the actress taking her first semi-naked photocall. Ageing, Woodward suggests, is not – and might not be – given more dignity: 'It's just that the ageing body is being remodelled, in an attempt to eliminate it' (p. 163).

The pursuit by the boomers of the surgically youthful body, which she sees as 'the postmodern version of Dorian Gray . . . the uncanny, ageing body-in-masquerade' (p. 164) does not promise an immediate change in attitude, the acceptance for which Woodward and so many others call. Those now on either side of 50 are in possession of much of the country's disposable income, which might easily be spent on fashionable garments and related goods, rather than merely on aids, drastic and otherwise, to maintaining an illusion of youth. Market researchers, trend forecasters and marketing journals both here and in America keep reminding us of this fact and of its implications. Within the marketing arena, as Kimberly Anne Sawchuk elaborates, 'what previously was assumed obsolete and without value is turning into gold' and advertisers attend seminars for advice in how to approach 'the new seniors' (Sawchuk 1995: 173–85).

But what, if anything, has actually happened, particularly within the UK retail sector? Most of us are aware that the 50-plus sector of the population is growing, and that by the year 2020, 50 per cent of all adults in the UK will be 50-plus. We all know too about the declining youth market – which so many high street retail outlets continue to target. Furthermore, the market research that has been done has, not surprisingly, shown that older women do *not* lose interest in their appearance. The Mintel Report *Third Age Lifestyles* (1993) showed quite clearly that older women were prepared to pay for quality, which they valued more than fashion. But this does not necessarily mean a loss of interest in style. Indeed, the report stressed the diversity of the segment studied and the high level of disposable income.

In February 1997, an article in the *Journal of Fashion Marketing and Management* (Belleau *et al.* 1997), which studied control groups of younger and older American women, made it perfectly clear that there were few differences in attitude between the groups. If anything, the older women were more media-aware. They paid more attention to fashion coverage – and found it inappropriate. They were more interested in comfort than the younger women, but equally demanding in fashion terms. The article states unambiguously, 'Future research should focus on the satisfaction/ dissatisfaction of older women with apparel currently available' (p. 167).

However, so much of the British fashion industry seems indifferent, unprepared, and even potentially hostile. Paradoxically, the success of 'British fashion' can be attributed to the members of this very generation and their past tastes and habits; yet, once they hit the magical age of 45 they seem to become invisible. Retailers, when describing their target markets, will conclude '35–45'; fashion magazines use similar patterning when describing their target readers. There is a growing media interest in the existence and the purchasing power of what has been recently christened in the media the phenomenon of 'middle youth' – those in their late thirties and early forties who are reluctant to abandon fashion, music, clubbing and football. The successes of certain magazines are indicative of the perceived purchasing power and fashionable tastes of this sector of the population. Yet in ten years' time, they too will suffer from the sudden withdrawal of commercial interest and opportunity. So far, the only movement in the 'older' magazine market has been worrying; the recent launch of the magazine *Aura*, whose first editorial proclaimed 'We're the generation that wore loons, screamed at the Monkees and read *Honey*.' On the cover was Susan Sarandon, actress and political activist, wearing fishnet tights and a feather boa (*Aura*, May 2000).

If they have money, of course, women over 50 may be ignored but there is still fashion to be found – small designer shops with their sympathetic ambience can offer them Jil Sander, Betty Jackson, Ghost and Nicole Farhi – female designers, themselves of a certain age, who are responsive to their needs. But these, of course, are often classic or dateless clothes. For those whose spending power is limited, a trip to M&S – or even BHS or Littlewoods (or previously C&A before its demise) – seems the only alternative. Somewhere in between lie the concessions in department stores favoured by their mothers – Windsmoor, Planet, and the like. Jaeger can dress those with money and modest pretensions to fashion.

Clothing, rather than fashion, is what seems to be on offer for the over-fifties. Furthermore, so many younger designers are currently unable to escape their obsession with retro – and these garments cannot be worn by those who wore them first time around. But these 'boomers' are the first generation to grow up with and within fashion, as *Aura* stressed. In the 1960s, fashion became for the first time youth-driven – and so it has remained. In fact, it could be argued that the only industry really geared up to respond to the needs of the ageing population is, as Woodward's work intimates, the beauty industry. Cosmetic scientists and surgeons are set to maximise their profits and allay the fears of their customers.

Yet some organisations, intended to produce changes in attitude and design, are already in place in Europe and the United States. The Hamlyn Foundation was set up in 1987 by Helen Hamlyn, who was distressed to find, when her elderly mother became ill, that this meant a room full of 'porridge-coloured objects' (Hamlyn 1990). Since 1991, the Foundation has funded the Design Age Project at the Royal College of Art. This enterprise, run by Roger Coleman, works from within the College to encourage, promote and inspire innovative design in all areas – including fashion and textiles – for an ageing population both here and throughout the world.

In 1993 the Royal College of Art Textiles and Fashion Department and Design Age hosted a seminar and workshop entitled 'Fashion and Textiles for our Future Selves'. Chaired by Jeff Banks, participants included journalist Brenda Polan and Bryan Godbold of Marks & Spencer, who discussed the company's perception of their 'mature customer'. The conference ended with a 'shopping list' of demands from the various workshop groups – 'new possibilities' as 'scenarios and concepts for environments, products and services'. These ranged from 'positive media coverage – more use of older models' through 'consideration of changing shape' to the need for an 'attractive ambience' and particular facilities within the retail environment (Coleman 1993). As yet, most of these demands are not being met at high street level – even Marks & Spencer, who obviously pride themselves on meeting the needs of older customers, do not have the suggested chairs. In fact, they don't even have the loos, which were on the 'shopping list' of demands and which are generally found in any department store.

Many of the speakers at the Royal College of Art symposium reiterated the demand for a 'fashionable, modern approach to designing for older people.' (Coleman 1993: 25). This, too, has not been answered – certainly not in most high street retail outlets. 'Positive media coverage' is still in its infancy – while the 'use of older models' has been so limited as to seem gimmicky and tokenist. Some of the more avant-garde designers, such as Jean-Paul Gaultier, have put older people on the catwalk – but for the most part, despite the efforts of photographers such as Nick Knight and Steven Meisel, whose 1987 Gap campaign was the first fashion campaign to feature mature women (and men), magazine journalism remains youth-dominated. During my own research, one (male) journalist said to me, 'You can't *really* expect young designers to think about older women – they'd rather think about sexy 20-year olds' (interview). Journalist Nilgin Yusuf was far more positive when interviewed, describing the design potential for the ageing population: 'With the growing popularity and use of fabrics such as Tactel and Tencel, older women can perhaps eventually have comfort *and* chic.'

Certainly this is taken into consideration at the upper end of the market – for example, in my interview with the manageress of a Whistles branch, she told me,

'I have customers in their sixties and seventies. Of course, the fact that I'm 47 and not 25 does help.' She told me that Whistles would be offering far more styles in size 16, something they have already begun to do.

Whistles was one of the shops mentioned with approval by my focus group and by David Shaw, a former director of the Burton Group. In an interview he told me,

> There's what I call 'information mythology' – it's particularly mis-leading here. There's a false correlation between youth and fashion ability. If the high street chains continue as they are, they'll go under. For a start, too many brand managers are too young to understand customer needs.

My chosen focus group was made up of women who are extremely stylish, very interested in clothes and in fashion, but not professionally involved in the industry. A/Bs all of them, they are aged between 47 and 52. They included a landscape gardener, a university professor, a publisher and a solicitor, and they live countrywide. I questioned them at length about their interest in fashion, shopping habits, preferences, and experiences.

They all said that they read *Vogue*, even if sporadically, and certainly follow fashion coverage in the broadsheets and Sunday papers. The publisher read *The Face* 'for the Belgian designers'. Most found it necessary to shop for clothes in London – those who lived elsewhere travelling to London for that purpose at least twice a year. The shops they visit? All mentioned Whistles, Agnes B, Jigsaw, Nicole Farhi, Harvey Nichols, Liberty, and Margaret Howell.

Outside London, all mentioned 'small shops' where the staff 'know your style'. Provincial department stores were not able to provide 'a suit for work . . . everything's so fussy – I suppose they're occasion suits for corporate wives.' All were critical of the high street: 'The only shop I feel comfortable in is Marks & Spencer – I feel positively young in there.' All mentioned negative experiences: 'I get paranoid in the Gap. I've always bought stuff there – but sometimes I feel they're thinking "Poor deluded fool" even if they're not.' Another confessed the need to pretend, in high street shops, that she was looking for 'something for my daughter'. All stressed the unpalatable nature of the high street 'offer': 'Badly made tat – all right if you're 20'.

Sizing was criticised: 'What will happen when most women my age can't get into a size 14 any more?' So, too, was the retail ambience – the harsh lighting, the changing rooms, the loud music. One commented, 'What will it be like when I'm 60, if I feel like this now?' Another took this idea one stage further: 'At the moment I'm pretty robust, and sometimes *I* can't face the shops. If I'm old and fragile, maybe I won't be able to cope.'

The message for most retailers is clear: if these stylish, financially comfortable women feel self-conscious, what about others in this massive age group with less money and less confidence? Why should they be made to feel unwanted and unwelcome? The seeming assumption that visual discrimination disappears with the onset of middle age must finally be abandoned. If anything, women of this generation will continue, in their fifties and beyond, to demand even more of retailers than they did when they were younger. In the 1960s and 1970s, they wanted inexpensive high fashion. Now they want fashion awareness and style. They understand and pay attention to quality and finishing. They know what to look for, and what to reject – in product and ambience. There must be some sensible, productive dialogue between high street designers, brand managers and those responsible for shop-floor design.

But above all, we need to rethink our attitudes to ageing. As the population ages, will these boomers be able to effect that change from within? This generation, who made youth synonymous with fashion, now have the responsibility of changing our attitudes once again. Middle age, now rechristened 'mid-life', may gradually lose its terror. But there is still a very negative perception of what gerontologists call 'deep old age'. This is partly a legitimate fear of the frailty of the 'fourth age', of the gradual loss of physical mobility. But so much of our fear is an irrational dread of our own mortality.

Our negative images of old age are constantly reinforced through film, television, and newspapers, where representation often resembles caricature. These images must be challenged, even replaced. It will be difficult, because they are so deeply entrenched, but it is imperative that we try. We must think of strategies to alter the negative, even hostile way in which we see, describe, and treat those of retirement age and older. The fashion industry, and fashion journalism in particular, has a part to play. Articles like Sarah Mower's account of the plight of her aunt, presumably in her sixties, who's now reduced to catalogue shopping, are not helpful. She ends 'Anyone with bright ideas, apply here' (Mower 2000). And Brenda Polan's article in *Red*, 'Style at any age', should be retitled 'Style at a price', given her advice. In the States, she tells us, there are books of tips with titles like 'Boomer Babes' (Polan 2000). But what of those who are already older? And poorer? I am not suggesting that retail therapy is any substitute for social policy; I'd like that, too. To quote from the ex-director of the Burton Group I interviewed: 'It won't be just retail suicide, to ignore the over-50s. It will be racial suicide – you can't ignore half the population.'

Coda

We should indeed engineer the changing of attitudes and push still harder for social and healthcare expenditure to benefit the elderly. Following this, we might change our retailing strategies so that the elderly are not confined to a shopping limbo. After all, many retired people have stated in interviews that they enjoy 'visiting the shops'. Perhaps the fashion industry could ensure that they find something worthwhile when they do so. One final footnote – as this volume was about to go to press, the tabloids were pressurising us to celebrate the centenary of the Queen Mother, the 'nation's favourite granny'. In one particularly telling photograph the Queen Mother is standing outside St Paul's Cathedral talking to two fellow centenarians, fetchingly garbed in a pale pink coat-dress and matching hat and standing on her own two feet, she reminded this particular jaundiced republican of Proust's description of the aged Duchesse de Guermantes as an ancient sacred fish. In the photograph, the other two ladies are both seated in wheelchairs wearing beige garments, limp cardigans and copious amounts of Tubigrip bandage. This is a sharp visual reminder of what money, private health care, preventative medicine and the ministrations of a good couturier can do.

References

Belleau, Bonnie, Didier, Jacqueline, Broussard, Louis and Summers, Theresa A. (1997) 'A comparison of older and younger women's attitudes towards apparel and media', *Journal of Fashion Marketing and Management*, February 1 (2).

Blaikie, Andrew (1999) *Ageing and Popular Culture*, Cambridge: Cambridge University Press.

Bourdieu, Pierre (1984) *Distinction: A Social Critique of the Judgement of Taste*, trans. R. Nice, London: Routledge & Kegan Paul.

De Beauvoir, Simone (1972a) 'Joie de vivre: on sexuality and old age', *Harper's Magazine*, January.

—— (1972b) *Old Age*, trans. P. O'Brien, Harmondsworth: Penguin.

Coleman, Roger (ed.) (1993) *Designing for our Future Selves*, London: London Royal College of Art.

Fairhurst, Eileen (1998) '"Growing Old Gracefully" as opposed to "Mutton Dressed as Lamb": the social construction of older women' in S. Nettleton and J. Watson (eds) *The Body in Everyday Life*, London: Routledge, 258–76.

Featherstone, M. and Hepworth, M. (1988) 'Ageing and old age: reflections of the postmodern life course', in B. Bytheway, T. Keil, P. Allatt and A. Bryman (eds) *Becoming and Being Old*, London: Sage.

Featherstone, M. and Wernick, Andrew (1995) *Images of Aging: Cultural Representations of Later Life*, London and New York: Routledge.

Featherstone, M., Hepworth, M. and Turner, B.S. (1991) 'The mask of ageing and the postmodern life course', *The Body: Social Practice and Cultural Theory*, London: Sage.

Greer, Germaine (1995) *The Change: Women, Ageing and the Menopause*, London: Penguin.

Hamlyn, Helen (1990) Interview in *Guardian Weekend*, September.

Hepworth, Mike and Featherstone, Mike (1982) *Surviving Middle Age*, Oxford: Blackwell.

Macdonald, Barbara, with Rich, Cynthia (1984) *Look Me in the Eye: Women, Ageing and Ageism*, London: Women's Press.

Mintel International Group (1993) *Third Age Lifestyles*, London: Mintel International Group.

—— (1995) *Marketing for Ages 45–64: Is there Life after 50?*, London: Mintel International Group.

Mower, Sarah (2000) 'A Grown-up guide to Getting Dressed', *ES Magazine*, 5 May.

Polan, Brenda (2000) 'Style at any age', *Red*, June.

Polhemus, Ted and Procter, Lynn (1978) *Fashion and Anti-fashion: an Anthropology of Clothing and Adornment*, London: Thames & Hudson.

Riviere, Joan [1929] (1986) 'Womanliness as masquerade', in V. Burgin, J. Donald and C. Kaplan (eds) *Formations of Fantasy*, London: Routledge.

Russo, Mary (1994) *The Female Grotesque: Risk, Excess and Modernity*, London and New York: Routledge.

Sawchuck, Kimberly Anne (1995) 'From gloom to boom: age, identity and target marketing', in M. Featherstone and A. Wernick (eds) *Images of Ageing: Cultural Representations of Later Life*, London and New York: Routledge.

Simon, Margaret (1986) 'In Memoriam', *Yale French Studies*, vol. 72 (86), New Haven: Yale University Press.

Sontag, Susan (1972) 'The double jeopardy of aging', *Saturday Review* (US), 23 Sept.: 29–38.

Woodward, Kathleen (1991) *Aging and its Discontents: Freud and Other Fictions*, Bloomington: Indiana University Press.

PART TWO

Catwalk and after

Chapter 6

Caroline Evans

YESTERDAY'S EMBLEMS AND TOMORROW'S COMMODITIES
The return of the repressed in fashion imagery today

Today, tomorrow, yesterday

IN 1991, WHEN THE FILM-MAKER Derek Jarman, already fatally ill, was canonised as Saint Derek of the Celluloid Knights by the Sisters of Perpetual Indulgence, an order of gay nuns, he wore a woollen hat by Joe Gordon embroidered with the words 'today, tomorrow, yesterday.' He also wore a six-foot long necklace set with gilded spring bulbs and porno pictures, made for him by the jeweller Simon Fraser. The necklace was to be planted in Jarman's garden in Dungeness. Although he was not expected to survive the winter, unexpectedly he did live and, when the bulbs came up in spring, took issue with the planting scheme, dug up some of the bulbs and replanted them, much to Simon Fraser's amused exasperation.

On his death, Jarman was buried in the hat; before then, the necklace had been buried in his garden but the artist cheated time and restructured the *memento mori*, leaving only traces of gilt from the original planting in the soil. This chapter is concerned with similarly unexpected reversals of, and loops in, time which characterised fashion from the 1990s, scrambling and re-ordering its chronology like the inscription 'today, tomorrow, yesterday'. The chapter maps out the way in which the past spools back into the present and reverberates into the future in contemporary fashion.[1] That this temporal scrambling could occur with particular intensity from the 1990s onwards was due, in part, to the pre-eminence of the image in contemporary culture. This chapter looks at the way in which fashion mutated in the digital culture of the late twentieth-century and, in particular, how history and image were imbricated in its new formations.

The conceptual Dutch designers Viktor & Rolf assert that 'fashion doesn't have to be something people wear, fashion is also an image',[2] and their work reminds us that designers are also semiotic tacticians. Like all the designers discussed below, I have privileged visual over verbal communication in my references to fashion images as, variously, emblems, 'thought-images', hieroglyphs, and, citing Walter Benjamin, 'dialectical images'. The exploration of fashion as a 'dialectical image' is the central crux of my argument, for it is intended to serve not only as an interpretative tool but also to offer a meta-narrative of the operations of fashion today through the process of historically referencing it. The way in which the fashion object mutated into image in the last ten years of the twentieth century gives us an insight into how the industry works, and the focus on image does not occlude 'the real' so much as recontextualise what 'the real' is in digital culture. Although I do not discuss them in depth, the industrial base of fashion and its relation to 'the real' underpin my analysis of the form and 'content' of contemporary design. As Lorraine Gamman and Merja Makinen have pointed out, the nature of commodity fetishism has shifted since Karl Marx described the mystification of the object itself in the nineteenth-century to a late twentieth-century form of fetishised representation of the object. They identify the way that, in Jean Baudrillard's writing, commodity fetishism is 'about more than just the disavowal of production . . . commodity fetishism occurs at the level of the sign' in post-industrial society. They also point out that Baudrillard's formulation, in its disavowal of 'real production of real commodities by real people in the real world', represents an epistemological break with Marx.[3] While acknowledging the recent past as having been characterised by just such an epistemological break, resulting from the proliferation of new technologies of the image and their impact upon commerce and culture, this chapter attempts to treat the commodity as 'sign' without simultaneously disavowing 'the real'.

Arguing that yesterday's emblems have become tomorrow's commodities, it uses 'dialectical images' to explain how contemporary fashion is part of a 'society of the spectacle' in the process of transformation. Of spectacle in general, Hal Foster argued in the 1990s that 'we become locked in its logic because spectacle both effects the loss of the real and provides us with the fetishistic images necessary to assuage or deny this loss.'[4] Yet I would argue that 'the real' is not irretrievably lost in such representations, only repressed. As such, it returns in contemporary fashion design when designers intuitively reinterpret past images of instability in the present. Kevin Robins has argued that the contemporary proliferation of images via new media signals a drive to disembodiment and a retreat from experience, and 'provides the means to distance and detach ourselves from what is fear-provoking in the world and in ourselves.'[5] Yet, in the 1990s the perfect body of mainstream fashion was progressively challenged by the abject, fissured and traumatised body of more cutting-edge fashion, another form of the return of the repressed, suggesting fashion as an important arena for articulating the complexities and contradictions of embodiment in the present day. And because all fashion is corporeal, the body, its pleasures, and its anxieties are rarely completely obliterated, even in the new digital culture. For even, perhaps especially, when fashion is at its most pictorial, it plays with images of two- and three-dimensionality, layering traces of bodies on fabrics, and vice versa. Olivier Theyskens clothed the body in a second skin like an anatomical drawing, appliquéd with arteries and a red lace heart. Two of Walter Van Bierendonck's menswear collections featured cutaway panels at the chest and crotch, under which the models wore thin body suits printed with *trompe l'œil* body parts.[6]

Spectacle

'In societies where modern conditions of production prevail, all of life presents itself as an immense accumulation of *spectacles*. Everything that was directly lived has moved away into a representation.' With these words, Guy Debord opened his *Société du spectacle* of 1967.[7] Debord characterised modern life as a world colonised by false desires and illusions, epitomised by the ubiquity of the commodity form. Although he demonised not vision but the way it operated in Western society, it is hard not to see a mistrust of the image itself in his writing.[8] Sometimes his writing suggests the puritanism of an author who is himself incapable of being ravished by the visible world. The spectacle is deathly for him because it is capital become an image; it is the other side of money:[9] it is death, or, rather, 'it is the visible *negation* of life'.[10] Debord wrote that 'the spectacle in general, as the concrete inversion of life, is the autonomous movement of the non-living'.[11]

However, at other times his gloomy prescriptions also read as descriptions, anticipating the deathly and spectacular effects of some 1990s fashion shows. The spectacle of the undead was made palpable in Antonio Berardi's 'Voodoo' collection, shown in London in September 1997, when models with dishevelled hair and dirty faces danced round a fire to the accompaniment of techno music and live African drumming. One in particular acted 'spooked': nervy but trance-like. The show was accessorised with celestial candle-holders with burning candles shaped into a crown, worn on the head, with shells and feathers plaited into long braids. A more Utopian spectacle of the 'undead' was exemplified by Jean-Paul Gaultier's cyber-collections of the mid-1990s, which mixed traditional elements from Asian and African dress with references to the European past and then added in elements of computer technology and club and festival culture. The visual reference to nomadic travellers who move in real space and time was transmogrified into an idea of cyberspace travellers who left spectral traces of their presence behind.

In these examples the fashion show could be construed as the paradigm of the modern spectacle which seduces us with the 'hyper-reality' of ravishing and perfect images. These fashion shows suggest that 'the society of the spectacle' that Debord identified in 1967 has merely intensified its effects, harnessing the new technologies of the image to do what it always did so well: visual seduction through fetishising the commodity form, succinctly demonstrated by the fashion photographer Richard Avedon's statement in 1984 that he saw his role at *Vogue* as 'selling dreams, not clothes'.[12] As Rosalind Williams describes in her book on nineteenth-century consumption, *Dream Worlds,* the seduction of the commodity form lies precisely in its ability to veil the real, commercial nature of the transaction with seductive 'dream worlds' in which the consumer loses him or herself in fantasy and reverie.[13] On the face of it, the contemporary fashion show, as one example of late twentieth-century spectacle, seems to be a very precise evocation of this principle, the starriest of star commodities: 'when culture becomes nothing more than a commodity, it must also become the star commodity of the spectacular society.'[14] Debord predicted that by the end of the century culture would become the driving force in the development of the economy, as the car was at the beginning of the century, or the railway in the second half of the last. Indeed, we do now refer to the 'culture industries', suggesting that culture is the new motor that drives the economy of our information society, just as coal and iron powered the economy of an earlier, industrial society. Yet, despite his prescience, Debord failed to imagine the developments in information technology which so transformed the late twentieth century from the 1960s when he was writing.

Although Debord located the origins of the society of the spectacle in the 1920s, his analysis has proved a fruitful model for understanding a number of other periods, from the origins of modernity in the Paris of the Impressionists, to the commodity culture of nineteenth-century London, and the image of woman as spectacle in relation to modernity.[15] Clearly it had a pressing relevance to the anti-consumerist left politics of the 1960s and 1970s. Yet today, for all its interesting academic applications, its sour denunciations of the image seem curiously redundant in relation to contemporary culture. I suggest this is because the nature of the commodity has changed since Debord was writing, so that his descriptions no longer chime with the world of spectacle we inhabit, a spectacle in perpetual transformation. Whereas Debord's descriptions of the commodity were rooted in Marxist critiques of the form as economic object, the overarching transformations of the 1990s (globalisation, new technology and communications) have radically altered its form. Indeed, Thomas Richards suggests that the days of spectacle are numbered, and that 'it may turn out that the semiotics of spectacle played a transitional role in capitalist mythology'.[16]

Current fashion participates in an economic system that is developing very differently from its nineteenth-century origins, which pioneered the techniques of retail and advertising to promote the garment. Now the fashioned garment circulates in a contemporary economy as part of a network of signs, of which the actual garment is but one. From its existence primarily as an object, the fashion commodity has evolved into a mutant form with the capacity to insert itself into a wider network of signs, operating simultaneously in many registers. Whereas it used to exist as, for example, a dress, which preceded its single representation in the form of an advertisement or fashion photograph, it is now frequently disembodied and deterritorialised. As such, it can proliferate in many more forms, within a larger network of relations: as image, as cultural capital, as consumer goods, as fetish, art exhibition, item on breakfast television, show invitation, or collectable magazine.

It is because the commodity form is evolving that we can talk about fashion signifying in a new way, as part of the circulation of signs and meanings in a global economy unchecked, since the fall of the Berlin Wall, by any alternative economic system. The development of the commodity is paralleled by many other kinds of social organisation. For example, Richard Sennett has described how management pyramids in the workplace are being replaced by 'flexible networks' and he differentiates this 'flexible bureaucracy' from 'Balzac-ian capitalism'.[17] In the same way, modern fashion is part of a network of themes, ideas and motifs that spread, virus-like, by contact with and colonisation of their subjects. Gilles Lipovetsky has argued that the development of business practices in nineteenth-century Parisian couture houses played a significant part in the bureaucratisation of the nineteenth-century;[18] similarly today fashion, that most spectacular sign, is at the vanguard of a new model of social and commercial organisation, the network.

Thus, in the technological and information revolution of the late twentieth century, the role of image in fashion shifted. No longer mere representation, the image frequently became the commodity itself, in the form of exclusive fashion shows, Internet web sites, television programmes and a new kind of fashion maga-zine, such as *Tank*, *Purple* and *Visionaire*. New media and increased fashion coverage made previously elite fashion accessible to a mass audience, but only as image, never as object. Throughout the 1990s the fashion show as a genre became increas-ingly spectacular, sometimes seeming to have evolved into pure performance in the extravagant shows of designers like Alexander McQueen and John Galliano, evoking Susan Sontag's claim that 'a society becomes "modern" when one of its chief activities is producing and consuming images'.[19] For the public, it became possible to acquire a high degree of familiarity with such contemporary fashions, even a kind of 'ownership' of them, through the power of the image. Alison Gill suggests that contemporary fashion is

> worn first by 'star' bodies on runways, in a continuing flow of new commodifiable themes, gestures and styles . . . Yet we must also acknowledge the immaterial domain that has arrived with the material forms of fashion and extends its effects beyond clothing; fashion both designs and is designed by an empire of signs that propel and commu-tate at an ever-increasing speed, a domain into which we are all interpellated as 'fashioned people' whether we like it or not . . . Within this empire . . . our bodies . . . are repetitively styled and styling across lived domains both spectacular and mundane.[20]

Her references to 'star' bodies in the first line, and to 'spectacular domains' in the last, clearly evoke Debord's identification of culture as a star commodity in the society of the spectacle. She suggests, however, that the spectacle, far from simply seducing us visually, has become a regime, or practice, through which we are 'fashioned' as modern subjects. Similarly, Foucault reminds us that

> Our society is not one of spectacle, but of surveillance; under the surface of images, one invests bodies in depth . . . the play of signs defines the anchorages of power; it is not that the beautiful totality of the individual is amputated, repressed, altered by our social order, it is rather that the individual is carefully fabricated in it, according to a whole technique of forces and bodies.[21]

To Foucault, the spectacle was simply another technique of surveillance or, more subtly, as is suggested in this quotation, one of the forms of the 'the care of the self'.[22] The passage expresses the germ of an idea which Foucault was later to explore in his study of ancient Greek and Roman etiquette and other pre-Christian practices which, he argued, revealed the origins of the modern idea of existence as being dominated by self-preoccupation. Anthony Giddens has termed this modern self 'reflexive'[23] and identified it as particular to modernity because specific anxieties and risks are attached to it. Foucault, too, when he writes about dietary regimes and sexual activity as producing a 'modelled self',[24] draws a parallel between the pre-Christian world he writes about and the modern period. He argues that both are periods of transition in which, with the collapse of conventional morality, people have to create new and appropriate codes of behaviour and ethics.[25]

Yet while the image plays a role in 'the care of the self' it also, simultaneously, functions as 'sign' commercially. In the 1990s such images were not free-floating signifiers but part of a network of signs which constituted an expanded 'society of the spectacle' promoted and disseminated through the media. John Galliano was described by the British fashion journalist Sally Brampton as 'the greatest 3-D image-maker alive'. Brampton argued that he was partly responsible for the greatly increased attendance at the Paris shows, which she described as 'a media feeding frenzy as newspapers and television stations around the world give increasing prominence to fashion'.[26] For these designers the spectacle of the fashion show, simultaneously enticement and advertisement, was 'the theatre through which capitalism acts'.[27] Stéphane Wagner, professor and lecturer in communications at the Institut Français de la Mode, said in 1997: 'If we accept that much of haute couture is about squeezing out maximum media coverage – good or bad – then the more spectacular the presentation and collection, the better.'[28] It follows that if the garment as commodity mutated into new and hybrid forms, so too did the fashion show in the 1990s. A Prada's menswear show took the form of a theatre play, with actors and dialogue. Helmut Lang put his show out on the Internet. Hussein Chalayan's shows were designed like art installations by an architect, and featured male voice choirs or avant-garde music. John Galliano's were based on theatrical fantasy and excess. Alexander McQueen drenched his models in 'golden showers' or surrounded them with fake snowstorms. By contrast to the theatrics of many London designers, the Belgian Martin Margiela pioneered the use of derelict urban spaces for his shows; on one occasion the show invitations so closely resembled a cheap publicity flyer that rumour had it that fashion editors threw them away without recognising what they were. While, on the one hand, Margiela's undoubtedly innovative show designs could be said to function as Situationist-style stratagems to evade the ubiquitous 'society of the spectacle', it could equally be argued that Margiela simply traded on a particularly exclusive kind of 'distinction' which required insider-knowledge of new fashion signs.

Perhaps it is because of the fashioned object's evolving status as 'sign' that so much was made in the 1990s of the affinities of art and fashion, an affinity charted by significant exhibitions,[29] coverage of fashion in art magazines,[30] academic discussion of the relationship of art to fashion,[31] and the evolution of a more 'conceptual' type of fashion designer[32] and design outlets.[33] One could also point to the establishment in Britain of the Jerwood prize for fashion, following the precedent set by the Jerwood prize for painting; the establishment in the USA and UK of *Fashion Theory*, the first academic journal devoted exclusively to that topic; and to the more general expansion of fashion studies in publishing and academia. Writing in *Fashion Theory*, the academic John Styles related the changing significance of fashion studies to:

the postmodern turn in the human sciences – a downplaying of long
historical trajectories and deep causes, a focus on surface phenomena
and on diversity, a concern with the personal, the subjective and with
identity. These postmodern priorities have worked to move the history
of dress from the wings to the centre stage . . . Questions of meaning
and interpretation now dominate the intellectual agenda . . . The
broader intellectual developments that have propelled the history of
dress to its new respectability have brought with them new ways of
conceptualising that history.[34]

History

Ironically, however, the 'downplaying of long historical trajectories' in the human
sciences was paralleled, in fashion design, by a renewed interest in historical citation. Just at the moment that the fashion commodity became image, it also became
more referential, more historically or conceptually 'themed', perhaps to adapt to
its additional role as bearer of ideas as well as socially constructed object. John
Galliano evoked the seductive and vampish women of the beginning of the last
century, mixing *belle époque* opulence with tribal imagery. Alexander McQueen's
designs revealed a dark, sometimes cruel sexuality which was also historically
nuanced, particularly in its play on the dark side of Victoriana, a theme also strikingly developed in the work of Belgian designers Olivier Theyskens and Veronique
Branquinho. Vivienne Westwood recycled the sixteenth to the eighteenth centuries,
particularly in her 'Britain must go Pagan' collections of the late 1980s to early
1990s.

  How did these images of the past resonate in the visual economy of the late
twentieth century? In the 1930s, Walter Benjamin wrote that 'every image of the
past that is not recognized by the present as one of its own concerns threatens to
disappear irretrievably'.[35] Later in the century, critics of postmodernism argued
that in the 1980s and 1990s history was plundered to make a postmodern carnival,
and that the incessant return to the past was itself a kind of deathly recycling of
history which emptied it out of meaning, rendering it bankrupt, good only for
costume drama and fantasy.[36] I would argue to the contrary, that contemporary
fashion has an unerring eye for the topical in its choice of historical imagery, be
it that of the sixteenth-century anatomist or the twentieth-century showgirl. Walter
Benjamin wrote:

> [To the French Revolution] ancient Rome was a past charged with the
> time of the now . . . blasted out of the continuum of history. The
> French Revolution evoked ancient Rome the way fashion evokes
> costumes of the past. Fashion has a flair for the topical, no matter where
> it stirs in the thickets of long ago; it is a tiger's leap into the past.[37]

  When John Galliano summoned up the luxurious dream worlds of nineteenth-
century Paris for Christian Dior, despite the nostalgia of his designs, his flair was
for the topical as it stirred 'in the thickets of long ago'. His designs evoked the

link between modernity, spectacle and consumption in the nineteenth-century city, a link that was exemplified in the ambiguous figure of the *femme fatale* in which desire was tinged with dread. But rather than literal re-creation, Galliano's 'tiger's leap into the past', fusing cultures and histories, reconfigured the past in the light of the present, 'a past charged with the time of the now . . . blasted out of the continuum of history' to echo current concerns.

Benjamin's text implicitly recognises the pictorial and, particularly, emblematic nature of fashion. If the fetishised commodity became image in the late twentieth century, it began to function more like a Renaissance emblem than a commodity *per se*, as the image became flooded with meaning. Like Renaissance and Baroque emblem books, modern fashion gives us a collection of dislocated images in which many narratives, histories and images are condensed. Fashion images, like emblems or metaphors, are by their very nature densely packed with meanings which may be both complex and contradictory. Their interpretation is inevitably marked by the author's subjectivity. Yet because they also function in the modern period as a 'semiotic consolidation of capitalism',[38] one can begin to trace connections, re-seeing the past through the filter of present concerns, allowing fragments from the past to illuminate the present.

Just before his death in 1985 the Italian writer Italo Calvino planned a series of lectures on the future of literature in the new millennium. Making an eloquent plea for the power of the image, he included visibility as a value to be saved in the future in order to preserve the faculty of '*thinking* in terms of images'.[39] He discussed the potentially debased value of the image in an image-saturated society but also stressed the connection between image and the imaginary. As a child of the 'civilisation of images', he had grown up 'daydreaming *within* the pictures' of children's cartoons. Reading pictures without words was, for him, 'a schooling in fable-making, in stylisation, in the composition of the image'.[40] As in Calvino's writing, so in a certain school of 1990s European fashion design. The spectacular fashion shows of the 1990s were characterised by these three things: fable-making, stylisation, and highly mannered, elaborately composed images. Like writers, these fashion designers were fabulists, for their work was profoundly narrative, structured around stories and fables to produce what the German writer Stefan George, in a discussion of Mallarmé, called the *Denkbild*, or thought-image, a way of writing with hieroglyphic clarity in which found objects are 'steeped in traces and energies, electric with significance'.[41] Calvino described the idea for a story coming to him as an image that was 'charged with meaning', even though he could not formulate it in discursive or conceptual terms. As it clarified in his mind, he set about making it into a story: 'Around each image others come into being, forming a field of analogies, symmetries, confrontations.'[42] Only then does the writer start to give concrete form to these images. This concept of the image has something of the quality of the emblem. For the designer it permits the image to remain charged, forever potential rather than fixed, so that its meanings are always immanent, 'electric with significance'.

Via the fashion show, the single collection is further distilled, through press and magazine coverage, into a few pixilated emblems for the twenty-first century. One such example is encapsulated by Vivienne Westwood's persistent fascination with royalty, particularly with styling herself as the British queen. Her Autumn–

Winter 1997–98 collection featured a black model as Queen Elizabeth I, and Westwood wore the same dress herself as Elizabeth I for a publicity photograph by Gian Paolo Barbieri. Jonathan Sawday interprets the lavish dress and bare chests of Elizabeth I and all her court ladies prior to marriage, in which each displayed her stomach and breasts, as a kind of female blazon; and he argues that where the queen teasingly revealed and then concealed her body before her courtiers, 'she appeared to control her own self-blazoning'.[43] A blazon was an erotic poem to a woman's body parts. The sixteenth-century blazon was a self-perpetuating poetic form; blazons produced counter-blazons and counter-counter-blazons in which male poets traded the images of their mistresses' body parts, turning erotic hymn into rivalry and, in the process, piling up images of body parts like contemporary anatomists. Sawday argues that the English blazon was produced in a forum that was more erotically charged than the French court, because of the sex of the ruling monarch, Elizabeth I, the 'virgin queen'.[44] To the image of Westwood as Elizabeth I, one could add another: the image of Westwood insouciantly blazoning herself outside Buckingham Palace, the home of the second Queen Elizabeth. As Westwood posed for the press outside Buckingham Palace where she had just received an OBE, her skirt blew up to reveal that she wore no knickers under her tights. The image of Westwood with her skirt blowing up also evokes the famous scene in *The Seven Year Itch* when Marilyn Monroe's skirt is blown up by a gust from a vent but with the difference that Westwood was in her fifties, amply at ease with her own body and, unlike the tragic Monroe, in charge of her own destiny.

In other respects, too, the sixteenth and seventeenth centuries were evoked in contemporary design. The shows of the London designers Alexander McQueen, Andrew Groves and Tristan Webber, evidenced a fascination with Baroque theatricality, artifice and the staging of perversion in the violence and drama of their stagecraft. Even where their themes were contemporary, such as the troubles in Northern Ireland or J.G. Ballard's *Cocaine Nights*, these were tinged with Jacobean cruelty and sexuality. For Walter Benjamin the fragmented nature of the German Baroque mourning play (a play about loss, ruination and transience) mourns the off-stage transition to capitalist modernity. As such, it helps us to understand the fragmented nature of modernity in the nineteenth century when, he writes, 'the emblems return as commodities.'[45] Something of this idea was caught in Alexander McQueen's second couture collection for Givenchy, 'Eclect Dissect', shown in Paris in July 1997, which was based on the story of a fictional *fin de siècle* surgeon and collector who travelled the world collecting exotic objects, textiles and women which he subsequently cut up and reassembled in his laboratory. The 'scenario' of the catwalk show staged the return of these gruesomely murdered women who came back to haunt the living. It was shown in a Paris medical school, swathed with blood-red velvet curtains and decorated with medical specimens.

'Eclect Dissect' fused seventeenth-century anatomical drawings and late-Victorian dress references with the entirely modern theme of the serial killer. For Benjamin, there was a link between nineteenth-century consumption and the rise of mercantile capitalism in the seventeenth century. The culture of the Reformation was a culture in the early stages of capitalist transition; that of the nineteenth-century one in which capitalist production was consolidated, expanded and modified through the processes of industrialisation and urbanisation. Both were cultures of transition, in which all fixed points seem to have been removed. Our own period of globalisation and fast-changing technology shares this characteristic, which may account for some writers' fascination with the themes of abjection, trauma and anxiety in the present.[46] In moments of rapidly changing fashion, mutability itself becomes charged with meaning because it can enact, or speak, anxiety through the process of change. Fashion 'acts out' transition in periods which feel, to their participants, unstable. Thus its 'tiger's leap' into what can seem over-the-top historical pastiche frequently reveals the same aesthetic and cultural concerns as the period which is seized on in the present, and can be construed as a kind of 'acting out' of current concerns as they are revealed through past images.

Dialectical images

Whereas fashion's transience guaranteed it a marginal role in historical accounts of more stable social periods, the emphasis on change, fluidity and risk in contemporary society[47] makes it an avatar of modern sensibilities. As such, fashion is a paradigm of a mutated commodity form in a society of the spectacle in transition. The new, and still evolving, visual economy in which fashion operates feeds on instability and alteration, always the defining characteristics of fashion. Now, however, those characteristics typify the modern world, not just fashion, so that it becomes an emblem of modernity itself. In this it functions as what Walter Benjamin called a dialectical image. In his unfinished *Arcades Project*[48] Benjamin fastened on certain images of the nineteenth century which he felt resonated in his own period, the 1930s: the figure of the prostitute, the city of Paris, its early nineteenth-century arcades and late nineteenth-century shop windows, urban consumption on the one hand and, on the other, urban dereliction and detritus in the form of the ruin, dust, and the ragpicker. These 'dialectical images' were not based on simple comparisons between past and present; rather, they created a more complex historical relay of themes. For Benjamin, the relationship between images of the past and the present worked like the montage technique of cinema.[49] The principle of montage is that a third meaning is created by the juxtaposition of two images, rather than any immutable meaning inhering in each image. Benjamin conceived of this relationship as a dialectical one: the motifs of the past and the present functioned as thesis and antithesis. The flash of recognition of the historical object within a charged forcefield of past and present was the dialectical image that transformed both.[50]

Onto the idea of *Denkbilder*, or 'thought-images', one could graft Benjamin's description of 'wish images' in which 'the old and new interpenetrate'.[51] One such example is 'passing fashions', which display both a desire to rid oneself of the unsatisfactory present, especially the recent past, and a utopian desire for newness.[52] As a dialectical image, fashion anticipates technological change by creating its effects through other means, which prefigure the technology of the future. Benjamin argues that fashion's mutability is a kind of semaphore of secret signals of the future: 'Whoever understands how to read these semaphors would know in advance not only about new currents in the arts but also about new legal codes, wars and revolutions.'[53]

Yet, at the same time that it looks forwards, fashion also looks backwards. For Benjamin, 'the true dialectical theatre of fashion' is due to its ability to refabricate the very old as the most up to the minute.[54] Ulrich Lehmann draws on Proust's and Benjamin's formulation of true memory as 'involuntary' to argue that 'in fashion, quotation is sartorial remembrance', and that fashion activates the past in the present by rewriting its own themes and motifs through historical quotation.[55] In Proust's 'mémoire involontaire', chance encounters with objects bring back experiences that would otherwise have remained dormant or forgotten.[56] Lehmann discusses how the turn-of-the-century designs of Jeanne Paquin evoked the revolutionary period of a hundred years earlier. Today Paquin's period furnishes the imagery for John Galliano's vamps, sirens and seductresses.[57] Yet the historicism of Galliano's evocations of the image of woman as 'commodity and seller in one', as Benjamin described the prostitute,[58] does not simply recreate the past nostalgically, but also brings it into the present by picturing the relationship between fashion, women, spectacle, and commodification today.[59] Esther Leslie argues that Benjamin jolts Proust's method into modernity by imagining memories as 'involuntarily summonised strips of montaged images' which flash past in rapid sequence, to provide 'an unexpected, shocking link between an experience in the present and one in the past. It disrupts linearity, confounds temporality.'[60]

For Benjamin, some historical images only 'developed' in the future:

> If one wishes to view history as a text, then it is valid to suggest what a recent author has said about literary ones: the past has deposited such images in them as can be compared with those that are caught on a light-sensitive plate. 'Only the future has at its disposal a developer strong enough to let the image appear in all its details.'[61]

The imagery of fashion today can be construed as the 'developer' of earlier moments of capitalist production and transition, be they the sixteenth, seventeenth or nineteenth centuries. Current fashion imagery is the means of developing the image in the 'light' (that is, the darkroom) of the present, whether those images are historical ones, such as Galliano's opulent fin de siècle evocations, or images of the passage of time itself, such as Margiela's use of decay and dereliction, discussed in the next section. And the afterlife of today's imagery will perhaps develop again, in ways we cannot imagine, in the future.

Jolted out of the context of the past, the dialectical image can be read in the present as a 'truth'. But for Benjamin it was not an absolute truth, rather a truth that was fleeting and temporal, existing only at the moment of perception, characterised by 'shock' or vivid recognition: 'the true picture of the past flits by. The past can be seized only as an image which flashes up at the instant when it can be recognised and is never seen again.'[62] It was not that the past simply illuminated the present, or that the present illuminated the past; rather, the two images came together in a 'critical constellation', tracing a previously concealed connection.[63] Fashion was one of the key tropes of nineteenth-century Paris identified by Benjamin as a 'dialectical image' precisely because of its capacity to reverberate in time, to obscure the linearity of history in favour of what Jean Baudrillard calls the 'cyclical time' with which fashion replaces linear time.[64] Citing the French historian

Michelet's epigram that 'each epoch dreams the one that follows', Benjamin wrote that 'every epoch, in fact, not only dreams the one to follow but, in dreaming, precipitates its awakening'.[65] And he argued that dialectical thinking was the organ of historical awakening.

Benjamin believed that conventional historical writing promulgated fictions which concealed the truth; indeed, he regarded such history-writing as having been 'the strongest narcotic of the [nineteenth] century',[66] a phrase that recalls Marx's categorisation of religion as the opium of the people. The role of the dialectical image was to rescue the historical object by ripping it out of the narratives of law, religion and art. Crucially, for Benjamin, his 'truth' was to be revealed through visual rather than linear logic. 'As in a flashing image, in the now of recognition, the past is to be held fast', wrote Benjamin.[67] His ideas offer art and design historians a complex and sophisticated model of how visual seduction works, because his ideas are predicated on an understanding of how visual similes function in an image-driven society, something which other historians have not privileged. Benjamin gives us a methodology particularly appropriate to fashion, and also particularly appropriate to the present moment, because of the way visual culture has developed in recent decades. His method allows us to perceive similarities across periods apparently separated by rupture and discontinuity, and to plot historical time not as something that flows smoothly from past to present but as a more complex relay of turns and returns, in which the past is activated by injecting the present into it.[68] Thus, for example, in the designs of John Galliano, we can 'activate' the excess and opulence of nineteenth-century Parisian consumer culture by 'injecting' it with the excess and opulence of Galliano's contemporary designs, to understand both in terms of 'modernity' and how it can resonate in the present.

Dereliction

Even where a designer does not explicitly use historical references, nevertheless the passage of time can be conjured up by the lustre, sheen or patina of a garment. Grant McCracken has argued that patina and fashion are inimical: in his analysis patina was a signifier of social status until the eighteenth century, when it was eclipsed by the consumer revolution that formed the bedrock of the modern fashion system in which status is marked by novelty rather than by the signs of longevity and age.[69] Thus, he states, fashion is the 'terrible rival' of patina. Yet at the end of the twentieth century, just as one group of designers began to play with historical citation in the most up-to-the-minute clothes, so too did another group begin to introduce the theme of patina into their more avant-garde designs. The signs of ageing, and the idea of a history, were replicated in the work of a number of designers whose work was not overtly historically themed but which, instead, drew on motifs of refuse, detritus, remnants from the past which were transformed in the present. Martin Margiela re-used second-hand clothing, which he described as giving it a new life, as did the New York designer Susan Cianciolo and the British-based Jessica Ogden whose clothes were patterned with biography. Made from second-hand fabrics, they bore the trace of the past in their stains, darns and hand-sewn seams. Where Ogden used new cloth she often stained it first, not to 'antique' it but to imbue it with feeling. She described her garments as if they were sentient, capable of bearing memory traces. Robert Cary-Williams too created a stage setting for the history and the life of a garment:

> My kimono dress is tattered so it will leave pieces behind everywhere it is worn until there is only a little bit left at the top, then it has had its life . . . Some pieces will be at a party and others will be at someone's house, like some of the spirit of the garment is left everywhere.[70]

Viktor & Rolf's second collection in 1994 consisted of twenty versions of the same white dress in early nineteenth-century style on which they had carried out various experiments: slamming it in a door, cutting it, burning it, and embroidered stains on it. Themes of death and disaster permeated some other collections: Robert Cary-Williams' Autumn–Winter 1999 collection was called 'Victorian Car Crash':

> the inspiration for this collection was a woman from the Victorian era who somehow ends up in the present day . . . She's run over by a car. She survives, but the clothes get damaged.[71]

Latex and leather jackets, dresses and full skirts were cut away so they fell from the body, leaving only an armature of seams and zips to trace the ghostly presence of the former garment in space. In the same period, the design team Boudicca produced shattered tailoring, inspired by genetically misshapen clothing forms, grafting jacket parts on to coats and dresses. Their Autumn–Winter 1999–2000 'Distress Dress', in high-visibility orange nylon, was based on the black box after a plane crash: 'In fact it is orange. We thought it was interesting because it contains the pilot's last words.'[72] These designs were predicated on the conceit that the supposedly inanimate garment assumed an uncanny life of its own, not unlike Max Klinger's series of etchings *The Glove* from the 1880s, which depict the proto-Surrealist adventures of the glove in episodes of abduction, seduction and abandonment.

For other designers, the theme of decay evoked the passage of time. As Marx wrote, 'in history as in nature, decay is the laboratory of life'.[73] Hussein Chalayan's 1993 graduate collection featured fabrics which had been buried with iron filings for several weeks before being dug up to reveal a veneer of rust. In 1997 Martin Margiela produced an entire exhibition where moulds and bacteria were 'grown' on his clothes. The London-based designer Shelley Fox gave her textiles a patina of decay and age; wool was felted and scorched, laser-cut and bubbled, or burnt with a blow torch. Her wrecked textiles, like Margiela's tracery of mould and decay, summoned up another of Benjamin's figures, the nineteenth-century ragpicker who scavenged cloth for recycling, recuperating cultural detritus cast aside by capitalist societies.

Although Margiela and Fox used the techniques of the avant-garde, their practice was rooted firmly in commerce. As 'dialectical images', their patinated textiles illuminated the parallels which underwrite the free-market economy of fashion, both past and present: between elite fashion and ragpicking, luxury and poverty, excess and deprivation. All the examples of late twentieth-century fashion design cited in this article are framed, symbolically, by two nineteenth-century emblems of the capitalist process: the woman of fashion on the one hand, and the ragpicker on the other. Though they seem diametrically opposite to each other, and the status of one was as exalted as that of the other was debased, yet both were part of the same economic process, equally locked into the fashion system by nineteenth-century *laissez-faire* policies. Fox and Margiela's images of melancholy dereliction are the flipside of capitalist excess, just as the nineteenth-century ragpicker formed an eloquent counterpoint to the woman of fashion. These are the twin ghosts of the past that today's designers call up: John Galliano, in his evocations of *fin de siècle* luxury and excess; Martin Margiela in the mouldy tatters of his more experimental practice. Margiela's mannequins and mouldy clothes draw our attention to the darker side of capitalist modernity, a darkness that also surfaces when earlier centuries of capitalist transformation are drawn on in contemporary design such as Alexander McQueen's 'Eclect Dissect' collection for Givenchy. As I have suggested, this is due in part to the sense of instability produced in a period of rapid change that leads it to track back to comparable images of instability in the past. However, this historical relay is an index not merely of sensibilities but also, and equally, of how such sensibilities are anchored in specific moments of capitalist production and consumption, and of technological change.

Trace

The haunting of contemporary fashion design by images from the past is a kind of return of the repressed, in which shards of history work their way to the surface in new formations and are put to work as contemporary emblems. The fragmented and episodic traces of the past that surface in contemporary designs are traces of instability and transience. These traces come back as fragments under the weight of some cultural trauma, which has been expressed by historians of modernity as 'shock' and 'neurasthenia'[74] and by writers about contemporary culture as 'trauma' or 'wound culture'.[75] In particular, contemporary fashion has fastened on the themes of instability and alteration, selecting past images of mutability which resonate in the present. Fashion imagery, itself semiotically unstable, thus fixes images of instability and change, but in ways that destabilise conventional history, and run counter to the idea of coherent narrative. They demand, rather, a re-evaluation of the imagery of the past in the light of the present – something that characterises the work of Michel Foucault as well as that of Walter Benjamin.

For Foucault, the breaks, ruptures, and discontinuities of history serve to unravel the straightforward relationship of causes and effects over time. All history is written about from the perspective of the present, in the sense that the present throws up the themes to be studied historically. Because the present is always in a state of transformation, the past must constantly be re-evaluated; and the past takes on new meanings in the light of new events in the present. This is 'genealogy': history written in the light of current concerns.[76] It is also something very like the actual process of fashion design. John Galliano and Alexander McQueen's work reveals complex historical relays between past and present. In one collection

McQueen explored the relationship between the nineteenth-century Arts and Crafts movement and what he called 'the hard edge of the technology of textiles.' Segueing between pre-industrial craft imagery and post-industrial urban alienation, the collection combined moulded leather body corsets with frothy white lace, punched wooden fan skirts and regency striped silk. The show was opened by the athlete and model Aimee Mullins in a pair of hand-carved prosthetic legs designed by McQueen (the model was born without shin bones and had her legs amputated below the knee at the age of one), and was closed by the model Shalom Harlow, who revolved like a music box doll on a turntable as her white dress was sprayed acid green and black by two menacing industrial paint sprays which suddenly came to life on the catwalk.

Juxtaposing the organic with the inorganic (a model that mimicked a doll, a paint spray that mimicked human motions, and an artificial leg that enhanced human performance), the collection skewed the relation of object and subject to evoke Marx's nineteenth-century commodity exchange in which 'people and things traded semblances: social relations take on the character of object relations and commodities assume the active agency of people.'[77] In the figures of these two young women the ghosts of Marx seemed to flutter up and live again at the end of the twentieth century, as the embodied forms of alienation, reification and commodity fetishism.

In such collections, fragments and traces from the past reverberate in the present. Reversing Foucault's idea of 'genealogy', that is, of history written in the light of current concerns, one might use the idea of the historical fragment to uncover traces from the past and to read the present through them. All the traces, or fragments, of history that surface in fashion design do so as images. This is how the connections made between past and present are tracked, by finding traces of the past in the present, articulated through visual means. Raphael Samuel's *Theatre of Memory* uses the idea that objects are emotion holders, traces of the past, and carriers of discourse from other times into the present.[78] The artist Joseph Beuys believed that materials, such as the felt and fat which he used, carried traces of the past with them.[79] In a similar way contemporary fashion images are bearers of meaning and, as such, stretch simultaneously back to the past and forward into the future. Not just documents or records but fertile primary sources, they can generate new ideas and meanings and themselves carry discourse into the future, so that they take their place in a chain of meaning, or a relay of signifiers, rather than being an end product of linear history.

In other words, images are a cultural archive which can be raided to make sense of the present. However, for an understanding of how visual similes work, we must turn back to Walter Benjamin because, as I have argued, only his analysis engages with the singular and complex nature of images themselves. In this context, his concept of the 'trace', from his Arcades project, could be used in a new kind of cultural analysis, more fragmented and less coherent than the historian's, in which the fashion historian and the designer alike are scavengers, moving through cultural history like the figure of the ragpicker sifting rubbish in the nineteenth-century city.[80] The historical fragment, or trace, can illuminate the present. Benjamin uses the term 'trace' to describe the mark left by the fossil (that is, the commodity) on the plush of bourgeois interiors or on the velvet linings of their cases.[81] Here, history turns into detective story, with the historical trace as a clue.

The figures of the collector, the ragpicker and the detective wander through Benjamin's landscape. Thus the historian/designer's method is akin to that of the ragpicker who moves through the city gathering scraps for recycling. Irving Wohlfarth argues that the ragpicker, as a collector of 'the refuse of history', is the incognito of the author: 'the historian as *chiffonier* unceremoniously transports these leftovers of the nineteenth century across the threshold of the twentieth.'[82]

I have assumed an equivalence here between the historian and the designer. Perhaps, however, the designer makes a better cultural *chiffonier* than the historian. Stephen Greenblatt has articulated the notion of a historical method of 'talking to the dead' and the dead themselves leaving textual traces.[83] Howard Felperin has taken him to task for his tendency to 'cultural poetics' rather than 'cultural materialism', and Graham Holderness has suggested that Greenblatt's approach tells us more about our own concerns in the present than about the period studied.[84] While such criticisms may legitimately be made of the historian, designers can take liberties and poeticise; Leila Zenderland talks about how the past can be put to use by non-historians, suborning ghosts to speak to contemporary concerns.[85] Citing the popularity in the 1970s, among both black and white Americans, of Alex Haley's book and television drama *Roots*, she talks about 'myth-symbol scholarship' where history becomes myth in the course of its redeployment. As such, it allows us to scan traces of the past for their mythic meanings, rather than their historical truths.

My descriptions of 'dialectical images' in contemporary fashion are not properly cultural materialism at all, but, rather, examples of how the traces of the past can be woven into the fabric of a new story to illuminate the present. Yet Benjamin's concept of 'dialectical images' serves as something more than a hermeneutic tool to interpret the work of a few designers. Rather, it unlocks the way in which the work of these designers – fragmented, episodic and emblematic – helps us to make sense of contemporary culture and its concerns. The designers I have discussed all practise a form of 'cultural poetics', evoked through visions of either capitalist excess or melancholy dereliction, the two opposing poles of nineteenth-century *laissez-faire* economic policies, both locked equally into the fashion system. I have suggested that this is due in part to the sense of instability produced in a period of rapid change that leads it to track back to comparable images of instability in the past. Perhaps this is connected too with the nihilism that characterises the present moment. Whereas modernism thought it could produce a brave new world, the postmodern period has been marked, rather, by the sense of an ending;[86] this shift is reflected in the 'cultural poetics' of today's designers, whose evocations of history and time suggest a sense of crisis or trauma in the present.

Acknowledgement

Thanks to the Arts and Humanities Research Board of Great Britain whose funding of the 'Fashion & Modernity' research group at Central Saint Martin's College of Art & Design, London, 1999–2000, facilitated the writing of this chapter.

Notes

1   I have used this opportunity to draw extensively on theory; this has precluded my giving as much space to contemporary fashion design as I would have liked. The fashion examples given are brief illustrations.

2   Stephen Gan, *Visionaire's Fashion 2001: Designers of the New Avant-Garde*, edited by Alix Browne, London, Laurence King, 1999.

3   Lorraine Gamman and Merja Makinen, *Female Fetishism: A New Look*, London, Lawrence & Wishart, 1994, 32–35.

4   Hal Foster, *The Return of the Real: the Avant-Garde at the End of the Century*, Cambridge Mass. and London, MIT Press, 1996, 83.

5   Kevin Robins, *Into the Image: Culture and Politics in the Field of Vision*, London and New York, Routledge, 1996, 12.

6   Olivier Theyskens, Autumn–Winter 1998–99. W. & L.T., Autumn–Winter 1996–7 and Autumn–Winter 1997–8. Illustrated in: Luc Deryke & Sandra Van de Veire (eds), *Belgian Fashion Design*, Ghent and Amsterdam, The Netherlands, Ludion, 1999, 202–3.

7   Guy Debord, *Société du spectacle*, Paris, Buchet/Chastel, 1967. English edn: *The Society of the Spectacle*, London, Zone Books, 1994, para. 1.

8   Martin Jay, *Downcast Eyes: The Denigration of Vision in Twentieth-Century French Thought*, Berkeley and London, University of California Press, 1993, 427. Debord, ibid., para. 4.

9   Debord, op. cit., para. 49.

10 Debord, op. cit., para. 10.

11 Debord, op. cit., para. 2.

12 Martin Harrison, *Shots of Style: Great Fashion Photographs Chosen by David Bailey*, London, Victoria & Albert Museum Publications, 1985, 13.

13 Rosalind H. Williams, *Dream Worlds: Mass Consumption in Late Nineteenth-Century France*, Berkeley, Los Angeles and Oxford, England, University of California Press, 1982.

14 Debord, op. cit., para. 193.

15 T.J. Clark, *The Painting of Modern Life: Paris in the Art of Manet and his Followers*, Princeton, Princeton University Press, and London, Thames & Hudson, 1984. Thomas Richards, *The Commodity Culture of Victorian England: Advertising and Spectacle, 1851–1914*, London and New York, Verso, 1991. Heather McPhearson 'Sarah Bernhardt: portrait of the actress as spectacle', *Nineteenth-Century Contexts*, 1999, 20 (4): 409–54. Thanks to Carol Tulloch for bringing this invaluable article to my attention.

16 Richards, op. cit., 258.

17 Richard Sennett, *Welfare after the Welfare State*, lecture at Bishopsgate Institute, London, 20 May 1999.

18 Gilles Lipovetsky, *The Empire of Fashion: Dressing Modern Democracy*, trans. Catherine Porter, Princeton, Princeton University Press, 1994.

19 Susan Sontag, *On Photography*, Harmondsworth, Penguin, 1979, 153.

20 Alison Gill, 'Deconstructing Fashion: The Making of Unfinished, Decomposing and Re-assembled Clothes', *Fashion Theory: The Journal of Dress, Body and Culture*, March 1998, 2 (1): 25–49, 27.

21 Michel Foucault, *Discipline and Punish; The Birth of the Prison,* trans. Alan Sheridan, Harmondsworth, Penguin, 1977, 217.

22 Michel Foucault, *The History of Sexuality, Volume 3: The Care of the Self*, trans. Robert Hurley, Harmondsworth, Penguin, 1984.

23 Anthony Giddens, *Modernity and Self-Identity*, Cambridge, Polity Press, 1991.

24 Michel Foucault, *The History of Sexuality, Volume 2: The Use of Pleasure*, trans. Robert Hurley, New York, Viking, Pantheon, 1985.

25 For a discussion of Foucault in relation to contemporary postmodernism and fashion see Elizabeth Wilson, 'Fashion and the postmodern body' in Juliet Ash and Elizabeth Wilson (eds), *Chic Thrills: A Fashion Reader*, London, Pandora Press, 1992, 3–16.

26 *Guardian*, 14 October 1998.

27 Richards, op. cit., 251.

28 Quoted in Stephen Todd, 'The Importance of Being English', *Blueprint*, March 1997, 42.

29 In 1983 the Costume Institute of the Metropolitan Museum of Art in New York showed a 25-year retrospective exhibition of Yves Saint Laurent, after which other museums gradually also began to mount fashion exhibitions, not always on the topic of single designers. These included: *Fashion and Surrealism* at the FIT Gallery in New York in 1987 and the Victoria & Albert Museum in London in 1988; *Infra-Apparel* at the Costume Institute of the Metropolitan Museum of Art in 1991; *Street Style* at the Victoria & Albert Museum, London, 1994. In the 1990s, three internationally reviewed exhibitions explicitly linked art and fashion thematically: *Mode et Art*, Brussels and Montreal, 1993; *Il tempo e le mode (Looking at Fashion)*, Florence Biennale, 1996, which was further developed as *Art/Fashion*, Guggenheim Museum, Soho, New York, 1997; and *Addressing the Century: A Hundred Years of Art and Fashion*, Hayward Gallery, London, 1998, and Kunstmuseum, Wolfsburg, 1989. In the same period there were also a range of smaller, innovative exhibitions linking art and fashion in Europe and New York.

30 The March 1982 issue of the New York magazine *Artforum* featured an Issey Miyake collaboration on its cover. Throughout the 1980s and 1990s art magazines such as *Artforum*, *Art in America*, *Flash Art* and *Frieze* began to give editorial coverage to more 'avant-garde' designers like Comme des Garçons and Martin Margiela and, subsequently, to feature advertisements from fashion companies like Helmut Lang and Prada. There is a list of some of this editorial coverage tabulated in: Sung Bok Kim, 'Is fashion art?', *Fashion Theory*, March 1998, 60–1. See, too, Michael Boodroo, 'Art and fashion', *Artnews*, September 1990, 120–7.

31 For example, Robert Radford, 'Dangerous liaisons: art, fashion and individualism', *Fashion Theory*, June 1998, 151–64.

32 Following on from the first wave of Japanese designers in the 1970s–80s, namely Issey Miyake, Comme des Garçons and Yohji Yamamoto, in the 1990s one could cite graduates of the Antwerp Academy of Design and London's Central St Martins College of Art and Design, such as Martin Margiela and Hussein Chalayan. In New York in the late 1990s Susan Cianciolo was a rare American practitioner of a more conceptual trend in fashion design.

33 Such as The Pineal Eye in London and Colette in Paris. While not a retail space, the Judith Clark Costume Gallery in London was also influential in promoting critical attitudes to fashion.

34 John Styles, 'Dress in history: reflections on a contested terrain', *Fashion Theory*, December 1998, 387.

35 Walter Benjamin, 'Theses on the philosophy of history', *Illuminations*, trans. Harry Zohn, London, Fontana/Collins, 1973, 257.

36   Fredric Jameson, *Postmodernism, or the Cultural Logic of Late Capitalism*, London and New York, Verso, 1991.

37   Walter Benjamin, op. cit., 263.

38   Richards, op. cit., from the acknowledgements, unpaginated.

39   Italo Calvino, *Six Memos for the Next Millennium*, trans. Patrick Creagh, London, Jonathan Cape, 1992, 92.

40   Ibid., 94.

41   Esther Leslie, 'Souvenirs and forgetting: Walter Benjamin's memory-work' in Marius Kwint, Christopher Breward and Jeremy Aynsley (eds), *Material Memories: Design and Evocation*, Oxford and New York, Berg, 1999, 112.

42   Calvino, op. cit., 89.

43   Jonathan Sawday, *The Body Emblazoned: Dissection and the Human Body in Renaissance Culture*, London and New York, Routledge, 1995, 198. Sawday quotes the words of the French ambassador in 1597 who described the queen as wearing: 'black tafetta, bound with gold lace...a petticoat of white damask, girdled, and open in front, as was also her chemise, in such a manner that she often opened this dress, and one could see all her belly, and even to her navel...she has a trick of putting both her hands on her gown and opening it insomuch that all her belly can be seen.'

44   Sawday, op. cit., 197.

45   Susan Buck-Morss, *The Dialectics of Seeing: Walter Benjamin and the Arcades Project*, Cambridge, Mass. and London, MIT Press, 1989, 181.

46   See Hal Foster, *The Return of the Real*, op. cit., for a discussion of 'trauma' culture by an art historian; Peggy Phelan, *Mourning Sex: Performing Public Memories*, London and New York, Routledge, 1997; Paul Aritze and Michael Lambek (eds), *Tense Past: Cultural Essays in Trauma and Memory*, London and New York, Routledge, 1996; and, for a characterisation of 'wound culture', Mark Seltzer, *Serial Killers: Death and Life in America's Wound Culture*, New York and London, Routledge, 1998, which discusses anxiety, change, fear and trauma in relation to contemporary culture. A number of cultural critics since the 1990s have adapted pathological terms such as trauma and anxiety to discuss wider formations of cultural anxiety and trauma. Frank Füredi, *Mythical Past, Elusive Future: History and Society in an Anxious Age*, London, Pluto Press, 1992, characterises contemporary nostalgia as a form of anxiety about the future. See, too, Sarah Dunant and Roy Porter (eds), *The Age of Anxiety*, London, Virago, 1996 and Jeffrey Weeks, *Inventing Moralities: Sexual Values in an Age of Uncertainty*, New York, Columbia University Press, 1995.

47   Anthony Giddens, *The Consequences of Modernity*, California, Stanford University Press, 1990 and Cambridge, Polity Press, 1991. Ulrich Beck, *Risk Society: Towards a New Modernity*, trans. M. Ritter, London, Sage Publications, 1992.

48   Walter Benjamin, *The Arcades Project*, trans. Howard Eiland and Kevin McLaughlin, Cambridge, Mass. and London, The Belknap Press of Harvard University Press, 1999.

49   Buck-Morss, op. cit., 250.

50   Buck-Morss, op. cit., 250, 219.

51   Benjamin, 1999, op. cit., 4.

52   Benjamin, 1999, op. cit., 4–5.

53   Benjamin, 1999, op. cit., 64. As a marginal note Adorno wrote, 'I would think, counterrevolutions.'

54   Benjamin, op. cit., 64.

55   Ulrich Lehmann, 'Tigersprung: fashioning history', *Fashion Theory*, September 1999, 308.

56   See Esther Leslie, op. cit., 116–17.

57   Colin McDowell, *Galliano*, London, Weidenfeld & Nicolson, 1997.

58   Buck-Morss, op. cit., 184.

59   Caroline Evans, 'John Galliano: spectacle and modernity', in Ian Griffiths and Nicola White (eds) *The Fashion Business: Theory, Practice, Image*, Oxford, Berg Publishers, 2000 discusses the relationship between nineteenth-century consumption, modernity and the 1990s fashion designs of Galliano.

60   Leslie, op. cit., 117.

61   Benjamin, cited in Leslie, op. cit., 109.

62   Benjamin, 1973, op. cit., 257.

63   Buck-Morss, op. cit.,185, 221, 250, 290.

64   Jean Baudrillard, *Symbolic Exchange and Death*, trans. Iain Hamilton, London, Sage Publications, 1993.

65   Benjamin, 1999, op. cit., 13.

66   Benjamin, 1999, op. cit., 218.

67   Benjamin, 1999, op. cit., 219.

68   For a discussion of fashion and Benjamin's historical method, see Ulrich Lehmann, 'Tigersprung: fashioning history', *Fashion Theory*, September 1999, 297–322. Hal Foster, *The Return of the Real: The Avant Garde at the End of the Century*, Cambridge, Mass. and London, MIT Press, 1996, is similarly concerned with the temporality of twentieth-century avant-gardes, and with what Foster calls 'the co-ordination of diachronic (or historical) and synchronic (or social) axes in art and history' (p. xii).

69   Grant McCracken, *Culture and Consumption: New Approaches to the Symbolic Character of Consumer Goods and Activities*, Bloomington, Indiana University Press, 1990, 31–43.

70   Robert Cary-Williams interviewed by Lou Winwood, *Sleazenation*, 7 Nov. 1998.

71   Stephen Gan, op. cit.

72   Quoted in Susannah Frankel, 'We want to be', *Independent Magazine*, 8 May 1999, 30.

73   Cited in Georges Bataille, *Visions of Excess: Selected Writings, 1927–1939*, ed. and trans. Allan Stoekl, Minneapolis, University of Minnesota Press, 1985, 32.

74   Walter Benjamin's concept of 'shock' and Georg Simmel's notion of 'neurasthenia' are summarised and discussed in Mike Featherstone, *Consumer Culture and Postmodernism*, London, Sage Publications, New Delhi, Thousand Oaks, 1991; Bryan S. Turner (ed.), *Theories of Modernity and Postmodernity*, London, Sage Publications, New Delhi, Newbury Park, 1990.

75   See Foster, op. cit., and Seltzer, op. cit.

76   Michel Foucault, *The Order of Things: An Archaeology of the Human Sciences*, trans. A.M. Sheridan-Smith, New York, Vintage, 1973; Michel Foucault, *The Archaeology of Knowledge*, trans. A.M. Sheridan-Smith, London, Tavistock, 1974.

77   Hal Foster, 'The art of fetishism', *The Princeton Architectural Journal*, vol. titled 'Fetish', 1992, (4): 7.

78   Raphael Samuel, *Theatres of Memory: Past and Present in Contemporary Culture*, London, Verso, 1994.

79   Caroline Tisdall, *Joseph Beuys*, Soloman R. Guggenheim Foundation, 1979, 7.

80   For an account of the historian as ragpicker, see Irving Wohlfarth, 'Et cetera? The historian as chiffonier', *New German Critique*, 39, Fall 1986: 142–68.

81   Buck-Morss, op. cit., 211.

82   Irving Wohlfarth, op. cit., 146.

83   Stephen Greenblatt, *Renaissance Self-Fashioning: from More to Shakespeare*, Chicago, University of Chicago Press, 1980.

84   See essays by Howard Felperin and Graham Holderness in Francis Barker, Peter Hulme and Margaret Iverson (eds), *Uses of History*, Manchester, Manchester University Press, 1991.

85   Leila Zenderland (ed.) *Recycling the Past: Popular Uses of American History*, Philadelphia, University of Pennsylvania Press, 1978, viii.

86   Francis Fukuyama, *The End of History and the Last Man*, London, Hamilton, 1992. Jean Baudrillard, *The Illusion of the End*, trans. Chris Turner, Cambridge, Polity Press, 1994.

Chapter 7

Nathalie Khan

CATWALK POLITICS

Introduction

CATWALK SHOWS ARE TRADITIONALLY perceived to be the
fashion year's defining moment. Now their spectacle far outweighs their
commercial significance and their crowning moment is no longer the emergence
from backstage of a casually dressed Ralph Lauren with a false, self-deprecating
smile, engulfed by his statuesque models. The emphasis has shifted away from this
cult of personality and on to the couturier as artist and the creation of spectacular, controversial and conceptual designs. As spectacle, the catwalk helps
determine ideals of physical beauty, its impact stretching far beyond the ten thousand dollar dresses on show. The shows are ritualised, frozen moments, aesthetic
performances severed from reality in which not just designers but photographers,
models, fashion journalists, make-up artists, and celebrity guests are quintessen-
tial components.

For the fashion industry itself, the importance of such shows remains beyond
doubt: 'the ready to wear shows make or break a designer's career' (Carter-Morley
2000: 11). And beyond the narrow confines of the industry itself, the significance
of the catwalk show is well recognised. Frey in particular argues that:

> however broad the theatrics, very often a show will contribute some-
> thing to the changing way we see fashion and the way we are likely to
> be seeing fashion in the future. Somewhat less frequently, it even tells
> you something about the way everyone will dress and look and feel
> about what they wear at some point twelve to eighteen months in the
> future.
>
> (Frey 1998: 39)

But establishing why the catwalk show continues to enjoy consistent and enduring appeal is not a straightforward task. This chapter will attempt to address this question by examining two recent and interrelated trends in its history. The first is characterised by the deconstruction of the very systems and structures of the catwalk show, as fashion designers have sought to take it from backdrop to centre stage. The second trend has seen the catwalk taken beyond the realm of fashion, as a small number of mainly avant-garde designers have sought to utilise the catwalk in order to forward a particular social cause or political message. In doing so, the chapter will seek to differentiate the use from the purpose of the catwalk show.

In an industry that relies so heavily on media hype, the catwalk show is seldom able to break out of its own realm and few events stand out as representing something of 'substance'. Yet despite the rigid structure and closeted environment, fashion does enjoy broad popular appeal. The chapter will therefore conclude by addressing the potential of this appeal, by asking whether the catwalk show can ever do anything more than just sell a product. Does fashion make us think and can fashion be powerful?

The social and political context of fashion

Within the history of late twentieth-century fashion, one can observe styles and trends that reflect upon the wider social landscape. While many of these have been short-lived, a number have survived as landmarks that helped to shape the image of their time. Fashion has influenced culture, in the same way that it has reflected cultural change. The relationship between the hemline, economic prosperity and social mores is, of course, well established and it was only ever a small step from the skirt to the T-shirt, as political consciousness became an explicit part of fashion.

One of the most familiar recent examples of fashion presenting the political was Katharine Hamnett's '58% don't want Pershing' T-shirt, which the designer famously wore when visiting the then Prime Minister, Margaret Thatcher. The origins of this 'fashion with attitude' movement of the early 1980s, championed by Hamnett herself alongside up-and-coming designers of the time such as Vivienne Westwood, can at least in part be traced back to the Che Guevara T-shirts of the 1960s. But the significance of what Hamnett and others did went beyond what had occurred then. First, it had become personalised. It was the designer and the fashion house that were making the statement, as much as the wearer. Second, it was intrinsically linked to the mechanics of the fashion industry itself. One must not forget that the '58% don't want Pershing' T-shirt was in fact taken from Hamnett's Autumn/Winter 83/84 collection entitled 'Choose Life'. Yet while such work clearly marked and shaped the idea of confrontational design, its significance appears to have been ephemeral, lasting no more than the duration of a particular fashion season. This may lead one to question the veracity of such apparently political statements. As Jean Baudrillard argues,

> [f]ashion represents what can least be explained: actually, the obligation that it presents of a renewal of signs, its continual production of

> apparently arbitrary meaning, its thrusting of meaning, the logical
> mystery of its cycle in reality – these all represent the essence of the
> social moment.
>
> (J. Baudrillard cited in G.M. 1998: 59)

More recently Benetton's controversial advertising campaign, which included
images of people with HIV on roadside billboards, the breast cancer awareness
campaign for which star models sport consciousness-raising T-shirts, and the high-
profile, anti-fur movement of the early 1990s, have all attempted to go beyond
the merely commercial. Yet it is difficult to avoid viewing most, if not all, of these
developments as reflecting popular sentiment, more than engaging in any profound
manner with the substantive issues at stake. Most pointedly with the anti-fur
campaign of the 1990s, is the ironic picture of a number of the models that had
volunteered their time in the name of the cause, latterly wearing fur on the catwalks
of Paris, New York and Milan. In this regard it appears that a new value system
can be rendered obsolete as and when the wider fashion industry discovers the
profitability of a new trend. Few designers have openly tried to resist the mood
of the moment.

> Art is all about permanency and fashion is all about the moment. Perhaps
> the art world's fascination with fashion is a recognition of fashion's
> ability to address everyday influence instead of the obsession with the
> heroics of creating history.
>
> (A. Rosen cited in Doe 1999: 4)

If fashion can do little more than reflect upon that which is current, it simply
confirms that any message it purports to forward will remain without meaning.
Fashion can therefore only promote a particular set of values if those values reflect
current trends. Constituted thus, fashion can reflect, but it cannot renew, society.
And if the fickle nature of fashion prevents it from creating history, then why
should one see its message as being of cultural or social significance?

In order to create a sense of the novel, fashion has increasingly been drawn
into addressing and then re-addressing the manner in which it acts. This is predicated on the assertion that while fashion changes every season, its inherent structure
does not; which leads to the realisation that fashion can only be radical where it
demonstrates the ability to challenge its own systems and structures. Through such
means may lie the potential for contemporary cultural expression and it is in this
light that recent developments in the catwalk show are best considered.

The catwalk show

The catwalk show is a public event, a marketing exercise, where each show guards
and maintains its own aura of exclusivity. Such exclusivity is part of its very
marketability, where the audience forms part of the spectacle and the product
portrays an image that is reflected only in its semblance:

> The absence of the final consumer at fashion shows meant that the
> designers were destined to see their messages ever interpreted, either
> in the pages of magazines – where film from the runway shows is
> clipped apart and rearranged, or where the clothes are simply reshot
> with an editor's notions of styling firmly in the fore – or in stores –
> where only sampling of the whole collection is purchased . . .
>
> (Frey 1998: 34)

The catwalk show has one purpose and one purpose only, which is *to be noticed*.
Within today's highly competitive environment this can present designer and
fashion house with a significant challenge. While there may be more than 850 journalists present each season at the Milan shows and 2,000 at the Paris shows that
follow them, competition for press attention is fierce. In Paris alone, more than
100 catwalk shows will take place in an eight-day period.[1] In order to gain the
attention of the world's press, designers have increasingly found the need to utilise
more fully the half-hour that they are given. The clothes themselves are now often
not enough to grasp the necessary media attention, which has led designers such
as Jean-Paul Gaultier and Vivienne Westwood to turn their attention to the catwalk
show itself. First, shows were taken out of traditional arenas to churches, ware-
houses and train stations (a move linking fashion in with performance art that was
parodied in Robert Altman's *Prêt-à-Porter*). Attention then turned to the design of
the shows themselves. Finally, even the traditional model came to be replaced
firstly by elderly and schoolgirl models and then, in a final ironic twist, by the
same celebrities that once made up their audiences.

In many ways, it might seem somewhat surprising that so few designers have
tried to leave the rigid confines of the traditional catwalk show. Yet such apparent
conservatism may well reflect upon the enduring strength of the underlying structure that has remained fixed and rooted in its own traditions. Such adherence may
give one an insight into why the catwalk has such enduring appeal. It also provides
us with a starting point from which to consider the designers who have attempted
to challenge and subvert its traditional conventions. 'Radical' catwalk then is an
event that not only seeks to attract the attention of the media, but which is in
itself reflective, if not critical, of the mechanisms it utilises.

The use of provocative imagery and sign systems is a constant element in
fashion design; indeed, catwalk shows that utilise such imagery can and do provoke
strong public reactions. Such was the case with Rei Kawakubo's Spring 1995 collection premier for Comme des Garçons, entitled 'Sleep'. The catwalk show featured
two tall young men with shaved heads wearing dressing gowns and striped pyjamas.
Given that the show was held on the precise date of the fiftieth anniversary of the
liberation of the Nazi concentration camp at Auschwitz, the public outcry that
followed was nothing less than wholly predictable. The problem with the use of
such emotive imagery lies in the apparently casual manner in which it is done; for
as Joanne Finkelstein (1998: 3) has commented, designers such as Kawakubo simply
'generate a sensation by stumbling into politically sensitive areas'.[2] As a form of
radical catwalk, such shows are attempting to be measured against something larger
and more important than fashion. Fashion's supposed superficiality becomes a
product of protest – a form of declaration, concept or contemplation.

The popular response to catwalk shows that play with socially sensitive issues such as the Holocaust is to accuse designer and fashion house of sensationalism. The media and fashion press feel both offended and confused, yet such a response may play into the hands of those who masterminded the event. Interest in the label may grow and the fashion house can project an image of being bold and self-assured. It is this level of confidence that gives the design a so-called 'edge', as well as an image of profundity that appeals to a specific kind of buyer. Sensationalism implies that the catwalk has been used subversively, but the use of challenging imagery does not necessarily mean that fashion must offend. Some designers have managed to adopt a radical approach to the catwalk, which is both serious and sensitive towards the issues it addresses. It is to three of these designers that we now turn: Alexander McQueen, Hussein Chalayan and Martin Margiela.

The emotional catwalk

Alexander McQueen's catwalk shows are visual spectacles of breathtaking theatrical quality and technical skill. He is a designer who enjoys a high public profile, which is in no small part a direct result of the manner in which he presents his radical designs to the public. That the medium of the catwalk provides McQueen's most immediate contact with the public, consequently offers him the potential of an unrivalled public platform. McQueen has used his catwalk shows to shock and challenge. Yet in spite of the provocative images that he has drawn upon for a number of his shows, McQueen has so far resisted the temptation to ascribe to his shows any obvious or predictable message. McQueen himself argues that his main concern is to make his audience react, be it with joy, sadness or disgust. He is on record as having said 'I don't want to do a cocktail party, I'd rather people left my shows vomiting' (McQueen cited in Frankel 1997: 8).

One of McQueen's most notorious shows was the Autumn/Winter 1995 'Highland Rape' collection. Press response at the time was hostile to his use of violent and sexual imagery.[3] Although the event was clearly staged to provoke, McQueen has sought to challenge the accusation that the show portrayed a negative view of woman and glorified violence. He has since explained his catwalk show as a statement on the eighteenth-century involvement of the British in the Scottish highlands.

> Scotland for me is a harsh, cold and bitter place. . . . I have no respect for what the English did there, they wiped whole families out. The reason why I am patriotic about Scotland is because I think it has been dealt a really hard hand. It's marketed the world over as, you know, fucking haggis, fucking bagpipes. But no one ever puts anything back into it. I hate it when people romanticise Scotland. There is nothing romantic about its history. What the British did there was nothing short of genocide.
>
> (McQueen cited in Frankel 1999: 10)

Following his 'Highland Rape' show, McQueen chose, in Autumn/Winter 1999, to highlight a second issue of concern to him, namely physical disability. The show's protagonist was Aimee Mullins, an American model and student born without fibula bones in her shins who had her legs amputated below the knee when she was one year old. Mullins and McQueen worked on a photo-shoot he art-directed for the British magazine *Dazed and Confused*. The fashion spread was photographed by Nick Knight and featured only self-elected models with severe disability, dressed in clothes by designers such as McQueen, Comme des Garçons and Hussein Chalayan.

For the purpose of the collection premier, McQueen designed a pair of prosthetic legs. Mullins' hand-carved and varnished legs were designed to complement the clothing she wore, but more importantly were shown as a symbol of both perfection and beauty. Mullins' appearance was deliberately downplayed. She was simply one of the models taking part in a fashion show. For McQueen the rationale for her inclusion in his show was straightforward:

> I'm not doing this to save the world. I suppose the idea is to show that beauty comes from within. You look at all mainstream magazines and it's all beautiful people, all the time.

One of the very basic movements of a catwalk show is that of young, classically beautiful and slim women walking up and down a runway. This tradition accedes to the idea of physical perfection – it is so elementary to the idea of the catwalk that it can easily be trivialised or undermined. In some way one might argue that by working with a model who is physically different, McQueen rejects this tradition. But while McQueen did question notions of physical beauty, he did not question the use or function of the catwalk. Walking 'beautifully' is an elemental part of this presentation of physical beauty and McQueen created a performance that both acknowledged this tradition, whilst simultaneously seeking to challenge it. McQueen's representation of physical beauty exceeded the physical. It was clear that what he had designed was not a commodity – the prosthetic legs were part of Mullins' body. But at the same they were a functional piece of clothing that had all the decorative qualities of a pair of boots. Through this functional purpose as well as aesthetic, lies a belief system that challenges the divide between body and clothing.[4] It is one that has found resonance amongst critics: as the *Guardian* (1988: 12) pointed out, 'Not only had McQueen broken the boundaries of what is and is not accepted as beautiful, he had also done so quietly, displaying a sensitivity and emotional complexity with which he has not often been credited.'

It was through his appointment as head designer of the couture house Givenchy in 1997 as much as the development of his own label Alexander McQueen, that McQueen has gained international recognition. Whether his appointment reflected primarily upon his credentials as a designer or on his ability to garner much-cherished press attention is open to conjecture. While the economic imperatives that underpin the operation of the haute couture business are of course well known, it must not be forgotten that this same system also offers the fashion designer an unrivalled position from which to develop ideas and ambitions. It is a business of contradictions, where creative freedom stands alongside tradition and restraint. Within such a setting everything appears possible, as McQueen's appointment appears to prove.

The runway of ideas

In contrast to McQueen, Hussein Chalayan's shows appear as meditations on fashion. His work is concerned with fashion in the sense that it is associated *with* the body and designed *for* the body. Since his final year degree show at Central St Martin's 1994, Chalayan has been acclaimed for creating clothing that goes beyond traditional commercial boundaries. He does not follow any specific trends, nor do his shows attempt to create them. Such shows are focused less on the clothes and more on the 'work' itself. Chalayan's shows are provocative. They challenge the idea of the catwalk, but they do so without appearing offensive in the manner of Kawakubo's show. Many of the garments he shows are not even meant to be sold or worn, but simply represent ideas and concepts carried through the collection as a whole.

Unusual, unrestrained design is not uncommon in fashion, but what is different about Chalayan's shows as well as their design, is that they stand separate from any wider fashion trend. His shows cannot be seen as a designer showing and it may be more appropriate to compare them to a medium such as performance art. Live music or live transmission of sound instead of soundtrack, unusual use of space and choreography that differs from the conventional parading up and down a catwalk, and most of all an overall sense of design that follows themes and ideas rather than any specific trend. This is what sets Chalayan's work apart:

> The way he presents his work is groundbreaking! – It's never just a designer showing clothes on the catwalk, or even an indulgent designer showing 'art'. His clothes can be as perplexing as his shows.
>
> (Holgates 1998: 43)

A number of Chalayan's shows have worked on the basis of visual theory, with the catwalk serving as a stage upon which he translates concepts into design. This has included dresses suspended by helium balloons, jackets lit up with red dots like a flight path, and electronically controlled petticoats, whose skirts opened out like aeroplane wings coming into land. Chalayan himself has tried to articulate what he is doing by making reference to the fashion industry today. He argues that, 'Fashion is so transient now. I'm trying to give my work constant development – both conceptually and aesthetically' (cited in Holgates 1998: 45). Conceptual design is an inherent element of the avant-garde and in the field of fashion forms an oppositional perspective to label or branded design. Thus what Chalayan describes as transient might best be related to the passing ideas within high fashion, or the label culture. Chalayan's designs are not 'fashionable', instead they embody ideas and concepts. His catwalk shows are direct extensions of these ideas and they occupy a stage on to which he brings not only his clothes, but the ideas that inform them.

Chalayan's shows are focused on particular themes, be that challenging religion and cultural identity, redefining conceptions of personal space, or addressing issues of freedom and sexuality. His Spring 1998 show, for instance, featured models who wore the traditional Middle Eastern Bulka head-dress, but who were naked from the waist down. Rather then exploiting this culturally sensitive area, the staging of his show saw the runway used in a self-conscious manner, which questioned underlying issues of fashion. Chalayan focused on conceptions of gender by using the garments to feminise social, political and moral issues. By confronting his Western European audience with half-naked but veiled models, Chalayan clearly comments on the cultural significance of dress and identity as denoting difference, devotion and defiance. Contrary to Western beliefs, Islamic culture does not see a contradiction between the religious and the sexual, but what Islamic culture does forbid is the public flaunting of the latter (Guindi 1999: 56). The veiled but exposed models unravel a very Westernised idea of dress; the use of female Islamic dress and loss of modesty stands in direct opposition to the idea of 'fashion being associated with sins of lust and pride' (Steele 1998: 68). A large number of designers have, often misguidedly and offensively, used religious dress on the catwalk, playing with the sacred symbols and signifiers of others. One of the most infamous examples is Karl Lagerfeld, who was widely attacked for using images of Islamic script from the Koran on the fabric for his Autumn 1994 collection. The criticism led Lagerfeld, not a stranger to political controversy, to withdraw the relevant pieces from sale. But the use of erotic religious imagery has rarely been used to challenge the ritualised display of the female body on the catwalk, and may even serve to make Chalayan's work appear rather modest, far removed from ideas of self-adornment or pride.

When examining the significance of the catwalk for Chalayan's design vision, it is soon apparent that the two are intrinsically linked. Like few other designers working today, Chalayan appears to build his entire collection around his collection premiere. The catwalk is then a stage, a platform to communicate his visual theory. Each garment plays a role, in the sense that it functions to elaborate on a particular aspect of the wider theme. But as with the Bulka show, Chalayan's emphasis is predominantly on providing a context for the wider body of work. His designs are concerned with ideas but they also function on a material level. Such was the case with his Autumn/Winter 2000 show, which centred on the function, meaning and use of the garment as object. The show itself took place in a traditional dance and performance setting – Sadler's Wells Theatre, London. Moving away from the traditional framework of the catwalk, he created a set that featured a group of models on the stage, standing behind grey armchairs and tables. As the show came to an end, the models removed the covers from the chairs and slowly dressed themselves with them. The covers were therefore turned into elegant and simple dresses with stunning sculptural details. The tables themselves were also transformed into garments, dismantled and worn by the models as skirts.

Within Chalayan's catwalk shows, the images presented are never given explicit meaning, leaving the spectator to interpret what they see. But like all of Chalayan's shows, the Autumn/Winter 2000 collection is still based upon an explicit theme, in this case the war in the former Yugoslavia:

> It was about times of war, when people's houses are raided and they are told to leave in five or ten minutes or they will be killed. It was about the idea of having to evacuate your home. So the idea was to take a horrific situation like that and contradict it – to represent it in

Figure 7.1
Hussein Chalayan, 'Table-dress', Autumn/Winter 2000.
Courtesy of Niall McInerney

an almost beautiful way. The idea was to hide those possessions that mean a lot to you: hiding the clothes on chairs, turning the chairs into suitcases, and carrying them away. So it's like you've carried your environment with you.

(Chalayan cited in Craik 2000: 4)

Chalayan's collection premier confronted its audience with images that are in no way related to any preconception of what a fashion show might be. Like the tables on the stage, the idea of the catwalk is turned on its head. Freed from its own convention, his work is suspended from meaning. Conceptual fashion, like conceptual art, is not about forms and materials, but about ideas and meanings. It cannot be defined in terms of any medium or style, but rather by the way it questions what fashion is. By presenting complex ideas in a performance setting, Chalayan creates an unmediated reality.

New realities

Chalayan has shown that there are few conventions as to how fashion can be represented, nor how garments are worn or what their significance might be. Another designer who has used the catwalk in order to question predetermined ideas of the runway presentation is Martin Margiela. Belgium-born Margiela is part of a group of designers who graduated from the Antwerp School of Fashion. Margiela's fashion events can be differentiated from conventional catwalk shows in four ways. First, his collections are not 'new', in that the pieces are either made up from second-hand materials or out of pieces from previous collections. Second, he never uses professional models, choosing instead to draw upon groups or individuals that have little or no connection with the fashion industry. Third, he also selects locations that are unfamiliar to the traditional catwalk show audience, which may challenge their understanding of both its function and purpose. Finally and most importantly, he rejects any notion of personality – referring to himself only as one member of a wider team of designers and avoiding the media limelight (Margiela has never given a face-to-face interview).

His fusion of ideas extends the potential of the dressmaker's art, using the field of fashion to develop his ideas of conceptual design. To this end Margiela has seen the catwalk show as providing an important means through which to realise his aims. His catwalk shows have often been compared to life or installation art performances, bridging the gap between art and fashion through the creation of a critical aesthetic that bears little relation to high fashion. Of course, the catwalk is a purely visual event, in which ideas come alive through the choice of location, performer, and the garments themselves. What helps define Margiela's work as art rather than design is that it offers reflexive commentary upon the very fashion industry of which he is a part.

In 1992 Margiela staged his Spring/Summer collection in a Salvation Army depot in Paris. Margiela, as someone who had become known for his use of second-hand materials and garments, had chosen a location that truly reflected the idea that lay behind his wider design concept. His work is constructed around a dialogue between the past and the future and represents the destruction of the old, in order to re-create the new. Each of the garments has an inherent history and aesthetic that forms an opposition between the functional and the exclusive. By using the setting of the Salvation Army depot, not only did Margiela go back to the source of his own inspiration, but he did so in a manner that confronted his audience with a reality that they would not usually encounter. Margiela's choice of venue stands in direct relation to his use and transformation of second-hand clothing. Apart from creating a specific atmosphere in which to display his designs, he created a setting in which the fickle world of fashion is brought into sharp contrast. This contrast is also mirrored in his design concept – the low status of second-hand clothing against the high value of a one-off designer piece.

> Many of Margiela's 'raw materials' are fashion detritus when he starts with them: second-hand or army surplus clothing is the commodity form with the lowest exchange value in the fashion system. Second-hand clothing has historically been associated with low economic status and class; the second-hand clothes trade clothed the poor long before there was a ready-to-wear industry . . . Most humiliatingly they were a type of charity to be endured as enforced 'gifts'.
>
> (Evans 1998: 82–3)

Within the setting of a high fashion collection premier, the creation of a 'new reality' is indeed a high goal. Margiela's catwalk shows appear to demonstrate that he wishes to make certain demands on his audience. Without a reliance on overt political imagery, he attempts to make the link between power and meaning within fashion. Margiela sees his own work as important and it is apparent from the few personal statements that he has made, that he believes fashion to have a wider social significance.

> I think everyone has to be aware these days. In this age, it's no longer possible to be a designer out of touch with reality . . . I think the whole business is in evolution. Fashion as a luxury is redundant and must eventually be replaced by a new reality.
>
> (Margiela cited in Buckett 1992: 12)

Margiela creates this 'new reality' in a manner that is detached from the high glamour of the Paris catwalks and it is this reality that forms the basis of his *œuvre:* abject and unfinished clothing alongside the rejection of the 'new' or of original design.

Margiela works with the idea of showing and selling high fashion and in doing so he treads a fine line between the exploitation of the poor and the entertainment of the fashion crowd. His catwalk shows are then performances that bring together each element concerned with the value and use of clothing, which simultaneously seek to make a statement on the futility of fashion. In this way he creates a vision that not only confronts two very different worlds, but which also sets an agenda in which he can contextualise his own role and that of the garments he displays. By working with and beyond the conventional, Margiela is able to create a distinct aesthetic.

Yet, while being highly critical of the fashion system in which he works, his commercial success makes him none the less an inherent part of it. His choice of venues such as the Salvation Army depot also opens up Margiela to the accusation of being exploitative, of turning an interesting idea into a radical marketing ploy. Margiela has been sensitive to such accusations and in the case of the depot show, not only did he pay for using the depot but also 'closed the circle', by donating the entire collection to the Salvation Army. In failing to present his clients with traditional saleable merchandise, while at the same time showing 'his dependence on the history of fashion' (Gill 1998: 31), Margiela's work does appear to represent a critique of fashion. In his work clothes are shown as a waste product that is reassembled, recycled and resold in a setting that points to the very superficiality of the fashion industry itself.

Conclusions

The catwalk show is a highly stylised and strictly regimented construct, which until recently varied little in terms of form or content. It is only since the late 1970s that designers and fashion houses have begun to see both the need and the potential to take the catwalk show to a new developmental stage. Change, where it has happened, has focused on each of the three central elements that go to make up the catwalk show; the venue, the spatial setting and the role of the model. What this chapter has attempted to do is to trace these developments by means of an examination of the work of three designers who may be considered to be at the forefront of the radical catwalk. Its aim has been to establish where the current boundaries of catwalk design have been drawn and to assess the extent to which it is in fact valid to talk about radical catwalk.

Breaking out from the constraints of the exhibition hall has for many designers been a necessary, if not a sufficient, first step towards challenging existing convention. Yet in the cases that have been examined in this chapter, a change of venue has done little more than to provide a framework and signifiers of how the designer or design house would like to see itself. McQueen's theatrical events have almost become traditional in their use of elaborately staged settings, where neither cost nor effect is spared. By contrast, Hussein Chalayan's Autumn/Winter 2000 show, set as it was on the stage of Sadler's Wells, brought fashion towards the world of culture and high art. The distance between the work of the designer and the audience might be interpreted as representing the gap between the meaning and the actual understanding of what is represented. However, even if such a meaning were to have been in the mind of the designer, it is far from certain whether this was readily understandable to the principal audience to whom it was addressed. Only very rarely does the environment within which a catwalk show is set play an integral role in conveying an underlying social or political message. However, this was the case with the use of the Salvation Army depot for Martin Margiela's 1992 show, where the choice of venue played an active part in the creation of the show's social significance.

The treatment of the model has always been central to the catwalk show, and recent history has seen a number of designers again challenge existing conventions. While mainstream fashion has given the star model a powerful position, the designers considered in this chapter have all, to a greater or lesser degree, subverted this tradition: McQueen's use of dummies, Chalayan's attempt to cover the models' faces and Margiela's refusal to employ 'real' models. All three approaches are united in their desire to draw attention away from the person presenting the clothes and towards the spectacle of the clothes themselves. On the traditional catwalk the star body of the model has the function to style the clothes, while at the same time being styled by them in a manner that represents what the industry considers to be the 'fashionable body'. The absence of the star body implies a refusal to conform to the idea of the fashionable body, which at the same time allows the designers and their clothes to reanimate the audience. The model is made obsolete by a process of depersonification that allows the clothing to become the body.

But when looking behind current trends, one cannot fail to notice the growing importance of brand image and personality. Designers are the new celebrities, taking over from the cult created around supermodels. Designers such as Tom Ford, Stella McCartney and Marc Jacobs have all been appointed in order to rebuild old and established fashion houses. Their role is to give these houses image and style – the two most powerful and profitable components in any fashion house. Their challenge has been to communicate a brand image that has the resonance to carry through to each niche of an ever more complex marketplace.

The catwalk plays only one small part in the creation of brand image and identity, but given the current fascination with designers as cult figures, those who are best able to maximise the potential of this revered institution will find themselves much in demand. Where this leaves the concept of the radical catwalk is less certain. To accuse designers such as McQueen, Chalayan or Margiela of cynical manipulation would be as far from the truth as to assert that for these designers the message is more important than the product. One must remember that each of the designers considered here has been and continues to be, commercially successful.

The catwalk show is likely to remain an integral part of the fashion industry's marketing armour. It provides a tried and tested method of presenting products and establishing trends. But as a means of social or political expression, the catwalk show is only ever going to be marginal, destined by design to be ephemeral. The fashion show is an important event, during which nothing is said – at least nothing of substance.

Notes

1   One recent industry calculation held that the week-long Paris showings generated 2000 pages of editorial and 120 radio and television shows internationally.
2   Rei Kawakubo's use of the Holocaust as 'inspiration' was either deliberately provocative or the result of genuine but hardly credible naïveté. The show might have been outrageous, but it misfired as many of Comme's Jewish buyers were deeply offended.
3   The British press talked about an 'anarchic freak-show' with models 'appearing wild and distraught, McQueen's collection showed pubic bones scything into sight and ripped bodice' (A. Veness, *Evening Standard*, 14 March 1995). 'The models on the catwalk could be seen as dishevelled escapees from the English soldiery of the eighteenth century' (C. McDowell, *Sunday Times*, 17 March 1995).
4   In 1999 McQueen took the idea of the clothing as body even further when he presented his Givenchy collection on fifty lifeless, glass-fibre mannequins, which were winched up and down through holes in the floor. McQueen's attention was clearly to draw attention away from the models and to the clothes on display.

References

Alexander, Hilary (1999) 'Dead fashion', *Telegraph*, July: 7.
Becker, Susanne and Schütte, Stefanie (1999) *Magisch Angezogen – Mode, Medien, Markenwelten*, Munich: Becksche Reihe.
Blau, Herbert (1999) *Nothing in Itself – Complexions of Fashion*, Bloomington: Indiana University Press.
Buckett, D. (1992) 'Martin Margiela', *Guardian*, 29 Oct: 7.
Cartner-Morley, Jess (2000) 'In fashion, it's autumn already', *Guardian*, 5 February: 11.
Doe, Tamasin (1999) 'Art on your sleeve', *Guardian*, 21 May: 4–5.
Evans, Caroline (1998) 'The Golden Dustman: a critical evaluation of the work of Martin Margiela: exhibition' in V. Steele (ed.) *Fashion Theory: The Journal of Dress, Body & Culture*, Oxford: Berg, 2 (1): 73–93.

Finkelstein, Joanne (1998) *After a Fashion*, Victoria: Melbourne University Press.

Frankel, Susannah (1997) 'The real McQueen' *Independent Magazine*, September: 6–15.

—— (1999) 'Martin Margiela' *Independent Magazine*, March: 37–42.

Frey, Nadine (1998) 'Mass media and the runway presentation' in Giannino Malossi (ed.) *The Style Engine*, New York: Monacelli Press, 30–9.

Gill, Allison (1998) 'Deconstruction fashion: the making of unfinished, decomposing and re-assembled clothes' in V. Steele (ed.) *Fashion Theory: the Journal of Dress, Body & Culture*, Oxford: Berg, 2 (1): 25–49.

G.M. (1998) 'What do you want to say today?' in Giannino Malossi (ed.) *The Style Engine*, New York: Monacelli Press, 58–9.

Guindi, Fadwa El (1999) 'Veiling resistance' in V. Steele (ed.) *Fashion Theory: The Journal of Dress, Body & Culture*, Oxford: Berg, 3 (1): 52–80.

Holgates, Mark (1998) 'Portrait – Hussein Chalayan', *British Vogue*, July: 43–5.

Hollander, Anne (1980) *Seeing Through Clothes*, New York: Avon.

Keenam, William (1999) 'From friars to fornicators: the eroticization of sacred dress' in V. Steele (ed.) *Fashion Theory: The Journal of Dress, Body & Culture*, Oxford: Berg, 3 (4): 389–409.

Kerwin, Jessica (1996) 'Alexander McQueen', *WWD*, March: 15.

Lurie, Alison (1992) *The Language of Clothes*, London: Bloomsbury.

Mendes, Valerie and De la Haye, Amy (1999) *20th Century Fashion*, London: Thames & Hudson.

Steele, Valerie (1998) 'Why people hate fashion' in G. Malossi (ed.) *The Style Engine*, New York: Monacelli Press, 66–71.

Chapter 8

Hilary Radner

ON THE MOVE
Fashion photography and the Single Girl in the 1960s

R ETROSPECTIVELY, FASHION PHOTOGRAPHY constitutes a historical document that offers us evidence of the practices and ideals of a given period. However, fashion photography is not merely a passive reflection of a period; it served as a vehicle for circulating new patterns of consumption tied to evolving notions of the self. In the 1960s, the role of fashion photography as the vehicle for a new ideal, the 'Single Girl', underlines 'the multiple ways in which clothing interacts with the body in the formation of identity' (Bruzzi 1997: 199). In the 1960s fashion photography and women's fashion was 'on the move' as a result of the confluence of a number of factors, which eventually would produce the very vocal feminisms of the 1970s. In the 1960s second-wave feminism was only beginning to understand itself as such; however, it was preceded by the consolidation of a new feminine ideal. Young, single, economically self-sufficient, the ideal incarnated the notion of movement, of a culture in transition. The degree of control that women had over this 'movement' that they embodied was ambiguous.

Fashion photography of this period expresses the paradoxes of the position of this new feminine, the 'Single Girl' as she would come to be called. Since she represented 'movement', her capacity to move was limited by the fact that her primary function was to signify the ideal of a period. This ideal is formulated through the publication of such popular works as Helen Gurley Brown's *Sex and the Single Girl* in 1962. Both in appearance, waif-like and adolescent, and in goals, to be glamorous and adored by men (in the plural) while economically independent, the Single Girl defines femininity outside a traditional patriarchal construction. At the same time, the Single Girl establishes consumerism as the mechanism that replaces maternity in the construction of the feminine.

Typical of the contradiction inherent in this new ideal is the evolution of fashion photography during this same period, which accords Helen Gurley Brown a prominent place in the public eye. Fashion photography in this period shifted stylistically, giving expression to the Single Girl ethos. The model is shot outside, often walking or running; she is 'active'. This activity is not, however, without its contradictions. The body as an object constructed through consumerism also becomes an important element in feminine culture that is transformed and sold. As often remarked by contemporary feminists, this body emphasises youth as the crucial characteristic of the new feminine ideal. Though fashion photography undergoes significant changes during this period, the meaning of these changes remains ambiguous. Tom Wolfe recalls:

> Once it was power that created high style, but now high style comes from low places, from people who are marginal . . . who carved out worlds for themselves, out of the other world of modern teenage life, out of what was for years the outcast corner of the world of art, photography, populated by poor boys.
>
> (Castelbajac 1995: 130)

Whether 'style' originated in the 'margins' of society is debatable; less debatable is that the 'look' of style, its vocabulary, its iconography, were reversed: 'low' became 'high'. Certainly, as art historian Martin Harrison observes, fashion photography underwent a transformation during the 1960s in terms of both its subject and its style. Like many phenomena associated with the 1960s, these changes did not suddenly erupt and transform social discourse; they were symptomatic of larger and gradual mutations in culture during the post-Second World War era. 'New-Wave' photography freed women from a domestic *mise-en-scène* and from the studio. It emphasised fluidity and movement, a certain style rather than a set of commodities. Harrison refers to this photographic mode as 'outside fashion', a mode that he sees as a representation of a new feminine ideal grounded in activity. These aesthetic and social issues were associated with economic changes in major consumer industries, clothing in particular, as well as such diverse events as the shifts in Hollywood that resulted in a fragmentation of the film industry and the rise of the independent film. This new cinema, characterised by young European film-makers, for example, had a marked influence on fashion photography and its reception. According to Harrison, '*Blow-Up* (1966) defined the public's image of the 1960s fashion photographer. Ironically, Antonioni's earlier films had strongly influenced many fashion photographers' (Harrison 1991: 187). Indeed, David Bailey (a primary exponent of New-Wave photography and the 'model' for Antonioni's protagonist) claimed that his work had been influenced by 'films like *Jules et Jim* and Fellini's *8½*' (Harrison 1991: 211).

If the film industry were reformulating itself in response to the Paramount decision in 1948, the rise of television and the move to suburbia, the fashion industry was also in the process of transformation, as was the woman's magazine. The 'working girl', for whom Helen Gurley Brown revamped *Cosmopolitan* in 1965, was the new preferred customer, rather than the socialite of the pre-war years. 1960s designer Mary Quant asserts in her autobiography:

> There was a time when clothes were a sure sign of a woman's social position and income group. Not now. Snobbery has gone out of fashion,

and in our shops you will find duchesses jostling with typists to buy
the same dress.

(Jackson 1998: 43)

Haute couture catered to the wealthy woman of leisure, who had the time and
money to afford a wardrobe. Ready-to-wear assumes a woman of limited time and
funds, for whom fashion was practical as well as pleasurable. *Funny Face* (1957) –
designer Givenchy's ode to his muse Audrey Hepburn – marks a transitional
moment in the move from haute couture to prêt-à-porter, seemingly anticipating
the new ideal promoted by Helen Gurley Brown. *Funny Face* is the working girl's
fantasy: a story in which a shopgirl becomes an haute couture princess. Yet it is
not Audrey Hepburn in designer Givenchy's gown at the film's conclusion that
will inspire future fashion. She is remembered for the black turtle-neck and capri
pants that she wears to frolic as yet unreformed in the cafés of Paris. Similarly
Jean Seberg's blue and white striped cotton sailor's jersey seen in *A bout de souffle*
(*Breathless*) (Godard 1959) will become an anti-fashion staple, from the boutiques
of agnès b. in the 1970s to the catalogues of J. Peterman in 1990s. This image of
a young woman, unattached and uninhibited, represents an ideal that continues to
dominate public imagination, from Françoise Sagan's *Bonjour Tristesse* in the 1950s
to US television's *Ally McBeal* in the 1990s.

The new ideal was young and single, but not necessarily economically or socially
privileged, seemingly as accessible to the typist as to the duchess. The 1960s notion
of 'the look' tended to undermine a concrete definition of style as ownership, something achieved through assembling a set of objects. 'The look' (a termed coined by
Mary Quant, one of its primary proselytisers) also emphasised the element of
surprise, of the unanticipated, of the continually new, as an attribute of the 'stylish'.
'Image, attitude and association – in other words, 'the look' – were as important as
the actual content of the product itself, whether this be a painting, a record, a dress,
or a chair', claims Lesley Jackson in *The Sixties: Decade of the Design Revolution* (1998:
38, 40). In the words of Terence Conran in 1965, one of the designers responsible
for Habitat, 'Expendability is no longer a dirty word', or more picturesquely: 'Taste
is constantly on the move' (Jackson 1998: 36). 'Activity' was a style, a mode of
representation, but it also implied an 'active' subject. Magazines stressed the importance of exercising and dieting. 'Underwear' and 'home appliances' highlighted
in the 1950s (Castelbajac 1995: 130) were supplanted by products that promoted a
body that was the result of self-control and that was ultimately concerned with its
'self' rather than others. Harrison (1994) argues:

> Women's fashion magazines were the first medium to present images
> of women for the consumption of women, rather than men, and the
> women depicted in these photographs – who after all represented their
> readers – began to be cast in active as opposed to the passive roles
> traditionally assigned to them in art.

Within Harrison's argument, the displacement of the fashion model from the
studio to the outdoor *mise-en-scène* signified the construction of an 'active' as
opposed to 'passive' feminine. This 'active' genre emphasises the contradictions

inherent in fashion photography, which hinge upon the coincidence of seemingly inconsistent terms such as 'street' photography and high fashion; spectacle and activity; provocation and commercialism. Unlike 'art', fashion photography obviously functions primarily within a marketplace that serves to sell clothes. Only belatedly does fashion photography sell itself as art, almost as an afterthought. The boundaries between art photography and fashion photography have always been blurred – photographers themselves crossing easily between genres. Institutions such as Condé Nast, a major publishing house that specialises in magazines, and women's fashion magazines in particular, were among the first to promote art photography as such in the twentieth century.

Ultimately, as a commercial genre that itself follows 'fashion' and the dictates of magazine editors, it resists the requirement of contemporary high art, which arguably sees the work's fundamental goal as the expression of individual genius. Harrison attempts to define certain photographers such as William Klein as having such a personal vision. Yet, if the photographer William Klein pioneered the 'street' look in fashion photography, it was the lesser known Frances McLaughlin or Karen Radkai who were equally responsible for furnishing *Vogue* with these images of a new urban femininity.[1] In his book *Appearances: Fashion Photography since 1945*, Harrison himself underlines the significance of McLaughlin's work: 'Liberman saw in Frances McLaughlin, then only 24 years old, the ideal interpreter of junior fashions' (Harrison 1991: 42). In fact, the 1933 image that Harrison claims provides the seeds for this genre, which would flourish in the post-Second World War years, was commandeered by editor Carmel Snow. Harrison comments that

> [the] burgeoning new commodity she had to propagate was sports wear.
> Of all aspects of clothing, sports wear most clearly exemplified the
> modernist fascination with speed – streamlining, motor-racing, air
> travel, movies – all testified to the faster pace of urban life.
>
> (Harrison 1994)

Martin Munkacsi, a sports photographer who 'creates' the historic image, at Snow's request 'not only instructed his model to move, but to run' (Harrison 1994). The genre developed in response to a 'client' that required a new aesthetic to promote a new type of clothing. The effect of spontaneity is a construction, designed to articulate this new aesthetic of urban life, produced through a hierarchy of 'instructions', of stage directions, geared towards creating a certain market. Stylistically, the genre exploits the techniques of immediacy (and disposability) that characterise the mass media in general. The Munkacsi photograph of Lucille Brokaw (according to Carmel Snow) is 'the first action photograph made for fashion' (Harrison 1994). This action is 'staged', 'made' rather than 'taken', affirming the duplicity of the moment. The model is 'to be looked at'. She 'sells' the new 'sports-wear' look as well as a set of specific items. She is not an athlete or soldier performing a designated task with an external goal. She represents something other than her 'self', even as she offers a model of this 'self' for the woman reader.

Yet, the contrast between this image and others of the period is undeniable. Brokaw seemingly moves outside the frame – her hand blurred, her leg extending beyond the formally inscribed field of the image. Her body is draped with a cloak

Figure 8.1   Martin Munkacsi (Howard Greenberg Gallery)

– some sort of after-bathing apparel. Both the details of what one must assume is a bathing suit and the cloak are obscured by the lines of movement. The body itself as an entity defined by specific physical attributes overwhelms the structural attributes and details of her outfit: the musculature of a thigh is sharply delineated, one white shoe visible at the bottom of the page, the neckline of the suit itself hidden, her crisp hair softened by air rushing past.

In clear counterpoint (as Harrison demonstrates), a series of fashion photographs shot by Edward Steichen that appeared in the 1 May 1927 issue of *Vogue* emphasises the image as a process of containment: the model is triply framed by the page and then within the page itself. The photographs portray a woman carefully posed for the camera, immobile, her body fully and conspicuously displayed,

Figure 8.2   Edward
Steichen (*Vogue*)

captured in its entirety. This body takes its identity from the clothes that cover
it. Rather than asserting its independence, the body is subsumed, rendered abstract,
by the clothes that cover it. Every detail is visible, including the details of jewellery
and hose. Here, the image functions as a means of enumerating a set of items,
which when assembled constitute the fashionable look. Stylistically the image draws
explicitly on fashion illustrations that offered similar portraits of an anonymous
model, or even actual details of hats, shoes, jewellery, accessories, etc.

   This transformation of the feminine began in the 1930s but did not take on
its full importance until after the Second World War. In post-Second World War
culture, mass-produced 'ready-to-wear' dominated the market. 'Style' was reinterpreted in terms of the new economy of non-durable consumer good. The 'new'
rather than the 'well-made', innovation rather than quality, became increasingly
the signifiers of 'style'. Ellen Leopold remarks:

> The mechanisation of tailoring skills did replace this attribute of clothing
> with an alternative idea of apparel as a consumer durable designed to
> be worn until literally worn out. Instead, it preserved the possibility
> for a high turnover of an unlimited elaboration of styles. Constant
> renewal of designs substituted for high levels of output.
>
> (Leopold 1993: 115)

In the 1960s the new 'ready-to-wear' lines replaced the individualised fashions of 'couture', in which a dress was made for a given client, as the expression of 'high style'. These 'ready-to-wear' lines were important not only in terms of how they were manufactured but also in terms of what they 'sold'. They represented a shift away from formal evening gowns and a European 'look'. Fashion increasingly concerned itself with day-wear and, in particular, 'working' clothes. This shift implied another setting for the fashionable woman. By the 1960s, it was the so-called 'working girl' (as Mary Quant observes above) who set fashion standards. For practical and aesthetic reasons the formal attire of the socialite (though still important to the scene of fantasy that fashion magazines offer their readers) no longer was constructed as the locus of 'correctness' and 'authority'.

Not coincidentally, the proper and the improper – the career girl and the working girl – the woman in the streets and the streetwalker – become less and less distinguishable. If the body that emerges is a minimised attenuated body, a childlike body, it is none the less a body that inhabits clothes as 'body'. 'Nipples reappeared as a normal part of the anatomy' (Castelbajac 1995: 130). The body refused effacement, asserting its identity much as does the model that can no longer be contained within the image. During this period models develop an independent identity, a signature. The model emerges, the supermodel, as a significant author in fashion discourse, as a recognisable and recognised agent in the production of the fashion spectacle. Harrison signals this transition by including the names of the models alongside those of the photographer in his attribution. Steichen's models remain anonymous, though the collection – the couture line – is noted.

Fashion photography illustrates that it was not the politics of the 1960s activism that wrought changes in contemporary social fabric, changes now associated with the 1960s. Rather it was popular culture itself, far from resisting change, that posited the personal rather than the political as the new primary arena of experience and citizenship. The formula 'the personal is political' comes to characterise the new feminist values of the 1970s and the 1980s. This position, however, far from challenging consumer culture, affirmed its continued attempts to collapse the public and the private, to eliminate the public sphere as the forum of a specifically political engagement. This is not to negate the feminist's legitimate contention that private space had a political dimension, but rather to question the direction that this assertion has taken in contemporary everyday life. Fuelled by consumer industries' increasing need for new markets, popular culture encouraged the emergence of discourses that formulated an individual whose major preoccupation was the fulfilment of his or her needs and desires as the significant expression of citizenship. Helen Gurley Brown and Betty Friedan, if divided in their sense of how best to achieve this objective, had in common their conviction that each woman had the right to fulfilment defined on her own terms. The 'sexual revolution' in this context is a logical extension of social transformations in the twentieth century that posit the individual as the location of identity and fulfilment.

The anxiety generated by the construction of a social hierarchy in which identity is assumed in the workplace rather than the home – in which the salaried individual rather than the family became the fundamental economic unit – has been well documented. Media scholar Lynn Spigel, among others, has mapped out the cultural anxiety surrounding the domestic status of the feminine in her studies on advertising in the late 1940s and early 1950s. She claims that from 1948–55,

> women's home magazines . . . held to an outdated model of femininity, ignoring the fact that both working class and middle class women were dividing their time between the family work space and the public work space. . . . the [1950s] witnessed a dramatic rise in the female labour force – and, in particular, the number of married women taking jobs outside the home rose significantly.
>
> (Spigel 1989: 34)

The Single Girl represents a strand in popular culture that embraces rather than denies work and 'singleness' as the emblem of a new sexual order. Helen Gurley Brown's enormously successfully transformation of the ailing *Cosmopolitan* in 1965 (a magazine that clung to the outmoded domestic ideal described by Spigel) into a publication that spoke to and legitimated the working woman, or 'girl' as she was more popularly known, testified to the importance of these changes.

Symptomatic of the solution was a conflation of the categories of woman/girl into the category of working girl. In *Sex and the Single Girl*, Brown thus proposes that a Single Girl whether married or not, 'is known by what she does rather than by whom she belongs to' (Brown 1962: 89). For the Single Girl, then, her identity is determined in the workplace rather than the home. The term 'girl' maintained or at least represented the woman's status as nubile – marriageable – long past her youth or even childbearing years. Significantly, Helen Gurley Brown never had children and, as Nora Ephron points out, she was 43 when she took over

Figure 8.3 Helen Gurley Brown in the 1960s.

Cosmopolitan Magazine in 1965 and revamped its format from women's service magazine to handbook for the working girl. In so doing, she increased circulation from under 800,000 to over one million copies a month in five years, from 259 advertising pages a year to 784 (Ephron 1970: 22, 23, 29).

If the transformation of *Cosmopolitan Magazine* into 'Cosmo' illustrates the social diffusion of a new ideal, the figures within the fashion world that best represent this shift – the culmination of which is largely a 1960s phenomenon – are David Bailey, the photographer and Jean Shrimpton, the model. A brief analysis of a few crucial images of this period illustrate how these multiple discourses operated in terms of a 'thick' representation of the new femininity and its relations to fashion. Here we can see the formalisation of the movement that we have traced from Munkacsi in the 1960s itself.

In the 1960s, fashion editors looked for a 'face' that was somehow 'new', or different, while focusing on a certain almost perverse image of girlishness. The elfin Twiggy, who was 5 ft 6 ins tall, weighed 91 pounds, and measured '31, 22, 32' at the time of her fame, was one of the first models to be identified with the 'youthquake' (Gross 1995: 179). Yet Twiggy, one might say, was also the victim of the same phenomenon which saw the new ideal as one that depended on 'the dichotomy of youth and very high fashion' in the words of fashion photographer Steven Meisel (Meisel 2000: 98). Twiggy epitomised the pre-fabricated face, the 'paper face', a face reputed to be constructed and managed by Nigel John Davies (aka Justin de Villeneuve). Twiggy lacked flexibility. In a sense, she could only sell her 'self', and thus she retired at the age of 19 (Gross 1995: 183). Shrimpton represented the new model. She was not anonymous. She had to be both recognisable as 'star' and capable of transforming her 'looks' in order to conform to the demand for the continually 'new'. Shrimpton continued to model into her thirties; she too, however, officially retired at the age of 26 (Liaut 1996: 108). Shrimpton as an icon functions as the synthesis between an older ideal of style as 'breeding' and the new ideal of style as 'disposable consumer object'. At 5 ft 8½ ins, weighing 118 lbs, her measurements were '34, 24, 35' (Liaut 1996: 103). In spite of her height, Shrimpton projected an image of youth, wearing her hair in braids, carrying toys, often appearing dishevelled, 'un-made'. Like Cindy Crawford in the 1980s and 1990s, Shrimpton had a certain wholesome quality that could be transformed but that never strayed too far from its origins. She always projected a defined and recognisable 'self'.

In contrast, Wilhelmina, later a successful agent, who was perhaps the most financially successful model of the period, was too anonymous in her presentation. Not coincidentally she was known as the 'last star of the couture era' (Gross 1995: 193). Her stature and dimensions also recalled an outmoded ideal. When she began her career as a model, she was 5 ft 9 ins, and her measurements were recorded as '36, 24, 37'. She claimed to weigh 132 lbs but in fact weighed 159, which was 56 lbs more than the emaciated Twiggy. Though by 1967 she was in such demand that designers were willing to rip open seams in order to accommodate her size, her image remained of less importance than the clothes she wore. Wilhelmina was an expert in the art of self-transformation. One of her admirers reported: 'I was fascinated by how fast she could change hairpieces' (Gross 1995: 193–8). While constructing herself as 'star', Shrimpton was also a 'working girl' who contrived a 'self' suited to a given occasion. She adapted to a given photographer while conveying a sense of identity, and continuity to the public. From the upper-middle classes, she moved easily between the demands of haute couture and the new ready-to-wear market. Yet with her wide-set eyes, her winged eyebrows, generous mouth, thick hair and almost coltish limbs, she appeared to be in a state of perpetual adolescence, a girl forever on the verge of womanhood. Though eventually she worked with most of the noted photographers of the period, her relationship with David Bailey marked her as a model. To a degree she, as his first 'star', 'made' him or rather legitimated him, assigning the photographer a new role, as star-maker. The figure of the photographer as star-maker in this period comes not only to have an economic significance but also a highly charged erotic connotation. David Bailey is himself of working-class origins and is presented as a photographer who saw fashion as primarily a means of achieving a certain economic status in the world:

> (F)or me, the sixties were really more about a class-structure thing anyway. It was about the emergence of a class that never had a voice before, the working class and kind of vaguely lower middle class. Until the sixties, the class structure here was almost like a case system in India. If things had gone on as they were, I would have ended up an untouchable. But that all broke down in the sixties.
>
> (Gandee 1999: 540)

He also frequently remarks on the erotic aspect of his work, his relations with his models. He is infamous for remarks such as 'The only reason I ever did fashion was because of the girls', or 'A model doesn't have to sleep with a photographer, but it helps' (Gross 1995: 165–7).

Bailey, though then at the beginning of his own career, helped Shrimpton to create her 'look'. Yet in another sense he discovered her as 'the beauty of the century in a kind of democratic way', claiming that she 'was the first super-model . . . At one point in the mid-sixties, she was on the cover of *Newsweek*' (Gandee 1999: 540). Twiggy's look underlined her status as a 'paper face'; however, Shrimpton's look was as a set of gestures, a vocabulary of the body as it was a specific hairstyle and make-up. This new vocabulary of the body emphasised the body as such, the fact that it could not be contained by the image. This code of movement and gesture would be something that Bailey would teach generations of models, each transforming the vocabulary to suit the specificity of a new body and face displayed for the camera gaze. Harrison elaborates in his study on Bailey:

> Motion had been a touchstone of modernism (rapidly appropriated in fashion photography throughout the twentieth century), and the emphasis on exaggeratedly angular and anxious permutations of the fluid body was a central component of the imagery that Swinging London presented to an intrigued world audience in the Sixties.
>
> (Harrison 1999: 27)

In order to represent this 'fluid body', to develop what Harrison calls Bailey's 'vocabulary of gesture', Bailey needed Shrimpton who was able to embody his particular vision, one that coincided with the historical moment (Harrison 1999: 28).

Bailey's genius, his acute sense of the moment, is caught in that same moment. To be caught in the moment is also his great failing as an 'art' photographer. William Klein, who more successfully makes the transition to artist than does Bailey, self-consciously plays with the codes of the fashion photograph. Bailey fixes and formalises these codes. Shrimpton, in his photographs, has escaped the confines of the family manor. She has other possibilities than marriage to 'a Mr Collins', the set of constrained choices presented to the heroines of a Jane Austen novel in which 'wife' or 'spinster' delineated the range of occupations open to a well brought-up young woman. However, she does not have the purposeful stride of Klein's models who seem fiercely intent on breaking through the frame. Shrimpton as a model and as a professional, as the agent of her own interests, remained 'caught' in her status as image. She never, for example, achieves the economic stability and flexibility of a Cindy Crawford, who is able to control her distribution as image. Similarly, Shrimpton seems captured by the photograph; she is its prey and never its mistress. The model in Klein's photographs appears to have a very different relationship to the camera.

In Klein's photograph of Simone d'Aillencourt, taken in 1960, the model walks directly towards the camera (Gross 1995: 184). She does not even flinch as a man on a scooter crosses behind repeating the horizontal movement of the white stripes painted across the street that she is crossing. Her inexorable passage is precisely perpendicular to the horizontal lines of movement literally inscribed upon the earth. The man on the scooter too seems unaware of her. Another woman, another model, turns back to look as she moves, we sense almost regretfully, across the street towards a point somewhere in the distance, at which the white stripes will form a tiny triangle, the point to which all representation in 'perspective' must refer – *le point de fuite*. In the right-hand top corner of the frame, two figures move along the white horizontal lines, cropped so that only their legs are visible. The world is 'in movement', in an ordered pattern, articulated if not explained by the formal composition of the photograph. At the bottom of the frame, we see the backs of the heads of men turned towards the woman who advances upon them, oblivious to the manner in which they seem to block her path. The heads are fixed, a moment of stasis which the movement of the image must eventually confront. Indeed, it is the position that we as the readers of this image must inevitably take – arrested in front of it, blocking the very movement of the image in our attempts to decipher it. The figure of the woman advances upon us, intent on her own goals it would seem.

A famous photograph of Shrimpton, which appeared in British *Vogue*, April 1962, presents her similarly caught in the nexus of urban life (Harrison 1999: 46). Instead, however, of a series of trajectories that lead the eye out of the frame, Bailey reinscribes, underlining as it were the frame through the telephone booth in which Shrimpton is literally encapsulated. The strong horizontal line of her black-gloved hand, even the black and white plaid of her suit, repeat the formal motif of the frame. If in some sense Shrimpton seems too small for her little box

– her sinuous limbs not quite mastered by the geometry of the phone booth, she is at least momentarily 'fixed'. Her immobility serves a certain purpose: that of displaying the details of her outfit, the hemline, the cut of the skirt, the shape of the collar. And as if to recall the little girl that she really is, her teddy bear is perched atop the phone looking down upon her. A man in a fedora (a big teddy bear perhaps himself) stops and looks at the camera. He seems to lack the sense of purpose and integrity that we note in Klein's figures.

In another photograph published in the same issue, from the same series 'New York: Young Idea Goes West', Shrimpton, still holding her teddy bear, stops at a corner and stares almost aggressively into the camera, though the crossing light clearly says 'Walk' (Harrison 1999: 47). Should we fail to understand, another sign barely attached to the post instructs us to 'Cross at the Start of the Green'. Shrimpton does not cross – rather she displays her outfit for us, for the camera, the clean lines of her coat, the rakish tilt of her hat, and the height and shape of her heel. We could say that there is a brutal honesty in her stare. It recognises her function, which is to sell clothes, and then more clothes – clothes that will go with a woman/girl wherever she chooses, but clothes that none the less must be constantly renovated 'on the move' themselves. Yet, something has happened. The comparison to the Streichen is remarkable. Shrimpton's stance aggressively calls our attention to her role as 'model'. Steichen's anonymous model is almost apologetic. Her eyes are modestly averted, looking off-screen, away from the camera, her legs are positioned in a lady-like manner, crossed one in front of the other, classical ballet's third position. Even in a studio shot such as that of Shrimpton and Terence Donovan that appeared in *Vogue* (15 September 1961) we notice a marked change in demeanour (Harrison 1999: 59). Shrimpton wears a neat little suit, her white gloves draped over her handbag (no teddy bears) which is placed on the ground. However, her stance – her legs akimbo, her torso off-kilter, her arms and hands extending awkwardly along the lines of the body – these suggest a body in all its viscerality, and a body in movement at that. In contrast, Terence Donovan seems constrained, his body muffled, as it were, by the frumpy and rumpled lines of his sports jacket and slacks. Yet we note again that if Shrimpton does not seem quite the proper lady, she is careful to display the details of the clothing and accessories she wears, down to the chunky bracelet that adorns her wrist. She may be independent but she knows her job.

Two details from American *Vogue* illustrate this contradiction at the heart of fashion photography represented by the careers and work of Klein and Bailey. In an unattributed series of photographs on 'rainwear', an unidentified model with Shrimpton's 'look' stops in mid-step as she crosses a street, adeptly displaying her coat, boots, gloves and hat (*Vogue*, 1 April 1962: 148). The motion of her foot serves to draw attention to the line of the boot, underlined, as it were by the curb. In spite of the poor quality paper and printing, the fashion 'commodity' is clearly recognisable as a silhouette: the length and shape of the heel, and the column of leather sheathing the calf, are highlighted against the asphalt. The model may be free to wander but it is in a direction that serves the purposes of that which she sells. In the 1 August 1962 issue (62) the photographs are attributed to Klein and again they feature women 'outside', on the 'street'. Even in a detail, we note how Klein plays with the conventions of fashion photography, using them

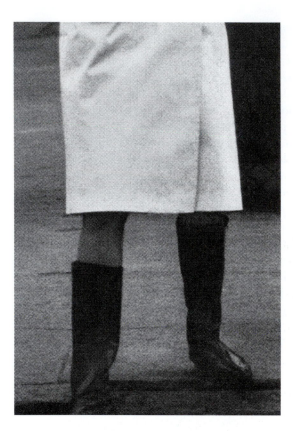

Figure 8.4 David Bailey, detail
(*Vogue*)

against the grain.[2] Here the image of the woman is that of her reflection in a series
of glass planes rather than that of her 'self', a process of reflection that is doubled
(a reflection of a reflection), so that woman and garments seem almost about to
disappear. This effect of the disappearing woman is intensified by the poor quality
of the paper and printing: she is strangely 'doubled' while ghostly and transparent
– she is too many but not entirely present. The human is not recuperated in the
work of Klein. Rather the aesthetic formal qualities of the model's face transformed through the camera render her beautiful as an art object, an *objet d'art* but
an object none the less that works hard in the service of consumerism. Thus even
the work of Klein finally says: with the proper cultivation of the face and body
through the use of consumer products, all women can improve themselves. Only
the camera, however, that renders them not 'themselves'– only reflections,
shadows, traces – can capture beauty, a beauty that is ultimately inhuman, a technological invention.

The careers of Bailey and Shrimpton illustrate how fashion comes to constitute 'a "popular" thing, rather than an "elite" thing, in post-1960s culture'
(McRobbie 1998: 8). However, the work of Klein as a photographer and cultural
critic should also suggest that noting this simultaneous reversal and conflation of
'high' and 'low' is 'merely a starting point' (McRobbie 1998: 8). The concept of
the Single Girl, who 'works' both to pay the rent and perhaps even more importantly as a consumer of non-durable goods, indicates the intimate connection

Figure 8.5   William Klein, detail (*Vogue*)

between an ideal portrayed in fashion photographs as 'aloof and distant' and 'the messy business of earning a living' (McRobbie 1998: 185). The Single Girl pays her way because she is a wage-earner but also because she 'buys' a certain look that is presented as both immutable (an ideal) and the result of the purchase and use of goods that are by their nature evanescent, ever-changing. The Single Girl is 'free' to consume but her 'freedom' is constrained by the field of consumer culture itself, in which consumption is the single imperative. This fraught relationship between consumer culture and the feminine requires that we refrain from assigning a fixed value to 'fashion' and the 'fashionable'. Rather this complicated relationship is by its nature 'in movement', allowing for moments that critique the very practices that make this initial relationship possible. An analysis of fashion photography requires us to think in terms of 'an ethics at one with the flight of time' constructed 'in the absence of the possibility of judgement in a timeless auratic culture' (Lash *et al.* 1998: 168). Fashion photography leads us elsewhere even as it directs us in a clear and unambiguous manner to embrace a culture of planned obsolescence and endless expenditure in the pursuit of an ever-receding ideal, 'on the move'.

Notes

1   For example, see *Vogue* (15 April 1947: 141) and *Vogue* (1 November 1954: 86).
2   Klein's film *Qui êtes-vous Polly Magoo?* (1963) is a vicious parody of the fashion world that none the less depends on the same aesthetic that it critiques for its effect.

References

Brown, Helen Gurley (1962) *Sex and the Single Girl*, New York: Random House.
Bruzzi, Stella (1997) *Undressing Cinema: Clothing and Identity in the Movies*, London: Routledge.
Castelbajac, Kate de (1995) *The Face of the Century: 100 Years of Makeup and Style*, New York: Rizzoli.
Ephron, Nora (1970) *Wallflower at the Orgy*, New York: Bantam.
Gandee, Charles (1999) '1960s: photographer David Bailey revisits Swinging London', *Vogue*, November: 540.
Gross, Michael (1995) *Model: The Ugly Business of Beautiful Women*, New York: William Morrow.
Harrison, Martin (1991) *Appearances: Fashion Photography since 1945*, New York: Rizzoli.
—— (1994) *Outside Fashion: Style and Subversion*, New York: Howard Greenberg Gallery.
—— (1999) *David Bailey: The Birth of Cool: 1957–1969*, New York: Viking Studio.
Jackson, Lesley (1998) *The Sixties: Decade of Design Revolution*, London: Phaidon.
Lash, Scott, Quick, Andrew, and Robert, Richard (1998) 'Introduction: millenniums and catastrophic times', *Cultural Values* 2 (3): 159–73.
Leopold, Ellen (1993) 'The manufacture of the fashion system', in J. Ash and E. Wilson (eds), *Chic Thrills: A Fashion Reader*. Berkeley, CA: University of California Press, 101–17.
Liaut, Jean-Noël (1996) *Cover Girls and Supermodels: 1945–1965*, trans. Robin Buss, London: Marion Boyars.
McRobbie, Angela (1998) *British Fashion Design: Rag Trade or Image Industry?* London: Routledge.
Meisel, Steven (2000) 'The Moving Image', *Vogue*, April: 98.
Spigel, Lynn (1989) 'The domestic economy of television viewing in postwar America', *Critical Studies in Mass Communication*, 6: 17–55.

Chapter 9

Elliott Smedley

ESCAPING TO REALITY
Fashion photography in the 1990s

I want to make photographs of very elegant women taking grit out of their eyes, or blowing their noses, or taking the lipstick off their teeth. Behaving like human beings in other words . . . It would be gorgeous, instead of illustrating a woman in a sports suit in a studio, to take the same woman in the same suit in a motor accident, with gore all over everything and bits of the car here and there. But naturally this would be forbidden.

(Cecil Beaton cited in Hall 1979: 202)

IN THE 1990S, THE DESIRES of that seemingly conservative fashion photographer, Cecil Beaton, are no longer 'forbidden'. Clothing manufacturer Diesel has produced advertising that imitates motor crashes, while models taking grit out of their eyes or lipstick from their teeth are perfectly normal – as in David Sims' pictures of supermodel Linda Evangelista, fingers in mouth, for a Jil Sander campaign in 1993. Behaving like 'human beings ' and documenting 'realistic' activities became a prominent feature of contemporary fashion photography in the early 1990s, and dominated the decade. The role of fashion photography as a commercial instrument, although still intrinsic to its purpose, seemingly became superseded in this decade by the need to reflect wider concerns, rather than just endorsing product placement. This became manifest in a gritty 'warts and all' realistic style that eclipsed the glossy, groomed fashion spreads of the past, which had served to convey a seemingly unattainable ideal of beauty. Such a shift may seem unsurprising, given the socio-economic conditions of the time and the perceived ability of fashion photography to 'capture the spirit of an era' (Craik 1994: 101). Yet those concerns that this style introduced and conveyed in the 1990s have implications both for, and beyond, fashion photography.

It is important to establish and understand the motivation for the prevalence of this style in the 1990s, since a 'recourse to the documentary and vernacular image is not entirely a contemporary phenomenon' (Williams 1998: 104). Periodically, there is an attempt by the fashion world to shed what it perceives as an overly commercial image – and its search for something new often results in a flirtation, even a courtship, between fashion and the art world. In this case, the 'art' concerned is documentary photography, a strand of photographic practice now accepted as a legitimate art form. This courtship is crucial to the realist aesthetic of the 1990s, with practitioners within both arenas crossing the boundaries – and thus blurring them. The concerns of documentary photography – 'the perfect tool for the representation of the human plight and experience' (Mack 1996: 232) – presented fashion photography with the chance to challenge its own role. While this role has traditionally been to create fantasy, fusing this notion with that of documentary has led to some misinterpretation.

Paving the way: historical precedents

Fashion photography emerged within and grew to dominate the commercial arena during the 1920s and 1930s, largely as a reaction against fashion illustration – or what Condé Nast, the publisher of *Vogue*, called 'wilful, wild, willowy, wonderful drawings'. *Vogue* readers, he exclaimed, 'were so literally interested in fashion that they wanted to see the mode thoroughly and faithfully reported – rather than rendered as a form of decorative art' (Seebohm 1982: 178–9). Photography was at first seen as a form of representation which possessed the ability to depict clothes realistically, without any artistic distortion.

However, rather than just providing an exact likeness of fashionable garments, in practice it constructed other forms of representation that held wider connotations. These were the same as those of the fashion illustration: the impression of a fashion ideal or chic – 'a far more tantalising and marketable idea than a precisely detailed photograph' (Maynard, quoted in Craik 1994: 98). In effect, early fashion photography was a continuation of this ideal, creating a visual fantasy to which women could aspire, and a standard that conventional fashion photography still pursues. The practice of using aristocrats or socialites further endorsed such a concept and it was not until art movements – surrealism, realism and modernism – surfaced within fashion and its photographic representations that such notions were challenged.

Certain fashion photographers borrowed from the different movements, creating a plurality of photographic styles. Modernism gave to fashion photography a graphic and geometric influence; surrealism inspired dream-like images. Realism, on the other hand, inspired a less formal approach: sometimes models were depicted (as never before) in action and in movement. Such a look came from 'the realist imagery of sports fashion photography which offered the modern woman a look she could apply to her own life' (Hall-Duncan 1979: 77). Static poses began to disappear, to be replaced by moments of narrative, fleeting impressions and relaxed actions. Elitist fashion imagery, which owed much to illustration, was superseded by more commercial pictures. While clearly shaped by the fashions of the day, such as the influence of sportswear, the impact of Hollywood was central to the construction of this new ideal. 'Films threw up the new role models, images of a consumer society, visually based fantasies and narratives, and new codes of representation' (Craik 1994: 101). These representations were plundered by fashion photography, most notably in the way models became 'blemish free' and 'uniformly youthful' while their potential as commodity increased (Craik 1994: 101).

While early fashion photography became less restricted, its capacity to reflect women realistically was not fully realised until the 1940s, and specifically during the Second World War. This furthered the transition to a realistic approach to photographing fashion, since magazines discouraged displays of excess and frivolity while fashion itself became more austere due to the rationing of fabrics. Lee Miller, the one-time partner of Man Ray, emerged as a key fashion photographer of this period, mainly working for British *Vogue*. Her photographs were as much a social documentary as a recording of fashion, showing women in wartime Britain in everyday situations. Condé Nast complimented her on one series for *Vogue* in 1942, asserting that:

> The photographs are much more alive now, the backgrounds more interesting, the lighting and posing more dramatic and real. You managed to handle some of the deadliest studio situations in the manner of a spontaneous outdoor snapshot.
>
> (Seebohm 1982: 244)

This emerging realist aesthetic was also felt in America; the art director at *Vogue*, Alexander Liberman, realised that 'the immediacy of the unopposed news photograph could be grafted onto fashion photographs to give them a wider appeal, greater realism' (Harrison 1991: 42). In the 1950s, Liberman commissioned photographers who used the techniques of social documentary, specifically Richard Avedon and Irving Penn, whose images contained a contrived spontaneity. Avedon captured the looks, mannerisms, and gestures of 'human beings', while Penn emphasised the anthropological and sociological elements of fashion (Hall-Duncan 1979: 140–54).

In Britain a similar style to that of the 'spontaneous snapshot' became a hallmark of certain photographers during the 1950s. While this trend contained an element of 'reality', signified by the use of locations rather than the studio, its limitations were seen in the continuing construction of an aspirational feminine ideal. In effect, many of these photographs contained a fiction of reality, idealised moments that enabled 'women to imagine what they would look like, to men, in this situation or outfit, without having to commit themselves in any way to that situation or that outfit' (Barnard 1996: 120). While this notion may hold true of much conventional fashion photography, consumed as it is primarily by women, it is not the aim of this chapter to challenge any notion of the 'female gaze' – although in the 1990s, it raises problems around fashion imagery.

In the 1960s, a shift in social attitudes and new directions in publishing – particularly the influence of the magazine *Nova* – traversed the boundaries customarily placed around the editorial fashion story in a defiant yet controlled way. These conventions extended the role of fashion photography into a larger debate which encompassed discussions of race, sexuality and class within fashion and style (see Williams 1998). The emphasis on sexuality in fashion photography was promoted by the self-styled 'Terrible Three' – David Bailey, Terence Donovan and Brian Duffy – working-class Londoners with an irreverent attitude to the world of fashion and the pretensions of its protagonists. Theirs was a vision that developed a theme of women's independence, yet also placed value on beauty, sexuality and success. In summing up their style, Brian Duffy stressed the fact that the three of them were 'violently heterosexual butch boys . . . We emphasised the fact that there were women inside the clothes. They started to look real' (Craik 1994: 96). This was evident in a look, a gesture, a way of wearing clothes – and in documentary observations taken from their East End roots. Models such as Jean Shrimpton and Twiggy typified this new ideal; indeed, Shrimpton attributed her success to 'ordinariness' (Craik 1994: 105).

They were also identifiable role models for a newer, younger audience who were more attuned to the rising success of the new designers and smaller boutiques which emerged as the dominance of couture waned. The liberated new woman, who was as much a *Nova* construction as a reflection of the time, was reinforced within fashion imagery by the influence of metropolitan youth culture. While much 1960s fashion imagery was resolutely positive in its construction and depiction of the 'liberated woman', Bob Richardson reflected another side of her personality that had rarely been seen in fashion photography. He incorporated images of despair, melancholy and anxiety, using images that clearly resembled snapshots, often within a wealthy or glamorous setting – such as the famous narrative sequence set on a Mediterranean beach. However, Richardson invariably used clearly constructed tableaux to portray these wider concerns; despite the fact that he developed realistic themes within his narratives, they cannot properly be described as 'realistic'.

In the 1970s some of these themes were taken up by photographers such as Helmut Newton and Guy Bourdin, whose style Jennifer Craik (1994: 108) calls 'brutal realism'. However, the glamorous fashions of the period and the highly stylised images in which they were portrayed could hardly be seen as documentary. But the issues they developed, mainly the eroticism of the women, involved wider cultural debates. They could be seen as reflecting the underlying tensions about the fantasies, myths and images of sexuality – and in many ways, therefore, there is a questioning of the dominant orthodoxy of the 'liberated woman' that was the creation and legacy of the 1960s. Their photographs were extraordinarily explicit; it has been suggested that 'it was difficult to imagine the spectator, whether male or female, identifying with anyone in the photograph' (Harrison 1991: 52). They therefore encountered charges of misogyny and sexism; the photographers were accused of being exploitative and regressive. Here, fashion photography encountered critical discourse – and entered the public consciousness – through feminist debate.

Yet a new strand of documentary photography was emerging, which recorded the street styles of the time, specifically the subculture of punk. This genre had originated in the 1960s, when photojournalists captured the upsurge in youth cultures for the newspapers and supplements of the time. Its purpose was not to record styles of dress but to document this new social phenomenon. Fashion photography had never even attempted this; it had merely tried to reflect and respond to the youthful spirit of the age and its attendant subcultural styles, while never fully abandoning its preoccupation with conventional ideals of beauty and with aspirational images of women. The powerful, growing influence of subcultures – and of increasingly subversive forms of self-presentation – was largely ignored by high-profile magazines such as *Vogue*, until in 1978 its then art director, Terry Jones, produced a volume entitled *Not Another Punk Book*; this featured portraits of punks on London's Kings Road (Williams 1998: 11).

In 1980 this work became the basis for the magazine *i.D.* which he founded. Its fashion editorials, known as the 'straight up', owed much to these portraits. The 'straight up' pages of photographs – featuring people spotted on the streets rather than using professional models – functioned both as portraiture and as social documentation. Yet, because of the use of credits informing the reader where the subjects had purchased their clothes, they were also within the domain of fashion photography. These images took as their point of reference and basis of style the notion of the 'ordinary person'. However, they still worked to create an ideal of the 'fashionable' self. This style, which *i.D.* and its competitor, *The Face*, made into the visual currency of the early 1980s, reinforced the credo that fashion was 'lifestyle'. This notion, which has continued within their fashion editorials, has acted as a formative influence on many of the most directional photographers of the last two decades – and other publications have followed where the 'style magazines' led.

While maverick tendencies within fashion photography and publishing were pioneering the idea that a fashionable lifestyle was accessible to many, rather than the prerogative of a favoured few, their traditional glossy counterparts continued to depict an upwardly mobile lifestyle based on the glamorous heritage of fashion photography. This was seen in the construction of an inaccessible ideal that perfectly reflected the excess associated with the 1980s, exemplified in fashion pages by the repeated use of certain models possessed of almost superhuman physical qualities. Later, these particular women were to be nicknamed 'supermodels' and they would become staple journalistic fare. It was the chasm between this unattainable ideal of beauty and the very different notion of the fashionable self previously created by *i.D.* and *The Face* that created a space, even a vacuum, within which the new realism in fashion photography could operate, and which it proceeded to fill. This was a realism never witnessed before within fashion photography. By breaking completely with tradition, it exceeded the confines which the unspoken politics of fashion had placed upon photography in the past, and thus called into question not only its role in the portrayal of the fashionable, but in a far wider social context.

Harsh reality: fashion photography in the 1990s

> Decisive moments and turning points in fashion photography have been identified as successive styles reflecting new moods. Fashion photography has constituted both techniques of representation and techniques of self formation. It has served as an index of changing ideas about fashion and gender and about body habitus relations.
>
> (Craik 1994: 93)

As the history of fashion photography shows, it has developed the ability to reflect the spirit of its time rather than merely to showcase the preferred modes of the day. However, a number of photographers – often subversives within their field – have tried to reflect this mood as realistically as possible. Such endeavours, whilst still servicing the needs of fashion, have questioned preconceived ideals in a way that their conventional counterparts have not. These successive attempts paved the way for a photographic practice within the fashion arena that captures the reality of everyday life in a defiant and deliberate 'anti-glamour'. This style, which has been labelled the 'school of London' (Muir 1997: 14), has stripped bare the fantasies and the superficial ideals that the fashion industry had formerly felt compelled to portray and disseminate. Iwona Blazwick (1998: 7) describes this 1990s style of realism: 'Constructed tableaux are rejected for a truth located in the artless, the unstaged, the semiconscious, the sexually indeterminate and the pubescent – the slippages between socially prescribed roles'.

The photographers who worked in this way, although not strictly London-based, had surfaced from within the innovative style magazines currently centred there. Among the most prolific were Corinne Day, David Sims, Juergen Teller and Nigel Shafran. While they each had their distinctive individual style, they all shared a similar aesthetic based around notions of realism. Their style had its roots in the insecure political climate of post-Thatcherism and global recession; there was a perceived platform for change. Fashion had reacted to this mood – designers presented expensive versions of the street style that the press quickly designated 'grunge'. In fashion photography, such a change was not just made manifest in its depiction of a particular reality, but also in its rejection of the precise photographic techniques which had helped to construct the ideal images of perfection of the past. Corinne Day, an ex-model turned photographer, was one of the first to define this change. She encompassed the mood of the new decade with a seemingly 'unprofessional' technique – exemplified by a series of photographs of Kate Moss (not then a 'supermodel') which appeared in *The Face* in 1990.

On a denotative level, the series shows a young, free-spirited girl, happily playing on a beach, in simple relaxed clothes or in a state of near-nudity. Her semi-nakedness signifies not an eroticism but a natural quality that is also denoted by her surroundings, her lack of grooming and the daisy chain that she wears in one particular shot within the series. Her laughing expression, her squinting eyes and playful gestures hold connotations of innocence, immaturity and a teen spirit that is further signified by her under-developed body. In some ways Moss's 'ordinariness' and waifish appearance parallels that of models such as Twiggy in the 1960s. Where they differ is that although the 1960s images reflected the new, 'liberated' woman of that era, who owed much to the sexual revolution, the photographs themselves were taken by male photographers, invariably the 'Terrible Three', who infused the images with their own sexual desire. In contrast, Day's images neither empower nor undermine Moss's sexuality, which remains passive; this is an image of a woman taken by a woman. The intimacy that is apparent within them, and the natural surroundings within the image, deflect any erotic interpretation and resemble more a private, unstaged moment being acted out before the camera – like a snapshot in a family photo album. That Corinne Day was at this time a close friend of Kate Moss adds credence to this feeling, as does

Figure 9.1   Kate Moss, 'The Third Summer of Love', *The Face* 1990. Courtesy of Corinne Day.

a photographic technique that clearly eschews the technical perfection of conventional fashion photography. Day explained, 'She was like my little sister; we'd go off, have a laugh, take some pictures' (Roux 1996: 12). In essence, this is what Day captures, combining a realistic documentation and a fashion photograph, thereby negating the strictures of a precise photographic technique and the false ideals of 'femininity' previously created within fashion imagery.

However, the title of Day's series, 'The Third Summer of Love' is of course a direct reference to the 1960s and the original 'Summer of Love' of 1967. The evocation of the hippie ethos of 'peace and love', and an alternative lifestyle that was a reaction against consumerism, in some ways reinforces the connotations of Day's images. Where it differs is in the impetus behind the second Summer of Love: the second time this term was used, in 1988, it was to describe the emergence of acid house and rave culture. Although vaguely similar in its ideals to its 1960s counterpart, it was rooted firmly in drug culture and hedonism, particularly in the use of Ecstasy, rather than in the counter-cultural philosophical concerns of the original hippies (Polhemus 1994: 64). While Day's images in this series do not directly draw on such references, apart from that implicit in its title, her realist style later explored the surrounding culture and therefore lost much of its optimism.

These pessimistic signs, which in some ways reflect Bob Richardson's style of the 1960s, can be seen in a series of photographs for *Vogue* in 1993 entitled 'Under Exposure'. Here Day's style switches from a sense of the abandonment embodied by her youthful models into one that evokes a feeling of loneliness and urban alienation. This is signified by Kate Moss alone, in her cold, starkly furnished flat, again in a state of undress. That it is cold is signified by Kate sitting on a radiator, in a dishevelled quilt that connotes poverty; so too does her pale thin body and the sparse surroundings. The sense of urban alienation is indicated by Kate looking out of her window on to the world outside, with a television and telephone as her only means of communication. Her expression is mainly blank as she stares

Figure 9.2   Kate Moss, 'Under Exposure', Corinne Day/*Vogue* 1993. Courtesy of Condé Nast.

out of the shot, or window, suggesting boredom; this is further connoted by her nonchalant poses, which may indicate a reference to drug culture, as could the Lou Reed cassette seen in one image.

The narrative of this series seems to suggest an awkwardness and uncertainty that are integral to youth; its grim reality likens it to a series of snapshots, further enhancing this feeling. But there is an ambiguity about these images. Writing in the *New Yorker*, Hilton Als remarked:

> The pictures in question were in some ways Day's apotheosis as a photographer. Besides being intensely moving – Day had managed to catch on film Moss's transition from young chum to commodity – they are a first testimony to the fashion industry's now pervasive flirtation with death. The naked bruised look in Moss's eyes was an apt expression of the brutality that Day was beginning to experience in the fashion world.
>
> (Als, quoted in Williams 1998: 114)

While Als notes that they are a form of documentation in the sense of Moss's career trajectory, like many other media commentators he saw them primarily as holding wider connotations – for him, these spoke of death and mortality. Such a message was conveyed by elements of despair within the narrative of this series – but that these images held such extreme connotations is largely due to their context in a glossy fashion magazine, and specifically within the pages of *Vogue*. Als's understanding of these images seems to be based on the perception of traditional fashion photographs, which is that they are designed to create an unattainable ideal and a fantasy, in other words to function as fiction. However, Day seems to challenge the notion of how fashion photography should be perceived by breaking with the previously accepted practices which created these impossible ideals. Robin Muir, picture editor of *Vogue* at the time, describes them as 'eerie stills from a gritty documentary or freeze frames from someone's home movie. Whatever they were, they weren't fashion photographs' (Muir 1997: 14). As Als and Muir both note, Day challenges what a fashion photograph should be by incorporating elements of documentary. She seems to back this up in her description of the pictures and of Moss herself:

> we were poking fun at fashion. Halfway through the shoot, I realised it wasn't fun for her and that she was no longer my best friend but had become a model. She hadn't realised how beautiful she was and when she did, I found I didn't think her beautiful anymore.
>
> (Day quoted in Muir 1997: 14)

Therefore these images are as much, if not more, about making a documentary of her friend, in her own flat, evolving into a model and consequently into a commodity, as they are a narrative of a typical teenage girl. Indeed, the fact that the photographs were shot in Moss's own flat further links them with documentary photographs. However, as this fact is not usually known to the spectator, they can only be understood within the context of traditional fashion photography. They are therefore seen to create not a realistic ideal but a narrative of misfortune. In doing this, Day pokes fun not only at fashion conventions – showing tights-over-knickers as never before seen in *Vogue* – but at the industry as a whole. Whatever the ambiguous function and possible readings of these images, whether they are seen as documentary or as realistically stylised tableaux, there is an element of discomfort about the possibly voyeuristic nature of viewing such intimacy that has led to misinterpretation. Their context, then, can be seen to confuse their meaning; indeed, if they had been placed within *The Face* or on a gallery wall, it is likely that they would not have caused any offence.

Testament to this assumption is the social documentary work of photographic artist Nan Goldin. Cited as a major influence for fashion photographers of the 1990s, Goldin has created a compelling photographic diary of her life that explores the depths and heights of human existence, recording the deaths of many of her friends and fellow-travellers from drugs and Aids-related illnesses. Michael Bracewell, writing in *Frieze*, notes that 'she records photographically, that portion of society which is divorced from the usual restraints and support systems that service and control contemporary urban life' (Bracewell 1993: 34). However, the apparent intimacy between Goldin and her friends in her photographs deflects the sense of voyeurism, while the snapshot aesthetic further averts such a feeling. It is as if we were invited to join and view her world with all of its highs and lows – above all because it is hung on a gallery wall, or seen within a book, and thus validated by the critical value that the art world places upon it.

In contrast, Day's images could – wrongly – be seen as exploiting her intimacy with Moss due to their primary use within a fashion magazine. It was never the job of fashion photography and fashion magazines to invite us into a private world; theirs has never been a domain of truth but rather one where the prevailing function is that of commerce. It therefore seems that the context in which photographic realism is seen confounds its meaning; seemingly 'art photography' and 'realist' fashion photography have ostensibly different roles. In fashion's case, this role is seen as promoting a destructive ideal, rather than the fantasy which it is normally expected to purvey; within an art context it is seen as making visible the situation and the needs of the less fortunate. As Scott William (1986: 9) writes, 'social documentary encourages social improvement. . . . It works through the emotions of the members of its audience to shape their attitude toward certain public facts. . . . It is that maligned thing, propaganda.'

With the blurring of these boundaries, both art and fashion photography are imbued with different meanings; fashion appropriates the richness of art, while art – in this case Nan Goldin – can fall prey to the fictitious values of fashion. Thus, when Goldin works in the fashion arena, the validity of her personal work has been questioned. Collier Schorr in *Frieze* comments that 'as much as we count on fashion to lie, perhaps we have begun to rely rather too heavily on art to be sincere' (Schorr 1997: 93). But while some question Goldin's work in fashion, her intentions are clearly that of the documentary photographer – to work on the viewer's emotions, to shape attitudes. In Goldin's fashion work, for Matsuda and Helmut Lang, she affronts her audience into questioning the preconceived ideals that fashion holds. In one advertising image for Matsuda, two fully clothed women are seen lying in a form of embrace on a bed. One of the women is wearing revealing, sheer clothing, while both have sweaty complexions. The photograph is entitled 'Sharon and Kathleen embracing, Bowery, NYC, 1996', furthering the ambiguous connotations; the Bowery in New York is synonymous with social depri-vation. These women could be prostitutes, lesbian partners or friends comforting each other, sharing an intimate moment. Their grimy complexions and setting also reference a drug-induced setting. Goldin's previous work, including her book, *The Ballad of Sexual Dependency* (1989), lend credence to such connotations, although its implications are apparent even for a spectator completely unaware of her other work.

The fact that this work is actually fashion advertising confuses the issue further since the role of fashion advertising (even more than that of the fashion editorial spread) has traditionally been to sell an ideal and a lifestyle. Therefore Goldin's images could be seen as an attempt to promote an ideal of deprivation. However, the idea that fashion photography could play an active role in influencing social habits and lifestyles is not wholly convincing, despite a plethora of media claims during the last decade. Indeed, such claims have never been substantiated – Goldin was not trying to promote prostitution or drug abuse; Corinne Day was not advocating anorexia. Such images can work as a conventional marketing tool when used in a context where their audience will understand the dominant conventions, especially in fashion advertising, where they can promote a completely different lifestyle to that actually depicted. The prospective clients are not buying into a world of deprivation but into the usual 'ideal that anybody can be fashionable',[1] however disenfranchised from society that person is. However the book *Fashion Photography of the Nineties* (Nickerson and Wakefield 1996) seems to suggest that such images do have a deeper meaning, other reverberations. Containing images culled from the fashion world, both traditional celebrations and their 'wilder coun-terparts', and using both 'art' and documentary photography, the book confuses fiction with reality by placing these various images within the context of a single volume. The very brief text claims that:

> in these photographs the body and its gestures report on the defining characteristics of a decade. . . . The ambiguity of gender and beauty lays bare our secret desires, dissolving the boundaries between what is worn and the way we wear it. . . . Out of the collision between style and the subconscious emerges a portrait of our time.
>
> (Nickerson and Wakefield 1996)

That it 'lays bare our secret desires' is an ambitious claim, but one image by Juergen Teller reproduced within this book consolidates many of the issues surrounding the realist fashion imagery of this decade. First published in the German broadsheet supplement *Suddeutsche Zeitung Magazin*, the image is taken from a series entitled 'Morals and Fashion'. In the series the model Kristen McMenamy is seen naked but for the word 'Versace' written in lipstick in a heart shape on her breasts and buttocks. In part of the series the poses replicate that of contrived fashion photography, in others she is walking around a stark room like a model preparing for a fashion show. Clearly a constructed tableau, although formally resembling a series of snapshots, Teller sends up the fashion ideals denoted by the use of the word 'Versace', whose clothing is generally considered to connote glamour and sex. McMenamy's skin is mottled, scarred and bruised, while a tampon string is clearly visible. Teller is surely questioning the value of Versace's sexy ideals by showing very different images of women within this tableau. In a sense, considering McMenamy's bruised body, Teller seems to go as far as suggesting that women are exploited by the fashion industry. That she appeared flawless in a glamorous high-profile advertising campaign for Versace, shot by Richard Avedon, in some ways substantiates this suggestion. Of the images, Teller said,

> I chose Kristen because I am fed up with the glorification of the model. You see her in so many magazines looking glamorous and polished, but she's not like that. She's wild and funny and more like an actress. I agree that the bruising is quite grotesque, but that shows the fragility of the body. And that fragility is more beautiful to me than any amount of retouching.
>
> (Roux 1996: 42)

However, the result of these images is almost a parody of his own work and of the realist fashion photographs of the decade. By mixing the realist snapshot aesthetic with contrived tableaux to make clear his own feelings about the fashion industry, Teller renders the images' likeness to reality inauthentic, since they are clearly as constructed as those criticised for conveying ideals of perfection. This questions the authenticity of other 'realist' images, and in doing so suggests this style has possibly lost its primary impact – the ability to shock. However, realism in fashion photography, although less prevalent now than in the early 1990s, has refused to go away and its proliferation in the 1990s raises certain questions.

Can we agree that out of the 'subconscious emerges a portrait of our time' (Nickerson and Wakefield 1996)? Can we consider this style, then, as a collective movement? Roland Barthes has said of documentary photography that it is an 'explosion of the private into public, or rather into the creation of a new social value, which is the publicity of the private' (Barthes 1981: 98). Surely realist fashion photography possesses this capacity and, in the 1990s, this rendering of the private into the public acted as a subconscious attempt to affirm what has been lost through increasing virtual reality, through the process by which technology and media take the place of society or community. This implication can be seen in Corinne Day's series 'Under Exposure' for *Vogue*, where a sense of urban isolation, physical loneliness and social alienation are forcefully conveyed through these particular images of Kate Moss in her sparse flat, where her television set connotes her only visible bond with the outside world. Yet while images such as these may be seen as disquieting and uncomfortable (as indicated by the hostile media reaction), the sight of these fundamental actions and private moments are 'reassuring in their familiarity' (Muir 1998: 105). In effect, they seem to reinforce the bonds of human community by 'reclaiming lost areas of compassion and humanity' (Bracewell 1993: 37).

Perhaps realist fashion photography has been successful in pointing to this aspect of our culture where photojournalism has, seemingly, failed. As Michael Mack writes:

> In an era dominated by the technological intrusion of the spectacular, the lament rings wide that such is our over-exposure to scenes of individual suffering and mass disaster that we are encompassed by a malaise and a hedonism which preclude their continuing significance.
>
> (Mack 1996: 232)

It therefore seems that realist fashion photography in the 1990s has that function that photojournalism has lost, perhaps through its sheer volume. Furthermore, realist fashion photography can reach a wider audience than social documentary or art photography could ever hope to achieve. Indeed, when President Clinton of the United States of America refers to fashion photography's ability to influence social behaviour, as in his attack on 'heroin chic' (11/10/1997), then clearly it has a deeper impact, even if it does not or cannot activate any radical social change. By complicating its formerly established role, and in its evident capacity to evoke both literal reality and the collective unconscious, fashion photography now has much more to say to us than is credited or acknowledged.

In its inherent search for the new, fashion stumbled upon this particular photographic practice, which, while rooted in the avant-garde, went on to penetrate the mainstream. Perhaps the images that proliferated did more than present a challenge to conventional ideals, suggesting that fashion was now more democratic and that anybody could be fashionable. Nan Goldin, among others, chose to document and depict 'real' people wearing fashionable clothes.

One cavil, however – realist fashion imagery did not, and does not, go as far as it might. The exclusion here as elsewhere of the non-slim, the non-young and those who are not able-bodied must have certain implications. The collaboration between Alexander McQueen and Nick Knight on the 'Fashion-Able' shoot for *Dazed and Confused* (October 1998) is notable within fashion photography precisely because it is without precedent and – so far – without parallel.

But this is not to detract, hopefully, from the implications and potential of 1990s realism. Yet, through the sheer velocity of the mechanics that constitute the fashion industry, this style will at some point be superseded. But its impact, its ability to cause controversy where photojournalism has lost that power, is undeniable. It can confront problematic issues, force us to ask questions and to address wider concerns. Susan Sontag's axiom makes a fitting conclusion: 'Great fashion photography is more than the photography of fashion' (Sontag 1978: 104).

Note

1   Interview with Charlotte Cotton, assistant curator of photography, Victoria & Albert Museum, 20/12/98.

References

Ash, Juliet, and Wilson, Elizabeth (eds) (1992) *Chic Thrills: A Fashion Reader*, London: Pandora.

Barnard, Malcolm (1996) *Fashion as Communication*, London and New York: Routledge.

Barthes, Roland (1977) *Image-Music-Text*, London: Fontana.

—— (1981) *Camera Lucida*, London: Jonathan Cape.

Blackwell, Lewis (1997) 'Man of the moment', *Creative Review*, April.

Blazwick, Iwona (1998) 'Feel no pain', *Art Monthly*, November: 7.

Bracewell, Michael (1992) 'A fine romance', *Frieze*, 3.

—— (1993) 'Making up is hard to do', *Frieze*, October.

Burgoyne, Patrick (1996) 'Beyond the supermodel', *Creative Review*, May.

CNN (1997) 'Clinton urges pop culture to stop glamorising drugs', posted 11 Oct. (http: //www.druguse.com./news.html)

Cooke, Rachel (1997) 'Curse of the catwalk', *Sunday Times*, Style section, 4 May.

Craik, Jennifer (1994) *The Face of Fashion*, London and New York: Routledge.

Devlin, Polly and Garner, Philippe (1994) *Essays from 'A Positive View'*.

Evans, Caroline and Thornton, Minna (1989) *Women and Fashion: A New Look*, London: Quartet Books.

Farrelly, Liz (1996) 'Fashion, art and rock'n'roll', *The Face*, October.

Goldin, Nan (1989) *The Ballad of Sexual Dependency*, London: Secker &Warburg.

Hall-Duncan, N. (1979) *The History of Fashion Photography*, New York: Alpine Book Co. Inc.

Harrison, M. (1991) *Appearances: Fashion Photography since 1945*, London: Jonathan Cape.

—— (1998) *Young Meteors, British Photojournalism: 1957–1965*, London: Jonathan Cape.

Howell, Georgina (1991) *In Vogue, 75 Years of Style*, New York: Random Century.

Januszczak, Waldemar (1998) 'The poor relation no more', *Sunday Times*, Culture supplement, 5 April.

Mack, Michael (ed.) (1996) *Surface: Contemporary Photographic Practice*, London: Booth-Clibborn.

McRobbie, Angela (1998) *British Fashion Design: Rag Trade or Image Industry?*, London and New York: Routledge.

Muir, Robin (1997) 'What Katy did', *Independent Magazine*, 22 February.

—— (1998) *Subverting the Genre, Addressing the Century: 100 Years of Art and Fashion*, London: Hayward Gallery Publishing.

Nickerson, Camilla and Wakefield, Neville (1996) *Fashion Photography of the Nineties*, New York: Scalo.

Polhemus, Ted (1994) *Street Style*, London: Thames & Hudson.

Rombough, Howard (1987) 'Fashioning reality', *Creative Review*, November.

Roux, Caroline (1996) 'Reality bites', *Guardian*, 2 November.

Schorr, Collier, (1997) 'A pose is a pose is a pose', *Frieze*, April: 63.

Scott, William (1986) *Documentary Expression and Thirties America*, Chicago: University of Chicago Press.

Seebohm, C. (1982) *The Man Who Was Vogue*, London: Weidenfeld & Nicholson.

Sontag, Susan (1978) 'The Avedon eye', *Vogue*, Dec.

—— (1979) *On Photography*, Harmondsworth: Penguin.

Stout, Lindy (1998) 'Breaking style', *Creative Review*, November.

Stungo, Naomi (1998) 'Representing fashion', *Blueprint*, May.

Wargnier, Stéphane (1993) '*Le style Anglais*', *Vogue Homme International*, Autumn/Winter: 137.

Williams, Val (1998) *Look at Me: Fashion Photography in Britain 1960 to the Present*, London: The British Council.

Windlin, Cornel (1996) *Juergen Teller*, Cologne and London: Taschen.

PART THREE

Images, icons and impulses

Chapter 10

Jane M. Gaines

ON WEARING THE FILM
Madam Satan (1930)

THERE WAS A TIME when a feminist approaching a film like Cecil B. DeMille's *Madam Satan* (1930) would have felt obliged to talk about its orgy of bodies in terms of objectification and fetishization. We are, however, arriving at a new moment in which many methodologies will bloom and a film like *Madam Satan* – a *tour de force* of art deco film design – will invite many analyses. At this moment, I have been emboldened by two developments, both of which bode well for the serious consideration of costume design. First, I am indebted to Stella Bruzzi's *Undressing Cinema*, which makes a passionate case for understanding costume in the cinema 'for its own sake', that is, not as a handmaiden to the narrative. I particularly like Bruzzi's admission that there are some costumes that make such a strong statement that they 'steal the show', so to speak. These 'iconic clothes', as she calls them, have the capacity to 'disrupt the normative reality of the text'. They are 'interjections' that declare themselves with visual exclamation marks (Bruzzi 1997: 17). And it has been such exclamation point designing that first drew me and my colleague Charlotte Herzog to the work of designer Gilbert Adrian, whose important tenure at MGM spanned the golden era from 1927 to 1941.[1] It is that visually exclamatory aspect of Adrian's *Madam Satan* dress that I want to explore here, and Stella Bruzzi's affirmation of the disruptive tendency of *tour de force* design inspires my decision to look exclusively at 'the dress' in this film (see Figure 10.1). Clearly, Adrian's black cut-out seductress costume is one of those extravagant iconic designs that monopolize the eye and transfix the viewer. The Kay Johnson character (Angela Brooks) wears the dress to seduce her own philandering husband, catching him in the act of seduction by planting herself as the bait in the trap.

If my first debt is to new feminist work on motion picture costume, my second is to new approaches to phenomenology from within film theory.[2] Elastic in its

Figure 10.1   Gilbert Adrian design for *Madam Satan* (dir. Cecil B. DeMille
1930). Courtesy of the Academy of Motion Picture Arts &
Sciences.

methodology, phenomenology is the philosophy of exhaustive detail and description.
Relevant for us, it has a concern with language and the body in common with
Lacanian psychoanalysis (so significant in the founding years of feminist film theory),
although in the existential phenomenology of Merleau-Ponty, for instance, even
more emphasis is placed on the body.[3] It could be said of this phenomenology that
it is deeply interested in the 'bodiness' of things. As Vivian Sobchack demonstrates,
the utility of Maurice Merleau-Ponty for film theory, the promise of this approach
is in its starting point in embodiment, a dense phenomenological concept, which, as
she shows, can be opened up into a thorough inventory of all of the parts of the
cinematic apparatus as well as an analysis of their functioning. For Sobchack, the
pertinent parts of Merleau-Ponty theorize the 'lived-body', that incarnation of
consciousness, the place where world meets self. As Sobchack describes this intersection, the 'lived-body correlates consciousness and the world, textualizing the
sensing body' (Sobchack 1992: 69). Our advantage here is in the efficiency of a
theory that runs everything through the body, the form that is made to assume
primary responsibility for meaning as it textualizes its own senses. There is further
economy in phenomenology's recognition of the double-sidedness of things. As

consciousness, the body is of the world or as body, consciousness is, in Sobchack's term, 'enworlded' (Sobchack 1992: 59). But that is not all. Abstracted out from the human sensate body, the *concept* of (material) body as place of intersection between consciousness and world has further utility as it explains other phenomena – for instance, as it explains the function of the moving picture machine.

Where is the application for a theory of costume design in the cinema? This is the theory that we have been inching toward over the past decade, a theory that is more than a theory of design, that is finally a theory of the relationship between the female spectator and the embodied screen design-in-motion. Because of the emphasis in feminist film criticism on spectatorship as well as consumer culture, one would expect that the key questions would have to do with the inter-section of on- and off-screen bodies, with embodiment and disembodiment, with emulation and imitation. Certainly the question of design in cinema privileges the female spectator, the spectator who is the measure of the star image. At least two recent feminist studies take seriously the question of the female consumer in regard to screen fashions and establish the importance of archival film industry research as well as theoretically informed empirical inquiries into the lives of female fans (Stacey 1994; Berry 2000). It is important to begin with an affirmation of these studies which provide the social grounding and the ultimate reason for theory. From there I want to see where the question of costume might be placed in the theoretical account, testing the claims of phenomenology as a method. For our purposes, there will be three branches of this phenomenological trunk that will prove significant for a theory of costume design in film: the seeing body as inex-tricable from the visible body; the cooperation of the senses; and the commutability or substitutability of things. From the last principle, I follow Sobchack in her approach to analogizing film and spectator as well as film and body, adding to these analogies a third, the analogy between film and costume. But first, why is *Madam Satan* such an interesting example? I want to address this with a short detour through the production history of the film.

Madam Satan: adultery and electricity

As one of only three films that producer-director Cecil B. DeMille made for Metro-Goldwyn-Mayer, *Madam Satan* is already somewhat of an exception in the way it fits into DeMille's career. However, it is also typical of him in terms of his repu-tation for promoting art directors, producing spectacle, addressing bedroom topics, and titillating audiences with racy scenes.[4] To quote Mitchell Leisen, assistant director as well as art director on *Madam Satan*: 'DeMille had no nuances. Everything was neon lights six feet fall: *Lust*, *Revenge*, *Sex*. You had to learn to think the way he thought, in capital letters' (Chierichetti 1995: 23). Although DeMille had won a reputation for dealing frankly with matters of marital infidelity in films such as *Don't Change Your Husband* (1919) and *Why Change Your Wife?* (1920) and had demonstrated an apparent relish for sexual abandon in films such as *Male and Female* (1919), in the history of Hollywood and censorship *Madam Satan* was on the borderline, looking backward to the tolerant 1920s and forward to the tempered 1930s, appearing as it did at this juncture. Actually, this proved to be an early test case for the Production Code (which went into effect in February 1930) during the time that *Madam Satan*, released in the fall of that year, was in production (Black 1994: 57).

The point of this production history is to situate the film as an example of an interesting problem for costume theory, since it presents us with a case where, although the narrative was found objectionable to censors, the solution to the problem of sexual representation was enforced at the level of the *mise-en-scène*. The narrative was not changed; instead, the costumes were modified. The MGM pressbook describes this story as that of a wife who wins back her husband by assuming the guise of a powerful seductress with a French accent who encounters him at the extravagant masquerade party aboard a giant zeppelin:

> The story, by Jeanie Macpherson, is a very simple one of a husband and wife who have grown apart because the wife is really too perfect, and too cold. Finding that her husband is slipping away from her, she resolves to fight for him with the weapons used by the women who have attracted him. The husband goes to the ball on board the Zep of his friend, and there he meets a particularly gorgeous and voluptuous creature, 'Madam Satan'.[5]

The script was sent to the office of Jason Joy who worked then for Will Hayes, president of the trade industry association, the Motion Picture Producers and Distributors of America.[6] According to one account, although Joy himself did not necessarily find the script objectionable, he was concerned about state censors who would want to 'protect young women of the country from the idea that they must employ "passion and deceit" in order to live successfully with their husbands'. Instead of altering the script, however, the compromise solution was an alteration of the costumes for the zeppelin party, invitations to which suggested that guests might arrive in either costume or 'nothing at all'. Angela Brooks (Kay Johnson), in the script, was to have worn a mask over her face but just as little as the other women (presumably mistresses and playgirls) on her body. To solve the problem of too much exposed skin, translucent fish nets and body stockings were added to costumes (Black 1994: 57–8).

Here, it would seem, is an admission of the cultural fear of the naked, the unsheathed. It is not as though the flesh on these women's bodies would be completely unmediated, however, filtered as it was through the lens and the screen of the photographic apparatus. The Hays Office dictum is interesting in this regard. Nudity, one might say, had to be *represented* by a modified semi-nudity. Further, it is a question as to whose modesty was the greatest concern – that of the actresses themselves, whose nudity was used to *represent* nudity, or that of the women (and girls) in the audience, whose modesty might have been offended by the nudity of another woman. The body stocking (nude soufflé or flesh-coloured silk) solved the problem of the representation of nudity by turning nudity itself into 'not the thing itself' but the representation of it. But finally, what this historical situation tells us is that this is a question not only of seeing (since the materials used were 'see-through') but a question of tactility, a problematic to which I shall return in my final examination of the way touching is implied in seeing.

Perhaps even more intriguing from the contemporary point of view is the Hays Office objection to the wife's elaborate deception, the masquerade she resorts to in order to keep her husband. Clearly the implication is that by 'taking off' her clothes she has 'put on' a sexuality that is not hers. He is sexual and she isn't, and she suffers under the burden of the knowledge that he has strayed because she is so icy cold. In order to keep him, she must be what she is not, even though she wins him back by proving that she *is* this, after all (else why would she be successful?). The contradictions inherent in the moral code at that historical moment may not be immediately evident because of the stubbornness of the cultural construct, 'sexless wife'. How can she be at the same time not sexual and sexual?[7] From the point of view of pro-sex feminism, I am going to argue for a reading of this film that resolves this contradiction in favour of female sexuality.[8] What, for instance, if we were to consider the wife as actually having the sexual desire that she is not supposed to have? Putting on the costume of Madam Satan, Angela disguises herself in her *own* sexuality, the sexuality that her husband Robert (Reginald Denny) does not recognize. Married women, for the most part in the last century, were expected to have no sexual desire at all and thus, since they had to hide their interest, the ice-cold wife was the real masquerade, not the brazen seductress. Perhaps in this desexualization the First World woman can be understood in terms of the Third World, where the phenomenon of the clitoridectomy dramatizes the husband's fear that bodily desire will cause the wife to stray.

Following this interpretation, the moment at the costume ball at which Angela removes her mask is actually the moment when she puts it on, removing the sequined devil's head to show the cold, contorted face underneath. This cold face of the wife is also the hysterical face, the face that Angela reveals in her abrupt change from the powerful self-confidence of Madam Satan to the frantic wife. A dramatic narrative development forces her to remove the mask. Party goers are abandoning the zeppelin which has been hit by lightning and is dropping to earth. In a flash, the 'electricity' thematic connects the disparate parts of the film: the metaphoric sexual charge that ignites the party is joined up with the literal bolt of electricity that wrecks the dirigible. In this second, the film changes genre, shifting from the light frivolity of musical comedy to the high hysteria of melo-drama. Angela confesses her love for her husband then throws herself at him. It is not clear at this point whether or not he will return the feelings since his mistress Trixie (Lillian Roth) interrupts and he is thrust into the role of rescuer, finding parachutes for the two women in the last desperate seconds of the balloon's descent. One of the visual highlights of *Madam Satan*, the sequence of revellers parachuting to earth, interrupts the dramatic complications of the triangle. In an epilogue, the couple are shown together at home. He laments that he had to 'wander so far from my own fireside in search of fire' but is irritated by her reprise of the siren song that she sings in the heavily French-accented voice of Madam Satan. Further, he criticizes the seductive black dress ('The most indecent thing I ever saw'). In regard to the issue of her sexuality, however, the final scene is ambiguous. Thus if we are going to resolve the question in favour of Angela's own sexual desire, we will need to look elsewhere – that is, we will need to look within the film but beyond the narrative.

The film's strategy for the expression and containment of sexuality is not unusual for the period and is fairly typical of DeMille in particular. Like the 'Cinderella Ball' in *Forbidden Fruit* (1921), the sack of Rome in *Manslaughter* (1922), and the Babylonian sequence in *Male and Female* (1919), it is a concentration of excess into a bounded sequence. The function here is analogous to the way, after the 1927 advent of sound, the musical of the next decade would use the song and dance number, cordoned off from the rest of the narrative, to express utopian or other-worldly aspirations.[9] The zeppelin world, floating above the city, is a world without wives or inhibitions, and in the history of the American musical, it exemplifies what I would call the quasi-musical. Within the parameters of the party sequence, several musical options are explored: dance numbers are choreographed by LeRoy Jerome Prinz, ranging from the vaudeville-like 'The Cat Walk' to 'Ballet Méchanique', ' a modernist exercise featuring Russian ballet star Theodore Kozloff as 'Mr Electricity' (see Figure 10.2). Both Kay Johnson and Reginald Denny sing ballads, and Roland Young as the host, Jimmy, half-sings, half-talks, his introduction to the female floor show that prefigures the Busby Berkeley musicals in its fascination with the visual crescendo of feathered and sequined females, as though his singing and rhyming could provide an acceptable alibi for the exhibition. The awkwardness of this staging defines for me the quasi-musical, an ungenre that is

Figure 10.2   'Mr Electricity', *Madam Satan*. Courtesy of the Academy of Motion Picture Arts & Sciences.

not certain what to do next before the development of the conventions that would smooth the transitions in and out of song.

More than anything, however, it is the stark modernism of the decor of the zeppelin interior that marks *Madam Satan* as well as gives visual voice to an alternative discourse. Here is where I would place emphasis on the subversive function of the *mise-en-scène* that the Hays Office attempted to tame. Already I have argued for an understanding of costume as a distracting discourse that industry practices in the classical era had to modify to serve narrative ends, a practice that produced in many cases a disappearance of costume design into unseen clothes (Gaines 1990). More recently, Charles and Mirella Affron have made a parallel point about set design, which, as it served the narrative, could be seen as an 'exercise in self-effacement, in self-denial, in disappearance' (Affron and Affron 1995: 45). The irony of course is that designers of both costume and sets worked to produce designs that were simultaneously 'to be seen' and 'not to be seen'. This, as I have argued before, is a by-product of the contradiction between the individualist artist and the dominant discourse of classical narrative construction (Gaines 1990). What interests me, as I stated at the outset, is 'interrogatory' costume (here working in league with the set design) that has the potential to threaten the narrative, competing, as it were, as its own distinctive discourse. To give only one example, on watching *Madam Satan* today, one is not struck by the parlour drama itself but by the incongruity between the adultery story and the angularity of the shining steel futurist sets reminiscent of Fritz Lang's *Metropolis* (1927). This design is not background but foreground. It is as though design and design alone is the driving reason behind the production. The zeppelin party sequence, at aesthetic odds with the rest of the film, features a streamlined art deco shell flaunting the exposed beams and architectural undergirding redolent of the factory interior. It is strange, in retrospect, that the icons of labour that stood for the modern city would come to connote the space of modern sexuality. It would seem that art deco, the marriage of the signifiers of art and industry, stood for 'decadence' as well as for 'decoration'.[10]

It is tempting to attribute the virtuosity of the design in this film to the confluence of talents, to the creative personnel who would have been interested in a new style of decoration. Taking this approach, one focuses on the fact that Cedric Gibbons, the head of the MGM design department between 1917 and 1955, attended the 1925 Paris Expo (Mandelbaum and Myers 1985: 10). One might then note that Gibbons, associated for so long with the MGM art deco look, shares the art design credit with Mitchell Leisen.[11] Or, one might look at producer-director DeMille's role in the evolution of design in films of the 1920s.[12] Even more difficult to resist is the tendency to want to explore the liaison between Leisen, who has the assistant director credit on *Madam Satan*, and Gilbert Adrian whom he claims to have discovered (Chierichetti 1995: 36). And the next step would be an exploration of the exquisitely excessive aesthetic of association with what might be called the gay sensibility.[13] We come now to a crossroads in our study of designers and designing. Until now, most studies of set as well as costume designers might be said to lapse into the cult of personality. Like the art historical approach to the master artist, the approach to a motion picture costume design talent such as Gilbert Adrian would seriously consider not only his famous transformations of Jean Harlow (the braless, bias-cut gown), Joan Crawford (the

Figure 10.3   Gilbert Adrian design for *Dynamite* (dir. Cecil B. DeMille, 1920).
Courtesy of the Academy of Motion Picture Arts & Sciences.

enormous shoulders), and Greta Garbo (the luxuriant slouch) but also his signature details (See Gaines and Herzog 1981–82). His interest in the whimsical, in
the starkness of modernism, and his characteristic uses of asymmetry, come to
mind. It is well known that he preferred to work in black and white and resisted
Technicolor (which he found gaudy) as long as he could (LaVine 1980: 55).

Yet even the facts of the histories of Hollywood production challenge the
auteur theory as applied to designers. If sources assert that the zeppelin number
was shot not in the black and white we see in the extant print and on VHS tape
but in two-colour Technicolor, an early process, we can't very well study *Madam
Satan* as Adrian's exercise in black and white (Chierichetti 1995: 39).[14] Publicity
for the film describes the *Madam Satan* gown as black with red and gold. Was it
the black and white effect on screen or the use of black and white fabrics that was
Adrian's forte? In addition to factoring technological developments into our
account, we also need to take the confluence of talents seriously. Consider, for
instance, the design work on *Dynamite* (1929; the DeMille MGM film completed
just before *Madam Satan*) and a costume such as the asymmetrically striped sports
outfit which I attribute to Adrian (see Figure 10.3). Although the bravura of the
design is vintage Adrian, we are given pause when we consider that the design
team credited on *Dynamite* is almost identical to the team that collaborated on

Madam Satan, namely DeMille, Gibbons and Leisen.[15] I should at least signal here the need not only to put costume designers in context but also to find a way of addressing the interrelation between scenic decor and costume decor. Yet this too may need to wait for even more sophisticated theoretical work on both the scenic and the sartorial. To this end, in the following I take *Madam Satan* as the inspiration for a phenomenological investigation of the dangerous and subversive discourse of design.

Seeing the film's seeing

Madam Satan presents us with a costume that consumes our seeing. Within the seduction scenes, all vectors direct our attention toward what is transpiring on the body as defined by the dress that sculpts out the space on screen. *Madam Satan* is an exploration of a body that is specially designed to see as well as be seen, the devil's head mask part of the costume (with its two eye holes) calling attention to this looking-out function. Curiously, this body design elucidates our paradigm, which, in Merleau-Ponty, is the principle of reciprocity between the body that sees and the body that is visible. The two are, as he says, 'intertwined'.[16] Note the divergence from traditional feminist film theory. This is a principle markedly different enough from the Freudian theory of voyeurism that it is able to take us around the theoretical dead-end that seems always to lead to the objectification of the female body about which so much has already been said.[17] If the seeing body and the visible body are reciprocal, then there is a circuit: the body that sees is seen, a distinctly different move from the one in which one body does and the other doesn't, the one-way trajectory of voyeurism.

But unless one goes the next step with Merleau-Ponty, it is difficult to appreciate the move away from the voyeuristic model. The next step demonstrates that the principle of reciprocity is as important as an intercorporeal (within the body) phenomenon as it is between bodies. Perhaps the novelty of his thinking here is best illustrated with Merleau-Ponty's concept of 'flesh', a concept that refers to much more than mere skin and even transcends materiality, suggesting a sensory structure or even system. To quote his clarification:

> Once again, the flesh we are speaking of is not matter. It is the coiling over of the visible upon the seeing body, of the tangible upon the touching body, which is attested in particular when the body sees itself, touches itself seeing and touching the things, such that, simultaneously, *as* tangible it descends among them, *as* touching it dominates them all and draws this relationship and even this double relationship from itself, by dehiscence or fission of its own mass.
>
> (Merleau-Ponty 1968: 146)

The body that 'sees itself, touches itself seeing and touching' is the synaesthetic body, the body that knows one sense always in terms of another. It is a body wrapped up in seeing and viewed in touching. The radical implications of this for film theory should be apparent. If the senses are not exclusive of one another, seeing is no longer the dominant mode of access to the world but will always be qualified by the other senses which may assert their own dominance. Further, the senses are both in accord with each other and interchangeable. Sobchack speaks of the 'cooperation' as well as the 'commutation' of the senses (Sobchack 1992: 76). And it is here that we find the opportunity for the consideration of costume. As Merleau-Ponty stresses the sympathetic simultaneity of touching and seeing, he anticipates the problematic of cinematic costume design: *to be seen wearing but also to wear seeing*.

Wearing seeing is a state of cinema enacted by stars and imagined, enjoyed, and anticipated by spectator-fans. It is characterized by the unity of tactility and visuality that knows and has known particular sense experiences. The importance of this 'having known' comes out in Sobchack's statement of how one translates the principle of synaesthetic seeing into a theory of cinema spectatorship. For us, she demonstrates new theoretical habits of thought, urging us to reform our understanding of seeing, to grasp seeing as not narrowly visual since it is always actually synaesthetic. Seeing as only 'one of many modalities of perception', she says, 'is not only a visual activity'. She goes on:

> Whether human or cinematic, vision is informed and charged by other modes of perception, and thus it always implicates a *sighted body* rather than merely transcendental eyes. What is seen on the screen by the seeing that is the film has a texture and solidity. This is a vision that knows what it is to touch things in the world, that understands materiality. The film's vision thus perceives and expresses the 'sense' of fabrics like velvet or the roughness of tree bark or the yielding softness of human flesh.
>
> (Sobchack 1992: 133)

I will return momentarily to the question of vision as either human or cinematic and for the time being let us assume that the sensory capabilities of the film are like those of a human being. It would seem, then, that Sobchack might mean here that the film is sensitive to profilmic tactilities and that it has known them; that it has, in *its* sense, felt. The film that both looks and says (that perceives and expresses) is intensely aware of the fabric of the world. It picks it up; it knows it. This, to return to Merleau-Ponty on the function of the flesh, is the phenomenon of 'touching itself seeing', a concept we are extending to a notion of the flesh of the film.

Parts of existential phenomenology can be somewhat disorienting, however – particularly if the reader forgets the foundational principle of commutability. One might wonder what Sobchack means by the 'seeing that is the film'. To clarify this, which will help us find the place of the dress design in the philosophical scheme, we need to move on to three provocative analogies to which I earlier referred, two of which are Sobchack's and one of which is mine. Basic to Sobchack is the concept that as you sit in the theatre you are seeing how the film sees. 'I see the film's seeing', she says (Sobchack 1992: 138). And by this she means not that the film, through point of view, is directing the seeing of the spectator but that the one seeing can be analogized with the other: the film's seeing '*duplicates* the structure and activity . . . of its spectator's vision'. Thus there are essentially two seeings, although not necessarily a shared vision. Seeing the film's seeing is like experiencing the seeing of some other who is '*like* myself, but *not* myself' (Sobchack 1992: 136). And so it is that the film is understood in terms similar to those we might use to describe another spectator, a separate spectator who sees similarly but does not necessarily view the same thing. The spectator sees a visible world; the film sees a visible world. The spectator looks from the inside out; the film looks from the inside out.

And all the while we are following this argument we are wondering how the film can be like the spectator who is defined by his or her body as well as consciousness. The phenomenological solution to this problem can be found in the concept of embodiment. This concept allows Sobchack to explore the ways in which the materiality of the cinematic apparatus functions like a body. To the degree that the film functions – to the degree that it sees, that it hears and makes sounds, that it makes meaning through the use of signs, that is the degree to which it is body-like. 'Insofar as a film is revealed as a similar commutative system and performs similar ontological functions in constituting the experience of consciousness and the consciousness of experience, it can be said to be "embodied"', Sobchack explains (Sobchack 1992: 162). The test of the degree to which the film is analogizable to a human body, however, comes in Sobchack's discussion of the limit case of film embodiment – the famous restricted point of view experiment, *The Lady in the Lake* (1946), a film shot almost entirely without reverse shots (Sobchack 1992: 230–47). The film has traditionally been analysed in terms of the disorientation produced by the way in which the body of actor Robert Montgomery (as the character Marlowe) is withheld from view, the camera positioned in the place of the actor's body. Sobchack reverses this, considering the way the film has attempted to disguise itself as the body of a human, concluding that the failure of the film to pass itself off as a body is significant as it reveals the limitations as well as the possibilities of the analogy. Whether or not one grasps the concept of the film's body, this is still a fascinating test of the methodology intent on exhausting the possibilities of metaphor and substitution. Most difficult to grasp is that the operative metaphor here is not mechanism (so that, as Sobchack says [1992: 171], the film is not considered as one might consider a water heater or a telephone). Again, the central concept, following Merleau-Ponty, is embodiment. Neither can the film be 'reduced to its mechanisms' as, according to Sobchack, human perception cannot be explained in relation to parts of human anatomy. Thus the film's body is neither the camera nor the lens, the projector nor the screen (Sobchack 1992: 169). The film's body is the sum (of the parts) that produces the functioning that constitutes the 'experience of consciousness and the consciousness of experience': this functioning a meaning-making process that relies on these parts in total (Sobchack 1992: 162).

Wearing the film

While Sobchack pushes us to think how the film's functioning is like the human body's functioning and how the film (with its own seeing) is like the spectator who views, I want to urge an adjacent analogy between the costume and the film: two embodiments, the one within the other. The two overlap. This I find in Merleau-Ponty, whose formulation of the seeing body intertwined with the visible body anticipates the problem of the spectator-fan, for whom seeing is always a being, a spectator whom I will assume to be female throughout the following discussion.[18] Another way of understanding the seeing body as intertwined with the visible body is to consider that a looking is connected with a fashion 'look'. Important here, thinking of our paradigm in the Madam Satan costume, is that the meaning of the looking figure (woman masked) is *not* to be understood as about 'returning the look', that old paradigm of voyeurism that posits all looking as between male and female. Instead of the sharp-edged directionality of voyeurism, there is a characteristic interior circularity in this looking that implies a 'look', the phenomenologist's 'coiling' of the body that 'sees itself, touches itself seeing', which returns us to Merleau-Ponty's definition, of 'flesh'. The 'two mirror arrangements of the seeing and the visible, the touching and the touched' are exemplified by this new paradigm or figure (Merleau-Ponty 1968: 146). This is the figure who looks as she is seen and touches herself seeing, in a gesture of mirroring that is mirrored back (re-mirrored) by the spectator who (in reverse now) is seen as she looks and sees herself touching. The Madam Satan figure, touching herself seeing, is seeing out from behind her costume, and to wear this design is without a doubt to touch oneself seeing. But it is a privileged position – the wearing of the Adrian design in this film. Only one actress gets to wear this dress which was tailor-made for her body. The wearing/seeing dialectic in which to wear is to see is to wear is strong, however, and recalls Sobchack who asserts that in relation to the cinematic image, the sighted body is always 'implicated' (Sobchak 1992: 133). It remains a crucial question in this phenomenology of film, as to whether or not this body is just anybody.

Two embodiments, the costume and the film. Two overlapping embodiments. But how and where? First, as flesh. Flesh, the stuff of the coiling visible in Merleau-Ponty and flesh as the screen itself in Sobchack, the flesh that is the material that 'allows perceptive activity' and that is unlike the flesh of the lived-body (Sobchack 1992: 211). What, then, do we do with the representation of flesh that so often defines the body of the female? And is the screen the flesh that is over this flesh or that which is under it? Adrian's costume reminds us of the ratio of flesh to fabric that is often the principle informing the design of the evening gown in this period. The Madam Satan dress works on the principle of reveal/conceal that is articulated in the film narrative as a discourse on the exposure of naked flesh. Jimmy's single word response to Trixie's question: 'How do you like my costume?' is 'overexposed' and it is this overexposure that reveals the scar that gives her away when another suitor identifies the intimately placed mark. Angela's concealment of her identity encourages her husband to commit adultery with her – his own wife. On the purely visual level, the costume's play on under- and overexposure of Kay Johnson's body repeats the problematic of the film negative, as the light and dark parts exchange places in the positive print that is the antithesis of the negative. The seduction sequences themselves are such pure play on light and shade, circle and square, that they verge on the cubism of Fernand Leger's *Ballet Méchanique* (1924). In fact, the seduction *mise-en-scène* could be classified with the

Salvador Dalì nightmare sequences in Alfred Hitchcock's *Spellbound* (1945) as among the more unforgettable outbreaks of modernism within the classical realist text in the history of Hollywood. In this, the set decor is of a piece with the dress, an aspiration toward unity of design principle that is so striking in some of the art deco films of this period. So the dress, intricately choreographed in the scene in which Angela the temptress dances provocatively with her errant husband, entertains the eye by creating abstract shadow patterns against the night sky backdrop as the zeppelin floats above the city. The dress summarizes the *mise-en-scène*: abstraction and surprise, texture and angle, starkness and whimsy. But in this *mise-en-scène*, more than anything it is the flesh in relation to the dress, this pattern of reveal/conceal, that dominates. And it dominates because of the way that the two distinctly different bodies move: the film's body and the body it 'presents'.

Cinematic movement is the function of the film's body (Sobchack 1992: 207). The film produces movement but in Sobchack is also seen to 'present' movement (Sobchack 1992: 226). Here, perhaps, a variation on camera movement and subject movement. What is important for our purposes is to note that among the types of movement presented by the embodiment that is the film is the movement of the Madam Satan dress itself. The dress moves and is moved: the train flapping in the wind as Angela parachutes to the ground, the glint of the trim tracing this movement. The strength of this particular Adrian design is its movement versatility, its exemplification of the costume that could only be worn to be photographed and is never properly worn but is rather hung and stuck on the actress who becomes something like a moving mannequin. Like Adrian's bugle-beaded red costume from *The Bride Wore Red* (1937), the Madam Satan dress is an impossible dress that one could only wear standing up, its movement restriction actually a mode of producing the silhouette, form, and shape. In fact, one could say that the *mise-en-scène* of this film was written by means of the sartorial shaping of human flesh. In this respect, the architecture of the gown itself is perhaps as important as the movement it allows.

Architecturally, the Madam Satan gown is not a dress. It is a creative solution to a difficult semiotic problem: how to render a volcano in fabric, or better, how to translate the literal volcano into the seductive female on metaphoric fire. Interestingly, the difference between Adrian's sketch and its realization in concrete fashion terms hints at the difficulty of this particular exercise, a commutation in which the substitutes broadly announce their status as stand-ins (Figure 10.4). The incongruity between the naturalistic erupting volcano and Adrian's fantasy rendering produces the humour in this exemplification of the masked ball costume genre. The costume falls so short of naturalistic reality that part of its fascination is the very impossibility of the project. The almost ridiculous aspiration (woman as volcano) is further confirmed by the sketch that represents the tendency toward literalization unchecked. Further, in the sketch, Adrian demonstrates his apparent disinterest in practical costume solutions as well as his signature indifference to the hard facts of the female form. The flaming forearms must be produced as black batwing-like gloves. One could also object to the tiny 'v' shapes that stand in for the foot, and a further improbability: the woman's breasts are both enveloped in flames and held up by them. Perhaps most intriguing in this comparison between drawing and realization, is the technology of nude soufflé, the flesh-coloured fabric

Figure 10.4   Gilbert Adrian costume sketch for *Madam Satan*. Courtesy of the
Academy of Motion Picture Arts & Sciences.

to which the dark, curling flame shapes are sewn on the bodice as well as the back
of the gown, producing the image of the naked body born out of the cone of the
volcano (See Figure 10.5). It is the long swath of nude soufflé run from her neck
past her hip to upper thigh in front and down to the small of her back on the
reverse side that produces the image of nakedness, helped along by the fact that
in this pre-production code film, Kay Johnson would not have been wearing underwear. Thus the architectural design feat is to produce the dress that looks like no
dress at all. (Angela's husband Bob later calls the dress 'outrageous' and the 'most
indecent thing I ever saw'.) Studio publicists must have been concerned, for in
some of the publicity images for the film, the photographs of the Madam Satan
dress have been touched up to create an illusion of opaque fabric in the places
where flesh showed through in the Adrian version, creating what appears to be an
entirely new dress design sketched over the original.

   Once again, I want to stress that this is not just a costume, that it is as much
a frame as a dress, the support for the illusion that Madam Satan is wearing nothing
but flames. ('She is on fire.') However, like many illusions, it is only partially
successful. Like cinematic illusionism, the flowing gown gives the impression of
being of a piece and neither cut up nor sewn, even suggesting that there are no
seams in this costume. But the viewer is curious about its construction, particu-

Figure 10.5   Gilbert Adrian design for *Madam Satan*. Courtesy of the Academy
of Motion Picture Arts & Sciences.

larly since this is a dress that has been literally sliced open up the front in such a
way that the viewer is invited to see into it, to observe the shape of the actress's
breasts under the cut-out flame figures. And so it is that this unusual dress invites
the spectator to imagine it from the inside out (as worn) as well as from the
outside in (as seen), epitomizing the synaesthetic circularity of the touching that
reaches over the seeing.

Inasmuch as the Madam Satan costume is at once a visible body that sees, it
represents the coiling of the tactile over the ocular (the seen touched and the
touched seen), illustrating what it might be like to touch seeing. And given that
to wear is to see is to wear, to touch seeing is to wear seeing. Our principle is
symmetrical. The actress who can be seen to wear seeing is mirrored by the spectator who is in the position to see wearing. In so far as the film body presents the
moving body and because the architecture of the dress succeeds in its illusion,
because the flesh of the film overlaps with the flesh framed by the film, the costumed
figure can be said to 'wear the film'. To wear the film is to move seeing, to reveal
and conceal through the patterning of light and shade. To wear the film seeing is
to see moving, to touch it where it moves. To see the film is to wear the film.

Notes

1   See my 'Costume and narrative: how dress tells the woman's story' (Gaines 1991: 195) in which I discuss the criticism of Adrian's designs as 'too up for the down moments'. Further, George Cukor's remark that if a costume 'knocked your eye out' it wasn't good for the scene or for the entire film, is meant as representative of the kind of discourse around costume that circulated during the years of Adrian's tenure at MGM. In retrospect, I would characterize this articulation as ambivalent, particularly coming from the director who was associated with such costume excess films as *The Women* (1939). In giving voice to this dominant Hollywood discourse (which played down costume all the while secretly relishing it), my co-author and I were describing this unmistakable discourse from the period. However, our own work should not be taken as advocating this approach to classical costume constraint and here we are definitely connoisseurs of the aesthetic of costume 'for its own sake'.

2   Here I want to avoid giving the impression that phenomenology is completely new as an approach to film. Emphasis on the renewed interest in recent years should now be at the expense of forgetting the debt of earlier theorists such as André Bazin and even the early Christian Metz. For an overview, see Sobchack (1992: ch. 1).

3   Merleau-Ponty has not been immune to criticism from feminism (see Sobchack 1992: 148–58 for an overview of the feminist critiques of phenomenology).

4   This was during the period in which, after his original affiliation with Famous Players-Lasky (later Paramount), DeMille left his own DeMille Studio to make three films for MGM. Of the three – *Madam Satan* (1930), the third version of *The Squaw Man* (1931), and *Dynamite* (1929) – only *Dynamite* made money. After the short stint at MGM, he returned to Paramount Publix where studio heads Jesse Lasky and Adolph Zukor were being repositioned in yet another power struggle (Higashi 1994: 200). As a kind of dress rehearsal for *Madam Satan*, *Dynamite* employed many of the same creative personnel.

5   Jeanie Macpherson was Cecil B. DeMille's main scenarist from around 1914 to 1930. DeMille's liason with her as well as with actress Julia Faye was well known at the time (Higashi 1985: 7).

6   In his autobiography, DeMille awards himself a place in history *vis à vis* the Code, aligning himself with its decisions and recalling that at the time *Madam Satan* was produced he was president of the West Coast chapter of the Motion Picture Producers' Association. Seeming to congratulate himself that the Production Code was based on the Ten Commandments, he says of *Madam Satan*: 'from Mount Sinai to Madam Satan may seem a long leap; it illustrates points about the Seventh Commandment in its clear statement of the fundamental laws of marriage . . . [that is the] need to help each other to keep the law' (DeMille 1959: 299–300). To clarify the history of the Production Code, it is important to recall that there were really two phases of censorship. The first beginning in 1930, involving industry self-censorship, and the later in 1934, a tightening move in response to pressure from the Catholic Church and other religious organizations who spearheaded the Legion of Decency campaign. The new censorship office, the Production Code Administration, directed by Joseph I. Breen, was given significantly more control over the content of films (Black 1994: 2).

I would not want to give the impression here that censorship is a concept that is particularly important in film theory. In my own considerations of this function, I have relied on a more Foucauldian understanding of the way censorship produces the proliferation of desires (see Staiger 1991: 224).

7   Richard Dyer has identified the cultural contradiction in the expectation that women be both sexy and innocent, as exemplified by his discussion of the Marilyn Monroe image (1998: 129–31).

8   I have elsewhere discussed this question of the importance of the pro-sex moment in the history of the Second Wave of feminism (see Gaines 1995). More recently, feminists have begun to return to sexuality studies with fresh eyes. See, for instance, Laura Kipnis on adultery (Kipnis 1998).

9   Rick Altman, for instance, discusses the way the narrative and the number represent two opposed realms and, as in the backstage musical, the performance represents an escape from the problems that surface only in the tough reality part of the film (Altman 1987).

10 Art deco has become an umbrella concept. First coined in 1966 in Paris at a retrospective of the 1925 Paris Exposition, the term has been used in reference to 1920s modernism, streamline moderne, Bauhaus, and even Russian constructivism. If we follow the current usage of art historians, then *Madam Satan* (1930), because it falls into the period from the 1925 Expo to the early 1930s, would be understood as art deco, whereas art from the mid- to late 1930s would be considered art moderne or streamline moderne (Mandelbaum and Myers 1985: 4).

11 It is important to note that although Cedric Gibbons, whose credits at MGM from 1917 to 155 numbered 1,500, was head of the design department, this did not necessarily mean that he was responsible for the designing itself (see Mandelbaum and Myers 1985: 22).

12 Robert LaVine credits DeMille in the Paramount years for getting Adolph Zukor to secure the renowned designer Paul Iribe from Paris to work with Gloria Swanson. (He had worked earlier as assistant to the important Paul Poiret.) Although he also says that Iribe was brought back to work on other films such as *Madam Satan*, this is not confirmed in other sources (LaVine 1980: 16–17).

13 There are also implications that Adrian and Leisen were lovers at one point. Chierichetti, in an author's note says: 'Leisen told me he once traveled from Los Angeles to New York in a stateroom on a train with his costume designing protégé Gilbert Adrian. Adrian woke him up in the middle of the night by tickling his nose with a feather and Leisen's raised eyebrows conveyed to me the idea that he and Adrian subsequently had sex' (1995: 7). Elsewhere I go into much further detail about the relationship between the gay male designer and the camp aesthetic and even stress the importance of the relationship between the gay designer and the lesbian director (Gaines 1992).

14 See Basten (1980: 29) for more on the history of the short-lived, two-strip Technicolor process.

15 I am indebted to David Chierichetti for suggesting that I consider Gilbert Adrian in the context of a group of other artists in these early years.

16 Merleau-Ponty, in *The Visible and the Invisible* (1968: 138), thus elaborates this interpenetration: 'My body as a visible thing is contained within the full spectacle. My seeing body subtends this visible body, and all the visibles with it. There is reciprocal insertion and intertwining of one in the other.'

17 The reference here is to Laura Mulvey's 'Visual pleasure and narrative cinema', which has been reprinted countless times since it first appeared and has been widely used in disciplines outside film studies.

18   Here I follow Stella Bruzzi, who has argued that female dress is not necessarily
      'for men'. Her suggestion that fetishization has the potential to 'de-eroticize' is
      a provocative new development in feminist studies (Bruzzi 1997: 24).

References

Affron, C. and Affron, M.J. (1995) *Sets in Motion: Art Direction and Film Narrative*, New
      Brunswick: Rutgers University Press.
Altman, R. (1987) *The American Film Musical*, Bloomington: Indiana University Press.
Basten, F. (1980) *Glorious Technicolor: The Movies Magic Rainbow*, South Brunswick, New
      York: A.S. Barnes.
Berry, S. (2000) *Screen Style: Fashion and Femininity in 1930s Hollywood*, Minneapolis:
      University of Minnesota Press.
Black, G. (1994) *Hollywood Censored*, Cambridge: Cambridge University Press.
Bruzzi, S. (1997) *Undressing Cinema: Clothing and Identity in the Movies*, London:
      Routledge.
Chierichetti, D. (1976) *Hollywood Costume Design*, New York: Harmony Books.
—— (1995) *Mitchell Leisen: Hollywood Director*, Los Angeles: Photoventures Press.
DeMille, C.B. (1959) *Autobiography*, ed. D. Hague, Englewood Cliffs: Prentice-Hall.
Dyer, R. (1998) *Stars*, London: British Film Institute.
Gaines, J.M. (1991) 'Costume and narrative: how dress tells the woman's story, ' in
      in J.M. Gaines and C. Herzog (eds), *Fabrications: Costume and the Female Body*,
      New York: Routledge/American Film Institute, 180–211.
—— (1992) 'Dorothy Arzner's trousers', *Jump Cut*, 36: 88–98.
—— (1995) 'Feminist heterosexuality and its politically incorrect pleasures', *Critical
      Inquiry* 2 (1): 382–410.
Gaines, J.M. and Herzog, C. (eds) (1991a) *Fabrications: Costume and the Female Body*,
      New York: Routledge/American Film Institute.
—— (1991b) 'Puffed sleeves before teatime: Joan Crawford, Adrian, and women
      audiences', in C. Gledhill (ed.), *Stardom: Industries of Desire*, London: Routledge/
      British Film Institute, 24–33.
Grant, B. (ed.) (1995) *The Genre Reader II*, Austin: University of Texas Press.
Higashi, S. (1985) *Cecil B. DeMille: A Guide to References and Resources*, Boston: G.K.
      Hall.
—— (1994) *Cecil B. DeMille and American Culture: The Silent Era*, Berkeley: University
      of California.
Kipnis, Laura (1998) 'Adultery', *Critical Inquiry*, Winter 24 (2): 289–327.
LaVine, W.R. (1980) *In a Glamorous Fashion: the Fabulous Years of Hollywood Costume
      Design,* New York: Charles Scribner.
Mandelbaum, H. and Myers, E. (1985) *Screen Deco*, New York: St Martin's Press.
Merleau-Ponty, M. (1968) *The Visible and the Invisible*, trans. Alphonso Lingis, Evanston,
      Ill.: Northwestern University Press.
Mulvey, L. (1975) 'Visual pleasure and narrative cinema', *Screen* 16 (3): 6–18.
Sobchack, V. (1992) *The Address of the Eye: A Phenomenology of Film Experience*, Princeton:
      Princeton University Press.
—— (1995) '"Surge and splendor": a phenomenology of the Hollywood historical
      epic', in Grant, B.K. (ed.), *The Genre Reader II*, Austin: University of Texas
      Press, 280–307.

Stacey, J. (1994) *Star Gazing: Hollywood Cinema and Female Spectatorship*, London: Routledge.

Staiger, J. (1991) 'Self-regulation and the classical Hollywood cinema', *Journal of Dramatic Theory and Criticism* 6 (1): 221–31.

Chapter 11

Rachel Dwyer

BOMBAY ISHTYLE

Meraa juutaa hai jaapaanii
Yeh patluun inglistaanii
Sar pe laal topii ruusii
Phir bhii dil hai hindustaanii

My shoes are Japanese,
My trousers are English,
On my head a Russian hat,
But my heart remains Indian.
(Shailendra, from Raj Kapoor's *Shri 420*, 1955)

Introduction

THE BRITISH COLONIAL GOVERNMENT set itself the task of measuring, mapping and categorising India, to produce knowledges of its empire. Region, religion, caste and gender were primary ways of classifying the imperial subjects, images of whom were produced in paintings and photographs. While the dubious science of anthropometry formed part of this analysis, the dominant features were clothing, ornamentation and dress: facial hair, headdresses, jewellery, veils, trousers and ways of draping cloth, made these people clearly distinct from one another. Drawings, prints and photographs, many published in books, models and toys, attest to the scale of this enterprise, while the deepness of its roots was seen in one of the great arenas for standardised costume – the army uniform. Indian soldiers were required to wear versions of their regional dress as interpreted by the British, notably the Sikh soldiers who wore full *khalsa* dress as their everyday uniform.

In the nineteenth century, many of the urban elites began to wear British clothing, at least for formal wear. However, beginning with the *swadeshi* campaign, a boycott of British goods, in 1905 and further impelled by Gandhi's adoption of Indian clothing on his return to India in 1915, the nationalist leaders, almost all of middle-class and elite origins, abandoned the Western dress that had symbolised their social status. While Nehru began to wear the Muslim *sherwani-pyjama* (a knee-length coat with 'Nehru' collar with tight trousers), many of the dominant Congress Party adopted a new uniform of *khadi* (homespun cloth), which came to represent the ideals of their movement. The meaning of *khadi* was exemplified in the person of Gandhi, who, leaving his caste and Western dress aside, began to wear only the simplest loin-cloth which he himself had spun, creating a form of clothing available to all. (However, his near nakedness was unacceptable to many who opted for the more generous covering afforded by the *kurta-pyjama* [long, loose shirt and trousers].) It was largely through his skill in manipulating symbols that Gandhi extended the base of nationalism from the elite to the masses, and clothing was among his principal successes. Fifty years after independence, *khadi* remains the Congress uniform for men, although it has come to be mocked in Indian cinema, where the *khadi*-clad politician is usually associated with civic corruption.

Early Indian cinema

Cinema is one of India's most vibrant cultural products and a major industry: now nearly 100 years old, it makes the largest number of films in the world, at its peak estimated at around 800 a year, that is, a quarter of the total number made in the world. India's 13,000 cinema halls have a daily audience of around 15 million and many of these films are hugely popular overseas, in Europe and North America, not only among the South Asian diaspora, but loved by much of the rest of the world. While its budgets are small in comparison with Hollywood, the sheer volume of employment (around 1 million people) and taxation (around $100 million) which it generates means that its economic importance is considerable. India has not one, but several cinemas which can be distinguished in terms of film-making (methods of production and distribution), the film text (technical and stylistic features, language) and by the film's reception (by the audience and by critics). I concentrate here on the Hindi-Urdu popular or commercial cinema made in Bombay (Mumbai), the most widely seen cinema in India, among the South Asian diaspora, which is popular in many other areas of Asia, Africa and the former Soviet Union.

Cinema in India began on 7 July 1896 with a screening of the Lumière Brothers' Cinematograph films in Bombay. The first entirely Indian made film, *Raja Harischandra*, produced and directed by D.G. Phalke, was released in 1913. Phalke was inspired to make a film about Indian mythology after seeing a film on the life of Christ: 'While the life of Christ was rolling fast before my eyes, I was mentally visualizing the gods Shri Krishna, Shri Ramachandra. . . . Could we, the sons of India, ever be able to see Indian images on the screen?'[1] Although Phalke did not record how he chose to dress his characters for this mythological and quasi-historical film, he drew on a wide range of scopic regimes and visual culture, including the emerging modern 'Indian' art, chromolithography and photography, religious processions and performances, folk and urban theatre, and foreign cinema.[2] (Footage of Phalke at work shows him dressed in entirely Western clothes.) This new hybrid created by Phalke became the norm immediately in three of Indian cinema's popular genres: the mythological, the devotional (films about the lives of saints) and the historical. However, other genres, grouped loosely as 'social films', set in contemporary India, had to address the question of costume anew.

Hollywood films were the most popular movies in India during the silent era, and Indian film-makers emulated their style of glamour, make-up, hairstyles and some of the men's clothing, although dress, especially for women, was largely local. For example, in Bombay most of the studios during the silent period were Gujarati, and a Gujarati *mise-en-scène* is the norm during this time, whereas in Calcutta, a Bengali style emerged. The evolution of an Oriental style in Hollywood, in the films of Valentino, the Douglas Fairbanks and the Cecil B. DeMille biblical epics, introduced a way of depicting the East that was often incorporated into the Indian films.

The coming of sound with the first Indian talkie, *Alam Ara* (1931), soon divided the cinema audiences. Bombay became the centre of the Hindi-Urdu film, using a form of spoken language that was understood at varying levels over much of north India, which was later to become the (contested) national language of India, as well as that of Pakistan. Although Bombay lies outside the Hindi-Urdu speaking area, Urdu was one of the major languages of the city, largely because of its sizeable Muslim population. By the 1930s, Urdu was becoming associated as the language of Muslims and the language of culture of Punjabi Hindus and Muslims, hence the high proportion of personnel in the film industry from these communities from the 1930s. Their language skills were in demand particularly as writers of dialogues and lyrics of the all-important songs, which were based in the Urdu lyric tradition, and as actors whose accents would be acceptable in north India. This further developed the cinema's hybrid nature, allowing it to evolve a style that would be seen as national, while the other cinemas began to be regarded as local or regional. Although the Partition of 1947 resulted in a decline of the Muslim population of Bombay, it saw the arrival of a number of displaced Punjabis, some of whom had worked in the Lahore film industry. The majority of these Punjabi refugees settled in Delhi, which replaced Lahore as their cultural capital, although their nostalgia for their homeland of Punjab never waned. Their north Indian style is of critical importance, for the Punjabis have continued to dominate the industry as producers, directors and male actors, inscribing their culture as the national culture of India.

The studio system in Bombay collapsed during the late 1940s with the emergence of the independent producer, often a Punjabi. They saw the star as the critical box-office factor, and began to chase the big stars for their movies, who in turn hiked their prices to unheard of levels, eating up most of the producers' budgets. The stars represented idealised forms of masculinity and femininity whose images circulated in film, photographs, gossip magazines, advertising and movie publicity to become national icons. The operation of a star system was further reinforced by the films' specific requirements of their heroes and heroines, allowing the stars to appear as ideals, rather than natural, psychologically plausible characters.

The norm of the film's characters is urban, upper-caste, north Indian Hindu. Characters from other religions, other regions and castes, are portrayed as 'others', their style of speech, their attitudes and their clothes are seen as humorous or exotic. It is not surprising then that the male stars have been mostly Punjabis, whose height and fair skin approximated ideals of physical beauty, an association reinforced by the British who created a myth of Punjabis as a martial race, notable for a predominance of 'masculine' qualities. The great stars of the 1950s were Dilip Kumar (Pathan), Dev Anand and Raj Kapoor (both Punjabi). All three were tall, light-skinned (Raj Kapoor even having blue eyes), slim, and lightly built; their bodies, which were barely shown, were not particularly muscular or athletic.

Reversing the nationalists' search for 'Indian' clothes, the post-independence period saw Western clothes becoming the norm again for the urban, upper-caste male, with 'Indian' clothes reserved for wearing in the home (the vest or *kurta* worn with a *lungi* or sarong) or for strictly formal occasions (the *bandgala* [lounge suit with 'Nehru' collar] or the *sherwani-pyjama*). The male star in the film wore largely Western clothes or stage-costumes for performances within the text loosely based on Western clothes. In the 1950s, Dilip Kumar, who took the widest range of roles, wore 'Indian' clothes in historicals and in films where he played a village character; Dev Anand's urbane style, including quiffed hair, earned him the tag of Debonair Dev; while Raj Kapoor identified with the 'man in the street', or famously adopted the Chaplin-look.

Case study: *Shri 420* ('The Fraudster', 1955)

The verse *Mere juutaa hai japaanii,* given above, exemplifies this film's constant references to clothing. The hero of this film, Raj (Kapoor), comes to the city from the village, his belongings in a bag on a stick like Dick Whittington. He is dressed like Charlie Chaplin, but Raj's clothes are too small for him rather than too large. The real crook of the film, Seth Dharamanand, wears a *dhoti* (sarong-type garment) and proudly announces he wears homespun cloth, to which Raj replies by repeating the chorus from his song above. Raj falls in love with a teacher, Vidya ('Knowledge'), played by Nargis ('Mother India'), who dresses modestly in a sari and who has had to pawn her bangles because of her family's poverty. She says he looks like a clown, to which he replies he is only wearing a mask, a recurrent theme in the film. Raj finds work in the Jai Bharat ('Victory to India') laundry, where he begins to borrow clothes. Returning laundry, he meets the vamp Maya ('Delusion'), who wears fish-tail gowns and smokes cigarettes in a holder. She persuades him to dress in black-tie and accompany her into a world of vice. He takes a sari to Vidya to wear to a party, where she is humiliated by Maya who accuses her of wearing the clothes she gave to the laundry. Raj becomes a conman and property developer, adapting to his new role as easily as changing his clothes, but when he becomes aware of how the homeless will suffer, he abandons this new world, and, with Vidya, sets off to a brave new world.

The modern male star

Shammi Kapoor, 'India's Elvis', brought in the Western casual look in the early 1960s, followed by a number of softer male stars, such as Rajesh Khanna, who adopted the boy-next-door, fashionable look. The greatest superstar of the Hindi movie, Amitabh Bachchan, very tall, thin and not conventionally handsome, set the trend which has continued to the present, for 'cool', for outrageously stylish, high-fashion for men, often eclipsing his female co-stars. Bachchan's representation was fetishistic, his first appearance usually being of his feet, in black leather, the camera slowly panning up his long body. His legs, which were used in the movie as weapons of destruction, were clad in the widest flares or bell-bottoms, often impossibly white. Bachchan often appeared in a vest, but his body was for action, not offered for display, while his fashionable clothing became his trade-mark. His roles were often masochistic, and he often died at the end of the film, in the arms of his buddy or his mother.

The action films of the 1980s saw the macho action-hero dominating the screen, who was replaced by the short, muscular hero with a pretty face in the 1990s. Salman Khan, one of the most popular, takes his shirt off several times in each movie to show his pumped body, frequently wearing gym-gear and American sportswear. The suburban look of Tommy Hilfiger and Nike trainers is the informal uniform, while the men wear double-breasted suits for formal occasions, showing that men's clothes as ever are designed for careers and leisure, although they are supplemented by a number of fancy outfits for the song and dance numbers.

One striking feature of the male stars, is that unlike most men under 40 in India, they are clean-shaven. Most young men wear moustaches, a sign of mascu-linity which has become proverbial: 'muuch nahin: kooch nahin' ('No moustache: no nothing'), although older men often shave. Only elite and middle class men and *jankhas* ('effeminate men') shave, a rule followed by the movie star even when playing a street guy.[3] This fashion is not followed by many movie fans, who do follow the fashion for haircuts seen in the movies. Just as the quiff and the crew-cut were fashionable in the 1960s, and the sideburns in the 1970s, the 1980s saw the rise in popularity of the short front and long back cut. In *Viraasat* ('Inheritance', 1997), the hero, Anil Kapoor, returns from the USA with long hair and designer stubble, but cuts his hair and grows a moustache after his father dies and he takes up his role as village landlord. Hairweaves and wigs are popular among the balding stars; beards are for intellectuals, baddies, Muslims and Sikhs.

The male at the end of the twentieth century is groomed, maintained, exer-cised, dressed in the clothes of consumer society, an object of his own narcissistic gaze while inviting the gaze of the audience on his often fragmented body in a way traditionally associated with women.

Female stars and female attire

Unlike the men, the female stars who play north Indian, upper-caste women, are often from other regions of India. Some of the top stars are Bengali, Maharashtrian and south Indian stars, most of whom are upper-caste (usually Brahmins), who are said to be lighter-skinned than the lower castes. The body shape of the stars has changed radically over the years. The early stars had big breasts and big hips, were often large, and rarely athletic. Although some were always slim, the 1990s has seen the star becoming increasingly thin, some even having a worked-out/gym look. Within films a different look is required for different types of heroine: the former models used for modern, Westernised women; the more curvaceous women for more traditional roles.

In patriarchal society, women's bodies belong not to themselves but to the patriarchal male. At the most extreme, couples do not meet before marriage, the family deciding on the choice of partner, where beauty is less important than the moral qualities of the bride and her family. In such families, the older members decide which clothes are important for the young woman; any attempts by her to exercise free choice can become a source of family conflict.[4] These rules have been relaxed considerably in recent years, although the romance followed by family negotiation, as seen in most films, glosses over many important issues in the ownership of women's bodies. This appropriation of the woman's body is further complicated in the cinema, where the woman is the object of gaze.[5] This being looked-at nature is reinforced in Indian cinema through the operation of the star system, which creates an image of glamour rather than a realistic depiction of women and may be further complicated by Indian scopic regimes.

The relationship between women's clothes in movies and in real life is not one of reflection, but the codes of cinema require clothing to fill particular semiotic functions, which I attempt to trace below. The sari is seen as the national dress of Indian women, but this is only a recent fashion. A taboo on wearing stitched clothing has meant that a variety of methods of draping different lengths of cloth have been practised in India for at least two millennia. Today there are two main lengths. One is the 9-yard sari, worn only by married women, now rarely by the upper-classes, being mostly restricted to the lower castes and classes. Instead the norm now is for the 6-yard sari, now found worn in two major styles, the so-called Gujarati-style, where the *pallu* (the patterned end) is worn draped over the front, but the sari is usually worn with the *pallu* hanging loose over the left shoulder. The saris themselves are very different, a whole variety of weaves, prints, borders, and textiles are made, many regionally marked. A widely understood grammar of wearing the sari exists, with specific occasions requiring different saris according to season, time of day and degree of formality. For example, a wedding in north India requires, if at all possible, a costly Banarsi sari (heavy silk, with *zari*, or gold thread), while any religious occasion demands a silk sari (some orthodox women still wear a silk sari for eating everyday). The choice of colour is also important: red, green and yellow are the choice for festive occasions; widows traditionally wear white or pale colours; black is not a popular colour, being worn largely as a Western fashion.

The sari is often seen as an eternal and unchanging dress, but not only is its widespread popularity and standardisation of drape recent, but it is as subject to changes in fashion as any other article of clothing. One year may see a trend for heavy weaves, followed by cottons with hand-painted designs, followed by chamois silks.

The *choli* (blouse) became popular in the nineteenth century, and has now become almost mandatory, with many styles of sari, including a blouse-piece in their fabric. Otherwise blouses are usually made in a fabric that matches the sari, but fashion sometimes demands a contrasting colour. Blouse styles change radically from season to season as regards degree of tightness, length of sleeves, shape of neckline and so on. Versions drawing on ethnic backless bodices, traditionally worn with skirts and veils, have remained popular among the more daring for several years, while other ethnic styles, such as the jacket-style, retain popularity as a heavily embroidered or beaded item, worn with a plain sari.

The sari is the orthodox form of Hindu dress, some temples refusing admission to women not wearing them. Other communities also wear saris, the Parsis preferring small borders and sleeveless blouses, although many wear Western clothes. Women in some Goan Christian communities also wear saris; they can be distinguished from others who only wear Western-style dresses. Some Muslims also wear saris, but it is increasingly regarded as an inappropriate form of dress for Muslims in terms of its association with Hindus and because it shows the body and the arms. Among Muslims the sari is largely confined to weddings, although the *sherara* (a long culotte-type skirt) is usually preferred for the bride. It is widely regarded as a particularly chaste dress,[6] despite its frequent showing of the midriff and cleavage and is regarded as the appropriate dress for women at home and at work.

Saris are important social markers as regards age, marital status and class beyond the mere fact of cost and maintenance of the garment. Saris are rarely worn by young, middle-class and elite women, except for formal occasions. These groups prefer Western-style clothes or the *salwar-khamees*. However, after marriage (see below), and especially after having children, the sari becomes increasingly popular, especially for middle-class girls who live with their in-laws.

The sari is heavily laden with cultural meanings of nostalgia, tradition, womanhood, nationalism and social status, the full range of which are developed in the Hindi movie. Mothers or mother-figures always wear traditional, sober saris. In older movies which contrasted the heroine with the vamp, the heroine almost invariably wore a sari as an emblem of her chastity and goodness. In recent years, the unmarried heroine, who is usually a teenager, wears Western clothes before marriage but changes into *salwar-khamees*, but more often the sari, after marriage. In one of the big hit films of 1999, *Biwi no 1* ('Wife Number 1', dir. David Dhawan), the wife and mother of two always wears a sari, although her rival wears Western-style fashion. When the wife decides to produce a portfolio of modelling shots, her unfaithful husband is outraged at her wearing the same clothes as his mistress, reminding her that she is married and the mother of two. The top film of 1998, *Kuch kuch hota hai* ('Something Happens', dir. Karan Johar), has the two young heroines both in Western clothes. The hero fails to realise he is in love with one, since she is his best friend and a tomboy and so marries the other. When they meet again after he has been widowed, the heroine has begun to wear a sari and the hero soon realises that he is in love with her after all. However, the heroine who is not a mother often wears a type of sari and sari blouse which would be unacceptable for a mother, most often a transparent chiffon sari. Thus the sari becomes a meeting point for the maternal and the erotic in the movies, a conjunction supported at many other points in the movie.

The *salwar khamees* or Punjabi suit, originally a Muslim dress which became popular in north-west India, has also become a national and even international dress made popular by Jemima Khan and Diana, Princess of Wales. The suit comprises trousers (loose *salwars* or tight *churidars*), a long shirt and a scarf. The materials and colours may be the same, contrasting or mixed. The stylistic variations are endless, the scarf alone carrying a range of meanings according to whether it is used to cover the head, the breasts or worn like a Western scarf.

This outfit is a popular option for younger women, being easy to maintain, comfortable modest in covering the limbs and even the head. Although Punjabi women and Muslim women of all ages and statuses wear this outfit, it has recently become the standard dress of many college girls, unmarried women, and working women. Regarded by many as a frumpy outfit, it has been glamorised largely within films. The films of the 1950s show it as a typically modest outfit, but the 1960s saw the introduction of the tight-fitting top, further glamorised by Sadhana's introduction of the *churidar* trousers in *Waqt* ('Time', dir. Yash Chopra, 1965). One of the most striking uses of the *salwar-khamees* in recent films was Manish Malhotra's outfits for *Dil to pagal hai* ('The Heart is Mad', dir. Yash Chopra, 1997), where they were worn by the 'traditional' heroine in contrast to the other heroine, the DKNY, sportswear-clad, best friend of the hero. Once again, the hero falls in love with the girl in Indian clothes, who only wears a sari for a dream sequence, her Western clothes being for holidays in Europe, nightwear and stage performances. In this film, the outfits have much transparent material, are cleavage-revealing and the scarf is used more for pictures of billowing material than for modesty.

While ethnic chic is a fashion associated with activists and intellectuals, although very popular at the beginning of the 1990s, the Hindi film has invented its own version of the village belle, the *gaon ki chori*, who usually appears in a skimpy version of a regional costume, with knee-length skirts and backless shirts. While some village women may show their backs, they do not show their legs and they usually cover their heads, if not their faces. Madhuri Dixit wore such an outfit in *Khalnayak* ('The Villain', dir. Subhash Ghai, 1993), for her infamous song *Choli ke peeche kya hai?* ('What's under my blouse?'). The heroine had her head covered for the opening of the song, but the camera's close-ups on her heaving breasts and her naked back dispelled any suggestion of modesty, despite her protest that her heart was in her blouse.

While many Hindu women veil themselves in the presence of older men, by covering their heads and sometimes their faces, the veil is largely associated with Islam. This is true in the films also, and it plays important roles in some genres, such as the Muslim social and in the courtesan films. In the Muslim social, the hero catches a glimpse of the heroine, but her veil (the full *burqa*) often leads to a tragedy of mistaken identity. In the courtesan film, the heroine may wear a veil, but her honour is not that of wider society. In *Pakeezah* ('The Pure One', dir. Kamal Amrohi, 1971), the heroine clings on to her honour (hence the name her beloved gives her, Pakeezah), accusing men of trying to rob her of it by removing her veil in her famous song *Inhe logon neo* ('Ask these people'). The veil is erotically charged by the idea of concealing and revealing, and numerous songs in Hindi films are about veils, even if the heroine no longer wears one herself.

Women in India took longer than men to wear Western clothes, which have remained restricted to certain groups. They are worn as uniforms by schoolchildren, nurses, police and so on. Certain communities, some Christian and some Parsis in particular, wear Western clothes, although the form varies from an old-fashioned 'frock' to the latest Western designers. They are also popular with modern, urban women, although mostly before marriage and children. Western clothes are seen as more sexy and more 'fun' by young urbanites, but it is felt that one has to have a good figure (i.e. be slim), in order to wear them. Western designer clothes, in particular sports clothes, cannot be purchased in India, adding a further element of glamour to their acquisition. In film, the sports clothes display their labels proudly, *Kuch kuch hota hai*, being emblazed with the Tommy Hilfiger and DKNY labels.

Perhaps more important than outerwear in India has been the impact of two parts of the Western wardrobe, namely underwear and nightwear. The bra, the strange erotic and chaste garment of the twentieth century, has been widely adopted in India at all levels, and although not shown directly in films, the recent fashion for the truss-like Wonderbra has been all too obvious. In India, one traditionally slept in one's day clothes, but now kaftans have become popular, along with a rise in Western-style nightdress/pyjamas or T-shirt with a gown. Nightdresses are often featured in movies, to provide a certain eroticism, in particular as preludes to songs of the 'dream sequence' type.

Although one rarely sees a nude or naked body in a Hindi film, there have been debates around this, sparked largely by a scene in Shekhar Kapur's *Bandit Queen* (1992), in which the heroine is stripped by her attackers. This proved a major attraction for some viewers, although the Hindi cinema's elaborate codes of eroticism are far more sensual than the presentation of a humiliated woman. The Hindi cinema's most controversial outfit is the swimsuit, popular in the films of Raj Kapoor, whether his 1951 *Awaara* ('The Vagabond') or his 1973 *Bobby*, but deemed unsuitable for a round in the Miss World contest held in India in 1996. However, this is far less erotic than Raj Kapoor's other device, the wet sari, which not only reveals the heroine's body to the point of nudity, but is also associated with the erotic mood of the rainy season and of sweat. It also allows a display of the parts of the body which are seen as most erotic in India, namely the trunk – breasts, waist, hips and the back. The limbs, although they must be covered, are not seen as particularly erotic but can be vulgar when displayed.

The film heroine's body must look good in all these outfits, for she is likely to be required to wear the whole range in a film. This totality of costume is similar to the fashion show, in which the Indian designer is required to present all types of clothes, from Western to a whole range of Indian (especially the wedding outfits), although she/he may specialise in one. These designers have come to world notice since their clothes were worn by several of the Oscar nominees in 1999. Many of these designers provide costumes for the films, sometimes being consultants for particular stars, and dressing these stars in their off-screen appearances.

Heroines wear a huge number of outfits in the films, not just for the occasions required by the script, but for song sequences, which may be fantasies allowing them to wear otherwise incongruous outfits, and nearly all of which often involve many changes of clothes. These changes of clothes have many functions, partly as the modern idea of romance is based around consumption, whether dress, travel or going out, but also to show the heroine's adaptability – both physical (in looking good in a variety of styles) and in her ability to don or remove clothes as masquerade.

Jewellery, hairstyles and bridal attire

Jewellery is not just a means of displaying wealth in India. Traditionally, a woman's only legal possessions comprise the jewellery which she is given on marriage, which never belongs to her husband. It has a whole range of religious meanings, as the mark of a married woman (see below), to astrological functions, notably in the use of stones as protection against malign planetary activity. A woman will almost always have her ears pierced in childhood; nose piercing is common among certain groups. Hair also has complex significance,[7] ranging from the erotic (long, loose hair), to the ordered (long, groomed, and tied back for women) and hair is covered for specific occasions. A whole variety of haircuts are also seen, often shown by using wigs in films, from sleek bobs to big, fluffy hairstyles. However, hair colour is usually a natural black, although streaks have become increasingly popular. Women never show any bodily hair in India, and for middle-class and elite women the beauty parlour is an important monthly visit, where the hair is trimmed, the face is tweezed, threaded, waxed and bleached, while exposed limbs and under-arms are waxed. Pubic hair is not shown on films, but is often removed for religious as much as cosmetic reasons. Manicures and pedicures are fairly commonplace, the latter being popular since the foot is regularly exposed in the standard footwear of the open sandal, from the flat to the platform. The foot is further decorated by anklets and married women of many communities wear toe rings on their second toe. Moreover, feet are decorated with henna at the time of family weddings. Given the ritual impurity of feet and footwear, and their consequent importance as a sign of submission, it is not surprising that many films exhibit foot fetishism to varying degrees.[8]

While Hindu men undergo various ritual initiations, a woman's only initiation is the rite of marriage. The importance of marriage in Indian society is hard to overestimate, whether in terms of religion, economics or society. This important event requires a particular form of dress for all participants, with the most costly clothes required. The spectacle of the wedding as much as its romantic associations have meant that most films incorporate a wedding, requiring the most sumptuous clothes and jewellery. Traditionally, the woman changes the way she dresses after marriage, to appear as the auspicious married woman (*saubhagyavati*), a form of dress in which she will be cremated if she dies before her husband, or which she will have to abandon on his death. The colour and form of outfit the bride wears vary between communities and regions. Given the Punjabi atmosphere of the Hindi movies, the dominant representation is of the Punjabi wedding, with many people referring to a 'Yash Chopra wedding', after the creator of the look in some of India's most popular romantic films. The film will show the bride in full red for her wedding dress, the groom with his face covered with flowers, wearing a turban.

After marriage the bride may or may not wear the complete outfit of the *saubhagyavati*, but will often begin wearing colourful saris, more jewellery, and always a *bindi* (auspicious mark on the forehead). The jewellery is an essential part of dress, marking wealth, religion and region. The absolute minimum will be earrings, a necklace (often the black-beads of the *mangalsutra*, or wedding necklace), bangles (red glass are traditional in north India as a minimum, but gold is worn when it can be afforded), and a ring (seemingly incorporated from the Christian tradition, but worn on any finger). The absence of jewellery is always a statement, usually of widowhood, but it has also been adopted by feminists and other activists, although some may wear some oxidised silver 'folk' jewellery rather than more costly gold.

Cross-dressing, film and fashion

A popular comic feature of Hindi movies is to have a hero appearing dressed as a woman. This is usually at some point in the story when the hero needs to pass himself off as a woman although it can be purely for comic effect. One of the most popular songs of the 1990s, *Didi tera dewar divana* ('Sister, your husband's brother is crazy'), from *Hum aapke hain kaun . . .!* ('What am I to you?'), involved men and women cross-dressing. The women of the house hold a six-month pregnancy ritual to ensure the birth of a son. This is attended only by women, so the men of the house try to get in by pretending to be women. The younger son dresses as a pregnant woman, while a female friend dresses as the younger son. This is seen as being pure fun and part of the happiness of the celebration, perhaps because the transgression of gender boundaries brings a further intimacy.

The purple dress worn by the heroine in this song is indicative of the wider effect of the fashion from the Hindi films. This dress became one of the most copied items from the films of recent years, with girls asking their tailors to make them this outfit for family functions. This is part of a trend which has been wide-spread since the earlier days of movies and observed in many other societies, such as by the female fans of Hollywood stars in the West, who copy clothes, hair-styles and make-up, along with gestures and ways of speaking.[9] Madhuri Dixit was the undisputed top box-office star when this outfit became widely copied, her popularity augmented by the phenomenal success of the film and in turn this partic-ular song. She is one of several stars who have always been top trendsetters. In the 1960s, Sadhana cut a fringe in her hair to conceal her broad forehead and this became a style copied by girls all over India. For the 1965 *Waqt* ('Time', dir. Yash Chopra), Sadhana wore *churidars*, which had previously been considered 'Muslim' dress and created a fashion for these which has endured for decades. Rekha, the star who transformed and monitored her appearance more than any other star, set a whole range of fashion styles from the clothes she herself selected for her film roles, such as 'the Rekha blouse' and her styles of make up.

Film has also been an important way of introducing Western dress styles to an Indian audience. Nowadays, the heroine can wear Western clothes, which no longer carry any negative implications, but represent a facet of her character, namely her ability to be at home anywhere in the world. Western clothes now mark her as modern and cosmopolitan but will usually form only a part of her wardrobe, and as in earlier films, all married women wear some form of Indian clothes and usually have long hair. The clothes worn by the stars in films are often from labels favoured by the new generation of film stars and film directors, who wear these clothes in their everyday lives as a variety of fashion statements: casu-ally informal yet markers of foreign travel and wealth; sporty as part of their new

healthy lifestyle; American sports clothes rather than European formal or eccen-
tric clothes mark the norms of the so-called transnational or global fashion.

The fashion of films has interacted with the growing consumer culture of 1990s
India, which has also seen an explosion of new media (cable and satellite television, the magazine industry, advertising, sex & shopping novels). Television in
particular has drawn heavily on film for its programmes, circulating images from
the film to ever wider audiences. The best-selling magazines are film-based and
show images of the film stars in film costumes and other outfits. Youth programmes
and Western television have increased awareness of Western designers, although
their clothes, perfumes and accessories still have to be purchased overseas, often
on shopping trips to Dubai or holidays in the US, UK or Australia. Many of the
Indian middle classes and elites have family settled abroad; this can create a circulation of goods through visits to India and overseas, allowing new forms of style
to emerge.

Fashion flows move in multiple directions as the Western clothes in film and
the clothes worn by the film personnel interact with 'street fashion', often originating in African American communities and subsequently adopted and adapted by
many British Asians. India has continued to remain a source for 'hippy chic' (and
not so chic) as well as for luxury items such as pashmina shawls, silks and jewellery.
The mixture of Indian and Western clothes remains eclectic: Indian jewellery may
be mixed with Western clothes, the *bindi* or vermilion mark has mutated into
stick-on motifs embellished with eye and lip pencil designs; the shawl can be worn
with formal Western clothing; sari-borders are found on jeans; toe-rings and nose-
rings are associated with Western 'grungy' styles.

The Hindi movie has eschewed these hybrid trends, the stars wearing a totally
different style in different scenes and even displaying several changes of style within
a song sequence. These outfits remain separate like in the Miss World contest,
with its evening wear round and its swimsuit round among others. The cinema
continues its fondness for songs about clothes even though it has changed its lyrics
from 'My red muslin scarf flew up in the breeze' (*Barsaat* 'Rain', dir. Raj Kapoor,
1949) to 'Even my shirt is sexy, even my trousers are sexy' (*Khuddar* 'Self-respect'
dir. Iqbal Durrani, 1994).

Notes

1   Quoted in Rajadhyaksha 1987: 48.
2   Rajadhyaksha 1987.
3   See Cohen 1995: 292.
4   See Tarlo 1996 on a major family dispute when a village woman wanted to wear
    a cardigan.
5   Mulvey 1975.
6   This respectability was demonstrated in a *cause célèbre* in Bombay in the early
    1990s, when two women dressed in saris were refused entrance to a nightclub
    on the grounds of dress, in that it would make people feel uncomfortable. See
    Loomba 1997 for details.
7   Olivelle 1998.

8   Uberoi 1997.
9   See Stacey 1993.

References

Cohen, Lawrence (1995) 'The pleasures of castration: the postoperative status of hijras, jankhas and academics', in P. Abramson and S.D. Pinkerton (eds) *Sexual Nature, Sexual Culture*, Chicago: University of Chicago Press, 276–304.

Dwyer, Rachel (2000) *All You Want Is Money, All You Need Is Love: Sex and Romance in Modern India*, London: Cassell.

Loomba, Ania (1997) 'The long and saggy sari', in *Women: a Cultural Review*. (Special issue: *Independent India*, guest editor A. Roy.) Oxford: Oxford University Press, 8 (3): 278–92.

Mulvey, Laura (1975) 'Visual pleasure and narrative cinema', *Screen*, 16 (3): 6–18.

Olivelle, Patrick (1998) 'Hair and society: social significance of hair in South Asian traditions' in A. Hitebeitel and B.D. Miller (eds) *Hair: Its Power and Meaning in Asian Cultures*, New York: State University of New York Press, 11–49.

Rajadhyaksha, Ashish (1987) 'The Phalke era: conflict of traditional form and modern technology', *Journal of Arts and Ideas*, 14 (5): 47–75.

Stacey, Jackie (1993) *Star Gazing: Hollywood Cinema and Female Spectatorship*, London: Routledge.

Tarlo, Emma (1996) *Clothing Matters: Dress and Identity in India*, London: Hurst & Co.

Uberoi, Patricia (1997) 'Dharma and desire, freedom and destiny: rescripting the man–woman relationship in popular Hindi cinema' in M. Thapar (ed.) *Embodiment: Essays on Gender and Identity*, Delhi: Oxford University Press, 145–71.

Chapter 12

Catherine Constable

MAKING UP THE TRUTH
On lies, lipstick and Friedrich Nietzsche

THIS CHAPTER WILL EXPLORE the philosophical implications of
make-up by examining different theoretical constructions of the relation
between the mask and the face and analysing their presentation within three films
that star Marlene Dietrich. The common-sense view of make-up defines cosmetics
as a mask which covers over the true face. This basic model of opposition between
the mask and the face can be seen to feed into a dialectical model of appearances
versus truth that begins with Plato and later informs the work of contemporary
feminist theorists such as Luce Irigaray and Laura Mulvey. The second section will
explore an alternative construction of make-up as a mask which signals the absence
of the face, beginning with Joan Riviere and ending with Jacques Derrida. Stephen
Heath connects Riviere's conception of masquerade with Nietzsche's view of femininity. In contrast, I will argue that Nietzsche and Baudrillard can be seen to offer
a more complex appreciation of make-up and the final section will focus on their
analyses of the mask as that which foregrounds its own constructedness and therefore possesses a kind of truthfulness.

Mask versus face

The film *Destry Rides Again* (1939; dir. G. Marshall) contains a good example of
the commonsense construction of make-up as a mask that covers over the true
face. It occurs at the end of a heated exchange between the deputy sheriff, Tom
Destry, played by James Stewart, and Frenchy, the chanteuse at the local saloon,
who is played by Marlene Dietrich. Tom has visited Frenchy at home in order to
investigate some rigged poker games and finds her *en déshabillé*. Frenchy's bottle
blonde hair falls in ruffled corkscrew curls and her heavy make-up, complete with

beauty spot, is still evident from the night before. As he is leaving, Tom comments 'I don't think you're half as bad as you make out.' Frenchy replies, 'Never mind what I am' and looks down, away from him, playing with the bow on her negligee. The gesture draws attention to her flimsy clothing and dishevelled appearance, clearly indicating her sexual availability and experience. Tom continues to stare at her adding, 'I bet you've got kind of a lovely face underneath all that paint there.' His right hand reaches for the corner of her mouth and he smears the lipstick down the side of her face with his thumb. Taking her into his arms he says, 'Why don't you wipe it off some day and have a good look?'

Tom's comments serve to present Frenchy's make-up as a superficial layer of badness that can be wiped away to reveal the true goodness underneath. His comments pit the mask of make-up against the truth of the face and clearly feed into the common-sense definition of the mask as a deceptive surface. Interestingly, Tom's remarks also play around with the usual formula in that the vamp's mask is said to hide her goodness rather than covering over her manipulative, devious nature.[1] Importantly, the opposition between the mask and the face can be seen to support and sustain a series of further oppositions, notably: outside/inside, surface/depth, appearance/truth and appearance/reality.

The congruence of the opposition mask/face and appearance/truth demonstrates that the common-sense appreciation of make-up feeds into a philosophical tradition that can be traced back to Plato. Plato's famous myth of the cave constructs appearance as the inverse of truth and reality, setting out the role of appearances in a purely negative way. The prisoners in the cave are said to be chained so that they do nothing but stare at the shadow play on the wall opposite to them. Their lack of movement means that they mistake the flickering images for reality. The philosopher is the one who breaks free of the chains and recognises that the shadows are cast by objects, which are, in their turn, being held by people walking up and down a pathway in front of a fire. The philosopher clambers up the pathway and out of the cave into the dazzling sunlight. The sun is said to symbolise the form of the good, a figure of eternal truth. The fire is a symbol of the world of phenomena. Phenomena are ephemeral copies of the forms, just as the fire is a pale imitation of the sun. The shadow play on the cave wall symbolises the realm of mere appearances. These images have no relation to the world of the forms because they are not caused by the sun. They are distorted views of phenomena that prevent people from searching for the truth. The cave analogy sets up a particular model of absolute truth, the eternal world of the forms, and positions appearances as its negation (Plato 1987: 316–25).

Plato's dialectical definition of appearances can also be seen to denigrate them as fake, superficial and trivial. In the mid-eighteenth century this pejorative definition takes on explicitly gendered overtones because woman comes to be positioned as the paradigm of the beautiful (Dijkstra 1986: 143). Woman's association with appearance and adornment means that she too can be denigrated for being superficial and trivial. This link between woman and appearance has been challenged by feminist philosophers who argue that it constitutes a patriarchal definition of woman. Luce Irigaray reads the literary and cultural constructions of woman as a beautiful surface as a series of figures which entrap woman within a patriarchal disguise:

Stifled beneath all those eulogistic or denigratory metaphors, she is
unable to unpick the seams of her disguise and indeed takes a certain
pleasure in them, even gilding the lily further at times. Yet ever more
hemmed in, cathected by tropes, how could she articulate any sound
from beneath this cheap chivalric finery? How find a voice, make a choice
strong enough, subtle enough to cut through those layers of ornamental
style, that decorative sepulchre, where even her breath is lost.

(Irigaray 1985: 142–3)

In this passage the decorative layers of appearance are seen to possess a deadening
weight in that they stifle the true woman underneath. Irigaray's argument can be
seen to remain within the dialectical model in that she pits the mask of patriarchy
against the true face of woman. The opposition pivots an image that is imposed
by another against one that is self-generated. Irigaray argues that the masks of
woman are carefully defined. Woman appears as a shallow surface in order to
secure man's positioning as the personification of depth and truth. For Irigaray,
the solution is to strip away woman's masks and thus end the patriarchal staging
that simply supports man's self-definition.

I am no longer the lining to your coat, your – faithful – understudy.
. . . You had fashioned me into a mirror but I have dipped that mirror
in the waters of oblivion – that you call life. . . . I have washed off
your masks and make-up, scrubbed away your multicoloured projections and designs, stripped off your veils and wraps that hid the shame
of your nudity. I have even had to scrape my woman's flesh clean of
the insignia and marks you had etched upon it.

(Irigaray 1991: 4)

Irigaray's position is a complex and poetic vision of the first-wave feminist
rejection of fashion and make-up as demeaning forms of objectification. Her critique
can be compared to Laura Mulvey's famous analysis of the representation of woman
as spectacle in Hollywood cinema. Mulvey argues that classical Hollywood cinema
typically presents woman as the object of the gaze. In contrast to the male characters, who are active and control the space of the action, female characters are
said to appear in moments of narrative stasis and are therefore defined as passive
(Mulvey 1989: 19–20). This mode of displaying female characters means that they
lack the range of qualities exhibited by male protagonists, simply connoting 'to-
be-looked-at-ness' (Mulvey 1989: 19). Mulvey argues that the representation of
woman as visual object supports a scopic regime that plays out the desires of the
male spectator. The glamorised presentation of female stars is said to offer the
male spectator a means of disavowing his knowledge of castration. The female star
thus functions as a fetish, an erotic object which reassures and restores the male
spectator. Mulvey argues that Dietrich's highly glamorised presentation in the films
of the von Sternberg cycle is a good example of fetishistic scopophilia (Mulvey
1989: 21–3).

For both Irigaray and Mulvey, the cultural construction of femininity as pure
appearance is a patriarchal strategy in which woman's role as visual object simply

serves to support the male subject. Both theorists therefore reject the masks of make-up and argue that the true face of woman is to be found elsewhere. This face is said to exist beyond patriarchal representation. For Irigaray, it is a question of radically 'disconcerting' the specular economy to map a different kind of space.

> But perhaps through this specular surface which sustains discourse is to be found not the void of nothingness but the dazzle of multifaceted speleology. A scintillating and incandescent concavity, of language also, that threatens to set fire to fetish-objects and gilded eyes.
>
> (Irigaray 1985: 143)

Mulvey argues in favour of alternative cinema as a space in which women could create their own modes of representation.

While the possibility of uncovering/creating a pure space beyond patriarchy is an enormously seductive vision of the power of art, it remains a problematic one. This is because the rigid dichotomy between the mask and the true face suggests that art is either purely patriarchal or revolutionary and therefore negates the ways in which texts operate as sites of contesting meaning. Moreover, Mulvey's sense of the revolutionary potential of film-making in the 1970s cannot be straight-forwardly shared today. The pervasive quality of female icons, such as Dietrich, suggests that their images need to be considered as more than a parade of patri-archal masks. This re/assessment requires a more complex appreciation of the mask itself.

The absent face

The take-up of Riviere's famous definition of femininity as masquerade within psychoanalysis and cultural studies offers a different conception of the mask as a surface which reflects the absence of a true face. Riviere's article, 'Womanliness as masquerade', offers an analysis of the behaviour of a female academic. After lecturing competently and professionally, the academic would immediately begin to flirt with male members of her audience. Riviere argues that the lecturer's show of intellectual competence constitutes a display of her possession of the father's penis. The woman therefore goes on to flirt with male members of the audience in order to avoid retribution for castrating the father. She assumes the mask of femininity, presenting herself as deferential and dependent, as a means of appeasing the audience and abolishing her own guilt (Riviere 1986: 36–7). Riviere famously refuses to distinguish between 'true' womanliness and the lecturer's exaggerated coquettishness, thus suggesting that all femininity is performance or masquerade (Riviere 1986: 38).

Stephen Heath's famous analysis of Riviere's concept of masquerade connects her work with both Lacan and Nietzsche. On the Lacanian model, the construc-tion of gender is seen to involve masquerade. Lacan outlines two positions: that of having or being the phallus. Both modes of psychic organisation can never be fully realised because they revolve around the subject's construction within language, an order which is always already foreign to the subject itself. While both subject positions are therefore fake to some extent, Lacan goes on to define the position of being the phallus as an empty masquerade:

> [I]n order to be the phallus, that is to say, the signifier of the desire of the Other, – woman will reject an essential part of her femininity, notably all its aspects through masquerade. It is for what she is not that she expects to be desired as well as loved.
>
> (Lacan 1982: 84)

Heath argues that Lacan presents alienation as 'a structural condition of being a woman' which operates over and above the alienation that is the basis of all subjectivity (Heath 1986: 54).

Heath also demonstrates that the definition of femininity as an act raises epistemological issues. He quotes from Nietzsche's writing in *The Gay Science*:

> Reflect on the whole history of women: do they not have to be first of all and above all else actresses? Listen to physicians who have hypnotized women; finally, love them – let yourself be 'hypnotized by them'! What is always the end result? That they 'put on something' even when they take off everything.
>
> (Nietzsche 1974: 317)

According to Nietzsche, woman's participation in the sexual act is just an act, thus the moment that woman should be 'laid bare', utterly revealed to her lover, she is still concealed. Mary Ann Doane picks up on the paradoxical definition of the moment of revelation that is also a mode of concealment in her later discussion of femininity as masquerade.[2]

> While the organisation of vision in the cinema pivots around the representation of woman – she is always aligned with the quality of to-be-looked-at-ness – it is also the case that in her attraction to the male subject she confounds the relation between the visible and the knowable.
>
> (Doane 1991: 46)

Doane reads the glamorous presentation of Concha Perez in *The Devil is a Woman* (dir. J. von Sternberg, 1935) as an example of femininity as masquerade. Dietrich plays Concha, a *femme fatale* whose numerous liaisons are traced across the film. One of her lovers, Antonio, is wanted by the police and therefore uses his carnival costume as a disguise. Doane contrasts the diegetic motivation for Antonio's disguises with Concha's flamboyant use of costume, arguing that her masks and veils 'take on the arbitrariness of the signifier in their apparent lack of any motivation beyond that of pure exhibitionism, pure show' (Doane 1991: 49).

A detailed analysis of the carnival sequence at the beginning of *The Devil is a Woman* will substantiate Doane's argument. Concha first appears wearing a dark filigree mask over her eyes as well as a dark, loose-weave mantilla decorated with pompoms which hangs down over her mask. Her hair is parted and a single kiss-

curl is visible in the centre of her forehead. Her mouth is unveiled and emphasised by dark lipstick. The presentation of her hair and lipstick show that the face
beneath the mask and mantilla can be viewed as yet another mask. Later on in the
sequence, Concha eludes Antonio, peering out from behind wrought-iron lattice-
work gates and glimpsing him from an upstairs window where she is framed by
lace curtains. The profusion of veils within the *mise-en-scène* can be seen to provide
a series of surplus surfaces that obliterate the concept of depth.

> The veil . . . reduces all to a surface which is more or less removed,
> more or less accessible. . . . Thus, the woman comes to confound the
> topology of Western metaphysics, its organisation of space and hierar-
> chisation of depth and surface in their relation to truth.
>
> (Doane 1991: 56)

Woman's construction as a play of surfaces can be seen to negate the dialectical
model of surface/depth, appearance/truth and appearance/reality that is set out
by Plato. The play of the veils marks the annihilation of the concepts of absolute
truth and an external, objective real. Derrida follows Nietzsche in arguing that the
moment of loss can be traced back to the rise of Kantian Idealism.

> Now the stories start. Distance – woman – averts truth – the philoso-
> pher. She bestows the idea. And the idea withdraws, becomes
> transcendent, inaccessible, seductive. It beckons from afar (*in die Ferne*).
> Its veils float in the distance. The dream of death begins. It is woman.
>
> (Derrida 1979: 87–9)

In this quote, the figure of woman represents the illusion of the possibility of truth;
she is the seductive veil that is always just out of reach. Ultimately, woman comes
to symbolise the impossibility of attaining the truth, she is the veil that is forever
suspended and cannot be lifted. Derrida's definition of woman as the 'untruth of
truth' is also used to convey the impossibility of attaining the one true meaning
of any text (Derrida 1979: 51).

The problematic aspects of Derrida's model are demonstrated at the end of
The Devil is a Woman. Concha's final encounter with Don Pasquale takes place in
a hospital. He has been badly injured in a dual over her. Concha wears a black
hat with a black brim that is angled down to the left of her face. The hat is covered
by a black mantilla which falls down over her shoulders, veiling her face and neck.
She is also shrouded by a black lace shawl that is draped across her shoulders.
Concha's costume indicates her status as Don Pasquale's dream of death. However,
the triple veiling also has the function of highlighting the impossibility of understanding her motives and desires, a reading that is substantiated by the considerable
critical dispute over the nature of Concha's feelings in this scene (Studlar 1988:
163). Derrida's model can therefore be seen to offer *the* meaning of woman's
masquerade. Woman's masks and veils are the means by which she lures the
reader/spectator into the project of attempting to decipher her.

The psychoanalytic and philosophical analyses of woman's masquerade as
demonstrative of the absence of a true face can be seen to have some radical

potential in that they undermine the dialectical structure in which woman's relation to appearance automatically results in her denigration. However, by defining
the mask in terms of absence, Riviere, Lacan and Derrida all pivot their definitions of masquerade around a moment of loss or negation. This is important because
the mask comes to be defined as emblematic of that loss and is therefore still
haunted by the traditional categories of truth and authenticity that it is used to
destabilise.

Masks of truth

While Baudrillard and Nietzsche both offer definitions of femininity as absence, I
want to focus on other aspects of their discussions of woman and truth in order
to generate a more productive model for thinking about the meaning of make-up.
In *Seduction*, the heavy make-up worn by the seductress is said to constitute 'a
solution by excess' (Baudrillard 1990: 15). For Baudrillard, the seductress draws
attention to her own fakeness and therefore becomes a figure of innocence:

> How can one mistake this 'exceeding of nature' for a vulgar camou-
> flaging of truth? Only falsehoods can alienate the truth, but make-up
> is not false, or else . . . it is falser than falsehood and so recovers a
> kind of superior innocence.
>
> (Baudrillard 1990: 94)

Baudrillard's analysis of the seductress's face as a mask that foregrounds its
own constructedness and therefore possesses a kind of truthfulness borrows from
Nietzsche. In *Twilight of the Idols*, Nietzsche criticises Plato's conception of objective truth, arguing that the world of the forms, the figures of eternal truth, must
be read as a fable. For Nietzsche, the fable of the true world is created to uphold
a particular ethical system. The use of the sun to represent both truth and goodness in the myth of the cave clearly demonstrates this interrelation; revealing
objective truth to be nothing more than 'a moral-optical illusion' (Nietzsche 1971:
484). A fable is mistaken for 'the truth' when its fictionality is forgotten:

> What then is truth? A moveable host of metaphors, metonymies, and
> anthropomorphisms: in short, a sum of human relations which have
> been poetically and rhetorically intensified, transferred and embellished,
> and which, after long usage, seem to people to be fixed, canonical and
> binding. Truths are illusions which we have forgotten are illusions.
>
> (Nietzsche 1979: 84)

Nietzsche valorises art which foregrounds its metaphoricity. 'Thus art treats illusion
as illusion; therefore it does not wish to deceive; it is true' (Nietzsche 1979: 96).

The loss of any objective truth or reality is not seen as a descent into nihilism.
Rather than accepting the metaphors which have gained canonical status through
cultural repetition, Nietzsche argues that the subject must create his/her own fables
and metaphors in order to live:

there simply is no *true world*. Thus: a *perspectival appearance* whose origin lies in us (in so far as we continually *need* a narrower, abbreviated, simplified world).

— That it is a measure of strength to what extent we can admit to ourselves, without perishing, the merely *apparent* character, the necessity of lies.

(Nietzsche 1967: 14–15)

On this model the process of creating a perspective is what constructs the subject and the world. As a result, both the subject and the world have the status of fictions which are created through the metaphors underpinning the perspective. What is important is that these fictions are necessary, the lies enable the subject to exist at all.

Nietzsche's conception of the necessity of lies feeds back into his arguments about the truthful illusion. While the world and the subject are both seen to be fictional, Nietzsche is not arguing that these constructions can be totally changed from one moment to the next. On this model, the perspective that is created over time will become the 'truth' of the subject. While the subject is still a mask, a fictional construct, s/he is created through patterns of repetition that come to constitute his/her truth. This perspectival truth is a specific mode of seeing particular to the subject that is not to be confused with objectivity. 'There are many kinds of eyes. Even the sphinx has eyes – and consequently there are many kinds of "truths", and consequently there is no truth' (Nietzsche 1967: 291).

The concept of the truthful illusion is illustrated in the film *Shanghai Express* (1932; dir. J. von Sternberg). A notorious prostitute, Shanghai Lily (Dietrich), has a series of encounters with her ex-fiancé, Captain 'Doc' Harvey (Clive Brook) during the long train journey. The character of Shanghai Lily is introduced as the subject of gossip and scandal and Lily's first confrontation with Doc shows her willingness to play up to her image. She is wearing a black dress, lavishly trimmed with black feathers and her posture within the train compartment, hand on hip, clearly serves to confront Doc with her new-found profession. Later, in the scene on the observation deck, Doc reveals that he still has the watch that she gave him. There is a portrait of Madeleine, from the time before she became the notorious Lily, in the lid of the watch. Madeleine's long hair and fuller features clearly contrast with Lily's fashionable bob and hollow cheekbones. The image sustains a series of contrasts between Madeleine and Lily, such as past/present and innocence/experience. As Doc begins to reminisce about his past regrets looking back into the darkness from the observation platform, it is clear that the image of Madeleine also functions as the representation of his ideal bourgeois wife. Lily's sceptical expression is visible from behind Doc's back and as he turns to face her he is forced to see the woman that she has become and therefore to acknowledge the gulf between his dream of Madeleine and Shanghai Lily.

The role of Shanghai Lily can therefore be seen to enable Lily to escape the fate of becoming Madeleine. The mask of Lily, which is clearly acted up for Doc's benefit at key moments across the film, therefore gains a kind of authenticity because it constitutes a refusal to become the woman of his dreams and later becomes a refusal to be held accountable to him. Thus in *Shanghai Express*, the masquerade of being Lily is repeatedly used to enable the female protagonist to escape patriarchy in so far as she escapes the roles of wife and mother that would have been imposed upon her. Importantly, the mask of glamour operates as more than a mere facade; its repeated mobilisation comes to constitute the truth of Lily's perspective.

The Nietzschean analysis of the mask as truthful illusion can therefore be seen to open up a more sophisticated way of analysing glamorous images of women in film texts. Once the mask is not viewed as purely patriarchal, or merely indicative of the absence of the truth, it becomes a construct that can be mobilised in a variety of ways. This means that the mask can be seen to generate a wide variety of possible meanings rather than simply and reductively indicating its status as 'untruth' or the 'untruth of truth'. Furthermore, the analysis of the mask as truthful clearly has important implications for feminism in that it radically destabilises the definition of glamour as objectification. This creates a space for thinking about the radical potential of the power to hold the gaze and the ways in which that power might be instantiated by a range of female icons. Thus, Nietzsche and Shanghai Lily can be seen to open up new possibilities for feminism and film theory.

Notes

1   See Janey Place's discussion of the ways in which the masks of the *femme fatale* serve to construct her as duplicitous (Place 1978: 47–8).

2   Doane discusses Nietzsche's conception of truth, paralleling his views with those of Lacan and Derrida (Doane 1991: 56–62).

References

Baudrillard, J. (1990) *Seduction*, trans. B. Singer, London: Macmillan Education.

Derrida, J. (1979) *Spurs: Nietzsche's Styles*, trans. B. Harlow, Chicago: University of Chicago Press.

Dijkstra, B. (1986) *Idols of Perversity: Fantasies of Feminine Evil in Fin-de-siècle Culture*, Oxford: Oxford University Press.

Doane, M. A. (1991) *Femmes Fatales*, London: Routledge.

Heath, S. (1986) 'Joan Riviere and the masquerade', in V. Burgin, J. Donald and C. Kaplan (eds) *Formations of Fantasy*, London: Methuen.

Irigaray, L. (1985) *Speculum of the Other Woman*, trans. G.C. Gill, Icatha, NY: Cornell University Press.

——— (1991) *Marine Lover of Friedrich Nietzsche*, trans. G.C. Gill, New York: Columbia University Press.

Lacan, J. (1982) 'The meaning of the phallus' in J. Mitchell and J. Rose (eds and trans.) *Female Sexuality: Jacques Lacan and the Ecole Freudienne*, London: Macmillan.

Mulvey, L. (1989) 'Visual pleasure and narrative cinema', in L. Mulvey, *Visual and Other Pleasures*, London: Macmillan.

Nietzsche, F. (1967) *The Will to Power*, trans. W. Kaufmann, New York: Vintage Books.

——— (1971) *Twilight of the Idols* in W. Kaufmann (ed. and trans.) *The Portable Nietzsche*, London: Chatto & Windus.

—— (1974) *The Gay Science*, trans. W. Kaufmann, New York: Vintage Books.

—— (1979) 'On truth and lies in a non-moral sense' in D. Breazeale (ed. and trans.) *Philosophy and Truth: Selections from Nietzsche's Notebooks of the Early 1870s*, New Jersey and London: Humanities Press International.

Place, J. (1978) 'Women in film noir' in E. Ann Kaplan (ed.) *Women in Film Noir*, London: BFI.

Plato (1987) *The Republic*, trans. D. Lee, London: Penguin.

Riviere, J. (1986) 'Womanliness as masquerade', in V. Burgin, J. Donald and C. Kaplan (eds) *Formations of Fantasy*, London: Methuen.

Studlar, G. (1988) *In the Realm of Pleasure: von Sternberg, Dietrich and the Masochistic Aesthetic*, Urbana and Chicago: University of Illinois Press.

Chapter 13

Edward Buscombe

CARY GRANT

IN *NORTH BY NORTHWEST* (1959) Cary Grant plays Roger Thornhill, a
smooth New York advertising man pursued by the police for a murder he didn't
commit. Escaping on a train he meets Eve Kendall, a seductive blonde who invites
him to her sleeping compartment. He can't believe his luck, unaware that she is a
spy, and takes it as a tribute to his good looks and charm. Locked in an embrace,
they trade compliments. He says she's a big girl, 'in all the right places'. She says
she ought to know more about him, besides the fact he's in advertising. 'What else
do you know?' he asks. 'You've got taste in clothes,' she replies. It's not the first
comment on his fashion sense. Earlier in the film, Thornhill meets the chief spy,
Philip Vandamm (James Mason), who praises him for being 'polished'. Vandamm
presents Thornhill to his henchman, Leonard (Martin Landau), who is subtly coded
as gay: 'Have you met our distinguished guest?' Leonard's eyes light up and he
responds with yet another compliment: 'He's a well-tailored one, isn't he?'

In his beautifully cut grey suit, matching grey silk tie, white shirt with discreet
cufflinks and shiny black shoes, Cary Grant's late-1950s elegance appeals to women,
straight men and gays. This is surely a priceless asset for a film star, the ability to
maximise the potential audience by being simultaneously an object of desire for
women, a role model for straight men, and either or both for gay men. Speaking
as a straight man, what seems to me especially admirable in Grant is his knack of
maintaining this elegance no matter what. Despite being shot at, rolled in the dirt
and doused with chemical fertiliser in the famous crop-dusting sequence of *North
by Northwest*, Grant returns to Chicago with his suit showing only the bare minimum
of wear and tear. Eve remarks that he'd better get it cleaned; 'You belong in a
stock yard looking like that.' Hardly; his tie is still perfectly knotted.[1]

It's not only his clothes, of course, that give Grant his style; it's the whole
ensemble. His movements are graceful; even running from a plane that's trying

to kill him, he still looks good. 'I find myself enjoying Grant's smooth stride and the sprinter's pump in his arms, chiefly because I can see that despite his age, he still runs beautifully,' writes James Naremore.[2] Later in the film we see him bare-chested, wearing only a towel. Despite being in his mid fifties when the film was made, he is still in good shape. Grant, of course, had been trained as an acrobat before he entered the movies, and he never lost his physical grace. But, though he could wear casual clothes or a uniform as well as any, what he did best was to wear a suit.

Appropriately, his father was a tailor's cutter. Grant took what might be considered, at least by straight, middle-class Englishmen of his generation, an inordinate, even prissy interest in the details of his clothes. Graham McCann in his excellent biography records that 'One of his long-suffering tailors said that he would measure the lapels of his jackets with a ruler, insisting on corrections if there was even a fraction of an inch between the angle of the cut and the lapel.'[3] Such fussiness may have contributed to the rumours that he was gay, rumours of which Grant himself was well aware.

> I've always tried to dress well. . . . I've enjoyed my success and I include in that success some relationships with very special women. If someone wants to say I'm gay, what can I do? I think it's probably been said about every man who's been known to do well with women. I don't let that sort of thing bother me.[4]

That suggests that men felt jealous of Grant, and perhaps some did. But much more common than envy, one would think, is admiration.

This admiration may owe much to a suspicion that the kind of aggressive masculinity which the cinema so often promotes, the kind we associate with Clark Gable and Gary Cooper, or more latterly with Mel Gibson or Bruce Willis, the rugged, hirsute, sweaty sort of manhood that spurns a neatly pressed trouser leg or crisp white shirt cuff, might not play so well indoors, where, in the movies at least, smart women are encountered. Grant is a conspicuous example of what can be achieved in that department by meticulous dressing, and the type of manhood that it implies. Cary Grant showed that being genteel, *soigné*, and well-mannered was an equally successful form of masculinity.

But looking good in a suit is not the same as being a stuffed shirt. Grant was always ready to lose his dignity in the cause of a funny scene. In *North by Northwest* he makes his escape from the train dressed in the ill-fitting borrowed uniform of a redcap, or porter. In the following scene he's obliged to shave with a miniature ladies' razor lent by Eve, and gets a funny look from a man at the next wash-basin. It's not easy to say exactly what the look means, but the implication is that only a man of dubious sexuality would use such an item. Grant was secure enough in his sexual identity to dress up in drag or have jokes made about his gender for most of Howard Hawks's *I Was a Male War Bride* (1949).

Grant made the occasional foray into the hyper-masculine world of the action film, convincingly enough in *Gunga Din* (1939) or *Only Angels Have Wings* (1939). But his outings in costume were mercifully few. It's impossible to imagine him in a Western. Cary Grant was nothing if not modern, and the lounge suit is, of course, the modern garment *par excellence*. It's adaptable to a variety of occasions, both business and leisure. It's classless, or at least relatively so; the plutocrat and the office worker wear the same uniform. The film star in the suit is dressed like the rest of us (men). Not that Grant is always suited; he could wear casual dress to great effect, relaxing in cravat and slacks in Hitchcock's *To Catch a Thief* (1955), where he plays a gentleman jewel thief retired to the south of France, a sort of Riviera Raffles. In *The Philadelphia Story* (1940) he's a rich socialite trying to woo back his estranged wife, Katharine Hepburn, who's planning to marry the *nouveau riche* owner of a coal mine, George Kittredge (John Howard). Kittredge is always stiff and awkward in his double-breasted suit, while Grant as C.K. Dexter Haven is relaxed, debonair and irresistible in sports jacket and slacks.

But if there is a certain egalitarianism about the suit, the superior elegance with which Grant wears one always gives him the edge. At the same time as being one of us, he's able to use his impeccable tailoring and the social confidence it imparts to put one over on others in a way which most of us can only envy. If there were any doubt that there are suits and then there are suits, look again at the crop-dusting scene in *North by Northwest*. A car approaches and deposits a man on the other side of the road. Grant approaches him. The man is wearing, in contrast to Grant's grey worsted, a cheap brown suit with a crumpled collar and an outsized hat (anticipating the trend, Grant seems to have abandoned head-wear early in the 1950s – or is it just that he's usually indoors?). The incongruity between the two men's clothes serves to emphasise how out of place Grant is, out on the prairie; yet at the same time it reinforces Grant's elegance and refine-ment. Elsewhere in the film, there are some good jokes which depend on the effortless sense of superiority which his tailoring seems to give him. When he is arrested by the police on a drunk-driving charge, he's allowed one phone call, which he makes to his mother. She wants to know the name of the policeman. 'Emile Klinger,' the officer replies. Grant starts to tell his mother the name, then does a double-take. 'Emile?' he says, with devastating condescension, as if to say, how could a mere policeman have such an exotic name?

Cary Grant retired at 62 with his looks still intact. He could have gone on, but doubtless he sensed styles of masculinity were changing along with fashion. To call someone 'a suit' has become an insult. Appropriately enough, he spent the rest of his professional life working for Fabergé, promoting a style of elegance he had done so much to define.

Notes

1   In fact, Grant had six identical suits made for *North By Northwest*.
2   James Naremore, *Acting in the Cinema*, Berkeley, University of California Press, 1988, 214. Naremore goes on: 'I have always been fascinated with Grant's socks, flashing elegantly from beneath the cuffs of his trousers as he dodges bullets from that low-flying plane. Some years ago, I was amused to discover that Raymond Durgnat had admitted to a similar preoccupation, and more recently Stuart Byron noticed the same detail. In 1985 Byron opened the *Village Voice*'s annual 'World's Most Difficult Film Trivia Quiz' with a multiple-choice question: 'In the crop-

dusting sequence of *North by Northwest*, the color of Cary Grant's socks is (a) blue, (b) orange, (c) red, (d) yellow.' (The correct choice is 'a', although for accuracy the socks ought to be described as bluish grey, in keeping with Roger O. Thornhill's darker grey suit and grey silk tie.)

3   Graham McCann, *Cary Grant: A Class Apart*, London, Fourth Estate, 1997, 178.
4   Ibid., 158.

Chapter 14

Stella Bruzzi

GRACE KELLY

IN 1962 ALFRED HITCHCOCK – whose direction of Grace Kelly in *Dial M For Murder* (1954), *Rear Window* (1954) and *To Catch a Thief* (1955) in effect created the Kelly mystique – commented:

> As for myself, I prefer a woman who does not display all of her sex at once – one whose attractions are not falling out in front of her. – It is important to distinguish between the big, bosomy blonde and the lady-like blonde with the touch of elegance, whose sex must be discovered.
> (Hitchcock cited in Gottlieb 1995: 95–6)

Clearly, Grace Kelly, in direct contrast to a Monroe or a Bardot, epitomised the latter category of blonde. Indeed, of Monroe and Bardot Hitchock, on another occasion, remarked: 'Poor Marilyn Monroe had sex written all over her face, and Brigitte Bardot isn't very subtle either' (Truffaut 1978: 278). An essential component of Kelly's allure for Hitchcock, then, was her ambivalent and subtle sexuality; that she appeared so demure, classy, sophisticated, untouchable and yet possessed a smouldering eroticism in a way that Audrey Hepburn did not. Hitchcock fetishised and utilised Kelly's duality. For *Rear Window*, he insisted upon twenty-seven takes of the close-up shot of her kissing James Stewart's forehead (and in addition shot an intentionally fetishistic close-up of her shoes that was never used). In *To Catch a Thief*, he said of the surprise on Cary Grant's face as it is Kelly who plants the first kiss purposefully on his lips that 'It was as though she'd unzipped Cary's fly' (Lacey 1997: 146; 177). Hitchcock knew he could get away with saucy and hardly over-subtle *double entendres* in *Thief* precisely because of the pervasive perception of Grace Kelly as 'pure'; he delighted, for example, in the incongruity of a classy dame asking the far more suspicious ex-cat burglar played by Cary Grant during their impromptu picnic 'Do you want a leg or a breast?'. *To Catch a Thief* becomes infected with this slightly puerile humour (which in turn works deliciously against the effortless suaveness of its stars) as in the sequence in which Kelly and Grant again kiss against a backdrop of intrusively over-active fireworks. Kelly's perfection is predicated upon her ability to sustain this duality; to be both sensuous and aloof, mysterious and straightforward, pure and sexy.

To continue with the comparison between Kelly and her bustier counterpart blondes, underpinning this suggestion of purity (itself an undoubted masquerade, for in private Kelly was credited with a prodigious romantic appetite) is a sense of naturalness. There is something contrived or manufactured about Marilyn, her metamorphosis from Norma Jean Baker into the 1950s girl of celluloid dreams so assiduously and consciously undertaken, her hair so bleached and her make-up showy, as if *who* Marilyn was mattered less than the way in which her image was to be received. For all the performative irony of *Gentlemen Prefer Blondes* (1953) or *Some Like It Hot* (1959), Monroe's flaunting of her assets implies a falsification or fragility (as the media has been wont to characterise it). Conversely, despite being associated with couture and refinement, Kelly projected an image that was always more 'natural'– one of the most beautiful images of Kelly is of her clearing her clothes off the MGM lot with her publicist just prior to her departure for Monaco and marriage to Rainier. Kelly is looking off camera, contemplative and not engrossed in pleasing our gaze at all, dressed in a casually tailored suit – slightly too ample as expensive clothes often are on the skinny – that's half hidden behind a voluminous screen gown. Like Audrey Hepburn, Kelly refused to wear falsies to pad herself out (thereby signalling the confidence to set trends rather than follow them) so her on-screen image was perceived to be an effortless extension of her real self. This has led to somewhat breathless assertions about her naturalness. Edith Head, for example, maintained, 'there was no pretense in her make-up or her clothes; she never dressed to attract attention; she never dressed like an actress; she dressed like Grace Kelly, and she was Grace Kelly' (Head and Ardmore 1959: 142–3), whilst Cary Grant said of her, 'Grace acted the way Johnny Weissmuller swam or Fred Astaire danced. She made it look easy' (Lacey 1997: 179). This fluid transition from woman to icon was an essential component of Kelly's appeal and lay at the root of Hitchcock's adoration. Conversely, the icons 'Monroe' or 'Rita Hayworth' were founded upon an unerasable split between their persona and their 'real' selves; in Monroe's case one can point to the fetishisation of her 'real' unhappiness or the masquerading of her 'real' intelligence; in the case of Hayworth, as she herself ruefully remarked, 'men went to bed with Gilda but woke up with me'. This cruel realisation is enacted in Welles's *The Lady from Shanghai* (1948), a noir in which the director transforms his then wife from voluptuous, red-haired siren to icy blonde, a version of femininity with which Hayworth appears totally ill at ease.

The Lady from Shanghai was made in 1948, and maybe was a sign of times changing. It might seem perverse to argue that it was Grace Kelly rather than Bardot, Monroe *et al.* who epitomised the 1950s, and yet, for many people (mainly women) it was. In large part this was her affinity with Dior's New Look, a style that Hollywood continued to adore long after the world (except perhaps the young British royals) had tired of it. The New Look ushered in a new femininity, and although the 1950s came to be seen as that most traditional of eras when men brought home the bacon to several children and a wife in an apron tending her mod cons, far more intriguing is the rich ambiguity of both the times and the femininity it spawned. Although I find it hard to agree with their conclusions, when both Elizabeth Wilson and Pam Cook focus on the New Look's androgyny (Wilson 1985: 46; Cook 1996: 58–9), perhaps what they're signalling is its complexity: that superficially the tight-bodied, small-waisted and full-skirted image might seem entirely compatible with a life of domesticity, no work and leisure but that it could equally well become the perfect masquerade for assertiveness and independence. Grace Kelly uses her femininity and concomitant intuition to dynamic effect in *Rear Window*, whilst Jane Wyman, condemned to far frumpier New Look gowns in *All That Heaven Allows* (1955), shocks her eminently shockable country club community by ensnaring hunky young gardener Rock Hudson. Furthermore, Kelly was associated specifically with fashion (as opposed to the more nebulous 'style') and had a Hermès bag named after her. This might seem an insignificant contribution to fashion by comparison with, say, Audrey Hepburn's tireless championing of Hubert de Givenchy and yet it remains a deeply telling one, for in this instance it was the fashion house that sought to emulate and reproduce the glamour of the icon rather than the star who strove to enhance her image by association with couture.

To return to the compliments Grant and Head paid Kelly's 'naturalness': she defined her iconic status rather than be defined by it. In this alone, Kelly posed a clandestine threat to men and their adoring eyes, as her femininity anachronistically implied she didn't exist to please them. A significant component of this power was fashion, or more precisely Kelly's interest in fashion as an articulation of her independence. As I have written before with regard to Grace Kelly in *Rear Window*, James Stewart/L.B. Jefferies rejects her at the outset of the film because she's too perfect: not only is she exquisitely beautiful, but she is a professional woman of means and she controls her life and the events around her (Bruzzi 1997). The location for this hyper perfection is her self-categorisation as fashionable, and so her involvement with fashion comes to symbolise the fact that she does not need or seek the approval of men to believe in her own identity. Within such a context, fashion itself becomes an exclusive discourse that proclaims a woman's self-containment and independence – even from her image and the manner in which it can be received. This division highlights another feature of Grace Kelly's attraction: that she appealed as much if not more to women as she did to men, not necessarily in a homosocial-as-a-masquerade-for-lesbian way, but because she challenged and deflected the traditional male consumption of the feminine image.

She made comparatively few films (11) and even fewer dud ones; she retired from movies to marry Prince Rainier of Monaco in 1956 and fans have tended to forget that, whether due to the consumption of alcohol or a difficult menopause, she grew very jowly and plain towards the end, set up an alternative home in Paris and surrounded herself with a motley variety of 'toy boys'. In 1964 Kelly was due to return to the screen in what eventually became the Tippi Hedren role in *Marnie*; like the out of character *Country Girl* (1954) for which Kelly won her Oscar, the part of a sexually repressed kleptomaniac would have perhaps stretched the image, especially if the film had been released under its provisional title: *I Married a Frigid Female Thief*. The appeal of Grace Kelly was always hard to pin down; she made a good princess, but she could equally well unzip your fly.

References

Bruzzi, Stella (1997) *Undressing Cinema: Clothing and Identity in the Movies*, London and New York: Routledge.

Cook, Pam (1996) *Fashioning the Nation: Costume and Identity in British Cinema*, London: BFI Publishing.

Gottleib, Sidney (ed.) (1995) *Hitchcock on Hitchcock*, London: Faber.

Head, Edith and Ardmore, Jane Kesner (1959) *The Dress Doctor*, Boston: Little, Brown & Company.

Head, Edith and Calistro, Paddy (1983) *Edith Head's Hollywood*, New York: E.P. Dutton Inc.

Lacey, Robert (1997) *Grace*, G.K. Hall and Co.

Truffaut, François (1978) *Hitchcock*, London and St Albans: Paladin.

Wilson, Elizabeth (1985) *Adorned in Dreams: Fashion and Modernity*, Berkeley: University of California Press.

Chapter 15

Jacqueline Reich

UNDRESSING THE LATIN LOVER
Marcello Mastroianni, fashion, and
La dolce vita[1]

IN GIUSEPPE TORNATORE'S 1990 FILM, *Stanno tutti bene* (*Everybody's Fine*), Marcello Mastroianni portrays an ageing widower, Matteo Scuro, who has decided to make a surprise visit to his children. The first stop on his journey is Naples, the home of his son Alvaro, who unbeknownst to him is in prison. As he futilely awaits Alvaro's return, Matteo is approached by a young prostitute, who, as she lifts her skirt to reveal her shapely leg, says, 'Grandpa, do you want some company? Look at these legs!' He slowly puts down his suitcases and pulls up his pant leg to reveal a thin, pale leg covered mostly by a dark knee sock and replies, 'Hey, look at mine!'

Although intended to comment on the character's state of innocence and zest for life, this scene constitutes one of the rare appearances of Marcello Mastroianni's naked legs on the screen. In fact, in his 160 odd screen appearances, Mastroianni's body is rarely eroticised. This lack of masculine secularisation, particularly in the 1950s when Mastroianni began his film career, is somewhat against the norm. This period in film history is in fact what Steven Cohan has called 'The Age of the Chest' in both American films, featuring such stars as William Holden, Marlon Brando, and Charlton Heston, and in Italian popular cinema, particularly the many biblical epics and peplum films (Cohan 1997: 164–200; Dyer 1997: 145–83.

If Mastroianni's body as imaged in Italian cinema does not depend on the secularisation and the eroticisation of the male form, how does one explain the attribution of the term 'Latin Lover' to Mastroianni, a label he detested and struggled against up to his death in December 1996? In what follows, I wish to argue that the image of Mastroianni as Latin Lover has as much to do with the Italian post-war economic boom and the commodification of Italy on an international level as it does with Mastroianni star persona. The Latin Lover is above all a *product*, a consumer icon, a cultural commodity offered up for consumption to an international public. Mastroianni was a symbol for Italian style, for a style of life that resonated with a national public experiencing greater prosperity after years of struggle and with an international consumer market hungry for all things Italian.

This chapter examines the interrelated phenomenon of the Latin Lover and 1950s consumer culture in the light of the film which came to epitomise this phenomenon, Federico Fellini's *La dolce vita* (1959). Both the genesis and the success of *La dolce vita* arose in part out of the post-war cultural climate of Rome as it evolved from 'open city' to the hot spot of the rich, famous, and beautiful. Fellini was inspired by this new Roman culture, particularly the Via Veneto, which in the 1950s came to symbolise the post-war economic rebound after years of struggle and reconstruction. It became a haven for the international jet set, the cultural elite, and the Italian and American film communities. As a result of this world-wide exposure, by the late 1950s Italy emerged as a cosmopolitan style-maker and trendsetter with the success of the Vespa, the Fiat 500, and, last but not least, Italian fashion.

In the end, Fellini's film unmasks the superficiality and the materialism of this growing consumer culture precisely through a baring of the fashion system. Through its critical presentation of fashion and clothing, *La dolce vita* subtly critiques traditional constructs of Italian masculinity, in particular the *bella figura*, the public manifestation of the private self through behaviour and appearance. In the film, Fellini dresses up the journalist Marcello Rubini, as played by Mastroianni, in the latest Italian fashion but ultimately strips him bare to reveal a man at odds rather than triumphant over a rapidly changing economic, social, and sexual environment.

La dolce vita recounts a week in the life of Marcello Rubini, a writer making his living stalking the rich and famous for the gossip columns in Rome. Critics have traditionally broken the film down into a series of seven episodes taking place over seven days and nights, with a prologue (the arrival of the statue of Christ in St Peter's square), an interlude (Marcello meets the young girl Paola at the beach), and an epilogue (Marcello's final encounter with Paola) (Bondanella 1993: 143–4). The film's narrative trajectory is that of a journey or a quest: a quest for meaning in the morally and spiritually vacuous milieu of late 1950s Rome. Rather than a mimetic representation, Fellini's portrait of the Eternal City is highly personal and allegorical. The image that emerges is a city that has lost its connection to its ancient roots, preoccupied instead with immediate gratification, be it sexual, personified in the character of Maddalena; exploitative, as with the *paparazzi*; or spiritual, in the sightings of the Madonna. This loss is also expressed in terms of the city's architecture. There is a stark contrast in the films between the old (the Trevi fountain, the Termi di Caracalla, San Pietro) and the new (the housing developments, the highways, the desolate industrial countryside), epitomising urban modernisation's corruption of a pre-modern innocence (Sparke 1990: 230).

Mastroianni, as a result of his role as Marcello, was labelled the newest incarnation of the Latin Lover. How did the Latin Lover tag come to be applied to Mastroianni, if, as I claim, the role that solidified that image deconstructs that iconic rubric? The reasons have little to do with Mastroianni himself (although his very public off-screen affairs with many of his co-stars helped to proliferate the image), and more to do with what exactly a Latin Lover is, and how it relates to both the international image of Italy and Italian masculinity. A cultural symbol of the Italian as other, the Latin Lover has become the 'imagined' embodiment of the primitive, whose unrestrained and exotic passion directly affronts the more civilised and restrained Northern European or American society (Allen 1997: 3; Dickie 1996: 19–33). Much of this differentiation is due to the fact that Italy has consistently been seen as a backward as opposed to a modern nation. The origins of this concept of backwardness lie, according to John Agnew, in Italy's many historical failings and inadequacies in achieving a modern state: its inability to fulfil the promises of Renaissance glory as well as its failure to develop into a concrete and stable political identity after the *Risorgimento*. Furthermore, Italy's late industrialisation, and consequential slow development of a bourgeois ruling class, its ties to a more traditional, family-based way of life, and its distrust of government have created spaces of difference between it and other more 'Westernised' countries (Agnew 1997: 23–42).

The Latin Lover is also a product of popular culture, a consumer icon turned real, which played off and exploited these cultural clashes (Malossi 1996: 24). The cultural archetype of the Latin Lover, despite coming to fruition in the 1950s, dates back to the literary, musical and theatrical incarnations of the Don Juan/Don Giovanni myth, which engaged European culture from the Renaissance onward (Forti-Lewis 1992: 11–31). On the screen, the hysterical fan culture surrounding Rudolph Valentino created the first international hybrid of Latin Lover: the Italian immigrant who achieves the American dream first through dance, then on-screen exoticism (Studlar 1996: 150–98). After Valentino's death, actors such as Alberto Rabagliati, the Italian winner of the 1928 studio-sponsored 'Next Rudolph Valentino Contest', the American John Gilbert and Ramon Novarro, the Spanish hybrid who failed to achieve the same status as Valentino in the eyes of the female public (Panaro 1996: 95–113), attempted to fill the void.[2]

After Valentino, just being an Italian male was often enough for future Italian stars in Hollywood to garner the label of the Latin Lover. Rossano Brazzi's roles in *Three Coins in the Fountain* (dir. Jean Negulesco, 1954), *The Barefoot Contessa* (dir. Joseph Mankiewicz, 1954) and *Summertime* (dir. David Lean, 1955) played off the fantasy of the exotic, erotic Italian seducing the prim, responsible American woman with his ardent behaviour and eulogies to love.[3] It was a fantasy that was rapidly becoming a reality. In 1955, the year of *Summertime*'s release (UK title: *Summer Madness*), more Americans visited Europe than ever before, and one of their main destinations, especially for female tourists, was Italy ('Love transforms a plain Jane' 1955: 55).

Thus the rubric of the Latin Lover was well established in the United States and just waiting for Mastroianni, in spite of the fact that the actor did not make a movie in Hollywood until 1992. His films, however, came to the United States at a time when the boundaries between mainstream and art-house cinema were beginning to break down. *La dolce vita*, Mastroianni's first big success in the United States, became the first cross-over hit in terms of both box office receipts and audience reception: it became the highest-grossing foreign film ever released. His popularity continued into the 1960s with *Divorce, Italian Style*, for which he was nominated for an Academy Award; Fellini's *8½*, an Academy Award winner; and his collaborations with Sophia Loren, many of which were dubbed and then released on the non-art house circuit.

As opposed to the extracinematic image of Marcello Mastroianni as Latin Lover, however, the character of Marcello Rubini in *La dolce vita* is representative of a more prevalent phenomenon which runs throughout the representation of masculinity in post-war Italian cinema: that of the *inetto*, the Italian incarnation of the *schlemiel* or anti-hero. For Sanford Pinsker, in his study on the *schlemiel* as metaphor in Jewish literature and culture, the *schlemiel* is someone 'who handles a situation in the worst possible manner or is dogged by an ill luck that is more or less due to his own ineptness' (Pinsker 1991: 2). As opposed to the *schlimazl*, who is more the victim of pure bad luck, the *schlemiel* is usually an agent in his own destruction.

Gian Paolo Biasin has traced the origins of the Italian version of the *schlemiel*, the anti-hero or *inetto*, to twentieth-century poetry and prose. Biasin notes how the modern and contemporary protagonists of Western literature have departed from the models of Greek and Roman epic hero. They are defined not by action but rather passivity, intellectualism and artistic sensibility; they are successes rather than failures, mired in bourgeois mediocrity rather than stellar achievement (Biasin 1989: 69–107).

The Italian *inetto*, while rooted in the comic tradition of the *commedia dell'arte*, does not, in its most recent incarnations in literature and film, necessarily fit within the genre of comedy. While the *inetto* does loom as the cultural antecedent to the incompetent, bumbling protagonists who populate the *commedia all'italiana* films (comedy Italian style) of the 1950s and 1960s (and Roberto Benigni's populist reincarnations in the 1990s), traces of his existence appear in the alienated, lost souls of Michelangelo Antonioni's modernist films, such as *La notte* (1960) and *Blowup* (1966), as well as the sexually and socially challenged Southerners who populate Lina Wertmüller's class commentaries. This modern incarnation of the *inetto* actively chooses passivity and ineptitude as a way of life – it is his strategy. Biasin states:

> When applied to the hero, 'strategy' has an active, aggressive conno-
> tation; when applied to the anti-hero, it has a passive, self-defensive,
> self-ironic quality . . . In any case strategy points to the environment,
> not to the subject, and this environment is definitely hostile, if not
> cruel and violent.
>
> (Biasin 1989: 78)

For Biasin, the anti-hero's circumstance in contemporary Italian culture is one of alienation, as well as the self-conscious ironisation of that condition.

The *inetto*, moreover, constitutes the negative binary opposite of phallic constructions of Italian masculinity, many of which have found representations in Italian cultural forms over the centuries: the valiant and brave soldier of the Roman Empire, the Machiavellian Renaissance prince, and the Casanova. Rather than active, he is passive; rather than brave, he is cowardly; rather than sexually potent, he is either physically or emotionally impotent. Thus the *inetto* articulates the traditional binary opposite of the masculine, that is the feminine, as it is constructed in Italian culture and society, and as it relates to sexuality: the cuckold, the impotent and feminised man.[4] Moreover, his shortcomings and failings correspond to the anti-masculine. His passivity, impotency and alienation are in direct opposition to the prescribed masculine norms of Italian culture.

How does Marcello Rubini become Fellini's version of the *inetto*? Throughout the course of the film, Marcello fails to accomplish anything. Incapable of making a choice between journalism and literature, he semi-prostitutes himself instead to the tabloids. Mired in mediocrity, he succumbs to the temptations of bourgeois and aristocratic decadence. He even chooses the wrong masculine ideal role models to turn to for potential guidance: the false intellectual Steiner, as well as his narcissistically absorbed, ageing father.[5] Marcello's passivity and metaphoric impotence also reveal themselves in his relationships with women. With Emma, Maddalena, Sylvia and Paola, he searches for some meaning to his existence but ultimately remains frustrated. He becomes prey, albeit at first willingly, to Maddalena's sexual games at the prostitute's house and the castle. He fails either to commit himself to or extricate himself from his relationship with his fiancée Emma. With Sylvia in the Trevi fountain, however, in what has become the iconic emblem of the film, the era, and Mastroianni's Latin Lover image, Marcello's constitution as the modern *inetto* fully exhibits itself.

Although the presence of the American actress Sylvia references the cultural climate of late 1950s Rome, specifically the large Hollywood community shooting films there, her character symbolically signifies much more. For Marcello, at the party at the Caracalla Baths, she is everything in a material sense: 'the first woman of the first day of creation . . . the mother, the sister, the lover, the friend, angel, the devil, the earth, the house'. She also personifies an animalesque physicality, not just in the corporeality of her statuesque figure, but also in her connections to the animal world (the cat, the howling along with the dogs, the fur stole she wears, her mane-like hair) and her proximity to the earth itself (she consistently appears barefoot). She stands out from her Roman counterparts and surroundings in both her Nordic features and her embodiment of an earthly sensuality lacking in the material city. Her primitive and uncontrolled, rather than 'civilised' and proscribed existence, offers a possible alternative to Marcello's bourgeois malaise.

In the Trevi fountain sequence, Marcello joins the modern incarnation of Nordic, earthly Venus as she bathes in the waters of the Eternal City, symbolised in the fountain's connection to both Ancient Rome (the ancient aqueduct is its source) and Papal Rome (it was commissioned by Pope Clement XII and completed by the sculptor Nicolo Salvi in 1735). Yet he is unable physically to touch and metaphorically to connect with his potential salvation. As she metonymically baptises him into this new world, the fountain shuts off, symbolising, for Bondanella, 'a clear sign of his spiritual impotence', or rather his incapacity to reject the material in favour of the sensual (Bondanella 1993: 147).

The abrupt cessation of the flowing waters, however, does have important implications for the representation of masculinity, and not just in terms of Christian iconography. This harsh interruption implies castration not only in the strictly Freudian sense: that the figure of the woman, here directly associated with the waters, personifies that threat. It also symbolises castration in more general terms: faced with sexual and sensual pleasure incarnated in Sylvia's body, Marcello is rendered immobile, rigid, and is denied release. His anxious reawakening from his sensual stupor once the flow of water is suspended intends a sexual and psychological frigidity in the face of both unbridled female sexuality and the salvific potential of abandonment to that earthly sensuality.

Marcello's narrative trajectory is the opposite of the classical Hollywood character arch: rather than passing from a state of darkness into an awareness and light, he ultimately descends further into that darkness. However, in keeping with the modern *inetto*, he actively chooses that strategy. Devastated by the Steiner murder-suicide, he plummets into a moral, spiritual and sexual abyss, epitomised by the orgy sequence near the end of the film. The carnivalesque setting, complete with transvestites, stripteases, and insinuations of homosexuality, cinematically codifies the scene as one of lascivious degradation and ethereal emptiness. Marcello's final rejection of Paola at the beach, framed by the encounter with the monstrous fish, underscores not only his alienation but also alienation as a dynamic decision.

This 'strategy' is marked throughout the film in terms of fashion. Fashion was in fact an inspiration for Fellini in *La dolce vita*, in particular the women's sack dress. The sack dress, a popular style in the late 1950s, was an unconstructed sheath-like dress which, according to Brunello Rondi, one of Fellini's collaborators on the film, possessed that sense of luxurious butterflying out around a body that might be (physically) beautiful but not morally so; these sack dresses struck Fellini because they rendered a woman very gorgeous who could, instead, be a skeleton of squalor and solitude inside (Bondanella 1993: 134).

The growing divide between surface and substance is a theme that runs throughout *La dolce vita*, and one that hinges, in many aspects, on the fashion system in general and the history and nature of the Italian fashion industry in particular.

The Italian fashion industry was integral to Italy's economic and cultural revival after the fall of the fascist regime. As Italian borders opened up to international markets, one of the main areas of interest for consumers and investors was Italian fashion and design (Ginsborg 1990: 72–5, 94). Italy had long enjoyed a reputation as being the site of superb craftsmanship, particularly in the accessories market of shoes and leather goods as well as with fabric, especially silk. The industry was aided by Italian financial groups who saw fashion as the best product to circulate in the global marketplace. They actively recruited the participation of Italian tailors and designers such as Oleg Cassini and Salvatore Ferragamo who had emigrated to the United States and enjoyed success there (Morelli 1985: 58–65). These designers set the stage for the wave of Italian fashion that would sweep the United States in the 1950s.

Another important factor that contributed to Italian fashion's rise to prominence was a series of financial and image problems afflicting the French fashion industry, long the dominant trend-setter for women's fashion (Settembrini 1994: 484–94). The first Italian designers, many of whom had worked behind the scenes in the Paris ateliers, preserved the lines of French style. However, they made their clothes with the high-quality fabrics for which Italy was known, with cheap labour as a result of the high post-war unemployment rate, and with a superb attention to line and form. Designs by Emilio Pucci, the Sorelle Fontana, and Emilio Schuberth reflected a simplicity in style, a focus on detail, and a sophisticated use of colour which would come to characterise Italian fashion for the next decade (Settembrini 1994: 485–7; Steele 1994: 496–506).

Moreover, the money invested in the Italian fashion industry after the Second World War did not exclude the male sector. The guiding principle for Italian designers, led by the Roman fashion house of Brioni, was to free the body from the often restrictive clothing of British designs. Rather than tying clothing to class and power, men's fashion on the Italian front came to be associated with a more relaxed way of life, liberating it from the rigidity of an aristocratic legacy and anchoring it firmly in the growing middle class. The idea was to project the new ideology of informality, leisure and pleasure, essential qualities of the new *dolce vita* which post-war prosperity allowed, and from which Fellini would draw inspiration (Settembrini 1993: 13–33; McDowell 1997: 94–5, 137–40; Chenoune 1993: 241–50; 1998: 6–15).

One key factor of the Italian style was its broad appeal to all classes, not just the rich and famous. According to Ted Polhemus, Italian men of differing social status considered dressing well both a privilege and a responsibility (Polhemus 1994: 45). This emphasis on projecting an Italian male style is linked to the cultural heritage of the *bella figura*, reflecting a taste for public display of self-worth through appearance, regardless of class or gender (Nardini 1998: 5–33). Akin to the Northern European figures of the English dandy and the French *flâneur*, the *bella figura* dates back to the Renaissance figure of the courtier and the concept of *sprezzatura*. In Castiglione's *Il libro del cortegiano* (The Book of the Courtier), *sprezzatura* is a courtly ideal – the opposite of affectation and the epitome of grace, denoting a naturalness in appearance that belies the effort that went into its preparation (Castiglione 1972: 61–2).

In the ideals of both *sprezzatura* and the *bella figura*, the performative aspect of Italian masculinity begins to reveal itself. The Italian male literally puts on a show for an admiring public. Like the dandy, the *bella figura* parades his sense of style, his masculinity, and his sensuality, regardless of his social and economic status. Both individual and national identity are written on the body through clothing and grooming and paraded for the community, be it urban or rural (Malossi 1993: 37–42). While the dandy is the object of the gaze and the *flâneur* the subject, the *bella figura* is at once both spectacle and spectator. His aim is both to be seen and be recognised as important and full of honour, as well as to see that others recognise these traits in him. This dual function is possible in part due to the site of the performance: public space, be it the piazza (such as the Piazza del Campo in Siena), or the main street of a town or city (in *La dolce vita*'s case, the Via Veneto).[6] The architectonics of the *bella figura* thus breaks the typical spectator/spectacle dichotomy – the structure of public space, as opposed to the private stage, allows for the simultaneous situation of looking and being looked at.

If the public arena is the *bella figura*'s stage, then fashion, in particular the suit, becomes his costume. According to Anne Hollander, suits, since their birth in the later seventeenth century, have been seen as 'naturally masculine'. She traces their modern evolution back to the Enlightenment, when, influenced as well by a rediscovery of classical antiquity, the suit began to adhere to the contours of the Ancient Greek and Roman male ideal. Broad shoulders, small waist, and long legs became the 'new anatomical foundation' for the modern man, 'expressed not in bronze or marble but in natural wool, linen and leather'. Hollander believes that the modern suit has survived because it has retained its ability to suggest that classical nudity and exude a 'confident male sexuality' (Hollander 1995: 63–113).

Hollander's use of Mediterranean models of masculinity in her analysis of the relationship between a man's clothing and his sexuality is particularly appropriate for the Italian scene. Her discussion, however, presupposes a unified and unconflicting definition of masculinity, as well as a definite correspondence between clothing and male subjectivity: that is, what a man wears necessarily reveals who he is socially and sexually. This theory is questioned if that correspondence is negated: what if a man's attire becomes instead his costume, a Pirandellian mask which not only conceals the fragmentary nature of male subjectivity but also projects a radically different social identity? Stella Bruzzi, in her work on fashion and cinema, notes that men's clothing in film often works against character. In her analysis of recent Franco-American gangster films, the emphasis placed on dressing well often masks unstable masculinity. When the gangsters don these suits, modelled in fact on *la linea italiana* (the Italian line) of the late 1950s, they are allowed to assume the traditional position of power and control. Without the costume, however, they may as well be naked. Vulnerable and frail, they reveal, as does Marcello Rubini's character in *La dolce vita*, the tendentious state of 'conventionalised masculinity' (Bruzzi 1997: 67–94).

Fellini takes this notion of a discontinuity between surface and substance in relation to fashion and clothing one step further. Although he dresses Marcello in the latest fashions, this costuming fails to mask his moral, spiritual and sexual failings. Throughout the course of the *La dolce vita*, Piero Gherardi, the costume designer, has clothed Marcello in a variety of stylish suits, intended to epitomise the suave, debonair urban bourgeois male and representative of Italian men's fashion at its best. He wears highly tailored, single-breasted jackets with thin lapels and a single flap; slim-fitting pleated but narrow trousers; clean-pressed white, thinly striped, or dark shirts with cufflinks and thin dark ties; and the requisite pointed Italian shoes and dark sunglasses. This stylish image further enhanced the extracinematic association of Mastroianni as Latin Lover. Costume and fashion, specifically Italian fashion, have always played an integral role in the 'imagined' figure of the Latin Lover. The Latin Lover's success on and off the screen depended on projecting a casual but 'elegant and refined manner,' epitomised by the cravat and open-necked shirt (Romano 1996: 60–3). Rossano Brazzi had a whole new wardrobe made for his 1957 trip to the US to film *South Pacific*, saying 'I must carry the bold flag of Italian elegance' ('A Titre de Revanche' 1957). In *La dolce vita*, Marcello Rubini's ubiquitous dark sunglasses, his cufflinks, and the style of the white linen suit with dark shirt he wears at the end of the film became fashion trends (Bagley 1994: 100). Mastroianni notes bitterly how after he made that film, producers and distributors only wanted to cast him as the Latin Lover because they 'only wanted to see me in the V-shaped jacket with gold buttons' (Mastroianni 1997: 61). As the latest incarnation of the Latin Lover, Mastroianni in *La dolce vita* became, like Italian fashion itself, one of Italy's greatest and most successful exports (Dewey 1993: 142–6).

Ironically, however, while the national and international public embraced the Latin Lover style and the Italian consumer culture, the text employs fashion, costume and make-up to subvert the material superficiality of that image and the

era. Signs of Marcello's moral emptiness and inevitable decay appear throughout
La dolce vita, and are marked precisely by fashion and appearance. Physically, Fellini
wanted Marcello to appear at once intense and hollow. His eyes were masked by
fake eyelashes and very little attention was focused on them. The lighting on his
face is full of shadows (Kezich 1996: 95). Hints of Marcello's impending demise
appear at Steiner's apartment after the murder-suicide: his tie is loose, his top
shirt-collar unbuttoned, his normally slicked-back hair out of place. In the final
scenes at the beach, fashion signals the *inetto*'s strategy as Marcello descends into
his moral, spiritual and sexual abyss. He wears the inversion of his original and
signature outfit: instead of the dark suit with crisp shirt, he opts for a rumpled
and dishevelled white linen suit with the dark shirt. The *bella figura* has become
the grotesque *brutta figura*: the fashion emblem of the Latin Lover, the cravat with
open-necked shirt, here serves as ironic commentary on the emptiness of that label
and the culture it embraced.

In the end, Mastroianni had this to say about the role of Marcello in *La dolce
vita* and the Latin Lover image ascribed to him as a result:

> Yes, from *La dolce vita* on, this label of the Latin Lover, which doesn't
> fit me, stuck to me. At first I played chauffeurs, ingenuous workers,
> modest but very nice young men. After this film new proposals for
> more intellectually committed roles started to arrive, but there was
> always some story in the middle involving the Latin Lover, with which
> I had nothing to do because I have never been one. In fact, I was always
> busy saying: 'Excuse me, but in *La dolce vita* this protagonist is not a
> lady-killer – he doesn't conquer anyone. If anything he is the one
> conquered. It's women who use him and he, being provincial, inno-
> cently falls for it every time! The foreign actress uses him; his mistress
> uses him, even though she may be the only one over whom he has the
> least bit of authority; the woman in the castle of aristocrats uses him
> – he is only the victim!' So, I'm not exactly sure what this idiotic term
> palmed off on me means. People have labelled me as such evidently
> because I wore a blue blazer in the film and moved in a circle with a
> lot of women.
>
> (Fofi and Faldini 1981: 17)

Mastroianni's comments address several important issues that I hope to have
stressed in this chapter. First, that the Latin Lover image, more than a direct reflection of the characters the actor portrayed throughout his career, is a consumer
icon, marketed to the international public who hungered for Italian commodities,
including sexualised images of Italian masculinity. What was being consumed in
La dolce vita in 1959 was not only the European Don Giovanni but also an Italian
style, based on the emergence of Italian fashion and design in the international
marketplace. Mastroianni as commodity was tied to other Italian products, specifically, as even he notes, Italian fashion, with the 'blue jacket' as indicative of the
relaxed Italian style of the 'sweet life'.

The film's emphasis on materialism, superficiality, and spiritual abandonment
has important consequences for contemporary masculinity. Marcello Rubini is far

from the masculine ideal of the *bella figura*. Rather he is the modern anti-hero and *inetto*, among the first in a long line that Mastroianni would immortalise on the screen. Passive rather than active, conquered rather than the conqueror, he reflects the crisis of masculinity in an Italy dominated by materialist conservatism and spiritual decadence. At odds with rather than triumphant over his environment, his final strategy is physical masochism, ethereal annihilation, and a major fashion *faux pas*.

Notes

1   I would like to thank Toby Miller, James Mandrell, and Eva Woods for their help on this article. All translations from Italian to English are mine unless otherwise noted.

2   Latin American actors also benefited from Valentino-mania. Figures such as Ramon Novarro, Antonio Moreno and Gilbert Roland of the silent era and later Ricardo Montalbán and Fernando Lamas came to fill the Latin Lover void created by Valentino's death. An essential difference between Italian Latin lovers and their Spanish-speaking counterparts was genre (the latter being almost exclusively relegated to the musical in the sound era) and class (with the Italians usually belonging to the professional ranks and the Hispanics the working class) (López 1997: 315–17; Noriega 1993: 52–66; Reyes and Rubie 1994: 1–20).

3   Even though Ava Gardner's character was Spanish in *The Barefoot Contessa*, her Hollywood glamour image was so ingrained in American popular culture that her 'Americanness' was never in doubt, despite her admirable attempt to reproduce a Spanish lilt to her English.

4   Freud's concept of innate bisexuality of the human subject lies at the crux of Dennis Bingham's work on stardom and masculinity. For Bingham, the deconstruction of the masculine persona reveals 'man's identification with his repressed femininity' (Bingham 1994: 9).

5   Marcello's passivity and state of impotence has not gone unnoticed by critics. Frank Burke notes the character's inability to change throughout the film, resulting in a creative negation, as opposed to *La notte di Cabiria*'s life-affirming ideology (Burke 1996: 98–103).

6   Donald Pitkin notes how Italians, as opposed to their European neighbours, have privileged and idealised the urban over the rural space, and that that very public space has been 'domesticated', thus blurring the distinction between public and private (Pitkin 1993: 95–101).

References

'A Titre de Revanche: Rossano Brazzi conjure le mauvais sort en faisant à Hollywood une rentrée en beauté', (1957) *Cine Revue*. Online. Available in English translation http://www.neponset.com/brazzi/party.htm.

Agnew, J. (1997) 'The myth of backward Italy in modern Europe', in B. Allen and M. Russo (eds) *Revisioning Italy: National Identity and Global Culture*, Minneapolis: University of Minnesota Press.

Allen, B. (1997) 'Introduction,' in B. Allen and M. Russo, (eds) *Revisioning Italy*, Minneapolis: University of Minnesota Press.

Bagley, C. (1994) 'The sweet life of Marcello Mastroianni', *Details Magazine* (November): 100.

Biasin, G.P. (1989) *Montale, Debussy, and Modernism*, Princeton: Princeton University Press.

Bingham, D. (1994) *Acting Male: Masculinities in the Films of James Stewart, Jack Nicholson and Clint Eastwood*, New Brunswick: Rutgers University Press.

Bondanella, P. (1993) *The Cinema of Federico Fellini*, Bloomington: Indiana University Press.

Bruzzi, S. (1997) *Undressing Cinema: Clothing and Identity in the Movies*, London: Routledge.

Burke, F. (1996) *Fellini's Films: From Postwar to Postmodernism*, New York: Twayne Publishers.

Castiglione, Baldassarre (1972) *Il libro del cortegiano*, Milano: Mursia.

Chenoune, F. (1993) *A History of Men's Fashion*, Paris: Flammarion.

—— (1998) *Brioni*, New York: Universe.

Cohan, S. (1997) *Masked Men: Masculinity and the Movies in the Fifties*, Bloomington: Indiana University Press.

Dewey, D. (1993) *Marcello Mastroianni: His Life and Art*, New York: Birch Lane Press.

Dickie, J. (1996) 'Imagined Italy', in D. Forgacs and R. Lumley (eds) *Italian Cultural Studies: An Introduction*, Oxford: Oxford University Press.

Dyer, R. (1997) *White*, London: Routledge.

Fofi, G. and Faldini, F. (1981) *L'avventurosa storia del cinema italiano raccontato dai suoi protagonisti 1960–1969*, Milan: Feltrinelli.

Forti-Lewis, A. (1992) *Maschere, libretti e libertini. Il mito di Don Giovanni nel teatro europeo*, Rome: Bulzoni.

Ginsborg, P. (1990) *A History of Contemporary Italy: Society and Politics, 1943–1988*, New York: Penguin Books.

Hollander, A. (1995) *Sex and Suits*, New York: Knopf.

Kezich, K. (1996) *Su* La dolce vita *di Federico Fellini. Giorno per giorno, la storia di un film che ha fatto epoca*, Venice: Marsilio.

López, A.M. (1997) 'Of rhythms and borders', in C. Frasier Delgado and J. Esteban Muñoz (eds) *Everynight Life: Culture and Dance in Latin/o America*, Durham: Duke University Press.

'Love transforms a plain Jane' (1955) *Life*, July, 39 (4): 55–7.

McDowell, C. (1997) *The Man of Fashion: Peacock Males and Perfect Gentlemen*, London: Thames & Hudson.

Malossi, G. (1993) 'La bella figura: Gli italiani e l'eleganza', in G. Malossi (ed.) *La regola estrosa. Cent'anni di eleganza maschile italiana,* Milan: Electa.

—— (1996) 'Introduction: the banality of the Latin lover,' in G. Malossi (ed.) *Latin Lover: The Passionate South,* Milan: Charta.

Mastroianni, M. (1997) *Mi ricordo, sì, io mi ricordo*, Milan: Baldini & Castoldi.

Morelli, O. (1985) 'The international success and domestic debut of postwar Italian fashion,' in G. Bianchino *et al.* (eds) *Italian Fashion*, Milan: Electa.

Nardini, G. (1998) *Che Bella Figura! The Power of Performance in an Italian Ladies' Club in Chicago*. Albany: State University of New York Press.

Noriega, C.A. (1993) 'Internal "Others": Hollywood narratives about Mexican Americans', in J. King *et al.* (eds) *Mediating Two Worlds: Cinematic Encounters in the Americas*, London: BFI.

Panaro, A. (1996) 'Mass-produced Valentinos: Rudolph Valentino's Doubles' in G. Malossi (ed.) *Latin Lover: The Passionate South*, Milan: Charta.

Pinsker, S. (1991) *The Schlemiel as Metaphor: Studies in Yiddish and American Jewish Fiction*. Revised and enlarged edition, Carbondale, IL: Southern Illinois University Press.

Pitkin, D.S. (1993) 'Italian urbanscape: intersection of private and public', in R. Rotenberg and G. McDonogh (eds) *The Cultural Meaning of Urban Space*, Westport, CT: Bergin & Garvey.

Polhemus, T. (1994) *Street Style: From Catwalk to Sidewalk*, London: Thames & Hudson.

Reyes, L. and Rubie, P. (1994) *Hispanics in Hollywood: An Encyclopedia of Film and Television*, New York: Garland.

Romano, C. (1996) 'Anarchy hurt the Latin lover: fantasy, decline and eternal fascination of the Latin lover,' in G. Malossi (ed.) *Latin Lover: The Passionate South*, Milan: Charta.

Settembrini, L. (1993) 'La regola estrosa. Cent'anni di eleganza maschile', in G. Malossi (ed.) *La regola estrosa. Cent' anni di eleganza maschile italiana*, Milan: Electa.

—— (1994) 'From haute-couture to prêt-à-porter', in G. Celant (ed.) *The Italian Metamorphosis, 1943–1968*, New York: Guggenheim Museum.

Sparke, P. (1990) '"A home for everybody?": design, ideology and the culture of the home in Italy', in Z. Baranski and R. Lumley (eds) *Culture and Conflict in Postwar Italy: Essays on Mass and Popular Culture*, London: Macmillan.

Steele, V. (1994) 'Italian fashion and America', in G. Celant (ed.) *The Italian Metamorphosis, 1943–68*, New York: Guggenheim Museum.

Studlar, G. (1996) *This Mad Masquerade: Stardom and Masculinity in the Jazz Age*, New York: Columbia University Press.

Chapter 16

Christopher Breward

THE DANDY LAID BARE
Embodying practices and fashion for men

I'm a fashionable beau
Just turned out the newest go,
So elegant, so exquisite, so handy o
My tip top style of dress
And my shape, my air, my face,
I'll prove beyond compare that I'm a dandy o.

A skeleton's the taste
Scarce five inches round the waist
My body-belt tight buckled is so handy o;
My pantaloons cossacks,
Puffed and swelling out like sacks,
I'm sure from head to toe I'm quite a dandy o.

Now do but view my coat
For 'tis meet that you should know't
My bosom here, so beautiful, so handy o;
My hair quite flat at top,
Thick and bushy like a mop,
My neck a foot in length, I'm all the dandy o.

My stays are laced so tight
That I'm forced to walk upright,
My chin pok'd out, my neck-cloth stiff and bandy o;
My whiskers neatly trimm'd,
And my hat so narrow-rimm'd
My spurs are all the kick – I'm quite a dandy o.

You see I've got the swell
Of Bond Street and Pall Mall
For quizzing all, and cutting some so handy o;
I lounge from street to street,
As my brother swells I meet,
Some stare, but all declare that I'm a dandy o.

At op'ra, rout and play
Then I hear the ladies say,
How stylish! lud, how handsome! how handy o!
He's got the Bond Street swing,
I declare he's quite the thing!
Do! do but see! now isn't he the dandy o.

Pretending not to hear
Then I modishly draw near
My ribbons sport, my rings display, so handy o
I read it in their eyes,
And I hear it in their sighs,
The ladies are all dying for the dandy o.
                              (Anon, *c.* 1820: 7–8)

CONTRARY TO CLAIMS that the original version of the dandy inhabited only an elite milieu, such was the ubiquity of his figure in the imaginative urban landscape of the early nineteenth century that its revolutionary characteristics were obsessively recorded across a range of popular media. The song reproduced above is only one example of countless products which profited from the dandy craze. His faintly ridiculous persona was considered a fitting subject for the entertainment of the masses, a guarantee for healthy sales. Thus a rather fantastical and overblown version of dandyism became the stock in trade for pantomime balladeers, print sellers and penny novelists; entrepreneurs whose output has provided a rich but compromised seam of commentary for future historians of fashionable masculinities (Laver 1968; Chenoune 1993; McDowell 1997). Indeed, if the archives were to be stripped of these distorted caricatures of sartorial behaviour and corporeal modification, a whole set of subsequent discourses relating to the rise of commodity culture, the experience of modernity in the city and the relationship between desire, clothing and the gendered body would remain unexplored and without example; for any evidence of the material practice of dandyism (and there is not much) counts for little when placed alongside its potent and more familiar role as a symbolic representation of less tangible cultural fears and concerns.

It is this ongoing mobilisation of the 'idea' of the dandy, as a cipher for a particular yet very fugitive version of masculine fashionability, bodily display and metropolitan neurosis that interests me in this chapter. I am concerned here with the ways in which the description, critique and analysis of a dandified subject-position are both embodied in the choices and actions of real consumers, yet also exist at a level of abstraction. They are thus held in a seeming tension with

immediate historical realities but illustrative of longer historical developments which
trace the role played by fashionable men in defining the tenor of metropolitan life
in the modern period. This double-bind might best be illustrated by isolating the
image and form of the dandy at three pivotal points in its evolution. Separated by
over half a century, each incarnation shares a locus in the West End of London and
finds its co-ordinates linked to a more general crisis in the articulation of acceptable
forms of masculine sexuality as represented through male bodies and their relationship to fashionable living. Such a trajectory has been traced before, largely through
the lens of literary and sociological enquiry (Moers 1960; Wilson 1985), but in the
light of recent investigations into the specific economic, political and aesthetic structures necessary for masculine fashion consumption and its representation (Hollander
1994; Mort 1996; Nixon 1996; Jobling 1999) the dandy terrain is ripe for revisit-
ing. In the self-consciously manufactured figures of the Regency Buck, the *fin de siècle* Aesthete and the neo-Edwardian Gent, fashion history has inscribed a remarkably
suggestive model for understanding the complex nexus of taste, longing and corporeality that constitutes a key definition of modern fashion culture itself. Their deliberately artificial performances, sometimes contradictory and sometimes interlinked,
form an echoing commentary on the obscured nature of masculine narcissism across
the years.

In the lines of the ballad 'I'm a fashionable Beau' (published by a Newcastle
printer some time around 1820 in a collection titled *The Dandy's Songster: Being a
Collection of the Most Charming, Exquisite, Popular and Most Approved Dandy Songs for the
Fashionable Dandies* and quoted at the opening of this chapter) all the identifying
characteristics of the breed are itemised for the ridicule of a broad audience. This
beau is first and foremost a victim of his commercial and material context, foolishly
prioritising the latest trends in an expanding market of fashionable goods to construct a vain and effeminate parody of genteel tastes. A susceptibility to new-fangled
fashions and urbane faddishness had been a staple target of the satirist for several
centuries, though it was more usually female consumers and their unpatriotic
partiality for foreign goods that attracted criticism (Breward 1995). In the late
eighteenth and early nineteenth centuries, British sartorial products aimed at men
achieved wide approval on a global scale, offering new possibilities for a satirical
focus on male consumers. The temporary eclipse of Paris as a centre for the production of luxuries including fine clothing during the Revolution and the Napoleonic
Wars left an opening for London to assert itself as the new source for a gentleman's
wardrobe that was more closely attuned to the philosophical and practical concerns
of the moment. The London dandy in his 'newest . . . tip-top style of dress' was
inevitably kitted out in plain, home-manufactured, fine wools and linens, designed
in deliberate contrast to the showy silks of the *ancien régime*, but in their overt
modernity still vulnerable to persistent critics of the fashion system. Dress historian
Anne Hollander makes a strong case for understanding this shift in the choice of
textiles and the rising importance of cut as an embodied process, reflecting concur-
rent academic and connoisseurial concerns with a re-evaluation of the antique, and
especially of the heroic nude male figure. The technology of new measuring and
construction techniques mastered by London-based tailors and a choice of materials
that subtly smoothed and emphasised muscularity, their neutral colours mimick-
ing the tones of naked flesh, eased an aesthetic transition from an aristocratic

concentration on elaborate but immobile surfaces to an idealistic celebration of 'individual moral strength founded on moral virtue'. This was made manifest through a clothing style which deliberately suggested the inherent nobility of the ideal male body (Hollander 1994, 90–1).

The fashionable beau of the ballad clearly fell some way short of the desired model, though his fixation on presenting a body that was moulded to fit fashionable expectations is clearly expressed. Corsets, collars and cravats constrain his upper form to skeletal proportions, whilst the adoption of flared cossack pantaloons, a wild and unruly hairstyle and athletic spurs pays some regard to the current romantic obsession with physical action and heroic deeds. In his enthusiasm the dandy has overshot any imitation of the natural athletic form promoted by re-appraisals of Greek statuary; instead his manipulation of proportion bears a closer relationship to the bodies and toilettes of his female counterparts. He has assumed the fussy and mincing mien of a fashionable courtesan. It is this mannered effeminacy and misplaced effort that caused most amusement, largely because the appearance of a casual effortlessness, though arrived at through laborious dressing rituals, was a central desideratum of the new dandy creed. This beau has completely missed the point. Most subsequent commentators credit the infamous socialite and trendsetter George 'Beau' Brummell as the originator of the 'correct' sartorial philosophy. Hollander sees his minimalist stance as a radical commentary on the breakdown of social hierarchies: 'In the new urban dandy mode, a man's heroism consisted only in being thoroughly himself; Brummell proved that the essential superior being was no longer a hereditary nobleman' (Hollander 1994: 92). Elizabeth Wilson notes that in his reversal of the usual dynamic of the dressing-room lie the seeds both of an anti-fashion stance, in which the undemonstrative gentleman's suit pioneered by Brummell gave rise to a notion of an unchanging 'classic' style, and an oppositional take on the politics of appearance:

> Hours were still spent on the dandy's toilette, now not in order to produce a painted and bedizened creature, but on the contrary in scraping, scrubbing and shaving the skin, in polishing boots to perfection and in tying the ultimate cravat to give an impression of indifference. The dandies invented Cool; but the blasé pose was of course arresting. There was both revolt and classic chic in the dandy style.
>
> (Wilson: 1985, 180)

Wilson also worries about the cold horror that lies at the heart of the dandy sensibility. Like Susan Sontag in her discussion of Nazi chic, she finds in the calculating distance and glorification of self that a Brummellian take on life dictated, a chilling premonition of the aesthetics of fascism:

> When politics becomes aestheticised, when, that is, political activity is evaluated in terms of its 'beauty' rather than of its effects, then this produces a fascist elevation of style above humanity and of effect over suffering, and a justification of cruelty and death in the name of style.
>
> (Wilson: 1985, 204)

Certainly in the context of the 1810s and 1820s, Brummell's celebration of hygiene, clean linen, perfect tailoring and supreme self-control accrued one level of meaning from the contrast between his pampered body and the ragged, emaciated bodies of the poor who littered London's streets. He may well have challenged the long-held assumption that aristocratic prerogative dictated the direction of fashionable taste, but his alternative promotion of style was no less feudal in its tight bracketing of sartorial display with worldly power. His apartments in Chesterfield Street and Chapel Street sat in the midst of an elite enclave marked by the extrav-agantly stocked shops of Bond Street and St James's Street, the well-appointed carriage driveways of Hyde Park, the exotic reception rooms of Carlton House, and the luxurious clubs of Pall Mall. Furthermore, all of these sites, their fittings and products, were serviced by a burgeoning empire and a thriving manufactur-ing economy whose trade also set the body of the dandy in stark relief against other even more compromised bodies, those of the enslaved and the indentured, whose exertions supported his pleasures and his indolence. Regardless of their pain and discomfort, the sparkling opulence of such a milieu provided a fitting setting for the proudly relaxed display of Brummell's well-turned tailoring and his sharp wit. As his contemporary Captain Gronow noted, Renaissance notions of princely magnificence paled besides Brummell's audacious appropriation of *ancien régime* splendour:

> In the zenith of his popularity he might be seen at the bay window of White's club, surrounded by the lions of the day, laying down the law, and occasionally indulging in those witty remarks for which he was famous. His house in Chapel Street corresponded with his personal 'get up'; the furniture was in excellent taste, and the library contained the best works of the best authors of every period and of every country. His canes, his snuff boxes, his Sèvres china, were exquisite; his horses and carriages were conspicuous for their excellence; and in fact, the superior taste of a Brummell was discoverable in everything that belonged to him.
>
> (Gronow 1862: 62)

Something of this realisation, that in its apparent levelling of distinction Brummel's simple wardrobe only succeeded in revealing social inequalities, also pervades Ellen Moer's assessment of its significance. She quotes Max Beerbohm's admiration for its beautiful understatement, citing his rather knowing and ironical belief that its ordered austerity formed the ideal costume for democracy. However, she goes on to affirm that 'there remains an irreducible firmness to the Brummell figure, something compounded of assurance, self-sufficiency, misanthropy, nasti-ness, even cruelty, that made him feared in his lifetime and will never be explained away' (Moers 1960: 38). The essential arrogance of the echt-dandy's body can be seen in the ballad's evocative suggestion of the way in which the 'fashionable Beau's' figure commanded a grudging respect as it moved through the city's public spaces. He lounged from street to street with a 'Bond Street swing', demanding attention, inspiring desire, and spawning a whole new vocabulary to describe dandyism as a physical practice. In all of the subsequent literature on consumption, gender identities and city life, with its valorisation of the prostitute, the *flâneur* and the middle-class female shopper as iconic tropes of modernity, the dandy has arguably remained something of a footnote, his reactionary posturing forcing him out of the frame and casting him in a nostalgic light. Yet in these contemporary descriptions, representations of his loud insistence on his own presence and an obsessive and constant remoulding of his image placed the dandy's body at centre-stage, yoked to other manifestations of corporeal spectacle whose apparent 'naturalness' helped to refine emerging and subsequent models for the performance of fashionable masculinities in an urban setting. If this early literature of dandyism tended to undermine the seriousness of the pursuit through humour and caricature, this was perhaps only an ameliorating response to the terrifying power of fashion as a medium for social and cultural change.

Hollander suggests that

> [this] perfect man, as conceived by English tailors, was part . . . country gentleman, part innocent natural Adam, and part naked Apollo the creator and destroyer – a combination with an enduring appeal, in other countries and other centuries.
>
> (Hollander 1994: 92)

In support of this claim, by the 1820s the dandified body was able to refute those accusations of effeminacy raised in satirical representations through recourse to its associations with a sporting virility personified in the pursuit of horse-racing, fencing, gambling, womanising and boxing. If the 'fashionable Beau' made himself ridiculous and effeminate through his too-eager pursuit of fashionable novelties, he could at least redeem his masculine pride 'at op'ra, rout and play', for it was in these more rowdy settings that the perfection of the male form was most profitably displayed and celebrated. Pierce Egan, the most assiduous recorder of – and apologist for – the perfected dandy lifestyle in his journalism and his picaresque novels of London life, presented the heroic figure of the boxing champion as the apotheosis of a desirable modern masculinity made material. Truly naked in action, aside from his leather breeches, the pugilist offered his body as a living model for the man who aimed for antique minimalism in his clothing and a modern rationalism in his philosophy (blurring the boundaries between homosocial discourse and homoerotic longing in the process). Writing about Bob Gregson, a famous fighter who retired in 1810 to take over the stewardship of the Castle Tavern in Holborn (a public house much patronised by the dandy classes), Egan noted that his 6 foot, 15 stone frame was the focus for much admiration.

> A finer or better proportioned athletic man could not be met with. . . . He was considered by the celebrated professor of anatomy at the Royal Academy a most excellent subject to descant upon. . . . He was likewise selected by the late Sir Thomas Lawrence as a fine subject . . . his general deportment was above all absurd affectation; nothing supercilious was to be found in his manner . . . [he] was always well, nay fashionably dressed.
>
> (Egan 1976: 159–60)

The valorisation of the pugilist marked a watershed in the honing of an appropriate and democratic representation of masculine sartorial desire in an urban context. As self-controlled as Brummell, but more wary of excess, his figure straddled the worlds of West End finery and a more demotic energy. This fusing of the heroic modern body with the promises of fashionable consumption set a template that Egan captured most forcefully in his portrait of 'the modern Corinthian' – the virile dandy. Here was a feisty and classless corporeal identity that rejected the foppery and elitism of previous incarnations and looked forward to an uncertain but longstanding role in the imaginative cityscape and sartorial language that constituted forms of masculine fashionability during the nineteenth and twentieth centuries. His genealogy forges a useful link to the re-emergence and re-definition of a dandy rhetoric fifty or more years later:

> I feel induced now to describe, for the benefit of posterity, the pedigree of a Dandy in 1820. The DANDY was got by vanity out of Affectation – his dam, Petit-Maître or Maccaroni – his grand-dam, Fribble – his great grand-dam, Bronze – his great great grand-dam, Coxcomb – and his earliest ancestor, Fop. His uncle, Impudence – his three brothers, Trick, Humbug and Fudge! and allied to the extensive family of the Shuffletons. Indeed this Bandbox sort of creature took so much the lead in the walks of fashion, that the BUCK was totally missing; the BLOOD vanished; the TIPPY not to be found, the GO out of date; the DASH not to be met with; and the BANG UP without a leader, at fault and in the background. It was only the CORINTHIAN that remained triumphant – his excellence was of such a genuine quality, that all imitation was left at an immeasurable distance.
>
> (Egan 1821: 42)

Moers sees the intervening years, between the disgrace of Brummell and the decline of first-wave dandyism in the London of the 1820s, and the rise of Oscar Wilde and the cult of aestheticism in the same city at the tail-end of the century, as a golden age when the practice of 'clothes-wearing' took on the guise of a moral philosophy. Transcending the actual acts of acquisition and dressing, dandyism in the 1830s and 1840s gradually becomes a disembodied stance, divorced both from the site of its birth (in London) and its meaning as a process rather than a position. Taken to its logical extremes by the Count D'Orsay, who combined Brummell's insistence on the perfection of cut and materials with Egan's sportiness and the satirist's taste for the outlandish, the material pursuit of dandyism simply came to connote an outrageous and privileged vanity, a deliberately trivial and voluptuous escape from reality. Further developed into a mannered exposition on artificiality by Honoré de Balzac, whose own unprepossessing body formed a rather bathetic prop for an elaborate and overblown dress code, the hollow shell of the dandified image found its polished surfaces more usefully detailed as a textual discourse in academic treatises and popular gossip columns than paraded in textural form on the streets. Dandyism as an abstract proposition reached its apogee with the publication of Jules Amedee Barbey d'Aurevilly's volume *Du Dandysme et de George Brummell* in 1845, a polemical discussion of dandyism as a political gesture in conflict with bourgeois values. This was closely followed by a series of poetic reflections by Charles Baudelaire on the capacity of the dandy's defiant stance to ferment rebellion and stand as 'a moral consciousness' in a corrupt modern world. By the 1850s the 'fashionable Beau' of 1820 might as well have hailed from another planet.

As Moers points out, Barbey

> minimises the place of clothes in Brummell's dandyism, not because he considers the art of dress negligible (on the contrary) but because he wishes to emphasise what he calls the intellectual quality of Brummell's irony, wit, impudence and poise. What he does say about Brummell's style of dress . . . is that it was so restrained and so natural as to be a triumph of mind rather than body.
>
> (Moers 1960: 262)

Similarly, Elizabeth Wilson underlines the cerebral and critical bias of Baudelaire's construction of dandyism, which he saw as 'a search for perfection, an exacting and stoical discipline, a form of spirituality and also a social response to those transitory epochs when democracy is not yet all powerful, yet aristocracy is only partially dethroned and debased' (Wilson 1985: 183). It would seem (despite Moers' protestations) that in the hands of the Parisian literati the rarefied practice of thinking about clothing ultimately succeeded in belittling any serious consideration of the physical traces of its very production and consumption, a phenomenon that would have amused a practical man of the wardrobe like Brummell no end. Yet putting aside tensions between the rival claims of French theory and English empiricism to the ownership and correct interpretation of dandyism (indeed of fashion history generally!), there is a significant point to be made here about the way in which the established historiography of the dandy has obscured his very physicality and material context. Indeed, it has hindered the application of his ideas and practices to a broader understanding of the historical relationship between men, their bodies and their clothing. Moers herself is guilty of just such a dismissive attitude (overlooking the fact that the dandy always was a creature prone to mass dissemination) when she asserts that following her 'golden age',

> Baudelaire's thought was transmitted to the *fin de siècle* through the feverish imagination of Huysmans and the juvenile imagination of Swinburne. Dandies and corruption, dandies and sin . . . would in the 1990s become partners in cliché . . . For the dandy was to go down to defeat at the hands not of decadence but of vulgarity. The fin de siècle made him over for a mass-audience.
>
> (Moers 1960: 283)

It was for a mass audience that the popular writer of contemporary fiction Richard Whiteing created the dandy figure of the young aristocrat Seton in his 1899 novel *No 5 John Street*. However, this in no way dilutes the sharpness with which Whiteing represents the dandy's body, rescued via Paris and transposed back to a much-changed London, the city and its society hovering with some sense of apprehension on the brink of the twentieth century. Some things though remain much the same, as the reader witnesses Seton's careful preparation, aided by his manservant, for a leisured ramble through the streets of Mayfair to Hyde Park. Here was a path towards self-adoration not so much changed from that previously followed by Brummell himself:

> Atkinson now comes in to put the finishing touches to his master for the morning promenade. He brings half a dozen cravats, and a whole trayful of scarf pins . . . Seton is to choose . . . puts a forefinger on a scarf of quiet grey; then again, laying it on a perfect pearl . . . retires to his dressing room, followed by his man. When he reappears, it is as the finished product of civilisation. He is booted, hatted, gloved and generally carried out in all the details of a perfect scheme . . . His valet regards him with the pride of the stableman who has just drawn the cloth from the loins of a flawless horse. 'Cigarettes, Atkinson, I think. Put the cigars in the bag!' The cigarettes are in a tiny case of enamelled gold, which bears an 'S' in inlaid diamond points on the lid . . . 'Which cane sir?' 'Let me see!' and he turns to a suspended rack at the door. There are as many canes as scarf pins. He hesitates between a trifle in snakewood, with a handle of tortoiseshell, and a slender growth of some other exotic timber, capped with clouded amber almost as pale as the pearl . . . Now we are out of doors, and skimming, in Seton's private hansom over the well watered roads . . . until we reach the flower shop in Piccadilly for the morning button hole . . . Our dandy looks at a whole parterre and points to one bloom, like the chess player who knows that he is pledged to the choice by touching the piece.
>
> (Whiteing 1899: 182–3)

Literary historian Lynn Hapgood characterises the style of *No 5 John Street* in terms of a dandified perspective, as 'a world of surfaces in a text full of sensuous detail that exposes the deceitful nature of what the physical eye sees . . . the upper class in particular is portrayed as all surface since its concerns are with life as art, in a deliberate evasion of reality' (Hapgood 1994: 185). Certainly the dressing-room rituals of Seton appear to conform to that commonly held notion of late nineteenth-century dandyism as the mannered denial of sordid realities (whether sexual or economic) through the deliberate manipulation of appearances, the construction of a protective and critical carapace of finely tuned sartorial exhibitionism. The 'life as art' performances of infamous aesthetes such as Robert de Montesquieu and James McNeill Whistler together with other fictionalised versions by Wilde and Huysmans are all reflected in Whiteing's description. Yet beyond the extraordinary poses of self-publicising celebrities or the exaggerating tendencies of decadent novels, Seton's self-presentation can be seen also to link with popular debates and widely held concerns over the moral state of masculinity, the advances of consumerism and the temptations of city life that informed a more generalised understanding of male corporeal behaviour, fashionable display and sartorial desire at the turn of the century. In the pages of popular fictions, tourist guides, journalistic accounts, music hall programmes, department store catalogues and advertising promotions, both real and imaginary men like Seton were seen to epitomise a tangible mood of assertive masculine acquisitiveness whose challenging potency has since been overlooked or misconstrued by historians of fashion, consumption and gender alike. Indeed the enduring supposition has been that shopping and dressing were the exclusive domain of middle-class and aristocratic women, or of men whose masculinity was in some way 'deviant' (Breward 1999).

Cultural historian Richard Dellamora (1996) has made connections between these disruptive models and the sexual upheavals of the 1890s, in which the figures of the New Woman and the homosexual were first consciously described and linked to dandified behaviour. He conjectures the reasons for the dismissal of popular characters like the dandy as anything other than incidental signifiers in broader and supposedly more 'serious' histories. He states that

> heretofore, political historians, by which I mean male political historians, have been blind to the significance of homosexual scandal in the 1890s . . . a less defensive approach . . . would acknowledge the crisis of masculinity at the time. And a less pure history, which permitted itself to be contaminated by literary scandal and gossip, would recognise how anxiety about gender roles inflects a wide range of interactions.
> (Dellamora 1996: 82)

Along with Regenia Gagnier (1986), Elaine Showalter (1992), Maurizia Boscagli (1996), and Rhonda Garelick (1998), Dellamora repositions the *fin de siècle* dandy at the centre of these interactions, in a manner which, while it illuminates the rhetorical intentions of a cosmopolitan minority, still perhaps ignores the day-to-day commercial and material significance of his type. In an echo of the paraphernalia, visual ephemera and 'gossip' which positioned the early nineteenth-century dandy at the centre of cogent debates on masculinity, national identity and conspicuous consumption, descriptions and appropriations of late Victorian dandyism have much more to tell us about the general relationship between men, their bodies and their clothes at this confusing time.

Recalling (though not repeating) the barely disguised homophobia of Moers, who sees only the corruption of a noble ideal in Wildean incarnations of dandyism, the decline of Brummell and Baudelaire's inheritance has been used portentiously by more recent theoreticians to reflect 'a loss of balance between the dual imperatives of leisure and work incumbent upon Victorian gentlemen. The dandy is too relaxed, too visible, consumes to excess while producing little or nothing' (Dellamora 1996: 86). In the spectacular and very singular body of Oscar Wilde, whose 1895 disgrace is generally quoted as precipitating the crisis over appropriate models of masculinity that informed twentieth-century attitudes towards the 'correct' performance of 'manliness', with all its connotations of denial and disavowal, the two models of dandy and gentleman are seen to have become dangerously confused (Cohen 1993; Sinfield 1994). Moers traces the sartorial and embodied patterns of Wilde's flirtations with the politics of dress from his early promotion of a rather rigorous aestheticism with the aid of green velvet and medieval posture, through the florid and bohemian adoption of an extravagantly furred and accessorised wardrobe of opera cloaks and fedoras, influenced by the example of D'Orsay and Balzac in the 1880s, to the strict (and rather Brummell-like) formality of correct evening dress taken up to mark his commercial successes in the theatre of the 1890s when 'he was content to express individuality (aside from his enormous and oddly proportioned bulk) with a single detail: a green boutonniere, a bright red waistcoat or a turquoise and diamond stud' (Moers 1960: 299). In this final incarnation he mocked the ideals of gentlemanly deportment with ultimately disastrous results for himself and for the future of an unproblematised relationship between middle-class men and the construction of their outer selves. But, beyond that affront to notions of bourgeois respectability, the dandy has been held to signify very little else, perhaps because it is difficult to extrapolate broad cultural or material meanings from the 'unreproducible' posturings of one man, or because the close association of dandified forms of presentation and behaviour with the image projected by Wilde has succeeded in limiting their application elsewhere.

There can be little doubt then that figures like Wilde had a decidedly unsettling effect on the literary, legal and medical construction of sexualities; indeed, this period at the end of the nineteenth century needs to be revisited as a crucial moment in the development of their 'modern' forms. However, one might argue for a clearer recognition of the less spectacular circumstances which gave rise to an identifiable 'dandified' style – such as that attributed to Seton – as being rooted in a more popular, generalised celebration of leisured urban masculinity, relatively untouched by high moral debate but linked materially and philosophically to that earlier circulation of representations of the heroic and self-adoring dandy which had marked Regency London. The adoption of a visibly relaxed and 'non-productive' sartorial rhetoric was not in itself transgressive; only the context and manner in which it was mobilised made it so. In equating an embracing of idle display too closely with sexual dissonance, some historians have been in danger of obscuring or distorting similar choices made by men who identified with the status quo. Furthermore, it could be claimed that the metropolitan dandy of the 1890s continued to draw on a thriving, self-consciously virile culture of cosmopolitan masculine consumption which had been in evidence since Pierce Egan's celebration of gambling dens and boxing tournaments at the opening of the century. This was a mode of living which re-colonised wider forms of popular culture at precisely the moment that Wilde's version was acquiring its problematic sexual reputation, sending the established version into partial eclipse. The two strands of dandified display – one associated with political, sexual and social resistance, the other with a commercial and corporeal engagement with the urban marketplace – require careful unravelling if the defining features of the latter are not to be subsumed by the polemics of the former.

The fictional figure of Seton, with his carefully judged appearance and assiduous collecting of fashionable possessions, is thus as much a reflection of what London's shops and catalogues offered the ambitious and stylish young man at the turn of the century as evidence of decline and decadence. His literary scopophilia may look to the obsessions of Dorian Gray in one direction, but in the other it finds a brighter resonance in the pages of a tailor's seasonal directory. That the mannered presentation of self could simply represent an unproblematic adherence to the rules of 'smart' society in an expanding arena of consumer choices is clearly communicated in retail and social guides such as *London and Londoners*, published a year before Whiteing's novel in 1898, where the author provided tongue-in-cheek guidance to the ways of modern society:

> It is fashionable to be radical in theory and advocate women's privileges. To have an inner knowledge of all classes of society. To know the latest club scandals. To have some particular fad. To wear some particular garment different from anybody else . . . To be up in the slang of the day . . . To know the points of a horse. To have an enormous dog in the drawing room . . . To know the latest music hall song . . . To go to Paris twice a year and at least once to Monte Carlo. Never to be in town after Goodwood or to return to it before November . . . To excel in one's special sport, fox hunting for preference, and be able to drive a tandem . . . To belong to a club and have some of one's letters and telegrams sent there. Always to fill one's rooms with more men than women.
>
> (Pritchard 1898: 323–4)

While such a list evidently revelled in the paradoxical nonsense of trivia, its pointed social observations map the co-ordinates of an accumulated cosmopolitan knowledge that defined the exalted status of the fashionable man and traced the limits of his finely tailored body. In its random citation of desirable adherences, it is possible to discern the more serious juxtapositions of high and low culture, reactionary posturing and avant-garde enthusiasms, artistic affectation and hearty philistinism, that influenced a prevalent model of fashionable masculinity at the turn of the century. Here was a dandified position that comfortably accommodated sexual conformity, advanced tastes and commodity fetishism within its remit. It also drew on the homosocial milieu of club life, hunting and gambling that alongside the insistence on the 'particular' as far as the wardrobe was concerned, would not have surprised a Regency beau. This corporeal engagement with the modernity of London positioned the dandy in the midst of a culture enthralled rather than repelled by the notion of masculine pleasures. More than this, his body had come to symbolise the assumption of a forward-looking and productive position in society. Sleekly clothed according to scientific measuring systems and mechanised construction processes which superseded even the revolutionary techniques of Brummell's tailors, its slim, sharp contours traced a hygienic and athletic profile that was as potent in commodity terms as the Gibson Girl, the Dollar Princess or the Music Hall Strong Man. His monocle, top-hat and morning coat embellished advertisements for products as diverse as shoe polish, cigarettes, and alcohol and reflected the glare of the spotlight in any West End revue worth its salt, providing a template of urban sophistication for any aspirant office-clerk or shop-counter worker who chose to adopt it.

In this sense the perfected (rather than the corrupted) body of the *fin de siècle* aesthete marks a transition towards dandyism as a truly commercial trope, moving away from the carefully guarded secrets of the Savile Row tailor and the arcane pronouncements of the society dictator to express a potential within sartorial taste

that was dangerously malleable and democratic and no longer so prone to the
ridicule of the caricaturist (in direct contradiction to Flügellian theories of renunciation). The fashionable man now took control of his body and his image in a
world where image was rapidly becoming a prime currency and in this action the
dandy still laid claim to a certain brand of heroism. Seton's skilled mastery of
the cutter's workshop and its products, related by Whiteing in a description of
the dandy's visit to his tailor, is thus a prophecy of the continuing, but increasingly compromised ability of dandified practices to describe masculine desire and
self-fashioning in the following century:

> Seton has so much the use and habit of the place that he passes at once
> to his favourite room. A lay figure, moulded exactly to his shape . . .
> stands in a corner, clad in his latest suit. The lugubrious effigy is a
> model for clothing only, so its representative functions stop short of
> the head which is but a block, and of the feet, which are but pedestals
> of iron. The rest is Seton to a hair, in shoulders, waist and hip . . .
> Then there ensues a most amazing discussion of experts, in which the
> dandy holds his own in fair give and take of technicalities with the snip
> . . . Such Mesopotamian terms as 'forepart', 'sidebody', 'middle-
> shoulder' and . . . the triply mysterious 'skye' are freely bandied about
> . . . From time to time, Seton seizes the chalk and makes drawings on
> the garment, or makes the figure spin like a prayer wheel. In vain is
> the cutter summoned . . . On the question whether a back seam should
> be convex or straight, our young blood takes the pair of them without
> yielding an inch, while the staff gather about the door as though to
> catch glimpses of a well-stricken field.
>
> (Whiteing 1899: 184–6)

By way of a conclusion, both to this chapter and to the genealogy of the
dandy's body which it describes, it is worth considering the manner in which the
obsessive structuring of the wardrobe and fetishisation of the surfaces of the formal
suit – which mark the *fin de siècle* aesthete's attitude to dress and life – translated
to what has widely been described as the last incarnation of Brummellian dandyism
in the decades immediately following the Second World War. Linking the two
epochs is the diminutive figure and biting wit of Max Beerbohm, the social satirist
and critic who in 1896 produced a definitive text (entitled *Dandies and Dandies*)
on the nature and history of the practice. Moers acknowledges the corrective nature
of Beerbohm's narrative and the antidote it provides both to the abstracting tendencies of a Baudelairean perspective and to the heady flamboyance of the decadence:

> The point of his essay is that the art of costume itself is the essence of
> Brummell's dandyism. Costume is not a mere outward show of some
> profound spiritual achievement. 'Dandyism', Beerbohm writes 'is ever
> the outcome of a carefully cultivated temperament, not part of the
> temperament itself.'
>
> (Moers 1960: 318)

In this sense Beerbohm returned to first principles, both in his interpretation of dandyism and in the conduct of his own affairs, which closely mirrored the dandified idea of expending great effort on outcomes which themselves betrayed the utmost simplicity through their surface polish. Literary theorist Robert Viscusi illustrates how the dandy as idea, body and text conjoin in Beerbohm's lustrous life as in his self-reflective publications:

> Dandies make themselves. Whatever they may be by birth and nurture, dandies are born anew as dandies when they first dress themselves according to the dandy code. The dandy self, naked and fresh, is a figure in black and white. Completely dressed, almost completely monochrome, he is, to put it simply, a written thing.
>
> (Viscusi 1986: 28)

Put even more simply, in Beerbohm's writings and epoch the original dandy spirit is finally made modern flesh. Though in setting him down, Beerbohm announces his eventual decline.

Beerbohm died in 1956 and his wardrobe, suitably monochrome, survives at the Museum of London. An evening suit impeccably tailored in black wool and a soft brown smoking jacket trimmed with chocolate braid suggest a life lived permanently according to the stylish rituals of the 1890s – in flight from vulgarity. The rather ironical modernity of such a position in the mid-1950s is not so surprising, for it was precisely at this moment in the history of menswear that a particular grouping of fashion designers and consumers made conscious reference to the picturesque heritage of the dandy style in the face of profound cultural and social change. The 'neo-Edwardian' style as it became known is displayed at its most self-assured in Norman Parkinson's iconic photograph of a group of financiers lounging in silhouette in one of the few remaining alleyways to survive in a blitzed City of London. Tightly kitted out in Savile Row suits, they have rejected the more capacious and baggy 'one size fits all' hang of the utility and demob clothing that served in drab post-war circumstances for a conscious celebration of swaggering fin-de-siecle panache. Bowler hats and tightly rolled umbrellas provide the glamour of the parade ground and the race track while velvet collars, covered buttons and turned-back cuffs recall the ostentation of the music hall. The couturier Hardy Amies, who was soon to turn from designing the wardrobe of the new Queen to designing a line of men's suits for the multiple tailoring firm Hepworth's, captured the complacent, wistful and undeniably elitist tone of the masculine new look in his autobiography of 1954:

> It seems to me that the basic principles of our way of life have not changed much. We still like to be ladies and gentlemen and if fewer succeed in so doing then at least more attempt it than would ever have dared to before. But all are fighting to preserve something they believe in. The young man who has just left his public school or the University dresses, when in London, in a neat dark suit, with well-pressed narrow trousers, cuffs to the sleeves of his jacket and possibly lapels to his waistcoat. Even if he doesn't indulge in such fashionable details, he

would feel uncomfortable in anything other than a hard collar and a
bowler hat. His more daring companions may flourish a flowered waistcoat and a velvet-collared coat; but if I mention too eccentric examples
I may frighten the reader out of my argument. Let us agree, however,
that the average young man of position tries to give an air of substance
without being stodgy: of having time for the niceties of life. His appearance may be only demonstrating wishful thinking: that he has several
thousand a year in the funds, and that income tax is only a shilling in
the pound; that he is prepared to be a good father to a large family.
But I think the wish is there all right.

(Amies 1954: 245)

In Amies's description of the conservative dress code of the aspirant young
man, the co-ordinates of the 'neo-Edwardian' style are clearly discernible, though
kept tightly reined-in by the prerogatives of a petit-bourgeois understanding of
respectability and an overriding concern with the tidy notion of 'gentlemanliness'.
Elizabeth Wilson has equated the look with a reactionary Tory stance against
'austerity' and the incursions of the Welfare State, an echo of the aggressive elitism
which had first inspired Brummell to use clothing as a social weapon (though in his
case the practice was allied to a more progressive brand of aristocratic politicking
than Anthony Eden's, the Conservative Prime Minister whose suave taste in tailoring provided a dominant template for the new gentleman) (Wilson 1985: 189).
In a parallel reading of the development of the style, cultural historian Frank Mort
looks beyond such 'aristocratic' bodies to trace the ways in which the tenets of
this late dandyism informed the marketing and design strategies of post-war multiple tailors 'Burton's'. Here provincial and subaltern consumers were presented with
a model of fashionability that was buttoned-up, upright and uncompromisingly
English; armour against the incursion of 'all those dissidents and unconventional
types who were marked out by improper dress'. By this, Mort is referring to the
increased visibility of homosexuality in popular discourse after the publication of
the Wolfenden Report in 1957 and the survival of older stereotypes of criminality
or subversion through the figure of the spiv or the bohemian (Mort 1996: 137–8).
There is something of this fear of change and suspicion of difference in Amies's
professed desire not to 'frighten' his readers by describing the more extreme characteristics of a renewed interest in the adornment of masculinity, repeated again in
his more recent celebration of The Englishman's Suit, where he states that:

The Edwardian look was helped by the narrow trousers and the shaped
coat, although it was too stuffy to last. [However] . . . it became acceptable that men discussed fashion seriously. The fashion shows I mounted
for Hepworth for seven years at the Savoy in London were eagerly viewed
by men in the City and not exclusively by those in the fashion press.

(Amies 1994: 33)

As Amies suggests, it was of course in a strictly metropolitan milieu, amongst
a close coterie of like-minded men, that the final versions of a purer dandyism
were played out. These were the inheritors of Beerbohm's attenuated minimalism.

Their starkly tailored bodies paid allegiance to a philosophy of life in which elegant repose and a certain withdrawal from the humdrum bother of living according to the dictates of the masses could be summed up in the placing of a button hole or the height of a shirt collar. Moving across a social terrain that encompassed the diverse worlds of choice guard's regiments, merchant banking, financial and property speculation (sometimes of a criminal nature), the theatre, publishing and the newer creative industries, theirs was an arrogantly confident pose, deliberately out of time and more profoundly subversive and deeply embodied than that peddled by weary politicians or high street outfitters. Cecil Beaton and Kenneth Tynan produced a celebration of such personalities in their publication *Persona Grata* of 1953. As an apt example, the theatrical entrepreneur Hugh 'Binkie' Beaumont sprawls in profile on a chaise longue across one of Beaton's photographs. Tynan's acerbic prose does him full justice:

> Beaumont, who is forty three years old . . . is the eminence grise of English Drama. Out of self defence, he has become an enigma, and it suits him, his was never an emphatic personality, and he has little truck with personal wealth or imperatorial whim . . . His social manner is flawless, twinkling without smugness, shining without slickness; the gestures are soft and self-effacing, inducing a gentle hypnosis . . . as he talks he smokes, insatiably but smoothly, never in nervous sucks . . . His trick of holding his cigarette between the middle two fingers while wearing a monogrammed signet ring on the little one, represents his only homage to dandyism. Vocally . . . favouring a lazy, glazed, leaning tenor, which irons out its sentences as if they were so many silk shirts. 'Terrible' is the universal epithet.
>
> (Beaton and Tynan 1953: 15–16)

Ultimately it is Beaumont's body, as much as his clothes, which marks him out as a 'true' dandy, the softness of his voice deputising for the luxury of silk shirts. But perhaps this is the logical destination for a sartorial practice which lost its visible potency at a moment when refinement, modernity, outrage and all those other dandified pursuits were opened up to a teenage market on an unprecedented commercial scale. In such a context distinction can only be marked by, rather than on the body. As pop journalist Nik Cohn states (his homophobia a product of the times):

> The Edwardian look . . . lasted til about 1954, by which time it had been taken up and caricatured by the Teddy Boys, who made it so disreputable that even homosexuals were embarrassed to wear it. Nothing could have been more ironic: having started as an upper class defence, Edwardiana now formed the basis for the first great detonation of male working-class fashion.
>
> (Cohn 1971: 27)

And so the rarefied version of dandyism inaugurated by Brummell and endorsed by Baudelaire finally dissolved from view, the possibilities for constructing a radical surface identity through the manipulation of a regimented wardrobe given over to the commodified realm of the boutique owner, the features writer and the pop celebrity in a logical conclusion to the processes set in motion during the period of Wilde and Whiteing. By 1965 the 'dandy-style' signified little more than the fancy-dress ruffles and military 'retro-chic' which cluttered the rails of Carnaby Street and the King's Road. The word itself now persists in fashion journalism as an adjective rather than a noun, and dandyism survives in the world of style magazines as a rather diffuse, but potent description of masculine glamour, effort and attitude, usually retaining some nostalgic connection to the style of the models excavated here/ (In the late twentieth-century spreads of *Arena* and *Vogue Hommes* the descriptive repertoire of dandyism is endlessly played out but with seemingly little direction.) In a literature where language evoking male sartorial desire is even more limited than that reserved for the meaningful description of fashionable femininities, its residual survival counts as a blessing, though it lacks the virulent energy which marked comparable early nineteenth-century commentaries.

A resistance to closure, together with an acknowledgement of the emptiness which lies behind the surface have always been pivotal characteristics of the dandy's repertoire, aiding and frustrating definitive categorisation. With this in mind I hesitate in drawing any firmer conclusions from the changing nature of dandyism over the course of the modern period, other than affirming that the dandy narrative forms a compelling commentary on the rise of consumer culture and its shifting relationship to the bodies of men. This is perhaps best expressed as a continuous tension between notions of elite and mass taste, between a controlled exercising of restraint and an abandonment to conspicuous consumption. It is pertinent then that we should hold on to the constant dialogue between fashionable clothing, corporeality and concerns with sexual and class identities which his figure represents as a mainstay of contemporary discourse. Above all else, as succeeding incarnations of the type have shown, the central identification of the dandy with his wardrobe is a visceral one, the suit as sensate a membrane as the skin. Through the historical actions of the dandy we remember what it is to wear fashion.

Acknowledgement

I am extremely grateful for the perceptive comments of Caroline Evans in the drafting of this chapter.

References

Amies, H. (1954) *Just So Far*, London: Collins.
—— (1994) *The Englishman's Suit*, London: Quartet.
Anon (1820) *The Dandy's Songster. Being a Collection of the Most Charming, Exquisite, Popular and Most Approved Dandy Songs for the Fashionable Dandies*, Newcastle upon Tyne: J. Marshall.
Beaton, C. and Tynan, K. (1953) *Persona Grata*, London: Allan Wingate.
Boscagli, M. (1996) *Eye on the Flesh. Fashions of Masculinity in the Early Twentieth Century*, Oxford: Westview Press.

Breward, C. (1995) *The Culture of Fashion*, Manchester: Manchester University Press.
—— (1999) *The Hidden Consumer. Masculinities, Fashion and City Life 1860–1914*, Manchester: Manchester University Press.

Chenoune, Farid (1993) *A History of Men's Fashion*, Paris: Flammarion.

Cohen, E. (1993) *Talk on the Wilde Side. Towards a Genealogy of a Discourse on Male Sexualities*, London: Routledge.

Cohn, N. (1971) *Today There Are No Gentlemen*, London: Weidenfeld & Nicolson.

Dellamora, R. (1996) 'Homosexual scandal and compulsory heterosexuality in the 1890s', in L. Pyckett (ed.) *Reading Fin de Siècle Fictions*, London: Longman.

Egan, P. (1821) *Life in London, or the Day and Night Scenes of Jerry Hawthorne Esq., and Corinthian Tom*, London: Sherwood, Neely & Jones.

Egan, P. (1976) *Boxiana, or Sketches of Ancient and Modern Pugilism*, ed. J. Ford, London: Folio Society.

Gagnier, R. (1986) *Idylls of the Marketplace. Oscar Wilde and the Victorian Public*, Aldershot: Scolar.

Garelick, R. (1998) *Rising Star. Dandyism, Gender and Performance in the Fin de Siècle*, Princeton: Princeton University Press.

Gronow, R. (1862) *Reminiscences of Captain Gronow*, London.

Hapgood, L. (1994) 'Regaining a focus: new perspectives on the novels of Richard Whiteing', in N. le Manos and M.J. Rochelson (eds) *Transforming Genres: New Approaches to British Fiction of the 1890's*, London: Macmillan.

Hollander, A. (1994) *Sex and Suits*, New York: Kodansha.

Jobling, Paul (1999) *Fashion Spreads: Word and Image in Fashion Photography since 1980*, Oxford: Berg.

Laver, J. (1968) *Dandies*, London: Routledge.

McDowell, Colin (1997) *The Man of Fashion: Peacock Males and the Perfect Gentleman*, London: Thames & Hudson.

Moers, E. (1960) *The Dandy. Brummell to Beerbohm*, London: Secker & Warburg.

Mort, F. (1996) *Cultures of Consumption. Masculinities and Social Space in Late Twentieth-century Britain*, London: Routledge.

Nixon, S. (1996) *Hard Looks*, London: UCL Press.

Pritchard, R. (1898) *London and Londoners*, London.

Showalter, E. (1992) *Sexual Anarchy. Gender and Culture at the Fin de Siècle*, London: Bloomsbury.

Sinfield, A. (1994) *The Wilde Century. Effeminacy, Oscar Wilde and the Queer Moment*, London: Cassell.

Viscusi, R. (1986) *Max Beerbohm, or the Dandy Dante, Rereading with Mirrors*, Baltimore: Johns Hopkins University Press.

Whiteing, R. (1899) *No. 5 John Street*, London: Grant Richards.

Wilson, E. (1985) *Adorned in Dreams*, London: Virago.

Chapter 17

Sarah Cardwell

DARCY'S ESCAPE
An icon in the making

DARCY CONSTITUTES A CURIOUS ICON for our times. Originating in Andrew Davies's 1995 BBC adaptation of *Pride and Prejudice*, Colin Firth's Darcy escaped the bounds of the serial and, lusted after by millions, became a 'free-floating signifier', as icons are wont to do. Darcy's appeal is primarily sexual, as is the case with 'traditional' icons. Yet it is the ways in which he differs from those predecessors that make him such a curious and important example of iconicity, and that, indeed, guarantee his salience in contemporary popular culture, despite the apparent hindrances of his fictionality and his 'birthplace' (television). What is also intriguing in this case is the role played by the text itself (*Pride and Prejudice*, 1995) in signalling Darcy's potential for escape into iconicity.

'Mr Darcy – sorry, Colin Firth – looks great in jodhpurs' (Brown 1997: 6) and a 'translucent Regency shirt' (Billen 1997: 6). Indeed he does. Colin Firth-as-Darcy was born to wear period costume: it flatters his figure, drawing attention to his muscular legs and his broad, though hairless, chest. In *Pride and Prejudice*, glowering, brooding, shooting icy looks and disdainful sneers all around, Darcy's near-silent display of manly characteristics means that we can gaze upon him without being distracted by having to listen to what he has to say. Lisa Hopkins notes that '*Pride and Prejudice* . . . is unashamed about appealing to women – and in particular about fetishizing and framing Darcy and offering him up to the female gaze' (Hopkins 1998: 112).

Of course, the appeal of Darcy is inextricable from his physical presentation within the text. Darcy without the trappings – the thigh-skimming jodphurs; the high collars that determine Darcy's haughty, aloof air; the dark curly hair, complete with sideburns, implying an unruly, wild streak – is Colin Firth. As Alison Graham writes:

as Mr Darcy in the BBC adaptation of *Pride and Prejudice* he was lusted after by millions of otherwise sensible women. All it took was for him to smoulder on a staircase or rise, dripping and fully clothed, from an impromptu dip in a lake, and women across the country – and later the world – melted like toasted brie. And there's the rub. It was Mr Darcy they were swooning over, not necessarily Colin Firth . . . Firth would be the first to admit that he doesn't turn heads when he walks into the pub. And even at the height of Darcymania, he was rarely stopped on the streets.

(Graham 1997a: 22–3)

Graham's unbecoming comparison of the rather average-looking Firth with his attractive, brooding alter ego Darcy verges on the offensive; to add insult to injury, the piece finishes with the note '[T]urn to page 126 for the second and final token for your Darcy poster' (Graham 1997a: 23). Obviously there cannot be the clear separation intimated by Graham between the dull Firth and the sexy Darcy, for they are inextricably physically linked in the unique way that actors always are with the roles they play. Yet Graham's comments suggest the importance to 'Darcymania' of maintaining a distinction between the performer (Firth) and the performed (Darcy).

Herein lies the first fundamental difference between Darcy and traditional icons. In an important sense, Darcy clearly does not exist. Although it is true that the veneration of an icon idealises and objectifies him/her, requiring a refusal to accept the existence of an ordinary, flawed human being behind the image, Darcy is even more obviously a fiction. Notably, critical and popular discourse flaunted an awareness of Darcy as fictional and overtly recognised his fictionality as a source of his appeal. Another contemporary, equally popular fictional creation, Bridget Jones, offers an intriguing ongoing analysis of the Firth/Darcy (real/fiction) distinction. On comparing her potential boyfriend Mark Darcy with Mr Darcy, Bridget observes that 'Mr Darcy was more attractive because he was ruder but [his] being imaginary was a disadvantage that could not be overlooked' (Fielding 1996: 247). Further, on seeing a photograph of 'Darcy and Elizabeth' (actually Firth and Jennifer Ehle) in the *Evening Standard*, she notes that she feels 'disorientated and worried, for surely Mr Darcy would never do anything so vain and frivolous as to be an actor and yet Mr Darcy *is* an actor. Hmmm. All v. confusing' (Fielding 1996: 248).

Whilst iconic film stars bring their own particular 'star persona' to the roles they play, their renowned iconicity overshadowing the roles they perform, the Darcy phenomenon reversed this familiar process. Colin Firth was overtaken by Darcy – Darcy became more famous, more significant than Firth. Indeed, Firth's exorcism of Darcy in later roles such as that of Paul Ashworth in *Fever Pitch* (1997) revealed Firth's body and identity, now uninhabited by the spirit of Darcy, to be rather dull and very ordinary.

The differences between Firth and Darcy, and the relative superiority of the latter as an icon, are central to the public's imaginative engagement with the Darcy phenomenon. Bridget Jones's problematic subordination of Firth by Darcy, and her excessive hero worship of the latter, continues into the sequel to her *Diary*, aptly named *The Edge of Reason*. This later book, published in 1999, is a testament to the enduring mythic power of Firth's Darcy, and to the extent to which his iconic status requires a misrepresentation or denial of the 'real' and a celebration of fictionality. When Bridget is assigned to interview Firth about his forthcoming film *Fever Pitch* (1997), she must finally overcome her desire to subsume Firth under his alter-image Darcy and instead recognise the fictionality of the latter and the personhood of the former. This is not achieved without a struggle. Bridget insists on referring to Firth as Darcy in the days preceding the interview, and their meeting itself constitutes a battle of wills as Bridget repeatedly questions Firth/Darcy regarding his intentions towards Elizabeth, his political beliefs, and (most frequently) the 'wet shirt' incident mentioned by Graham, above. Meanwhile Firth wrestles to reclaim himself from Darcy's identity, eventually pleading 'Can we talk about something that isn't to do with Mr Darcy?' The close of the interview sees Bridget finally vocalise her confusion between Darcy and Firth, and Firth deny any meaningful links between the two:

> BJ   But do you think you're not like Mr Darcy?
> CF   I do think I'm not like Mr Darcy, yes.
> BJ   I think you're exactly like Mr Darcy.
> CF   In what way?
> BJ   You talk the same way as him.
> CF   Oh, do I?
> BJ   You look exactly like him, and I, oh, oh –
> [*Protracted crashing noises followed by sounds of struggle*]
>
> (Fielding 1999: 178)

As Bridget recognises that her worship of the iconic Darcy is based only on superficial features of voice and appearance, her clumsy expression of desire and confusion – '*protracted crashing noises followed by sounds of struggle*' – echoes the destruction of her long-admired icon through her failure to maintain any level of belief in his independent existence.

The 'Darcy phenomenon', noted by popular writers like Graham and Fielding and explored by academics like Hopkins (1998), extrapolated Darcy/Firth from his place within a text, and placed him as a 'free-floating signifier' within a wider cultural context. Darcy 'enter[s] a moment of autonomy, of a relatively free-floating existence, as over against its former objects' (Jameson 1991: 96). This postmodern aspect of the *Pride and Prejudice* experience undermines Jonathan Miller's assertion that

> The fact that someone is in a novel . . . does not mean that they are *in* the novel in the same way that someone else might be *in* Birmingham or *in* a cubicle. They cannot be taken out of the novel and put in a film of it.
>
> (Miller 1986: 238–9)

Darcy, by contrast, was not only concretised in the 1995 adaptation to the extent that Firth-as-Darcy became a more familiar Darcy than Austen's one, but was also freed from the programme to reappear elsewhere (such as in the BBC TV licence and Heineken adverts): in other words, he gained the freedom necessary to become an icon.

As suggested at the beginning of this chapter, Darcy's birthplace was also untraditional. Unlike most icons, who arise within the glamorous fields of cinema or fashion before bursting into a wider cultural sphere, Darcy was born in the domestic medium of television, which one might imagine would limit his potential for iconicity, the latter commonly implying a rejection of the mundane, the domestic, the quotidian. Yet it is the specificities of television that ensured (or at least increased the likelihood of) Darcy's release into the extended cultural community as an icon – not just because of the widespread distribution of his image, but because of the particular nature of our attachment to television and to 'television events' like *Pride and Prejudice*. His appearance in a programme marked as 'special' – as 'a television event' (Graham 1997b: 122) – enhances his cultural significance. Fan Bridget Jones recounts,

> Just nipped out for fags prior to getting changed ready for BBC *Pride and Prejudice*. Hard to believe there are so many cars out on the roads. Shouldn't they be at home getting ready? Love the nation being so addicted.
>
> (Fielding 1996: 246)

Thus she articulates a desire for a shared national viewing experience, dependent upon a simultaneity of broadcast possible only in the televisual medium, which also endows Darcy with a 'presentness-to-us' not available to icons born and existing elsewhere.

Darcy is thus a man struggling for release – a feat he accomplishes quite spectacularly and on many levels, succeeding, as an icon, in escaping textual boundaries, and even the actor who plays him. Finally, *Pride and Prejudice* appears deliberately to construct Darcy as a potential icon – not just by making him 'sexy', but by figuring in the text his desire to escape the text(s), medium and the actor playing him. *Pride and Prejudice* (1995) could have been subtitled 'Darcy's Bid for Freedom'. The overwhelming sense garnered is of a man struggling to contain his passions, trying to resist the urge that drives him to express the wealth of emotions he feels. Darcy, the *real* Darcy, it is suggested, longs to escape the bounds of conventional behaviour imposed upon him by 1800s society; within the framework of a traditional classic novel adaptation, this desire for escape is reconfigured in generic terms. Darcy's attempts to gain his freedom here require his escape from the limitations imposed upon him by the genre itself. His struggle against the expectations of generic character is represented directly as he determines to escape conventional codes of behaviour, traditional modes of representation, and even his clothes.

Textually, Darcy is frequently represented as imprisoned. Taking the place most often designated for women in these adaptations, he is often physically confined. Traditional classic novel adaptations are 'organized around the viewpoint of bourgeois female characters who are both actually and metaphorically "housebound"', and display the 'woman at the window', ever gazing out from her confined space (Pidduck 1998: 382). *Pride and Prejudice* offers a reversal of this convention, as Darcy gazes longingly out of windows, or from a distance, at Elizabeth, unable to follow his instincts and express his feelings for her; in addition, he is frequently shown in profile, particularly during the early stages of the adaptation, emphasising the containment of his viewpoint within the text (Hopkins 1998: 113–14). Darcy is a man frustrated by his confinement, whether that confinement is configured as physical or emotional. The effects of this imprisonment, and of Darcy's struggle to escape it, are manifested in and displayed by his body. Darcy displays an excess of sexual energy, through scenes of him jousting, horse-riding, pacing restlessly, and so on. Specifically, as Hopkins observes, during salient moments 'the visual imagery is structured by a heady mingling of two *leitmotifs*: heat and sex' (Hopkins 1998: 116).

Darcy's escape is a slow one, building to a moment of release from the text-as-adaptation, generic norms and Darcy's own repression of his desire. In the moments when Darcy lets his guard down, and releases some of the pent-up energies described above, he is literally shown to be cooling down his heated passions. We see Darcy taking a bath, and the removal of his formal period costume emphasises his vulnerability, his emotional being, under the clothes the genre places him in. Later, as he expresses in a letter to Elizabeth all that he has been longing to say, the emotional exertion of breaking down his own restrictive behaviour necessitates the action of splashing his face with water to cool down his overheated desire for expression. Finally, and most famously, Darcy's desires build to such a degree that he finds himself impulsively, and symbolically, flinging off his outer garments, tearing open his shirt and diving into the lake at Pemberley, emerging 'in a state of some blousoned transparency' (Billen 1997: 6). As Hopkins writes, 'the fever-heat of his passion, it seems, is still in need of cooling' (Hopkins 1998: 118).

However, this scene has significance beyond this diegetically related concern. Thus divesting himself of the manifest vestiges of restrictive nineteenth-century clothing and modes of behaviour – at least in so far as they are commonly depicted in traditional classic novel adaptations, Darcy simultaneously discards generic convention. In addition, in breaking away from the book (in all three instances, but so vividly in the last), Darcy also breaks free from the dogma of fidelity that underlies faithful adaptations, cutting himself away from the source novel, from Austen's text and her characterisation of his character. The importance of this famous lake incident is thus revealed: it marks Darcy's escape to iconicity.

References

Billen, Andrew (1997) 'Fan fatale', *Observer*, 30 March: 6.

Brown, Maggie (1997) 'Provocations: Pride not Prejudice', *Guardian*, 1 February: 6.

Fielding, Helen (1996) *Bridget Jones's Diary*, London/Basingstoke: Picador.

—— (1999) *Bridget Jones: The Edge of Reason*, London/Basingstoke: Macmillan.

Graham, Alison (1997a) 'My goodness, how they've changed', *Radio Times*, 12–18 July: 22–3.

—— (1997b) 'Confessions of a belated Darcy fan', *Radio Times*, 26 July–1 August: 122.

Hopkins, Lisa (1998) 'Mr. Darcy's body: privileging the female gaze' in Linda Troost and Sayre Greenfield (eds) *Jane Austen in Hollywood*, Kentucky: University of Kentucky, 111–21.

Jameson, Fredric (1991) *Postmodernism; or, the Cultural Logic of Late Capitalism*, Durham, NC: Duke University Press.

Miller, Jonathan (1986) *Subsequent Performances*, London: Faber & Faber.

Pidduck, Julianne (1998) 'Of windows and country walks: frames of space and movement in 1990s Austen adaptations', *Screen* 39 (4): 381–400.

Chapter 18

Sarah Gilligan

GWYNETH PALTROW

'CHARMING, ELOQUENT, BEAUTIFUL AND DIVINE' (Corry 1998: 18). Neil Corry's gushing depiction of Gwyneth Paltrow in his review of *Sliding Doors* (dir. Peter Howitt; 1998), epitomises the way in which the press tend to describe Paltrow. She is rarely described in terms of her acting abilities, but rather in terms of her 'look'. Julia Roberts has described Paltrow's look as 'incredibly interesting' a look which 'transcends time':

> She can look very today, she can look very Sixties, she can look very period. And also she can go from being incredibly, exquisitely beautiful to being just plain interesting-looking. She's got a face you want to look at for a very long time; you want to absorb it.
>
> (Julia Roberts quoted in Hochman 1996: 32)

In April 1995, Paltrow was described as 'the luckiest girl in the world'. She was 'the woman Brad Pitt has fallen for' (Pearce 1995: 10). For the London premiere of Pitt's *Legends of the Fall* (dir. Edward Zwick; 1994), she chose an outfit from the three that Calvin Klein had sent from LA, via Federal Express (Pearce 1995: 10; Watson 1996: 2). In 1996, with the release of *Emma* (dir. Douglas McGrath), Paltrow became the 'It girl' of the moment. Her leading role enabled her to move another notch up the celebrity hierarchy, to become a 'star' (Lim 1996; Katz 1996). She was on the front cover of American *Vogue* in the August, which as Ian Katz notes is 'a rare distinction for a non model' (Katz 1996: 2). *Vogue*'s editor Anna Wintour wrote that Paltrow was 'well known as the actress every designer wants to dress' (Katz 1996: 2). Calvin Klein personally asked Paltrow to be the model for the print campaign that Autumn. She turned him down and in an interview told Lesley O'Toole that:

I was going to do it, but literally couldn't. I had no time. That would
be fun but I don't know. . . . I really feel that if there are any more
pictures of me anywhere people are going to kill themselves.

(O'Toole 1996: 9)

Despite her supermodel beauty of 'long blonde hair, perfect angles, waifish thinness and angelic face', writers such as David Hochman saw it as offset by 'a healthy
(and refreshing) dose of goofiness' (Hochman 1996: 33). Paltrow in her interview
with Hochman declared:

Calvin Klein asked me to do some runway stuff, but I just couldn't do
it . . . For me, it's far more difficult to cultivate that silent-mystery-
model thing than go, 'Oh hi, howahya?' You can't have a personality
when you're sashaying down the runway. I could never walk down that
thing.

(Hochman 1996: 33)

Despite her apparent increasing star status, just after the US release of *Emma*, *Entertainment Weekly* undertook a survey on the streets of New York; when asked to
identify pictures of Paltrow, the most common response was 'Brad Pitt's girlfriend' (Lim 1996).

It was not until early 1998 that Paltrow moved from being a celebrity girlfriend or the current 'next big thing', to being a fully fledged Hollywood fashion
icon. In the February, her new look was launched on the cover of British *Vogue*;
a messy 'undone' look, of an ear-length, tousled blonde bob, which promptly
caused a 'stampede to the hair salons' by women clutching the magazine and
wanting 'a Gwyneth' (Maxted 1998: 22). *Vogue* wanted to put her on the cover,
because of her 'contemporary feel' (Maxted 1998: 22). With the UK release of
Great Expectations (dir. Alfonso Cuarón) in April and *Sliding Doors* in May, this
contemporary feel and 'look' was further perpetuated. Both films enabled a shift
away from the costume drama look of *Emma*,[1] to contemporary fashion wardrobes
provided by Donna Karan and Calvin Klein. In both films the look is classic and
understated, a focus upon clean lines and the way the fabric skims the body, rather
than upon showy spectacular excess. Together with the clothes were yet more
haircuts to be copied; from long and straight to short and styled.

Paltrow from then on existed not as a single iconic image, but as a multiplicity of images, a ceaseless flow of self transformation and masquerade. This
notion of masquerade pinnacled at the 1999 Oscars when she 'dressed up' in a
pink Ralph Lauren dress, with shoe string straps and full skirt. 'With her goldie
locks, regal jewels and snow-white skin, Gwyneth looked like a fairy tale princess
. . . The only thing missing was a tiara' (Comita 2000a: 94). Jenny Comita in *US
Weekly*, proposed that the image of Paltrow in her Lauren dress embodies a return
in Oscar style, to 'pretty dresses reminiscent of Hepburn's and Kelly's'. The article
juxtaposes the image of Paltrow with an image of Grace Kelly from the 1955
Oscars (Comita 2000b: 93). Indeed, there is some likeness between them, an air
of refinement, of sophisticated femininity. Yet Paltrow's androgynous body
contrasts with Kelly's feminine curves. The wearing of the Lauren dress with her

hair scraped back and minimal make-up, can be seen to epitomise the understated, classic style of Ralph Lauren, making her the ideal mannequin for his designs. Yet simultaneously, Paltrow has an air of 'dressing up', the smiling face contrasting with the awkwardness of the body, the dress although beautiful, doesn't quite fit, and instead draws attention to just how thin Paltrow actually is. At the 71st Oscars, her 'look' the previous year was parodied by Matt Stone of *South Park* fame, wearing a pink, ill-fitting slip with sunglasses and stubble.[2] Although looking nothing like her, the dress instantly signified Paltrow the fashion icon. At the same ceremony, Paltrow wore a grey embroidered Calvin Klein dress; it was surpassed in the media by the showy, flesh-revealing Versace dresses worn by Liz Hurley and Cameron Diaz. Paltrow's look was more understated, less overtly sexy; she embodied the chic of classic fashion as espoused by designers such as Klein.

The representation of Paltrow as a refined and understated fashion icon can be seen as constructed through a combination of text and images. Column inches describe her upper-middle-class upbringing, Hollywood 'family' and education in a manner that represents her as the ideal all-American girl, the 'product of all American health and wealth' (Nadelson 1998). In a similar way to Grace Kelly, she becomes the 'ideal mate' rather than the sexualised 'playmate' (see Harris 1957: 42). Paltrow's body language also echoes that of Kelly; the straight back and raised chin highlight the long neck and well defined bone structure of her face.[3] The posture creates an air of grace and refinement, reinforced by the huge smile and penetrating gaze which dominates so many images of her. The body language serves to create a look that seems timeless, an image that is dominated by class and femininity. It seems apt therefore, that Anthony Minghella developed the part of Marge in *The Talented Mr Ripley* (1999) specifically with Paltrow in mind, as she was the only person to him who could evoke 'a well-bred, well-to-do, American ex-patriate in the 1950s – who could inhabit the costumes, the voice' (Minghella quoted in Schneller 1999: 56). Paltrow in *Ripley* has a casual look that evokes the confidence of the very rich (see Hodgkinson 2000: 4). As the 'Official Film of London Fashion Week', its influence was seen from Harvey Nichols to Etam; with mid-length skirts, capri pants and fitted tops filling the shop windows and rails (Armstrong 2000: 39). With the LA premiere of *Ripley,* Paltrow publicly presented yet another image of herself; instead of her trademark blonde she appeared with chestnut brown hair.[4] This new look sparked a surge of articles: 'Look like Gwyneth for just £6.99'; 'The year in Gwyneth'; 'Gwyneth reveals her style'.[5] The dramatic difference in her look can be seen as an attempt to move away from the image of herself at the 1999 Oscars:

> There is this image that I feel is not me. I don't feel connected to it. I feel the need to point out there is a difference between me and this person that everybody projects all this stuff on and everybody has all these opinions about. And I feel that it's not based on criteria that are real or that I've contributed to putting out there. In a way, I wish this wasn't my real name. It's nice for people who change their name because they can separate the two. You know in real life they're Betty Whoever and then they're Lauren Bacall or something. I wish I'd done that. . . .

I dyed it for a role in a film called *Bounce*. The director was very tired of the blonde Gwyneth Paltrow person. And I was too. I'm tired of her. So now there's a new Gwyneth Paltrow person.

(Paltrow cited in Palmer 2000: 18)

By getting 'rid of' the old Gwyneth Paltrow person, she has in turn become more 'real', more obtainable. As a fashion icon, it is not only the glamorous star self that is of interest, but also the 'real self':[6]

I'd be happy to wear a cashmere tank, a pair of jeans, cargo pants or khakis every day . . . I always pack Turnbull & Asser men's pyjamas, leather pants and a big, soft sweater. I never wear one person's clothes head to toe. Right now I'm wearing my favourite T by Marc Jacobs. The jeans are Diesel. My boots are D&G, the coat is Armani. Mixing the elements is what personal style is all about.

(Paltrow cited in Rubenstein 1999)

Despite her status as a fashion icon, Paltrow claims the sexiest thing in her wardrobe is her pyjamas: 'they're lovely and loose and made of flannel' (Pearce 2000: 33). In representing Paltrow in such a way, we are encouraged to identify with her, attempt to copy her look, produce a new idealised image of ourselves.[7] Although we can attempt to copy the look, it is never fully achieved, there is always something missing. Perhaps the something that is missing is the essence of Paltrow. With her beaming smile she possesses supermodel looks without the sullen attitude, an Upper East Side refinement merges with the ordinariness of the girl-next-door. Through watching her in films, going through newspaper and magazine cuttings, production stills, photoshoots and 'real life' photos, Paltrow exists as a ceaseless flow of images. Perhaps it is here that her appeal resides for audiences and designers, not in a single image that 'is' Paltrow, but in the multiplicity of images. Past and present, character, stars and the 'real', merge into something ever recognisable, yet somehow never stable.

Notes

1   For discussion of the costume design for *Emma*, see Douglas McGrath (1996: 74–77, 117).

2   For a copy of the image online see: http://www.oscars.com/redcarpet/red_026.html

3   *A Perfect Murder* (the remake of Hitchcock's *Dial M for Murder*) provides another point of comparison between Paltrow and Grace Kelly, together with another example of Paltrow 'dressing up' in an evening dress.

4   See Lanani (1999: 15). There are some 'snap-shot' images of Paltrow in the autumn of 1999 with red and also chestnut hair, but these did not really get mass coverage until the surge of articles following the LA premiere of *Ripley* in Dec. 1999.

5   See *New Woman*, March 2000; *Now!*, 2 Feb. 2000; *US Weekly*, 3 April 2000 (amongst others).

6   Richard Dyer argues that we never actually know stars 'directly as real people, only as they are to be found in media texts' (Dyer 1999: 2). Therefore even the 'real' images of Paltrow can also be read as signifying constructions.

7   For a discussion of women copying the look of stars as an idealised self, see Stacey (1998: 167–8).

References

Anon (2000) 'Oh Gwyneth, now you're just showing off!', *New Woman*, March: 72–6.

Armstrong, Lisa (2000) 'The talented Miss Roth', *The Times*, section 3, 14 February: 39.

Comita, Jenny (2000a) 'The year in Gwyneth', *US Weekly*, 3 April: 94.

—— (2000b) 'Awards night rewind: eight decades of Oscar fashion highlights', *US Weekly*, 3 April: 92–3.

Corry, Neil (1998) *Sliding Doors* – review, *Film Review*, June: 18.

Dyer, Richard (1997) *Stars* (new edn with supplementary chapter and bibliography by Paul McDonald), London: BFI.

Gandee, Charles (1996) 'The luckiest girl alive', *Vogue*, August. Online at http://www.gwynethpaltrow.org

Harris, Thomas (1988) 'The building of popular images: Grace Kelly and Marilyn Munroe' in Christine Gledhill (ed.) *Stardom: Industry of Desire*, London and New York: Routledge. (Original article written in 1957.)

Hochman, David (1996) 'She's got it. She's got him. She's got everything', *Daily Telegraph*, *Weekend* magazine, 7 August: 30, 32–3.

Hodgkinson, Will (2000) 'The stylish Mr Ripley', *Guardian*, 'The Guide' section, 19–25 February: 4–7.

Katz, Ian (1996) 'Hollywood's smash Its', *Guardian*, G2, 14 August: 2–3.

Lanani, Shiraz (1999) 'A look to dye for', *Mirror*, 14 December: 15.

Lim, Dennis (1996) 'The making of a movie star', *Independent on Sunday*, 8 August.

McGrath, Douglas (1996) 'Raising Jane: a diary of the making of *Emma*', *Premiere*, September, 10 (1): 74–7, 117.

Maxted, Anna (1998) 'Getting to grips with the Gwyneth', *Daily Telegraph*, 13 March.

Nadelson, Reggle (1998) 'If looks could kill', *Tatler Magazine*, November. Online at http://www.gwynethpaltrow.org

O'Toole, Lesley (1996) 'A cute accent', *Guardian*, G2, 3 September: 8–9.

Palmer, Martyn (2000) 'A star is re-born', *Times* magazine, 12 February: 14–21.

Pearce, Garth (1995) 'The woman Brad Pitt has fallen for', *Mail on Sunday*, *You Magazine*, 4 April: 10–11.

Rubinstein, Hal (1999) 'Gwyneth when she glitters', *Instyle Magazine*, January. Online at http://www.gwynethpaltrow.org

Schneller, Johanna (1999) 'Gwyneth Paltrow', *Women in Hollywood 2000: Premiere Special*, 52–56, 102.

Stacey, Jackie (1998) *Star Gazing: Hollywood cinema and Female Spectatorship*, London and New York: Routledge.

Walson, Shane (1996) 'The Pitts', *Evening Standard*, 7 June: 2.

PART FOUR

Spectacle and subculture

Chapter 19

Angela McRobbie

FASHION AS A CULTURE INDUSTRY

WHEN THE NEW LABOUR government came to power in May 1997, there were few signs that the culture industries would so quickly be propelled to the political centre-stage as representing the great hope for economic recovery and job creation as well as the symbol of a modernised Britain. Granted, Tony Blair had expressed his desire to overturn John Major's traditional and nostalgic image of Britain, the land of spinsters on bicycles and warm beer. Instead the UK was to become a 'young country' (Blair 1996). It was ripe for social change, and young people were the key agents for bringing about this social transformation. But this did not suggest the wholesale endorsement of the culture industries which followed the election of the new government. The Cool Britannia episode, a media and politics publicity jamboree to promote UK creative talent internationally, at once marked the start of the government's bid to turn British-made culture into global commodity and the extent to which such media-led initiatives could so easily rebound. The photo-opportunities at No 10 Downing Street with pop star Noel Gallagher and his wife Meg Matthews were an accident waiting to happen. As soon as government attempted to prove its 'cool' credentials, the unruly 'youth' felt called upon to dissociate themselves from such endeavours. It was reminiscent of the would-be trendy teacher attempting to show his talents on the floor at the school disco and the floor quickly emptying as pupils exchange embarrassed glances and decide to sit this one out. Some months later when actress Emma Thompson was called upon to be a mentor and role model for young women, she acted in exactly the same way. No way, she ungratefully replied, she'd much rather be identified with the bad girls.

But since then, though with less socialising with musicians, fashion designers and celebrities, the emphasis on the culture industries have continued to grow. Minister of Culture Chris Smith claimed in the annual report of the Creative

Industries Task Force that more than one million people were now employed in the sector. The new so-called guru to Tony Blair, economist and journalist Charles Leadbeater has talked about the future Hollywoodisation of the UK labour market (Leadbeater 1999). He was referring to the process by which many scripts are written but only a few make it into production. Leadbeater wanted young British 'cultural entrepreneurs' to adopt a more resilient approach, where failure in one venture becomes an incentive to succeed in the next. At the same time, up and down the country, local councillors discuss 'cultural regeneration'. In de-industrialised regions the prospect of attracting some artists with the lure of cheap studio space is the most desirable of outcomes for policy-makers. It creates interesting stories for the press, it holds the promise of gallery owners and more mainstream media companies moving in and with these the whole panoply of coffee shops, bars and restaurants, i.e. the 'Shoreditch effect'. Such high hopes are not wholly restricted to urban areas; one recent report in the *Guardian* described an attempt to encourage creative and artistic skills among the nation's farming and agricultural community, as they too face the same threat to their livelihoods as did industrial workers twenty years ago (Gibbons 1999).

The new centrality of the arts and culture is now evident almost on a daily basis, from the grand opening of the Tate Modern (11/5/2000) to the ongoing debates about what art works should be displayed on the 'vacant plinth' on Trafalgar Square. Indeed on BBC2's *Newsnight* programme (12/5/2000) an architect argued for the whole of the Trafalgar Square space to become a traffic-free site for public art. There is almost a sense of national euphoria as art becomes a topic of discussion not just for the few but for the people as a whole, as Blair put it when asked his thoughts on the opening of Tate Modern. Art critics have become the most called upon experts to give their opinions and explain to this public the thinking behind conceptual art. But it is not just art that attracts this kind of news coverage. The media also report on a regular basis on the numbers of young authors, many still in their teens, signed up by publishers offering huge advances on the basis of a half-finished manuscript. Stories of writers like J.K. Rowling moving from 'rags to riches' as a single parent writing her world best-sellers (the Harry Potter series) on a notepad in Edinburgh cafés while her baby slept in her pushchair have become commonplace. Such swings in fortune have led sociologists to comment on the new lottery-style cultural labour market as evidence of the 'chaos of reward' (Young 1999) or else as a windfall of 'easy money' (Beck 1999). This kind of success is also presented as evidence of the new meritocracy, with many talented young artists and writers and designers coming from poor or working-class backgrounds (Damien Hirst and Tracey Emin are usually offered as examples). British film-making has also been the focus of enormous attention, resulting in the recent setting up of a new Film Council led by film-director Alan Parker with a governmental brief to support scripts which have popular box-office appeal.

The recent successes of British-produced cultural forms has led some commentators like Leadbeater to celebrate the possibility in the UK of a new, more open society where 'everyone has a chance to make it'. One of his models of success is fashion designer Alexander McQueen whom he describes as an East End boy with no formal qualifications. In fact McQueen studied for a Masters at Central St Martin's College of Art and Design. Leadbeater's error is indicative of his desire to insist on the way in which traditional barriers have been broken down, allowing talent to shine through. In fact the success stories of UK-trained fashion designers have been relatively restricted to Stella McCartney, John Galliano and McQueen, with Vivienne Westwood achieving status as a kind of national icon. In the final section of this chapter I shall consider the issues which make it more difficult for fashion designers to sustain both recognition and success in significant numbers and the questions that fashion as a culture industry poses for governmental policy. I shall also argue that fashion design increasingly finds itself forced into re-definition as 'fine art fashion' in order to attract the kind of media attention needed to create names and generate contracts. The new climate for working as a fashion designer in the UK following the high rate of failure and bankruptcy in the mid-1990s has forced a change in practice for most young designers which I will describe in greater length later in this chapter.

It is noticeable, however, that the various articles and essays which have appeared in the last few months on the new prominence of the culture industries have had little or nothing to say about the experience of those working in this labour market, be it fashion or fine art. Instead the focus has been on broader issues, including the idea of 'cultural governance' as marking a new kind of political strategy. Valentine, for example, has described the way in which culture and the arts have been defined as socially beneficial, as healthy for the nation, even a better way of encouraging social inclusion (Valentine 2000). The work of the 'yBas' (young British artists), British fashion designers and others have been packaged and exported abroad by the British Council as a sign of the vitality of contemporary British culture and, as Valentine also puts it, as 'interesting' in an ethnographic sense. Valentine's list could be extended, with the BBC Radio World Service regularly commenting on and describing this new cultural field for its listeners across the world (13/5/2000). This argument is implicitly Foucauldian with culture in a dispersed and positive sense marking a new modality of power, one that operates through appeals to the social body to enjoy and find pleasure in these practices. Other commentators have seen in New Labour's culture policies a cruder attempt to put the arts in the service of 'social goals and political aims'. The arts are thereby disciplined, re-cast not as a sphere for dissent but as a 'command culture' to achieve social inclusion and community (Brighton 1999). McGuigan suggests that, drawing on Raymond Williams, the new culture industries operate for government as 'display' (McGuigan 1998). They have been utilised by Blair to achieve a 'governmental project of national aggrandisement'.

As far as I can ascertain, there have only been two less critical assessments of New Labour's cultural policies. Simon Frith correctly draws attention to Chris Smith's background in the municipal politics of the 1980s and his endorsement of the Comedia work of that time which recognised the future of culture as industry, commodity and also as 'way of life' (Frith 2000). This, argues Frith, contributes to Smith's current vision for culture as participative, non-elitist, a field to which more people must have access and also a popular phenomenon. This is an entirely different view of culture from that of the Tories. Likewise even though Liz Greenhalgh recognises the attempt to subject the arts and culture to the language of business and new managerialism, none the less the kind of work initiated by the GLC in the 1980s which addressed issues including audiences and distribution of cultural goods and services are now also central to New Labour's vision of widening participation (Greenhalgh 1998). This is highly ironic in that the GLC is demonised by New Labour as one of the main causes of the electoral failure of the Labour Party through the 1980s. Greenhalgh reminds us that one of the persons behind these GLC policies, Geoff Mulgan, is now himself a policy advisor to the PM. In many ways it was the radically left-wing GLC which reinvented the term 'culture industries' to refer to the small businesses that provided different kinds of cultural expression from those found in the multinationally owned record companies, film and television corporations and big high street fashion retailers.

It is also the case that it was the GLC which first established 'fashion centres' in London to enable lesser-known designers, especially those from ethnic groups, to work in subsidised spaces alongside machinists and to create a more viable design sector less associated with sweatshop wages and exploited immigrant labour. Greenhalgh points out that much of the investment and resources behind the current government's support for the culture industries actually comes from the public purse. Thus it could be argued (though Greenhalgh does not pursue her analysis this far) that despite all the rhetoric about public–private partnerships (and, I would add, despite the flow of funds from corporate sponsors to young British artists), the infrastructure of support for the new culture industries comes from the public sector. The high cost of training in the art schools and universities, 'the use of public funds for large-scale cultural facilities in city regeneration [and] the public promotion of cultural activity abroad' (Greenhalgh 2000), all of these suggest that New Labour is in fact implementing the same policies as those spearheaded by the GLC and also by radical city councils in Sheffield and elsewhere during the long Thatcher years, but this time 'by stealth'. These are left-wing policies reconfigured to maintain the support of Middle England through the emphasis on wealth and success and on the 'Hollywood effect' embodied by the new Film Council.

I would propose that in fact there are two things happening simultaneously, and represented in the different personas of the PM and the Minister of Culture. The former endorses the model of culture and the arts as a source for moral and spiritual regeneration and also for creating better citizens. The latter, in contrast, recognises the existence of cultural inequalities and the domination of culture by the large multinationals and the stranglehold it operates over alternative or independent production, hence the recognition of cultural diversity. But the Minister of Culture is also party, at least as far as public statements are concerned, to the new euphoria about successful cultural entrepreneurs. When I asked him as a participant in a round table discussion (Royal Television Society, February 2000) to comment on the fact that as my research on fashion designers showed, not all cultural entrepreneurs were high wage-earners and in fact most of them were barely scraping a living, unable to take a holiday, never mind take time off to have children, he replied with three short points. First, that it was not the role of government to provide the kinds of support I was suggesting in relation to new forms of social insurance. Second, that government was providing business start-up funding and advice. Third, that these young cultural workers do this work 'because they love it, and they know what they are letting themselves in for'. This raises a final point. Does the money currently being directed towards encouraging cultural regeneration in run-down areas such as Deptford in South-East London find its way to alleviating the real difficulties faced by young creative workers to sustain themselves on the longer term, or is this support more about creating part-time or semi-employment for a wider range of culture intermediaries whose role is managerial, administrative and thus 'supportive' of the artists and designers? Is it also about creating jobs for people who will train the artists on how to present a better business plan, and if so, is this culture industry as employment policy? The answer to this has to be yes. These are presented as enjoyable jobs, close to the media and arts and thus sharing in the glamour and in the limelight. They are typically part-time 'portfolio' jobs, which are often undertaken on a freelance basis. Under such conditions the worker takes on full responsibility for his or her own insurance and other costs, thus lessening the burden to the 'contractor'. By this means the entire cultural labour market comes to be a fragile web, loosely held together, buoyed up by a network of semi-independent producers and contractors all engaged in short-term projects and for whom the juggling of two or three jobs at the same time makes it difficult for them to plan more than six months in advance. The question of policy then, is how will these new occupations turn out, not in the distant future, but simply in the next few years? To what extent can the 'opaque futures' described by Giddens (1997) be a sustainable working reality for so many people?

Working in fashion design

The manuscript for my study of the career pathways of young British fashion designers was being completed in the months following the election of New Labour (McRobbie 1998). Indeed, it was only in the course of doing the research and interviewing the designers that policy began to strike me as important. The questions that informed the work in its initial stages were far removed from the world of government and policy. Let me briefly rehearse some of those questions. First, there was the appearance from the mid-1980s onwards of a cultural phenomenon which seemed unique to the UK; the rise of the art school-trained fashion designer, whose work belonged neither to the haute couture world of the European fashion houses nor to the fashion end of the high street, nor was it simply an expression of the street or youth subcultures.

My instinct was that the art schools, as peculiarly British institutions, played a major role in producing this new kind of creative person. But alongside this hunch which I duly explored both historically and sociologically, was another set of questions. Fashion design, apart from the handful of male stars, was a resolutely feminised field. And despite all the media attention it received from the mid-1980s onwards, it was possible to detect a lack of confidence about how it placed itself and understood itself in the hierarchy of the arts and culture. There was a defensiveness and an anxiety about insisting on the relevance of traditional fine art values and vocabularies. The available language for discussing fashion design, and the criteria for excellence were seemingly under-developed, assertive, somehow unconvincing. In journalism it seemed to be simply a matter of proclaiming this or that designer a genius, and adopting a kind of 'auteur' approach, with different fashion moments, periods or epochs, understood in terms of the distinctive style of a range of acclaimed designers. There was very little engaged criticism, or outright disagreement. Fashion design appeared to be a conflict-free zone, both in academic terms and in the wider world of journalistic commentary. This is not to suggest that there was not a substantial and extremely rich body of scholarship in fashion history and in contemporary debates about fashion and consumption, and fashion and the body. But what was entirely lacking was a debate about, let us say, the status of John Galliano and the meaning or value of his work. Why had he achieved such prominence? What was it that marked his work out as so special? Was the success and the acclaim justified? Was the work idea-based and conceptual in the manner of Damien Hirst? Is it the case that the UK fashion designers have been playing with the same kind of ideas and utilising the same kind of self-promotional strategies for years before the *yBas* suddenly came to the attention of the world media?

There was a gender dynamic in fashion's collective lack of confidence. The male designers flamboyantly cut through this by casting themselves almost as dramatists, as masters of spectacle, as theatre directors. This was a bid to disconnect fashion from its lesser status in the art schools where, as the historical research showed, it had to struggle to attain degree status and thus the respect and recognition of the fine artists who ran most of the art schools. To them fashion remained associated with a range of less elevated practices, with dressmaking, with the decorative arts, with embroidery and overall with the degraded field of the feminine. In the book (McRobbie 1998) I describe the various stages which marked fashion's ascendancy, and in particular the role of pioneering women fashion academics from Muriel Pemberton to Madge Garland to Lydia Kemeny. I argue that it was particularly important for fashion design to dissociate itself from the dressmaking tradition and also from manufacture, since the latter carried unwelcome connotations of the 'rag trade'. In short, fashion had to look upwards. It had to assert its leading figures as comparable to great artists and designers in the European tradition. It had to be able to locate itself within modernism and then post-modernism, writing its history to fit with the existing trajectory of art and design history. In actual fact, despite all these efforts, the eventual recognition came more from a pragmatic realisation that the art school sector had to demonstrate a connectedness with the changing world of commercial culture, and it was decided that fashion could be the envoy of change. The emergence, from the mid-1960s, of popular culture as a serious subject for debate outside the art schools, including the attention being paid to fashion photography in the new colour supplements, and the wider more sociological interest in fashion designer-retailers like Mary Quant and the Biba store, gradually won round the principals and vice-chancellors.

I was proposing that a sociological and cultural studies approach might be able to offer better insight into fashion as a cultural practice, fashion as something more than the possession of unique insight, vision, talent or even genius. After all, the limitations of this vocabulary were increasingly apparent to designers who were finding themselves described in euphoric terms one season, and completely ignored by the press the next. There was recognition of the disparity between receiving pages of publicity, even becoming household names while struggling to make ends meet, and existing on a virtually non-existent salary. This called for greater understanding of the various intermediary processes which 'created the creator' (Bourdieu 1993). Could the self-representational strategies of the designers as seen on the catwalks (the work, the collection) be better understood as the result of the deployment and orchestration of a series of design practices which, in turn, were gleaned through the repertoire of available fashion discourses? Thus Galliano's trademark style is one that 'plunders history'. He is famous for staging a particular historical moment not by producing costume drama but by exaggerating or distorting the period piece to give it some degree of visual intensity or even brilliance – what Sally Brampton described as 'lyricism' (Brampton 1996).

Was it the case that the excitement which accompanied the emergence of a new fashion design star could be traced through a series of precise promotional strategies involving fashion editors, fashion writers, fashion buyers (who need something avant-garde to liven up a window display) as well as an array of stylists, photographers, models and friends from college, all of whom might be said to constitute a 'network'? These ideas led me to trace design practice back to the distinctive pedagogies with which the designers, as students, had been familiar. And sure enough what I found was great emphasis on networking, on gaining experience by working for nothing as a student as a way of making contacts. Likewise, the importance of achieving a distinctive style with a noticeable 'signature' is as much a way of attracting the attention of the media, and thus of getting work, as it is a mark of design talent or integrity. I also wanted to understand how the designers navigated their way through the fashion business once they had graduated, and how they perceived their own design practice. These kinds of questions, about how they got set up in business, what kind of turnover they needed to keep going, how they managed to meet deadlines and ensure that orders were finished in time to get them shipped off to the US, all of this meant that the study became a work of sociological demystification.

It was the rhythms of their working days, the patterns which gradually built up across the experience of all of those I interviewed, and the extent to which they attempted to reconcile an inner desire to retain a commitment to imagination and vision with the requirements of packaging, branding and marketing their names and labels, which provided the backbone of the study. Romantically they saw themselves as led by inspiration, ideas, intuition and dreams; practically though, they knew they had to sell a look and a combination of ideas. With skill they deployed the right kind of art vocabulary as a means of branding their own work. This was also a way of locating their work in an ideal retail environment. If a designer described her work in a press release statement or in an interview as 'evoking memories of Matisse', this pointed not only to the kind of customer she had in mind but also the kind of store she hoped would buy her range. Slowly it became clear that fashion design was a multi-layered practice combining design and drawing skills with a much broader range of activities. It was also apparent that the designers I interviewed, despite being well known and having received a good deal of publicity, were in fact working on very small budgets. None of them had really managed to move into the global marketplace, most operated with annual turnovers of less than 1.5m, and all had either experienced or come close to bankruptcy.

What role did this work of sociological demystification play? What was the point of bringing fashion down to earth by inspecting its less glamorous practices?

I argued in *British Fashion Design* that many elements of the present system were anachronistic and detrimental to the long-term success of the sector. As a feminist I was interested in the energy and enthusiasm with which these young women pursued their careers, but it was also apparent that the culture of the fashion design sector, in particular its resistance to opening itself up to self-scrutiny and to promoting wider debate about its internal politics and organisation, made it more difficult for them to succeed. For example, its model of success hinged round the notion of competitive individualism. There was also a rigid hierarchy and whole set of rituals of deference and authority in relation to the high-powered fashion leaders, the key journalists who were able to make or break careers, the 'prima donna' designers who had made it to the top, the carelessness in regard to ensuring good working practices, and basically the existence of a non-democratic culture which allowed snobbishness and elitism to prevail.

In the above respects the fashion designers actually have a lot to learn from their fine art counterparts, especially the infamous *yBas*, whose collaborative and mutually supportive strategies were what made it possible for them to produce their own shows, pull their resources to attract the right kind of publicity, and demonstrate a kind of public loyalty to each other by helping out in each other's shows (McRobbie 1999). While the outcome was also a new celebrity culture of artists on a scale unknown, none the less there was a rejection of authority, hierarchy and tradition. There was also a repudiation of the snobbish patrician values associated with fine art: the 'Sensation' exhibition as almost all commentators pointed out, was anti-elitist, even populist in its overall presentation. Art had become 'ordinary' while fashion design was still aspiring to being 'extraordinary'. Most of the designers I interviewed described feeling isolated and cut off from any opportunities for collaboration. Despite the existence of the 'networks' which functioned more as a means of keeping in touch, there was an expressed need for some form of association which as yet did not exist. No single designer I interviewed had any experience of the kind of group support which has served the *yBas* so well.

But it was also the case that the distance their training had encouraged them to stake from the manufacturing end of fashion design, for fear of being mistaken for a dressmaker or rag trade manufacturer, also did them little good. By having so little hands-on knowledge of the process of production, they were often financially exploited by the middlemen. Often they were over-charged or else discovered too late that their orders were put to the back of the queue when more lucrative ones came in from bigger companies. Beholden to these middlemen, who took charge of the production and farmed out the work on a sub-contractual basis to very low-paid workers, there was little the designers could do when a late delivered order was then cancelled by a big retailer. It was the designers who paid the costs and this practice alone accounted for the majority of bankruptcies. In short, I recommended that the designers get their hands dirty by visiting the factories, learning about production and even finding new ways of sharing facilities with other designers and also pooling manufacturing costs by bringing in direct labour on better wages rather than on relying on exploitative chains.

Finally I argued that it was also important to challenge the rigid and conservative practices of the fashion press. They wielded their power arbitrarily and also drew up a strict agenda about what were and what were not 'fashion stories'. Socialising with the top designers as part of a whole glamorous and international fashion circuit, gratefully receiving all sorts of fashion freebies, and fearful of being left out in the cold for filing a poor review, fashion journalists rarely step out of line. It has been a marked feature of recent news stories about racism and sexual exploitation inside the fashion industry that they have been written by news journalists. The fashion world quickly closes ranks as soon as questions about sweatshops, the employment of under-age children or the widespread existence of racist attitudes are aired in public. This too marks it out as inward-looking, politically conservative, and seemingly unwilling to engage in public debate about its own internal organisation and reluctant to adapt to the place which fashion could play as a major culture industry.

Looking to the future

There were a number of problems which the young designers faced on an almost daily basis. There was no doubt that there existed an enormous disparity between the high levels of talent and commitment and the ensuing publicity the whole sector received, and the fragile, indeed shabby infrastructure which saw bankruptcy if not as a norm or a rite of passage, then at least as part of the cycle of expectations. This places fashion design in the realm of what the sociologist Ulrich Beck calls 'risk work' (Beck 1992). But need it be so risky, I asked? Need the future be so opaque for these highly trained designers? Is there not an element of fatalism in the theorists of the new world of work which actually lets the government and others off the hook? It did not seem, as I completed the book, so unrealistic to search for better ways of supporting graduate designers after they left college and, given the huge investment already made in their education and training, to make some provisions available to them in the early years. This could take at least two inter-connected forms: access to a series of fashion design and production units or centres which in turn might be in partnerships with art schools and colleges. These would provide on a subsidised basis, expensive high-tech equipment, production facilities as well as shared publicity and promotional resources, business and other training, and also space to work and space to show the work. Equally important might be the ethos of collectivity and sharing, so that the rather vacuous idea of the network becomes something more than just a series of names and telephone numbers.

There are two further issues that needed addressing. First, there was the seeming inability of all the designers I interviewed who were 'independents' and working on a relatively small scale (i.e. employing less than twenty people, selling collections to up to a dozen retail outlets) successfully to break into foreign markets and to consolidate that presence on a long-term basis. Second there was the question of their own personal economies, which showed how narrow their margins were, how easily a bout of illness or a family crisis could destroy the entire business. These remain of central importance three years on. While the first of these issues calls for more serious debate about the viability of small-scale designers surviving in a global market, the second inevitably raises the question of how the career pathways of freelance and self-employed creative workers will be sustainable not just into middle age but also into old age. It might be imagined that this would be the stuff of the Creative Industries Task Force, but sadly not. The two key figures from the fashion world who have played an advisory role are Paul Smith and Caroline Coates. These are both highly knowledgeable and experienced people, but there are not many others who have developed such commitment to policy and to improving the fashion sector as a place of work. The British Fashion Council clearly has a role to play, but so far this has been disappointing, restricted to fund-raising for London Fashion Week and otherwise supporting business start-up programmes.

Nor does there seem to be evidence of the 'joined-up thinking' so encouraged by New Labour. The DTI sees the fashion design sector as small fish, the DfEE is more concerned with (yet again) start-up programmes (and graduate designers are not necessarily a priority) and the Creative Industries Task Force has been dominated by film and popular music. Fashion has no lobbyists as loud and outspoken as Alan McGee (former owner of Creation Records), or indeed Lord Puttnam. In short, fashion does not do itself credit on the political front, despite the valuable efforts of its two key representatives. At present fashion experts claim that the newly recommended pathway for young designers is actually working better. That is, instead of being encouraged into going it alone in the early years, a new model is emerging. This sees the majority of graduates going for more sensible jobs in industry in the hope of gaining experience and setting up alone at some point in the future. But will this ever happen, and is it fair to train students to think of themselves as designers only to then encourage them on graduation to get experience with BHS? And is it not the case that the early years after graduation are the best time to explore talent and imagination more fully? If it doesn't happen then, maybe it never will. This recommendation is therefore politically safe, seemingly sensible but ultimately self-defeating. British fashion design is renowned for its uniqueness, adventurousness and creativity. If this is stifled as soon as the students leave college, then that reputation will be lost. The other solution is that the chain store will step in, offering contracts to 'star' designers to produce collections under their own labels but for the mass-market. So far Top Shop has pioneered this with most success, but as I point out (McRobbie 1998), this can be a short-term fix. Come a recession or even simply a downturn in sales and the contract can be ended. What is more, to win such a contract in the first place the designer has to have a 'name', a 'label' and a reputation. How can this be achieved if the early years are to be spent playing safe and working for a large company? Of course, many graduates will want to opt for this route in any case; the fashion industry is big and important enough to absorb trained designers in many roles. But there is a danger of this becoming the official pathway and of thus either throwing the baby out with the bathwater, or else of adopting an 'I told you so' mentality when the ambitious designers come up against difficulties.

In conclusion there seems to be a real and urgent need for the fashion design sector as creative industry to be addressed in more depth and with greater seriousness at every level. But this requires that the fashion world shows itself willing not to turn away from the field of political economy but towards it. It has to become more 'socialised'. This also has to start early, indeed in training. The ethos of art for art's sake is of little help when people's working lives are at stake. The crudely promotional and collaborative strategies learnt by the yBas have at the very least improved the annual incomes of young artists in Britain for the first time in recent history. Granted those at the top now can command stratospheric amounts for their work, but there has been a trickle-down, and the artists have themselves become more aware of what it takes to keep a budget ticking over. Perhaps there is also another lesson here. We may be asking too much of designers to train them as artists (in the mode of 'fine art fashion'), and then expect them to make their way in a global market dominated by cheap suppliers and companies now able to 'translate' the look from the catwalk on to the rails at Kookai within a couple of weeks. Why not let them work as artist-designers who have shows in the same way as Damien Hirst *et al.* do? And why not also invite them to apply for Arts Council, British Council, Lottery and whatever other funding is available, including designer-in-residence posts, and then to eradicate the elitism and snobbery for once and for all, to encourage them to think of what they do as not 'extraordinary' but as 'ordinary'? As Damien Hirst has said on may occasions, 'I'm no genius' (quoted in Frith 2000).

References

Beck, U. (1992) *Risk Society: Towards a New Modernity*, London: Sage.
—— (1999) 'Die Zukunft oder the political economy of uncertainty'. Lecture delivered at the LSE, London, February.
Blair, Rt Hon. PM (1996) *New Britain: My Vision for a Young Country*, London: Fourth Estate.
Bourdieu, P. (1993) *The Field of Cultural Production*, Cambridge: Polity Press.
Brampton, S. (1996) 'Flight of fantasy', *Guardian*, weekend edn, 2 February.
Brighton, A. (1999) 'Towards a command culture: New Labour's cultural policy and Soviet socialist realism', *Critical Quarterly*, Autumn 41 (3): 24–36.
Creative Industries Mapping (1998), London: Department of Media, Culture and Sport.
Frith, S. (2000) 'Mr Smith draws a map', *Critical Quarterly*, Spring, 41 (2): 3–8.
Gibbons, F. (1999) 'Old Macdonald had a vision', *Guardian*, Saturday review, 24 July: 5.
Giddens, A. (1997) 'Runaway worlds'. Lecture delivered at Runaway Worlds Conference at the ICA, London, February.
Greenhalgh, L. (1998) 'From arts policy to creative economy', *Media International Australia*, May, 87: 84–94.
Leadbeater, C. (1999) *Living on Thin Air: the New Economy*, London: Viking.
McGuigan, J. (1998) 'National government and the cultural public sphere', *Media International Australia*, May, 87: 68–83.
McRobbie, A. (1998) *British Fashion Design: Rag Trade or Image Industry?*, London and New York: Routledge.
—— (1999) *In the Culture Society*, London and New York: Routledge.
Valentine, J. (2000) 'Creative Britain', *Critical Quarterly*, Spring, 41 (1): 9–17.
Young, J. (1999) *The Exclusive Society*, London: Sage.

Chapter 20

Noel McLaughlin

ROCK, FASHION AND PERFORMATIVITY

Introduction

POPULAR MUSIC AND FASHION are frequently used interchangeably in 'everyday' discourse. As Simon Frith puts it, 'pop is nothing if not fashionable (drawing attention to its transience, to the ever familiar shock of the new)' (Frith 1996: 157). In this respect, the popular music and fashion industries are regarded as sharing a close relationship: popular music is taken to play a powerful role in 'shop-windowing' and selling clothes (with certain rock and pop stars regarded as 'fashion leaders') and, in turn, clothing has been viewed as a central part of how popular music signifies. However obvious this may seem, the relationship between popular music and fashion has been much neglected and both areas have been radically under-theorised, especially in comparison to other areas of contemporary culture. If 'dress', as John Street puts it, 'is perhaps the most obvious way in which the formally inarticulate speaks volumes' (Street 1997: 36), then this 'silence' about the dynamic between popular music and fashion is somewhat regrettable as clearly clothing and dress are an important part of how popular music functions and, indeed, a central aspect of popular musical pleasure. In this regard, the lack of detailed consideration about the relationship between popular music and fashion is somewhat surprising, given the centrality of music and clothes to pop's broader 'aestheticisation of everyday life' (McRobbie 1999).

There are a number of reasons for this silence. In relation to fashion, many writers have pointed to how an 'old style' leftism is suspicious, even contemptuous, of fashion and indeed popular culture, seeing these as essentially transient phenomena. Even within the elaborated field of film studies (which has occupied the canonical place in the contemporary study of culture), there has been a reticence to consider the significance and pleasures of costume. As Church Gibson (1998) has poignantly observed:

Only in the last decade or so has fashion really established itself as a serious academic discipline and as an important area of theoretical debate. The reasons, of course, are well documented: the centuries-old belief in the essential frivolity of fashion, reinforced by the puritanism of many on the left, for whom fashion is the most obvious and . . . objectionable form of commodity fetishism, and the conviction of the majority of second-wave feminists that fashion is an arena in which women . . . display themselves in order to gratify male desire.[1]

(Church Gibson 1998: 36)

This chapter seeks to explore the pop–fashion relationship, to make some general points about how clothing works in popular music culture. This means assessing some of the main debates about both fashion and pop before moving on to offer a case study of the rock/pop band, Suede.[2] I will be focusing primarily on the performance of gender in pop and the role of clothing in the popular music matrix. This is because rock and pop are taken to be 'about sex' (sex, rhythm and the beat and so forth). Before moving on to this, I want to make a few general points about pop and fashion.

Popular music and fashion are casually used terms, but their everyday sense of transparency conceals their complexity. It is frequently claimed 'anything can be fashionable'; that any music can be 'popular'. However, the problem with this type of relativism is that, to paraphrase Richard Middleton, we empty the terms of the meanings which they carry in actual discourse (Middleton 1990: 3). Both pop and fashion cannot be defined in isolation, and the two terms respectively act as 'other': first, pop is other to rock – which can today mean a variety of musics in an increasingly elaborated subcultural field of discriminations (see Thornton 1995) – and second, to something (as yet unnamed – perhaps antifashion or 'normal' dress) that transcends or stands *above*, or is unconcerned with fashion.

Rock culture has been underpinned by ideologies of authenticity which are antifashion in outlook. As rock was apparently unconcerned with fashion, it could mark itself as superior to a more fashion-centred (and 'superficial') pop. Fashion, then, became associated with 'mere' entertainment and the perceived corrupting ('inauthenticating') effects of consumer capitalism. Put differently: rock culture's difference from pop and the world of fashion enabled rock 'to matter' (Grossberg 1993: 201). Furthermore, as Frith and Goodwin surmise, this distinction between rock and pop

is a matter of gender, with female (pop) consumers being described as essentially 'passive', in contrast to the discriminating, engaged, male audience for rock . . . The essential male address of 'real' rock is thus taken for granted and embodied in the standard history of rock as a succession of bold male heroes.[3]

(Frith and Goodwin 1990: 370)

'Close to home?': pop, fashion and the academy

At the risk of causing offence, academia has never been renowned as a Mecca of male fashion. But, if anything, male dress in the academy has been caricatured as a 'fashion disaster-zone' of tweed jackets and elbow patches, ill-fitting, worn corduroy trousers and Hush Puppies (or their more modern equivalents). Despite the superficiality of this remark, it conceals what is an important point: the masculine academy could be characterised as a host of omniscient spectators – analogous to the male gaze in cinema – who like to look outwards at the world imagining that they cannot be seen in return. Male academics have liked to see themselves (much in the manner of Michelangelo's David) as having their minds on 'higher' things than the flippancy and vagaries of fashion. Moreover, this has been accompanied by a sense that they (we) are beyond scrutiny.[4] This is indicative of a broader trend, where men and male dress have liked to go unnoticed, to function, in Richard Dyer's words, as an 'absent centre' (Dyer 1997) around which 'others' – gay men, women, blacks and Asians (and those 'low' enough to be duped into conspicuous consumption) – revolve. It is important therefore to turn the spotlight back on the masculine academy and on to intellectual agendas themselves. When brought into view, the history of male 'fashions' can prove illuminating. As Fred Davis points out, male dress codes were designed not to be noticed, to be 'not fashion at all':

> [M]en's dress became the primary visual medium for intoning the rejection of 'corrupt' aristocratic claims to elegance, opulence, leisure, and amatory adventure . . . Men's dress became more simple, coarse, unchangeable, and sombre, sartorial tendencies that in many respects survive to the present.
>
> (Davis 1992: 39)

Fashion has functioned as 'other' to the 'serious' and mainly masculine world of work. Accompanying this is the lingering sense that fashion and pop can be equated within the feminine. As Bruzzi has argued in her detailed study of clothing in the movies, 'discussions of costume have tended to exclude men and masculine identities, as if attention to dress is an inherently female trait' (Bruzzi 1997a: xv). Similarly, Jennifer Craik has concluded, in surveying the field of fashion literature, that 'most studies of contemporary fashion emphasise female fashion and marginalise attention to male dress'. Accompanying this is the sense that 'men who "dress up" are peculiar' consolidating the 'myth of the "undecorated" male' (Craik 1994: 176).

This, however, goes against the tide of history where, since the 1980s in particular – the period of accelerated de-industrialisation and the development of a 'feminised' service sector – masculinity has increasingly come into view, making it no longer feasible to assert that clothes and fashion are essentially a 'feminine' preserve and 'not worth bothering with'. With it, the idea of a 'crisis in masculinity(ies)' has gained increasing currency (see Rutherford and Chapman 1988; Easthope 1992). A key aspect of this has been the introduction of a number of glossy 'style' magazines aimed at men – *The Face*, *Arena* and latterly *loaded* –

which in their different ways have constructed and placed the male body under the spotlight as an object for sexual consumption (see Mort 1996; Nixon 1996).[5] As a consequence, 'men . . . are now more than "disinterested observers"' (Bruzzi 1997a: xv).

This is somewhat general, because it doesn't tell us very much about how masculinities have changed (and the reasons for my diatribe against the masculine academy is that by ignoring clothes and music, we may miss the progressive possibilities these so-called superficialities may afford). Furthermore, there has been a reluctance to consider the way that pop has articulated gender identity from the early 1980s onwards; as well as the role of clothing and dress within this. As Frith has argued,

> the academic study of popular music has been limited by the assumption that sounds somehow reflect 'a people' . . . too often attempts to relate musical forms *to* social processes ignore the ways in which music is *itself* a social process . . . [I]n examining the aesthetics of popular music we need to reverse the usual academic argument: the question is not how a piece of music, a text, 'reflects' popular values, but how – in performance – it produces them.
>
> (Frith 1996: 269–70)

While masculinity has come under the spotlight, Frith's insight takes us towards considering the ways this has occurred and what is at stake. He begins to question how different combinations of music, clothing and body in performance articulate different masculine identities. There are obvious but significant differences between performers such as Soft Cell, Boyzone, Oasis and Culture Club, but frequently these are not registered let alone explored in contemporary cultural criticism, where there is an unfortunate tendency to be panglossian in the treatment of pop.

Andrew Goodwin has referred to (and this is the other side of pop nostalgia) a form of 'secret hatred' of popular music within the academy (Goodwin 1993). While popular music studies (which has become a discipline in its own right in recent years) can contribute greatly to an understanding of the role of clothing in contemporary culture, there has been a reluctance to consider this. In fact, rock ideology and popular music studies have colluded together in treating clothes and fashion as the 'gloss' on a performing pop culture that has valued the organic, the natural and the spontaneous.

The notable exceptions have been discussions of punk and subcultural 'style' (Hebdige 1979, 1988). Here, the 'oppositional' moment punk was taken to embody has blinded the academic study of popular music to later moments, which were found 'wanting' contrasted to punk's vitality and authenticity. Indeed, punk has been the subject of more academic nostalgia – both simple and reflexive – than any other period or genre in pop history (see Rabin 1999). However, what was important in Hebdige, for example, was the serious consideration of the clothed body in popular music culture and its role in the politics of resignification. But there is a significant absence in this work when it comes to exploring the clothed body *in* popular musical performance (see McDonald 1997: 281). The other exception is the longstanding debate about Madonna (cf. Fiske 1992; Kaplan 1987) – what Frith has termed the 'academic Madonna business' (Frith 1996: 14) – which has been important in opening up discussion about the performance of gender and introducing the role of clothing and fashion in pop performance (against a rock culture suspicious of both pop and fashion). Here though there is a neglect to consider the relationship between clothing and performance within the specificities of popular music culture.[6]

Authenticity

Authenticity is a central issue in discussions about the value of clothing in popular music culture, as it is a central issue in contemporary cultural studies more broadly. But the notion of authenticity is also a problem and clearly presents difficulties in discussions of popular music (see Thornton 1995). These are most apparent in the extreme ways the term is used: between its unselfconscious use in everyday discourse; and as one of the most perplexing concepts in contemporary cultural criticism. This critical self-consciousness has not extended into popular music culture itself and, indeed, the value judgement that a sound, a performance, the way a particular group is dressed, is 'real' or 'authentic' is a routine designation often made with no more justification than 'I feel it in my gut' – an assertion frequently offered by journalists, musicians and audiences. These inconsistent judgements (about music, performance and dress) take their power from this type of definitional imprecision and, as a consequence, their routine use in day-to-day discourse is obscured and their force left unchallenged.

In rock and popular music, this lack of justification and perpetual mystification of the term makes analysis all the more difficult – a version of 'don't analyse it, feel it!' However, as authenticity is more used of rock and pop than any other cultural form, it is clearly important to investigate the ramifications of these apparently unselfconscious descriptions and judgements. We could ask, following Judith Butler: 'what does "transparency" keep obscure?' (Butler 1999: xix).

Despite the increased prominence of theoretical anti-essentialism in cultural criticism, essentialist ideas and arguments have played a powerful and defining role in the history of popular music. What makes music particularly susceptible to essentialist notions of identity is that music has often been valued within rock ideology precisely for its ability to release repressed desires, to strip away the layers of 'artifice' and reveal the core personality, the essence of race, humanity or sexuality obscured underneath (see Middleton 1990). In 'orthodox' rock history, this ability to facilitate the emergence of an essence of identity has led to certain musical attributes – the 'grain of the voice' (Barthes 1977: 181), the characteristics of a performance or body – to be read as the expression of a unique identity. Middleton, for example, has drawn attention to how forms of sexualised or libidinal authenticity have invoked essentialist conceptions of the 'pure' sexual body. This is a common position in rock ideology and 'here libidinal energies are thought to be channelled into musical forms . . . radical rock was supposed to provide a direct route to the unconscious, a way to plug in your libido' (Middleton 1990: 259). While this may be powerfully *felt* in certain quarters, its attempted universality masks its situatedness, and frequently sexual authenticity in rock has been underpinned by a particular heterosexual and masculine discourse (see Frith and McRobbie 1990; Frith 1990). Therefore, the discourse of authenticity may serve to erect a false naturalism (with masculinity as its centre), sustained by a sex-gender essentialism that maintains unequal power relations and closes off other ways of envisaging identity, other possibilities of pleasure and performing.

This distrust of fashion is closely related to rock culture's suspicion of the emergence of music video; which has made 'fashion' and 'image', in Will Straw's words,

> more important than the experience of music itself, with effects which were to be feared . . . the potential difficulty for artists with poor 'images', the risk that theatricality and spectacle would take precedence over intrinsically 'musical' values . . . [This is part of] a longstanding caution about the relationship between rock music as a culture of presumed resistance and television as the embodiment of mainstream show business and commercial culture.
>
> (Straw 1993: 3–4)

However, against the thrust of the positions described by Straw, other commentators have pointed out that rock has always depended on visual images, on fashion, theatricality and spectacle. Shumway (1992) has argued against the orthodox narrative, and suggested that even the early performances and success of Elvis Presley were attributable as much to his visual performance and the significance of the clothed body as to 'the music' itself.

The 'birth' of Anglo-American rock culture marks something of paradigm shift in the history of fashion, with popular music taking over from cinema as the main source of fashion influence. However, the orthodox narrative of rock history conceals the significance of performers like Little Richard, who played a formative role in articulating the gender-dissonant complexities of performance, the body and dress. Indeed, the performative possibilities of black performers have been overlooked by a more general rock discourse that has validated black music as the authentic expression of racial 'essence', and a key aspect of this has been the long-standing 'necessary connection' forged between black people, black culture (clothes and performance styles) and music-making: between blackness, the body, rhythm and sexuality. This emphasis on validating black music as *the* marker of sexualised authenticity has overlooked the way that black music cultures have used clothes both to undermine conspicuous consumption and to question essentialist notions about the body, gender and sexuality.[7]

What I am describing here is the tendency within a rock culture concerned with authenticity (of music, sexuality, identity) to see clothes as the 'veneer', as essentially fickle, to 'look through them', to value what is *inside*. For rock culture, it is 'others' who wear masks, others who dress up, '"we" just are'. As Paul McDonald has observed, unravelling masculinity is difficult, its false universality hard to pick apart:

> [T]he production of feminine appearance has required cosmetics and clothing to create a glamorous surface – so that it is known that

> femininity is 'made up' . . . [D]efinitions of masculinity are in contrast
> imagined as apparently unconstructed authentic identities . . .
> [A]ttempts to read masculinity as performance may be actually more
> difficult than seeing femininity as a construction.
>
> (McDonald 1997: 283)

However, as Bruzzi points out, 'clothes and superficialities *are* identity' (Bruzzi
1997a: 143; emphasis added) and cannot be swept aside by some dubious appeal
to the transhistorical body underneath. Even clothing that appears to be unconcerned with fashion, or that seeks to establish itself as beyond (or 'outside')
fashion and not draw attention to itself, still has to be 'read' as significant on such
terms: 'unconcern' has to be carefully constructed to be read as unconcern.
Therefore, those clothing styles which attempt to conceal their constructedness
warrant the most analytical attention (as these are the styles that have sought to
evade 'capture').

Tensions in the pop matrix: 'bring "the noise"'

Riviere's idea of femininity-as-masquerade has acted as a powerful challenge to the
essentialism that underpins 'commonsense' thinking about the inter-relationship of
sexuality and gender (Riviere 1986 [1929]). Essentialist discourse posits that sex
and gender go together: determine, explain and express one another. This, a
primary example of Stephen Heath's 'sexual fix' – the way we are *fixed* by the
discourse of sexual authenticity – suggests an imaginary unity between biological
sex, anatomy, gender, clothing and behaviour (Heath 1982). In other words, gender
is the outward expression of some inner sexual 'essence'. As we have seen, 'dress
codes have been conditioned by a belief that clothes should solidify gender identity, not question it'; where clothes are simply 'reflective of the dominant,
established and unquestioned sex of the wearer' (Bruzzi 1997a: 149).

What has been important about Riviere's argument to debates about gender,
clothing and the performing body is that there is no 'original', 'authentic', or
primary sexuality behind the mask. If, as Bruzzi asserts, there is 'no difference
between womanliness and masquerade' and 'no such thing as "genuine" womanliness, then there is no such thing as "genuine" manliness or a stable subjective male
position' (Bruzzi 1997a: 129) untouched by changes in fashion, culture and history.
A recognition of the performative aspect of gender helps foreground the 'constructedness' of both sex and gender, prizing open their mutually sustaining necessity
and making apparent their relationality; holding sex and gender *apart*. As sex and
gender are performative, they must be continuously re-enacted in social situations.
'Identity', as Frith puts it, 'comes from the outside, not the inside; it is something we put or try on, not something we reveal or discover' (Frith 1996: 273)
and popular music plays a powerful role in how we *learn* to be sexed, gendered
subjects. However, as Frith moves on to argue, while clothes are

> social signs . . . written on the body itself, on its shape, its size, its
> texture, its curves and bones and flesh and hair . . . [s]tage clothes . . .

do not transcend physical circumstances . . . [but] depend, for their
effect, as much on the musical relationships between a group's members
as on their design features. How musicians look . . . clearly affects how
at first we hear them . . . But we don't just experience a musician's body
as costumed.

(Frith 1996: 219)

Put differently; the issue in popular music performance is not clothes, but clothing
in performance; popular music is about clothes *and* stars, clothing on bodies
performing popular music. This means that the *meaning* of dress will be inflected,
altered, amplified or contradicted by the musical and performing conventions and
associations within which they are placed. Furthermore, clothes work not only
within and against musical and performance conventions (the internal conventions
of the song) but externally, as contrasted to other work by the same group or
singer, as well as along chains of similarity and difference with other music, clothes
and performance styles. Popular music has its own history of performances, its
own performing discourse, its own way of organising meaning and value. In validating and finding pleasure in popular music performers, in their music, in their
clothes, their bodies, we are considering a performance, not in isolation, but as a
performance within a history of performances, the enactment of identity within a
series of identities. And often the most interesting, most disruptive music works
by articulating the historically and culturally salient contradictions.

Not only does the performance of gender need to be understood within pop-
specific discourse, but a further problem in evaluation is the 'artifice-authenticity'
binary itself. This binary mutates and changes, meaning that performative artifice
may itself be continually reclaimed and ghettoised by essentialist, 'naturalised'
heterosexual (and gay) discourse (see Smelik 1998).[8] In this respect, performance
that works at a distance from the organic paradigm of the masculine rock centre
can be seen as just 'gay music' conforming to the most sedimented notions of gay
culture. Gayness may be linked with modes of performing artifice (types of clothing
and gesture) and 'playfulness' that may in particular contexts serve the needs of
essentialism. Even pop performers such as Divine, Erasure, Boy George, and Marc
Almond, who had an historically important role in articulating sex-gender dissonance, may be seen as 'safe', conforming to the broader expectations of
heterosexual hegemony. While, as Bruzzi argues, 'lang, Madonna, Lennox and
Harvey all, in different ways, are performative; in that they are constantly putting
on show the moment of gender construction' (Bruzzi 1997b: 198), this misses
telling which performances by the artists mentioned above are performative, for
whom, why and how?[9]

A further issue relates more specifically to authenticity and performance. As
Frith argues,

[P]erformance involves gestures which are both false (they are only put
on for the situation) and true (they are appropriate to the emotions
being described, expressed or invoked). . . . [Certain performers] have
grasped the camp point that the truth of a feeling is an aesthetic truth,
not a moral one; it can only be judged formally, as a matter of gestural

grace . . . 'Sincerity' . . . cannot be measured by searching for what
lies *behind* the performance; if we are moved . . . we are moved by
what we *immediately* hear and see.

(Frith 1996: 215)

And even though some performers seek to overcome tensions (of gender, sexuality,
authenticity and artifice), every performance is at least potentially a combination
of sincere and insincere elements.

What I am arguing then is that there is no master performative template.
Performativity in pop can only be understood with attention to pop's specific
modes of performance and value. In pop, some forms of drag, cross-dressing and
androgyny may be overwhelmed by the discursive, rendered 'safe', and seen as
the 'innate' expression of 'others' on essentialist terms. Put differently: certain
artists may lend themselves to being valued as 'authentically gay'.

Furthermore, as Bruzzi argues, we need to differentiate between terms like
'drag', 'cross-dressing' and 'androgyny' (as these may be used interchangeably),
but we need to do so in a popular musical context (Bruzzi 1997a: 149). Also, we
need to consider differentiations within these key terms: between misogynistic and
anti-misogynistic drag and cross-dressing; between naturalised and performative
androgyny. Not all acts of 'drag', cross-dressing or gender-blurring are subversive
or radical; not all performances hold sex and gender in distinction. Stella Bruzzi
(1997b), for example, in a discussion of k.d.lang, differentiates between that
singer's conventional 'naturalised' androgyny after 'coming out', one which has
been recouped to essentialist discourse ('fitting "the truth" about lesbians') and a
performative, dissonant androgyny that 'signals and re-signals the space between
subject and construction' (Bruzzi 1997b: 205). The knowledge about 'coming
out', Bruzzi further argues, creates a narrative within which lang's performance
and meaning are anchored – a 'shift in not knowing to knowing' (Bruzzi 1997:
205), a move from suspense, noise, 'inbetweenness' to coherence, closure and
naturalisation.

Importantly, Bruzzi's reading pays attention to both the associative semiotics
of lang's clothing and how these interact with music conventions, such as genre,
as well as discourse about lang (star biography, the music press). In terms of
authenticity, what is significant about lang is the 'space' created: how she simultaneously inhabits and departs from these conventions in a combination of sincere
and inauthentic elements. 'The pleasure [or lack of it] is in not knowing why and
how these elements fit together' (Bruzzi 1997b: 192).

A major part of my argument centres on the importance of considering the pop
'text'. Pop's mobile and shifting textuality (of which clothing and fashion are an integral part) may itself problematise the idea of authenticity, as the rock 'text' is not
quite as clear as in other cultural forms. Moreover, rock and pop's mobile inter-
textuality may set up tensions amongst its various levels.[10] This occurs in three main
ways. Tensions may be set up between music, performance, clothing, the body,
video and 'star text', where some areas may be regarded as 'authentic' and other
areas less so (as between music and video; rock and fashion). Second, tensions may
operate historically when a group or performer begins to change sound and style (as
in k.d. lang pre- and post- 'coming out'). Third, as Frith has argued, any pop per-

formance occurs within a 'history of performances' and what these, over time, are taken to mean, prompting us to consider how performers interpret past perform-ances, evaluating their 'usefulness' to the context in which they find themselves.

This is in part why I have elected to discuss two moments of the fashion–pop nexus in particular (and they are both connected). The first is the so-called New Pop period of the early 1980s. The second is the pop group Suede and in partic-ular their self-titled debut album (*Suede* 1993) and its performance in the video *Love and Poison* of the same year.

New Pop

New Pop has borne the brunt of rock scorn, regarded as exhibiting an excessive dependence on fashion, and treated with suspicion and disdain – in many ways the popular musical equivalent of the women's picture in film studies. In this respect, pop that was discursively linked to consumer culture was seen as essentially 'femi-nine' and at odds with the machismo of most mainstream rock. Moreover, rock's 'subsequent corruption and "emasculation" are understood as a straightforward effect of the rock business's attempt to control its market . . . The decline of rock 'n roll rested on a process of "feminisation"' (Frith and McRobbie 1990: 383). Hence the 'sell-out' narrative of punk's (rock) decline into the consumer co-option of New Pop.

In this way, New Pop was seen as the popular musical counterpart of Thatcherism, as the outward manifestation of Thatcherite ideology, as a cultural form whose 'real' meaning lay in the celebration of conspicuous consumption. There are two problems with this argument. First, it depends on a simple corre-spondence theory: rock discourse has viewed the music of the period as simply embodying the values of an era. This tendency of seeing music as corresponding to eras in such a way is, of course, problematic. As John Hill has argued, there is a danger of 'reading off' meanings in culture from the presumed politics of Thatcherism (Hill 1999: 28–9). Second, after the 'heroic' resistance to consumer capitalism embodied in punk, New Pop could be constructed as *bourgeois* to punk's apparent proletarianism (or is it with hindsight punk's masculinity to new pop's 'femininity'?). As punk dress was understood within subcultural theory as 'not really "fashion" at all', the operation of clothing and make-up in punk could be held at some distance from the 'feminine' world of fashion.[11] Even critics such as Peter York could retrospectively join in and attack New Pop's femininity, its 'bad' music, and assert that the significance of the early 1980s was merely as a period for 'dressing up' (York and Jennings 1995). In both cases, this served to displace what was 'noisy' about New Pop – namely New Pop's 'play' on gender expecta-tions. As Paul McDonald has warned,

> the difficulty with limiting the reading of gendered performance to items of costume is that it can suggest that while forms of dress are obviously something put on, it could be presumed that the body which lies underneath is a natural and inevitable fact.
>
> (McDonald 1997: 282)

What this does is conceal a number of significant changes that the period began to articulate in musical, performance and clothing terms. Here any subversion at the level of clothing and performance is displaced by an appeal to an underlying gender naturalism – clothes are again just the veneer. Of course, the music and performance helped support this, as much of New Pop was defined by a suppression of libidinal conventions. As opposed to strutting, prowess, chest hair, genitals, inconspicuous clothing and the 'bump and grind' of 'the hard rock beat', guitar solos and phallic posturing, New Pop performers comprised a different semiotic: stillness, immobility and camp gestures, and favoured the 'plastic', the 'artificial', the shiny, the conspicuously feminine, over the organic and the natural. Discursively, however, this 'playfulness' was peripheralised and issues about gender and performance were displaced (meaning that New Pop was spoken about within a discourse of kitsch nostalgia – as an era of bad music and making money).

But what was significant about aspects of New Pop was the manner in which clothes came to the fore – not as a layer of 'artifice' that left naturalised (hetero)sexuality intact underneath, but the manner in which gender assumptions were problematised. But New Pop was by no means reducible to the discourses of gender and sexuality. An important feature of New Pop fashion was its 'play' on heritage costume. This was more than nostalgia. As McRobbie has argued, styles such as these 'are neither nostalgic in essence nor without depth. Nostalgia indicates a desire to recreate the past faithfully, and to wallow in such mythical representation' (McRobbie 1989: 41). Therefore, heritage costume was appropriated, rendered excessive, and this was signalled by pop fashion's more general 'knowingness . . . wilful anarchy . . . irrepressible optimism . . . colour, exaggeration, humour and disavowal of the conventions of adult dress' (McRobbie 1989: 42). In this way, New Pop was able to draw attention to the constructedness of heritage, to 'make strange' its pleasures (especially as these clothing styles occurred within a very modern, artificial soundscape and performance mode). Aspects of costume were not only rendered 'strange' by the excessive manner of their 'style' (exaggerated scale, colour and the manner in which they were re-signified with other elements), but in their utilisation on performing bodies in the context of sounds that connote the 'future', modernity and so forth. In performance, New Pop artists favoured strategies that downplayed, even exposed, the traditional masculine signifiers required to perform 'powerfully'. As Stan Hawkins has argued, artists such as The Pet Shop Boys 'remind us that music can function as a key vehicle in deconstructing fixed notions of gendered identity in everyday life' (Hawkins 1997: 118).

Thus, the New Pop semiotic worked to form a 'fit' among the different areas of pop's textual matrix, to carefully construct the signification of 'artifice'. This was based on a self-conscious critique of rock in order to counter the organic conventions and masculinist ideology with which rock had become associated. But in time this mode itself became devoid of tension, of contradiction – in other words, the conventions on which signalling the performative depend have to be refreshed, lest they become ghettoised into serving the needs of essentialism.[12]

Suede: beyond camp?

Suede emerged in the early 1990s, a period marked by the rise to prominence of 'the lad' and a new type of 'old' masculinity (see Mort 1996). This, of course, was personified in the rock group Oasis and the 'movement', termed 'New Rock' (Brit-rock) or 'new authenticity', which marked a retreat into a more conventionalised and conservative masculinity and its accompanying rock performance style.[13]

Suede's eponymous debut album went to Number 1 in March 1993, and such was the controversy that the band's every move became much debated in the music press (Savage 1996: 341). The cover, borrowed from the 1970s book of lesbian erotica, *Stolen Glances*, which featured two people of indeterminate gender kissing, announced much of what the band were about: Suede were regarded as offering a 'gleeful trashing of sex and gender boundaries' (Savage 1996: 342), one that is all the more significant given the context into which they emerged. Discourse in the music press plays a powerful role in framing discussions and interpretations about popular music, mediating between star and audience. The significant and much quoted example here is Brett Anderson's (Suede's lead singer) controversial claim to *Melody Maker* in February 1993, that he 'sees himself as a bisexual man who has never had a homosexual experience' (quoted in Wise 1998). The

Figure 20.1   Maybe, maybe it's the clothes we wear
The tasteless bracelets and the dye in our hair
(Suede, 'Trash', *Coming Up*, Nude Records, 1996)

band here could be recouped to the orthodox position – that Suede are in a long line of male heterosexual pop performers who have colonised aspects of an 'excessive femininity' and the iconographies of 'gay culture' (see Reynolds and Press 1995). However, this accusation of gender-tourism is too neat as it drags us back to essentialism – that sexuality, gender, identity, performance and musical expression all go together.[14] Alternatively, Judith Butler's concept of drag as performative is useful in understanding the group's performance and its significance.

In one vital sense, Anderson's pronouncement supports the indeterminacy of Suede's performance of gender, not in a way that supports heterosexual masculine complexity, but rather undermines it, foregrounding the dissonance between sex and gender and revealing their constructedness. Suede destabilise the naturalised heterosexism of rock, de-essentialising it. We could follow Bruzzi (1997b) and argue that if Brett Anderson were to 'come out', this would anchor the narrative about Suede into ontological sex-gender security: to 'fit the fit' ('oh, Anderson is gay, therefore . . .' and the music and performance become explained).[15] We can get a glimpse of this line of argument in Suede's debut review in *Village Voice*. The reviewer, Barry Walters, teases out some of the complexity of Suede but argues that he'd 'prefer it if Anderson was a bona fide homo, rather than merely an enthusiastic student' (Walters 1995: 769).[16] But surely the point is that there is no arrival into the essentialised, naturalised world, no point of closure, of sex and gender certitude. We could already conclude that Suede have successfully put on 'the show of gender construction'. However, what interests me is why and how, in what way? How are Suede different from Madonna, New Pop, The Pet Shop Boys or k.d.lang – artists who are taken to be, in some way or other, performative?[17]

To understand this we have to turn to consider the specificities of popular music culture itself. Here, it is important to bear in mind that popular music can be disruptive owing precisely to the tensions set up amongst its various levels and their attendant associations. As we have seen, a great deal of rock and pop strives to form a 'fit' among all the elements concerned, whether into the discourse of authenticity, or of artifice.

There appear to be two main dynamics at work with Suede in their relationship to pop history, costume and performance. The first involves a dynamic with New Pop and a recognition of the limitations of its particular discourse of 'artifice'. The second is a musical appropriation (and critique) of masculinist rock naturalism, the 'New Rock' or 'new authenticity' associated with, say, Oasis. Similarly, in musical terms Suede (circa 1993) did not use synthesisers, sequencing or other forms of 'electronica', which runs in contradistinction to New Pop.

Suede are something of a hybrid of aspects of New Pop performance styles and the codes of British counter-cultural rock and, significantly, occupy the hinterland between rock and pop (between masculine and feminine, authenticity and artifice). A major influence here is David Bowie – perhaps the most famous singer associated with gender-blurring.[18] While, in one way, Bowie is regarded as something of a 'pioneer', it could be argued that for some time he has been valued primarily within a discourse of hagiographic artistry; that Bowie's 'experiments' are subordinate to Bowie as 'great figure'. Pleasure in Bowie's chameleonic elasticity and role-playing, therefore, could be viewed differently: he, more than any

other artist, has been able to colonise other identities and their associations, elaborating the already-elaborated subjectivity of the white male (see Dyer 1997).
Suede, in the period I am discussing, are, by contrast, a first album band without
the same prominent 'auteur' myth, and no narrative security to ground what is
dissonant.

Similarly, Suede's difference from New Pop needs to be understood in relation
to the changing dynamics of popular culture and readings of performance, clothing
and their performative value. While Suede could be located within a more widely
discussed heritage pop/rock trend, exhibiting a self-consciousness about both
English pop's (great) past and the codes of counter-cultural rock, this is by no
means all they are about and such a critical trajectory reduces the complexity of pop
pleasure and meaning. While these heritage elements are, without doubt, in place,
they are utilised in a manner that reveals an increased critical self-consciousness
about how popular music makes meaning and, in particular, what music, clothing
and the body together signify. Suede's 'gender-as-masquerade' offers few of the
traditional signifiers of drag and cross-dressing and is, perhaps, based on an implicit
recognition of the limitations of particular drag/cross-dressing practices and their
(in)ability to signify sex-gender dissonance.

What is immediately noticeable about the way Suede are dressed is the absence
of a conspicuous or clearly signalled male 'dandyism' and its associated shiny, 'inauthentic' apparel. In one sense, Suede avoid the usual camp tropes of dress as
'feminine excess'. What Suede (particularly Anderson) wear is not conspicuously
high fashion, or novel or shocking. Anderson is dressed simply in black (black
being, of course, the favoured colour of subcultural Bohemia): loose-fitting Levis
and a tight-sleeved top with a low-cut circular neck, and only the latter has feminine connotations. Elsewhere, in terms of music and dress, Suede owe a great deal
to rock's past. With regard to movement and posture, hair and clothes, Bernard
Butler invokes the image of 'legendary' rock guitarist, Jimmy Page.[19] Sonically, in
addition to Page, Butler owes a great deal to Jimi Hendrix (particularly so on the
track I have chosen for discussion, 'He's Dead'). This sense of rock traditionalism
is carried through to video release, *Love and Poison* (1993): Suede elected to release
a 'live' performance video as opposed to video compilation or experimental film,
in the manner of their New Pop antecedents.[20]

Musically, 'He's Dead' is convincing (i.e. 'authentic') rock with counter-
cultural connotations, with an extended Hendrix-style guitar solo of swirling
feedback and distorted 'wah-wah' effects. However, the conventional meanings
associated with the form are offset and a number of tensions/contradictions opened
up. The first of these relates to the song's address – the use of 'I', 'you', 'we',
'she' – with Anderson unambiguously singing, mournfully, about a 'he'.[21] The
second is how the clothing is inhabited on the performing body in question within
this music-performance context, with the tall and slim Anderson invoking the
image of the feminine 'modelesque'.

Anderson's Levis are not figure-hugging or tight, but styled to gather around
the hips. Together with his body posture and the figure-hugging top, these tend
to signify traditional notions of 'womanliness' (i.e. wider hips and thighs to the
normative masculinity). In movement, the singer's style runs against the territorial
strut associated with rock and men performing 'powerfully'. Importantly, during

the guitar solo – that rock cliché of masculine phallic prowess – Anderson turns his back to the audience and begins a series of non-normative movements. This 'turning away' works in opposition to the thrust of most phallic rock. Attention is taken away from the front of the body, most particularly the genitals, to which, as I argued previously, attention is not drawn either in the framing or by Anderson's dress-code. This fits the more general discourse of avoiding traditional markers of the 'authentically' male.[22]

Instead, Anderson offers his backside to the audience, pushing it out, slowly wiggling it. He also pulls his legs together to construct and accentuate a feminine body shape (traditional sexualised 'womanliness'). Most significantly, utilising the low-cut top, he pushes his shoulder-blades together to form 'breasts', creating the image of a cleavage (significantly swapping the plunged front of orthodox performing masculinity for a plunged back that reveals the constructedness of sexual desire and creates a gap between sex and gender).[23] This invites the gaze on to the cleavage as signifier of male heterosexual desire while simultaneously problematising it, foregrounding its constructedness, its role in the idea of 'femininity-as-masquerade', as well as revealing the performative aspect of the sexualised, gendered body (Riviere 1986; Bruzzi 1997a, 1997b). Anderson becomes a 'back-to-front' woman, a distorted, 'cubist' composite of constructed sexualised fragments. In this way, Suede signify gender dissonance/gender confusion, staving off the either–or binary between straight and gay; masculine and feminine; authenticity and artifice. This is accompanied by a self-conscious use of the microphone,

Figure 20.2   Suede in concert.

which is played with suggestively, with the cable used as a whip at the song's beginning and also pulled, suggestively, across the singer's backside.

In one sense, Anderson is adopting the performance conventions of certain strands of pornography to generate a whole series of uncertainties around the construction of desire: Is this symbolic of anal sex? is this drag? is he creating the image of the sexualised woman? Is he gay? Are we, the audience, supposed to feel desire? This confusion is amplified due to an avoidance of traditional drag, as any elements of drag utilised here avoid the 'traditional' signifiers of 'feminine excess' at the level of make-up and costume, and offer a more modern, 'everyday' 'femininity'.[24]

The image here is not simply of transvestism, drag or androgyny, but is something of a hybrid of aspects of all three categories. If the image is mainly androgynous it is not a conventionalised androgyny, but one that simultaneously invokes the constructedness *and* the 'polymorphous perversity' of sexual desire. As Bruzzi argues,

> the blurred ambiguity of the image . . . makes androgyny a far more erotic form of transvestism . . . than cross-dressing, because it is not defined by an acceptance of the fixity of gender binaries, but rather by the effect of ambiguity.
>
> [. . .]
>
> The androgynous body is never complete because it is innately unstable; it always possesses the capacity for mutability and transformation, And unlike the cross-dressed body, does not hold onto the notion of its single, 'real' sex.
>
> (Bruzzi 1997a: 199)

It was certainly rare to see the musical conventions associated with masculine prowess inhabited in a way that rendered ambiguous the performance of masculinity. However, the Suede performance is not just 'playful'; they do not inhabit the conventions of counter-cultural rock in a simple ironic, or merely 'playful' way (both of these terms are often used in a way that shuts out their complexity in order to forge a sense of progressiveness). In fact, musically, these conventions are heavily invested in and inhabited convincingly. It can be countered that there is nothing essential in rock's sound that makes it the natural expression of heterosexist masculinity. As Frith and McRobbie (1978: 386) have argued, 'rock's hard beat may not, in itself, speak in terms of male domination, power or aggression'. The musical conventions and their articulation, in their links to authenticity, invoke 'seriousness' which works outside of the conventional discourse of camp. Rather, the conventions of sex-gender blurring are pulled to where they wouldn't normally belong – into organic masculinist rock. The gender dissonance created is forceful precisely because it occurs in a 'naturalised', masculine rock space.

Thus, Suede are the more radical for not wholly working within the discourse of artifice, but in their articulation of sincere and inauthentic elements; between clothing and the body, the body and performance, clothing and sound, and so on. In one way, rock's 'hard beat' is being 'reclaimed', dislodged from its essentialist masculinist moorings. As Frith and McRobbie (1978: 371) claim in relation to pop, performance and gender: 'the best writers on the subject state the contradictions

Figure 20.3   Suede in concert.

without resolving them'; it is just as interesting, and more provocative, when popular musical performers do the same.[25] As Judith Butler has argued:

> The moment in which one's staid and usual cultural perceptions fail, when one cannot with surety read the body that one sees, is precisely the moment when one is no longer sure whether the body encountered is that of a man or a woman. . . . When such categories come into question, the *reality* of gender is also put into crisis: it becomes unclear how to distinguish the real from the unreal.
>
> (Butler 1999: xxii–xxiii)

Performers such as Suede represent a brief, if crucial, break 'in the compulsive repetition of normative heterosexuality' and have played a not insignificant part in 'interrogating the binary divide between men and women' (McRobbie 1999: 86).

Notes

1   A significant feature of this 'fashion-neglect', as Church Gibson moves on to point out, is that camera angles and lighting styles have occupied much more serious scholarly attention than the semiotics of costume. This, in one sense,

may be read as part of a masculinist agenda that has valued 'the labour of the technical' over fashion labour and the development of a semiotics of dress. In other words, within the history of the academic 'culture disciplines', some codes have been given priority over others.

2   I am greatly indebted to the members of Suede and to Mehelli at Nude Records for their enthusiasm, support and the use of images of Suede in performance.

3   While masculine attire in rock may have been used for sexual display, it was never reducible to this; male rock could set itself up as being about more than 'just clothes and sex'.

4   As Angela McRobbie has pointed out, cultural studies itself has been seen as 'merely fashionable', as 'feminine', within the masculine academy; that much of the study of culture is focused on the 'trivial' compared to, say, the serious study of 'hard' economic realities (McRobbie 1999: 99). Again, this is regrettable because it overlooks the possibility of where changes might emerge.

5   It is important to point out here that even though I have discussed these magazines together, their construction and treatment of masculinity, in terms of the body and dress, vary greatly.

6   However, not only has the Madonna debate dominated discourse about popular music and gender, it has like punk before it, pushed out to the margins discussion of other artists' performative moments.

7   For a more detailed discussion of the issues of black musical expression and the operation of authenticity see Gilroy (1993).

8   Smelik notes that essentialism is a powerful discourse within areas of gay culture. By contrast it is important to assert that 'sexuality is not a given of nature but a construct of culture. Thus, the debate shifts from realizing a shared essence to understanding homosexuality as a product of social forces' (Smelik 1998: 144).

9   This is not to dispute that each of the artists mentioned above has at some time articulated radical sex-gender dissonance, but we could take Bruzzi's argument about lang and apply it to Annie Lennox: if there was a performative moment it was *Sweet Dreams*, not the later *Diva*.

10 The study of popular music has needed to be multidisciplinary and attuned to the different areas that comprise popular music culture – audience studies, various forms of textual analysis (performance, video, musicology, the semiotics of clothing: subcultural style) and studies of discourse (debates about popular music, both routine [the music press, the rock biography] and specialist [the journal and textbook]). Here, the role of clothing is clearly of great significance, but needs to be considered in relation to specific musical and discursive contexts and theorised as belonging to a body *in* musical performance. Arguably, 'reading' the role and function of costume in film and theorising text–subject relations is less problematic in film studies – the audience's relationship to the form is taken to be clearer. In the cinema the audience is conceived as centred – seated in the dark, fixed and facing the screen. Fashion and popular music by contrast are less anchored in a single (relatively), discrete experience and may be viewed and enjoyed in a variety of different contexts – on the street, club, catwalk, live performance and so on.

11 As Davis argues, much of the objection to fashion within subculturalism is based on 'utilitarian outrage' (Davis 1992: 168), with fashion seen as the height of 'wastefulness, frivolity, impracticality, and vanity' (ibid.). Fashion is constructed

as working against the modernist impulse of 'form following function'. Hence, within Hebdige's narrative, punk has to be anchored to its 'function' as subcultural resistance, and distance itself from the 'feminine' (whereas, of course, much of punk (anti)fashion was extremely 'impractical' and expensive).

12   As Richard Middleton has argued, the association of particular musical sounds (guitars signifying warmth, passion and emotion; synthesisers, carrying connotations of coldness, modernity and the future) have particular ideological associations attached to them that once consolidated, become very difficult to dislodge (Middleton 1990: 90). We could add clothing and performance styles to this list: clothes that are shiny and 'feminine' carry connotations of the orthodoxly 'camp' and so forth.

13   In many respects the performing style of Liam Gallagher could be construed as articulating a type of hysterical masculinity; one defined by a lack of movement, an avoidance of anything vaguely 'feminine' and an attempt to stave off sex and gender ambiguity. Liam in performance (as in interview) was surly, sullen and disinterested. As with other types of masculinity that seek to absent themselves, Liam's performance becomes interesting through what it is not. In this way, the masculine boorishness of Oasis relates to Bruzzi's description of 'manliness as masquerade' which can be regarded as 'a desperate, embarrassing, hysterical reaction to encroaching insignificance' (Bruzzi 1997: 130).

14   As Frith and Goodwin have argued, these assumptions about a 'natural' relationship between sounds, performance and identity 'began to be unpicked by feminists concerned to expose the gender prejudice of 1960s theories of "liberation" through sex, drugs and rock 'n roll' (Frith and Goodwin 1990: 370).

15   Bruzzi argues that there is an anchorage, a closing down brought about by 'the character coming out the disguise . . . revealing who s/he really is' (Bruzzi 1997: 157). Here, any 'noise' is swept away and the performance fixed within the narrative of ontological sexual authenticity.

16   John Gill in his book *Queer Noises* notes the importance of Bowie, who for Gill is evidently 'not gay', in articulating Queer possibilities. Despite this, Gill still relies on a 'you have to be one or the other' position and rarely moves beyond the either/or binary into questioning the constructedness of both sex and gender.

17   It is important also in debates about popular music to consider differentiations *within* dance culture, as dance is often held up as more 'progressive' in terms of the articulation of gender and sexuality. While 'dance culture', in many areas, offers a more asexual iconography than masculinist rock, this is not always the case. For example, the sounds and fashion iconography of 'boozy Big Beat' were criticised for their masculine boorishness by more 'progressive' quarters of the dance music press. Also, aspects of dance culture have valued strains of hip hop, not as a challenge to notions of rootedness and authenticity, but precisely as a marker of masculine and racial authenticity (see Gilroy 1993: 99–101). Therefore, it is not enough simply to celebrate the artistic creativity of contemporary dance culture wholesale in the manner that Angela McRobbie (1999) does (even if I agree). While the turntable is not phallic-shaped in the manner of the electric guitar, it has been put to similar uses, where the DJ skill of mixing may be valued in much the same way as the guitar solo of yore – as an index of predominately male skill. Even though dance presents DIY opportunities, these may become animated by older aesthetics and values. The old codes of prowess and control haven't disappeared, they have just become transferred into new areas (areas where, it is often predicted, they won't belong).

18   For a discussion of Suede's relationship to Bowie and English suburbia, see Simon
      Frith's (1997) essay, 'The suburban sensibility in British rock and pop'.

19   He significantly also plays the same two guitars most favoured by Page: the
      Gibson Les Paul and the Gibson ES335. Suede musically favour the authenticity
      of the pentatonic Blues scale over the decidedly un-R&B inauthenticity of elec-
      tronic New Pop.

20   Neil Tennant, for example, disliked playing live, and, by contrast, liked to boast
      about not being able to 'cut it' live as part of the New Pop critique of rock.
      The Pet Shop Boys and Soft Cell both experimented in terms of video release,
      as with much of New Pop, avoiding the associations of the 'live'.

21   In discussions of queer artists a frequent criticism, as in Bruzzi's discussion of
      k.d. lang, concerns the absence of gender-specific address in favour of a universal
      one (see Bruzzi 1997b).

22   The guitar solo and its conventionalised links to musical and sexual climax are
      well known. In the video this is acknowledged and parodied: when the solo hits
      its peak (climax) we see a shot of what we 'read' as cum hitting glass. This,
      presumably, is included to help expose and undermine the masculinist conven-
      tions of 'phallic' guitar rock.

23   As an index of pop's ability to play with and subvert naturalised (heterosexual)
      notions of desire, Frith argued in 1985 that 'the sexiest performer' he'd seen
      'was, in fact, a boy in Depeche Mode, a dyed blonde in mini-skirt and skimpy
      top. His shoulder straps kept slipping, leaving me a "heterosexual" man, breath-
      lessly hoping throughout the show to get a glimpse of his breasts' (cited in Frith
      and Goodwin 1990: 419).

24   Significantly, the singer doesn't wear a wig; rather his hair is cut into a bob –
      cut up at the back and at one side, and with a long fringe at the front that falls
      over his face – on the fault line between male and female.

25   This discussion of Suede in performance is greatly indebted to David Dunn's
      paper 'What does it take to turn you on?: Suede, gender & performativity' at
      The School of Art, the University of Northumbria in May 1998. As is customary,
      the interpretation of the argument here is entirely my responsibility.

References

Barthes, R. (1977) *Image, Music, Text*, trans. S. Heath, London: Fontana.

Bruzzi, S. (1997a) *Undressing Cinema: Clothing and Identity in the Movies*, London:
      Routledge.

—— (1997b) 'Mannish Girl: k.d. lang – from cowpunk to androgyny' in S. Whiteley
      (ed.) *Sexing the Groove: Popular Music and Gender*, London: Routledge, 191–206.

Butler, J. (1990) *Gender Trouble: Feminism and the Subversion of Identity*, New York:
      Routledge.

—— (1999) 'Preface to new edition', *Gender Trouble: Feminism and the Subversion of
      Identity*, London and New York: Routledge.

Church Gibson, P. (1998) 'Film costume' in J. Hill and P. Church Gibson (eds) *The
      Oxford Guide to Film Studies*, Oxford: Oxford University Press, 36–42.

Craik, J. (1994) *The Face of Fashion: Cultural Studies in Fashion*, London and New York:
      Routledge.

Davis, F. (1992) *Fashion, Culture, and Identity*, Chicago: Chicago University Press.

Dyer, R. (1997) *White*, London and New York: Routledge.

Easthope, A. (1992) *What a Man's Gotta Do: The Masculine Myth in Popular Culture*, London and New York: Routledge.

Fiske, J. (1992) 'British Cultural Studies' in R.C. Allen (ed.) *Channels of Discourse, Reassembled*, London and New York: Routledge.

Frith, S. (1990) 'Afterthoughts' in S. Frith and A. Goodwin (eds) (1990) *On Record: Rock, Pop and the Written Word*, London: Routledge, 419–24.

—— (1996) *Performing Rites: On the Value of Popular Music*, Oxford: Oxford University Press.

—— (1997) 'The suburban sensibility in British rock and pop', in Roger Silverstone (ed.) *Visions of Suburbia*, London and New York: Routledge, 269–79.

—— and Goodwin, A. (eds) (1990) *On Record: Rock, Pop & The Written Word*, London: Routledge.

Frith, S. and McRobbie, A. (1990) 'Rock and Sexuality' in S. Frith and A. Goodwin (eds) *On Record: Rock, Pop & The Written Word*, London: Routledge, 371–89.

Gill, J. (1995) *Queer Noises: Male and Female Homosexuality in Twentieth-Century Music*, London: Cassell.

Gilroy, P. (1993) *The Black Atlantic: Modernity and Double Consciousness*, London: Verso.

Goodwin, A. (1993) *Dancing in the Distraction Factory: Music Television and Popular Culture*, London: Routledge.

Grossberg, L. (1993) 'The Media Economy of Rock Culture: cinema, post-modernism and authenticity' in S. Frith, A. Goodwin and L. Grossberg (eds) *Sound and Vision: the Music Video Reader*, London: Routledge, 185–209.

Hawkins, S. (1997) 'The Pet Shop Boys: Musicology, masculinity, banality' in S. Whiteley (ed.) *Sexing the Groove: Popular Music and Gender*, London: Routledge, 118–34.

Heath, S. (1982) *The Sexual Fix*, Basingstoke: Macmillan.

Hebdige, D. (1979) *Subculture: The Meaning of Style*, London: Methuen.

—— (1988) *Hiding in the Light: On Images and Things*, London: Routledge.

Hill, J. (1999) *British Cinema in the 1980s: Issues and Themes*, Oxford: Clarendon.

Kaplan, E.A. (1987) *Rocking Around The Clock: Music Television, Postmodernism and Consumer Culture*, New York and London: Methuen.

Kureishi, H. and Savage, J. (eds) (1995) *The Faber Book of Pop*, London: Faber & Faber.

McDonald, P. (1997) 'Feeling and fun: romance, dance & the performing male body in the Take That videos' in S. Whiteley (ed.) *Sexing the Groove: Popular Music and Gender*, London: Routledge, 277–94.

McRobbie, A. (1989) 'Second-Hand Dresses and the Role of the Ragmarket' in A. McRobbie (ed.) *Zoot Suits & Second-Hand Dresses: An Anthology of Fashion and Music*, Basingstoke: Macmillan, 23–49.

—— (1999) *In the Culture Society: Art, Fashion & Popular Music*, London: Routledge.

Middleton, R. (1990) *Studying Popular Music*, Milton Keynes: Open University Press.

Mort, F. (1996) *Cultures of Consumption: Masculinities and Social Space in Late Twentieth-Century Britain*, London: Routledge.

Nixon, S. (1996) *Hard Looks: Masculinities, the Visual and the Practices of Consumption*, London: University of London Press.

Reynolds, S. and Press, J. (1995) *The Sex Revolts: Gender, Rebellion & Rock 'n' Roll*, London: Serpent's Tail.

Riviere, J. [1929] (1986) 'Womanliness as masquerade' in V. Burgin, J. Donald and C. Kaplan (eds) *Formations of Fantasy*, London: Methuen.

Rutherford, J. and Chapman, R. (eds) (1988) *Male Order: Unwrapping Masculinity*, London: Lawrence & Wishart.

Sabin, R. (ed.) (1999) *Punk Rock: So What? The Cultural Legacy of Punk*, London: Routledge.

Savage, J. (1996) *Time. Travel. From the Sex Pistols to Nirvana: Pop, Media and Sexuality, 1977–96*, London: Chatto & Windus.

Shumway, D.R. (1992) 'Rock & Roll as a Cultural Practice' in A. DeCurtis (ed.) *Present Tense: Rock & Roll and Contemporary Culture*, Durham; London: Duke University Press, 117–33.

Smelik, A. (1998) 'Gay and lesbian criticism' in J. Hill and P. Church Gibson (eds) *The Oxford Guide to Film Studies*, Oxford: Oxford University Press, 135–47.

Straw, W. (1993) 'Popular music and postmodernism in the 1980s' in S. Frith, A. Goodwin and L. Grossberg (eds) *Sound and Vision: The Music Video Reader*, London: Routledge, 3–21.

Street, J. (1997) *Politics and Popular Culture*, Cambridge: Polity Press.

Thornton, S. (1995) *Club Cultures: Music, Media & Subcultural Capital*, Cambridge: Polity Press.

Walters, B. (1993) 'Take it like a man' in H. Kureishi and J. Savage (eds) *The Faber Book of Pop*, London: Faber & Faber, 767–70.

Wise, N. (1998) *Suede: an Illustrated Biography*, London: Omnibus Press.

York, P. and Jennings, C. (1995) *Peter York's Eighties*, London: BBC Books.

Supplementary materials

Suede, 'He's Dead' from *Love and Poison*, 1993, Nude video.

—— *Suede*, 1993, Nude Records, LP.

Chapter 21

Stella Bruzzi

THE ITALIAN JOB
Football, fashion and that sarong

IN 1990 ITALY HOSTED their first World Cup since 1938, then under the shadow of Mussolini and the Fascist statues around the Stadio Olimpico in Rome. Italia 90 would be different, a chance to cut a fine figure and, more importantly to Italian football fans, win a third World Cup (*Mondiale*), thus going ahead of Brazil. Expectations were high, Italian club teams had just won all the European trophies, they had in Roberto Baggio – whose recent sale by Fiorentina to Juventus for $20m had prompted riots in the streets of Florence – the new Paolo Rossi, their hero of 1982, and they were playing at home. Things started well – to a superstitious Italian maybe too well – as Italy, thanks ironically to their new Sicilian striker Toto Schillaci, arrived unproblematically at a 1–0 lead in their semi-final against an inferior Argentina. Then Argentina scored and the home team choked, losing eventually 4–3 on penalties, ensuring Germany an improbable number of *tifosi* (fans) for the Final. Like the Victorian gentleman who shouted out to Othello before the end of Shakespeare's tragedy that Iago was not to be trusted, this disaster wasn't part of the script. Italy weren't supposed to end their World Cup campaign slugging it out in a lacklustre, also-rans, third-place play-off in Bari (albeit in a sumptuous, new Renzo Piano-designed San Nicola stadium) against an England team bereft of Gazza, tears and flair; they were destined for the reinvigorated Stadio Olimpico. It was not for this that Italy had designed, redesigned and renovated twelve stadiums, held a national poll to decide the official mascot's name ('Ciao' beating off the challenge of 'Dribbly' and 'Bimbo') and commissioned its film-makers to direct short films about their home towns and cities. As the despairing headline in *La Gazzetta dello Sport* declared the day after the calamitous defeat in the semis: 'Italia Noooo'.

Despite the resulting anticlimax for the host nation and the choice of Giorgio Moroder's *Un Estate Italiana* as the championship's accompanying pop song, Italia

90 was a turning point for how football was perceived, particularly in the UK where, in its wake, football became synonymous with style, desire, melodrama and spectacle. 'Football' had a new aura; the Pavlovian response to the word was no longer to think of bobble hats and beery, leery men in smelly sheepskin and scarves swaying on the terraces like tinless sardines between other 'white males of little education and even less wit' (Ian Taylor in Williams 1995: 243) on wet, wasted afternoons. Although the pre-Hillsborough and Heysel image of the fan is as much a cliché as the new man with muscles and Italian-cut suits who has replaced him, the shift is monumental and irreversible. Significantly, it wasn't all footballers whose images altered and the new-found football chic was firmly rooted in Italianness – or rather the British reconfiguration of Italianness. There is a marked difference in British attitudes to, for instance, David Ginola's 'Eurotrash' look of jacket, T-shirt, jeans, loafers and no socks than to Gianluca Vialli, player and ex-manager of Chelsea. Ginola is coded as sexy but available: he advertises hair products, he appears with monotonous regularity in the pages of *Hello!*. The Premiership reincarnation of Vialli, though, is another matter. On the eve of Chelsea's FA Cup Final against Aston Villa in May 2000, the *Guardian*'s Jim White remarks upon the club's final press day. Unexpectedly for a sports pages feature, perhaps, White begins by dwelling upon the 'Giorgio Armani' press pack that was handed out, in which the squad were pictured donning natty 'three-button, single-breasted suits in charcoal-grey wool worn, according to the blurb, "with light grey tone on tone shirt and tie combination"' (White 2000: 1). White here seems proud of his ability to describe, with admirable accuracy, the Armani garb, whilst simultaneously sneaking in that the journalists themselves were dressed 'in the standard fashion-free manner'. He reserves his greatest admiration, however, for the manager, commenting 'no one wears the ensemble as well as Gianluca Vialli'. This is a curious thing – prior to Vialli's departure from Juventus to Chelsea as a player under his managerial predecessor, Ruud Gullit, Vialli was a favourite target of the Italian sports press, not for his style but his lack of it. As Vialli started to thin on top, so he began tinkering with his mane and his facial hair: from wild curls to crew cut, from clean-shaven chin to designer stubble goatee (ostensibly illustrating the old truism that if you want to change something about your appearance that you'd rather went unnoticed, divert attention to some other feature at the same time). In England, Vialli's very Italianness ensures his fashion status.

Vialli took over at Chelsea from another Serie A export, Dutchman Ruud Gullit. Gullit's arrival at Stamford Bridge under Glenn Hoddle was another key post-Italia 90 moment of transition, although he was nearing the end of his career and had got a bit stocky, slow and ungainly on the pitch. Gullit, however, descended in his Milanese suits (and his own clothes line) and transformed the image of the team of Dennis Wise, London's Gazza. Several factors united to make Gullit such a key icon: his legendary status as a player, particularly at AC Milan; his sartorial panache; his intelligence both as a player and a TV pundit. The English reverence of Gullit (I distinctly recall several minutes of *Match of the Day* being given over to a discussion of the correct pronunciation of his name, as if Alan Hansen *et al.* just liked saying it) was relatively short-lived as he left Chelsea under a cloud and had little managerial success subsequently with Newcastle United. Alongside his 'culturedness', the other significant facet of Gullit's appeal was that he was black, and like English football has sought a patina of Italian finesse, so it has often been a place for acknowledging black stylishness. Storm, the London model agency, started signing up footballers in 1995 and those on its books by 1998 included Ruud Gullit, Les Ferdinand and Ian Wright. The common factor, of course, is that all three are black, more effortlessly cool and inherently stylish than their pasty-skinned colleagues. Another high-profile footballer-cum-model is David James, the Liverpool then Aston Villa goalie who has done Armani catwalk shows and, in 1996, appeared on a 50ft high poster wearing only Armani underpants. Chelsea's transformation from a parochial, technically crude squad pre-Hoddle to one that starts the 2000 FA Cup Final with only one native player is Gullit's lasting legacy. As if to render himself more stylish, Chelsea's only Englishman, Dennis Wise, went up to receive the cup clutching the new century's latest male fashion accessory – his baby.

It was thus more than Gazza's iconic tears of Italia 90 that have cemented the notion of fashionable football in the UK. At the time of the championships, the choice of Pavarotti's rendition of Puccini's *Nessun Dorma* as the BBC's official Italia 90 anthem was extremely influential in reconstructing football spectatorship as a couch activity worthy of the chattering classes. Although Pavarotti was the masses' opera star, and, alongside Placido Domingo and José Carreras, has become a fixture of British World Cup coverage since, *Nessun Dorma* was a far cry from Chelsea in 1971 grunting 'Blue is the Colour' or Glenn Hoddle and Chris Waddle appearing on *Top of the Pops* sporting spangly 1980s jackets, feathercuts and quiffs. During the BBC's 1990 coverage there was also the unusual side-tracking commentary by its pundits on the gorgeousness of the Italian stadiums, asides that inevitably contextualised football within society and culture at large. Italy and football were perhaps the significant if unconscious catalysts for the attitude change elsewhere; perhaps it was evident simply from how even designer-clad, middle-class Italians treated football as a significant part of their cultural lives that the sport could be sexy. Certainly in the aftermath of Italia 90 in Britain more women started to watch and be interested in football, Channel 4 began broadcasting live Serie A action and the accompanying *Gazzetta Football Italia* and footballers became fashion icons. To become fashionable, British football has had to become less parochial and less male, for this was the rite of passage that enabled footballers in general to become objects of pulchritude and aspiration.

There are other less frivolous factors that may have contributed to the need to find the chic in football, the most socially significant being the immediate call for all-seated stadiums after ninety-six fans – the majority from Liverpool – died at Hillsborough, Sheffield on 15 April 1989. The need for such measures had already been signalled by the violence that erupted between Liverpool and Juventus fans at the 1985 European Cup Final at Heysel Stadium where thirty-nine, mainly Italian, fans died. These ugly scenes (that led to English clubs being banned from Europe for five years) have been interpreted as the result of English fans' xenophobia, which is ironic considering their subsequent obsession with the European game. Lord Justice Taylor's official inquiry after Hillsborough stipulated that all stadiums in England, Scotland and Wales would need to become all-seated by the start of the 1994–5 season. The drop in attendances that this entailed meant in turn that ticket prices had to rise (Manchester United's average receipts per spectator, for example, rose by almost 223 per cent between 1988–9 and 1992–3) and 'raised the spectre, for some, of the sport increasingly becoming distanced, socially and spatially, from its "traditional" audience and being played in soul-less "production-line" concrete bowls in front of passive and affluent consumers (not supporters)' (Williams 1995: 225).[1] This, ironically, is more akin to the dominant European model for viewing football already in place by 1989–90, and it is significant that many commentators on the continental game cite as an important difference between the game in England (or Germany) and France or Italy the fact that in the latter countries it has traditionally been a cross-class activity, for spectators and players alike (Mignon 1999: 82; Lanfranchi 1994: 152–3). The changing image of football chic in the UK coincided, therefore, with the general poshening of the national game. An accurate gauge of this is the changing responses to Graham Le Saux's *Guardian*-reading middle-classness: whereas now he is deemed to fit in, earlier in his career he was ridiculed for being a boffin.

What then happened in the UK during and immediately after Italia 90 that was so radical? First, there was 'Gazza', the contradictory, loaded icon of 1990s English football: a Geordie genius whose famous tears at being issued with another yellow card in England's semi against Germany (which would mean, if England got there, that he wouldn't play in the Final) made him into a national institution, epitomising the British fixation upon the 'if only' brand of glorious sporting failure. Gazza's image, though, was a complex one; he was likewise renowned for his stupidity, bigotry and bad behaviour, and it was Gazza who declared to Terry Wogan 'I'm norra poof, like', who beat up his wife and got legless on the eve of Glenn Hoddle's selection of England's France 1998 squad. Gazza never lost his Englishness but it was also he who transferred to Lazio in the aftermath of Italia 90 and who, much more than David Platt who went to Serie A at the same time, exemplified the continuation of the British love affair with *calcio*.

Symptomatic of the essential ambiguity of Gazza's image, the dream combination of Gazza and Italy never took off: at Lazio he was plagued by injury and bad press, he never made efforts to learn Italian and he was swiftly marginalised from his 'news round-up' slot on *Gazzetta Football Italia*. Gazza was as much a symbol of the old image of football as the new; like Maradona and Schillaci, two of the other stars of Italia 90, he was the epitome of the working-class boy made good. There were also parallels to be drawn between Gazza and George Best (with his line of boutiques in the 1970s, one of the few footballers of the pre-1990s era to cash in on the football/fashion intersection): both were resonant icons for their respective generations, both squandered their talents by boozing, womanising and generally going off the rails. Herein lies the first of many contradictions pertaining to the renaissance of football in the 1990s: that the stylish, fashionable and image-obsessed game is in part a re-fashioning or reclamation of the old drab one. When *Hello!* magazine featured Gazza's wedding to Sheryl in July 1996 (white morning suits and stretch limos), it did so because there was a voracious audience for its kitsch appeal, not because Gazza had suddenly been immortalised into the incarnation of good taste. It was Gazza, the cheeky chappy who farted and belched at the Italian press, who was canonised by the intelligentsia in the UK, and to whom Ian Hamilton dedicated over half an edition of *Granta* in 1993 ('Gazza Agonistes').

As with Gazza's image, the whole issue of football's relationship to style is fraught with anomalies. First, in the fashion pages of men's 1990s style magazines it is often the old image of football that is evoked, obviously out of nostalgia for 1966 and all that but also out of an understanding that 'football chic' will remain a complex and equivocal term to do, for instance, with the inherently ambivalent ways in which designer leisure wear labels have been reappropriated and universalised. The rise of leisure wear as chic is very different from the smartening up of football by an association with more formal designer wear. As Robert Elms writes in *Arena*, the 'genesis of the footballer as style god' is the sartorially challenged footballer of the 1970s with his collar-length hair and floral shirts, but the 'real style icons' of the mid-1990s football fashion scene are 'the lads on the terraces'; these rather than the Ginolas or the James's on the catwalks are what football chic is about (Elms 1996: 142–4). However much Armani Gazza has worn – and for a 1991 cover article for *GQ* he reputedly wanted a £5,000 fee plus £3,000-worth of Armani clothes – there's still something of the shellsuit brigade about him.[2] This is still where British football chic and its Italian equivalent diverge. In the run-up to USA 94, British *Esquire* ran a fashion article in which several Italian players modelled exclusive ready-to-wear Italian designs by Gucci, Cerruti, Zegna, Armani, Dolce and Gabbana, Valentino and Versace. It's not that all the players selected (who include the hardly stunning – though brilliant – AC Milan defender and national captain, Franco Baresi) are beautiful, nor that they are all super-successful. Indeed, one of the intriguing features of the article, which in June 1994 was prepared reasonably close to team selection time, was that it chose as its models several players – such as Roberto Mancini and Marco Simone – whom few Italians would have tipped to feature in the World Cup squad. The significant 'it' factor seems to be that the footballers are Italian. It's hard to imagine a comparable Italian style monthly running a feature in which David Beckham, Nicky Butt and David Seaman model Paul Smith, Katharine Hamnett and Nicole Farhi.

In Italy there is a clear history of football being seamlessly integrated into the nation's style and culture, and this became one of the lasting legacies of Italia 90 in Britain. Again in June 1994 as their prelude to that year's World Cup, *GQ* studies the form of the countries involved (who didn't include England) in terms of what it calls 'elements of style'. For many of these countries their 'element of style' is related to their footballing chances, so the Cameroon are labelled 'uncontrollable' and the Irish 'optimistic' (although it was Ireland who beat the fancied Italy in their group's opening match). When it comes to the Italians, under 'Style' *GQ* identifies 'Michelangelo, Da Vinci, Verdi, the lot', under 'Strength' it singles out 'gorgeousness' and under 'Weakness' it mentions 'insane media'. Obviously, very little of this has to do with football and much of it has to do with style. This automatic assimilation of leisure and social activities such as football into what's generally held to be attractive about Italy (its art, architecture, people, food, cars) is a recurrent theme in *GQ*. In October 1994, the magazine ran a piece 'Gran Turismo' on Italian cars and clothes featuring the juxtaposition, sensually photographed, of details of the fabric and cut of loose Italian tailoring with close-ups of Alfa Romeo dashboards: the cars are vintage; the clothes soon will be. Then, in December 1998, *GQ* ran a short article again in praise of Italian design in which it yokes together by a sometimes unseemly violence, such eclectic manifestations of this as Leonardo, the Lira notes, the Alfa Romeo badge, the Fiat 500, the Beretta, the Romans, the *Cosa Nostra* and the Juventus kit. This arbitrary list that ranks Sicilian organised crime alongside a Renaissance artist crudely illustrates the point that Italy is innately fashionable and that we in England want to emulate it. Intriguingly, of the Juventus kit *GQ* says it is as 'Subbuteo as shirts come, which would seem appropriate given that their inspiration came from a visit by Notts County' (*GQ*, December 1998: 262). Although the same 'inspiration' on the similarly clad Newcastle United would, perhaps, have been treated ironically, the contradiction of retro English league non-fashion having influenced Agnelli's slick winning machine is what creates the strip's aura of chic. It is hard to imagine that same British men's style magazine praising the very similar Newcastle monochrome strip, which makes the reverence towards Italian style seem totally uncritical.

In 1982 Mick Jagger, while performing with The Rolling Stones at the Stadio Comunale in Torino after Italy's World Cup victory that summer, donned a Paolo Rossi Number 20 shirt. There is a sense of Italian football having always been cool and evoking effortlessly a whole aura and lifestyle – despite many a naff haircut (Roberto 'the divine ponytail' Baggio's of USA 94 being the most obscene) or the potentially emasculating shots of an entire team in baby blue vests during the shirt-swapping ritual with Brazil after the 1978 third-place play-off. A distinction can be made between the 'full' and the 'empty' footballer as fashion icon image. Whereas a picture of David Beckham in Gucci, for example, is 'empty' because it is just a picture of David Beckham in Gucci, a picture of Gianni Rivera at the height of his fame and powers in the late 1960s/early 1970s, nonchalantly propped up against a bookcase perusing a hefty tome in slim-line black suit and patent Gucci brogues, is 'full' because it evokes not just Rivera and football but an aspirational lifestyle. Beckham's clothes too often wear him, he doesn't look natural in his designer casuals, his 'intellectual' spectacles or indeed posing shirtless on the golf course; he's always self-conscious, always performing and demanding to be looked at. That Italian golden boy Rivera is reading and ignoring us is significant, and the way in which we are invited to view that image (used, for instance, in an *Homme Plus* feature on the fifty most stylish sportsmen of the twentieth century [*Homme Plus* 1996: 89–99]) is as evocative of an unmeasurable cool, a certain lifestyle. The Rivera image is symptomatic of Britain having also caught the Italian need to take football itself so seriously. *Calcio*, one writer suggests, is automatically placed alongside Fellini, Ferrari and wine as something quintessentially Italian, but it is given disproportionate sobriety by, for example, programmes such as RAI 3's weekly post-mortem football analysis programme *Processo del Lunedì* ('Trial on Monday') in which experts adopt absurdly 'lofty tones and flowery language' in their discussion of the matches held the day before (Lanfranchi 1994: 155). The treatment in Britain of football by mainstream culture (as opposed to legitimately interested sports academics) is too frequently ironic or knowing, Nick Hornby being a notably sincere exception. So men's magazines, alongside articles genuinely praising the pervasiveness of Italian style, run features on awful 1970s football haircuts (Kevin Keegan 'the Permed Prince of the Park' [Webb 1998]) and the gaudiness of goal-keepers' strips (see *GQ*, June 1994). It is this equivocal response to the pairing of football and style that informs the distressed, trendified Parka image of Fat Les, the trio of Damien Hirst, Keith Allen and Alex James who had a 1998 World Cup hit with *Vindaloo* and brought out a version of *Jerusalem* for Euro 2000.

The emergence of football chic in Britain, therefore, has continued to be double-edged. Sartorially speaking, even the more recent history of English football's relationship with fashion is characterised by disasters rather than successes. There was, for instance, the scorn poured on the Liverpool team's emergence for the FA Cup Final of 1996 wearing (ironically) pale beige Giorgio Armani suits. One journalist likened the team to ice-cream salesmen (Greenberg 1998) whilst a fan commented, 'I held my face in my hands in shame. From the moment they stepped out in those suits, I knew we were going to lose' (Blanchard 1998). Then there was the scrutiny of Glenn Hoddle's managerial decision to put the England squad for France 98 in darker beige (or taupe) suits designed by Paul Smith. Smith had suggested navy for the suits but Hoddle wanted something more 'summery'. Not often has what the England squad elected to wear off the pitch been front-page news, but in this instance the matter was treated with earnest interest, one journalist making the preparation for the big day when the suits would finally be unveiled sound like an important nuptial:

> Final fittings will take place shortly. Because of their training pro-gramme, players change shape in a matter of weeks and can only be certain of their final sizes just before the tournament starts.
>
> (Kennedy 1998)

Here the England squad are described in more feminine terms than normal; more common were references to Paul Ince's thighs bursting out of the flimsy linen-viscose mix trousers or comments such as, 'If the players had their way, they'd arrive [in France] looking like the bad guys in a Tarantino heist movie' (Greenberg 1998). Just as Glenn Hoddle was nicknamed 'Glenda' during his days at Tottenham Hotspur for his silky skills and dainty, leggy appearance, so the unmentionable implication of 'those suits' was that the England team's collective machismo and potential coolness were under threat. In October 1999, David Beckham was stung with a £50,000 fine (later revoked) by the Manchester United coach Alex Ferguson for breaking the club curfew before a Champions League game and turning up at a London Fashion Week show. Although Beckham assured Sir Alex that he and his wife Victoria Adams were in bed by midnight, a taste for fashion has become, like sex before crucial encounters, a factor that can detract from a player's footballing skills. As *The Mirror* put it, 'pictures of him [Beckham] wearing a trendy headscarf put him and United on the spot' (Nixon and Harris 1999).

Apparently most of the squad of France 98 had favoured blue, the colour of the suits Paul Smith had designed for England's Euro 96 team, and although the players were given both the beige and the blue versions of the 1998 suit, this wasn't sufficient — except for the ever-diplomatic and dull Alan Shearer, who thought the beige looked fine against his lads' tanned skin. Although many a critical journalist who attended the taupe extravaganza recalled the Armani/Liverpool embarrassment, none of them seemed to remember Glenn Hoddle's last notable fashion decision as a manager — to put his Chelsea squad for their doomed 1994 FA Cup Final against Manchester United in pale purple because it was, as Hoddle commented at the time, a little bit 'different'. Indeed Paul Smith, who two years previously had simply been given the go-ahead by then England manager Terry Venables, was surprised at Hoddle's interference, remarking, 'I don't think he's well known for his dress sense' (Lee 1998). Several points of emphasis emerge from the coverage in June 1998 of the unveiling of the England's off-pitch uniforms: that beige reflected Glenn Hoddle's taste (after all, Hoddle on the touchline was often to be seen in tracksuit bottoms hitched up just a tad high, which made him look like a relaxed version of Reeves and Mortimer's King's Singers); that the suits did not reflect the players' keener fashion sense and masculinity; that this choice suggested the team would fail. Journalists vied with each other to heap the most withering insults on the beige creations: they were not as sharp as the 1966 World Cup winners in 'slim, dark razor-cut' suits – although better than the off-the-peg Burton's numbers of 1970 or the sporty blazers of 1990 (Mouland 1998); they looked like a 'convention of double-glazing salesmen' or a 'pack of Scout leaders at the annual jamboree' (Spencer 1998); they weren't a patch on the French team dressed by Daniel Hechter or the FIFA officials in their Yves Saint Laurent. Even the dubious 'Gallic flair' of the 'former French internationals Eric Cantona and David Ginola' (Webb 1998) were dragged in for comparison. The realm of football and fashion overflows with such exquisite ironies: for Euro 2000 England reverted to suits by Burtons Tailoring, so that they were seen to be wearing clothes that the average fan could afford to emulate.

Paul Smith himself was never blamed for the France 98 sartorial *faux pas*, perhaps because he was Britain's favourite designer and because football coverage is, above all, patriotic (some journalists and fans, for instance, had taken umbrage at both Arsenal and Newcastle walking on to the Wembley turf the day before their FA Cup Final clash just a month before wearing unpatriotic Hugo Boss suits rather than designs by 'local' designer Katharine Hamnett [Blanchard 1998]).[3]

As proof of Smith's worth, it's significant that several of the June 1998 articles estimated the cost and exclusivity of the beige ensemble (£600 suits, £95 dark blue shirts, £55 pound cufflinks, a £50 tie and blue suede shoes from Cheaney of Northamptonshire) as if to deflect criticism. The England team could have – for once – been stylish, but 'Glenda' had thwarted their ambitions. The real problem with the men in beige was that they raised the ugly spectre of the pre Italia 90 football fashion dark ages, a stigma that the English game has never quite been able to shake off. For whilst the England 98 squad would dearly have liked to resemble their Italian and French counterparts, the images most often evoked throughout the discussions of the beige suits were fellow disasters: John Barnes's shiny suits and unconventional tailoring, Barry Venison's debut as a TV pundit in a silver waistcoat and sporting a 'mop of straggly bleached hair' (Webb 1998) – since dispensed with and replaced with a sombre crop and yet another pair of unshowy 'intellectual' glasses – and Gazza's hair extensions. These were painful reminders of old football and the ridiculously tight shorts of the 1980s, summoning up from the murky depths of fan memory those images of Keegan missing a sitter against Spain in the 1982 World Cup. The *Sun* had asked of David Beckham after the Manchester United midfielder had been spotted in the South of France wearing a sarong, 'Is he trendy, or a twit?' Those suits precipitated a crisis precisely because the English press didn't know what was good fashion and what was Venison fashion and they needed to be told. The maligned Barry Venison himself self-effacingly admitted to being in the dark about this; when questioned about why he'd chosen to look so awful for his television debut, he admitted 'I was not trying to look silly on purpose, it was purely down to my bad taste' (Webb 1998).

Two approaches to the fashion and football intersection have dominated British responses: that footballers are the new Hollywood stars – free, over-exposed and influential clothes horses – and that English football is still 'a style disaster waiting to happen' (Webb 1998). As always, it's a fine line between clever and stupid. Fashion, as the Ferguson–Beckham conflict illustrated, is perceived as a threat to football as well as the salvation of its image, despite the suggestion that the feminisation of the male is an essential component of the macho footballer image: Gazza crying, David Beckham wearing a sarong or the Italian Euro 2000 defence keeping their fringes out of their eyes with dainty hair bands. Real men accessorise. However, as Ginola modelled for Cerruti and David James for Armani, or as Marilyn Gauthier Models (MGM; the leading model agency in France), sent scouts to France 98 with the specific brief to get fresh footballing talent on their books, a definite sense emerges of the image being more important than the game. MGM signings include Thierry Henri, Patrick Viera, Emanuel Petit, Ibrahim Ba and Zvonimir Boban, but as a spokesperson for the agency comments, 'Footballers are sexy when they're doing well on the field because they exude confidence and the camera picks that up' (Grey and Lang 1998). No matter how much fashion has radically altered football's public face, nor how differently a wider audience has perceived it since Italia 90, the relationship with the players' real performances on the pitch is still paramount – the bad kits, tight shorts and vests won't go away.

The most prevalent English example of fashion dominating the image of football and concomitantly of it being hard to erase the negative connotations of football and football chic is David Beckham. He is the archetypal football-fashion icon: successful on the pitch, with a famous and even wealthier wife – Victoria Adams (aka Posh Spice) – a penchant for shopping and bland, malleable good looks. There is, however, the ominous suspicion that, just as his wife is more Essex than posh, Beckham might be more John Barnes than Paolo Maldini: mutton dressed up as lamb. Gianni Rivera later became an MP (for the Christian Democrats); this is probably a fate not awaiting David Beckham, despite the recent lowering, it seems, of his falsetto voice. So, is he trendy or a twit? The Beckham's wedding on 4 July 1999 at Luttrellstown Castle, near Dublin, would imply the latter (although the ostentatious glamour of the event was not without its fans). Posh went down the aisle in a champagne-coloured Vera Wang satin gown (made of Clerici Duchess satin, 'the finest Italian satin in the world', as *OK!*'s 'David and Victoria: their complete story' Special breathlessly informs us). David wore a complementary three-piece designed by English designer Timothy Everest and shoes by Manolo Blahnik. For the Robin Hood theme reception, the couple changed into matching head to toe purple Antonio Berardi outfits: he wore a double-breasted jacket with quite wide leg trousers over a splayed (shades of George Best) collar shirt, whilst she wore a slim-line, strapless gown of stretch satin with a thigh-high slit that revealed a red lining (to match the swathe of red and purple roses tumbling off her right shoulder) and silver Blahnik strappy sandals. Their uncomprehending baby Brooklyn had matching baby get-ups (two copies of each – in case he was sick down the first); particularly memorable is the purple sheriff's hat he was forced to wear for the reception. Victoria Adams maintained that many of the touches were 'tongue in cheek' (*OK!*, 1999: 24), but she omitted to mention walking to the reception marquee to the theme tune from Disney's *Beauty and the Beast* or intertwining 'VD' on their specially designed coat of arms.

The entire voracious relationship between the press and the Beckhams exemplifies the current state of the relationship between football and fashion that seems to dictate that we forget the Italian, tasteful aspirations and accept football chic's ambiguity and innate tackiness. Apart from feeding us a limitless supply of photos of Posh, Becks and Brooklyn, the contract with *OK!* is characterised by twin revelations: the extent of the couple's designer shopping and how much their respective outfits cost. In the 31 March 2000 edition, under the headline 'David and Victoria's style sensation', the family step out to reveal their radical new haircuts: Beckham and Brooklyn's crew cuts and Victoria's blonde spikey look. In a typically insipid accompanying article, Victoria reveals that she doesn't expect her husband's £300 shave to jeopardise his contract with Brylcreem (*OK!* 2000: 10) and hairdresser Nicky Clarke is quoted as stating the very obvious – that Beckham's style 'looks like a number one or a number two' (*OK!* 2000: 9). Posh and Becks have made themselves into consumable fashion icons; what's really on sale in this *OK!* feature is thus a composite image and its concomitant price tags: his Timberlands cost £130, his Hilfiger jacket £100, his Diesel jeans £80, her Gucci leather jacket over £1,800 and her Maharishi orange trousers (or are they Gap Kids as one caption says?) £100. Itemising and costing their clothes in this way is symptomatically tacky; as Chanel once remarked, good fashion doesn't draw attention to itself, if clothes are truly well designed what they do is subtly and unobtrusively compliment their wearer. The delicious perversity of Chanel has always been that its real signs of class (the braid concealing the join between lining and outer fabric) often remain concealed. This clearly couldn't be further from the point in the case of the Posh 'n Becks phenomenon; their designer labels give them an identity rather than vice versa. They are contemporary signifiers of power and success, not of taste. Their combined image is an ambivalent one; on the one hand, we know that Beckham and Adams have courted *OK!* and the kind of paparazzi fame it offers, on the other they're rather sweetly gooey, particularly about each other and Brooklyn. One would like to simply hate them for their scowling, posturing expressions when caught on camera, their affluence and their exhibitionism. There is, though, something endearing – if, again, terribly current – about Beckham's tattooed homages to Brooklyn: the boy's name across his lower back, the guardian angel across his shoulder blades watching over him and the promise that 'Et Animus Liber' (Free Spirit) is to follow. As with so many football and fashion fusions, however, there is the hint of a design hiccup here: having told the *Sun* (10 May 2000) and *Esquire* (June 2000) that he intends to have the names of any other offspring likewise tattooed under the angel (presumably between 'Brooklyn' and it) where is 'Et Animus Liber' going to go unless it consciously spoils the symmetry of the design? The Latin could, writ small, go above the angel, but this might look messy peeking out from underneath Beckham's football shirt.

The Beckhams, for all their appropriation of Gucci, are the style descendants not of the Italian aristocracy but of the floral shirts and fast cars of Rodney Marsh and the gold-laden 'Big' Ron Atkinson. The marriage of Gucci in particular and football has a certain resonance. In an interview since his retirement in March 1999, Vinnie Jones the ex-Wimbledon player mentions that he used to have his clothes made for him at Mr Ed in Berwick Street, London (one of the notable 'flash Harry' Soho tailors), and that the Gucci-Versace style of young football celebrities leaves him cold as he's not a label but an 'if I see something I like I buy it' person (Alexander 1999). He since became the 'unofficial ambassador' for Yves Saint Laurent in the UK ('I just go in and tell them what I want and they make it'). Vinnie Jones has classically been pigeon-holed the hard man of British football, an image immortalised by the snap of him squeezing Gazza's scrotum during a match and refined through many adverts and his acting debut in *Lock, Stock and Two Smoking Barrels*. His conscious distancing of himself from Gucci is especially significant because Gucci in particular epitomised the anomalous affiliation of a certain type of Italianate stylish dress and violence – British football hooligans in pristine Sergio Tacchini, Louis Vuitton and Gucci.

This is all a far cry from the veneration of Rivera, Verdi and Valentino Couture. What has happened as we start the new millennium is that football's fashion-conscious image has once again either dumbed down or got confused. With speculation about a forthcoming David Beckham module at the University of Staffordshire or the domination of the British Premiership by foreign players (in 2000 they numbered approximately 200), the identity of British football chic – whether it's related to the gentrification of the game through an association with Serie A and the rest of Europe or to the continued supremacy of home-grown football wide-boy fashions – is ambiguous. But then, with Vinnie Jones as YSL's unofficial ambassador and jockey Frankie Dettori as its official one, perhaps the relationship between football and fashion in this country was doomed never to be taken too seriously.

Acknowledgements

I would like to thank Mick Conefrey, Stephen Gundle, Barry Langford and Zara Bruzzi for their assistance in the researching of this chapter.

Notes

1   The Italian model would refute British Premiership claims that lower attendance figures coupled with soaring player salaries has forced ticket prices up: you can still get into a Serie A game for £10.
2   Ironically, Jim White maintains that Armani himself in the Chelsea FA Cup Final press pack 'appears to be wearing a shellsuit' (White 2000: 1).
3   Hamnett, at the time this comment was made, lived in Highbury.

References

Alexander, Hilary (1999) 'Fashion: Mr Jones strikes again', *Daily Telegraph*, 10 May.
Blanchard, Tamsin (1998) 'The fashion victims of football', *Independent*, 16 May.

Davies, Pete (1990) *All Played Out: The Full Story of Italia 90*, London: Heinemann.

Elms, Robert (1996) 'Saturday best', *Arena*, June: 142–4.

Fulton, Tamara (1996) '*Arena*'s essential guide to style and fashion', *Arena*, June.

Greenberg, Simon (1998) 'Three lions, the pitch and the wardrobe', *Evening Standard*, 8 June.

Grey, Toby and Lang, Kirsty (1998) 'Model footballers kick into fashion', *The Sunday Times*, 31 May.

Hamilton, Ian (1993) 'Gazza Agonistes', *Granta*, 45, Autumn.

Homme Plus (1996) '50 most stylish sportsmen of this century', *Homme Plus*, Spring/Summer: 89–99.

Kennedy, Dominic (1998) 'Team in red, white and blue wears Paul Smith', *The Times*, 15 May.

Lanfranchi, P. (1992) (ed.) *Il Calcio e il Suo Popolo*, Naples, Rome and Milan: Edizioni Scientifiche Italiane.

—— (1994) 'Italy and the World Cup: the impact of football in Italy and the example of Italia 90', in John Sugden and Alan Tomlinson (eds) *Hosts and Champions: Soccer Cultures, National Identities and the USA World Cup*, Aldershot: Arena.

Lee, Adrian (1998) 'Players get the blues over Hoddle's beige', *The Times*, 9 June.

Mignon, Patrick (1999) 'Fans and heroes' in Hugh Dauncey and Geoff Hare (eds) *France and the 1998 World Cup: The National Impact of a World Sporting Event*, London and Portland, Oregon: Frank Cass.

Mouland, Bill (1998) 'The men in beige', *Daily Mail*, 9 June.

Nixon, Alan and Harris, Harry (1999) 'Football: fashion victim', *Daily Mirror*, 1 October.

OK! (1999) 'David and Victoria: their complete story', *OK!: The Premium Millennium Edition*.

—— (2000) 'David and Victoria Beckham', *OK!*, 21 March, 206: 4–11.

Pennaccia, Mario (2000) *Il Calcio in Italia*, Torino: UTET, 2 vols.

Redhead, Steve (1991) *Football with Attitude*, Manchester: Wordsmith.

—— (ed.) (1993) *The Passion and the Fashion: Football Fandom in New Europe*, Aldershot: Avebury.

—— (1997) *Subculture to Clubcultures: An Introduction to Popular Cultural Studies*, Oxford: Blackwell.

Spencer, Mimi (1998) 'How can England score in beige?', *Evening Standard*, 8 June.

Walker, Howard (1999) 'In boots and boutiques George was always the best', *The Journal*, 3 August.

Ward, William (1990) 'Letter from Rome', *The Face*, May: 50–1.

Webb, Ben (1998) 'You'll never score in that kit, boys', *The Times*, 6 June.

White, Jim (2000) 'FA Cup Final', *Guardian*, 20 May, Sport Section: 1–2.

Williams, John (1995) 'English football stadiums after Hillsborough', in John Bale and Olof Moen (eds) *The Stadium and the City*, Stoke-on-Trent: Keele University Press.

Williams, John and Wagg, Stephen (eds) (1991) *British Football and Social Change: Getting Into Europe*, Leicester: Leicester University Press.

Chapter 22

Carol Tulloch

'MY MAN, LET ME PULL YOUR COAT TO SOMETHING'[1]
Malcolm X

People are always speculating – why am I as I am? To understand that of any person, his whole life, from birth must be reviewed. All of our experiences fuse into our personality. Everything that ever happened to us is an ingredient.

> (Malcolm X 1968: 243)

From the eighteenth century to the present, the techniques of verbalization have been reinserted in a different context by the so-called human sciences in order to use them without renunciation of the self but to constitute, positively a new self.

> (Foucault 1988: 49)

Epiphany

MY READING OF THE BOOK, *The Autobiography of Malcolm X*[2] is as a document that traces the renewal of a self and its spirit, following a series of life experiences and transformations. The tone of the book veers from anger to joy, and is reflective and informative, always couched in passion. This poignant testimony of self-telling was undertaken to counteract in the public mind the apparition of 'Malcolm X'[3] as simply 'the angriest man in America', divorced of a 'true' context. He wanted the public to gain access to his 'whole' life and persona so one could gain a better understanding of 'why am I as I am?'

By publishing *The Autobiography of Malcolm X*, the subject provided future generations with the contextual material with which he should be considered. So an exercise that focuses on the dressed body of Malcolm X, whose hagiographic status increased during the late twentieth century owing to extensive critical and poetic reference to him, is not to reduce his effective and affective cultural currency and political prowess to that of mere fashion icon, but it is an attempt to augment his iconic status in the presentation of another aspect of him, the dressed-Malcolm X. I argue that this aspect of Malcolm X was and is constituent to his telling-of-self, a technique he applied to produce a new self out of a life he defined as 'a chronology of changes' (Malcolm X 1968: 454) . Alexandra Warwick and Dani Cavallaro have declared that the analysis of an individual through dress can lead to a broader intelligent understanding of that individual:

> [I]t could be argued that it is only by analysing the superficial language of dress that one may arrive at certain, albeit provisional, conclusions regarding both singular and group identities. Ignoring the surface would leave us with no hints as to the cultural and psychological significance of a sign system which is by definition superficial and whose depth lies precisely on the surface . . . Dress, in this respect, is a manifestation of the unconscious at work, in that it is a superficial phenomenon, like symbolic language, which, also like language, speaks volumes about submerged dimensions of experience. Clothing, then, does not just operate as a disguising or concealing strategy. In fact, it could be regarded as a *deep surface*, a manifestation of the 'unconscious' as a facet of existence which cannot be relegated to the psyche's innermost hidden depths but actually expresses itself through apparently superficial activities.
>
> (Warwick and Cavallaro 1998: xxiii)

In my reading of the dressed Malcolm X, I want to blend the political and the sartorial aspects of his life and character with his personal reading of himself and hopefully see 'the unconscious at work [that] speaks volumes about the submerged dimensions of experience' (Warwick and Cavallaro 1998: xxiii). Malcolm X placed the *whole* of himself centrally in his pursuit for civil and metaphysical rights of equality and pride for the African American community at the zenith of the civil rights and Black consciousness movement of the 1960s, and clothes played a metaphysical, as well as technical part in this pursuit.

Malcolm X was acutely aware of the powerful poetry of self-adornment. To look at some of the ways he used and analysed his dressed body in *The Autobiography of Malcolm X*, is to situate dress as a technology of self-telling. This cogent remembering and verbalisation of why he was as he was, is peppered with what Michel Foucault called *Technologies of the Self*. For Foucault, the system is a study of the transition from one state of the self to another, and the necessity to understand the need and process of that transition. Equally, this change can impact on other areas of one's life or the lives of others, whether public, private or political, in this life or the next (Foucault 1988: 19–23). This knowledge and understanding of the self leads to the caring of the self through concern for the self, which Foucault argued is subject to four types of technology:

(1) technologies of production, which permit us to produce, transform, or manipulate things; (2) technologies of sign systems, which permit us to use signs, meanings, symbols, or signification; (3) technologies of power, which determine the conduct of individuals and submit them to certain ends or domination, an objectivizing of the subject; (4) technologies of the self, which permit individuals to effect by their own means or with the help of others a certain number of operations on their own bodies and souls, thoughts, conduct, *and way of being, so as to transform themselves in order to attain a certain state of happiness, purity, wisdom, perfection, or immortality* . . . Each implies certain modes of training and modification of individuals, not only in the obvious sense of acquiring certain skills but also in the sense of acquiring certain attitudes.

(Foucault 1988: 18; my italics)

Though Foucault's treatise is lodged in ancient Western traditions, the 'technologies' he presents are none the less associated with techniques used by Malcolm X to understand himself in order to care not only for his temporal, physical self but, as a Muslim, his spiritual self. Therefore Foucault's thoughts act as a guiding principle for this chapter, which is not solely located in the political thinking and activity of Malcolm X, but as an analysis of his process of becoming. The chapter is structured around epiphanies, 'turning point moments' that serve as revelations in an individual's life. In an epiphany, an individual's character is revealed during either a crisis or a significant event that is confronted and often leaves marks on lives (Denzin 1989: 70–1).

The autobiographical text materialises the person, 'the very self, the body, the figure' (Steedman 1992: 7). This is made more powerful by the representation of the self in photography. I argue that the 'autobiographical performance' of Malcolm X expounds the styling of the dressed-self as one of the 'technologies of the self'. To support this, the photographs of Malcolm X from 1961 to his death in February 1965 are another genre of self-telling utilised by him to compound the issues and aims raised in *The Autobiography of Malcolm X*, which he wanted to communicate to readers. As early as 1960, the astute Malcolm X put into place counter-strategies to combat such occurrences. He commissioned Robert Higgins as his personal photographer, and allowed photographers such as the white American Eve Arnold and the African American Gordon Parks, to photograph him in public and private. Throughout he remained guarded as to how he was to be presented, always in control.

The photographs visualise the resonance of his memories, his past *lives*, as to how he *became*. When 'read' in conjunction with *The Autobiography of Malcolm X*, then another technology of self-telling occurs, another way of telling lives. This chapter also considers the projection of Malcolm's various stages of transformation through the written and visual presentation of the dressed-self as autobiography. The consideration of styling techniques used by Malcolm X in the presentation of himself to the public, as a leading member of the Muslim community and political activist, placed his body as a 'projection surface' (Warwick and Cavallaro 1998: 47) for political aims and his spiritual beliefs.

Reading between the lines

> And it might be an interesting question to ask of an autobiography:
> who is its implied ideal reader, and what is the catastrophic reading it
> is trying to avert?
>
> (Phillips 1994: 71)[4]

Autobiography is a genre of 'self-telling'. Adam Phillips has examined the similarities between psychoanalysis and autobiography. He overrides Freud's theory
that an autobiography cannot be successful if the author has not undergone psychoanalysis. Phillips deems that it can be successful in the sense that the writer has
made some kind of recovery and come to 'know themselves and their history'
(Phillips 1994: 66). Phillips argues that there are connections between autobiography and psychoanalysis. Both want to uncover the past through the recounting
and analysis of memories. Phillips argues that there are connections between autobiography and psychoanalysis. Both are systems of self-telling that can uncover the
past through the recounting and analysis of memories. These methods of self-
knowledge also share the methodology of the interpretation of memories through
free-association and clarification of the results. In the case of the production of
the *Autobiography of Malcolm X*, a strong relationship was established between the
storyteller, Malcolm X and the guide, Alex Haley,[5] to unlock and interpret 'screen-
memories', 'as a way of putting us closer to the truth' (Phillips 1994: 67).[6]
An individual's life is not one life, but a multiplicity of lives. Therein lies the
problematics of autobiography. How does one get at the 'real', the 'truth'?: 'the
autobiographer is always having to manage the fact that too many autobiographies
make a life; that one's autobiography might be different at every moment' (Phillips
1994: 75).

The elusive quality of 'the real' and the 'whole truth' does not deter, in the
example of Malcolm X, the reader from being guided through the series of transformations that shaped his life by varying discourses of power and resistance. The
autobiography can help us to understand the operations of power and resistance,
namely the two different systems of power: that of White America and the Nation
of Islam. Power and resistance are so pervasive in his very existence and interaction with these systems that they become who he is. Power and resistance then
feature in the self-imaging of Malcolm X. But what I want to foreground in this
study is the importance of transformation in the making of Malcolm X, and the
pivotal part played by dress in the technology of self to complete the transformation in spite, though often because of, the persistent need to attend to the issues
of power and resistance.

There are numerous poetic and critical readings of *The Autobiography of Malcolm
X* that augment the different facets of his character and achievements. In her essay
'Sitting at the feet of the messenger: remembering Malcolm X', bell hooks focuses
on his search for spiritual awakening and fulfilment born out of his endurance of
the 'processes of dehumanization [that] warp, distort, and when successful break
the spirit' (hooks 1990: 80). It was his devout religious convictions that liberated
his mind and soul, particularly following his pilgrimage to Mecca in 1964, and
these provide an insight into the persona that was Malcolm X. The autobiography

partially informs a second work by hooks on the reassessment of the expansive critical scholarship on Malcolm X (hooks 1994). On this occasion, she conducts a reading of texts on and by Malcolm X from a feminist perspective to reach a new way of looking at the Muslim political activist in order to 'understand the complexity of his thinking about gender' (hooks 1994: 183). She charts his transition from a misogynist to a progressive in the last few years of his life, when he argued that *all*, not just male, intelligent human beings can fight for freedom (hooks 1994: 193). hooks pleads with the present and future generations to see Malcolm X in the round.

This is in contrast to the views held by Michelle Wallace on the 'spectacle of Malcolm X's reification, fetishization, and commodification' (Berger *et al.* 1995: 306). Wallace fears that Black youth will latch on to the wrong aspects of Malcolm X and ignore his temperate qualities. Reading between the lines of the final chapter of his book, Malcolm X warns that his life had been governed by 'such qualities as courage, heroism, militance, aggression, competitiveness, coolness, grace, elegance in battle, rigidity' (Berger *et al.* 1995: 306) – qualities that were to lead to his death – but he had produced his book to quell the kind of fears expressed by Wallace (Malcolm X 1968: 497). The posthumous accreditations to the memory and image of Malcolm X are part of the committed assembling of the history of heroines and heroes of the African diaspora to establish a history that has, until the 1970s, been hidden. To deny the whole life of Malcolm X, is to deny the African diaspora the pleasure of having him as (and to come to understand why he is) a political and cultural icon. Spike Lee's 1992 film portrayal of the life of Malcolm X is also based on *The Autobiography of Malcolm X*, and is one of the key players in the celebration of the life of Malcolm X.

Lee produced a poetic rendering of the African American hero told through the voice and eyes of others. Gamilah Shabazz, the daughter of Malcolm X, believes that the average African American in her home space of Harlem, New York, had forgotten who Malcolm X was and what he stood for until the film *Malcolm X* was released. This film repositioned her father into the hearts and minds of what he himself had called his home town.[7] Malcolm X hysteria did seem to take over Black communities in America and elsewhere on the release of the film. The London Borough of Hackney, for example, the thoroughfare of Kingsland High Street, pulsated under the plethora of baseball caps and T-shirts festooned with the grey, silver or white logo 'X', on Black (and some white) bodies, in the window displays of clothes shops or the market stalls of Ridley Road Market.

The film opens with a carnivalesque night-time vibe of a boisterous, noisy Boston street with all the glamour of Black city life in the early 1940s. The teenager Malcolm Little, or 'Red' as he was rechristened by fellow street revellers, strides across the screen with his 'Homie' Shorty in an outlandish, meticulously styled light blue Zoot suit ensemble:

> the young salesman picked off a rack a Zoot suit that was just wild: sky-blue pants thirty inches in the knee and angle-narrowed down to twelve inches at the bottom, and a long coat that pinched my waist and flared out below my knees. As a gift, the salesman said, the store would give me a narrow leather belt with my initial 'L' on it. Then

he said I ought to also buy a hat, and I did – blue, with a feather in the four-inch brim. Then the store gave me another present: a long, thick-lined, gold-plated chain that swung down lower than my coat hem.

(Malcolm X 1968: 135)

Malcolm X devotes a whole page of his autobiography to being 'schooled' in the etiquette of Zoot suit assemblage. The next page details the initiation process of the do-it-yourself 'conk' to complete the transformation of Malcolm Little into Red. In recollection, it was his 'conked' hair, not the image of himself in the Zoot suit, that 'was my first really big step toward self-degradation . . . I admire any Negro man who has never had himself conked, or who has had the sense to get rid of it – as I finally did' (Malcolm X 1968: 138). To go beyond 'the natural' hairstyle and to chemically transform one's birthright and identity as 'black', caused Malcolm X pain that extracted from him a lengthy sermon on racial pride. To wear the Zoot suit, on the other hand, and the elaborate accompanying accoutrements of hat and chains, and lindy-hopping at the Roseland Ballroom, was part of being 'Black'. Malcolm X saw the wearing of the Zoot suit by Black men as staying 'real', 'being their natural selves', not diluting their identity with 'phoney airs' like the 'negroes breaking their backs trying to imitate white people' (Malcolm X 1968: 122–5).

I believe that to straighten one's hair, at this historical moment, and to wear an outlandishly cut and coloured suit were both techniques of self-imaging that did not inhabit different degrees of 'Blackness', but when combined they produced a new, alternative aesthetic of 'Black' cultural experience. None the less, Malcolm X's adherence to a demarcation of ethnic divide based on an authentic Black body aesthetic remained in his analysis of this period of his life. In the opening sequence of *Malcolm X* Lee tried to capture the quintessence of styling and dressing-up amongst young Black men in the early 1940s. It was part of the street culture and camaraderie of these youths who revelled being in the spotlight, and saw themselves as the 'connoisseurs of styles'. As Malcolm X instructed: 'In the ghetto, as in suburbia, it's the same status struggle to stand out in some envied way from the rest' (Malcolm X 1968: 153). When you are 16, as Malcolm X was, the dressed body, the white girlfriend and the dancing were the technologies used in this battle of street status amongst one's peers.

None the less, this exuberant and popularist opening into the very serious issue of who Malcolm X was and is, focuses on his immersion into urban dress and style, and being at the centre of one of the most radically subversive ensembles. An underlying agenda of the Zoot suit was to critique the Second World War, and to question America's moral stance in its defence of other races from inhumane crimes, when it was guilty itself of such occurrences in its own country, such as lynching and the Jim Crow system, against non-whites. To wear such an expanse of fabric as the knee-length, wide-shouldered jacket and voluminous trousers, was to flout the rationing regulations. In the eyes of 'right thinking Americans', this caused one to question the patriotism of its wearer (White and White 1998: 249). From March 1942 the Zoot suit was effectively an illegal ensemble, following a dictate from the War Production Board that 'rationed cloth to a 26 percent cut-back in the use of fabrics', calling for a more meagre use of cloth in the form of the 'streamlined suits by Uncle Sam' (Schoeffler and Gale 1973: 24). Indeed, as Cosgrove put it, 'The regulations effectively forbade the manufacture of Zoot suits' (Cosgrove 1989: 9). Malcolm X makes no direct reference to these social and political issues in his autobiography. Indirectly, the point is made when 'Harlem Red' (the nomenclature signalling his acceptance by Harlemites, that was to become his home) exploits his 'clown outfit' to 'tom fool' his way out of being drafted into the army and fight for Uncle Sam:

> I dragged out the wildest suit in New York. This was 1943. The day
> I went down there, I costumed like an actor. With my wild Zoot suit
> I wore the yellow knob-toe shoes, and I frizzed my hair up into a
> reddish bush of conk.
>
> (Malcolm X 1968: 193–4)

As mentioned above, in his later life the conk may have acquired connotations of denying one's 'Blackness', but in 1943 it was part of the visual symbols of Black self-fashioning, as part of a complete wardrobe that was part of an urban Black trend.

The Zoot suit was vehemently un-American, solely entrenched in African American or Mexican culture, therefore non-white. Effectively, in this stage of his life as a Zoot-suit-wearing youth from 1942 onwards, Malcolm was undoubtedly one of 'the stewards of something uncomfortable' (Ellison 1947: 381). Lee was perhaps right to launch into his biography of Malcolm X with a highly charged performance of ghetto adornments. The Zoot suit was not just about high-rolling, and hanging with the 'Homeboys', it was about the attainment of power and control of the self by the wearer. Here was Black Power some twenty-odd years before the official counter-discourse of the movement of the same name, tailored into a specific style of suit, an attitude in opposition to White Power constructed in the authoritarian and patriotric garments of the military uniform of the streamlined, rationed suit. One could say that here, in the fabric and cut of three suits – the Zoot suit, the 'streamlined suit by Uncle Sam' and the military suit of the soldier – the social tension that has marred the texture of American society was played out in the public arena of the actual streets of America or the panoptic plane of the draft board.

Foucault, then, is useful in an attempt to understand the importance of dress in the life of Malcolm X as a political and cultural icon of this panoptic situation. Dress for Malcolm X not only provided and linked him with 'pleasure and individual freedom [in] the control over the self in one's regulated relations with others' (Lechte 1994: 114), but during his self-construction during his Zoot suit period, and most importantly coupled with the conk hairstyle, he was linked to the extended socio-political meanings of that subcultural dress. This was a successful technology of the self that doubled as a counter-discourse. Clothes then provide the instruments that empower the body to counteract a dominant ideology.

Talking pictures

I was amused recently at an International Center of Photography group show of pictures of Malcolm X. The lead picture was one of mine: a huge smiling profile of him looking smart; hat, gold watch and Masonic ring worn jauntily. A group of young black photographers came over to talk to me. 'Thank you, ' they said, 'for making him look like a dude.' 'It was a collaboration, ' I said.

(Arnold 1996: 63)

Figure 22.1   Eve Arnold, 'Malcolm X', *Life* 1961. Courtesy of Magnum.

In 1961, four years before the original publication of *The Autobiography of Malcolm X*, the White American photographer, Eve Arnold, took this photograph of Malcolm X (Figure 22.1). It was part of a series of images Arnold produced on assignment for *Life* magazine to document the Nation of Islam. Thirty-five years later, she remembers Malcolm X as an 'imaginative professional' who knew how to use the power of photography as an affective tool of positive representation: 'He knew his needs, his wants, his best points and how to get me to give him what he required' (Arnold 1996: 63). The question is, what did Malcolm X want out of this portrait? The photograph has become one of the most poetic and iconic portraits of the man who feared in the closing pages of his autobiography that, following his death, the image that would remain, engineered by 'the white man, in his press' would be one of 'a convenient symbol of "hatred"' (Malcolm X 1968: 500).

Arnold's portrait dominates the front cover of *Malcolm X: The Great Photographs*, an impressive photographic essay of the public life of Malcolm X from 1960 to the aftermath of his death in February 1965. The profile barely discloses the clean-shaven, facial features of Malcolm X, but there is no denying it is him, the face of Malcolm X is so much a part of the history and ideology of Black Struggle and Black history, Black pride and Black ideals. The suffusion of his image and ideologies within popular culture *per se*, is so entrenched that the symbol 'X' on a baseball cap, or a solitary pair of horn-rimmed glasses initiates a ricochet of image references, teachings and beliefs that *is* Malcolm X.

Garments and accessories dominate this monochromatic vignette of intimacy and intensity. They are linked to a pivotal period of transformation in a life that 'had been a chronology of *changes*' (Malcolm X 1968: 454) that was Malcolm Little, Red and Harlem Red, Malcolm X and El-Hajj Malik El-Shabazz. Days after his release from prison in August 1952, where he converted to the Nation of Islam, Malcolm X purchased three things:

> I remember well, I bought a better-looking pair of eyeglasses than the pair the prison had issued to me; and I bought a suitcase and a wrist-watch. I have thought since, that without fully knowing it, I was preparing for what my life was about to become. Because those are three things I've used more than anything else. My eyeglasses correct the astigmatism that I got from all the reading in prison. I travel so much now that my wife keeps alternate suitcases packed so that, when necessary, I can just grab one. And you won't find anybody more time-conscious than I am. I live by my watch, keeping appointments. Even when I'm using my car, I drive by my watch, not my speedometer. Time is more important to me than distance.
>
> (Malcolm X 1968: 289)

What relevance does the prominence of these items have in the photographic portrait of Malcolm X? In his autobiographical voice of self-telling and in the visualisation, through portraiture, of the essence of Malcolm X, his watch and glasses were part of the aesthetic tools that defined him as a man on a spiritual and political mission. This was a 'new man' who had come to know himself and took himself seriously enough on leaving prison to enter a new phase of his life. Here in this example of processing a 'screen-memory' Malcolm X shows, as Foucault argued, that 'the knowledge of oneself appeared as the consequence of taking care of your-self' (1988: 22). By addressing the importance of the purchase of the spectacles and the watch in his autobiography, and to include their practical and personal meaning of professionalism, Malcolm X could take control of representations, through a skilful blend of memory, dialogue and visual documentation as a route to a kind of 'truth'. The portrait achieves for Malcolm X and his projected self what Graham Clarke defines as the possibilities of portraiture; that it is

> not so much a portrait advertising a self as a general idea consumed . . . [but] each slightest difference suggests a distinction which has its place, its meaning, in a context outside the photograph. The result is a complex intertextuality between photographic significance and the social and cultural codes which defines status and power.
>
> (Clarke 1997: 105–12)

The practicalities of his horn-rimmed spectacles, or the affiliatory marker of the Nation of Islam in a ring, did not prevent Malcolm X from looking as cool as a crooner such as Frank Sinatra, another icon affiliated with the trilby worn by Malcolm X, who affected the same kind of 'cool' pose. The urban aesthetic that the young Malcolm X had cultivated on the streets of Harlem had not been lost to him in later life, despite the culture of conservative uniformity amongst the brothers of the Nation of Islam. The image suggests the effects of the passage of time on an individual and the results of transition.

Through an analysis of the dress code for men and women of the Nation of Islam in her book *In Retrospect* (1996), Arnold tried to gain some insight into how and why ordinary, working-class African American men and women, who joined the Nation of Islam, had attained an intense aura of dignity and pride. The uniform distinguished their sense of pride and self-respect given to them as Sons and Daughters of Allah, instilling a feeling of belonging and worth, though it segregated men and women through orthodox systems of gendered clothing and colour symbolism. An extreme example was the bands of monochrome seating arrangements Arnold photographed, which Malcolm X also described in his autobiography. At a rally of all the chapters of the Nation of Islam at the Uline Arena in Washington DC,

> The balconies and the rear half of the main floor were filled with black people of the general public. Ahead of them were the all-Muslim seating sections – the white-garbed beautiful black sisters, and the dark-suited, white-shirted [and bow tied] brothers.
>
> (Malcolm X 1968: 351)

In the everyday dress of the Black Muslims there was no place for ostentation or individual expression, 'the men were quietly, tastefully dressed' (Malcolm X 1968: 292). A sense of worth was carved into the close-shaven haircut; dignity and pride encircled the frame of the Black Muslims, trapped in the buttoning of an inconspicuous single-breasted suit and moderately shined shoes. What is expressed in the Malcolm X portrait is the release of emotion, a felt dimension of an individual life amongst the uniformity and orthodoxy of the Nation of Islam.

Dead man walking

To read *The Autobiography of Malcolm X* is to walk with him to his death. The interview process between Alex Haley and Malcolm X began in 1963. On 21 February 1965 Malcolm X was murdered. The emotional intensity of his whole life up to February 1963 imploded in the last four chapters of the book, as a new phase of his life unfolded and was recorded simultaneously. In December 1963, as documented in Chapter 16, Malcolm X was suspended for ninety days from the Nation of Islam, the Muslim organisation to which he converted in 1947 whilst in prison. He was 'silenced' from making any public comments on social issues by the leader of the Nation of Islam Elijah Mohammed, following the inflammatory comment he had made on the death of President John F. Kennedy, 'the chickens coming home to roost' (Malcolm X 1968: 411).[8] Malcolm X maintained that this was not the real issue behind the silencing. He believed it was his established status as one of the leading spokesmen on the human rights issue of African Americans, winning the respect of Muslims and non-Muslims, and his outstanding work in the growth of the Nation of Islam and the possibility of him replacing Mohammed that had engendered envy amongst members of his own religion. His disbelief and sense of betrayal at this order from Mohammed, whom Malcolm X had once placed higher than his own life, and the violent repercussions that he believed were to be put in place by the Nation of Islam, were the catalyst for his pilgrimage in 1964 to Mecca. The trip was to be a 'broadening [of] his knowledge of that religion' (Malcolm X 1968: 430). It came to provide him with the final act to sever his relationship with the Nation of Islam.

   The shared documentation of a life as it was experienced by Malcolm X and Haley, the daily witnessing of its roller-coaster ride to its end, attained synchronicity as the interviewer in the foreword to *The Autobiography of Malcolm X* and the interviewee individually documented the period of transformation for Malcolm X into El-Hajj Malik El-Shabazz, particularly through his dress. Prior to his departure to Mecca, Malcolm X wore the conservative attire befitting a member of the Nation of Islam of a plain, single-breasted suit, shirt and tie and classic horn-rimmed glasses, part of the iconography that *is* Malcolm X. Meeting El-Hajj Malik El-Shabazz on the day he returned from his pilgrimage, Haley can only express the change in Malcolm X through his appearance:

> When the blue Oldsmobile stopped, and I got in, El-Hajj Malcolm, broadly beaming, wore a seersucker suit, the red hair needed a barber's attention, and he had grown a beard . . . There must have been fifty still and television photographers and reporters jockeying for position, up front, and the rest of the Skyline Ballroom was filling with Negro followers of Malcolm X, or his well-wishers, and the curious . . . They picked at his 'racist' image. 'I'm *not* a racist. I'm not condemning whites

for being whites, but for their deeds. I condemn what whites collectively have done to our people collectively.' He almost continually flashed about the room the ingratiating boyish smile. He would pick at the new reddish beard. They asked him about that, did he plan to keep it? He said he hadn't decided yet, he would have to see if he could get used to it or not.

(Malcolm X 1968: 38–9)

Malcolm's choice of casual presentation to address a press conference some two hours after arriving in the country was change indeed. In this instance he had marked his individuality and chronic desire for temporal and spiritual change, to dislocate himself from his recent past as Malcolm X, the Minister of New York Muslim Temple No. 7 of the Nation of Islam, into El-Hajj Malik El-Shabazz, the founder of two new organisations in June 1964: Muslim Mosque Inc. and the Organization of Afro-American Unity. The aesthetic codes for men of the Nation of Islam, in regard to the presentation of the public self, was to be immaculate and unassuming: clean-shaven, well-maintained hair, plain conservative suit, well-polished (not highly shined) shoes. Abjection is perhaps the best explanation of this ambiguous self-presentation:

the abject is above all the ambiguous, the in-between what defies boundaries, a composite resistant to unity. Hence, if the subject's identity derives from the unity of its objects, the abject is the threat of unassimilable non-unity; that is, ambiguity. Abjection, therefore, is fundamentally what disturbs identity, system and order.
(Lechte quoted in Warwick and Cavallaro 1998: xvi–xvii)

Could the ambiguity inherent in the identity of Malcolm X be based on his past personas and the new words being spoken, effectively changing much of what had gone before? As a member and leading figure of the Nation of Islam, his immaculate, business-like attire underscored his orthodox Muslim practices, and his stringent views on race and racism – essentially a mistrust of 'the white devils' (Malcolm X 1968: 302). In the Hotel Theresa his views had become more inclusive, no longer the binary struggle between Blacks and whites, them and us. His clothing transmitted mixed messages of ease and control, the space for difference and creativity.

In this very public presentation and production of his self, Malcolm had controlled how he would be visually represented in the media. His relaxed attire of unkempt hair, the nonchalant, decorated self in the 'blustered' ornamented feature of a seersucker suit, was indicative of the confidence Malcolm had in himself to be himself. The cotton summer suit is a respectable item of the male wardrobe, but not on equal terms as the woollen summer suit, as it is prone to crease and therefore unable to retain its shape and the smart appearance of the wearer. The aura of elegance is lost. Its ability to keep the wearer cool overrides such sartorial drawbacks (Roetzel 1999: 115–16). A prosaic reading of the seersucker suit would foreground its function as effective summer wear, due to its cool and light-weight properties. In the heated context of a press conference, where El-Hajj Malik

El-Shabazz had to explain himself anew on religion, politics and physical appearance, the suit was not only a sign of a new Malcolm, relaxed yet in control of his future, but also the correct clothing in order to function in such artificially heated conditions. He kept his cool to be cool. In addition, looking cool in the face of the media, which can so easily show one 'looking like a fool' (Malcolm X: 418)[8] was of primary importance to the media-wary Malcolm X. It was significant that he should present himself in this way, unpolished and unconventional, voicing new opinions indeed, he was fully aware that he had 'an international image no amount of money could have bought' (Malcolm X 1968: 420), and he wanted to maintain his credibility as a representative in 'the American Black man's struggle'.

That ephemeral quality of cool is generally linked with urban lifestyles, the avant-garde, the unconventional. The exacted expression of cool that Malcolm possessed had the power to entice the generally apolitical, self-obsessed 'ghetto hustlers' and 'ghetto youths' – themselves, connoisseurs of cool – to political issues. After all, by 1964 Malcolm X had amassed such support from Black Americans that he was described as 'America's only negro who could stop a race riot – or start one' (Malcolm X 1968: 423). He was successful in the construction of a dressed image and a social and political standing, whilst his expressed empathy with *his* people, by 'being real' and keeping in touch with his origins, had paid off:

> The ghetto masses already had entrusted me with an image of leadership among them. I knew the ghetto instinctively extends that trust only to one who had demonstrated that he would never sell them out to the white man.
>
> (Malcolm X 1968: 424)

To be cool then, is not only what Gabriele Mentges defines as part of a modern form of self-construction predicated by street consciousness (Mentges 2000: 1), but in the case of Malcolm X, a modern way of political thinking and being, to combine the urban with the intellectual to result in a particular form of pride in being Black.

The goatee beard, though, was the fetishised marker of his particular transformation. The decision regarding whether he was or was not going to keep the beard had a profound spiritual meaning for Malcolm X and his experience of the Hajj:

> Standing on Mount Arafat had concluded the essential rites of being a pilgrim to Mecca. No one who missed it could consider himself a pilgrim. The *Ihram* had ended. We cast the traditional seven stones at the devil. Some had their hair and beards cut. I decided that I was going to let my beard remain. I wondered what my wife Betty, and our little daughters, were going to say when they saw me with a beard, when I got back to New York. New York seemed a million miles away.
>
> (Malcolm X 1968: 451)

Malcolm X kept the beard until his death in 1965.

The name Malcolm X was already known and unique in the public consciousness. To style himself in this new, easy liberated guise, was exacting a personal confirmation of this change in his life, on a course that was more inclusive of other people, of other ideas, political and personal. This relaxed, minimal image was not an original image, as the so-called 'Modernists', jazz artists and followers had perfected the look during the 1950s (Polhemus 1994: 38–9). The image was not far removed from the discreet style he had adopted and adapted when he was part of the Black Muslims. In this new phase of his dressed-self, the worldly undertones of his Muslim style so clearly suffused in the Arnold portrait was foregrounded. This style treatment to individualise the self, in the fine-tuning of El-Hajj Malik El-Shabazz, enabled Malcolm X to dissociate himself from the members of the Nation of Islam, break away from being a 'Zombie – like all the rest of them' (Parks 1990: 234). Newness in the form of a new self had taken centre-stage. This particular constellation of body, the self and dress provided the interface between new directions in his political and religious thinking in order to take care of and know the self.

The use of dress as metaphor for transformation, to present himself as El-Hajj Malik El-Shabazz, harked back to the edicts of street culture and philosophy of his time as a 'hustler' in Harlem, New York, 'that in order to get something you had to look as though you already had something' (Malcolm X 1968: 193). There at the Hotel Theresa amid people who knew him well (namely his wife and Alex Haley), and people who thought they knew him (America's press, and through their newspapers and television news articles, all America and beyond), Malcolm wanted to be accepted for who he was now. The conflation of the visual presentation of himself and the words he spoke, a transformed individual now stood in their presence:

> My pilgrimage broadened my scope. It blessed me with a new insight. In two weeks in the Holy Land, I saw what I never had seen in thirty-nine years here in America. I saw *races*, all *colors*, – blue-eyed blondes to black-skinned Africans – in *true* brotherhood! In unity! Living as one! Worshipping as one! No segregationists – no liberals . . . In the past, yes, I have made sweeping indictments of *all* white people. I never will be guilty of that again – as I know now that some white people *are* truly sincere, that some truly are capable of being brotherly toward a black man. The true Islam has shown me that a blanket indictment of all white people is as wrong as when whites make a blanket indictments against blacks.
>
> (Malcolm X 1968: 479)

Here in this moment of unveiling a new self, Malcolm X had attained the pride he had longed for. In 1931, following the murder of his father, the Reverend Earl Little, his family had begun to sink under the weight of poverty. The overriding value that Louise Little, his mother, tried to preserve in the midst of all this was pride, but it too dissolved like escaping gas. Malcolm X marks 1934 as the year of acceleration of this erosion, ending with the desegmentation of his family, the children sent to different families, and Lucille Little to a mental hospital where she stayed for twenty-six years.

This relaxed image could also be read as Malcolm X placing his dress as secondary to his change in political ideologies due to spiritual fulfilment. But I find this hard to entertain. Throughout *The Autobiography of Malcolm X* clothes and accessories are at the juncture of change for him. He enters into evocative descriptions of dress as metaphors for pride in oneself or as a combative system in the street or political arena. During his life as a hustler, the gun and the tie were necessary self-defining objects to his character and identity. In order to function correctly in his chosen environment, to *be* 'Red' and to survive on the Streets, clothes were a vital component: 'As I have said, a gun was as much a part of my dress as a necktie' (Malcolm X 1968: 240). They were the necessary and correct tools to complete a job professionally, more fundamentally, in order to survive.

The power of clothes to reveal the internal strengths and weaknesses of an individual were not lost on Malcolm X. Whilst he was in prison his brother Reginald, who had introduced Malcolm X to the Nation of Islam, was expelled from the organisation for transgressing their rules of morality. Reginald visited his incarcerated brother, and now a devout Muslim, Malcolm X believed he saw 'the chastisement of Allah – what Christians would call "the curse" – come upon Reginald' (Malcolm X 1968: 283), materialised in the very assemblage of his dressed body. 'When he had been a Muslim he had been immaculate in his attire. But now he wore things like a T-shirt, shabby-looking trousers and sneakers. I could see him on the way down' (Malcolm X 1968: 283). Reginald's easy street dress, and Malcolm's coming-out style premiered to the world at the Hotel Theresa, were kindred styles, though distanced through years and causation. This was dressing up to demonstrate one's styling capabilities and disdain for convention-making and taking pleasure in the presentation of the new self. This is not to say that Malcolm did not exercise the latter during his years with the Nation of Islam, the portrait taken by Eve Arnold extols this. He exuded there his maverick character, and his ability to set himself apart with the aid of a hat, a pair of glasses and watch.

Conclusion

> [D]ress may be treated as a deconstructive instrument for the interrogation of ideas of difference and differentiation, of their ideological fabrication and attendant demystification. By inviting a shift from an analysis of the signified to an analysis of the signifier, through its emphasis on the superficial, rather than deep, character of all processes of signification, the language of dress may help in the questioning of time-honoured metaphysical categories (origin, truth, presence) and hence in the subversion of all binary mythologies.
>
> (Warwick and Cavallaro 1998: xxiii)

To dress and style the body in a particular way to meet certain needs, places garments and accessories as a metaphor to address issues faced by an individual or group. Of course this is not new, these are observations made by subcultural theorists. What has intrigued me in the case of Malcolm X is his use of clothes and the dressed body to project himself as a legitimate, though unconventional and fiercely autonomous, political leader. His seersucker suit, for example, was not merely an object of desire but formed part of a new language of self used to signify the desire of his political objectives.

I disagree then with Ted Polhemus that Malcolm X would not want to be remembered for his innate dress sense (Polhemus 1994: 39). I think he would. As the opening quote intimates, Malcolm X wanted *all* of him, 'his whole life' to be reviewed, 'from birth . . . All of our experiences fuse into our personality. Everything that ever happened to us is an ingredient' (Malcolm X 1968: 243). I have tried to blend the political and sartorial aspects of Malcolm X, as the *whole* of him was placed centrally in his pursuit for the equal rights and the psychological liberation of the African American community – a right to pride. And for himself, may he no longer be consigned to a place in history as just an 'angry young man'.

Acknowledgements

Thanks to the Arts and Humanities Research Board of Great Britain whose funding of the 'Fashion and Modernity' research group at Central Saint Martins College of Art & Design, London, 1999–2000, facilitated the writing of this article.

Notes

1   Malcolm X used this street phrase as a metaphor to go 'fishing' for new converts as part of his recruitment drive for the Muslim organisation The Nation of Islam.
2   *The Autobiography of Malcolm X* was originally published in the United States of America in 1965.
3   Malcolm X had various names throughout his life, only one of which he chose himself, El-Hajj Malik El-Shabazz. They all equated with different stages of his life. The other names: Malcolm Little, Red or Harlem Red and El-Hajj Malik El-Shabazz will be used only to signify a specific historical moment. 'Malcolm X' is used here to acknowledge the fundamental juncture of transformation from his past life as 'Street Hustler' to Muslim and political activist.
4   I am grateful to Paul Antick for bringing this work to my attention.
5   In the foreword to *The Autobiography of Malcolm X* Alex Haley recounts how at the beginning of their relationship, Malcolm X only trusted him 20 per cent. Towards the end of his life, it had increased to 70 per cent (1968: 17–26).
6   The weekly interview sessions between Malcolm X and Haley, processed what Freud calls a 'screen-memory, a waking dream of the past' in order for it to be realised as a memory. The trusting relationship that developed between Malcolm X and Haley helped Malcolm X to retrace his past, with prompting from Haley to encourage associations – free or structured – in order to make sense and build a narrative of the life of Malcolm X. This is all very speculative on my part, but Malcolm X's blending of current events with the past encourages such assumptions.
7   Interview conducted with Gamilah Shabazz at her home in Harlem, New York, in September 1999.

8   Malcolm X explains in his autobiography that he was referencing the damage that can be caused by hate if 'spread unchecked', as it was in America at this time.
9   Malcolm X was referring to how he should present himself as a member of the audience at the Cassius Clay (Mohammed Ali) and Sonny Liston boxing heavy-weight championship of the world in Miami (1964).

References

Arnold, Eve (1996) *In Retrospect*, London: Sinclair-Stevens.

Berger, M., Wallis, B. and Watson, S. (eds) (1995) *Constructing Masculinity*, London and New York: Routledge.

Clarke, Graham (1997) *The Photograph*, Oxford and New York: Oxford University Press.

Cosgrove, S. (1989) 'The Zoot suit and style warfare' in Angela MeRobbie (ed.) *Zoot Suits and Second-hand Dresses: An Anthology of Fashion and Music*, London: Macmillan.

Davis, Thulani (1993) *Malcolm X: The Great Photographs*, New York: Stewart, Tabori & Chang.

Denzin, Norman K. (1989) *Interpretive Biography*, London/California/New Delhi: Sage.

Foucault, Michel (1988) *Technologies of the Self: A Seminar with Michel Foucault*, ed. L.H. Martin, H. Gurtman and P.H. Hutton, London: Tavistock.

hooks, bell (1990) *Yearning: Race, Gender and Cultural Politics*, Boston: South End Press.

—— (1994) *Outlaw Culture: Resisting Representations*, New York and London: Routledge.

Lechte, John (1994) *Fifty Key Contemporary Thinkers: from Structuralism to Postmodernity*, London and New York: Routledge.

Malcolm X (1968) *The Autobiography of Malcolm X. With the Assistance of Alex Haley*, London: Penguin.

Mentges, Gabriele (2000) 'Cold, coldness, coolness: remarks on the relationship of dress, body and technology', *Fashion Theory*, 4: 10.

Parks, Gordon (1990) *Gordon Parks: Voices in the Mirror. An Autobiography*, London/New York/Toronto/Sydney/Auckland: Doubleday.

Phillips, Adam (1994) *On Flirtation*, London and Boston: Faber & Faber.

Polhemus, Ted (1994) *Streetstyle: from Sidewalk to Catwalk*, New York: Thames & Hudson.

Roetzel, Bernhard (1999) *Gentleman: A Timeless Fashion*, London: Konemann UK Ltd.

Schoeffler, O.E. and Gale, W. (1973) *Esquire's Encyclopedia of 20th Century Men's Fashions*, New York: McGraw-Hill.

Steedman, Carolyn (1992) *Past Tenses: Essays on Writing, Autobiography and History*, London: River Oram.

Warwick, Alexandra and Cavallaro, Dani (1998) *Fashioning the Frame: Boundaries, Dress and the Body*, Oxford and New York: Berg.

White, Shane and White, Graham (1998) *Stylin': African American Expressive Culture from its Beginning to the Zoot Suit*, Ithaca, NY and London: Cornell University Press.

Chapter 23

Moya Luckett

PERFORMING MASCULINITIES
Dandyism and male fashion in
1960s–70s British cinema

MUCH OF THE RECENT WORK on national identity has followed
post-colonial theory's lead in exploring the relationship between gender
and national identity.[1] Cinema's important roles in helping form and inform national
consciousness in both established and emerging nations has led to careful and
systematic rethinking of the roles genre, narrative and film style play in articulating national difference. These analyses tend to ignore fashion, highlighting its
associations with superficiality as well as its tendency towards invisibility as the
significance of its details fade away with time. Yet fashion is perhaps the most
obvious marker of national and sexual difference, and one of the seminal products
in the battles for international popular culture hegemony. Fashion often identifies
the nation currently dominating pop culture, while its specific details hint at the
balance of gendered power and reveal the nation's particular gendered articulation of itself at that precise moment.

During the late 1960s and early 1970s, British national identity was in flux as
the nation saw itself on the cusp of three separate possible destinies – as part of
a European Common Market (associated with a utopic and progressive inter-
nationalism); allied with America but essentially independent (a vision that combined nostalgia for a recent past marked by international dominance in the sphere
of popular culture and a desire to recapture a greater lost heritage spanning back
centuries); and as a neo-colonial power through its Commonwealth (a conservative vision of an already lost empire). Within popular culture, the former two
identities vied for prominence, both creating their own essentially gendered visions
of nation. While the international articulation of the proto-European Britain became
increasingly linked to the new, active yet glamorously feminine (epitomised in
Swinging London heroines and their fashions), the latter image of a revived yet
independent Britain was more forcefully expressed in masculine terms.

As this brief sketch suggests, national identity resists easy gendered binaries, particularly in times of crisis or rapid transformation. Further interrogation reveals that this masculine/feminine grid was further complicated by the ways in which the period's male and female styles both reworked and incorporated traditional concepts of the masculine and feminine for both genders. In terms of women's dress, the adoption of more masculine designs has generally not been considered that remarkable. While 1960s and 1970s girls might have favoured more unisex styles, like the trouser suit, or simple, unadorned shift dresses, these do not imply femininity's eclipse but rather express the emergence of a more mobile and powerful feminine that lays claim to public, national life. The incorporation of the feminine in male dress is usually more contentious, suggesting both a social and cultural over-feminisation and the erasure of male power. The emergence of the 1960s and 1970s male dandy, however, challenges these oversimplifications, while suggesting another, more radical vision of nation, that severs Britain's dependence on America and even breaks its possible future links with Europe to create a counter-narrative of national male power. Following in the besuited steps of the Beatles and the confidence of the beruffled late 1960s and early 1970s young male, its dandies seize on the past to express contemporary male agency and national power.

Fashion revivals mount a complex social commentary on nation, gender and ideology. Unlike their female counterparts, the sartorial extremes of men's fashion revivals seem to require support from other cultural phenomena, like film and popular music, suggesting that breaking with conventions of male dress is far more radical than transformations in female style. This is as true today as it was in the 1960s. In September 1998, for instance, a nine-page *loaded* fashion spread devoted to *Performance* (dir. Donald Cammell/Nicolas Roeg, Warner Bros, 1968/70) featured clothes based on Chas's (James Fox's) suits and the more 'peacock' costumes that he and Turner wear later in the film.[2] Four months later, the magazine featured similarly ornate fashions in a pop music and television-influenced layout accompanied by the following copy: 'It's the '70s. It's a groovy soirée. And the heppest cats have turned up in Marc Bolan's old threads.'[3] Amidst wide-lapelled, loudly patterned 1970s style suits, elaborate gold rings, decorative watches and bracelets, puffed-sleeve dark blue shirts, gold lamé jackets with blue lamé lapels, fur coats, gangster-style blue and black suits, comedian Vic Reeves posed in a '1967 pink satin feather-trimmed dressing-gown by Biba'.[4] Clearly this joke comes from Reeves's completely masculine look, although its allusions to *Performance* are clear: the pink satin is the same shade as Pherber's (Anita Pallenberg's) trousers, while the look parodies Turner's (Mick Jagger's) many decorative dressing-gowns. Elsewhere, the rings recall Chas's jewellery while the suits resemble those worn by Jack in *Get Carter* (dir. Mike Hodges, 1971, UK). *loaded* fashion spreads usually focus on three distinct styles: an everyday sportswear look; 1960s/70s gangster-influenced highly tailored suiting, and the extremely flouncy and decorative 'peacock' look – the latter two usually photographed with the addition of female models.[5] These highly self-conscious styles suggest masculine concern with fashion, detail and fantasy, representing extremes of male dandyism, a phenomenon that dates back to antiquity.

Recent British films like *Lock, Stock and Two Smoking Barrels* (dir. Guy Ritchie, 1998, UK), *Velvet Goldmine* (dir. Todd Haynes, 1998, UK/USA) and *Face* (dir.

Antonia Bird, 1997, UK) foreground the importance of male fashion as a component of contemporary national identity. Their allusions to older cult hits, like the
recently re-released *Get Carter* and *A Clockwork Orange* (dir. Stanley Kubrick, 1971,
UK) also suggest a specific history of male style. In order to understand why this
dandy look is popular today in discourses around fashion, if not in men's actual
attire, we need to consider the relationship between masculinity and national
identity in the late 1960s, early 1970s and in contemporary Britain.

Costume historian, Diana de Marly, asserts that fashions must be read in the
context of the 'gendering' of a historical period, taking into account such issues
as the sex of the monarch, degrees of cultural and social change, whether a nation
is at war, its international relations, political stability and the amount of power
designated to each sex.[6] She notes:

> History shows that human society swings between the male and the
> female principle, so that some periods consider themselves to be mascu-
> line, while others regard themselves as more feminine. This redefinition
> of identity affects the way society determines its ideal males, for a
> masculine age will insist on heroic and martial qualities, while a feminine
> one will allow more sophisticated and artistic qualities. Consequently
> the changes to be seen in men's clothes reflect the changes in the defi-
> nition of what is masculine, which successive periods promote. Thus
> the question of whether a man ought to wear frills and jewels will
> depend upon how far a given period in history considers them appro-
> priate for the image of masculinity in which it believes.[7]

This does not necessarily mean that 'feminised' or ornate male dress denotes a
feminine age: in a masculine period (as that of Henry VIII), decoration highlights
the male body's supreme ability to resist feminisation – like Vic Reeves in a pink
Biba dressing-gown. In their day, tight tunics, short knickerbockers and codpieces
similarly foregrounded male strength, hypermasculinity and (allied) social status,
although they were not necessarily functional. As perhaps the most historically
relative practice, fashion needs to be placed in context: the increased masculinity
that de Marly sees in Regency dress would today seem excessively feminine.

The social and sartorial revolutions of the 1960s raise a number of questions
about how this age might be 'gendered'. Like many other commentators, de Marly
sees it as essentially feminine, but her explanations do not rely on fashion alone
but reach out to larger social, national and economic transformations:

> By 1962 the *Women's Mirror* was complaining that 'Men aren't what
> they used to be'. While the end of the Victorian paterfamilias dictating
> to the whole family was a good thing, modern man was leaving all the
> decisions to his wife. Granted, 4,000,000 wives were now wage-
> earners, too, but it seemed unfair to leave all the problems to them as
> well. Why, 50% of husbands had not even asked their wives to marry
> them; they just 'drifted into it'. The article pleaded for the return of
> a stronger man, but this did not happen. With more women working,
> a man's economic ability to dictate was on the decline.[8]

In his study of British post-war male style, Frank Mort offers an alternative interpretation, suggesting that men's increased interest in fashion indicated their upward mobility. Men's growing interest in fashion (tutored by a more advertising-aware fashion industry) highlighted instead a new, more fluid class structure and a concomitant multiplicity of acceptable masculine identities, offering men greater freedom. He finds

> a self-conscious attempt to encourage the idea of fashionability by manufacturers and retailers alike. It was a litany which went through endless permutations from the mid-1950s across all sectors of the market. Later manifestations of the trend included the promotion of Italian styling in 1959, fashion designer Hardy Amies' slogan of the 'peacock revolution', coined in 1965, culminating with the quintessential image of sixties 'swinging London'. At the heart of this commercial formula was a particular regime of retailing, advertising and marketing aimed at younger men.[9]

During the 1950s, dress had been affected by 'anxieties over male homosexuality, brought to a head in the government's publication of the *Wolfenden Report* in 1957 [which] frequently focused on the issue of whether homosexual men could be identified by their extravagant mannerisms and flamboyant clothing'.[10] By contrast during the mid-1960s, a certain masculine confidence around sexuality and dress was most strongly epitomised in the rise of 'peacock' fashions.

The rise and fall of Burton's foregrounds these changes and the splintering of British male style. Started by Montague Burton in 1930s as a midmarket brand, the store emphasised conventional attire until the 1950s, offering shoppers a discrete homosocial space to try on clothes or be measured for a suit. Sir Montague Burton's death in 1952 led to a change in management, and the chain, now led by the more trend-conscious Lionel Jacobson, began to refit their stores, modernise their advertising and concentrate more on the 16 to 30-year-old man. The new Burton's was not aggressively fashionable but it accommodated subcultures with some of its tailors making and fitting Teddy Boy suits. As Mort points out, there was no 'coherent identity' for the new young customers and Burton's was left behind by the mid-1960s.[11]

The thrift stores, market stalls and boutiques that emerged in the 1960s were the beneficiaries of this changed fashion climate. As de Marly notes, '[i]n 1957 John Stephen opened [Blades] a boutique for men in a backstreet called Carnaby. By 1966 there were 17 boutiques in the street, of which no less than 13 were for menswear'.[12] Young men's rejection of Burton's easy options highlighted their increased attention to the politics and diversity of fashion, a movement that led to the dandy's revival. Although the term 'dandy' dates from the late eighteenth century, the phenomenon it described – a man excessively concerned with dress – predated this period.[13] The figure most associated with the term was Beau Brummell, but while the dandy is conventionally associated with excessively fussy and decorative dress, he was more concerned with simplicity, smartness, elegance and quality, although the different standards of the time make his dress appear excessive today.[14] As the dandy is by nature fashion-conscious, there can be no

single model for his dress. It might be cutting-edge, expensive but, most importantly, it had to be meticulously put together, paying close attention to details.
Whether besuited like Chas in *Performance*, favouring decorative robes like Turner,
or experimenting with costume like Alex and his droogs in *A Clockwork Orange*,
the dandy flies in the face of conventional assumptions about men's fashion, which,
as Bruzzi notes,

> is usually considered . . . innately stable and to lack the 'natural
> tendency to change' of women's clothes, displaying instead, by virtue
> of being functional rather than decorative, a tendency to 'stereotype
> itself' and 'adopt the uniform of a profession' . . . There is also, there-
> fore, the suspicion with which flamboyant male dressers like dandies
> and dudes have traditionally been viewed, because 'real men' are not
> supposed to be narcissistic.[15]

Beau Brummell's eighteenth century evokes the dandy perhaps more than any
period, and these very styles were central to the mid-1960s dandy revival, especially
the peacock attire. This look influenced British male style throughout the next
decade, reaching its apogee in glam rock (as recently revived in *Velvet Goldmine*).[16]
Similarly, Stanley Kubrick's *Barry Lyndon* (1975, UK) creates an eighteenth-century
hero for the mid-1970s, whose masculinity is represented through clothing, wigs
and make-up as he rises and falls through the social classes. In his characteristic
study of the follies of masculinity, Kubrick foregrounds how excessive decor and a
strong interest in fashion highlight male power. While Lady Lyndon is submerged
in her costumes, wigs and make-up, Barry has a more visceral joy in dress, as seen
when he first meets the Chevalier de Balibari and falls under his spell. As Stella
Bruzzi has observed, period clothes are often fetishistic: 'Too often period costumes
are presumed to signify sexual repression as opposed to an active sexual discourse',
but here Kubrick sexualises its clothes – particularly its male attire.[17] *Barry Lyndon*
fetishises its Oscar-winning costumes on another level, with the pressbook foregrounding their obsessive authenticity, 'Kubrick has painstakingly captured the feel
and texture of the times . . . carefully duplicating the dress and manners of
Thackeray's characters.'[18]

Kubrick also plays on the potent connotations of eighteenth-century male attire
in *A Clockwork Orange*. Anti-hero Alex deLarge idolises Ludwig van Beethoven,
whose image decorates his bedroom. As Alex masturbates to the Ninth Symphony,
the film highlights the dandy-esque qualities of his image (his white shirt is open
at the neck and his big hair is styled like his hero's), foregrounding Beethoven's
influence on his look with a cut to his portrait. Masculinity's investment in
masquerade is further highlighted in Alex's fantasies, which feature him in Arabian
nights-style garb, as a Roman soldier and as a vampire straight from a Hammer
horror film.

Increasing colour and frills on male dress emerge around 1964 in the UK,
with the dandy-peacock look emerging as a national archetype in marked contrast
to 'classless' American style, epitomised by jeans.[19] In all its incarnations, the dandy
suggested a return to *British* youth culture (the Beatles conquered America in suits
not jeans) and a new national dominance in fashion and youth culture. The peacock

look also had upwardly mobile, even aristocratic connotations, recalling the aristocratic dress of yesteryear and being popularised, in part, by Lord Litchfield, the Queen's cousin and man-about-town. The dandy represented not the predominance of the elite but rather the coming together of youth of all classes, suggesting the possibility of social movement across various social strata in ways that the static classlessness of jeans could not, precisely because they mask differences in class, income and gender.

During the early 1960s, as aristocrats and members of the establishment flirted with East End gangsters like the Krays, the classes appeared to converge, although each none the less maintained their own identity.[20] Unions of tough men, glamorous idols and the establishment brought together diverse aspects of masculine power in the face of a sexual revolution that threatened men's position at the top of a gendered hierarchy. This convergence clearly influenced *Performance*, as Colin MacCabe has shown, with its crew including gangsters and aristocrats and its cast headed by James Fox, 'an old Harrovian as an East End gangster . . . crossing class as transgressively as Pherber was to encourage Chas to cross gender'.[21] It also informs *A Clockwork Orange* with its union between working-class convict, Alex, and the Minister, Fred. In both films, then, costume suggests the crossing, but *not* collapse, of social hierarchies.

Performance and *A Clockwork Orange* specifically articulate dandyism in relation to social changes affecting young white men. A similar critique/deconstruction of contemporary masculinity is at the centre of the recent release *Fight Club* (dir. David Fincher, 1999, USA), which, like *Performance*, features two protagonists with different approaches to dress – one conformist, the other, thrift-store bohemian – who morph into one, like Chas and Turner in *Performance*. The influence of past, present and future on male fashion in 1960s/early 1970s films like *Performance* and *A Clockwork Orange* similarly foregrounds how clothes articulate masculinity's frustrations, celebrations and limitations. Significantly, these might all be categorised as gangster movies, falling into a genre which, as Bruzzi observes 'equated [clothes] with status, money and style'.[22] As gangster films, they address themselves to an audience who anticipate that clothing will take on a certain narrative and iconographic importance, and who will also gain pleasure from looking at men's clothes. The current popularity of British gangster films from the 1960s to the present with young British male audiences needs to be understood, then, in the privileged role fashion plays in these movies.

From its first shot of the false-eyelash-wearing Alex and his white-clad droogs in their stylised frozen poses at the Korova Milkbar, *A Clockwork Orange* foregrounds a masculine investment in appearance while it takes on the look of avant-garde fashion photography. The whiteness of the droogs' dress contrasts with the film's post-apocalyptic dystopia, while the non-functional nature of their attire is augmented by the slightly visible smears and bloodstains on all the droogs' shirts – particularly Dim and Georgie's. As leader, Alex wears the most pronounced make-up (false eyelashes around one eye), a decorative touch that will later be lost when he is interrogated in the police cell. Like Dim with his red lipstick, Alex is not feminised by cosmetics, which instead denote the individual signatures that typify gang attire. His dandy-like investment in appearance is further evidenced in the care he takes when disrobing after the night's play: he delicately removes

his false eyelashes, placing them at the side of his bedroom mirror, using a deliberate gesture that highlights his investment in grooming. Narrative cannot contain
these gestures – similar ones are also found in *Get Carter* and *Performance* when
male heroes dress/undress – as they present themselves directly to the spectator
for admiration and possible emulation.

The purple outfit Alex wears to the record store in the next scene is his most
elaborate peacock-style costume and the only one that represents his individual
style. This is the one time we see Alex alone and with total control over his dress.
The droogs' attire is based on a larger template that each member personalises
with their own finishing touches (like Alex's eyelashes, choice of white shirt, hat
and jewellery). For his restful interlude of record-shopping and seduction, Alex
wears a long Edwardian-influenced, purple, double-breasted jacket that falls almost
to his ankles, trimmed with silver snakeskin at the bottom half of its large rounded
collar, its elbow-length cuffs, its deep pocket flaps and the sides of its skirt. Its
six silver buttons are fastened and he wears matching grey narrow trousers underneath. In keeping with this revamped Edwardian style, he wears a fully buttoned,
yellow, long-collared shirt. His dress is notably brighter than that of the other
men in the shop – the assistant wears a black and white op-art tunic shirt, one
customer wears a hippie-like brown suede jacket and matching trousers tucked
into his furry trapper-style boots, while the man on the phone wears a tan leather
jacket and beige polyester trousers.

The Edwardian fashion revival was central to both of the leading dandy-esque
looks of the 1960s and 1970s – the besuited man and the peacock. The first
Edwardian dress revival occurred in the late 1940s, when colour was added to the
earlier template, first by older style icons like Cecil Beaton and Alec Guinness and
later by South London Teds. De Marly suggests that the look was revived at this
time because the young Queen's consort, the Duke of Edinburgh, was not a fashion
leader, and there was no British male icon to counter the influence of American
fashions, disseminated through Hollywood films and popular music.[23] Edward VII
had been preoccupied with style and had been a major global influence on male
fashion throughout his long nineteenth-century tenure as Prince of Wales and his
shorter reign as King. Edwardian fashions were form-fitting but not tight, with
longer coats (often worn open) and full jackets, all designed to camouflage the
King's portly figure.[24] He was quite meticulous – in many ways, a dandy – advocating a highly rule-bound dress code with different costumes for different
occasions. Of course, this meant that men of a certain class had to have more
clothes, which opened up a gap between those who could and those who could
not afford such a wardrobe. The late 1940s/early 1950s Edwardian revival
expressed nostalgia for this supreme male power while it simultaneously (and
possibly defensively) acknowledged the shadow of a greater feminine presence
(whether that of Queen Victoria, Queen Elizabeth or the rumblings of a nascent
feminism).

Form-fitting suits and different clothes for different events testified to the new
affluence that made fashion possible for working-class youths. In *A Clockwork Orange*,
a new social order makes it possible for Alex and his droogs to have an appropriate costume for every event – white for fighting, blue suit for official business,
purple for seduction. Edwardian style also marks the culmination of Alex's fantasies

and his victorious union with the establishment as the film ends with his daydream featuring him naked and wrestling with a woman while men and women in Edwardian evening dress watch over him, very much in the style of Cecil Beaton's Ascot sequence for George Cukor's *My Fair Lady* (1964). This Edwardian allusion suggests the persistence of a particularly frightening brand of spectacular attractive, aggressive and highly sexual masculinity at the centre of society.

Performance further reinforces dandyism as a structural part of British heritage and its institutions in its focus on the law – represented here by barristers in their eighteenth-century wigs and hats. Like the barristers, Turner's status and profession (he is a pop star) are defined through masquerade. We first see Turner dressed after his bath wearing an outfit that combines strong masculine and feminine associations: red dressing-gown, a black sweater, a studded neck-band, black hipster belted trousers, Arabic-style gold and silver pointed-toe slippers (heightening the Orientalist discourse already present in the *mise-en-scène* of the house), a long chain necklace and pendant. Turner's studded neck and wristbands are non-functional but they articulate an aggressive masculinity that undermines concepts of essentially utilitarian masculine attire, suggesting that if masculinity were that stable, it would not require such props. When Turner later takes off his dressing-gown and turns on the microphone to 'perform', reciting over a non-diegetic music track that suggests his artistic collapse, Chas comments on his flawed performance of masculinity: 'Comical little geezer. You'll look funny when you're 50.'

The importance of male dress is highlighted in Chas's transformation into a Turner-esque peacock – a masquerade motivated by survival. He has to change his appearance to evade his boss, Harry Flowers' death squad, out to avenge Joey Maddocks's murder at Chas's hands. First Chas escapes by mixing toothpaste and red paint together, carefully smearing it over his hair and transforming his face into a mask. After finding sanctuary in Turner's mansion, he delicately removes the colour and then, with characteristic fastidiousness, cleans his jacket. As he phones his cousin Tony to arrange a new passport under a false identity, he tells him that he doesn't need to grow a beard – he can obtain a new look in this house. Already, the house appears to be working its spell as Chas wears his clothes with a new informality – his shirt is unbuttoned and his sleeves rolled up. After the phone call, he encounters Turner, who recognises that Chas has blow-dried his hair, revealing the film's concern with male grooming while demonstrating men's interest in each other's beauty routines.

At first Chas believes he controls his transformation, actively using Pherber and Turner to get his desired passport photo. But Pherber is in control, feeding him hallucinogenic mushrooms, revamping first his appearance and then his inner self. From the moment Chas arrives at Powis Square, Pherber's power is underscored as we see her playing with cameras, looking after money and doling out drugs. She paints Turner's lips while he lies prone in bed, puts her wig on Chas and powders his torso as he reclines on their bedecked bed wearing beads, wig, make-up and precious little else, all the while asking him 'Do you feel like a woman?' A mirror reflects her breast off his chest, stimulating Chas to sudden anger.

Pherber controls the machinery of cinema and inscribes sexual difference within the house. Cammell and Roeg knowingly flaunt her metacinematic powers within the narrative, all the while drawing on Pallenberg's own well-known, off-screen image as style-maker (she would later train to be a fashion designer), the lover and image-consultant to at least two Rolling Stones (the effete dandy Brian Jones and the dangerous, leather-clad Keith Richards, as well as a rumoured affair with Jagger on the set of *Performance*). On-screen and off, she creates the multiple masculinities that redefine the national moment, but she does so from outside, from the all-powerful position of European, international feminine that the dandy itself wished to counter.

The hypnotic strength of this feminine position is articulated in Pherber's reworking of Chas's identity. At first he is seduced by an ostensibly masculine transformation, dressed in full 1930s-style gangster regalia with a light grey trilby hat, dark grey suit, white shirt, red tie and a false moustache. The latter were common accessories in the late 1960s, and usually underscored active heterosexual masculinity of the kind characterised by television's Jason King, but this image is queered as we see Lorraine – the little girl who plays old – wearing a false moustache earlier in the film, while Chas's image is further feminised through the use of soft-focus. Both men's dress subsequently becomes more ornate: Turner wears a white frilly shirt, cream silk-embroidered waistcoat and white trousers, while Chas is dressed in increasingly baroque attire, including a markedly Orientalist cream and grey candy-striped silken hippie robe, beads, turquoise sash and red necklace. As Turner plays guitar wearing his characteristic black sleeveless shirt and studded wrist cuff, the film foregrounds the resemblance between this bracelet and Chas's gold wristwatch, linking the men through their jewellery (both wear rings) and prefiguring their eventual morphing into each other. Pherber then transforms Chas into an even more elaborate Turner, dressing him in a white, open-necked, flouncy shirt (in the mode of the day's regency-influenced dandy fashions) as she plays with Chas's guns (highlighting her power) while Turner talks about drugs, going into Chas's brains and the importance of performance – emerging briefly with a quiff, leather jacket, open-necked shirt before instantaneously turning back into his former self.

Abrupt changes characterise the film, its concern with appearance governing its form and narrative. The film foregrounds Chas's narcissism from the opening shots, where he watches his reflection while having sex, adjusting the mirror to get a better view. As his girlfriend, Dana, puts on her make-up and her underwear, he shows more interest in the reflection of the back of his neck in the hand mirror. Returning to the bathroom mirror, he adjusts his gun, belt, tie and checks his nails. Chas's meticulous concern for detail and appearance is echoed in the *mise-en-scène* and through his gestures: one of his drawers contains neatly folded white underwear, another is filled with a row of neatly arranged open jewellery boxes, and his freshly laundered shirts are folded in clear plastic wraps. Chas's gestures – like Alex's – are elegant, expressive and seem to break through the diegesis as he moves his hand carefully across his rows of rings before alighting on one. As he checks his appearance in front of the mirror, his gestures call attention to themselves and invite the stylish male viewer to follow his lead.

Chas's power and status are threatened as Joey Maddocks's men spray-paint and destroy his well-tended flat, following in the generic convention where 'Even . . . apparently innocuous damage to the gangster's appearance signals his vulnerability.'[25] Red paint is everywhere, suggestive of blood, violence and Turner's house with its red-painted lounge. After destroying his furniture, the intruders pick up Chas's rings from the floor, their different shapes and jewelled surfaces suggesting baroque decadence and a remarkable financial investment in his looks. Appearance is once again linked to sexuality as the gangsters paint 'Poof' on the wall and shots of Chas's torture are intercut with images of him having sex with Dana, which are followed by a dissolve to Turner's house. Previously, Harry had warned a minion that Chas is 'out of date'– a comment with connotations (not intended by Harry but available to the audience) that his style, unlike Turner's, was not cutting-edge. Appropriately, Chas's punishment is disfigurement: he is tied up and whipped by Joey as one mobster asks if he can cut his hair, recalling the punishment meted out to the barrister's chauffeur earlier in the film. This threat to his looks is intended to keep Chas in his place, but instead provokes him to greater violence. The gangsters have not considered the strength of his narcissism, his upward mobility, his resistance to punishment, his strength and cunning. Instead, he feigns a collapse and kills Joey but not without giving him false hope, letting him first plead for his life.

Even in a group of similarly dressed men, Chas stands out. Throughout the first half of *Performance*, he is better dressed than other gangsters. Harry's minions wear cheaper suits and pay less attention to details. Joey Maddocks, for instance, has a crooked tie and leaves the top button of his shirt open, while Harry's characteristic three-piece brown suits do not fit properly. (Chas prefers the more classic two-piece, single-breasted, grey and black suits.) When, in a drug-induced fantasy, Turner takes Harry's place and sings 'Memo from Turner', his multiple guises include an ill-fitting, three-piece, brown suit like Harry's. Turner looks similarly ill-groomed – his greasy, slick-backed hair compounding his déclassé appearance and acting as a suitable counterpoint to Harry's hairy back, seen when he wears his string vest.

These differences reveal that the suit is not just a bland, default option. As Chas demonstrates, its cut, drape and colour and the choice of accessories make it a central part of the dandy's wardrobe. In *A Clockwork Orange*, the suit functions differently, almost suggesting a dereliction of self and image. Alex's cheap, unfashionable, single-breasted, crumpled navy suit contrasts with his carefully detailed droog outfit and elaborate purple jacket, destroying his posture and screen presence. This suit articulates his loss of control and is worn during some of his worst moments: as he checks in and out of jail; when he is humiliated to prove the success of the Ludovicio experiment; during his period of depression and degradation after leaving jail; and while he is tortured by the tramps, Georgie and Dim and Mr Alexander's associates. He pays no attention to the details of his appearance when he wears this suit, highlighting his depression. As he checks into jail, for instance, the thin bottom of his tie hangs carelessly while his trousers are crumpled and drag beneath his shoes.

Alex's suit resembles the prison officers' and inmates' uniforms with their belted navy tunic jackets, patch pockets, navy trousers, blue and white candy-striped shirts and navy ties. The differences between inmate and officers' uniforms lie in details – the prison guards have gold buttons, their tunics have stripes, their buckles are centred, not off to the side, the fabric is higher quality and they wear hats. Alex is merely identified by the red armband he adopts as a Christian. After we see him wearing this for the first time, we see his biblical fantasies where he plays a sadistic Roman who engages in Orientalist sexual dalliances, suggesting that the acquisition of an identifying detail in dress might return his subjectivity and herald his (temporary) resurgence.

The grey, three-piece, single-breasted suits worn by the government officials who visit the prison almost blend in with the navy prison uniforms, with only Fred, the minister, standing out by virtue of the light silver grey of his suit and the additional decoration of a handkerchief poking out of his breast pocket. Their navy suits and uniforms align the inmates, the convicts and even the police, suggesting minimal difference between governmental, legal or cultural elites and the gangs that roam the streets. As Dim and Georgie, now both police officers, attack Alex near the end of the film, the viewer is struck by the strong resemblance between their policeman's uniform, Alex's suit and our memories of the prison service garb.

Crucially, the logic of these suit-like uniforms is not very different from the more image-conscious and dandy-like costumes favoured by both the gangs and the other cultural groups. The costumes worn by Alex's droogs, Billyboy's gang, the 'sophistos from the TV studios', the droogs in the Ludovicio films, prisoners and prison officers, hospital inmates and staff and government officials are all structured according to a principle of overall similarity with different details. Similitude establishes group allegiance, class, culture and social purpose, while details reveal identity. The two 'Sophistos' at the Korova on the woman's left are both dressed in black, two-piece, single-breasted evening suits and white shirts, but one wears a red bow tie, the other a blue. The man on her right is in a cream, two-piece, single-breasted evening suit with a white shirt and black bow tie, while the man on the far right in a similar black suit, white shirt and black bow tie. Billyboy's droogs all look the same in their camouflage jackets, military hats and leather trousers but a closer look reveals telling differences. All wear different brightly coloured ruffled shirts: Billyboy's is green and the others are respectively pink, bright blue with white flounces, yellow and orange worn with matching scarf. The droog in orange wears khaki trousers – the others all have tight leather trousers with different decorative embossed trims. All wear belts either over or under their jackets, none wears make-up, while their hats are drawn from different periods, branches and ranks of the armed forces (Billyboy wears an RAF officer's cap giving him an aura of power and class) and even different nations (the blue-shirted droog wears a round Nazi helmet). Their costumes demonstrate the masculinity of contemporary 'peacock' clothes, such as ruffled shirts, while deliberately drawing on their military garb's ideological connotations to blur rank, nation, class and political ideals. Meanwhile, Alex and his droogs have a look that combines the archaic (codpieces, collarless shirts, old vests, braces, canes, hats) with the futuristic (the codpieces are moulded out of plastic, while their make-up and overall look suggest a futuristic masculinity). All wear jewellery decorated with a severed eye and its seeping bloodstains. Their trousers are tucked up into their lace-up boots (at the time, a sure signifier of violent, aggressive and alienated males) reminiscent of the period's skinhead wear. Billyboy's droogs appear less futuristic in their army surplus attire, an effect compounded by the impact of the setting (we see them in a baroque hall whereas we first see Alex's droogs in the futuristic Korova Milkbar). These subcultures are clearly playing a semiotic game, revealing their mastery of the connotations of their dress, the history and meanings they represent. Such careful attention to detail is central to the logic of fashion, which Kubrick uses here to represent social, legal and cultural stratification. His nexus of fashion/agency/society foregrounds the structural role of appearance and costume and facilitates his larger critique of society, individualism, law and crime.

If the suit is variously a uniform, the garment representing an abnegation of interest in clothes or a central part of the dandy's wardrobe, then the dressing-gown – another garment prominently featured in both films – is usually, as Bruzzi notes, 'the uniform of a loser, a nobody, a garment that is not just ordinary, but one that frequently signifies a character who cannot be bothered to get dressed'.[26] This liminal, passive garment has these connotations strategically put into play and undermined in both *Performance* and *A Clockwork Orange*. *A Clockwork Orange* explores Mr Alexander's passivity and failed masculinity through the red and white dressing-gown which he wears over his white trousers and black shoes while Alex's droogs rape his wife and beat him. This first time we see him, he is typing at home, his dressing-gown is worn over outside dress to suggest a fusion of public and private, connoting comfort and highlighting the late hour. Its colours echo his interior decor, pick up the red of his wife's catsuit and the whiteness of the droogs' outfits (especially his legs, clad in white with black shoes), implicating him in his wife's violation. This same dressing-gown covers Alex later as he consumes the drug-laced wine that Mr Alexander and his cohorts use to prepare him for his ultimate torture, indicating that he too is in this position of fragmented masculinity.

Performance presents the dressing-gown's liminality in a quite different way, presenting it as a transformative costume. The garment of androgynes throughout the film, favoured by Turner and Lucy, the dressing-gown reveals the permeability of sexual difference and identity. Near the end of the film, Chas is in bed with Turner, who wears a blue and white muslin dressing-gown. Chas seems to kiss Turner, sliding the gown off his shoulder, but as the freckled skin and delicate limbs emerge, we realise this is Lucy (wearing the same garment); the garment and their similar hairstyles masking and straddling sexual difference. Earlier dressing-gowns, especially those worn by Turner and Chas, have been exotic garments, resembling Oriental dress or peacock fashions, the kinds of clothes that could be worn outside. The inversion of the dressing-gown thus explores the logic of dress as social change.

Unlike American hippies and Yippies, the 1960s and 1970s male dandies and their cinematic counterparts were not using clothing to make *radical* racial or political statements.[27] Instead of pointing to continuities between races, they use fashion to enact the merger of different historical and class regimes to make a statement about masculinity. Both *Performance* and *A Clockwork Orange* are dominantly concerned with white male power – although both films flirt with the exoticism of other nations, ethnicities and cultures. *Performance*'s gangsters share a defensive, working-class xenophobia, in a film that highlights Britain's increased multiculturalism with its shots of turbaned men in the street and Middle Eastern/Southern European victims of Harry's protection racket. Chas calls the latter 'a stinking foreign parasite', revealing his fear of the 'contaminating' influence of the other which he also expresses when he describes the residents of Powis Square to Tony as 'beatniks, drug addicts . . . foreigners'.

Yet ironically it is precisely these foreigners (Pherber and Lucy), beatniks (Turner) and non-whites (Noel) that Chas reaches to for temporary safety and possible salvation. As he waits for a train out of London, he overhears Noel, a mixed-race young man, telling his (white) mother that he is leaving Turner's place in Notting Hill because he owed rent and is going to Liverpool (a city with a strong black heritage and obvious rock connections). Noel wears green crushed velvet with a cream lace trim, has an afro and a goatee. His guitar case is plastered with images of naked women, highlighting his heterosexual potency and suggesting an alternative strong masculinity for a new, multiracial Britain. Significantly, Noel's appearance strongly evokes Jimi Hendrix, an American-émigré who came to fame while also living in London's multiracial Notting Hill, making a statement about a changed Britain, now the self-proclaimed international pop-culture capital. Male dandy fashions played an important and instrumental role in this transformation, as de Marly notes: 'The tolerant British allowed a man to be more unusual in his dress, but American men were more self-conscious. To them, colour and frilled shirts suggested homosexuality.'[28] The dandy-oriented Edwardian styles – both in suits and in the more peacock fashions – deliberately resisted American influence, making this fashion revival part of the discourse of a new Britain, emerging from rationing and Empire with a new and unprecedented sense of youth style. Male fashions celebrated otherwise potentially threatening changes, adopting feminine styles and moving far away from utility to articulate a more elastic masculinity that confronted the possibility that the working-class male body may soon no longer be necessary.

Unlike Britain's 'Angry Young Men', these new masculine fashions participated in the fantasies of dressing-up and the possibilities they offered for more flexible identity. But, at the same time, the dandy's very presence – his poachings from feminine culture, and, within these films at least, his seemingly inevitable dependence on the international, suggested the instability of this figure, and the impossibility of the independent, yet youthful, national identity he sought to represent. In *A Clockwork Orange*, for instance, Alex's fantasies reveal this figure's close associations with the Oriental (itself a Western construction, but one that depends on the lure of the exotic, non-native Other), while in *Performance*, the European Pherber masterminds all masculine play with gender, supported by the French androgyne, Lucy, as Chas himself is on the run for freedom – in America. While this dream is impossible, the alternative lies in the hyper-confinement of Powis Square, a piece of London that is itself under European, feminine rule.

Similarly, today's dandy revival provides a site for the interrogation of and play with masculinity in a culture where its relationship to national identity is under threat, where definitions of masculinity, rather than questions of the feminine, have become the problem. From a more utopian nostalgic perspective, these 1960s and 1970s images offer themselves up as material for new fantasies. Now predominantly a masquerade, intended for visceral contemplation rather than participation, the dandy's more plastic identities are used to hold out the possibility that the male might emulate both the pleasures, discipline and the flexibility of the modern woman, whose ability to keep up with fashion increasingly parallels her ability to maintain a dominant place in the social hierarchy.

Notes

1   See, for example, Anne McClintock, Aamir Mufti and Ella Shohat (eds), *Dangerous Liaisons: Gender, Nation, and Postcolonial Perspectives*, Minneapolis, University of Minnesota Press, 1997; Caren Kaplan, Norma Alarcón and Minoo Moallem (eds), *Between Woman and Nation: Nationalisms, Transnational Feminisms, and the State*, Durham, NC: Duke University Press, 1999.

2   'Enhanced *Performance*', *loaded*, September 1998, 53: 132–41. The spread also features girls dressed like Pherber and Lucy.

3   'Party people in the place to be', *loaded*, January 1999, 57: 136–45.

4   Ibid., 139.

5   Social historian, Frank Mort notes that the feminine figure (as in *Playboy*) is often used to reassert heterosexuality in male fashion advertising, offsetting the homo-erotic attraction of the male body. Frank Mort, *Cultures of Consumption: Masculinities and Social Space in Late Twentieth Century Britain*, London, Routledge, 1996, 143.

6   Diana de Marly, *Fashion for Men: An Illustrated History*, London, B.T. Batsford, 1985.

7   Ibid., 11.

8   Ibid., 134.

9   Mort, op. cit., 133.

10   Ibid., 139.

11   Ibid., 142, 134–42.

12   De Marly, op. cit., 132.

13   Ibid., 83.

14   Ibid., 83–6.

15   Stella Bruzzi, *Undressing Cinema: Clothing and Identity in the Movies*, London, Routledge, 1997, 68.

16   De Marly comments on the revival of Regency dress with its ruffles in the late 1960s; De Marly, op. cit., 136.

17   Bruzzi, op. cit., 37.

18   Pressbook, *Barry Lyndon*, (Warner Bros, USA), 1976, 4.

19   De Marly, op. cit., 133–5.

20   In *The Krays* (Peter Medak, 1990, UK), the brothers' rise is marked by their acquisition of Savile Row suits and monogrammed shirts.

21   Colin MacCabe, *Performance*, London, BFI Publishing, 1998, 39.

22   Bruzzi, op. cit., 67.

23   De Marly, op. cit., 131.

24   Ibid., 109.

25   Bruzzi, op. cit., 67.

26   Ibid., 86.

27   Leerom Medevoi, 'A yippie-panther pipe dream: rethinking sex, race, and the sexual revolution' in Hilary Radner and Moya Luckett (eds), *Swinging Single: Representing Sexuality in the 1960s*, Minneapolis: University of Minnesota Press, 1999, 133–80.

28   De Marly, op. cit., 135–6.

PART FIVE

Modes and methodologies

Chapter 24

Rèka C.V. Buckley and Stephen Gundle

FLASH TRASH
Gianni Versace and the theory and practice of glamour

W HEN HE WAS KILLED in July 1997, Gianni Versace was hailed worldwide as the master of glitz and glamour. News stories and obituaries referred
to the brashness and ostentation of his fashion, to his love of celebrities and his
taste for publicity. According to the *Daily Telegraph*, he established a huge fashion
empire 'by following Oscar Wilde's dictum that nothing succeeds like excess'. For
The Times, he was 'the king of glitz', the man who 'combined beauty with vulgarity',
while *The Independent on Sunday* suggested that, unlike the understated style of his
rival Armani, Versace's style catered to those Italians who preferred 'Middle
Eastern flashy'. The word that recurred most frequently in the press was glamour.
The designer's penchant for opulent beauty, the dramatic eye-catching nature of
his gowns, the mingling in his work of street style and high fashion, the heavily
sexual element, his invention of the supermodels of the 1990s, his flamboyant
lifestyle and professional and personal relationships with the famous all contributed
to the definition of him as the leading practitioner of glamour. In 1995, to convey
the sort of women the designer might have dressed, the *Financial Times* wrote that
'Cleopatra, Jezebel, Delilah, Mme de Pompadour, Jean Harlow, Jane Russell, Lana
Turner, Gina Lollobrigida, Marilyn Monroe, Brigitte Bardot, Claudia Cardinale,
Cher were all Versace girls, glitter queens to a woman'.[1]

Like many fashion buzzwords, glamour does not have any precise meaning;
rather it conveys an idea, in this case an approximate notion of wealth, excitement, beauty, sexuality and fame. As long ago as 1947, lexicographer Eric Partridge
described glamour as a 'vogue word'. Like other such terms, it had been invested
with high status and picturesque connotations by authors and journalists. 'Such
words', Partridge observed, 'gain a momentum of their own, whatever the primary
impulse may have been'. In disapproving tones, he asserted that

a girl or a gigolo may possess *glamour*: and it makes no matter whether the girl is glamorous in her own right or by the catch-guinea arts of her dressmaker or her cinematographic producer. *Glamour* has para-trooped its way over the stage gossip, film 'pars', and the rest of current journalism. It has even invaded the vocabulary of the most reputable novelists.[2]

Glamour's inherent slipperiness, its imprecision and vacuity have meant that it has existed in the interstices of studies of fashion, celebrity and the image of women without ever being investigated in its own right. For example, both Camille Paglia in *Sexual Personae* and Jackie Stacey in *Star Gazing* use the term frequently, but neither seeks to define it or give it a conceptual status.[3] Yet precisely glamour's concern with surface, appearance and the ephemeral gives it an importance in the aesthetics of postmodernity that needs to be addressed.

The aim of this chapter is to explore the origins and uses of glamour. An attempt will be made to develop it as a concept and to illustrate its application in the 1980s and 1990s in relation to the work of Versace. It will be shown that fashion has always been a central component of glamour in so far as it possesses an unrivalled capacity to express or enhance status, allure or notoriety. Indeed, Jeanine Basinger regards fashion and glamour as virtually synonymous.[4] But it will also be shown that, with the erosion of traditional social hierarchies, fashion became increasingly reliant on the mass media to perform its function of attracting atten-tion, staging the famous and arousing wonder. Versace understood this very well and it may be argued that his reputation as 'the king of glamour' derived from his masterly exploitation of the possibilities and contradictions of modern mass fashion.

Glamour theory

Despite the vagueness of its usage, the etymology of glamour is reasonably clear. According to *The New Fowler's Modern English Usage* (1996) the word was originally Scottish. It was an alteration of the word 'grammar' that retained the sense of the old word 'gramarye' ('occult learning, magic, necromancy'). The *Oxford English Dictionary* (1989) also highlights its Scottish origins and derivation from 'grammar', although this is indicated to mean magic, enchantment and spells rather than necromancy and the occult. According to *Fowler's*, glamour passed into standard English usage around the 1830s with the meaning of 'a delusive or alluring charm'. For *Webster's Third New International Dictionary* (1961), glamour is 'an elusive, myste-riously exciting and often illusory attractiveness that stirs the imagination and appeals to a taste for the unconventional, the unexpected, the colourful, or the exotic'. In its secondary meanings glamour is said to be 'a strangely alluring atmos-phere of romantic enchantment; bewitching, intangible, irresistibly magnetic charm; . . . personal charm and poise combined with unusual physical and sexual attractiveness'.

Walter Scott is indicated by nearly all sources as the author who first intro-duced glamour into literary language. As the inventor of the historical novel and a great promoter of Romanticism, Scott specialised in illusion and visual deception.

He blended historical fact and fiction to offer a romanticised vision of a medieval past that thrilled nineteenth-century readers and fired their imaginations. In novels including *Ivanhoe* and *Waverley*, Scott recounted stories of violent passions, terrible feuds, great loves, chivalrous acts and deadly battles, all of which took place in a setting of lakes, mountains, forests, castles and towers. 'Everything was depicted in high contrast', notes Mark Girouard. 'Even the sounds were strong and simple; armour clanged, teeth gnashed, maids shrieked, spirits groaned, hounds howled, and every knight lived in imminent expectation of "the bursting crash of a foeman's spear as it shivered against his mail".'[5] Scott's romanticised Scottish Middle Ages enjoyed enormous popularity throughout Europe. In particular, a middle-class reading public found in his novels a vehicle for its dreams and desires.

In a highly original work, Colin Campbell has explored the significance of this emphasis on fantasy and its link to the development of modern consumerism. For all its puritanical image, Campbell argues, the bourgeoisie did not renounce pleasure or desire.[6] On the contrary, insatiable desire, often expressed in day-dreaming or fantasy, was a crucial part of the individual bourgeois experience. Words, pictures or sounds all enable individuals to construct 'as if' worlds for themselves to inhabit. Campbell stresses that literary fantasies worked by using settings and events that were 'realistic' while eliminating inconveniences, employing coincidences and beautifying individuals such that the 'imagined experience' came to represent 'a perfected vision of life'.[7]

Between the late nineteenth and the early twentieth centuries, not just literature, but products became associated with the dreams people were acquiring of themselves as beautiful, attractive, successful, wealthy and healthy. Products were enjoyed not purely for their practical benefits but at an imaginative level through representations, with creative and entertaining experiences informing the act of purchase and bringing a variety of added values. The continuous nature of the bourgeois approach to consumption was different from the finite aristocratic approach. The root of bourgeois desire and the continuous pursuit of pleasure is not properly explained by Campbell, but he suggests that it may have been sexual. Whereas the paradigm for the aristocratic pursuit of satisfaction was food-seeking, the paradigm for the 'modern autonomous imaginative hedonism' that marked bourgeois experience was 'the initiation of sexual activity following the encounter with a potential mate'.[8] Atmosphere and responsiveness to sensations were crucial parts of the experience. In contrast to the hunt for food, such an idea was dynamic and boundless.

Several pre-conditions of what is understood today by glamour can be seen to have derived from this shift. Bourgeois consciousness facilitated the emergence and articulation of ideas, images and figures that were alluring and enticing. It also heralded a new role for fictions and narratives in sustaining the economic system. However, in order to understand the place of glamour in modern society, it is necessary to relate this development to a broader set of transformations. The displacement of an aristocratic concept of finite consumption was merely one of a complex set of trends and shifts which accompanied the decline of the aristocracy and the rise of the bourgeoisie. Other relevant factors included the growth of cities and the repositioning in the marketplace of some aristocratic attributes including style, taste and beauty. Also important were the opening of high society to exponents of the arts, showbusiness and the world of money, and an increased role for appearances in social relations.

There are no theories of glamour, although authors as diverse as David Bond and Clive Scott have attempted to examine its functioning in the fields of fashion and photography.[9] Some fragmentary considerations, however, may assist in the development of a more theoretical approach. Peter Bailey has related glamour to modernity and identified it as a property involving public visibility of a desirable object.[10] When they were appropriately managed or controlled, he argues, such objects became commodities which acted as markers of class difference. Bailey's argument is related to the enormous expansion of visual culture that was occurring due to advances in printing, photography, lighting, and techniques of display and packaging. In the modern city, magazines offered images, advertisements decorated walls, theatres were illuminated and shop windows were full of tempting goods. He makes the point that, while the visual horizons of the public were being widened, magazines and shop windows also functioned as distancing mechanisms. By serving to prevent immediate access, they fuelled envy and desire.

In contrast to Bailey, it can be argued that desire was not stimulated by distance but rather by the novelty of access. Exclusion and distance were conventional and were perpetuated by differential incomes. Rather, desire was stimulated by attractive presentation; for example, by using colours, exotic themes, lighting effects and a phantasmagoria of abundance. First developed in publications and commercial presentation, the world of dreams subsequently witnessed a significant expansion with the development of moving images and the cinema. All the techniques of visual seduction that had been formulated and deployed in product marketing were transferred into the new medium.

A further step towards a general theory of glamour can be taken by drawing on Walter Benjamin's analysis of consumption and of art in the industrial era. In his essay 'The work of art in the age of mechanical reproduction', Benjamin argued that, by being diffused more widely, art was losing its uniqueness and hence its aura.[11] The contemporary masses, he said, had 'a desire to bring things "closer" spatially and humanly'; this desire was 'just as ardent as their bent toward overcoming the uniqueness of every reality by accepting its reproduction'.

> Every day the urge grows stronger to get hold of an object at very close range by way of its likeness, its reproduction. Unmistakably, reproduction as offered by picture magazines and newsreels differs from the image seen by the unarmed eye. Uniqueness and permanence are as closely linked in the latter as are transitoriness and reproducibility in the former.[12]

Elaborating freely from Benjamin's insight, it might be suggested that the new reality, the emergence of which was marked by the advent of the mass media, permitted the 're-embedding' of qualities that had been 'disembedded' from their social context. Up to the eighteenth and early nineteenth centuries, the social bearer of glamour was the aristocracy. But increasingly this class, which was losing its political and economic power, offered only a paradigm. More important was the semblance, or reproduction, of distinction, stylishness, wealth and breeding that could be manufactured by commercial culture or through the media. This artificial aura, detached from the class that had created it and turned into a manufactured property, was the essence of glamour. Visibility redefined social relations and assisted the emergence of a new elite, which consisted of those who were photographed, painted, talked about in the press or noticed at public gatherings. Access to this elite was achieved by various means. Social status was important but so too were notoriety and photogenic beauty. Furthermore, artifice played an important part in attracting and holding attention and in creating the effects of dazzle and excitement. From the 1920s, movie studios excelled at the production of luxury, the exotic, beauty and sexuality.

This shift was secular rather than revolutionary, as aristocracy had long before turned the capital cities of Europe, the centres of court life, into sites of luxury and consumption. Werner Sombart argued that this pursuit of luxury actually gave rise to capitalism in so far as it stimulated international trade, money-lending, the growth of industries producing refined goods, and urbanisation.[13] Thus courts never had a monopoly on the trades they stimulated. Fashion, jewellery, perfumes, architecture, interior design and so on were always available to whoever could afford them. Yet the strong association of luxury with court life meant that the disarticulation or displacement of the court, as a unique concentration of style, ceremony and opulence, was none the less significant. As Norbert Elias wrote,

> As a central configuration of [this] stage of development, which after a long struggle gave way abruptly or gradually to a professional-bourgeois-urban-industrial stage, this aristocratic court society developed a civilising and cultural physiognomy which was taken over by professional-bourgeois society partly as a heritage and partly as an antithesis and, preserved in this way, was further developed.[14]

The 'heritage' element was apparent in the continuing importance of luxury production and its association with status, the canon of taste being formed by aristocratic modes. Also, as the American sociologist Thorstein Veblen noted, leisure conserved its association with privilege and status well into the industrial age.[15] The 'antithesis' was evident in the abolition of the significance of blood lines, freer social mobility, the wider visibility and accessibility of luxury.

Although aristocrats continued to play a role, the new, burgeoning culture increasingly took its cue from another source: the courtesans. The hybrid figure of the courtesan was in part *grande dame*, actress, professional beauty, fashionable woman and common prostitute. The courtesans were invariably beautiful and ambitious young women of lower-class origins who masqueraded as society women, taking part in all the public, money-related rituals of the *beau monde*: theatre, restaurants, shopping, races, sitting for portraits, visiting couturiers, etc. Courtesans, or at least a handful of them, were known to the public by name, but they also enjoyed a powerful fictional representation in novels, plays, opera and painting. The courtesan, as Christopher Prendergast has argued, was represented more than the street prostitute because she was an acceptable, glamorised version of a troubling phenomenon: the commercialisation of sex. As T.J. Clark writes,

> Prostitution is a sensitive subject for bourgeois society because sexuality and money are mixed up in it . . . There are obstacles in the way of representing either, and when the two intersect there is an uneasy feeling that something in the nature of capitalism is at stake, or at least not properly hidden.[16]

In the eyes of the ordinary public, there was probably little difference between the *demi-monde* and the *grand-monde*, or at least the two were not mutually exclusive. After all, in what was *seen* of the *beau monde*, the courtesans were prominent and they possessed precisely the qualities of beauty, desirability, fashionableness and wealth that attracted attention. The courtesan fitted so well with the new order because she was a professional of make-believe and illusion in an era in which appearances became substance. Clark asserts that

> her business was dominance and make-believe. She seemed the necessary and concentrated form of Woman, of Desire, of Modernity (the capital letters came thick and fast). It was part of her charm to be spurious, enigmatic, unclassifiable: a sphinx without a riddle, and a woman whose claim to classlessness was quite easily seen to be *false*.[17]

The play-acting, the pantomime aristocracy, the facade of elegance and refinement, which was cultivated by the courtesan and the racy crowd of *bon viveurs* who joined her in making over the image of the city, had a profoundly confusing, but vibrant and exciting effect – especially as far as the lower classes and outsiders were concerned. For the latter, the message transmitted by these groups was one of hedonism and consumption that found a counterpart in the arcades and the department stores. As David Frisby argues,

> The social life of the interlocking circles of foreigners, the world of fashion and the aristocracy was endlessly displayed whilst at the same time, with increasing economic development, there were underlying democratizing influences at work, at least on the boulevards.[18]

In the interstices of this glittering display of image, ostentation, sex, commerce and culture, modern glamour was born.

Versace and the contemporary fashion business

Before these points can be related to Versace, some general considerations on contemporary fashion must be advanced. In the 1970s, Italian fashion underwent a significant evolution. With the closure of many conventional couturiers and the development of a mass taste for fashionable clothes, textile companies gave rise to ready-to-wear lines that were significantly more expensive and 'fashionable' than the functional garments of the 1960s. In order to capture a growing market of well-off, middle-class people, these companies resolved to produce high-quality, ready-made clothes that would enjoy the prestige of a recognisable brand name.

Figure 24.1
Gianni Versace, 'Warhol Dress',
Spring/Summer 1991. Courtesy of
Niall McInerney.

Already in the 1950s, a company like Max Mara had produced quality garments in series for middle-class women, and in the 1970s fashion companies including Genny, Complice and Callaghan followed a similar course. Large enterprises such as Gruppo finanziario tessile (GFT), however, decided to take the process a step further by calling on experts who would assist them not only in responding to the market, but in leading it. The designers (*stilisti*) who emerged at this conjuncture were men (usually) with experience of the marketing and selling of clothes as well as with their manufacture. Giorgio Armani, for example, whose first collection was launched in 1975, had worked as a window-dresser and as a designer for Nino Cerruti before being offered the opportunity by GFT to develop a line bearing his own name.

The new category of *stilisti* enjoyed an unprecedented role. Their task was to interpret the humours and aspirations of the market and to create seasonal collections of garments that corresponded to the requirements and expectations of customers. This was not a straightforward task, since Italian society in the late 1970s was evolving rapidly following the impact of ten years of social protest and cultural change. Although interest in politics was waning fast by this time, the erosion of rigid social hierarchies, the entry into the labour market of large numbers of women, higher levels of education and stronger desires for individual expression all made for a fluid situation in which conventional class patterns of dress no longer applied. As the small and medium businesses of the 'third Italy' of the Veneto and Emilia-Romagna led the way out of the recession and Italy entered from 1983 what would be termed 'the second economic miracle', consumer aspirations for the first time became the driving force of the economy and society.

The designers made their names by identifying and engaging with social trends. The needs of professional and managerial women, the general interest in status symbols, the role of fashion in communicating identity, the greater willingness of men to take an interest in clothes, the erosion of once firm boundaries between the formal and the casual all provided extraordinary opportunities for designer-branded fashion. In the course of the 1980s Armani, Gianfranco Ferre, Gianni Versace and Valentino (all Milan-based save the last-mentioned, a couturier who made his name thanks to VIP clients including Jacqueline Kennedy Onassis and Audrey Hepburn) established themselves as style leaders with an unprecedented purchase on collective dreams and lifestyles. Although they catered primarily to the comfortably well-off, their astute use of the mass media and deployment of 'diffusion lines' and licensing arrangements ensured that they were positioned in the realm of desire, even for those on average or lower incomes.

Versace, a southerner from Reggio Calabria who worked in Milan for Genny and Callaghan before launching his own brand name, was always the least bourgeois of the quadrumvirate of leading designers. His early designs for his own label, launched in 1978, were relatively subdued, with only a slight Japanese flavour and a touch of sophistication giving his creations a modern edge. But in the 1980s, he developed the lavish, luxurious, overtly sexual style that became his trademark. He used the most varied materials, black leather appliquéd with velvet, rhinestones and lace, quilted satin, grey flannel doubled with shiny silk. Like his colleagues, Versace invested most of his energies in developing a clear and recognisable design signature through his main ranges. The expansion and promotion of the Versace label was driven by the business brain behind the company, Gianni's brother Santo. From one store in Milan's Via della Spiga in 1978, the company grew by 1995 into an empire of 138 boutiques in cities worldwide. These were all lavish emporia, each positioned strategically in locations such as London's Old Bond Street and Los Angeles's Rodeo Drive. In addition there were 340 other outlets and 2,660 shops which sold secondary lines.[19] In 1996, it was estimated that Versace had a global turnover of £600m and that pre-tax profits amounted to £60m.[20]

The expansion was fuelled mainly by three things. First, Italy's lax tax system: creative accounting and bribes to tax officials enabled a high percentage of profits to be channelled into expansion.[21] Second, the Versace company remained independent and retained control of all phases of design, production, distribution and retailing. The decision-makers in the company were all family members. In addition a complex range of secondary and tertiary lines were developed while licences for perfumes, accessories, sunglasses and homeware generated further profits. Among the clothing lines were Istante, Versus, Versatile, Versace Jeans Couture, Versace Classic V2, Young Versace, Versace Sport. Following the launch of Donna in 1981, the Versace fragrance range grew to include The Dreamer, Versus, Blue Jeans, Red Jeans, Versace l'Homme and Blonde. Hats, shoes, handbags, scarves, costume jewellery, ties, belts and umbrellas were the main accessories, while the Home Signature Collection included lamps, vases, picture frames, china, carpets, quilts, cushions, fabrics and linens. Versace offered not just clothing but a lifestyle package.

The designer's primary clients were the new rich. The international, the wealthy and the famous constituted a large enough base for the Versace group to have little fear of recessions. Among the 'jet-set maharanis' for whom he designed were Ivana Trump, Bianca Jagger and Lynn Wyatt.[22] His eye-catching style and the exorbitant cost of his creations appealed to their desire for ostentation and display.

Image and celebrity

Versace, it has been said, 'sold sex and glamour and he sold it with the gusto of the most garrulous second-hand car dealer'.[23] For any modern fashion house, advertising and promotion are crucial to the sale of the product. Advertising ensures a brand retains visibility and can be identified by consumers; it also distinguishes the product from competitors and weaves around it a mythology which arouses interest and envy. The Versace label distinguished itself by its emphasis on excess: of volume of advertising, of colour, of celebrity. A higher percentage of profit than any other designer was invested in promotion and the cultivation of image. According to British *Vogue* editor, Alexandra Shulman,

> Versace believed that fashion should be fun, fearless and, most of all, new. If he could make the whole experience colourful and exciting, people would talk about it, write about it, photograph it. The more exposure that a designer could have, the stronger that he would become. He understood that publicity is the oxygen of the fashion business. Today, the symbiotic relationship between fashion and fame is evident. But the Versace family put the most conviction behind it.[24]

The centrepiece of fashion promotion is the catwalk show. In the course of the 1980s, thanks in part to the innovations heralded by Versace, these evolved from restricted events aimed at the fashion press, buyers and selected clients into showbusiness events which captured newspaper headlines, generated magazine coverage and therefore impacted on popular culture. In every aspect they were conceived and choreographed to attract attention. Versace's shows won a reputation for being the 'flashiest events in the fashion calendar'.[25] As Gina Bellafonte explained in *Time*:

> The spectacles he created, replete with the blaring sounds of rockers like George Michael and clothes that were just as loud, earned the designer all the publicity they were meant to garner. As a result, he hastened the transformation of fashion from a rarefied interest of the elite into an object of bottomless mass-cultural fascination.[26]

Fashion professionals were no less impressed. As Alexandra Schulman wrote:

> The first time that I saw a Versace show was the first time that I understood the power of fashion. The combination of beautiful models strutting the catwalk, dresses that often appeared moulded to the body and a wonderful rock and roll soundtrack was completely seductive.

> For Versace there was no 'warts and all', everything was larger than
> life, everything was totally desirable.[27]

His shows, added another journalist, 'had all the production value of a Busby
Berkeley extravaganza, [they] telegraphed three simple messages: glamour, excitement and sexiness'.[28] The salesmanship continued after the shows, at parties that
were reported to be wild and hedonistic.

Central to the appeal of the shows were the 'supermodels', who Versace
himself was credited with creating. The original supermodels – Linda Evangelista,
Christy Turlington, Claudia Schiffer, Cindy Crawford and Naomi Campbell – were
photographic models whom Versace turned into celebrity clothes-horses in order
to attract attention to his garments. Their apotheosis came when he put them on
the catwalk together in 1991, breaking the established custom of sending one model
down the runway after another. This unprecedented gathering of faces and bodies
that were already known from their regular appearances on magazine covers and
fashion spreads marked the emergence of the supermodel as popular icon and won
Versace the reputation as a modern-day Svengali. 'Without Versace, we would
not have the cult of the supermodel, the Eighties catwalk stars who became celebrity
clothes-horses photographed wherever they went in the unmistakable siren dresses
that were the designer's trademark', wrote one journalist.[29] Versace flattered the
models with unprecedented fees; for example he once paid Turlington $50,000
to model exclusively in his show. He also lavished them with attentive personal
treatment. In return, they praised his creativity and generosity in every interview.

There was a world of difference between the courtesans of the nineteenth
century and the supermodels. But the latter too came to occupy a central place
in the collective imagination. Their lives and loves were the object of widespread
interest, as were their diversifications into acting, singing, writing, photography,
television-presenting and even fast-food sponsorship (Fashion Café). The supermodels were one-dimensional – no one heard them speak, but they none the less
dazzled as protagonists of a world that had all the features of glamour. They became
'stars of a new firmament in which they gravitated between the catwalk, cinema
and millionaire love affairs'. They were figures of that world which exists only for
the photographer's flash, the front page of the newspaper and the gossip column.
Like the courtesans, their fame rested on their desirability and sexuality, their
beauty contributing to both; but publicity and fashion were also central. The link
to money came through their commercial origins. Versace knew, it was said, that
'if the clothes make the woman, supermodels make the sales'.[30] The distancing
mechanisms were their silence, their cosmopolitanism, their belonging to a world
with socially exclusive connotations. Their accessibility derived from their visibility
and presence in the press, their ordinary origins, and their lack of any talent other
than their beauty. The public, attracted by their beauty and photogenic qualitites,
was drawn into their exciting profession, their magnificent wardrobes and the
narrative of their lives.

Versace advertising was also pioneering. He used top photographers, Richard
Avedon, Bruce Weber, Mario Testino and Helmut Newton, who photographed
supermodels and celebrities for spreads that could fill up to twenty pages of a
magazine. Versace insisted that his advertisements should have a full-length message

so uncompromising as to be totally compelling. He piled bodies high, one on top of the other, in a pagan display of the perfection of flesh, Colin McDowell argued. 'Young studs and supermodels intertwined naked limbs to make a statement about sex, power and money'.[31] The advertisements conjured up an image of a fantasy life of opulent sensuality and hedonism. It was not always easy to distinguish between advertising and editorial material where the coverage of Versace was concerned. The company granted magazines exclusives of photographic spreads, often featuring celebrities, which appeared as though they were part of a feature. This confirmed the impression that the company was not merely selling goods, but was shaping the culture.

Versace used stars from both the rock and the film worlds as well as super-models in his advertising campaigns. Elton John, Madonna, Jon Bon Jovi, Lisa Marie Presley, Courtney Love and Sylvester Stallone all appeared in commercial spreads – Stallone naked and John in a figure-hugging evening gown. But, aside from friends who became walking advertisements, Versace dressed numerous figures in the public eye, aware that in this way publicity could be won that was worth far more than even the costliest advertisement. By designing for Princess Diana, the most photographed woman in the world in the 1990s, he achieved enormous recognition. In Britain he was not widely known to the general public until he created 'that dress', an extraordinarily revealing black gown held together with safety pins, for Elizabeth Hurley's appearance at the world premiere of *Four Weddings and a Funeral*, the 1995 film starring her partner Hugh Grant. Front-page colour pictures in the *Sun*, the *Mirror* and the *Evening Standard*, as well as the broadsheets, turned Versace into a household name that functioned as a byword for show-stopping, sexy clothes.

Unlike his colleague and rival Armani, who worked within a bourgeois idiom of understatement and tastefulness, Versace's fashion was all about well-knownness. Just as celebrities are constructed as attention-grabbing commodities, so Versace offered customers the promise of standing-out, being noticed and, almost, of wearing a price tag. 'His designs shout wealth and status proudly from the rooftops', observed Susannah Frankel.[32] This was achieved by the use of bright colours, revealing cuts and shiny, luxurious fabrics. It was enhanced by advertising which ensured label recognition and public identification of the style. It was further charged by the identification of the style with movie and rock stars – here there was a reciprocal effect of adding drama and value. 'Stars loved wearing his clothes', observed Mario Testino, 'because for some of them, putting on a Versace dress was the first time they *felt* like stars'.[33] At the same time, they set the seal on Versace glamour. Finally the association with the supermodels added connotations of expensiveness, beauty and extraordinariness as well as publicity. Versace was well aware of the modern public's thirst for fame and often used references to it in advertising spreads. For example, in 1996 Bruce Weber shot for Versus a series of black and white photographs that used the idea of young stars arriving somewhere, dressed up for an event and surrounded by paparazzi.[34] None of the faces in the photographs, however, was well known. Like Andy Warhol, from whom he occasionally drew inspiration (witness his design based on Warhol's Marilyn), Versace was in thrall to the aura of celebrity. He was 'unashamedly star-struck, so unashamedly that it became endearing', noted Lisa Armstrong.[35]

In the diffusion and fragmentation of modern celebrity, few actors or performers felt they compared well with the great stars of the past. Packaged and presented by the Hollywood studios, the stars of the middle decades of the twentieth century basked in an aura of glamour that it seemed almost impossible to replicate. If Versace was one of the preferred designers of starlets and Oscar nominees, it was because he was able to work a certain magic. It was observed in the Italian women's magazine *Anna* that

> It is not only the models who owe him a lot. Stars like Madonna and Lady Diana turned to him when they wanted to rediscover their feminine side. The operation succeeded perfectly with Courtney Love too. The rockstar known for her excesses, the wife of Kurt Cobain, who was relaunched by cinema in *Larry Flynt*, tried to get rid of all her old photographs. Versace helped her to play a woman that, for her, was completely new: the Hollywood star.[36]

The Versace style

Old-style couturiers occasionally formed part of the circle of their aristocratic clients, but usually by courtesy and only if they were deemed socially acceptable. More frequently they moved in the café society but still as secondary figures. With the rise in the 1970s of the business-oriented fashion designer, men like Versace acquired great wealth and celebrity in their own right. Thus they could live in a style that not even the most successful of movie stars could enjoy. It was not Madonna and Elton John who offered hospitality to Versace but vice versa. It became common for designers to open their houses to magazine photographers but only Versace systematically developed a lifestyle that was designed to be photographed and to serve the ends of his business.

The designer owned four notoriously lavish houses, in Milan, on Lake Como, in Miami and New York. Here he established himself as a sort of monarch. According to one journalist, 'he lived like an emperor and surrounded himself with paid courtiers who kept the baying hordes away'.[37] 'The Italian Renaissance is not only a paradigm of dress for Versace, but also his model for life', writes Richard Martin.

> Versace aspires to Medici aesthetics and authority; his synthesis is found now not only in clothing that has the distinct colours and silhouettes of Renaissance pageantry, but also in his intellectual cultivation of neo-Platonism and his dispersal of an aesthetic voice into every aspect of living, from clothing to home furnishings, fragrances, music and houses. Versace does not inhabit old palazzi; he makes their contemporary equivalents. His publication of sumptuous books is the indulgence of a prince. His great houses are equipped with equally great libraries. His ubiquitous Medusa is not a label in the fashion sense, but an insignia in the Renaissance tradition.[38]

Versace lived in these houses with his extended family who appeared to live a life of golden leisure and privilege. 'The lifestyle had a direct correlation with the clothes; when you saw Donatella and her eight-year-old daughter wafting round the Roman-style pool in their leopard-print swimsuits and mules, it made sense', wrote British *Vogue*.[39] When Madonna stayed at the Lake Como villa with her entourage, she was entranced. As she wrote after Versace's death:

> We all had to keep pinching ourselves to make sure we weren't dreaming. Every sunset we were served fresh Bellinis, which we sipped under the giant magnolia tree at the edge of the lake. . . . the Sri Lankan servants waited on us with white gloves . . . Dirty clothes would never stay on the floor for more than a few seconds, and beautiful Versace gowns kept arriving. A new batch every day. . . . I had this fantasy that I was in an Antonioni film and the shoot was going on indefinitely. I felt like a spoiled princess. 'The Versaces really know how to live!' we kept repeating this over and over like a mantra.[40]

The whole Versace lifestyle was photogenic, not just the collections. Famous and beautiful guests were photographed and the results published, making it unclear where real life ended and publicity began. The transition from family album to major campaign was seamless.[41] The *dolce vita* image was played up, with reports appearing continually of how much Gianni loved life and lived it to the full. All this served to enhance the commercial appeal of the brand. Breathtakingly opulent parties were held to mark collections, open stores and launch the books in which the Versace *oeuvre* was recorded for posterity. The party held in Versace's Bond Street shop to launch *Men without Ties*

> had all the very high-glam ingredients – women soignée and sexy, men smooth and even sexier, the most beautiful bodyguards in the world, society dames, pop stars and assorted groupies, all of them celebrating . . . being lucky enough to be invited to a money-no-object bash thrown by the king of money-no-object bashes.[42]

Gender and sexuality

Versace was often accused of dressing women as whores. In particular his use of leather, lurex and rubber, often in combination with rhinestones or studs, signified a willingness to draw inspiration from fetish wear.[43] 'The hallmark of Versace's clothes is an overpowering sexuality that turns men into studs and women into hookers', wrote Fiammetta Rocco.[44] 'They have an exaggerated, almost cartoon glamour that celebrities the world over, especially the US, seemed to adore.' Versace himself cultivated this image. In interviews he referred to the impact the prostitutes of his native Reggio Calabria had on him as a boy. He claimed to have found their assertiveness and confident sexuality a source of inspiration.

This connection with the sexual underworld, far from being *outré*, situated Versace in the mainstream of a long tradition of glamour. As was shown above, if one stream of glamour was the aristocracy and the world of elegance, another was the world of commercial sexuality. These two first joined in the courtesans, who had a far-reaching impact on the development of a burgeoning consumer culture. However, there was a difference. In the past glamour involved a masking of sexuality with luxury, that is to say, the costumes and sets of Hollywood films were rendered rich and opulent precisely to deflect accusations of immorality in the same way that the high luxury of the courtesan was intended to create a facade of respectability. If something was rich, then it was also moral, argued Metro-Goldwyn-Mayer boss Louis B. Mayer.[45] In reality the unrespectable could only partially be masked and glamour came to be marked by a relationship between the classy and the sleazy. Versace rendered this tension more explicit than many designers and, in the less hypocritical climate of the 1980s and 1990s, tilted the balance towards a more explicit emphasis on sexuality.

However, the sexuality – or sexualities – that inspired Versace and which marked his work, were heavily conditioned by image, and tended towards the stereotypical. According to Colin McDowell, Versace's 'Roman inspirations seem to stem from nothing more ancient than Fifties gladiator films starring Victor Mature and Gina Lollobrigida in the romanticised Technicolor world of Hollywood. That's why Versace's is a raunchy and ersatz version of the ancient past'.[46] Although references to the strong women of Italian cinema of the 1940s and 1950s like Anna Magnani and Sophia Loren, were not as explicit in Versace as they were in designers such as Dolce & Gabbana, the influence was none the less apparent. As *The Sunday Times* once wrote,

> His models often look like fifties film stars, with their *maquillage* equal to that role. They have slanted eyes rimmed with kohl, faces powdered pale, their lips slippery, shiny, show-girl red. Christy, Naomi, Linda, Cindy – all dressed up with somewhere to go, but somewhere that a respectable middle-class mother might not *quite* approve of – in public, anyway.[47]

'Versace traded on sex, and made no bones about it. The women who wore his dresses looked instantly fabulous, as though they were the life and soul of the party', observed Tamsin Blanchard.[48] As fellow designer Jasper Conran put it, 'There's the Versace woman who dresses for men, *sans doute*. Versace girls make a career of sex; they don't have girlfriends, they're too much competition. The Armani woman dresses for herself.'[49] Versace used to claim that fabric could not be sexy, only women, but in reality it was the combination of the two. 'A strappy Versace evening dress which curves around the body before flaring out into a flirtatious kick, slashed to the thigh and with the deepest neckline in the business, is quite the most sensual garment any woman could hope to wear', one woman journalist claimed. In this way he transmitted a *joie de vivre*.

> When women and teenagers were depressed and humiliated, when they felt used and tired, betrayed or abandoned, thanks to him they rediscovered the joy of a happy and desacralised eroticism. Versace was the gluttonous life, the daily party, the posh quarter adventure.[50]

Versace liked anti-conformist women and was attracted by self-assured rebels. 'He gave women and men the ability to express themselves rather than abide by the rules. His women, in particular, are fantastically sexy, with a capital S', noted Marcus von Ackermann, the fashion editor of French *Vogue*.[51] In some respects, Versace was able to impart the confidence he admired in the women he elected as symbols.

> He didn't so much design clothes for ordinary people as create glorious carapaces to hide the emptiness that lurked behind all the golden glory he commanded. His clothes exuded the power and certainty, the sexual confidence and authority of a world he tightly controlled . . . his creations always trailed clouds of richly imagined dreams of beauty, albeit seen with a Hollywood eye.[52]

It was no accident that Versace prospered in the post-feminist climate of the 1980s and 1990s. Armani built his empire catering to the needs of career women, bourgeois professionals who wished to be able to convey an image of sobriety and elegance that matched the seriousness of their male-dominated working environments. Versace, by contrast, catered to the demands of women who wished to stand out or to seduce. This included the famous or the aspiring-to-be-famous, but it also appealed to women who were successful in their careers and who did not find any incompatibility between this and the exhibition of their femininity. This is another reason why the supermodels were so important. They were ordinary young women of exceptional beauty who stood in Versace's world view as symbols for all women who worked for their living and who aspired to be noticed and adored.

Versace caught a mood, but he also played a formative role. As an influential designer, he shaped tastes and aspirations. The editor of Italian *Vogue*, Franca Sozzani, observed that,

> together with the clothes, Gianni helped women discover a taste for glamour. He wanted them beautiful and happy to be so; he dreamed of women who wanted to please men. The Versace woman does not dress for her own pleasure: her aim is to conquer men.[53]

This is a view endorsed by Alexandra Shulman shortly after the designer's death.

> 'Yesterday, I was wearing a scarlet Versace cardigan. Made of clinging viscose and rayon, it had a sensuous quality and intensity of colour that you don't find in any old red cardigan. You couldn't help but have a good time in it, and that's what Versace wanted to achieve.[54]

The statements of these fashion magazine editors confirm Richard Martin's view that 'What Versace in fact created was a sensual contemporary woman who despite her short skirt has the powerful authority of a traditional menswear paradigm. And he created in her the template of courtly elegance.'[55]

Although Versace was accused of anti-feminism, a more accurate charge is that he fuelled a new elitism-based bodily appearance.

Taking the if-you've-got-it-flaunt-it principle to its ultimate degree, he designed clothes for men and women who were toned and tanned (in Versace's world, no other sort existed), who wanted their superb sexuality to be clothed in a way that didn't hide their firm, strong flesh, but did everything possible to enhance it.[56]

The designer created his own sphere of 'beautiful people' who, like the jet-setters featured in Françoise Sagan's precocious novel *Bonjour Tristesse*, were charming, decadent, golden-skinned and irresponsible. Their perfect bodies were primarily a source of social distinction and exclusion.

Conclusion

The analysis of Versace confirms a number of the features of glamour outlined in the opening section. The paradoxical combination of the elegant and the vulgar that characterises so much of the designer's work is entirely within the mainstream of glamour. The showy facades and the emphasis on desirable images can also be related to the emergence of glamour in the nineteenth century. Finally, the emphasis on women and the attempt to construct artificially alluring models of femininity also recall glamour's origins. But there are also several novel features that show how glamour has evolved and become a burden as well as a resource for contemporary fashion. In the first place, Versace's strategic investment in the alluring reveals that glamour was a process that required constant reinvention and renewal. If it is to be current, glamour has to be nourished constantly with new faces, new occasions, new images and new garments. This dovetailed well with the fashion world's link to cyclical novelty and also met the needs of the press, stores and consumers for constant novelty. However, in a media-saturated world, in which the competition to stand out as glamorous is intense, alluring images risk cancelling each other out by constantly raising the average level of opulence and luxury. The huge resources required to sustain the primacy that Versace achieved can only be obtained and invested as long as a brand can maintain its global popularity.

Although Versace experimented with new materials, combinations of colours, forms of fashion promotion and linkages with the press, ultimately his idea of glamour was highly derivative. Whereas nineteenth-century glamour retained a linkage of sorts to an objective social referent, and the Hollywood studio system forged a new mass language of glamour, Versace could only work off old images and established stereotypes drawn from the movies and popular culture. This derivative quality, which he shared with Warhol, enabled Versace to develop a strikingly shallow and self-referential aesthetic that distilled glamour into a familiar repertoire of gestures and stereotypes. This helped make his fashion instantly recognisable and adaptable to many contexts and personalities. The promise that any woman could look and feel like a star in a Versace gown was testimony not so much to the designer's creativity as to his predictability.

As far as the theory of glamour is concerned, the analysis of Versace confirms the paradox of accessible exclusivity. It also confirms that glamour is a visual language of the enticing that seduces through the deployment of images of theatricality, luxury, sexuality and notoriety. In Benjamin's terms, this language can be regarded as the artificial aura that mass society requires to substitute the decayed aura of uniqueness and authenticity. Fashion is not the only industry with access to this language, but it is certainly that which today uses it most systematically and effectively.

Notes

1 Brenda Polan, 'Is glamour glitter – or a graceful line?', *Financial Times*, 31/12/94–1/1/95, Weekend supplement, vii.
2 Eric Partridge, *Usage and Abusage: A Guide to Good English*, London: Hamish Hamilton, 1947, 361.
3 Camille Paglia, *Sexual Personae: Art and Decadence from Nefertiti to Emily Dickinson*, London, Penguin, 1992; Jackie Stacey, *Star Gazing: Hollywood Cinema and Female Spectatorship*, London, Routledge, 1992.
4 Jeanine Basinger, *A Woman's View: How Hollywood Spoke to Women 1930–1960*, London, Chatto and Windus, 1994, 114–59.
5 Mark Girouard, *The Return to Camelot: Chivalry and the English Gentleman*, New Haven and London, Yale University Press, 1981, 34.
6 Colin Campbell, *The Romantic Ethic and the Spirit of Modern Consumerism*, Oxford, Blackwell, 1987.
7 Ibid., 84.
8 Ibid., 69–71.
9 David Bond, *Glamour in Fashion*, London, Guinness, 1992; Clive Scott, *The Spoken Image: Photography and Language*, London, Reaktion, 1999.
10 Peter Bailey, 'Parasexuality and glamour: the Victorian barmaid as cultural prototype', *Gender and History*, 1990, 2 (2): 148–72.
11 Walter Benjamin, 'The work of art in the age of mechanical reproduction' in Benjamin, *Illuminations*, London, Fontana, 1973.
12 Ibid., 225.
13 Werner Sombart, *Luxury and Capitalism*, Ann Arbor, University of Michigan, 1967. (First published 1899.)
14 Norbert Elias, *The Court Society*, Oxford, Blackwell, 1987, 40.
15 Thorstein Veblen, *The Theory of the Leisure Class*, Boston, Houghton Mifflin, 1973. (First published 1899).
16 T.J. Clark, *The Painting of Modern Life: Paris in the Art of Manet and his Followers*, London, Thames & Hudson, 1990, 102.
17 Ibid., 109.
18 David Frisby, *Fragments of Modernity*, Cambridge, Polity, 1985, 180.
19 *La Repubblica*, 7/3/95, 26.
20 Clare Longrigg, 'On the rack', *Guardian*, 20/9/97, 5.
21 Lowri Turner, *Gianni Versace: Fashion's Last Emperor*, London, Essential, 1997, 44–5.
22 *The Sunday Telegraph*, 24/7/94.
23 Ibid., 35.
24 Alexandra Shulman, 'Versace and the power of fashion', *Daily Telegraph*, 16/7/97, 22.

25   Shane Watson, 'Viva Versace', *Elle*, November 1996, 76.
26   Gina Bellafonte, 'La Dolce Vita', *Time*, 28/7/97, 28.
27   Shulman, op. cit., 22.
28   Lisa Armstrong, untitled, *Vogue*, September 1997, 249.
29   Tamsin Blanchard, 'Versace: very sexy', *Independent*, 16/7/97, 12.
30   Watson, op. cit., 292.
31   Colin McDowell, 'The show must go on', *The Times Magazine*, 6/12/97, 39.
32   Susannah Frankel, 'Show a girl a good time', *Guardian*, 16/7/97, 15.
33   Armstrong, 'Gianni Versace', *Vogue*, October 1997, 292.
34   'The limelight club', *The Times Magazine*, 24/8/96.
35   Lisa Armstrong, untitled article, *Guardian*, 16/7/97, 15.
36   Claudia Costa, 'Naomi e le altre', *Anna*, 20/7/97, 37.
37   Armstrong, 'untitled article, *Guardian*, 16/7/97, 15.
38   Richard Martin, *Versace*, London, Thames & Hudson, 1997, 7.
39   Armstrong, 'Gianni Versace', 288.
40   Madonna '"I'm going to miss you, Gianni"', *Time*, 28/7/97, 33.
41   Armstrong, 'Gianni Versace', 288.
42   Colin McDowell, 'Midas touch', *Sunday Times Style*, 20/7/97, 8.
43   See, for example, Brenda Polan, 'The corrupted genius who demeaned women', *Daily Mail*, 16/7/97, 5.
44   Fiammetta Rocco, 'Death of an Italian dream', *Independent on Sunday*, 20/7/97, 17.
45   For a discussion of these issues, see Stephen Gundle, 'L'eta d'oro dello Star System' in Gian Piero Brunetta (ed.), *Storia del cinema mondiale*, vol. 2, *Gli Stati Uniti*, Turin, Einaudi, 1999.
46   McDowell, 'The Show', 42.
47   *The Sunday Telegraph*, 24/7/94.
48   Tamsin Blanchard, 'Versace: very sexy', *Independent*, 16/7/97, 12.
49   Quoted in Sally Brampton, 'Who do women really dress for?', *Vogue*, October 1995, 180–3.p   348   348

50   Denise Pardo, 'Filosofia della vistosita', *L'Espresso*, 24/7/97, 52.
51   Colin McDowell, 'The Midas touch', 8.
52   McDowell, 'The Show', 43.
53   Quoted in Sandra Cecchi, 'Un nemico del perbenismo noioso', *L'Espresso*, 24/7/97, 54.
54   Shulman, op. cit., 22.
55   Martin, op cit., 6.
56   McDowell, 'The Show', 8.

Chapter 25

Pamela Church Gibson

REDRESSING THE BALANCE
Patriarchy, postmodernism and feminism

THE PURPOSE OF THIS CHAPTER is to consider some of the points of intersection – past, present and possible – between fashion and feminist discourse. It grew out of a desire to discuss the perceived and gradual relaxation of feminist attitudes to dress over the past twenty years when located within the context of the parallel recognition of fashion as a respectable academic discipline, as a site of important cultural debates. For despite the seeming relaxation, the new legitimation, there remains a continuing scepticism, even hostility, towards fashion within certain strands of feminism. My aim, therefore, is to try and negotiate a path between some of these opposing positions and offer a way forward, building on the links previously made between fashion and postmodernism, to indicate a route that might make connections, resolve certain difficulties. There seems at the moment to be something of a stalemate or an impasse; fashion and feminism are still uneasily circling each other, not yet properly reconciled. Lest there be confusion in this chapter over terminology, I would like to stress that I am using the word 'fashion' to encompass both 'high fashion' and what Jennifer Craik describes as 'everyday fashion (clothing behaviour in general)'. I share, too, her desire to map the 'complex, disjointed or oppositional' relationships between the two (Craik 1994: ix).

In observing the dress codes both within and outside the academy, at meetings, conferences, meetings and any gathering advertised as 'feminist', it has been possible to chart, over the past two decades, the emergence of new perspectives in the gradual proliferation of different styles. It would, of course, be simplistic merely to observe that, as the second-wave feminism of the 1970s splintered and fragmented, so the different strands that emerged within feminism established their own dress codes, homogeneity duly becoming heterogeneity. Nor would it be correct to assume that a feminist condemnation of fashion belongs completely in the past and that there is now some relaxed, postmodern, third-wave consensus. Rosalind Coward writes in *Our Treacherous Hearts*: 'if anything, the concern with appearance, body shape and desirability seem to have grown' (Coward 1992: 154).

'Young women', she continues, 'flocked to buy Naomi Wolf's *The Beauty Myth* as if hearing for the first time the feminist message that women are coerced by the tyranny of slenderness' (Coward 1992: 154). Her belief that the fashionable image is one of 'desirability', that it involves a 'female obsession with rendering oneself the aesthetic sex, with making oneself sexually attractive' seems to me to be at the very heart of such feminist objections to fashion (Coward 1992: 154–5). It is, surely, fundamentally mistaken; the 'aesthetics' of fashion are not primarily sexual in nature, nor are they designed, necessarily, to attract the male gaze. Rather, 'fashionable' dress is a complex lexicon where the intention of sexual enticement may be absent altogether, or, if present, be unimportant in comparison with other criteria. Women, it is often observed, dress 'for each other': this colloquial observation contains, compressed within it, a number of important truths which include an awareness of the rituals of shopping, dressing up, adolescent identity parades, masquerade and the concept of same-sex looking. Since the Great Masculine Reclamation, that began in the 1960s and reached its apogee in the 1980s, men too can shop, gaze at other male bodies and forms of dress, and participate in a series of activities which may or may not include the attraction of potential sexual partners.

Certainly, Coward was right to intimate that much of *The Beauty Myth* was a contemporary reworking of ideas first presented in *The Female Eunuch* as long ago as 1971. Greer has been the dominant figure in defining feminist anti-fashion rhetoric, fuelling dialogues around dress and particularly in her reinforcement of the erroneous conflation of high fashion, notions of femininity and the quest for sexual desirability that I have outlined above:

> [F]ired with hope, optimism and ambition, young women study the latest forms of the stereotype, set out in *Vogue* . . . and other glossies where the mannequins stare from among the advertisements for fabulous real estate, furs and jewels . . . The stereotype is the Eternal Feminine. She is the Sexual Object sought by all men and all women . . . There are stringent limits to the variations on the stereotype, for nothing must interfere with her function as sex object.
>
> (Greer 1971: 58–9)

Greer's polemic not only gave vital impetus to the radical feminism of the early 1970s, but it has remained central to wrangles and disagreements around dress and self-presentation. However, her observations concerning the 'fashionable' are, nevertheless, part of the feminist fallacy around 'fashion'. The high heels, nail varnish and ostentatious jewellery that, for her, are signs that 'the Eunuch has set up her camp' are not always 'in fashion'. They are, of course, an integral part of the accoutrements of sexual pursuit – which is not to be confused with fashionability.

Nevertheless, in *The Whole Woman*, Greer returns to and reasserts her original lines of argument. There is a tendency to universalise, even essentialise: 'There are a few male fashion victims: all women are victims of fashion. Men will not buy cosmetics' (Greer 1999: 179). She fiercely attacks recent developments within fashion, seeing the new forms of self-adornment, piercing and tattooing, as new methods of 'mutilation'. For Greer they are 'a continuation of the incessantly stimulated desire in the little girl to bedizen herself, to change her hair colour, to paint her face and her nails' (Greer 1999: 127). Even for the purposes of rhetoric, clitoridectomy should not be bracketed together with the vogue for navel-piercing.

Greer has not shifted her attitude or her stance – and nor have others. Proof, if needed, that the smouldering antagonism surrounding questions of self-presentation and personal style can erupt, with ferocity, at any moment is provided constantly. For example, in December 1997, Camille Paglia's London lecture was interrupted, and eventually stopped, by vociferous heckling, soon after her claim that Madonna, the late Princess Diana and the Spice Girls were excellent role models for women. Paglia gave her account of the affair in an article in the *Guardian* – and, in a letter to the same newspaper, so did one of the women whose interruptions had provoked the furore. She explained that it was the choice of role models that had so antagonised her – she deplored their 'vanity'. The use of this word gave an extraordinary, Old Testament flavour to her denunciation, which was – presumably – directed at the preoccupation of these women with their appearance, their continuing changes of hair, make-up, clothes and their pursuit – within the gym or wherever – of a taut, toned physique. Paglia's article was entitled 'Why British feminism sucks' and claimed that Greer is the only 'British' feminist of any substance or distinction (*Guardian*, December 1997).

Professor Greer herself became involved in an acrimonious public dispute when she chose to attack the appearance of a feminist fellow-traveller. She famously reproached her chosen adversary, the feminist author and journalist Suzanne Moore, for the wearing of red lipstick, high heels or what Greer described as 'fuck-me shoes' (a phrase apparently favoured by Marilyn Monroe) and for 'displaying three inches of . . . cleavage' (*Guardian*, 1997).

This attack is – paradoxically – misogynist in its violent tone and reminiscent of the strident puritanism around dress that characterised Anglo-American feminism in the late 1960s and early 1970s. Indeed, it has never really gone away – a banner at a feminist meeting in the early 1980s apparently proclaimed 'Fashion = Control = Violence Against Women' (Walter 1998: 13). Obviously, every emergent political force is likely to be as purist – Maoist China, for instance. But just as in China today, fashion designers are speedily exploiting the opportunities offered them as the puritanism of the Mao years recedes, so the new, diverse feminisms in the West have no need to proclaim their identity by the imposition of uniforms. Furthermore, as the effects of feminism are increasingly felt within the dominant culture, and the struggles are no longer felt to be taking place from the margins, so the sense that women must declare themselves through an oppositional style has faded. But it is important to enter a caveat: as certain kinds of feminist activity are co-opted and even hijacked by patriarchy, so other regulations (and dress codes) come into force. The 'power suit' of the 1980s has been softened and modified slightly, but various forms of 'power dressing' and the corollary 'power bob' – surely the reverse of empowering – dominate most spheres of professional activity.[1]

It is vital, then, that we do not opt too quickly for a naïve and uncritical post-modernist celebration of a new diversity in the relations between feminists and fashion. It was surely Elizabeth Wilson's pivotal text *Adorned in Dreams*, which in 1985, finally made fashion a legitimate sphere of feminist scholarship. Wilson, vitally and accurately, defines fashion as a 'performance art' which acts as a 'vehicle' for the 'ambivalence . . . of contradictory and irreconcilable desires' (Wilson 1985: 246). In the final chapter, she focuses specifically on the troubled relationship between fashion and feminism. She credits Janet Radcliffe Richards, whose book *The Sceptical Feminist* had been published five years earlier, with clearly identifying and elaborating the feminist confusion around a notion of 'the natural' which is confused with 'authenticity' – a misunderstanding about 'the "natural" person being "the real thing"' (Radcliffe Richards 1982: 239).

It is this confusion of the 'natural' with 'authenticity' that seems to inform Greer's discourse; wearing high heels and red lipstick is unacceptable, but to pose naked – for a photographic portrait published in two national newspapers and which is to hang in the National Portrait Gallery – is perfectly permissible, because 'natural'. Indeed, the picture was published to illustrate an article entitled 'Why I loathe lingerie' which appeared in both the *Observer* and the *Daily Mail*, to coincide with the opening of an exhibition of undergarments at the Design Museum in London. Here she explained that her abandonment of underwear was politically motivated; it was 'part of my feminist battle against pornography, that I would not "tackle up"' (Greer, *Observer/Daily Mail*, May 2000). The article concludes by yoking together the 'synthetic marketing of babyfood, lipstick and high-heel shoes' as showing how 'the imagery of the mother retreated in the face of the onward march of prostitution'.

Wilson's text identifies another central problem which has contributed to the continuing disagreements around the question of fashion. The observation is as relevant now as it was at the time of writing:

> It is difficult to discuss fashion in relation to the feminism of today, because the ideologies about dress that have circulated within the women's movement seem never to have been made explicit. This may be one reason for the intense irritation and confusion that the subject provoked from the beginning . . . and still provokes.
>
> (Wilson 1984: 230)

This seems to be, indeed, the crux of the matter – that there has been no real academic confrontation, as there has in the case of, say, pornography. As an equally vexed area of passionate dispute and contradictory views, it is nevertheless far easier to debate for the simple reason that sides have been taken, positions declared – we usually know exactly where a particular feminist stands on, say, the question of censorship. Our own views may be dissimilar – but open discussion, in print and in person, is possible, because so many women have taken sides, have stood up to be counted. Fashion and its attendant disagreements have never been thus privileged – arguably because they do not have equal weighting. So divergent views and notions of difficulty coexist in silence. Although third-wave feminism may celebrate diversity and spectacle, may examine the politics of identity, the nature of consumerism in general and female consumerism in particular, may contemplate the body-as-text, there is no knowing when a voice of second-wave puritanism may intrude – and, as we have seen, do so quite forcefully. And yet, arguably, fashion – and its associated industries – play a part in the lives of all women. Whether women follow current trends, ignore them and create their own style, are relatively uninterested in 'fashion' as such, or have little, if any, money to spend on clothes, they nevertheless, by the simple act of getting dressed in the morning, participate in the processes of fashion.

Arguably, all women are not involved in, or even perhaps touched by, the pornography trade (unless, of course, you subscribe to the view that all men have been so brutalised by the pornographic climate in which we live that all women are, therefore, at risk). And yet the pornography debate is prolific in contributing to the literature of gender studies, while texts focusing on feminism and fashion can be ranged on a single shelf.

Nevertheless, there have been dramatic changes since 1984. Wilson's book concluded:

> Fashion is ambivalent – for when we dress we wear inscribed upon our bodies the often obscure relationship of art, personal psychology and the social order. And that is why we remain endlessly troubled by fashion – drawn to it, yet repelled by a fear of what we might find hidden within its purposes, masked by the enigma of its Mona Lisa smile.
>
> (Wilson 1985: 247)

The terms of reference here were determined by the state of feminist theory at the time – and so much has changed (or at least shifted) – since then, that it is now possible to restate some of the issues the author raises in other terms, provided by different (feminist) theoretical parameters. Wilson herself has responded to these changes in at least two articles, published in 1990 and 1992, and this essay owes a great deal to the way in which Wilson has developed and elaborated her work on fashion in recent years. First, she argues against cultural critics who, for all their allegiance to postmodernism, continue merely 'to ignore or denounce fashion' – even though fashion seems precisely to be at the heart of the post-modern (Wilson 1990: 209–10). Second, she argues, as a feminist, for a fuller grasp of the 'ambiguity' of postmodernism and emphasises the danger of 'a one-dimensional, over-simplified account' of it (Wilson 1990: 233–4). Third, she argues for a movement 'away from the simple, moralistic rejection of fashion which has characterised so many left-wing, radical movements' and towards a grasp of the constitutive 'ambivalence' of fashion itself 'as cultural phenomenon' (Wilson 1992: 14–15). As Jennifer Craik points out, for Wilson the ambivalence of the concept of postmodernism and that of fashion are necessarily intimately related. For post-modernism has not only 'opened up the space' in which the study of dress can be rescued from its 'lowly status' (Craik 1994: 8). It has also begun to account for dress as at one and the same time 'a powerful weapon of control and dominance' and *simultaneously* possessed of 'subversive qualities' (Wilson 1992: 14).

In the remainder of this chapter, I seek to pursue this way of thinking fashion a little further. But I also want to shift what for Wilson (1992: 3) is a 'mood of ambivalence' further in the direction of dialectics – dialectics, in particular, as deployed by Fredric Jameson (1991) as a strategy for thinking through the cultural contradictions of postmodernism itself. Wilson, of course, had already described fashion in these terms eight years previously: 'with dress: the thesis is that fashion is oppressive, the antithesis that we find it pleasurable . . . no synthesis is possible' (Wilson 1985: 232). She has also discussed Jameson's arguments on postmodernism as 'the cultural logic of late capitalism' at some length, taking issue with Jameson's account on several counts: most notably, perhaps, in the case of what she calls his 'conservatism', which she seems to equate with certain aspects of his particular Marxism, as in her reference to his 'reflexionist' notion of 'ideology' (Wilson 1990: 232). I shall end by arguing that it is surely by reaccentuating Marxian dialectics, as Jameson seeks to do, that we can make further progress with Wilson's conception of the 'ambivalence' of fashion. To do so, however, may mean that I also reaccentuate the left-wing, moral critique of fashion to a greater extent than Wilson would perhaps wish, but only as one side of the dialectic in question.

The relaxations in attitudes to fashion, where they exist, overlap with the directions that certain kinds of feminist theory have recently been taking. But I want to begin with the crisis in postmodernity, or better, postmodernity *as* crisis. If the grand narratives have been collapsing or have collapsed – if the enlightenment project is now threatened or at an end – then the question is whether the issues at stake are not gender-specific. A crucially important strain in contemporary feminist theory would argue that the postmodern crisis is a crisis in the structuring of male reason with which women have no need to feel much concerned. Indeed, the demise or at least the interrogation of the *logos*, of male reason, is precisely women's opportunity. This is the burden of work by feminist philosophers such as Luce Irigaray and Rosi Braidotti. Take, for instance, this passage from Irigaray's *This Sex That Is Not One*:

> When women want to escape from exploitation, they do not merely destroy a few 'prejudices', they disrupt the entire order of dominant values, economic, social, moral, sexual. They call into question all existing theory, all thought, all language. Inasmuch as these are monopolised by men and men alone, they challenge the very foundation of our cultural and social order whose organisation has been prescribed by the patriarchal system.
>
> (Irigaray 1985: 165)

Irigaray's whole philosophy is built on the assumption that women's thought, and with it women's values, 'economic, social, moral, sexual', have still to be created. All we know of women's thought and women's values thus far is as they have emerged in, and been determined by, terms dictated by men and a world constructed by men. What Irigaray calls 'the female genre', the world of women's thought, is necessarily future-oriented and still radically incomplete. And this means that it is radically at odds with masculine thought, which will always be backward-looking, in the sense that a long tradition already exists for it. Patriarchal thought is complete – or, if you like, finished.

Similarly, Rosi Braidotti has written of feeling 'the need for a qualitative leap of the feminist political imagination', of believing in 'the empowering force of political fictions' proposed by certain feminist thinkers – what she calls 'alternative figurations' – as a way out of the old schemes of thought (Braidotti 1994: 3). 'Figuration' is a key concept in Braidotti's work, though in the first instance she borrows the term from the work of Donna Haraway. Braidotti says that 'figuration' is precisely the challenge for women today – a challenge to find 'new images, new modes of thought' to help feminists think about changes and changing conditions that they have contributed to bringing about (Braidotti 1994: 1). It is precisely this interest in 'figuration' or 'new images' of thought that has come to seem so much more important to feminist theory in the past decade or so.

But how might it begin to shift approaches to some of the issues raised earlier? In the first instance, we need to ask whether attitudes to fashion have not hitherto been comprehensively determined by idealist assumptions that are intrinsic to patriarchy and what Irigaray calls its 'cultural order'. And that would be true of attitudes to fashion taken up by women, too. The French philosopher Michèle Le Doeuff quotes a line from Hegel as one of a host of examples of the misogyny so frequently apparent in Western philosophical tradition: 'Women have culture, ideas, taste and elegance, but they cannot attain to the ideal' (Le Doeuff 1989: 37). On the one hand, the order of the ideal is what truly matters in the end. On the other hand, women have no place in it. And they have no place in it because they belong irretrievably to the bodily world, the material world, the fallen world of matter. And this world is precisely the world of 'taste and elegance' that we might call the world of fashion. The classic and most familiar feminist attitude to fashion – the second-wave attitude, if you like – is precisely that women must struggle to dispute this definition and depreciation of their place and value. But this kind of high-minded rejection of the world of fashion as trivial and superficial is arguably in danger of relapsing into the very idealist mode of thought that it claims to oppose. A mode of theorising fashion that looked to more recent developments in feminist theory – to Braidotti, Irigaray, Le Doeuff and others – might at least consider the possibility of theorising or 'figuring' fashion on its own terms, by beginning with the material as the realm rejected by masculine tradition as the world to which both women and fashion belong. And fashion *is* material, in two senses: on the one hand, the world of fashion is a world of material things; on the other it is a world of constant change, transformations, shifting surfaces.

Postmodern culture, of course, has frequently been described as one of transient phenomena, of fleeting and ephemeral surfaces. Craik, explaining why fashion is of such interest to postmodernists, describes its 'slipperiness – the ambivalence, polyvalence, semiotic smorgasbord and excess' which 'fits into a world view of consumerism, pluralism and masquerade gone mad – the unfettered circulation of free-floating signs' (Craik 1994: 8). We've lost a conviction of the existence of the 'deep strata' that were supposed to underlie these surfaces: what the philosophers in their idealism called universals and essences, for instance, and thought of as changeless substances. So the world of fashion might indeed seem to be the epitome of postmodern culture. To begin to think about fashion in terms derived from theorists like Irigaray and Braidotti is at least to consider the possibility that feminism can best resist patriarchy by insisting that women's involvement with fashion – women's identification with fashion, the identification of women with fashion – can actually be read positively, as identifying women with a world of contingent material surfaces, as opposed to the world of ideas and the spirit that has constituted the intellectual world of patriarchy.[2]

However, it is precisely this world of contingent material surfaces that needs to be 'figured' anew, in Braidotti's sense; that needs to generate and be articulated in the new forms of thought for which Braidotti calls. To give a single instance: one such 'form of thought' might be some version of the concept of 'performativity', as elaborated by Judith Butler in the context of gender politics (Butler 1990: 134–41). In Butler's account of matters, gender is precisely a free-floating construct which has no necessary or inexorable ontological root in biology or corporeality – 'sex, and desire, or sexuality generally' (Butler 1990: 135). The gendered body is performative: that is, 'it has no ontological status apart from the various acts that constitute its reality' (Butler 1990: 136). Here reality is fabricated as an interior essence, interiority itself becoming an effect of a public and social discourse, the public regulation of fantasy through the 'surface politics of the body'. But the politics of fashion, of course, is intrinsically related to the 'surface politics of the body'. Fashion itself supplies the constituent elements of an indeterminate number and range of social performances or self-constructions. Fashion is a storehouse of identity-kits, of surface parts which, assembled, determine the 'interior essence' which is subsequently taken to determine the assemblage itself.

A material politics of fashion, then, might involve a positive (rather than a moralistic or critical) thinking of fashion, in so far as it recognises and works with fashion as an instrument crucial to the destabilisation or deconstruction of identity politics. Rather than raising questions of and for fashion, it might use fashion itself to raise questions: What are the functions of fashion as a complex determinant of identity and identities within postmodernism? What is the political force of a Barthesian recognition of the complex relations between the economy of fashion and the economy of identity within advanced capitalism? How exactly – and within what strictly defined limits – does an understanding of ourselves, women, as 'creatures of fashion' work to disturb or subvert a set of assumptions about the self-sameness of an entity in and through time – a metaphysics, that is, and an ontology which has underpinned the patriarchal understanding, not only of gender relations, but of a whole system of social relations? What might be radical – newly radical – in a theory of fashion as a 'surface politics of the body'? Might thinking fashion in this manner be, precisely, a way of instituting what Braidotti calls a 'truly radical materialism'? If so, how does it connect up with other radical materialisms (Braidotti's own, Irigaray's, Deleuze's) that have recently been appearing?

But another question emerges at this point: is such an approach not in danger of looking like just another species of heady, postmodern fallacy? And, furthermore, wouldn't that mean complicity with patriarchy, all over again? Does it not mean, after all, simply a continuing acquiescence in the exploitation and oppression of women? If we are to think the materiality of women properly and fully, don't we also need to keep reflecting on its material conditions?

We might begin with a consideration of consumption, since it was the subject of so much debate within cultural studies during the 1980s (and, at times, so much seemingly unproblematic – and therefore worrying – celebration within that discipline). Barbara Kruger's well-known billboard piece, 'I shop therefore I am' surely has a number of different levels of meaning. It is, after all, from the Cartesian *cogito* that Irigaray traces the modern forms of phallocentrism. Braidotti suggests that, post-Freud and post-Nietzsche, the Cartesian *cogito* should be reformulated, to acknowledge the existence of the unconscious, as *'desidero ergo sum'* – I desire, I wish for, therefore I am (Braidotti 1994: 13). Kruger's work obviously expresses, among other things, a specificity of female desire. But it also ironically alludes to its continuing connection with a male formula. The precise nature of Kruger's artwork – a huge billboard dominating urban space – provides, of course, an ironic comment on the culture of relentless consumption which characterised the 1980s. This consumption – as mentioned – became perhaps too much of a preoccupation with the cultural theorists of that decade. It was as if – after so much puritanical self-denial – some members of the academy were overwhelmed by the hedonistic possibilities opened up to them.

John Fiske is perhaps the most extreme example of this trend: he seems to believe implicitly in the subversive power of the consumer, and, following de Certeau, in the consumer-as-guerrilla. The young unemployed are 'guerrillas par excellence' within the space of the urban shopping mall, but women too are adept operators within these spaces, often spending the money of the supporting patriarch in a further act of resistance – against the structure of marriage (Fiske 1989a, 1989b). I don't entirely accept that a woman buying a designer garment in the 1980s (or, indeed, today) whether she is spending her own money or that of some male authority figure, is striking a death-blow at the very roots of the patriarchal structure.

I also feel that it is not only the wilder exploits of cultural historians in the 1980s that need to be revisited. It is important to note the developments around subcultures. *Resistance through Rituals* (Hall and Jefferson 1976) claimed, rightly, that subcultures have the power to subvert and disrupt, as did Dick Hebdige in *Subculture and the Meaning of Style* (1979). However, Hebdige also described the processes of incorporation, whereby the subversiveness of a subculture was recuperated by the dominant culture through processes of ideological assimilation and the transformation of subcultural styles into mass-produced commodities. As Evans and Thornton put it (with reference to Hebdige): 'All subcultures establish trends which feed back into the dominant culture and in fashion as elsewhere, nonconformist space must be continually renegotiated. By a process of symbiosis, cultural "deviance" is disarmed' (Evans and Thornton 1989: 31).

The power of subcultural style has, surely, been significantly eroded; this began during the 1980s and has continued throughout the present decade. It's not just the fact that subcultures were recouped and utilised by both couture designers and mainstream retailers. Rather, subcultural styles themselves became victims of the 'designer' decade, where that noun became an adjective to describe everything from mineral water to stubble. The desired street wear became designer-label sportswear, and the 'right' trainers – Nike, or whatever are mandatory – have taken over. Even a 'new' subcultural style such as rave culture demanded the wearing of particular trainers. And 'New Age travellers' have inspired emulation at high-street level: trend-spotters from the industry even trek to the Glastonbury festival. 'Grunge', of course, moved swiftly from the margins to couture collections and the 'dirty realism' that became so popular in fashion photography. This process of emulation and recuperation has been accompanied by an ironic development within the industry – subcultural and 'street' prediction, if you like. Massive corporations such as Nike employ self-styled 'cool consultants' – young people whose task it is to patrol the streets, see what the 'coolest kids' are currently buying and discuss with them their future wants, in order to have them available for purchase. The notion of fashion-as-subversion surely takes a knock here.

And the industry provides plenty of other very real problems that feminists should – and must – consider. The entire process – the cycle of prediction, design, manufacturing, retailing, advertising and consumption – is problematic for feminists. How can positive thought about fashion avoid the risk of colluding with the oppression of women? Fashionable clothes in the developed world are often produced in sweatshops where underpaid women, frequently from ethnic minorities, work in cramped and sometimes very dangerous conditions. Or they may be the products of the deplorably paid 'outworkers' – women working at home, paid at risible rates for skilled work. More and more, Western manufacturers depend for production on the Far East, where labour can be rewarded with a pittance and workers are not only female, but female children. Angela McRobbie's intervention, first published as an article in *Feminist Review* (June 1997) and later reprinted in her book on the 'culture industry' (McRobbie 1999) was a timely reminder that in the flourishing debates about consumption, production had seemingly disappeared from the agenda, together with any mention of poverty – the inability to survive, let alone to consume. And yet so much of the labour force within the fashion industries is female – the menial labour, that is. McRobbie focuses on the garment and retail industry in this country, and emphasises also the growing poverty in this country which makes the consumption of fashion a total impossibility for so many women. Frequently, women with very little if any disposable income have sole responsibility for bringing up a family; any luxuries that they can afford will be purchased for their children. She discusses, too, the working conditions of the shop assistant, strangely absent, as she notes, from recent feminist debates around shopping. She calls for 'greater integration across the production/consumption divide' (McRobbie 1997/1999) and for the development of policies to make this sector a better workplace for women and children.

McRobbie followed the first article with a book which set out to scrutinise the British fashion industry. Here she not only traces the career pathways of young fashion designers, but describes the workings of the linked 'image industries' – the fashion magazines and the fashion press who operate 'within an economy of looking' (McRobbie 1998: 172). She outlines the contribution of journalists, editors and stylists. Interestingly, she blames the 'celebratory' style of mainstream fashion journalism for helping to reinforce the 'marginalised, trivial image of fashion' which 'only serves to keep fashion journalism in the ghetto of femininity, while in almost every other sector of public life femininity and gender issues are increasingly coming to occupy the political centre stage' (McRobbie 1998: 174).

This, together with her necessary, pragmatic calls for legislation designed to safeguard those women working within the low-paid, higher-risk sectors of the industry, is another much-needed reminder that we should not simply be discussing these issues within the academy. As Braidotti (1991) stresses in her essay on Irigaray, a commitment to and involvement in the practical struggles of women's lives is vital for the feminist academic. Irigaray, she reminds us, concludes her theory of difference in 'a defence of feminism as a political movement' (Braidotti 1991: 251). Irigaray, after all, was formerly an advisor to the Italian Communist Party.

But the fashion industry does not only involve the manufacture of garments. It is now an enormous and complex industry with a number of interlocking sectors. One of the problems, of course, has been that academic discussion has not always looked at the sector as a totality. The existence of, say, fashion forecasters and the entire workings of the 'prediction' sector are not even recognised; the work of stylists, make-up artists and hairdressers has been virtually ignored within cultural studies debates, even those around fashion photography. So, too, has the fact that seemingly ephemeral garments are the end-product of a solidly established, eighteen-month-to-two-year cycle which begins, say, with dye consultants and manufacturers involved in the dyeing process, and moves on through fabric fairs to a final selection of fabrics – and only then to the design, manufacture and retailing of clothes.

The fashion industry, which depends for its success on the mass circulation of images of women, has perhaps to admit responsibility for a very particular sort of image, targeted primarily at women – the image of the young woman of excessively slender build. There must be some appropriate recognition within the world of fashion of the recent alarming increases in anorexia and especially in bulimia. Some feminist studies of eating disorders minimise the links with the fashionable image, focusing mainly on the renunciation of sexuality involved – but as Lorraine Gamman explains in chapter 4 of this anthology, although fashion is not responsible for anorexia and bulimia, it doesn't help.

Attempts to contest the dominant images within the fashion media seem merely to take on a novelty value. The iconography of fashion still excludes the non-slim, those no longer young, those who are not 'able-bodied', and there is, still, even today a predominance of white faces.[3] The process of exclusion finds its apotheosis in the phenomenon of the supermodel, where what is involved seems to be actually a double gesture of patriarchy. On the one hand, supermodels are fantastic creations: women of unusual height, of slimness that is in some cases almost prepubescent, but often possessed of the breasts of a mature woman, presumably as a result of silicone implants. They are so successfully marketed that they have fed through into mainstream, non-fashion journalism, where their private lives are lovingly chronicled. On the other hand, the actual women are palpably manipulated and often, perhaps, damaged in the process. Thus, in the case of the supermodel, patriarchy triumphs twice over women. Women might seem, often and in so many ways, to be in fashionspeak, 'victims' of the very industry which not only employs many of them, and clothes all of them, but which paradoxically can provide so much, harmless, guilt-free and specifically female pleasure.

I don't see why it can't be acknowledged that these are areas of concern for feminists without there being a wholesale embargo on our participation in, and examination of, the 'performance art' that is fashion. Kaja Silverman suggests the creative recycling of second-hand clothes – as a feminist solution (Silverman 1986). While we may be very happy to do this, it doesn't prevent the industry from continuing the relentless production–consumption cycle of the new. So what might be a possible way forward? For a start, there must be more informed feminist writing about fashion. It should be foregrounded, not ignored or glossed over. There should be more specifically feminist investigation of under-researched areas; one example might be the collective, ritual nature of so much fashion-related behaviour – women shopping together, trying on clothes together, painting each other's faces and nails, doing each other's hair, in private and public spaces. 'Fashion' can play a particular role in intergenerational rituals. Natasha Walter's book, although journalistic in style and content, does at least acknowledge this arena of collective female pleasure (Walter 1998: 47–9). Now that it is at least voiced by some – albeit in a rather tentative way – that women do not necessarily dress with men in mind, the resultant compression and confusion around 'femininity', sexuality and fashion must be thoroughly examined. There must, finally, be more overt recognition of the very real social problems and ideological tensions that are raised in this essay – surely they should be central to any feminist study of fashion. To ignore pragmatic questions – and to overlook these theoretical difficulties between feminists – is to ensure that the practical problems, and the nagging sources of conflict, remain. Women working in certain parts of the industry will stay in danger and discomfort, while within the academy the tensions will erupt from time to time, often in a disturbing way.

Lastly, a particular style of writing is needed which can encompass all this. Braidotti (1994) calls for 'a new kind of theoretical style, which involves "trans-disciplinarity" and which has as a particular feature "the mixture of speaking voices or modes"'. It rejects the traditional division between the 'logos-intensive' and 'pathos-intensive' discourses and attempts to mix the 'theoretical with the poetic and lyrical mode'. She explains that in her writing she rejects the 'functionalism' of language in which she was trained as a philosophy student: 'I would much rather fictionalize my theories, theorize my fictions and practise philosophy as a form of conceptual creativity.' She goes on to talk of the 'collective project of feminism', and the strategy of quotation citations as advocated, post-Derrida, by Gayatri Spivak: 'Letting others speak in my text is not only a way of inscribing my work in a collective political movement, it is also a way of practising what I preach.' Finally, her project involves a 'critique of the conventional distinction between "high" theory and "low" culture' (Braidotti 1994: 36–8).

Although Braidotti herself has not discussed fashion – presumably she is not at all interested – it does seem to me that her particular mode of discourse, a varied style ranging across disciplines, which is also exemplified in the cultural writings of Meaghan Morris, would be the mode in which to conduct any future feminist consideration of fashion. The spaces in which these debates might take place are also problematic – which genres and what medium might provide a forum for these dialogues? Academic writing, as I have intimated, does not necessarily reach the widest possible constituency – but could a debate of this nature take place within mass journalism? Should it coexist within the popular press, women's magazines and academic publishing? This may sound utopian and fanciful, while attempts to straddle divides have not always been successful. Elaine Showalter published an article 'The Professor Wore Prada' which called for an end to the academic rejection of the pleasures afforded by fashion. Unfortunately, it was published in this country in *Woman's Journal* – not the most suitable forum, given its claimed reader profile (Showalter 1998).

Finally, I would suggest that if we are going to produce a new, materialist mode of theorising fashion, that mode must have two sides, must of necessity be dialectical. Fredric Jameson argues that a dialectical analysis of postmodern culture is '"beyond good and evil" in the sense of some easy taking of sides' and he goes on:

> The point is that we are *within* the culture of postmodernism to the point where its facile repudiation is as impossible as any equally facile celebration of it is complacent and corrupt. Ideological judgement on postmodernism necessarily implies . . . a judgement on ourselves as well as the artefacts in question; nor can an entire historical period, such as our own, be grasped in any adequate way by means of global moral judgements.
>
> (Jameson 1991: 62)

I'm suggesting that a feminist theory of fashion today needs to position itself somewhere between what Jameson calls celebration and repudiation – or in an oscillation between them.

Notes

1   In the British General Election of 1997, a record number of women were elected as Members of Parliament. To ensure popularity with the electorate, they were instructed to dress for their public appearances in a particular way – in smart jackets of a bright colour. When they gathered together for a photocall in the aftermath of the election, one astringent right-wing journalist wrote that they resembled 'a convention of Avon ladies' (Lynda Lee-Potter, *Daily Mail*, 1997).

2   There are, as Christopher Breward has suggested, interesting parallels to be made here with materialist discussion of femininity and decoration – he mentions the work of Sparke, Carter and Wigley White Wallis.

3   The attempts by certain photographers to use older or larger models are notable, and noticeable, because they are the exceptions to prevalent norms, whilst among the most highly paid models, only a handful are dark-skinned. Steven Meisel has used older models, as has Nick Knight – the latter has also put an unknown girl who was a size 16, on the cover of Vogue. He also collaborated with Alexander McQueen on the 'Fashion-able' issue of *Dazed and Confused* of October 1998. Here a number of people who were not 'able-bodied' took part, as volunteers, in a fashion shoot where designers made clothes to their exact specifications and Knight photographed them for the pages of the magazine.

References

Braidotti, Rosi (1991) *Patterns of Dissonance: A Study of Women in Contemporary Philosophy*, Cambridge: Polity Press.

—— (1994) *Nomadic Subjects: Embodiment and Sexual Difference in Contemporary Feminist Theory*, New York: Columbia University Press.

Butler, Judith (1990) *Gender Trouble: Feminism and the Subversion of Identity*, London: Routledge.

Coward, Rosalind (1992) *Our Treacherous Hearts: Why Women Let Men Get Their Way*, London: Faber & Faber.

Craik, Jennifer (1994) *The Face of Fashion: Cultural Studies in Fashion*, London: Routledge.

Evans, Caroline and Thornton, Minna (1989) *Women and Fashion: A New Look*, London: Quartet Books.

Fiske, John (1989a) *Understanding Popular Culture*, London: Unwin Hyman.

—— (1989b) *Reading the Popular*, London: Unwin Hyman.

Greer, Germaine (1971) *The Female Eunuch*, London: Paladin.

—— (1999) *The Whole Woman*, London: Paladin.

Hall, Stuart and Jefferson, Tony (eds) (1976) *Resistance through Rituals: Youth Subcultures in Postwar Britain*, London: Hutchinson.

Hebdige, Dick (1979) *Subculture: The Meaning of Style*, London: Methuen.

Irigaray, Luce (1985) *This Sex Which is Not One*, Ithaca, NY: Cornell University Press.

Jameson, Fredric (1991) *Postmodernism, or the Cultural Logic of Late Capitalism*, London: Verso.

Le Doeuff, Michèle (1989) *L'Étude et le rouet: des femmes, de la philosophie, etc.*, Paris: Éditions du Seuil.

McRobbie, Angela (1997) 'Bridging the gap: feminism, fashion and consumption', *Feminist Review*, Spring, 55: 73–89.

—— (1998) *British Fashion Design: Rag Trade or Image Industry?*, London: Routledge.

—— (1999) *In the Culture Industry: Art, Music, Fashion*, London: Routledge.

Morris, Meaghan (1988) *The Pirate's Fiancée: Feminism, Reading, Postmodernism*, London: Verso.

Radcliffe Richards, Janet (1982) *The Sceptical Feminist: A Philosophical Enquiry*, (Harmondsworth: Penguin). (First published 1980, London: Routledge & Kegan Paul.)

Showalter, Elaine (1998) 'The Professor Wore Prada', *Woman's Journal*, June.

Silverman, Kaja (1986) 'Fragments of a fashionable discourse', in Tania Modleski (ed.) *Studies in Entertainment: Critical Approaches to Mass Culture*, Bloomington, Ind: Indiana University Press.

Walter, Natasha (1998) *The New Feminism*, London: Little, Brown.

Wilson, Elizabeth (1985) *Adorned in Dreams: Fashion and Modernity*, London: Virago.

—— (1990) 'These new components of the spectacle: fashion and postmodernism' in Roy Boyne and Ali Rattansi (eds) *Postmodernism and Society*, Basingstoke: Macmillan.

—— (1992) 'Fashion and the postmodern body' in Juliet Ash and Elizabeth Wilson (eds) *Chic Thrills: A Fashion Reader*, Berkeley: University of California Press.

Chapter 26

Clare Lomas

'I KNOW NOTHING ABOUT FASHION. THERE'S NO POINT IN INTERVIEWING ME'

The use and value of oral history to the fashion historian

ANYBODY WORKING IN THE FIELD of fashion or film, knowingly or unknowingly, relies very heavily on undocumented sources. After a period during which the voices of 'ordinary people' were rejected by professional/ academic researchers, the importance of oral history has begun to be acknowledged in the humanities and it is now being recognised as a valuable research tool for accessing first-hand experience. Researchers in the field of dress and textiles have realised its value and over the last ten years have used oral testimony to great effect. This chapter intends briefly to discuss the origins of oral history and reference some specific texts which deal with the achievements and problems associated with the use of oral history; it will also highlight some case studies of work involving oral testimony in dress and textiles.

Oral history has grown in academic value from its early developments as a form of 'democratic' history. Groups which found it most beneficial were those that found it gave them a 'voice' and offered a form of empowerment, such as women's groups, ethnic minorities, gay and lesbian groups, and local and family historians. For example, the Gay Men's Oral History Group, in collaboration with the Hall-Carpenter Archives,[1] published *Walking after Midnight: Gay Men's Life Stories* (Hall-Carpenter/Gay Men's Oral History 1989). The introduction states:

> Oral history, which is found in memory and not in documents, can uncover much which is hidden, neglected or dismissed by the traditional focus of history. By recording the personal and political events which have shaped the lives of people whose experiences are not normally recorded by official history, we become the active participants

of our own history and have more control over its interpretation. A richer more intimate picture of the past can be revealed, not only for ourselves, but to share with others.

(Hall-Carpenter/Gay Men's Oral History 1989: 1)

The achievements of oral history as well as the practical elements of ethics and copyright, the planning of an interview, and the number of people needed to represent adequately a certain period of time have been written about extensively[2] and as with any oral history projects, these elements are essential to protect both the interviewee or respondent and the interviewer and their work. Other considerations, such as what the material will be used for, are also extremely important and need to be agreed upon. For example, it should be established at the outset, whether the interviewee or respondent will have any further input after the initial interview takes place. Problems and conflict have arisen when the interviewee or respondent feels that 'their' narrative is not being used and represented as they wished.[3] There is also the role of the interviewer to be considered. Oral historian Mary Stuart (1993) discusses sharing one's own memories and states that 'the interview process is an intimate one. We are all aware as oral historians that we are sharing personal experiences. This process cannot be one way' (Stuart 1993: 82).

What then can oral history give to fashion historians or those interested in the history of dress and textiles? I would suggest that it can offer supplementary descriptions of objects and their contexts, and provide the opportunity for historians to engage with their subjects and question their sources first hand. Second, anecdotal material which is more specific to the narrator and their own personal life stories, can often be of great significance as they make history 'come alive' for the listener. This is certainly how it appears to have been used to great effect, to document that of the everyday, such as how and why people did things and what they thought of them – to record, in other words, the voice of personal experience. This is greatly important for recording, for example, experiences of mill life before those sources are lost to us in a rapidly changing world.[4]

There are many examples of work where these questions have been addressed and it is important to cite a few of these. One example is the chapter by Angela Partington in *Chic Thrills: A Fashion Reader* (1992) in which she investigated how working-class women in the late 1940s and early 1950s used the New Look (which had a nipped-in waist, soft rounded shoulders and long full skirt) to articulate class and gender identities that were not necessarily those intended by the fashion industry or the design profession. She stated that she wanted 'to reconsider post-war femininity as a source of contradiction and conflict, by considering the working-class women's adoption of New Look fashion' (Partington 1992: 147). The working-class women she described took a design which had been produced by the dominant classes and which communicated the values of that class, and appropriated and incorporated it with the utility look (square shoulders and short straight skirts) and the shirt-waister dress (worn by the housewife or homemaker of the period). Partington used a photograph of her mother wearing Utility fashions and New Look combined, taken at the Festival of Britain, to highlight this point, and challenged the assumption that women were manipulated by consumerism. It is interesting to note that the photograph of Partington's mother which shows the Utility and New Look combined is 'read' differently by her mother who

> insists that the wide-brimmed hat was not part of the New Look Style (but only bought as a souvenir) and that the style was free and comfortable rather than restrictive and ornamental, allowing it to be worn in an 'everyday' way rather than for evenings or special occasions.
>
> (Partington 1992: 159)

It is this anecdotal piece of information which 'contradicts the assumption made by fashion historians that the New Look was inappropriate for work or active pursuits' (Partington 1992: 159). Working-class women took aspects of the two styles and adapted them to suit their own needs and it is this appropriation that gave the clothing a new set of meanings and values. By doing so, they were, according to Partington, articulating class and gender in a new way.

Barbara Burman's oral history project on home dressmaking took place in the Spring of 1995.[5] The subject of home dressmaking had been seen very much as a 'Cinderella' subject, partly due to its domestic setting. Documentary evidence does exist, for example, in department store archives such as John Lewis, and Burman had been doing 'conventional' research on the Edwardian period and the area of home dressmaking, such as studying magazines. It was this documentary evidence that highlighted developments such as improvements to the sewing machine, paper patterns and the use of popper-studs. Burman chose to use oral history because she maintained that it could capture certain aspects which other recording methods (primarily written) cannot capture, whilst giving her the opportunity to ask people who were alive at this time specific questions such as: How early did people learn to sew? How old were you when you got your first sewing machine? Where was the sewing machine kept? Questions such as these helped to establish ideas around the 'gendering' of space and the nature of activity within the home. Burman (1999) interviewed eighteen elderly ladies, which was particularly problematic as people relived very painful emotional experiences such as losing spouses and children in the World Wars. However, one of the important things that she gained from her research was that home dressmaking was linked to self-esteem and it was not, as has often been suggested, just a cheaper way of doing things.

Frank Mort uses oral testimony in *Cultures of Consumption* (1996) in a chapter entitled 'Some conversations'. Here he sets out very clearly why he uses oral testimony and describes his selection process by stating that he 'charted a number of inter-linked narratives of economy and culture – [tracing] the ways in which a specific regime of commerce generated a number of personas offered to young men in the 1980s' (Mort 1996: 183). He goes on to state that his 'exploration of gender and consumer culture demanded some engagement with the personal testimonies of the young men who participated in city life'. He then includes extracts of 'autobiographical sketches' from twenty interviews which he collected throughout 1987 in Soho and adjacent areas of London:

> These were loosely structured, taped interviews with men, aged between 16–25. The chosen age range followed one of the most significant

consumer segments identified by contemporary market research. Visual
appearance was an important criterion for interview selection . . . there
was also an attempt to nominate a sexually and ethnically mixed constituency of young men.

(Mort 1996: 185)

Mort asked these men about their lifestyle, their age, occupation, about the way
they dressed and why, and specifically why they frequented that particular area of
London (Soho) where a new consumer culture was being established. Mort uses
these testimonies to highlight that there were 'more than the established boundaries of organising and regulating men' (Mort 1996: 198).

Shaun Cole, a museum curator, has also used oral testimony in his work on
gay men's dress. In his article 'Corsair slacks and bondi bathers: Vince Man's Shop
and the beginnings of Carnaby Street fashion' (Cole 1997), he specifically set out
to look at the clothing sold at Bill Green's shop Vince in the 1950s and 1960s.
He used the methods of oral history to interview John Hardy, who was a model
for Vince's mail order clothing catalogue, and assessed why gay men shopped at
Vince and wore the continentally influenced clothing associated with the shop. This
work is expanded in his chapter in *Defining Dress*, 'Invisible men: gay men's dress
in Britain, 1950–1970' (Cole 1999) where he again uses oral history to establish
what gay men wore and the emergence of specific clothing codes, for example,
suede shoes and bright coloured socks, that were used to express sexual orientation, or how men went to great lengths to hide their homosexuality and 'pass' in
the heterosexual world before the partial decriminalisation of homosexuality in
England and Wales in 1967.

My own work using oral history has allowed me to address certain issues that
oral history raises particularly for the fashion historian.[6] Certainly, the use of oral
testimony allowed me to fill a 'gap' in the literature on contemporary menswear
which Christopher Breward highlighted in a review of Sean Nixon's book *Hard
Looks* (1996):

If *Hard Looks* were to be extended one might look for the inclusion of
other male bodies, flesh and blood ones, who did the looking, the shopping, the browsing, and the posing. Ultimately this is a book that masters
explanations for male fashion consumption and its representation whilst
leaving the consumer himself out of the picture.

(Breward 1997: 336)

My aim was to access the experiential voice of the British male. The first stage
was a pilot questionnaire, sent out to twenty men aged between 24 and 36. The
main issues I wanted the pilot questionnaire to help answer were, first, to test
whether men would respond to any of the questions, and second, to obtain an idea
of how much men knew about their own clothes. The questionnaire was completed
by post, and a stamped addressed envelope was included. However, the responses
were anonymous in the sense that names were not written on the replies.

Identification of the group was through date of birth, which ranged from 1964
to 1974, because I was particularly interested in the experiences of this age group

over the last ten years. Specifically, I was interested in the period associated with the rise of the 'new' man; and in the academic field marked by the large amount of literature written on men and masculinity following the 1987 conference, 'Men Breaking Out: A Sexual Politics for the 1990s' (Chapman and Rutherford 1988).

The lack of response from my pilot questionnaire (after a great deal of persuasion fourteen were returned between the period July 1997 and November 1997) was followed by a lack of response from the potential male interviewees, many of whom felt they knew nothing about fashion and that it was not a subject that they, as men, should be interested in; certainly it was not one they wanted to be recorded discussing. Comments such as 'I know nothing about fashion. There's no point in interviewing me!' were frequent. The 'problem' of locating men prepared to be interviewed and recorded was also an issue highlighted by Steve Humphries and Pamela Gordon in their book, *A Man's World* (1996):

> Getting men . . . to open up and talk honestly and intimately has not been easy. They are simply not used to talking about themselves and their lives in the way that women are . . . Precisely how representative or typical it is has to remain a matter of conjecture – there are just too many silences to say with certainty.
>
> (Humphries and Gordon 1996: 9)

Following this initial lack of respondents and a very tight timeframe in which to conduct my research, I successfully completed six interviews.[7] The formats for the interviews I conducted were not rigidly structured, and allowed the interviewee to elaborate on any points they wished. I also utilised responses from four Directives (which totalled a further thirteen respondents) held at the Mass-Observation Archive[8] at the University of Sussex: 'Shopping in Britain', sent out in the Summer of 1995; 'Managing Money', sent out in the Autumn/Winter of 1993; 'Clothing' sent out in the Spring of 1988; and 'Waste, Thrift and Consumerism', sent out in the Spring of 1987.

One of the first issues to be addressed arose from having all this descriptive and anecdotal information in the form of quotations from interviewees and extracts from respondents from the Mass-Observation Archive and establishing a suitable framework in which to present this material. Lunt and Livingstone's *Mass Consumption and Personal Identity* (1992) was very helpful as they had been able to outline shopper profiles and certain characteristics portrayed by each consumer 'type' from the responses they received, including the emotions experienced; for example, whether the act of shopping was a 'pleasurable' experience.

I was able to divide the information gathered from my research into five sections based on divisions from Lunt and Livingstone's investigation: the prospect and pleasure of shopping; the male shopper as a decision-maker; everyday finances and the purchasing of garments; the relation between men and their clothes; and lastly, shopping as a 'gendered' experience. Within these five categories, I was also able to weave in some information from the pilot questionnaire and from the M-O A Directives. The findings of the research project were qualitative rather than quantitative. However, what they did highlight was the variety of opinions and views held by six men between the ages of 26 and 34 years, living in the

Greater London area, and consequently the difficulties in categorising consumers. The interviewees and correspondents had their own strategies for acquiring clothing yet rejected the broader idea of fashion consumption which they strongly linked to femininity.

In conclusion, oral testimony provides an insight into personal lives and, as Paul Thompson (1978) suggests, it does 'illuminate ordinary experience', particularly that which is highly descriptive and full of anecdotal material but which is so often ignored by the history books of dress and textiles – those that document the successful fashion designers and shops, and chart the changing silhouettes and length of hemlines, but leave the all-important consumer out of the picture. By accessing the voice of 'ordinary' people, the interviewer can 'engage' with history, question sources first-hand before those valuable sources are lost, whilst also raising many issues pertaining to the value of both the spoken and written word.

Acknowledgements

The author would like to acknowledge the oral history module which is part of the MA History of Textiles and Dress, Winchester School of Art, Southampton University, and particularly Dr Judy Attfield, Barbara Burman and Dr Lesley Miller. The author would also like to thank Dr Christopher Breward for his helpful comments.

Notes

1   Hall-Carpenter Archives, the national gay archive, is named after the authors Marguerite Radclyffe Hall and Edward Carpenter, and contains organisation records of various gay and lesbian groups and periodicals (stored at the British Library of Political Economy and Science at the London School of Economics), a press cutting collection (housed at the Art and Design Library at Middlesex University) and taped interviews (stored at the National Sound Archive at the British Library).

2   Those who are interested in oral history should refer to publications such as: S. Caunce, *Oral History and the Local Historian*, London, Longman, 1994; D. Henige, *Oral Historiography*, London, Longman, 1982; S. Humphries, *The Handbook of Oral History: Recording Life Stories*, London, Inter-Action Inprint, 1984; P. Thompson, *The Voice of the Past*, Oxford, Oxford University Press, 1978; P. Thompson and R. Perks *Telling It How It Was: A Guide to Recording Oral History*, London, BBC Education (n.d.); J. Tosh, 'History by Word of Mouth', in John Tosh, *The Pursuit of History: Aims, Methods and New Directions in the Study of Modern History*, London, Longman, 1999, 193–210; A. Ward, *Copyright Ethics and Oral History*, Essex, Oral History Society, 1995.

3   There are two articles which are valuable in highlighting this. First, L. Echevarria-Howe. 'Reflections from the participants: the process and product of life history work', *Oral History*, 1995, 23 (2):40–6, which highlights how the author took her work back to the field and had her participants' full agreement on how she intended to use their life stories for a future publication and educational purposes rather than the thesis she was working on at the time. The author sent copies

of the transcripts for their corrections, additions and comments and gave them both copies of their tapes as well as sharing her interpretation. The author considered that this exchange was a critical part of the work. Second, K. Borland, '"That's not what I said": interpretative conflict in oral narrative research' in S. Gluck and D. Patai (eds), *Women's Words: The Feminist Practice of Oral History*, London, Routledge, 1991, 63–75. This text highlights a very different response from an interviewee. It is a case study in the variability of the meaning in personal narrative, Borland, feminist, states in her text:

> For feminists the issue of interpretative authority is particularly problematic, for our work often involves contradiction. On the one hand, we seek to empower the women we work with by re-evaluating their perspectives, their lives and their art in a world that has systematically ignored or trivialised women's culture. On the other, we hold an explicitly political vision of the structural conditions that lead to particular social behaviours, a vision that our field collaborators, many of whom do not consider themselves feminists, may not recognise as valid. My own work with my grandmother's race track narrative provides a vivid example of how conflicts of interpretation may, perhaps inevitably do, arise during folklore transmission process. What should we do when women disagree.
>
> (Borland 1991: 64)

4   For example, O. Howarth (ed.), *Textile Voices: Mill Life this Century*, Bradford: Recording Unit/Bradford Libraries and Information Service, 1989.

5   This information was taken from the lecture given by Barbara Burman, Winchester School of Art (28/2/1997) and B. Burman, 'Made at home by clever fingers: home dressmaking in Edwardian England', in B. Burman (ed.), *The Culture of Sewing: Gender, Consumption and Home Dressmaking*, Oxford, Berg, 1999.

6   Unpublished MA dissertation, Clare Lomas, 'Inside Leg, Outside Gear' Winchester School of Art, Southampton University, 1998.

7   The minimum number of interviewees required for a project has been debated. However, Esther Newton suggests that 'To describe adequately a given historical period, between five and ten narrators' stories need to be juxtaposed in order to develop an analysis that is not changed dramatically by each new story', (Newton 1993: 304).

8   The Mass-Observation Archive (M-O A) is stored at Library at the University of Sussex. Mass-Observation initially began in the 1950s. The 'correspondents' for the M-O A were (and still are) self-selected volunteers, recruited through the national newspapers. The 1980s/1990s project is

> the second phase [which] began in 1981. Professor David Pocock and Mass-Observation archivist Dorothy Sheridan recruited people from all parts of the UK to write about their lives either in the form of a diary or more often in the form of detailed replies to questions on specific themes [called a 'Directive']. Since 1981 an enormous amount of written information about life in the UK has been accumulating including over 400,000 pages of hand written material representing a combined contribution of 2,500 volunteers.
>
> (Bloome *et al.* 1993: 3)

References

Bloome, D., Sheridan, D. and Street, B. (1993) *Reading Mass-Observation Writing: Theoretical and Methodological Issues in Researching Mass-Observation Archive*, Sussex: University of Sussex.

Borland, K. (1991) '"That's not what I said": interpretative conflict in oral narrative research' in S. Gluck and D. Patai (eds) *Women's Words: The Feminist Practice of Oral History*, London: Routledge, 63–75.

Breward, C. (1997) *Journal of Design History*, 10 (3): 336.

Burman, B. (ed.) (1999) *The Culture of Sewing: Gender, Consumption and Home Dressmaking*, Oxford: Berg.

Chapman, R. and Rutherford, J. (ed.) (1988) *Male Order: Unwrapping Masculinity*, London: Lawrence & Wishart.

Cole, S. (1997) 'Corsair slacks and Bondi bathers: Vince Man's Shop and the beginnings of Carnaby Street fashion', *Things*, Summer, 6: 26–39.

—— (1999) 'Invisible men: gay men's dress in Britain, 1950–1970', in A. de la Haye and E. Wilson, *Defining Dress: Dress as Object, Meaning and Identity*, Manchester: Manchester University Press, 143–54.

Echevarria-Howe, L. (1995) 'Reflections from the participants: the process and product of life history work', *Oral History*, 23 (2): 40–6.

Hall-Carpenter Archives/Gay Men's Oral History Group (1989) *Walking After Midnight: Gay Men's Life Stories*, London: Routledge.

Humphries, S. and Gordon, P. (1996) *A Man's World: From Boyhood to Manhood, 1900–1960*, London: BBC.

Lunt, P. and Livingstone, S. (1992) *Mass Consumption and Personal Experience*, Buckingham: Open University Press.

Mort, F. (1996) *Cultures of Consumption: Masculinities and Social Space in Late Twentieth-Century Britain*, London: Routledge.

Newton, E. (1993) *Cherry Grove, Fire Island: Sixty Years in America's First Gay and Lesbian Town*, Boston: Beacon Press.

Nixon, S. (1996) *Hard Looks*, London: UCL Press.

Partington, A. (1992) 'Popular fashion and working-class affluence', in E. Wilson and J. Ash (eds) *Chic Thrills: A Fashion Reader*, London: Pandora Press.

Stuart, M. (1993) '"And how was it for you Mary?" Self, identity and meaning for oral historians', *Oral History*, 21 (2): 80–3.

Thompson, P. (1978) *The Voice of the Past*, Oxford: Oxford University Press.

Chapter 27

Fiona Anderson

MUSEUMS AS FASHION MEDIA

Introduction

THE 1990S SAW THE MOVEMENT of fashion into hitherto unlikely venues. Museums and galleries with their own specialist focus such as the Imperial War Museum and the fine art-based Hayward Gallery in London, held major exhibitions of dress for the first time. This period also saw the consolidation of the 'new' fashion history and the 'new' museology, both of which have had far-reaching implications for the study, interpretation and display of fashion. In broad terms these changes have involved a greater emphasis on analysing the meanings invoked by cultural objects and practices and a questioning of traditional approaches and methodologies. Published research which comments on the overlap between these disciplinary shifts has been minimal, despite the vibrant activity around fashion in museums and galleries and a flood of academic publications involving both of the above-mentioned disciplines. In this chapter I wish to extend debate in that area, which I hope will encourage further publication.

The increased academic focus on fashion has principally occurred within Britain, the USA and to a lesser extent France and Australia. Although this study embraces an awareness of the significance and influence of developments within this wider context, it must necessarily follow a narrower remit. Due to the specificity of the historical development of museum practice in Britain and the interlinked importance of the art school system to the role of museums which display dress, the chapter will primarily focus on the British context.

The chapter will look at three case studies of museums and galleries in London, namely, the Victoria and Albert Museum (V&A); the Judith Clark Costume Gallery; and the Hussein Chalayan 'Echo Form' exhibition held at the Atlantis Gallery in 1999. These have been selected in order to compare and contrast the approaches taken by a leading national museum, a small independent gallery, and a designer who co-curated an exhibition of his own work. This choice has allowed the examination of approaches developed from traditional museological practice and also that of more experimental approaches firmly located outside of traditional curatorial contexts, but similarly located within the contemporary fashion system. There are not only marked similarities between the methods revealed in the chosen case studies, but also the need to acknowledge the intermingling influences of both academic and commercial ideas and practices. I shall finally examine the broader question of how museums and galleries as forms of media engage with, and contribute to, the complex circulation of visual and textual information involved in the contemporary fashion system.

These issues are explored through interviews with curators and with reference to museology, dress history, cultural studies, sociology and material culture texts. The chapter will also draw on my experiences as a curator and lecturer of fashion.

Museums as fashion media – context and convergence

In the 1980s, and more particularly the 1990s, there was a substantial climate of change within British museums. This new climate was partly the result of changing governmental attitudes, which in turn stimulated anxieties about funding and declining visitor numbers. Eilean Hooper-Greenhill in *Museum, Media, Message* (1995) expresses the profound level which the concern had reached: 'If museums are not seen and felt to be part of the daily life of society, they will not survive' (Hooper-Greenhill 1995: 2). This pressure to 'survive' led in the 1990s to the adoption of marketing strategies, marketing language and a more corporate culture, even within publicly funded museums. The need to address an 'audience', to target specific social groups, carry out visitor surveys, and evaluate the success of the range of a museum's activities, have all become fundamental parts of the climate in which many curators of dress are working. However, not all of these shifts had their origins in the commercial sphere: academic research methodologies, in particular those taken from media studies, cultural studies and ethnography, played a significant role in changing the way museums worked in the 1990s (Hooper-Greenhill 1995; MacDonald 1998). This influx of ideas has led to the focus of current museological debate being not just on how museums work, but on a more fundamental level, what they are and what they should be in order to be relevant for the twenty-first century.

A key part of these debates is the identification of museums as media, which raises the question of how museums are distinct from other types of media. This will be examined by exploring how museums and galleries engage with, and contribute to, the fast-moving circulation of information involved in the contemporary fashion system.

Fashion is surely *the* fastest changing source of new ideas in contemporary visual culture. It also has widespread popular appeal; even designer-level fashion has much greater accessibility than the equivalent products, images and texts of equivalent designer industries. The editorial of *The Face* in August 1997 stresses this appeal and highlights some of the potential opportunities and problems which curators of fashion face:

> Many people have been paying fashion more and more attention through-out this fast, bright, jumbled-up decade. . . . Thanks to the designer boom, oft-controversial fashion photography, in the form of adverts, now looms large in our towns and cities. Catwalk shows are no longer the province of the cognoscenti, but staple light-entertainment fare. Reporters analyse the shows and the stories and turn them into news, so often that we now think nothing of seeing a story about a model's age or weight on the front page of a national newspaper. All this means that fashion has now accrued all the celebrities, merchandising, empty spectacle, dubious morality and media coverage that it now takes to become a fully-fledged entertainment medium.
>
> (*The Face*, August 1997: 18)

These views underline key issues relating to the display of contemporary fashion in museum contexts, notably the consideration of fashion as entertainment and the persistence of the historically negative moral associations of fashion. They also high-light the central role of the body and the image to contemporary fashion design and the public's day-to-day engagement with the fashion system.

Paul Greenhalgh in his essay, 'Education, Entertainment and Politics' (Greenhalgh 1989) discusses the entertainment versus education dichotomy in rela-tion to the Great Exhibitions of the late nineteenth and early twentieth centuries. Although the origins of his argument are foregrounded in a specific historical context, his comments are extremely illuminating regarding the contemporary scenario. He states in relation to the aforementioned exhibitions: 'The separation of education from entertainment in Britain was emblematic of the divide between work and pleasure and as such it had been a seminal issue for moralists throughout the nineteenth century' (Greenhalgh 1989: 86). He further elaborates on these tensions with reference to the ideas of the utilitarian John Stuart Mill who had:

> agonised endlessly over the relation between what he termed the higher and lower pleasures. The higher pleasures represented the arts, human-ities and all areas of human endeavour; the lower pleasures were associated with the base functions, including sexual activity.
>
> (Greenhalgh 1989: 86)

Fashion, then, occupied a precarious position between its status on the one hand as a creative product of labour and an illustration of the good taste of its wearer, and on the other that invoked by its intrinsic relationship to the body, which solidly damned it as linked to the base, the sexual and most definitely the 'lower pleasures'. The social and cultural shifts which have led to the current postmodern epoch, have significantly raised the cultural status of fashion and trans-formed connotations of the body, and pleasure generally, into largely positive ones (Wilson 1992; Featherstone 1991). However, it is notable that the editor of *The Face* magazine, a publication at the cutting-edge of postmodern youth culture, should comment on fashion as 'empty spectacle' and symptomatic of 'dubious morality', terms John Stuart Mill would have applauded.

This highlights the complexities and contradictions which persist in our culture around perceptions of the fashioned body and the fashion industry. These contradictions are starkly apparent in some museums, which represents the persistence of what might appear as an outmoded ideological battle between 'high culture' and popular culture, or what may also be presented as the education versus entertainment (or pleasure) dichotomy discussed by Greenhalgh. Prejudice, fear and suspicion still surround the status of fashion within many museums and galleries. This sometimes takes the form of fashion being tolerated as a form of 'entertainment' which will 'pull the crowds', with no acknowledgement of the serious contribution it also makes to the educational role of the museum.

The larger picture is, however, extremely positive; fashion now has a higher profile within international museums and galleries than ever before. Even more encouraging is that many new developments in the curatorship of contemporary fashion indicate that ideological barriers around the status of fashion continue to be broken down in a most deliberate and exciting manner. Some notable British examples of this include work done at Brighton Museum and Art Gallery, the National Maritime Museum at Greenwich and those quoted in my three case studies.

Recent developments within the university-based study of dress have led to a multiplicity of new approaches to the study of fashion. Key to many of these diverse approaches has been an increased focus on representation and the body and a shift of emphasis from production to consumption. The arguments of the sociologist Mike Featherstone, in *The Body in Consumer Culture*, neatly encapsulate how these debates have legitimised the concept of the fashioned body as a site for serious cultural analysis. He states:

> Consumer culture imagery and advertising cannot be dismissed as merely 'entertainment', something which individuals do not take seriously. . . . Individuals may of course choose to ignore or neglect their appearance and refuse to cultivate a performing self, yet if they do so they must be prepared to face the implications of this choice within social encounters.
>
> (Featherstone 1991: 192)

This new body of research has influenced many British art school trained fashion designers, through tuition in either cultural studies or design history. A similar period has also seen shifts in the international fashion industry and in education, whereby a designer's remit increasingly includes not just thinking about garments, but also about their associated imagery and advertising. In tandem with these complex and interlinking developments, the work of museums and galleries engages directly with that of contemporary designers and design students through displaying and inspiring their work. These links and the efforts of curators to make their practice reflect on external intellectual, commercial and educational developments, has meant that museums and galleries not only have been profoundly influenced by but have also actively contributed to the above-mentioned developments.

The involvement of curators with the fashion industry has traditionally been more complex than that of university or college-based academics, who tend to comment from a safely demarcated distance. The broad and diverse publics addressed by curators and the nature of their exhibition and display work mean that (as Valerie Steele, Chief Curator at the Museum at the Fashion Institute of Technology in New York, noted in a recent article) they have often been accused of outright commercialism (Steele 1998: 334). She quotes from a critic of the Costume Institute at the Metropolitan Museum in New York: 'Fusing the Yin and Yang of vanity and cupidity, the Yves Saint Laurent show was the equivalent of turning gallery space over to General Motors for a display of Cadillacs' (Storr cited in Steele 1998). It is undeniable that the motivations of designers to co-operate with curators in having their work displayed in museums are largely about prestige, self-promotion and profit. This, allied with the fact that fashion designers are understandably fiercely protective of their all-important brand image, presents curators with persistent and sometimes delicate realities to negotiate. However, despite the complexities of this scenario, scholarly curatorial work must embrace an acknowledgement of the commercial character of the fashion industry. Attempts to avoid or eliminate this aspect will only lead backwards to approaches which decontextualise objects (Saumarez Smith 1989: 19).

Object and image?

Within museums and galleries approaches to dress have traditionally differed according to the overall focus of the institution, whether that be social history, military history, science and technology, ethnography, or the connoisseurial approaches one associates with museums of fine or applied art. What unites the treatment of dress within most museums and galleries is that it has generally focused around the study of garments as objects. In 1997, a conference called 'Dress in History: Studies and Approaches' was held at the Gallery of Costume, Platt Hall, Manchester. Several of the conference papers which were later published, in a special 'Methodology' issue of *Fashion Theory* (1998, vol. 2 issue 4), placed the object-based study of dress as a contentious issue, which has been at the centre of debates on 'old' and 'new' approaches to fashion history.

Lou Taylor's paper in that journal 'Doing the laundry? A reassessment of object-based dress history', and Naomi Tarrant's book *The Development of Costume* (1996) embrace a full historical account of the development of object-based approaches to dress in British museums, so I will not repeat those points here. However, it is worth stressing that much of the upsurge in academic work on fashion has been influenced by cultural studies approaches which focus on representation and linguistic texts. These have therefore been to some extent at odds with object-based approaches. Criticism of object-based approaches taken by museums has centred around the traditionally empirical, descriptive nature of the study of dress in those institutions, and has largely been presented as coming only from those engaged in 'new' fashion history. However, I would argue that the fact that many of these criticisms have been taken on board by curators has also been due to the rise of the 'new' museology, which similarly focuses on more sophisticated analytical approaches. The rise in material culture and design historical methodologies with their predominant focus on objects, has played a significant role in these shifts. To an extent, approaches from these disciplines have crossed over directly into 'new' museological theory and practice. Evidence of this is contained in Valerie Steele's article 'A museum of fashion is more than a clothes bag', in which she expresses her belief in the value of material culture methodologies to the study of fashion. She states:

> Because intellectuals live by the word, many scholars tend to ignore the important role that objects can play in the creation of knowledge. Even many fashion historians spend little or no time examining actual garments, preferring to rely exclusively on written sources and visual representations. Yet of all the methodologies used to study fashion history, one of the most valuable is the interpretation of objects. Naturally, scholars must also employ standard historical research methods (working in the library), but object-based research provides unique insights into the historic and aesthetic development of fashion.
> (Steele 1998: 327)

The study of garments can indeed be extremely valuable, but images, whether paintings, drawings or photographs, are objects too. The use of representations and a focus on garments as objects need not be contradictory, but can in fact be highly complementary and even revelatory. For example, placing garments produced by a designer like Calvin Klein alongside one of his advertisements gives a much more thought-provoking context to his work than if the garments were displayed by themselves. It also provides opportunities to relate directly to the wider public's daily experience of high-level designer fashion, which is most usually through images rather than the garments themselves. Despite the validity of approaches that focus exclusively on garments as objects, this is not necessarily the best approach to each and every display.

The Victoria and Albert Museum: tradition and postmodernity

The Victoria and Albert Museum is the national museum of art and design in Britain and has one of the leading dress collections in the world. In addition to a permanent display of dress, it also organises major temporary exhibitions and smaller displays of fashion. Since its founding in 1852, the V&A has enjoyed many innovations, yet it retains the legacy of its origins as a nineteenth-century decorative arts museum (Burton 1999).

The history of the role of dress within the V&A has been well documented by Lou Taylor in 'Doing the laundry' (Taylor 1998), in which she notes that the museum has always collected dress, yet only in a minor way until the 1950s. Taylor attributes this to the fact that: 'In the eyes of male museum staff, fashionable dress still only evoked notions of vulgar commerciality and valueless, ephemeral, feminine style' (Taylor 1998: 341).

A principal emphasis on historical dress was retained until 1971, when 'The exhibition "Fashion: an Anthology" organised by Sir Cecil Beaton at the request of the then Director Sir John Pope Hennessey' firmly established the role of the Museum as a collector and exhibitor of contemporary fashion (interview with Valerie Mendes, 1/3/00). Since that time the collection of dress has grown according to the Textile and Dress Department's policy to 'collect design which leads'. This has involved a predominant emphasis on designer-level fashion, though prior to the 1993 'Streetstyle' exhibition the execution of this policy was adapted to acknowledge the external realities that style is not universally led from the catwalk down (Mendes *et al.* 1992: 1).

Recent major display initiatives have included the 'Streetstyle' exhibition (1994) and the 'Cutting Edge: Fifty Years of British Fashion 1947–1997' exhibition (1997), both of which were curated by Amy de la Haye, who was then the curator responsible for post-1900 fashion. These exhibitions embraced new theoretical ideas on subcultural dress and post-war masculine fashionable consumption, thus reflecting the responsive approach expressed by Valerie Mendes, Chief Curator of the Textiles and Dress Collection at the V&A:

> While we have a pathway largely determined by the policies and thrust of an enormous and wide-ranging Decorative Arts Museum, we are inevitably influenced by developments and innovations in the world of academe and the ever-changing face of the international fashion industry and fashion press. We are not afraid of welcoming in and learning from commercial concerns.
>
> (Interview with V. Mendes, 1/3/00)

A range of exciting new developments within the V&A illustrate further this openness to new ideas. Their radical nature forms a direct assault on any lingering nineteenth-century notions that education and entertainment within museums are always separate and antithetical concerns. The recent projects which I now wish to discuss in further detail are 'Fashion in Motion' (Figure 27.1) and 'Wear on the Street'. Both were devised by Claire Wilcox, the curator currently responsible for post-1900 fashion at the V&A, who describes the first initiative thus:

> 'Fashion in Motion' is a monthly event that bridges the gap between live catwalk shows and static museum displays. Conveying the energy of fashion as performance, models walk around the Museum's galleries wearing the latest collections by top designers.[1]

The programme since 1999 has included the work of 'Philip Treacy, Alexander McQueen, Deborah Milner, Matthew Williamson, Arkadius, Christian Lacroix, Anna Sui and Vivienne Tam' (interview with Mendes, 1/3/00). In addition to the appearance of models wearing clothes by the designer in question, 'Fashion in Motion' also regularly features a video of their most recent catwalk show and a small static display of their work on mannequins. The project represents radical innovation for three main reasons; it brings *live* bodies into otherwise static museum display space; it disturbs the idea of the museum as an objective, neutral space by

Figure 27.1   V&A 'Fashion in Motion' exhibition, 1999. Courtesy of the V&A.

connecting it with the outside world in a most active manner; and by incorporating moving images of fashion in its unadulterated commercial context, it
represents a move away from purist object-based approaches towards a greater
contextualisation of the collection.

Through its use of live bodies wearing clothes which are lent by designers,
'Fashion in Motion' cleverly circumvents what has been a persistent conundrum
for the Museum's dress curators and for those at other institutions. Conservation
considerations prohibit the placing of any items in the collection on live bodies,
so eliciting criticisms from visitors who feel frustrated with the static and 'disembodied' nature of clothes worn by 'dead' mannequins (Mendes *et al.* 1992: 1–2).
Similar criticisms were voiced by the sociologist Elizabeth Wilson in her essay
'Fashion and the postmodern body', in which she comments on the 1991 'Pierre
Cardin' exhibition:

> Strangest of all were the dead, white, sightless mannequins staring
> fixedly ahead, turned as if to stone in the middle of a decisive move-
> ment . . . The clothes themselves were brilliantly coloured, clear,
> incisive of cut, fancifully futurist, yet simple. But without the living
> body, they could not be said fully to exist. Without movement they
> became oddly abstract and faintly uncanny. Nothing could have more
> immediately demonstrated the importance of the body in fashion.
>
> (Wilson 1992: 15)

Since these comments were made there has been a significant increase in the amount of work on the body, within both sociology and cultural studies. 'Fashion in Motion' has enabled the V&A to respond to these developments and criticisms from the Museum's visitors in an entertaining way which embraces the trend towards interactive museum displays, now common on the international scene (Barry 1998). It is also in tune with the current political and museological climate with its emphasis on 'social inclusion', as it enables more democratic access to an elite element of designer level fashion (*Independent*, 9/6/99: 9; *Guardian* supplement, 27/1/00: 10).

'Fashion in Motion' also allows the V&A to confront a key issue addressed in much of the recent museological literature. As Charles Saumarez Smith, currently Director of the National Portrait Gallery in London stated in 1989:

> One of the most insistent problems that museums face is precisely the idea that artefacts can be, and should be, divorced from their original context of ownership and use, and redisplayed in a different context of meaning, which is regarded as having a superior authority. Central to this belief in the superior authority of museums is the idea that they will provide a safe and neutral environment.
>
> (Saumarez Smith 1989: 9)

This acknowledgment that museum displays are no more or less objective or contrived than a runway show or a fashion photograph and are something which 'can itself be independently enjoyed as a system of theatrical artifice' has opened the way for approaches like that taken with 'Fashion in Motion' (Saumarez Smith 1989: 20). Therein lies the radical nature of the project, which due to its theatricality, interactivity and origins in the commercial world, actively disturbs traditional notions of the museum.

A similarly increased emphasis on contextualisation is evident in the fashion video component of 'Fashion in Motion' and the recent introduction of two video displays to the gallery featuring the permanent display of dress. Many of the fashion exhibitions held elsewhere in recent years have featured the use of video displays. However, although fashion videos have been collected for several years by the V&A, showing these within the permanent gallery space represents a major departure from previous, more 'purist', object-based approaches. This change in attitude by a major world player on the museological scene is evident in the following comments by Valerie Mendes:

> My feeling is that contemporary garments plus promotional fashion imagery are vital for an up-to-the-minute display. The public are accustomed to them and this familiarity helps to put visitors at their ease in a museum setting. Properly displayed and described, such garments and promotional material will enhance other exhibits. They help users understand clothes of the past and make their experience of dress in a museum both pleasurable and educationally rewarding.
>
> (Interview with V. Mendes, 1/3/00)

An even more significant move away from the traditional concerns of dress curators was the 'Wear on the Street' display of early 2000, which again was the idea of Claire Wilcox. This involved no garments at all and instead featured photographs of people wearing their own clothes, accompanied by a brief explanation as to why they had chosen to wear those clothes that day. The photographs were shown in a gallery belonging to the V&A's Prints, Drawings and Paintings department and were also reproduced as a series of posters which lined the tunnel leading from the local underground station to the Museum. The idea borrows somewhat from the approaches adopted by British *i.D.* magazine when it was launched in 1980, as a means of recording streetstyle fashions. However 'Wear on the Street' distinguished itself by taking a specific theme, outlined thus:

> This exhibition of posters features the work of ten photographers invited by the V&A to mark the beginning of the millennium. These informal portraits record the diversity of clothes people were wearing at the end of one century and the beginning of the next . . . The intrepid photographers approached friends, family, and complete strangers to capture a wide range of looks . . . The photographs were taken in London, Argyll, Brussels, Swindon, Norfolk, Cologne and Manchester.[2]

The project, with its focus on streetstyle and links with previously established documentary approaches, does not offer anything new in itself. However, it represents the breaking down of traditional barriers around the remit and status of dress curators within large institutional museums. It is an encouraging example of cross-departmental, cross-disciplinary curatorial work, which acknowledges that capturing something of the essence of the impure, perverse and contradictory medium of contemporary dress may require the adoption of a range of different approaches. Like 'Fashion in Motion', it combines this embrace of recent developments in academia with a firm commitment to wider accessibility and more democratic appeal.

Judith Clark Costume Gallery

This innovative, non-commercial gallery was set up by Judith Clark in February 1998 and is located in a quiet street in the fashionable Notting Hill area of London. The Gallery has since then been devoted to holding temporary exhibitions of dress and textiles, almost exclusively at designer level and with a major though not exclusive emphasis on contemporary fashion. It is the only small, independent gallery on the international scene which is devoted exclusively to the study and display of fashion. It therefore represents a tiny but vibrant experimental force within the curatorship of dress.

The Gallery is run almost entirely by the deeply committed and energetic Clark, who occasionally receives help and support from volunteers. Clark was born in Rome and prior to setting up the Gallery, she trained as an architect in London and then studied at the Architectural Association, London, taking a History and Theory diploma. She subsequently worked for a series of small arts organisations.

The gallery's display area is on the ground floor and consists of a small space painted white with natural stripped floorboards and a large mirror at one end. The serious intentions and keen fashion awareness of the Gallery's curator are evident in the range of literature available, which includes *Fashion Theory*, *Tank*, *Purple*, *Visionaire*, *Bloom* and a range of fashion books. Below the exhibition space is a library area dedicated to the study of dress, and a slide archive of Paris, Milan and London designer collections.

Although a key feature of the Gallery is its small scale and independence, the work of curators at large institutions played a central role in its founding. Clark pinpoints a visit to the 'Fashion and Surrealism' exhibition, which was curated by Richard Martin and brought to the V&A from the Fashion Institute of Technology in 1988, as the key inspiration to open her own dress gallery. Realising this ambition required not only commitment but also funding and confidence that this imagined gallery would be a sustainable exercise. Clark gained belief in her idea through observing the heightened attention fashion received in the 1990s, as she explains:

> What gave me the cue that perhaps it was an appropriate time to set up the gallery was increasing evidence of public interest in visiting exhibitions of dress within larger institutions and the obvious need for more. For example, huge audiences at the 'Cutting Edge: Fifty Years of Fashion' [V&A], 'Forties Fashion' [Imperial War Museum, London], the start-up of the Biennale of fashion in Florence driven by important curators such as Germano Celant, and the publication of *Fashion Theory* journal. Still I felt there was a gap for an experimental space free from the obvious restrictions of institutional or commercial briefs.

The above-mentioned freedom is a defining feature of the Judith Clark Costume Gallery, which has no permanent collection of objects to be built, preserved or made accessible. Similarly, this framework allows Clark to respond immediately to developments in the fast-changing world of fashion. Curators in larger institutions have to wait for their ideas to be assessed by committee within the context of a range of competing priorities. These freedoms are also linked to certain limitations, in that Clark operates without the range of specialised staff and facilities relating to education, marketing, publishing and research which are available within large museums. Furthermore, operating on a small scale means that exhibition space is extremely limited and without a collection, all of the objects for temporary exhibitions must be researched and gathered from scratch.

Clark sensibly realises the limitations of her resources and concentrates on the many advantages of the framework she has chosen and built. For example, it allows her to escape some of the criticisms of dress in museums which Valerie Steele highlights as follows: 'If fashion is a "living" phenomenon – contemporary, constantly changing, etc. – then a museum of fashion is *ipso facto* a cemetery for dead clothes' (Steele 1998: 334). The gallery launches a new exhibition every six weeks and as most of these feature specially commissioned or newly contemporary work, it operates with the atmosphere of a living, breathing space, a veritable laboratory for experimentation. However, the collaborative nature of many of the

Gallery's projects means that the designers with whom Clark works must constantly be reined in according to what she calls 'the brief'. She thus refers to the overall aims of the Gallery which she identifies as follows:

> The aim of the gallery is to promote the study of dress and to draw attention to its role within a broader history of ideas, projects, themes . . . Through a series of modest exhibitions, suggestions can be made about curatorial possibilities regarding dress; not definitive, comprehensive exhibitions, that is up to other people. I particularly wish to highlight the relevance of historical dress to contemporary projects through themed shows.

This focus on 'the study of dress' has helped attract some of the funding necessary to run the Gallery. It is a registered charity and is funded through a combination of sponsorship, individual donations and grants. This system of funding has enabled Clark to run the Gallery successfully, but as she stated in the interview (1.3.00), 'it has been very tough'. Despite these pressing difficulties, Clark remains in a different position to those who work in larger museums, whose work has been increasingly underpinned by mounting pressure to increase visitor numbers, as prompted by reductions in government or local authority grants. The greater degree of autonomy which Clark retains means that many of the 'on-the-ground' developments which have prompted much of the recent debate within museology are not relevant to her. However, it is clear that there is substantial cross-over with developments in the 'new' museology and the 'new' fashion history and approaches taken within the Judith Clark Costume Gallery. As Clark states with regard to her influences:

> There is a growing body of academic work on dress, its history and theory which I try to engage in. It has largely been the people producing this work who have been interested in the Gallery and its possibilities. Of course I am influenced by fashion to try to harness general interest or trends for academic and educational purposes.

Since opening the Gallery, Clark has been successful in forging excellent links with other curators, academics, fashion students and many fashion designers and photographers. These links have fed into approaches taken in the Gallery, often through direct collaborations with designers, lenders or collectors. For example, exhibitions held so far include; 'Pampilion – Dai Rees Millinery, Autumn/Winter Couture 1998'; 'Details from a Private Collection, Baroness Fiona Thyssen-Bornemisza 1950s Couture' and 'Pre-Inca Feather Dress'.

Clark is keen to encourage debate through the activities of the Gallery and also wants to 'highlight the relevance of historical dress to contemporary projects through themed shows'. However, I feel that in one show in particular, 'Parure de Plumes', which 'paid homage to James McNeill Whistler's Peacock Room', Clark took the emphasis on the contemporary too far. The exhibition featured a 'muslin "Peacock Dress" dating from the 1850s [which] was styled by contemporary milliner Dai Rees and jeweller Katherine Clark'.[4] Displaying historical dress in this way takes too far an attitude which acknowledges the obvious theatrical artifice of museum displays and leads one to ahistorical approaches that disturb and distort the educative potential of historical dress. The exhibition does, though, raise key points of discussion as to the relationship between the display of contemporary and historical fashion in the postmodern epoch.

Similarly interesting points of debate are raised by the role of the garment as object, the use of representations, and the portrayal of the body within the gallery. Clark comments as follows:

> Imagery has to take second place within the space I suppose, as there are photographic galleries etc. and I am quite protective of the object-based research I am promoting. However, images have been used in the window as panels, and of course whenever I can afford to print a catalogue I try to do so and commission new images by photographers

Figure 27.2   Detail of *Pampilion: Dai Rees* exhibition catalogue, February 1998. Photograph by Matt Collishaw. Courtesy of the Judith Clark Costume Gallery.

who can add something, who are not only documenting . . . like with
Pampilion (Figure 27.2), Mat Collishaw's work was in the catalogue
only, as a visual essay.

These views show similarities and differences to approaches taken at the V&A.
Both organisations now favour the use of static and moving imagery, in addition
to a primary focus on garments as objects. The use of specially commissioned

Figure 27.3   Detail of private view invitation to the 'C41 Simon Thorogood'
exhibition, September 1998. Photograph by Tim Bret-Day.
Courtesy of the Judith Clark Costume Gallery.

fashion photography has also been used at the V&A and the Judith Clark Costume Gallery. However, the imagery used by Clark in her catalogues is almost exclusively cutting-edge fashion photography of clothes worn on live bodies. The V&A and other large institutions with permanent dress collections though tend towards more conservative images of objects on mannequins. This is a further illustration of the freedom to experiment, which Clark optimises in relation to interpretation and display, as she states:

> The Gallery in some way, I think, can afford to make mistakes which perhaps everyone can learn from; it is a locus of experimentation regarding display. Mannequins, for example, are developed in the gallery. I know museums don't have budgets for trial and error mannequins.

These comments are interesting, as despite innovative developments regarding the use of representations and live bodies, static displays of garments will presumably continue (for conservation and scholarly reasons) to be the norm for most permanent displays and exhibitions of dress. Clark's work with mannequins has involved designing tailor-made ones to go with each show. For the 'C4i Simon Thorogood' exhibition (Figure 27.3) she worked with him to create wooden mannequins which were taken directly from his toiles. This experimental work is very worthwhile. However it is difficult to assess how influential it might be on larger British museums with their tiny budgets for such crucial items.

Hussein Chalayan 'Echo Form' exhibition. Atlantis Gallery, Brick Lane, London (27/7/99–10/8/99)

This exhibition of representations of Hussein Chalayan's work was co-curated by Chalayan and the photographer Marcus Tomlinson and held at an art gallery in London's East End.[5] It was clearly intended as a promotional exercise for Chalayan's Autumn/Winter 1999/2000 collection, also entitled 'Echo Form'. As Chalayan commented at the packed opening night preview, 'Tonight was an extension of this year's fashion shows' (British *Elle*, August 1999). After that night, the exhibition was open to the public free of charge for a two-week period.

This example has been chosen as it illustrates approaches taken by those in the commercial sphere, who are completely unfettered by museological traditions or responsibilities. Also, Chalayan's work typifies the shift towards the conceptual in contemporary fashion, a development which raises new questions as to how such work should be displayed in museums and galleries. Also, it was an exciting and stimulating exhibition, so analysing the reasons for this will hopefully yield some interesting answers to the broader questions explored in this chapter.

Hussein Chalayan is a designer renowned for creating fashion shows which look like art installations, so perhaps it is not surprising that he decided to go one step further to co-curate an exhibition of his recent work. The decision to portray Chalayan's work on the body, through both moving and static imagery, is in stark contrast to most museum displays of fashion, both historical and contemporary.

Through this emphasis on the body and the image, the exhibition raises many fascinating issues regarding the character, promotion and display of contemporary fashion, not to mention the nature of the creative process.

After selling his 1993 graduation collection from Central St. Martin's to the leading fashion retailer Browns, Chalayan launched his own label the following year (de la Haye 1997: 202). He has since developed a reputation for designing so-called 'difficult' clothes, the challenging nature of his designs stemming from his intellectual approach to fashion. The exhibition allowed Chalayan and his collaborators to express this approach in new and stimulating ways.

Turkish Cypriot-born Chalayan chose to show in the Atlantis Gallery, which is a large, white ex-industrial space with exposed metal pipes. Despite this unremittingly harsh environment, its airy, dark and deserted atmosphere, combined with high ceilings and the use of contemplative, Middle Eastern music evoked the atmosphere of a Turkish mosque as much as it did inner-city industria. The calm atmosphere inspired by the background music was disturbed at regular intervals by the soundtrack to a short film, directed by Marcus Tomlinson. The film began with a black screen, from which a white woman emerged wearing a white moulded plastic dress which rigidly encased the body like a piece of aeronautical engineering and which appeared simultaneously to protect and constrain her. Her legs appeared as black shadows, rather than as flesh, though her arms were exposed. Slowly the woman moved her hands from her waist to her sides. She then clenched them into fists, at which point a section of the dress mysteriously disengaged from the rest of the moulded form and dropped several centimetres to reveal part of the model's stomach and left hip. This naked patch of torso communicated a distinct, new level of bodily vulnerability and frailty. The woman then began to rotate, slowly at first, then increasingly quickly, until she was spinning at breathtaking speed. Gradually she slowed down, then stopped and both her dress and her hands came to rest in their original position. The film provoked thoughts on the sometimes pleasurable and often bewilderingly rapid rate of change within late twentieth-century society, and within the contemporary fashion system. The human body and the self, though protected by technology, were also seen to be fragile and at risk from technological change.

Chalayan used other images in the exhibition to comment on Western and Islamic attitudes to the female body, thus repeating a familiar theme in his work. The designer's observations on the nature of a creativity which is channelled into making sometimes beautiful, yet always ephemeral products were presented in two interrelated images. In a projected image Erin O'Connor appeared wearing a very simple, sleeveless, denim shift dress. Upon this blank canvas, top-stitching, pockets and other style details slowly and progressively appeared, and then dissolved away again in the same progression. This theme was repeated, but exaggerated, in a metallic print which again featured Erin O'Connor in the same denim dress. The style details appeared, then disappeared, then appeared and finally disappeared, as one walked from the right to the left side of the print. Chalayan highlighted the ambiguity and ambivalence of fashion and of the creative process itself. He looked directly at the process of designing, the adding of detail, the removal of it, the empowering, fulfilling and occasionally agonising nature of the creative process.

The multiplicity of meanings evoked by fashion were then explored through a rectangular brown box, which was open at one side and painted with surreal images inside and out. The left exterior of the box featured a headless woman's body standing on a raised, white shelf; it appeared as if her head had disappeared inside the box. She was dressed in black leather tights with feet, over which were shiny lycra knickers in a dull mauve (these reminded one of theatrical costumes worn by acrobats, or nineteenth-century strongmen rather than normal underwear). Just visible at the waist of these was the elastic of a pair of greying white knickers. The woman's back and arms were slender and shapely but were marked by several moles. At the back exterior of the box the woman seemed to have also lost part of her right arm to the inside of the box. The right exterior of the box featured the woman in yet a different pose, whereby her head, shoulders, arms and the lower half of her legs had disappeared. Most of the woman had now disappeared to the exterior world, where her appearance was not as one might expect. On the left inside of the box the head of a perfectly groomed model appeared. At the inside back of the box her arm and more of her brown tailored coat were also visible. We then saw the whole image, where in her chic brown tailored coat and black leather boots she comprised an image of formal fashionable perfection, fit for any glossy fashion magazine.

The box suggested a stream of meanings and practices regarding the body, both adorned and unadorned; performance, masquerade, fantasy, the need to reveal and conceal one's body and oneself, the frailty, beauty and imperfections of the body concealed, the tawdry, the perverse, and the mundane, to name but a few. Chalayan and his collaborators managed to say in a most refreshing and inspiring visual way what it would take an academic pages to explain. Therein lies the cleverness of this exhibition in that in purely visual form it provoked thoughts on the multi-layered, complex meanings associated with contemporary fashion, the body and representation. It met the challenge of capturing the ambiguity, ambivalence and speed of change which is the essence of contemporary fashion, something which is no mean feat (Davis 1992). Perhaps, though, the pertinence of the observations expressed is not surprising, as it derives from the cultural production with which Chalayan and Tomlinson are involved on a daily basis. That fashion industry context and the curators' art school training provide some explanation for the fact that the focus of the exhibition on the body, representation, and the production of meaning is entirely in tune with recent debates in both museology and fashion history. In fact the exhibition met very successfully most of the criteria suggested by Charles Saumarez Smith, as to what the characteristics of 'new' museum displays should be. He states that

> [t]he best museum displays are often those which are most evidently self-conscious, heightening the spectator's awareness of the means of presentation, involving the spectator in the process of display. These ideas can be formulated into a set of requirements: that there should be a mixed style of presentation; that there should be a degree of audience involvement in the methods of display; that there should be an awareness of the amount of artificiality in the methods of display; and that there should be an awareness of different, but equally legitimate, methods of interpretation.
>
> (Saumarez Smith 1989: 20)

Conclusion

An active process of cross-fertilisation between the 'new museology' and the 'new fashion history' has clearly had a significant impact on the curatorship of contemporary fashion within Britain. The similarities between developments in the three case studies also reveal the close and mutually stimulating exchanges between museums and galleries, and others engaged in the contemporary fashion system, from designers and photographers to the wider public. A new emphasis on the body and the image has been established even within traditional curatorial contexts, thus enabling design-led institutions (who are often characterised as elitist) to engage more closely with the public's day-to-day experience of designer level fashion. Similarly, the new approaches discussed have led to an increased contextualisation of objects, thus providing entertaining and increasingly non-didactic, educational experiences about fashion.

Acknowledgements

With grateful thanks to Sarah Hodges, Valerie Mendes, Claire Wilcox, Chook Sitbain, Sonnet Stanfill, Judith Clark and Marcus Tomlinson.

The section on the Hussein Chalayan exhibition, 'Echo Form', appears by kind permission of the editors of Fashion Theory: the Journal of Dress, Body and Culture.

Notes

1 Postcards featuring this text are available free to V&A visitors.
2 This text accompanied the display of posters in the tunnel leading from South Kensington underground station to the V&A.
3 This section of the essay and the quotations by Judith Clark derive from an interview I conducted with her on 1 March 2000.
4 Source: list of Past Exhibitions, courtesy of Judith Clark.
5 Source: conversation between the author and Marcus Tomlinson, 22/3/00.

References

Barry, Andrew (1998) 'On interactivity: consumers, citizens and culture' in Sharon MacDonald (ed.) *The Politics of Display: Museums, Science, Culture*, London: Routledge.
Burton, Anthony (1999) *Vision and Accident: the Story of the Victoria and Albert Museum*, London: V&A Publications.
Davis, Fred (1992) *Fashion, Culture and Identity*, Chicago: The University of Chicago Press.
Elle UK, August 1999, London: Hachette-EMAP Magazines Ltd.
Featherstone, Mike (1991) 'The body in consumer culture' in Mike Featherstone, M. Hepworth and B. Turner (eds) *The Body: Social Process and Cultural Theory*, London: Sage.

Frankel, Susannah (1999) *Independent*, Wednesday Review, 9 June.

Greenhalgh, Paul (1989) 'Education, entertainment and politics: lessons from the Great International Exhibitions' in Peter Vergo (ed.) *The New Museology*, London: Reaktion Books.

De la Haye, Amy (1997) *The Cutting Edge: Fifty Years of British Fashion 1947–1997*, London, V&A Publications.

Hooper-Greenhill, Eilean (1995) *Museum, Media, Message*, London: Routledge.

MacDonald, Sharon (1998) *The Politics of Display: Museums, Science, Culture*, London: Routledge.

Mendes, Valerie, Hart, Avril and de la Haye, Amy (1992) 'Introduction' in Natalie Rothstein (ed.) *Four Hundred Years of Fashion*, London: V&A Publications.

Saumarez Smith, Charles (1989) 'Museums, artefacts and meanings' in Peter Vergo (ed.) *The New Museology*, London: Reaktion Books.

Steele, Valerie (1998) 'A museum of fashion is more than a clothes bag', *Fashion Theory: the Journal of Dress, Body and Culture*, Methodology issue, 2 (4).

Tarrant, Naomi (1996) *The Development of Costume*, London: Routledge.

Taylor, Lou (1998) 'Doing the laundry? A reassessment of object-based dress history', *Fashion Theory: the Journal of Dress, Body and Culture*, Methodology issue, 2 (4).

Wilson, Elizabeth (1992) 'Fashion and the postmodern body' in Juliet Ash and Elizabeth Wilson (eds) *Chic Thrills: A Fashion Reader*, London: Pandora.

Index